PSYCHOLOGY

PSYCHOLOGY

ROBERT M. LIEBERT STATE UNIVERSITY OF NEW YORK AT STONY BROOK

JOHN M. NEALE STATE UNIVERSITY OF NEW YORK AT STONY BROOK

JOHN WILEY & SONS, INC.
NEW YORK LONDON SYDNEY TORONTO

Library of Congress Cataloging in Publication Data

Liebert, Robert M.   1942–
   Psychology.

   Bibliography: p.
   Includes indexes.
     1. Psychology.   I. Neale, John M., 1943–   joint author.
II. Title.   [DNLM: 1. Psychology.   BF139   L716p]
BF121.L47   150   76-54530
ISBN 0-471-53431-5

Printed in the United States of America

10 9 8 7 6 5 4 3 2

PREFACE

Psychology is not a required course in most colleges and universities, yet every year introductory psychology has a larger college enrollment than virtually any other subject. Almost certainly, one reason for psychology's popularity is that it promises to tell us something about why people think and act as they do. There is no doubt that a course in psychology can provide a student with this kind of information, but that is usually not the principal aim of instructors or text-writers. Their feeling is that psychology is a science and an academic discipline, and that a proper introduction to it at the college level should attempt to explain the basic ideas, theories, and discoveries that comprise the body of psychological knowledge. Often, it seems to be an "either-or" proposition: either one gears a text toward the students or one gears it toward the discipline, but not both. This book was written because we believe one *can* do both.

In the chapters that follow, we have described the various subareas of psychology—from psychobiology to psychotherapy—and explained the concepts and major findings that have emerged in each. This has been the traditional approach in introductory psychology, and here we have stuck close to tradition because we believe this information is of great value.

But we also believe that it is incumbent upon us to demonstrate the value of this knowledge, rather than merely claiming that it is of value. Thus, the major continuing theme of this book is that the basic findings of all areas of psychology are related to forms of behavior and experience that are familiar and of concern to everyone. This theme is reflected not only in the amount of space we devote to topics such as child development, personality, and abnormal behavior, but also in the way we treat the core areas of psychological science. Throughout the text we have tried to show the connection between the findings of the laboratory and the potential areas of application. In the field of psychobiology, for example, we focus on how the brain structures relate to areas of practical concern such as aggression and obesity. In addition to selecting our research examples to illustrate the operation of basic processes in meaningful situations wherever possible, we end each chapter with a section, "Psychology and the Problems of Society," in which we apply the basic ideas of the chapter to an area of immediate social importance such as perceptual discrimination and racial prejudice, and the application of learning principles to educating the mentally retarded.

In Chapter 1 we begin with a short explanation of the roots of psychology as a science, providing an overview of the various areas of psychology—somewhat like a roadmap of where our journey will lead. Chapters 2 through 5 describe the core processes of interest to experimental psychologists, beginning with the biological functions of the brain and nerves and then going on to perception, learning, and finally the cognitive processes. In Chapter 6 we return to the biological approach again, but now that we have already discussed the basics, we turn to an examination of the individual in terms of physical development (Chapter 6), mental development (Chapter 7) and social development (Chapter 8). Chapter 8's focus on the social behavior of the child leads to a discussion of the social behavior of adults (Chapter 9), including the processes that underlie it. The last three chapters focus attention on the whole person, beginning with some of the major conceptualizations of personality (Chapter 10), and then going on to the nature, causes, and treatment of abnormal behavior in Chapters 11 and 12.

From a pedagogical perspective we have tried throughout the book to explain how psychologists think about behavior and why psychological investigations take the form they do. To allow the student to check his or her insight into the psychological point of view, readers are periodically invited to think about selected research problems in psychology, set off as boxes for "Testing Your Understanding." These boxes are *not* tests of how well facts have been remembered; indeed, we have often included material in these boxes that had not been presented before. Our intention is to let the reader see whether he or she can anticipate how a psychologist would approach certain problems or apply various principles in research situations. After posing a question and inviting the reader to consider possible solutions, an "answer" is given, providing an opportunity to learn immediately what was actually done and found.

We have also attempted to involve the student as much as possible in the real excitement of psychological puzzle-solving. We have presented research in sufficient detail so that the student can see how questions arise and what forms solutions can take. Our emphasis on the applications of basic research findings takes research out of the "simply an academic exercise realm." Our "Testing Your Understanding" boxes have a similar goal.

Each chapter in the book is somewhat longer than comparable chapters found in most other introductory psychology texts. Although more than one sitting may be required to finish each chapter, the materials are presented with convenient breakpoints. Furthermore, we think that this format, which adheres to the traditional divisions within the field, allows a better appreciation of how the various parts of psychology as a science fit together than when the material is fragmented into several dozen mini-chapters.

Like other sciences, psychology has its share of technical terms. We have intentionally tried to limit these terms to those that are essential. When they appear, technical terms are explained in context and are also defined explicitly in the Glossary at the end of the chapter in which they first appear. The reader will probably note that our chapter summaries are somewhat longer than most. This was by design. Rather than merely reminding the reader of a few of the chapter's highlights, these summaries are designed to recap the flow of ideas within the chapter itself as a further aid to study and understanding.

As a final pedagogical aid, R. A. Vachon has prepared a *Study Guide*. The guide contains summaries of the chapters and a variety of questions. For the instructor, we have prepared a *Resource Manual* that includes supplemental lecture materials and an extensive test-item file.

This book has been more than 4 years in the making, and we would like to acknowledge the role of everyone who contributed to this memorable experience. Throughout the development of the manuscript, members of the Wiley Advisory Board and numerous anonymous reviewers offered valuable comments and criticisms; Gretchen Daly provided secretarial assistance; and R. A. Vachon and Susan Franzblau contributed valuable research and editorial assistance. Of the Wiley staff, the exceptional efforts of Stella Kupferberg are acknowledged with special thanks.

October 1976   **Robert M. Liebert**
John M. Neale

CONTENTS

CONTENTS

ONE

OVERVIEW

Marketing Manager of a Toy Company: We need to develop a commercial that will really sell this new doll. Some market sampling research we've done shows that kids don't like it much. They don't appreciate the fine facial details and quality of workmanship; they just think it's too small and uninteresting.

Ad Man: There are a lot of ways we can counteract those impressions in a TV commercial. First, of course, we'll have children playing with the doll and expressing great delight. We can do close-ups to accentuate the fine de-

tail and workmanship you mentioned. And we can also use small children and scale down the size of other objects that will be on the set. Size perception is pretty relative, you know. So if we make everything but the doll smaller, the doll will appear larger.

• • •

The half-time score was 14 to 14. In the locker room Toby Jones, the Bulls' awesome defensive end, went on the rampage. Storming to the front of the room, the usually quiet Jones proceeded to heap abuse on his teammates for their sluggish first-half play. The spirit of the whole team lifted. Final score: 35 to 14 in favor of the Bulls.

• • •

Dear Dr. Sisters,
    Ever since I was a teenager I have been nervous, especially when I'm around men. I am now a college senior and the problem doesn't seem to be getting better. When I am with men I get worried about what they will think of me and just clam up. But that doesn't really help because then they just think I'm dull. What can I do?

Troubled

Dear Troubled,
    Overconcern with the impression we make on others is a frequent cause of nervousness. You can't expect everyone you meet to like you, but, by being yourself, you will find that some men will like you exactly the way you are.

• • •

The trial was in its second week. The defendant, accused of murder, had already been in jail for more than 2 months; an initial plea by his attorney to have him judged incompetent to stand trial had not been granted. The case for the defense rested not on whether the accused was descriptively guilty—several people had been eyewitnesses to the murder—but on a plea of diminished responsibility for the act due to the defendant's temporary insanity. The next witness, a psychologist, had visited the defendant in his cell and had administered a battery of personality tests. The psychologist had "taken him back" to the moment of the crime under hypnosis and was prepared to testify that at the time of the murder the defendant did not know what he was doing.

What do all these situations have in common? They show how psychology might be applied to a variety of practical issues and problems. Today advertisers use psychology to sell their products, and sports championships are often won or lost depending upon which team was most effectively "psyched up" by a coach who understood the principles of motivation. Some newspapers carry regular columns by psychologists who offer advice to those who write in with problems. Not infrequently, these same newspapers carry accounts of grisly crimes, allegedly committed by emotionally troubled individuals who are then tested and often treated by psychologists.

During the past 30 years psychology has moved more and more into public awareness as a science that touches the lives of everyone. And, because of its relevance to many of our contemporary social problems (overpopulation, interpersonal and international violence, and the changes brought about in people's life styles and values due to technological changes), many people believe that psychology and the other related social sciences will be even more important in the years to come.

But what, exactly, is psychology? When beginning psychology students are asked this question, their answers differ widely. Some think psychology is the science of the mind, others believe that it is the art of dealing with people effectively, and usually at least a few have heard that psychology is the study of behavior—often the behavior of laboratory animals such as rats or pigeons. All of these definitions have also been suggested by psychologists themselves at one time or another because the definition of psychology has changed several times during the course of its history and is still changing today. In order to have a real understanding of what psychology is, it is necessary to know what it used to be in earlier times and how it has developed into its present form. As an introduction to the field, therefore, we will present a brief history. In the next few pages you will probably notice that the definitions of psychology have changed and that conflicting viewpoints have developed. This has led to disputes about theory and method that still prevail today, as between the Freudians and behaviorists. Undoubtedly you will also recognize the names of several important persons whose work has made psychology what it is today, and see how their crude methods of study have now developed into rather sophisticated research techniques.

BRIEF HISTORICAL BACKGROUND   **THE ORIGIN OF PSYCHOLOGY.** Until the eighteenth century, only philosophers made systematic observations of nature and speculated about the causes of natural events. However, the accumulation of knowledge and technical advances soon limited what any one philosopher could know or do; consequently, certain schools of philosophy whose primary interest was in specific natural phenomena began branching into areas that are now separate disciplines, such as physics, chemistry, and biology.

For the most part psychology is also concerned with certain natural phenomena, and it, too, emerged from philosophy. But psychology did not emerge as an independent field distinguished from philosophy until the late nineteenth century, when physics and chemistry were already well established. The separation of psychology from philosophy can be traced to two major lines of thinking—one *rational* (based on reasoning and logic) and the other *empirical* (based on direct observation and experience). When these two approaches to the nature of man finally converged, psychology was born.

One rational philospher who made a significant contribution to the emergence of psychology was René Descartes (1596–1650). Descartes believed that man's body, like that of animals, should be thought of as a machine but that man was unique because he also possessed a conscious soul that was entirely separate from his body. From Descartes we inherited the view that biologists, who study only the body, neglect a central part of human existence, that is, conscious experience. This omission now constitutes an important part of the field of psychology. Descartes also believed that many of our ideas about the world are inborn, being determined by the innate structure of the conscious mind itself.

This view was challenged by John Locke (1632–1704), founder of the school of philosophical thought known as British empiricism, or associationism. Locke asserted that the mind at birth was a *tabula rasa* (blank slate) and that experience, transmitted through the senses, molds each mind to make it unique. His view paved the way for a science of psychology that emphasized the effects of experience; and the related processes of perception, learning, and memory are still important and fascinating to psychologists today. Locke and his followers within the British associationist school also believed that complex ideas were formed as a result of combining experience with simpler ideas. For example, they thought that a person's concept of a wall was created from the simpler ideas of bricks, mortar, quantity, and position; a wall is no more than a quantity of bricks and mortar in a certain position. Such a view suggested that the mind could be understood by analyzing its complex components into simple and basic elements. As we shall see, this view was important at the time psychology became an independent discipline.

Figure 1.1
John Locke

Although Locke and his followers favored an empirical approach to a purely rational one and challenged the idea of a dualism between mind and body, it was not until the emergence of experimental physiology that the link between mental and physical events was explored directly. Several discoveries by experimental physiologists during the early nineteenth century were particularly important for the future of psychology. One was the discovery by Pierre Flourens (1794–1867) that distinct parts of the brain controlled different and distinct functions of the body. Another, made at about the same time by Sir Charles Bell (1774–1842) and François Magendie (1783–1855), was that most nerves in the body were concerned with *either* sensory functions (sending information to the brain) *or* motor functions (taking messages from the brain to the muscles and other structures) but not with both. Together with Johannes Müller's (1801–1858) conclusion that we do not experience the world itself directly, but only the state of our own nerves, these discoveries suggested strongly that a true experimental science of the mind could be developed. The mind was no longer seen as merely something spiritual, but rather as a biological reality as well, which could be explored through research. Physiological psychology (or psychobiology, as it is sometimes called today) is now a thriving branch of psychology and owes an enormous debt to these early investigators.

STRUCTURALISM: ANALYZING THE CONTENTS OF THE MIND THROUGH INTROSPECTION. When these rational and empirical lines of thought converged in the late nineteenth century, the time was ripe for psychology to become an independent discipline. Most historians agree that modern psychology dates from 1879, when Wilhelm Wundt (1832–1920) established a laboratory at the University of Leipzig in Germany for the purpose of studying psychological processes. Wundt's studies followed rather closely those of his predecessors in philosophy and physiology, for he, too, was interested in the structure of the mind. His unique contribution was in establishing a school of psychology—*structuralism*—to guide his efforts, and in using *introspection* as a research technique.

Wundt defined psychology as the study of conscious experience. To examine consciousness, Wundt and his followers gave trained observers various stimuli and asked them to describe their experiences in great detail. This method—introspection—was used to relate varying stimulus conditions to the experiences they produced. The subjects had to be trained to examine their own experiences carefully because they would be asked to describe each element or quality of the sensation produced by, for example, a sweet taste. Wundt hoped that by analyzing the content of the mind in this way he would be able to understand its structure. One of Wundt's students, Edward Bradford Titchener (1867–1927), brought the structuralist school of psychology (as Wundt's views came to be called) to America. Structuralism, though, flourished only briefly, for it soon became apparent that it was not possible to rely upon introspection; disagreements could not be settled by hard fact. But the importance of empirical research had been established. Psychology was finally separated from philosophy. This separation and the emphasis on research that brought it about are both still evident today.

With the passage of time, new developments finally emerged in the fields of physiology and psychiatry; these together with disagreements that arose among some of Wundt's followers, eventually led to the creation of a number of schools of thought within the field of psychology. Among the most important of these schools were functionalism, behaviorism, and psychoanalysis.

*Figure 1.2
Wilhelm Wundt*

Figure 1.3 (Right)
Darwin's theory of evolution, showing the descent of man from simpler forms of life.

Figure 1.4 (Below)
This 1872 cartoon ridiculed Darwin's views of evolution by showing man's descent from pig to bull to man.

THE FUNCTIONALIST SCHOOL AND ITS HEIRS. Structuralism was soon replaced as the dominant school of psychology by *functionalism*, a point of view that owed much more to biology than to philosophy. Charles Robert Darwin (1809–1882), a biologist, naturalist, and writer, had theorized that various forms of life had gone through a gradual process of adaptive evolution during the course of millions of years and that only those species that were most fit had survived. Early psychologists who were attracted to Darwin, such as the American William James (1842–1910), thought psychology should concern itself primarily with the adaptive functions of behavior. They viewed the mind as a functional organ that contributes to survival. Functionalism emphasized what the mind *does* rather than what it *is*.

Functionalism radically changed the focus of psychologists' studies. In turning away from questions of structure and consciousness, the

Figure 1.5
William James

Figure 1.6
Ivan Pavlov

functionalists broadened the field of psychology by emphasizing the importance of *behavior,* a major focus of psychological research today. Equally significant, the functionalist/educator John Dewey (1859–1952) and others began to ask practical questions, and the public became interested in the new science of psychology for the first time. With the advent of functionalism, psychology became more relevant to practical, everyday human concerns. For his contributions in this respect, Williams James is sometimes called the "father of contemporary psychology."

THE RISE OF BEHAVIORISM. Ivan Petrovich Pavlov (1849–1936), a Russian physiologist, became an important figure in the history of psychology quite by accident. Pavlov was studying the digestive processes and wanted to measure the salivary flow of dogs when they were fed. The dogs had to have a special apparatus attached to their mouths and head, and since experienced dogs accepted this situation much more readily then inexperienced ones, Pavlov used the same dogs over and over. But the highly experienced dogs developed the habit of salivating even before they received their food. At first Pavlov asked his assistants to use introspection to try to understand why this was happening from the dog's point of view. However, bitter arguments resulted, and Pavlov soon stopped such introspection and began to perform objective experiments to determine how the dog would behave in a particular situation rather than trying to imagine how he would feel about it. Pavlov found that stimuli associated with meat powder, such as the sound of a bell, could later cause the dog to salivate when no food was presented; he called this phenomenon a *conditioned response.*

At this time psychology in America was beginning to have its troubles with both the structuralist school and the psychoanalytic movement. The time seemed ripe for a new approach, and John Broadus Watson (1878–1958) took up the call. Following Pavlov's lead, Watson rejected introspection entirely as a method of inquiry and brushed the study of consciousness aside. He said that psychology should be concerned *only* with the study of behavior, and founded the school of *behaviorism.* Watson wrote:

Psychology as the behaviorist views it is a purely objective experimental branch of natural science. Its theoretical goal is the prediction and control of behavior. Introspection forms no essential part of its methods, nor is the scientific value of its data dependent upon the readiness with which they lend themselves to interpretation in terms of consciousness [Watson, 1913, p. 158].

To replace introspection, Watson saw conditioning, as Pavlov's discovery was eventually called, as the logical explanation for how behavior develops and changes. Watson believed that Pavlov's research showed that *all* forms of behavior, regardless of their complexity, could be reduced to a series of stimulus-response patterns conditioned by experience. He believed that psychology's task was to be able to determine

what stimulus would produce a particular response. Although one might start with simple problems, Watson was convinced that behavioristic psychology could have an important impact upon society, and he excited or infuriated audiences with his enthusiasm:

Give me a dozen infants, well formed, and my own specific world to bring them up in, and I'll guarantee to take any one at random and train him to become any type of specialist I might select, doctor, lawyer, artist, merchant-chief, and yes, even beggar-man and thief, regardless of his talents, penchants, tendencies, abilities, vocations, and race of his ancestors [1924, reprinted 1970, p. 104].

Although Watson's views sounded a little improbable, his claim that conditioning, properly understood and managed, could turn any baby into any kind of adult was irresistible, especially to Americans. Within a few years behaviorism was the most widely accepted school of psychology in America. Numerous experiments on conditioning and learning were done in the 1930s and 1940s with many species, including human beings, and by the early 1950s many of these ideas had been applied to the real-life problems of individuals and the community.

Although many psychologists today do not believe that behaviorism provides a complete description of learning processes, this movement has had a lasting impact upon the discipline of psychology. Researchers remain committed to a "methodological" behaviorism, that is, they believe that all hypotheses about human functioning must be framed so that they refer to objective and reproducible behavioral events. Even current experiments on internal mental events or cognitive processes depend upon behavioral measures such as reaction time, as will be described in a later chapter.

PSYCHOANALYSIS: UNCONSCIOUS MOTIVATION. Sigmund Freud (1856–1939), a contemporary of Pavlov and Watson, also made a significant impact on psychology, but in quite a different direction. A Vienna-born physician and psychiatrist, Freud discovered that many of his patients had strong emotional feelings of which they were unaware and that when these feelings were released it was therapeutic. Freud came to the conclusion that the forbidden wishes of childhood, particularly sexual wishes, are pushed out of people's awareness, but that they still motivate people unconsciously; he believed that these wishes could only be understood by means of *psychoanalysis*—Freud's method for revealing the unconscious by analyzing thoughts, dreams, and fantasies. An imaginative genius, Freud developed a theory of the structure of personality, including the importance of early experience and the nature of a psychological cure—in short, a complete theory of consciousness and behavior! His psychoanalytic theory offers an explanation of love and hate, of dreams and nightmares, and of life and death. Although Freud's views, like Watson's, were quite controversial, some form of psychoanalysis was soon being practiced by therapists in every country of Europe and in the United States as well.

Freud's belief that people could be understood only by examining

Figure 1.9
Alfred Binet

their unconscious motives was directly opposed to the behaviorists' emphasis on observable behavior. However, the very early behaviorists were not yet ready to apply their concepts to the needs of human beings directly, and their studies were largely aimed at understanding the simple problem-solving behavior of rats, cats, and pigeons. Therefore, almost all psychotherapists (whose concern is with people's emotional health and well-being) looked to Freud for answers until fairly recently. It should not be surprising that psychoanalysis is still important in the training and thinking of many clinical psychologists and psychiatrists.

Academic psychologists, on the other hand, were generally not willing to accept Freud's views in their entirety, but many saw that his propositions could be tested in some form, either in the laboratory or in the clinic.

OTHER INFLUENCES. If the ideas of Locke, Darwin, Wundt, Pavlov, Watson, and Freud formed the great rivers of psychological thought, there were also significant tributaries that contributed to the development of modern psychology. One of these was the demand for psychological measurement.

Measurement. Darwin had said that within a species individuals will differ in "fitness," and psychologists have long been interested in measuring these differences. Alfred Binet (1857–1911), a French psychologist, was commissioned by his government to prepare a test that would identify children who had special educational needs. Binet himself doubted that his test could measure an underlying trait of intellectual fitness, but the modern IQ test that later developed is obviously being used in that way. Comparable tests of mental fitness were soon being given to army recruits, would-be immigrants, applicants for executive positions, and children everywhere. These new IQ tests, which were developed by psychologists, were soon being examined by other psychologists for the soundness of their execution and their underlying theories. Measurement-minded psychologists also developed personality tests and these, too, became as controversial as the IQ tests. The entire field of psychological testing is still hotly debated.

The Gestalt School. A group of German psychologists who were contemporaries of Wundt objected from the beginning to the structuralist view that the contents of the mind could be divided into its constituent parts. Since they believed that the most important aspect of human experience was its wholeness, they attempted to demonstrate that patterns rather than isolated events were the raw materials of thought and feeling. Early Gestalt psychologists were interested in perception, thinking, reasoning, and problem-solving. They did not utilize the ideas of Pavlovian conditioning, behaviorism, or psychoanalysis. Nonetheless, modern cognitive psychologists, who are interested in how people remember information, have recently learned that whole meanings rather than isolated words strung together are the units of memory.

This finding is quite consistent with Gestalt psychology.

Comprehensive Learning Theories. From Locke through Pavlov to Watson psychologists have wanted to understand the process of learning. In the 1920s and 1930s many comprehensive theories about learning flourished, and there were arguments over the relative importance of motivation, reward, and various components of the stimulus-response relationship. Clark Leonard Hull set forth a quasi-mathematical theory of learning, emphasizing the importance of innate drives and habits acquired through reward. His followers vigorously debated the students of Edward Chase Tolman, who believed that learning did not require motivation or any direct reward at all.

From the perspective of today, many of their arguments seem strained, especially since most of their studies were done with small groups of rats and then generalized to human beings. But the controversy was not without benefit. Psychologists learned to sharpen their research skills and to examine their theoretical premises rather closely. Since the 1950s, the theories of Hull and Tolman (as well as others) have had less influence than more limited theories designed to explain less but to do it better. Psychology has branched into many subareas, revealing much new knowledge and insight. Although the rest of this book will deal with these new developments, the issues being researched have been with us for a long time.

CONTEMPORARY PSYCHOLOGY. As we have seen, the definition of psychology has changed several times as its focus of interest has shifted. For many years, standard textbooks defined psychology as "the scientific study of behavior." Since the word "behavior," as used by psychologists, refers to any observable activities performed by a living organism, this definition encompasses a tremendous range of possibilities. The field of psychology is still changing, and today there is a growing interest in such mental functions as thinking. Many psychologists are now willing to go beyond the stimulus-response links of the behaviorists to include consciousness among their psychological data. Other psychologists are investigating the relationship between physiological functioning and learning—as in biofeedback studies— to see how man might learn to control such bodily processes as heart rate and blood pressure. Therefore, contemporary psychology is best defined as *the scientific study of behavior and related mental and physical processes.*

FIELDS OF SPECIALIZATION To have a better understanding of psychology, it would be helpful to mention the areas of specialization within the field today. We will briefly describe these areas here, although they will be discussed in greater detail in later chapters.

Clinical Psychology. In this field psychology is applied to the needs of the individual who is in conflict with society or himself. More than one-third of all psychologists are clinical psychologists, trained in the diagnosis, treatment, and study of disturbed or maladaptive patterns of behavior. In contrast to psychiatrists, who are medical doctors, clinical psychologists receive their education in graduate departments of psychology and then serve an internship in a mental hospital, clinic, or similar institution. *Counseling psychologists,* who usually have clinical training, assist individuals with various personal problems such as marital and family difficulties or academic and career choices, but they do not generally try to work with individuals who show seriously disturbed patterns of behavior. *Abnormal psychologists* or, *psychopathologists,* also typically receive clinical training, but they differ from practicing clinicians in that they devote most of their time to research on the origins of abnormal behavior or the *processes* that underlie treatment rather than on doing therapy or assessment per se.

Experimental Psychology. Psychologists in this field do basic research on a wide variety of processes, including sensation, perception, motivation, learning, and cognition (although cognitive psychology is fast becoming a separate specialty). Many of the chapter titles in this book are named for these subdivisions of experimental psychology. The name of this field may be misleading, for it seems to suggest that only experimental psychologists use the experimental method in doing research. In fact, experimental research is conducted in all areas of psychology.

Educational Psychology. This field comprises the study and application of psychological processes as they relate to schooling. Educational psychologists are usually found in universities, where they study how the principles of learning, motivation, and development can be utilized in various school settings. *School psychologists* are most often employed directly by elementary and secondary schools, where they assess the difficulties and potentialities of individual students, as well as provide counseling.

Physiological Psychology (Psychobiology). This is the study of the biological bases of behavior, especially the role of the brain and the nervous system in controlling action and thought.

Developmental Psychology. This field describes and explains the behavioral, emotional, and intellectual growth of humans from the time of conception to death.

Social Psychology. This field focuses on how people behave when interacting with others and the processes that influence these interactions. Topics include aggression, cooperation, attraction, and conflict, as well as the processes of attitude formation and change.

Personality Psychology. In this field, the individual is studied, especially with respect to adjustment to the environment and the underlying dimensions of complex feelings and behavior. More than in most other specialty areas, personality psychology relies heavily on theory (such as psychoanalytic theory).

12

Applied Psychology. Here, psychology is applied to a number of fields. *Engineering psychologists,* for example, might be hired to prepare the most efficient design for a particular instrument panel; *industrial psychologists* are often brought in to help settle management-labor disputes; and *personnel psychologists* typically assist in the selection and evaluation of employees in many large corporations.

Methodology. This field includes the design of measurement instruments, research models, and statistical procedures for psychological research. Methodologists may focus on logic, statistics, or the philosophy of science, and many specialize in a particular research area as well.

SCIENCE AND PSYCHOLOGY

An important part of the definition of modern psychology is that it is scientific; psychology emerged when laboratories were founded and research began. But what does it mean to be scientific?

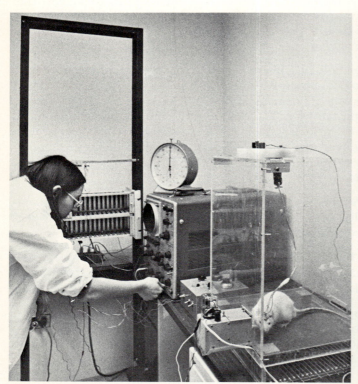

Figure 1.10
Psychologists study many things, ranging from simple responses in laboratory animals to complex social behavior.

The goal of any science is to be able to understand and explain events that fall within its particular domain; in the case of psychology, this means behavior and related processes. However, to be able to offer explanations and provide information that will be acceptable to other scientists, one must adhere to the investigative procedure that is called the *scientific method*. The first step in this procedure is to express the question or state the problem in a concrete way. The problem could be to test some aspect of a theory, or to try to resolve a practical difficulty, or to explain the results of earlier research. After thinking about the problem and finding out what others have already discovered, the scientist will formulate a hypothesis. A hypothesis is a proposition stating the expected relationship between two or more events of variables; for example, "if A occurs, then B will result." A more concrete example would be: "Exposure to TV violence increases the likelihood that a child will act aggressively." Finally the scientist selects a research method that is appropriate for the hypothesis and begins an investigation. The hypothesis will be accepted or rejected depending upon the resulting research evidence. The process is usually not this simple, however, because the information from any one study will rarely be sufficient to solve the original problem entirely. The same scientist or others will need to test the idea under many similar and different situations before the finding will be accepted as a general fact by the scientific community.

The scientific method differs from common sense in several important ways. A scientist must strive for explanations that are a result of, and can be modified by, publicly observed evidence. This means that all ideas, theories, and hypotheses, regardless of how true they seem, must be systematically tested in the public arena. Moreover, the results of these tests—the observations—must be reliable. The finding of a single individual or laboratory is not enough; the event must be reproducible, under the circumstances stated, anywhere, anytime, and anyplace. If the event cannot be reproduced in varying situations, scientists become doubtful about the original observation and feel that it has only limited usefulness. Only the scientific method of attaining knowledge has this system of self-correction, demanding many built-in checks to assure objectivity.

A number of research tools are available that follow the requirements of the scientific method but differ in the way in which one can obtain information from them and the degree to which one can generalize and draw conclusions from them. Psychologists use the following three basic strategies: the experimental method, the correlational method, and the case-study method.

THE EXPERIMENTAL METHOD. With this method, the researcher manipulates some aspect of the environment and then measures the effect of this manipulation (or treatment, as it is sometimes called) by comparing the behavior of individuals who have received it with the behavior of otherwise similar individuals who have not. When properly used, the experimental method is the psychologist's most effective tool because it permits one to draw direct conclusions about cause and effect. As an example of the method, let us consider an experiment conducted by Liebert and Baron (1972) to test the general hypothesis that viewing violence on TV will increase the aggressive behavior of children. A group of 136 children (5 to 9 years of age) participated in the research. Each child was first taken to a room with a television set and then was told that he or she could watch a program that was on for a few minutes until the experimenter was ready. For the first 2 minutes all of the children saw two commercials. Then, some of them viewed a 3½-minute sequence from "The Untouchables," which showed a chase, two fist fights, two shootings, and a knifing. The rest of the children looked at an exciting sports event for the same length of time. Then, for the last minute, all of the children saw another commercial.

Each child was then escorted to another room and seated in front of a large box from which wires extended into another room. The box had a white light on it, beneath which there was a green button labeled "HELP" and a red button labeled "HURT." The experimenter explained that the wires were connected to a game a child in the other room was going to play. The game required turning a handle, and each time the other child did this the white light would go on. The experimenter explained that by pushing the buttons the subject could either help the other child by making the handle easier to turn or hurt him by making the handle hot. The more he pushed the buttons, the more he helped or hurt the other child. The subject was told that each time the white light went on he had to push one of the buttons. (In fact, there was no child in the other room; the white light was automatically set by the experimenter to come on a total of 20 times for each subject.) After making sure that the child understood the instructions, the experimenter left the room.

The results of the study, presented in Table 1.1, show the average duration of pushes on the HURT button among the two groups of children—those who saw the segment from "The Untouchables" and those who saw the sports event. Clearly, those who viewed even the brief sequence of violence on television were somewhat more aggressive than those who had not.

Major Components of an Experiment. The Liebert and Baron study is a true experiment, that is, it incorporates all the necessary aspects of the experimental method. From the general hypothesis that viewing violence on TV will increase the aggressive behavior of children, the investigators deduced a *specific experimental hypothesis:* that children who had just watched an excerpt from a highly violent TV program would be more willing to hurt another child in a game situation than would those who were otherwise similar but had just viewed a nonaggressive show.

TABLE 1.1

Duration of aggressive responses among children in the Liebert and Baron experiment.	
Type of TV program viewed	**Average duration of HURT responses (in seconds)**
Aggressive ("The Untouchables")	9.92
Nonaggressive (sports)	7.03

Source: Liebert and Baron (1972)

Next, the factor that was believed to have influenced the children's behavior—the content of the television program—was manipulated by the investigators: Some of the children were shown an aggressive program and others a nonaggressive one. The factor that is manipulated is called the *independent variable,* and the way in which it is done is called the *treatment.* The purpose of the experimental method is to identify one factor or variable that contributes to behavior by manipulating it while eliminating or holding constant all other distracting or extraneous variables. If manipulating the independent variable is associated with differences in behavior between groups that are otherwise comparable, the scientist can be certain that there is a direct cause-effect relationship between the manipulated variable (watching violence on a television program) and the behavior to be measured (hurting another child). The general term for the behavior that is to be measured is the *dependent variable* because the measure will *depend* in part on the treatment if the experimental hypothesis is correct. Thus, in the Liebert and Baron experiment, the dependent variable was the length of time that the children pushed the HURT button. This aggressive response was expected to depend in part on whether the children had seen the aggressive or the non-aggressive program.

The children who saw the aggressive program constituted the *treatment group* in Liebert and Baron's study, while the children who saw the nonaggressive program constituted the *control group.* The behavior of the control group provides a standard for comparing the effects of the independent variable. The comparison is only valid when the participants are assigned to the treatment or control group on a random basis (such as by drawing their names from a hat) so that each person would have an equal chance of being assigned to either group. With a large number of participants, *random assignment* will balance out the various characteristics other than the independent variable that might make a child aggressive. As we will see, it is precisely this random assignment to different treatments that distinguishes the experimental method from the correlational and case-study method.

Statistical Significance and Inference. Typically the results of an experiment such as Liebert and Baron's are presented so that the reader can note the average or mean score for each group (see Table 1.1).[1] A difference between the means indicates only that the particular groups

[1] A more detailed discussion of this and other statistics can be found in the Appendix (page 439).

in the experiment differed after receiving the treatment. This difference could be due to chance, in which case it would not repeat itself if the experiment were done again. (For example, even if both groups had seen only commercials, their scores probably would have been somewhat different simply because of chance.) Before deciding that we have a real effect, it is necessary to know if the finding is reliable. Although we can never be entirely positive about this, tests of statistical significance will enable us to determine how confident we can be of our inference that a particular outcome applies to children other than those who were in the actual experiment.

Essentially, *statistical significance* is the likelihood or probability that the outcome of a given experiment was produced by chance factors (in which case inferences drawn from the study would not be valid). A *significant difference*, an expression used in reporting the results of an experiment, means that there is a very low probability that the results occurred by chance, usually less than one chance in 20. Because one in 20 is the same as 5 in 100, this is often called the .05 level; it is usually written as "$p < .05$" and read as "probability less than point-oh-five." A result that would occur by chance only once in 100 times is written "$p < .01$" As used by psychologists, then, the word "significance" does not mean the importance of a finding but rather its trustworthiness. The difference shown in Table 1.1 is significant at $p < .05$.

Internal and External Validity. Not all the experiments conducted, even by trained researchers, provide valid information for answering the scientist's original question. An experiment is said to possess *internal validity* only when the result can be logically tied to the manipulation of a certain factor and to nothing else. Although chance error is handled by imposing statistical tests, other questions can also arise. Suppose, for example, that a researcher wanted to find out whether businessmen's headaches can really be relieved by aspirin, as the ads suggest. He randomly assigns his businessmen-subjects to two groups; those in the experimental group are asked to take two aspirin when their next headache appears, and those in the control group are asked not to take aspirin or any other medication. Each of the participants might also be requested to write down the exact time when his headache began and ended, and the difference between these two times for each individual would be his score on the dependent measure—duration of headache. But suppose that those in the experimental group washed down their aspirin with a beer, while those in the control group drank nothing and took no medication during their suffering. This would make the experiment internally *in*valid. Even if the two groups differed substantially in the length of time of their headache, with the experimental group suffering much less, the difference might be due to the beer and not with the intended independent variable—the aspirin. Possibly aspirin works alone, but any reasonable doubt makes this study invalid as a test of the hypothesis.

The extent to which the results of any particular piece of research can be generalized beyond the immediate experiment is the measure of their *external validity*. For example, in the Liebert-Baron television experiment, the researchers supposed that their findings would also apply to the effects of other violent programs on TV as viewed by other children. The external validity of the results of an experiment, unlike their internal validity, cannot usually be determined unless one goes beyond the limits of the experiment itself. This can sometimes be done by performing other experiments in different and preferably more natural contexts. But sometimes methods other than experimentation must be used to show that a finding is externally valid. Providing this type of confirmation or disconfirmation of experimental findings is one important use of the correlational method.

THE CORRELATIONAL METHOD. With this method, the researcher does *not* manipulate variables or introduce treatments, but only observes and measures the existing characteristics of people and events. In a correlational study of viewing TV violence and aggressive behavior, for example, the investigator would first determine the amount of violence shown on the TV programs individual children were watching at home. Next, each child's usual aggressiveness would be measured in his natural environment, perhaps by observing the child at a playground or by obtaining teacher's records of aggressive behavior in various school situations. Then, by examining the two variables together, it would be possible to see whether they were related. This method is not only inexpensive, compared with experiments, but attractive because it makes use of natural situations without disturbing them. There is a problem, however.

Suppose that a correlational study disclosed that viewing TV violence and aggressive behavior do go together. Children who look at a lot of TV violence are more aggressive in real life than those who see little or none of it. Does this mean that watching violent programs on TV causes increased aggression? Not necessarily. Since children may vary in their natural aggressiveness, relatively aggressive children may be more likely to enjoy TV violence *and* more likely to be aggressive with other children. In this case, viewing TV violence and aggressive behavior would go together (that is, they would be correlated positively), but we could not logically conclude that one was the *cause* of the other.

In general, then, we would say that the correlational method is useful in answering questions about relationships: "Do variable X and variable Y go together or vary together?" Psychologists ask many questions of this type: "Are child-rearing practices related to adult personality?" "Is one's anxiety level related to his scores on college examinations?" "Is the use of marijuana related to the later use of heroin?" "Are men more likely to perform well on math problems than women?" By testing, interviewing, surveying, and making field observations, we can answer these questions without manipulating anything.

But in none of these examples will the mere existence of a relationship, however strong, prove anything about cause and effect. A large correlation between two variables simply tells us that they are related or tend to covary with one another, but we do not really know whether one is caused by the other, or whether both might be caused by something else. Here is an example we have used before.

One regularly finds a high positive correlation between the number of churches in a city and the number of crimes committed in that city. That is, the more churches a city has, the more crimes are committed in it. Does this mean that religion fosters crime or does it mean that crime fosters religion? It means neither. The relationship is due to [another variable]—population. The higher the population of a particular community the greater . . . the number of churches and . . . the frequency of criminal activity [Neale and Liebert, 1973, p. 86].

The Meaning of Statistical Correlations. The correlational method requires pairs of observations on each member of a group of subjects, such as amount of TV violence viewed and frequency of aggressive behavior, or height and weight, or gender and math scores. Once these pairs of observations have been made, psychologists will usually ask two questions: "What is the *magnitude* or strength of the relationship between the two variables?" and "What is the *direction* of the relationship between them—positive or negative?" In other words, it is not enough to say that two variables are correlated; it is important to know *how much* and *which way*.

To measure the strength of a relationship, a numerical value, or statistic—the *correlation coefficient*—is usually computed. It may range from $+1.00$, which indicates a perfect positive relationship, to -1.00, which indicates a perfect negative relationship. The higher the value of the coefficient, whether positive or negative, the larger or stronger the relationship between the two variables; the $+$ or $-$ sign only indicates the direction. For example, a correlation of $+.87$ between people's annual income and their cash contribution to charity would indicate a strong positive relationship between these two variables; as annual income increases, so does the amount given to charity. On the other hand, a correlation of $-.87$ between annual income and attitude toward welfare programs would indicate an equally strong but negative relationship; as one's annual income rises, one has a less favorable view of welfare.

To have a better understanding of a particular relationship, it is often helpful to plot it graphically; several types of correlational relationships are diagramed in Figure 1.11. Each point on the graph corresponds to the two values that have been determined for the given subject—the values for Variable X and Variable Y. In perfect relationships ($+1.00$ or -1.00) all of the points fall on a single straight line:

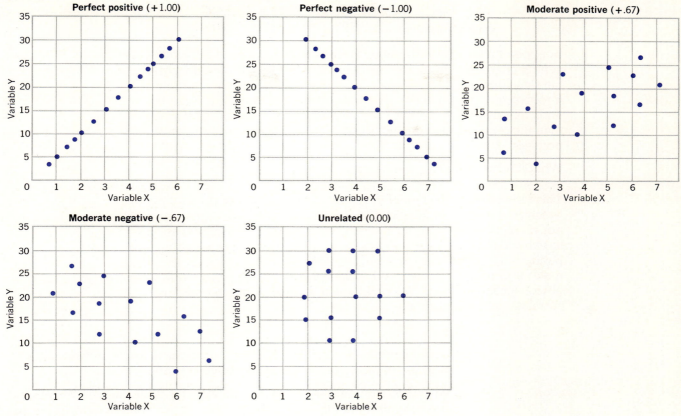

Figure 1.11
Various correlational relationships.

If we know the value of only one of the variables for a given individual, we know exactly what value we will have for the other variable. Similarly, when there is a relatively large correlation, there is only a small degree of scatter about the line of perfect correlation. As the correlations decrease, the values tend to become more scattered. When the correlation reaches 0.00, however, what we know about a person's score on one variable tells us absolutely nothing about his score on the other. In this case, the pattern will often look circular.

THE CASE-STUDY METHOD. Apart from introspection, most people only learn about human nature by observing others closely: "If you know someone well," it is said, "sooner or later you will find out what makes him tick." Understandably many psychologists are hesitant about calling the case-study method scientific. After all, there is no control group to act as a check on a single subject, and the person who does serve as a subject cannot be randomly assigned to a particular experimental situation. Also, any generalizations that could be made may actually apply only to a unique aspect of this one person. Hence, it would appear that studying a single individual would not be likely to yield any findings that would have internal or ex-

TESTING YOUR UNDERSTANDING
WHAT KIND OF RESEARCH IS THIS?

Suppose that a researcher hypothesizes that disordered thinking is the central characteristic of a particular type of psychosis—schizophrenia. He develops a test to measure thought disorder and then administers it to two groups of people—schizophrenics and normals. Then he finds that the schizophrenics actually do perform worse on the test than the normals and concludes that he has obtained support for his hypothesis.

What kind of research strategy has he used?

This research is *correlational* in nature. The variables of primary interest —schizophrenic-normal and disordered-nondisordered thinking—were not manipulated nor could the subjects have been randomly assigned to either condition. Psychologists often do this type of research in comparing naturally existing groups; for example, children of varying ages, males and females, blacks and whites. These correlational studies are obviously subject to all the problems that arise in interpreting any correlational investigation.

ternal validity. But, as we shall see, studying a single subject can be of *some* use as a research technique for certain purposes.

With this method, the researcher gathers together current, historical, and biographical information about one person. These descriptive accounts have been used in studying abnormal behavior and personality in at least four ways: (1) to demonstrate important, often novel, methods or procedures for interviewing, diagnosis, and treatment; (2) to provide a detailed account of a rare or unusual phenomenon; (3) to disconfirm allegedly universal aspects of a particular theoretical proposition; and (4) to generate hypotheses for future controlled research.

A famous case history of *multiple personality* reported by Thigpen and Cleckley in 1954 illustrates several of the foregoing purposes. The investigators studied a patient, "Eve White," who displayed at various times three very distinct personalities. Eve White had been seen in psychotherapy for several months because she was experiencing severe headaches accompanied by blackouts. Her therapist described her as a retiring and gently conventional girl. One day during the course of an interview, however, she changed abruptly and in a surprising way:

As if seized by sudden pain, she put both hands to her head. After a tense moment of silence, both hands dropped. There was a quick, reckless smile, and, in a bright voice that sparkled, she said, "Hi there, Doc!" The demure and constrained posture of Eve White had melted into buoyant repose. . . . This new and apparently carefree girl spoke casually of Eve White and her problems, always using she *or* her *in every reference, always respecting the strict bounds of a separate identity. . . .*

When asked her name, she immediately replied, "Oh, I'm Eve Black"
[1954, p. 137].

After this rather startling revelation, Eve was observed over a period of 14 months in a series of interviews that totaled almost 100 hours. During this time a third personality, Jane, emerged. The case of Eve White, Eve Black, and Jane constitutes a valuable classic in the psychiatric literature because it is one of only a few detailed accounts of a rare phenomenon—multiple personality. Besides illustrating the phenomenon itself, Thigpen and Cleckley's original report provides valuable details about the interview procedures that they followed and sheds light on the way in which this multiple personality may have developed and how one case was ultimately resolved.

Despite its value in the case just described, the case-study method has an inherent scientific weakness. Specifically, it has no controls for logically ruling out alternative explanations. To illustrate this problem, we will briefly describe a case study that received much public attention in its day—the case of Bridey Murphy.

Under hypnosis, a New England woman "regressed," apparently beyond her early childhood and back into an earlier life in which she was Bridey Murphy, an Irish girl. When hypnotized she was able to report many remarkable details of a town in Ireland that she had never visited, speaking in a Gaelic brogue while giving her description. Her case history supposedly demonstrated a true instance of reincarnation. Later, however, it was learned that the woman had been reared, in part, by an Irish maid from whom she had learned about Ireland. The maid's own accent had provided an excellent model for the brogue that the woman later produced under hypnosis as convincingly as if it were her own. At least in this instance, it is apparent that the hypothesis presented by the case history lacked validity.

PLAN OF THIS BOOK In this chapter we have briefly touched on the history of psychology and on its contemporary areas of interest and methods.

Subsequent chapters will discuss each of the basic processes (such as perception, learning, and cognition) and each of the present-day specialty areas (such as the study of social and abnormal behavior). Each chapter contains a brief glossary for easy reference as well as a summary of the major ideas and findings presented. Other features of the book are less traditional: Periodically we invite readers to test their understanding of some of the material (in this chapter, see page 20). Because learning is most effective when it is an active process, we want to encourage immediate reflection on certain ideas.

In all areas, we have purposely tried to emphasize research with human beings (rather than animals) and to include studies that have been done in interesting or imaginative ways. Psychology can be fun for its practitioners and should also be enjoyed by those who read about it. But beyond this, the entire discipline may help us learn how to cope with or even avoid certain human problems and suffering. Toward this end, each of the following chapters concludes with a section entitled "Psychology and the Problems of Society," illustrating how a basic psychological concept has been successfully applied to a practical social issue.

SUMMARY

Psychology is a relatively new science that emerged from philosophy in the late nineteenth century. Two major lines of thinking—the rational (based on reasoning and logic) and the empirical (based on direct observation and experience)—converged to lay the foundation for psychology. The first psychology laboratory was begun by Wilhelm Wundt in 1879. Wundt also founded the first school of psychology—structuralism—which attempted to study conscious experience through introspection. Other early schools included functionalism, which, influenced by Darwinian thinking, examined the adaptive functions of the mind and behavior, and Gestalt psychology, which focused on the patterns and relationships that constitute a whole event. Watson, who was influenced by Pavlov's conditioning experiments, redefined psychology in the early twentieth century as the science of behavior. Behaviorism rejected subjective experiences (such as consciousness) as inappropriate for scientific study and discarded introspection in favor of objective observation of external events. Sigmund Freud's therapeutic method of psychoanalysis led to the development of a theory of personality that emphasized the importance of unconscious motives. Other significant factors include the influence of Alfred Binet, the father of the modern IQ test, and the influence of Hull and Tolman, whose grand-scale learning theories failed to explain behavior adequately and therefore discouraged others from following in their footsteps.

The definition of psychology has varied over time. In its early years, psychology was the study of consciousness; with the advent of behaviorism (which is still among the most widely accepted approaches), it was simply defined as "the scientific study of behavior." Renewed interest in both the cognitive processes and the biological basis of behavior suggests that an appropriate contemporary definition would be "the scientific study of behavior and related mental and physical processes." Today there are many different kinds of psychologists, each with a particular specialty or area of interest. Some psychologists primarily do research and teaching at the college level, while others work in applied settings.

Science represents an agreed-upon method for solving problems; there are specific procedures for collecting and interpreting data in order to build a systematic body of knowledge. Scientific statements must be testable in the public arena and must be based on reliable observations. There are three specific methods of investigation used by psychologists.

In the *experimental method*, independent variables are manipulated and their effects on dependent variables are carefully measured. An experiment begins with a hypothesis to be tested. Generally, subjects are assigned at random to at least two groups: an experimental (or treatment) group, which experiences the manipulation of the independent variable, and a control group, which does not. Random assignment tends to ensure that the two groups do not differ from each other at the beginning; then, if differences are observed in the dependent variable between the experimental and control groups, one can conclude that the independent variable was the cause. Statistically significant results are those that have a low probability of occurring simply by chance (usually less than one chance in 20) and are therefore acceptable as evidence. If all these conditions are met and one has manipulated the independent variable properly, the experiment will be internally valid. However, the external validity of the findings, that is, their generalizability to other situations, can be assessed only by performing similar experiments under other conditions and also by checking the findings against those obtained with other methods.

When variables that interest psychologists are difficult or impossible to manipulate experimentally, the *correlational method* is often used. Correlation refers to the extent to which two or more variables go together or vary together. A correlation coefficient is the statistic indicating the degree of relationship and ranges from $+1.00$ to -1.00. However, unlike experimental findings, the results of correlational studies alone do not indicate cause and effect.

Finally, the *case-study method*, while containing numerous sources of bias that are inevitable when the behavior of only one person is examined, nonetheless permits the psychologist to study rare phenomena in all their complexity.

GLOSSARY

Behaviorism: The school of psychology, founded by John Watson, which asserts that the relationship between observable stimuli and responses is the only appropriate subject matter of psychology.

Case study: A research procedure by which current, historical, and biographical information is collected for a single individual.

Control group: An essential part of any experiment, this group of subjects does not experience the researcher's manipulation and thus constitutes a standard against which the treatment effects can be compared.

Correlation coefficient: A statistic or numerical value indicating the degree of relationship between two sets of data (for example, height and weight).

Correlational method: A research procedure for finding the relationship between variables; causality cannot be inferred in studies using this method.

Dependent variable: In an experiment, the behavior that is expected to vary with (or depend upon) the independent variable.

Experimental hypothesis: A testable statement of the relationship between two or more variables.

Experimental method: This is the most effective research technique because it allows causal relationships to be determined; this method includes at least one control group and random assignment.

External validity: The extent to which experimental findings can be generalized to other populations, settings, treatments, and so forth.

Functionalism: An early school of psychology that focused on the adaptive functions behavior and consciousness.

Gestalt psychology: An early school of psychology that emphasized the patterns, organization, and wholeness of human experience.

Independent variable: In an experiment, the factor that is controlled by the experimenter and is expected to influence the subject's behavior.

Internal validity: Quality attributed to experiments that have been designed and conducted so that competing explanations of their findings are implausible.

Introspection: A procedure used by early psychologists to try to describe the contents of the mind; accordingly, trained observers reported the experiences produced by various stimuli.

Psychoanalysis: A therapeutic method developed by Freud for treating mental patients. Freud's theory of personality, which stresses the importance of unconscious motives, was based on his experiences with the psychoanalytic method.

Psychology: The scientific study of behavior and related mental and physical processes.

Random assignment: The procedure used in experiments to make sure that each subject has an equal chance of being assigned to any of the groups.

Science: Systematized knowledge that is secured by means of observation, experimentation, and theory construction.

Statistical significance: Research results that have a low probability of occurring simply because of chance.

Structuralism: An early school of psychology that emphasized introspection to reveal the basic elements of consciousness and the structure of the mind.

Treatment group: In an experiment, the group of subjects that is exposed to the researcher's manipulation (as opposed to the control group which is not).

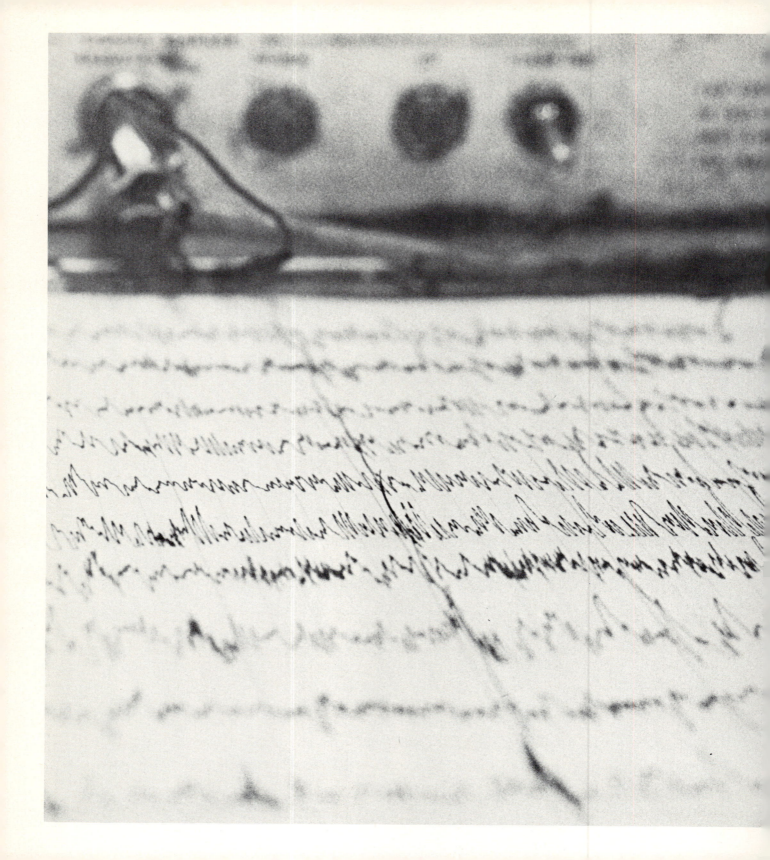

TWO

PSYCHO-BIOLOGY

What confused me, and Woody himself, in the early stage . . . was that he was a rather moody person. As early as 1948, we began to notice that he was more reflective, and often depressed by trivial things. . . . [Later] Woody developed a peculiar lopsided walk and his speech became explosive. He would take a deep sigh before breathing out the words. The moods and depression became more exaggerated and more frequent. . . . [Within the next four years] the disease was making rapid progress. Woody found it increasingly difficult to control his movements, appearing to be drunk

28

even when he wasn't drinking. Friends watched him with apprehension as he dived into traffic, oblivious to danger, Chaplinlike, warding off each car as it sped toward him [Yurchenko, 1970, pp. 139ff.]

In the preceding passage, Marjorie Guthrie relates the onset of Huntington's chorea, a genetically determined brain disease, in her husband Woody, the famous American folksinger. This tragic example clearly illustrates the close relationship between the brain and behavior. Emotions, speech, and motor movements are all affected by this disorder.

Although we are often interested in the relationship between various aspects of the environment and behavior, we recognize that the biological systems of the organism intervene between these two classes of events. Therefore, it can be more productive to try to understand the relationship among biological functioning, environment, and behavior. We will now survey the broad field of psychobiology, focusing on the relevance of various biological factors to certain important types of behavior.

STRUCTURE OF THE NERVOUS SYSTEM

NEURONS AND TRANSMISSION. The nervous system is composed of two types of cells: *Glial* cells provide a framework for the other cells, insulating them from one another, absorbing nutrients from the bloodstream, and removing dead cells. More important are the nerve cells or *neurons*, the active elements for internal communication. Each of the billions of neurons in the body, although differing in some respects, has four major parts: (1) the *cell body*, (2) one or more *axons*, (3) several *dendrites*, and (4) *terminal boutons* (endings) attached to the end branches of the axon(s) (see Figures 2.1 and 2.2). The neuron, which is stimulated at its cell body or through dendrites, transmits a nerve impulse along its axon to the terminal endings. The speed of the nerve impulse varies from 10–25 mph, depending upon several factors including the diameter of the axon. The nerve impulse, itself an electrical event, is produced by chemical changes in the axon and cell body. Nerve impulses follow an all-or-nothing principle; that is, they do not vary in strength. Once an impulse is started it follows through to the end; also, a strong stimulus will elicit exactly the *same kind* of nerve impulse as a weak one. The nervous system, though, can respond differently to strong and weak stimuli; strong stimuli will generate nerve impulses at a *faster rate* (Gardner, 1963).

Information, in the form of nerve impulses, is transmitted from one neuron to another; however, since neurons are not in direct contact with one another, a mechanism is needed to bridge the gap. Thus, we have the *synapse*—a 0.00002 mm. cleft between adjacent neurons (see Figure 2.3). The terminal bouton of the axon contains *synaptic vesicles*, small structures that are filled with chemicals called *transmitter substances*. Nerve impulses cause the synaptic vesicles to

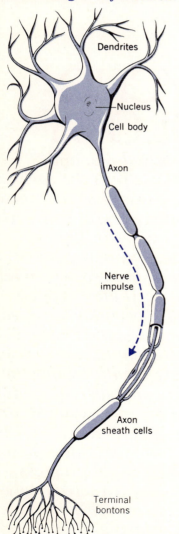

**Figure 2.1
Schematic diagram of a neuron.**

Dendrites
Nucleus
Cell body
Axon
Nerve impulse
Axon sheath cells
Terminal bontons

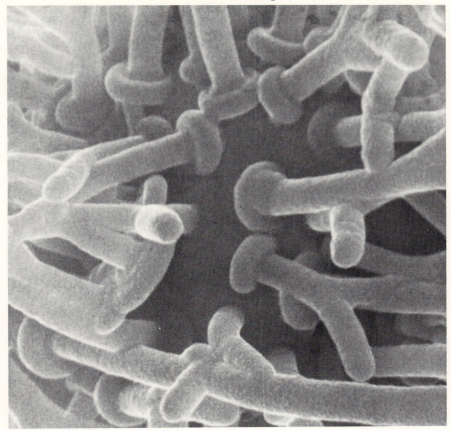

Figure 2.2
A scanning electron micrograph of the knob-like endings of a sea slug's axons.

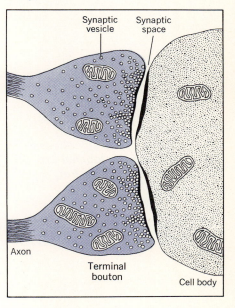

Figure 2.3
A synapse, showing two axons in close contact with a single cell body.

release their transmitter substances which then cross the synaptic cleft. At that point the transmitter substances will affect the adjacent neuron in either of two ways—excitation or inhibition. In the first case the rate of firing of the neuron is increased; in the second case it is decreased. Generally, transmission across a single synapse can either excite or inhibit another neuron, but not both.

THE CENTRAL NERVOUS SYSTEM. The nervous system is believed to have two major components—the central and the peripheral. (The structure and function of the peripheral nervous system will be described later.) The central nervous system is viewed as being made up of two major parts: *the spinal cord* and the *brain*. About 24 inches in length in the adult, the spinal cord extends from the brain to the lower back. A cross section of the cord is shown in Figure 2.4. Note the H-shaped area of *gray matter* surrounded by so-called *white matter*. The gray matter is composed mainly of nerve cell bodies, while the white matter contains the axons of cell bodies.

The brain, which is located within the protective covering of the skull, is enveloped in three layers of nonneural tissue—membranes

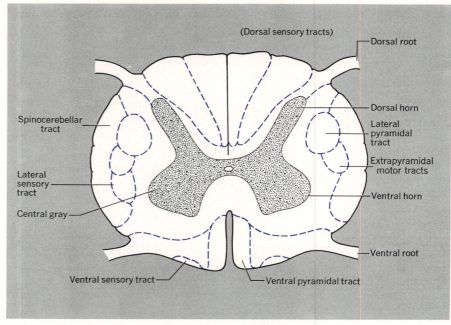

Figure 2.4
Cross section of the spinal cord. The tracts that are labeled are bundles of nerve fibers that serve particular functions.

that are called *meninges*. Viewed from the top, the brain is divided by a midline fissure into two mirror-image *cerebral hemispheres*—in man these constitute most of the *cerebrum*. The two hemispheres are connected by a band of nerve fibers called the *corpus callosum*. Figure 2.5 shows the surface of one of the cerebral hemispheres. The upper, side, and some of the lower surfaces of the hemispheres constitute the *cerebral cortex*, which is made up of six layers of tightly packed neuron cell bodies with many short interconnections. These neurons, about 10 to 15 billion in number, comprise a thin outer covering of

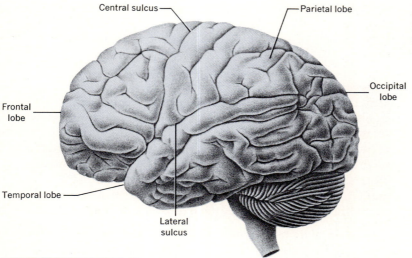

Figure 2.5
Surface of one of the cerebral hemispheres, showing the principal areas of the cortex.

the so-called gray matter of the brain. The human cortex is very convoluted; the ridges are called *gyri* and the depressions between them *sulci* (or fissures). Deep fissures divide the cerebral hemispheres into several distinct areas called *lobes*. The *frontal lobe* lies in front of the central sulcus; the *parietal lobe* is behind it and above the lateral sulcus; the *temporal lobe* is located below the lateral sulcus; and the *occipital* lobe lies behind the parietal and temporal lobes. Different physical and mental functions tend to be related to particular areas of the lobes—vision seems to be controlled in the occipital; discrimination of sounds in the temporal; reasoning and other higher mental processes, as well as the regulation of fine voluntary movements in the frontal; sensations from the muscles in a band in front of the central sulcus; sensations from the skin in a band behind this sulcus; and so forth.

If the brain is sliced in half vertically, separating the two cerebral hemispheres (Figure 2.6), additional important features can be seen. The gray matter of the cerebral cortex does not extend throughout the interior of the brain. Much of the interior is white matter and is made up of large tracts (or bundles) of myelinated (insulated) fibers that connect cell bodies in the cortex with those in the spinal cord and in other centers elsewhere in the lower brain. These centers are additional pockets of gray matter, called *nuclei*. Some cortical cells project their long fibers (or axons) to motor neurons in the spinal cord, while others extend them only as far as nuclei deeper in the brain. Many of the axons originating on one side of the brain descend to the opposite side of the spinal cord. One important implication of this fact, which will be discussed later, is that the right side of the brain tends to control the left side of the body, and vice versa.

There are four nuclei deep within each hemisphere, called collectively the *basal ganglia*. Other important areas and structures of the brain

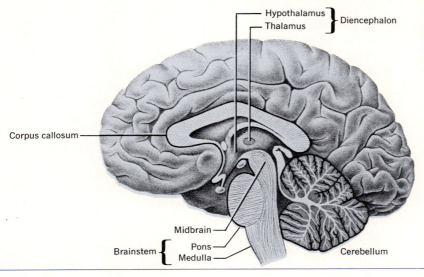

Figure 2.6
Slice of brain through the medial plane, showing the internal structures.

Hypothalamus
Thalamus
} Diencephalon

Corpus callosum

Midbrain
Brainstem { Pons
Medulla

Cerebellum

32

also contain nuclei. The nuclei serve as way stations, connecting the tracts from the cortex with other ascending and descending tracts, as well as integrating motor and sensory control centers (Gardner, 1963).

In addition to the corpus callosum, the four important functional areas of structures depicted in Figure 2.6 are:

1. The *diencephalon*, which is connected in front with the two hemispheres and at the back with the midbrain, contains the *thalamus* and the *hypothalamus*. The thalamus is a relay station for all sensory pathways except olfaction, that is, the sense of smell. Its nuclei receive nearly all impulses that arrive from the different sensory areas of the body before passing them on to the cerebrum, where they are interpreted as conscious sensations. The hypothalamus is the highest center of integration for many visceral processes; its nuclei regulate metabolism, temperature, water balance, sweating, blood pressure, sleep, and appetite.

2. The *midbrain* is a mass of nerve-fiber tracts that connect the cerebral cortex with the pons, the medulla oblongata, the cerebellum, and the spinal cord.

3. The *brainstem*, which is made up of the *pons* and *medulla oblongata*, serves primarily as a neural relay station. The pons contains tracts that connect the cerebellum with the spinal cord and the cerebellum with the motor areas of the cerebrum. The medulla oblongata is the main connecting link for the spinal cord tracts that ascend to or descend from the higher centers of the brain. It also contains nuclei that maintain the normal rhythm of the heartbeat, the diaphragm, and the constricting and dilating blood vessels. At the core of the brainstem is the *reticular formation,* which is sometimes called the reticular activating system because of the role it plays in arousal from sleep and maintenance of alertness. The tracts of the pons and medulla have fibers that connect them with the profusely interconnected cells of the reticular formation which, in turn, have fibers connecting them with the cortex, the basal ganglia, the hypothalamus, the septal area, and the cerebellum.

4. The *cerebellum*, like the cerebrum, is largely made up of two deeply convoluted hemispheres with an exterior cortex of gray matter and an interior of white tracts. The cerebellum receives sensory nerves from the vestibular apparatus of the ear as well as from the muscles, tendons, and joints. This information, which is received and integrated, relates to balance, posture, and the smooth coordination of the body when in motion.

A fifth important part of the brain, which does not appear in Figure 2.6, is the *limbic system*—lower parts of the cerebrum that probably came into existence at an earlier evolutionary period than the mammalian cerebral cortex. It is made up of a cortex that is phylogenetically older than the so-called neocortex that covers most of the cerebral hemispheres. The limbic system controls the visceral and physical expression of emotion—quickened heartbeat and respiration, trembling, sweating, and alterations in facial expressions—and the expression of appetitive and motivational drives—hunger, thirst, mating, defense, attack, and flight. We will have more to say about the structure and function of the limbic system later.

Figure 2.7
Examples of areas of the brain that influence various emotions and reactions.

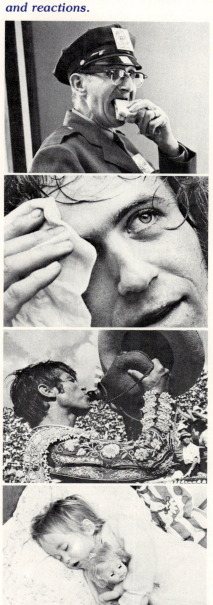

Hypothalamus
(controls hunger, sweating, thirst, sleep)

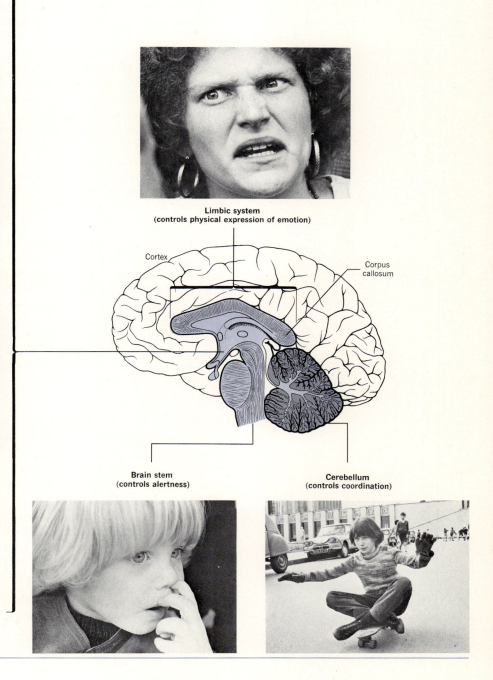

Limbic system
(controls physical expression of emotion)

Cortex

Corpus callosum

Brain stem
(controls alertness)

Cerebellum
(controls coordination)

34

THE BRAIN AND BEHAVIOR

We will now examine several of the ways in which psychologists have attempted to relate brain functioning to specific kinds of behavior. In so doing we will discuss three research strategies that have been used. The first, and most molar, is the study of brain waves produced by the firing of thousands of neurons; the second is the stimulation and/or destruction of discrete areas of the brain; and the third, the most molecular, is the examination of the activity of single nerve cells within the nervous system.

BRAIN WAVES. The brain is now known to be continuously active, chemically and electrically, throughout life, even during sleep. Individual neurons are firing, creating differences in electrical potential (that is, fluctuations in voltage). In 1924 Hans Berger, a German psychiatrist who had become interested in brain research following an apparent instance of telepathic communication between himself and his sister, recorded these electrical potentials in a patient with a congenital opening in his skull. In his early work Berger found what appeared to be regular patterns of brain activity. Today, it is no longer necessary to record directly from the brain; research can be done on brain rhythms using an electroencephalograph.

The electroencephalogram (EEG) is a graphic recording of the electrical activity of the brain. The fluctuations in voltage in the cortex, that portion of the brain that is directly below the skull, can be picked up by two or more sensitive electrodes pasted to the scalp. The recording machine, the electroencephalograph, amplifies the pulsations 1–2 million times and connects them to a pen recorder (or recorders) that registers them on graph paper as a pattern of oscillations. Although the EEG can only provide us with gross information about brain function since it reflects the net result of the activity of millions of neurons, certain interesting relationships between EEG and behavior have been observed.

In a normal adult subject who is awake but resting quietly with his eyes closed, the dominant rhythm has a frequency of between 8 and 13 pulsations or cycles per second (cps) and an amplitude of from 40 to 50 microvolts. This low-frequency, high-voltage wave is called the *alpha* rhythm. When a stimulus is presented, the alpha rhythm is replaced by a high-frequency (14 to 25 cps), low-voltage pattern—the *beta* rhythm. If very low-frequency waves predominate in the awake adult, they are considered abnormal. These slow waves are called *theta* (4 to 7 cps) and *delta* (less than 4 cps) rhythms. Delta rhythms occur during deep sleep; theta waves are recorded from subcortical parts of the brain. These rhythms are illustrated in Figure 2.8.

The Alpha Rhythm. Because of the recent popularity of biofeedback, there has been an interest in the alpha rhythm, which is produced by most people only part of the time. In the 1960s J. Kamiya began a series of investigations on self-control of the alpha rhythm. First, he

A	Three-day-old infant	
B	Six-month-old infant	
C	Four-year-old child	
D	Adult, relaxed wakefulness (alpha waves) interrupted by attentiveness (beta waves)	
E	Adult, deep sleep (delta waves)	
F	Adult, abnormal slow wave (theta waves)	

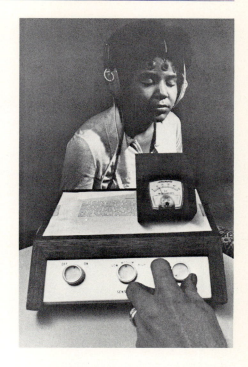

Figure 2.8 (Above)
Patterns of electrical activity in the brain as recorded by an electroencephalograph. [Source: Hare (1970)]

Figure 2.9 (Right)
Subject participating in a biofeedback experiment.

asked people whether they could discriminate alpha from non-alpha; the subjects were connected to the EEG machine and simply asked at various times whether their brain waves were in state A (alpha) or state B (non-alpha). With appropriate feedback most people could readily learn to distinguish between them. Later on he also demonstrated that people can learn either to enhance alpha production or to reduce it (Kamiya, 1969). Significantly, Kamiya also found that, subjectively, his research participants preferred alpha to non-alpha and that those with previous training in meditation were particularly good at producing the alpha rhythm.

These findings eventually led to the current popularity of trying to increase alpha. Portable machines (many of them promising much more than they can deliver) are now available, permitting those who hope to attain expanded consciousness, tranquility, or an improved self-image to try to increase alpha in the comfort of their own homes. What seems most appealing about the technique is that it may be a shortcut to the elevated states of consciousness that are usually possible only after many years of tutelage by a guru or a master of Zen. Does alpha really hold this much promise? At this point we cannot say. Although alpha is obviously pleasant and relaxing, it is not clear whether it can help us reach a different level of awareness of ourselves and our world.

Sleep. What happens when we sleep and why is it a necessary part of life? In doing some early work on this topic, Nathaniel Kleitman, a

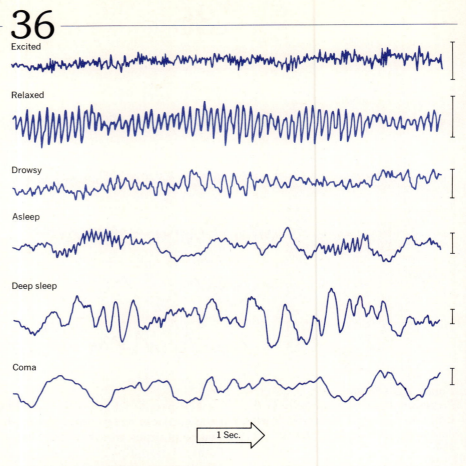

Excited

Relaxed

Drowsy

Asleep

Deep sleep

Coma

1 Sec.

Figure 2.10
EEG wave patterns that occur in different states of arousal and during the various stages of sleep. Note the sleep spindles that begin to appear during Stage 2 (asleep). [Source: Milner (1970)]

physiologist at the University of Chicago, observed cyclical changes in the EEG during sleep. At times the EEG showed a pattern that looked like wakefulness and was accompanied by restlessness. His early observations and the subsequent studies they inspired allow us to identify five stages of sleep:

Stage 1. This is the beginning of sleep. The eyes close, breathing deepens, the muscles relax, and the body slows down. This stage lasts from 1 to 7 minutes and is accompanied by various EEG rhythms (see Figure 2.10).

Stage 2. This is the beginning of true sleep. The EEG slows down and the first *sleep spindles*, short bursts of heightened activity, appear.

Stage 3. Now, 30 minutes after sleep has begun, it would be more difficult to awaken our sleeper. Bodily processes have slowed down even more and delta waves begin to appear.

Stage 4. At this time the delta waves have become the predominant EEG pattern. During this period of deepest sleep, bodily processes are at their slowest; sleepwalking and sleeptalking may occur.

Stage REM. About 90 minutes after entering Stage 4, the EEG returns to a pattern resembling Stage 1. This is the wakeful pattern associated with restlessness that was first noticed by Kleitman. The name of this stage is derived from the fact that it is accompanied by *R*apid *E*ye *M*ovements. During this stage dreaming occurs; when awakened from a period of REM sleep, about 80 percent of the subjects reported that they had been in the midst of a dream (Dement and Kleitman, 1957).[1] After a period of REM, the entire sleep cycle repeats itself, but Stage 4 becomes less frequent as sleep proceeds.

Sleep Deprivation. We began by asking why sleep is necessary. Now we can partially reformulate that question by considering the necessity of various sleep stages. To study this issue, a participant would be systematically awakened over the course of a number of nights only when he was in the particular stage being studied. A pioneering study of this type was conducted by Dement (1960) on REM sleep. Some participants were awakened whenever the EEG and eye movement recording indicated that they had entered REM. Others were awakened for equivalent periods but only during non-REM sleep. The importance of REM sleep was demonstrated by the fact that REM-deprived subjects showed a sharp increase in REM sleep following the deprivation period. Further, after several REM-less nights, the subjects became anxious, irritable, and tired, and had difficulty concentrating. Why is REM sleep necessary? One answer links the absence of REM to the associated lack of dreams. Perhaps, as Freud suggested, dreaming fulfills certain essential psychological functions.

[1] All of us apparently dream, but unless we awaken shortly after REM sleep, the dream has already been forgotten. In addition, it is not clear that dreaming takes place only during REM sleep. Foulkes (1967), for example, has reported the substantial recall of dreams from non-REM stages. One difficulty lies in defining the word "dream." Studies reporting high frequencies of non-REM dreams typically have used less stringent criteria.

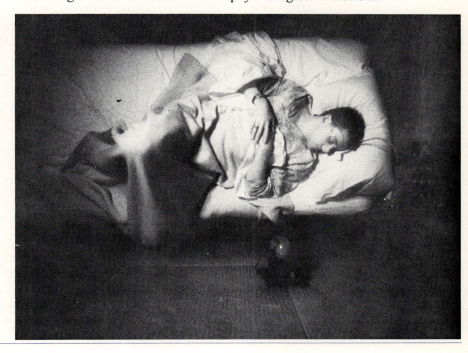

Figure 2.11
Subject participating in an experiment on sleep and dreaming. When he awakens he will use the telephone to call the experimenter.

Stage 4 sleep, like REM, appears to be biologically necessary. Selective deprivation of Stage 4 sleep leads to a "rebound effect" on subsequent nights (Agnew, Webb, and Williams, 1964), and several nights of Stage 4-deprived sleep produces disruptive effects on behavior (Luby, Frohman, Grisell, Lenzo, Cohen, and Gottlich, 1960). At present it is believed that Stage 4 may be a recovery period. The synapses become biochemically fatigued during one's waking hours and finally trigger inhibitory mechanisms that lead to sleep. Then, during Stage 4, the body restores the necessary chemical components so that the person can begin the next day refreshed.

DESTROYING OR STIMULATING DISCRETE BRAIN AREAS.

Having examined correlations between behavior and brain rhythms produced by the firing of thousands of neurons, let us now turn to studies where specific areas of the brain are either surgically destroyed or stimulated chemically or electrically in order to explore the particular function of those areas. At a simple level the results of such studies seem to be easily interpretable: If an animal becomes a glutton, for example, after parts of its hypothalamus have been destroyed, it would be tempting to conclude that the hypothalamus is a "center" that controls hunger. This conclusion, however, would not be justified. The destroyed area could control the jaw movements that are used in eating but have nothing to do with hunger as such. As we turn to an example of this kind of research, we must keep in mind the complexities in interpreting the data.

Aggression, the Limbic System, and the Hypothalamus. On the night of July 31, 1968, the following letter was written:

I don't really understand myself these days. I am supposed to be an average, reasonable and intelligent young man. However, lately (I can't recall when it started) I have been a victim of many unusual and irrational thoughts. These thoughts constantly recur, and it requires a tremendous mental effort to concentrate on useful and progressive tasks. In March when my parents made a physical break I noticed a great deal of stress. I consulted a Dr. Cochrum at the University Health Center and asked him to recommend someone that I could consult with about some psychiatric disorders I felt I had. I talked with a Doctor once for about two hours and tried to convey to him my fears that I felt overcome . . . by overwhelming violent impulses. After one session I never saw the Doctor again, and since then I have been fighting my mental turmoil alone, and seemingly to no avail. After my death I wish that an autopsy would be performed on me to see if there is any visible physical disorder. I have had some tremendous headaches in the past and have consumed two large bottles of Excedrin in the past three months. . . .

It was after much thought that I decided to kill my wife, Kathy, tonight after I pick her up from work. . . . I love her dearly, and she has been a fine wife to me as any man could ever hope to have. I cannot rationally pinpoint any specific reason for doing this. I don't know whether it is selfishness, or if I don't want her to have to face the embarrassment my actions would surely cause her. At this time though, the prominent reason in my mind is that I truly do not consider this world worth living in, and am prepared to die, and I do not want to leave her to suffer alone in it. I intend to kill her as painlessly as possible.

Later that same night, after killing both his mother and his wife, he wrote the following:

I imagine it appears that I brutally killed both of my loved ones. I was only trying to do a good, thorough job.

If my life insurance policy is valid please see that all the worthless checks I wrote this weekend are made good. Please pay off all my debts. I am 25 years old and have never been financially independent. Donate the rest anonymously to a mental health foundation. Maybe research can prevent further tragedies of this type.

The following morning Charles Whitman barricaded himself in a tower at the University of Texas. Armed with a high-powered rifle, he proceeded to shoot 33 people, killing 15, until he was shot and killed. An autopsy revealed a walnut-sized tumor located in the amygdala (Sweet, Ervin, and Mark, 1969). Certainly we should not conclude that all or even most violent behavior is due to brain tumors. Cases like Whitman's, however, as well as animal research suggest that an area of the brain known as the *limbic system* plays a role in aggression.

The limbic system is a collection of structures located in the upper brain stem and cerebrum; they are interconnected and also closely linked to the hypothalamus. The major structures in the limbic system are the *amygdala,* a large nucleus deep within the temporal lobe; the *hippocampus,* a long structure in the cerebrum; the *septal region,* a nucleus in the deep forebrain; the *olfactory projection areas,* which receive information from the sense of smell; and several areas known as "old cortex," which means that they are also found in more primitive organisms (see Figure 2.12). At one time it was believed that this part of the brain was only concerned with the sense of smell, and so it was called "rhinencephalon" (nose-brain). By the mid-1930s, however, it became clear that these limbic structures had additional functions.

In 1938 Kluver and Bucy produced widespread lesions in the temporal lobes, including the amygdala, of monkeys. After recovery the monkeys became playful, nonaggressive, and oversexed, and appeared to have a memory problem (one, for example, put a lit cigarette in its mouth, let the cigarette fall out while howling with pain, and then picked the cigarette up again and put it right back into its mouth).[1] Much of the research that followed Kluver and Bucy's original finding focused on the reduction of aggressiveness after removal or destruction of the amygdala. This research also showed that other areas of the brain that are closely connected with the limbic system could produce aggression when they were electrically stimulated; the most significant of these is the hypothalamus, a set of nuclei lying below the thalamus at the base of the forebrain.

[1]Subsequent research showed that the crucial feature of the so-called Kluver-Bucy syndrome was the removal of the amygdala.

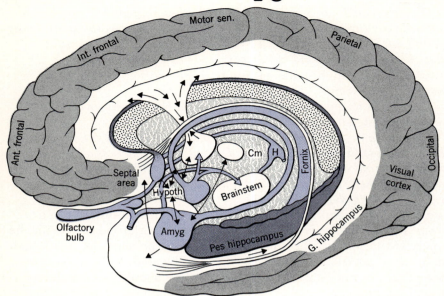

Figure 2.12
Major structures in the limbic
system.

Wasman and Flynn (1962) decided to study a group of cats that normally behaved in a nonviolent way toward rats. Small electrodes were implanted in the lateral (side) areas of the hypothalamus. It was found that high levels of electrical stimulation produced "quiet biting attacks." With no apparent signs of rage (for example, back arching or hissing), a stimulated cat would walk calmly over to a rat and kill it. A different pattern, however, emerged if the medial (mid-section) hypothalamus were stimulated. The cat would launch an "affective attack"; with hissing noises, wide eyes, and hairs erect, it would attack anything and everything—even inanimate objects (Egger and Flynn, 1963). As might be expected, because of the close connection between the limbic system and the hypothalamus, the effects of stimulating one structure depend, in part, on the state of the other. For example, when the amygdala has been destroyed, stimulating the hypothalamus can more easily provoke attacks (Egger and Flynn, 1963). Thus, from the data reviewed so far it would appear that the amygdala and hypothalamus are neural control centers for aggression.

Problems in Asserting That a Neural Control Center Has Been Identified. Earlier we mentioned that problems arise in interpreting the results of surgical removal or stimulation studies. Now, with our data on aggression in hand, let us return to these issues and see how well the facts stand up under closer scrutiny. First we must note that the degree of control and predictability is somewhat less than is usually implied in textbook presentations. Some animals do not respond to stimulation, and surgical removal of what appears to the same area produces different effects in different animals (Valenstein, 1973). Next we must ask to what extent the results have general applicability or external validity.

Kling, Lancaster, and Benitone (1970) have reported how an amygdalectomy has affected the behavior of monkeys who were returned to their natural habitat after the surgery. As in the classic Kluver and Bucy report, the authors found that the animals became more friendly and less aggressive during their period of confinement after the operation. But once they were returned to the wild, the animals seemed to be somewhat confused and fearful and they often behaved inappropriately. Instead of staying within the hierarchical social order that prevails among monkeys, they sometimes attacked higher-status males while acting submissively toward those of lower status. Most soon became social isolates, and all eventually died of starvation or were killed.

With such evidence, it is difficult to maintain that the primary effect of removing the amygdala is to reduce aggressiveness. Perhaps the animal becomes less able to link new stimuli with past experience (recall Kluver and Bucy's monkey who repeatedly put the lit cigarette into its mouth). Such reduced ability may make a monkey less likely to display aggression toward humans, but the principal result of the operation is interference with cognitive processes, including memory.

Splitting the Brain. As you will recall, the brain consists of two hemispheres joined together by a band of nerve fibers called the *corpus callosum.* Thus, the two hemispheres can communicate with one another. In general, most brain structures can be found in both hemispheres. But are certain functions located in one or the other hemisphere, and what exactly is the function of the corpus callosum? To answer these questions, we must close off communication between the hemispheres; thus, we come to research on so-called split brain preparations—organisms whose corpus callosum has been severed.

The first research on split brain animals was initiated by Roger Sperry, who wanted to learn where in the brain knowledge of a visual discrimination was stored. Sperry got a graduate student, Ronald Myers, interested in the problem. Myers began a series of studies in which cats who had been operated on so that information from one eye went only to one hemisphere would learn a discrimination problem with only one eye. Later testing with the previously covered eye (and the untrained hemisphere) revealed that the information had somehow been transferred, for the animals performed well. To try to learn how this happens, Myers performed various operations, destroying areas of the brain to see what would affect transfer. He finally hit upon the corpus callosum. After the corpus was severed, the animals could not perform the discrimination when they were tested with the "untrained" eye. Although the operation produced no apparent abnormalities in the animals' day-to-day behavior, the corpus callosum seemed to be the vehicle of communication between the two hemispheres (Sperry, 1961).

Later, Sperry became interested in a 48-year-old veteran whose brain had been injured by bomb fragments during World War II. After the injury, he started to suffer from epileptic seizures that were both severe and unresponsive to treatment. Finally, his physicians cut through his corpus callosum in an attempt to stop the seizures from spreading from one hemisphere to the other. The surgery was remarkably successful: the seizures stopped, and although initially he had some difficulty speaking, this soon passed.

Another of Sperry's students, Michael Gazzaniga, was able to perform a series of studies on this patient that revealed a great deal about the different functions of the two hemispheres (Sperry and Gazzaniga, 1967). At first, when the patient was asked to carry out a verbal command, he could do so only with the right side of his body. The left hemisphere, which generally controls the right half of the body, understands speech and is able to follow through on a command. The right hemisphere, which controls the left half of the body, apparently could not understand speech. Similarly, only the left hemisphere could read; the patient could only understand words that appeared in the right half of his visual field, which in turn project to the left hemisphere (see Figure 2.13). Conflict between the two hemispheres was also noted: On one occasion the man threatened his wife with his left hand (the right hemisphere), while his right hand (the "rational" left hemisphere) came to the rescue (Pines, 1973).

The presence of language, speech, and presumably other aspects of thought in the left hemisphere seem to justify labeling its functions "rational." But what of the "silent" right hemisphere? One area in which it seems to be superior is perception. Even though Gazzaniga's patient was right-handed, he was more adept at copying geometric figures with his left than with his right hand.

[Similarly, in a film the patient is] seen trying to arrange some colored blocks according to a diagram. He has no trouble at all doing this construction test with his left hand. But when his right hand tries, it gets hopelessly mixed up. Impatiently, his left hand shoots forward to help him, but the experimenter pushes it back. The right hand continues turning the blocks this way and that, achieving nothing. Again the left hand tried to come to the rescue, only to be pushed back. Peeved, [the patient] sits on that hand to keep it quiet. But he still can't do the block design with his right hand. When he is told he can try it with both hands, however, the situation grows worse: the two hands seem to fight for control, with the right hand tearing down whatever the left hand has built [Pines, 1973, p. 172].

Imaginative and creative activities may also be related to the right hemisphere. The famous Russian psychologist Luria, for example, reported the case of a musician who lost his speech after a stroke but who then composed even better music. Many creative people describe the creative act in ways that provide support for this possible role of the right hemisphere. Einstein, for example, said that his concepts first appeared as "physical entities—certain signs and more or less

Figure 2.13
With this apparatus, which has been especially designed to test split brain patients, visual stimuli can be presented to one or the other hemisphere exclusively. Touching can also be tested by allowing the subject to explore objects that are presented to either hand out of sight. To test right-hemispheric function, pictures or words are quick-flashed to the left visual field. The subjects invariably say that they saw nothing or else they guess. Yet the left hand, which sends its touch information to the right hemisphere, will be able to retrieve the object described. After the task has been correctly completed, the subject will still deny knowing anything about the specific aspects of the event because the activity was carried out by the right hemisphere, which is now disconnected from the left (speech) hemisphere, which is the half-brain talking to the experimenter.

clear images." The right hemisphere can also experience emotions. One of Sperry's subjects was shown a picture of a nude in her left visual field (which would "register" in her right hemisphere). Although she smiled in an embarrassed way when the picture was shown, she said that she had seen "nothing" when queried about it.

Thus, we appear to have two brains, each with different functions. Under normal circumstances, we experience a unified consciousness and have no awareness of the conflicts and differences between the two hemispheres. Research done on the split brain, however, has shown how much the hemispheres differ and that the "silent" right hemisphere actually has great creative powers.

SINGLE UNIT RECORDING. We turn now to much more microscopic research on brain functioning in relation to behavior. With

TESTING YOUR UNDERSTANDING
A HALF-ASLEEP BRAIN

Gazzaniga (1973) tested two patients who were about to have an angiogram, a tumor-detection procedure in which the brain's blood vessels are X-rayed after a special dye has been injected. In addition to the dye, a small dose of anesthetic was injected into the left hemisphere, which effectively put it to sleep and paralyzed the right side of the body. With the left hemisphere anesthetized, Gazzaniga briefly placed a common object (such as a cigarette) into each patient's left hand but out of sight. After the anesthetic wore off two tests were performed. First, the patient was asked what had been put into his hand. Second, he was shown a series of objects and asked "which one was it?" What results would you expect from each test? Why?

Recall that the left hemisphere, which had been anesthetized, controls speech. Thus, with the left hemisphere "asleep," the patient could not be expected to code the object verbally. But the alert right hemisphere was functioning and so when the patient was simply asked to select the object, he did so correctly.

Later, though, after the anesthetic has worn off, the information that the right hemisphere processed should transfer to the left hemisphere through the intact corpus callosum. Remarkably, though, even when the anesthetic had worn off the information was not transferred to the left hemisphere and the patient could not name the object. These results suggest that information that can influence behavior can be stored in the right hemisphere in such a way that it is inaccessible to the left hemisphere. Gazzaniga speculates that this observation may be related to our common failure to recall events before 2 or 3 years of age. Since these events occurred before we could speak, they may be stored but in such a way that they are not available once language has been acquired. This research may also be relevant to Freud's concept of the unconscious control of behavior (see Chapter 10).

the development of microelectrodes, thin, needle-like instruments with diameters much smaller than one-tenth of a millimeter, the electrical activity of single nerve cells can be recorded. Thus, it has become possible to determine whether stimulation will excite or inhibit a single neuron and what the precise effects of different stimuli are on different cells.

The best example of this type of research is in the visual field. Therefore, it seems advisable to describe the eye briefly at this time, even though it will be discussed at greater length in Chapter 3. The light sensitive cells at the back of the eye comprise the retina. Fibers from these cells are bunched together, forming the optic nerve in each eye. At the optic chiasma there is a crossover (see Figure 2.14) so that fibers from the right half of each retina project to the right lateral ge-

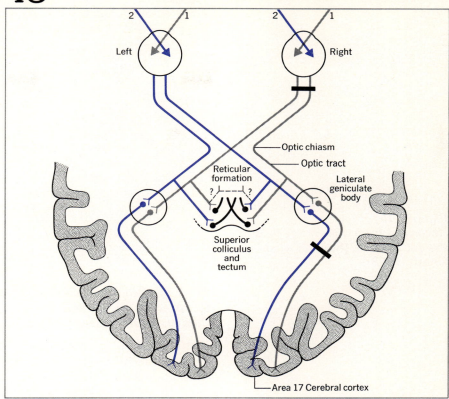

Figure 2.14
Schematic diagram of light falling on the retinas of both eyes and the neural pathways from the retina to the visual cortex. [Source: After Gardner (1963)]

niculate nucleus, an area within the thalamus. Similarly, fibers from the left side of each retina project to the left lateral geniculate body. From the lateral geniculate, there are fibers going to the occipital area of the cerebral cortex.

Microelectrode Recordings of Noncortical Cells in the Visual System.
Hartline was the first to isolate surgically and then record (with microelectrodes) single fibers in the frog's optic nerve (1938, 1940). The receptive field of a single fiber is defined as the area of the retina that will cause the fiber to fire when appropriate stimulation is applied. Because several receptors from the retina converge to form whatever optic nerve fiber is being studied, the activity recorded in an optic nerve fiber reflects the activity of many retinal receptors. In his early work Hartline discovered three different kinds of optic nerve fibers: "On" fibers, responding to light, show a quick burst of activity which slows to a steady rate as the light remains on. "Off" fibers show a burst of activity when a light goes off. "On-off" fibers show bursts of activity when a light goes on *or* off. Later research suggests that the frog's optic system is even more complex. Granit (1959), for example, showed that the same units can give "on," "off," or "on-off" responses depending upon the intensity of the stimulation. These findings provide information about how changes in brightness are coded in the retina (see Fig-

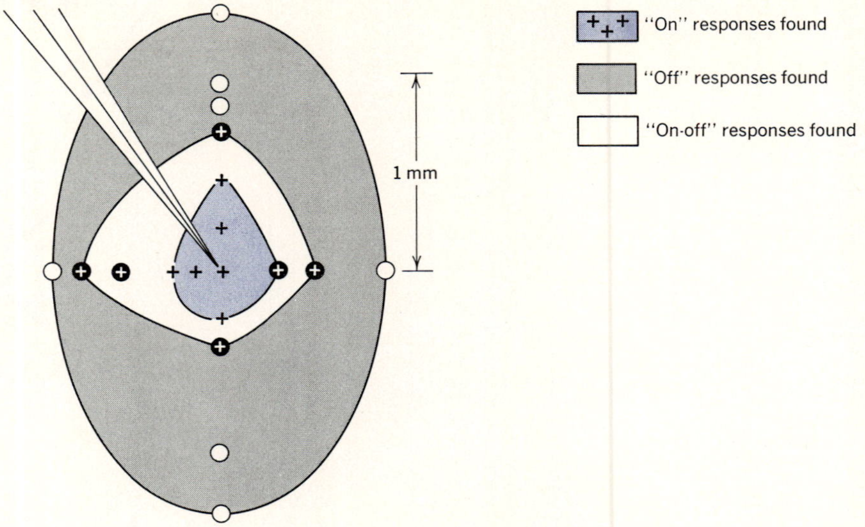

"On" responses found

"Off" responses found

"On-off" responses found

1 mm

Figure 2.15
Recording from a receptive field in the cat's retina. [Source: After Granit (1962)]

ure 2.15). But what about more complicated visual stimuli such as forms and objects? Does the retina have separate neural codes for them as well? At least for some species the answer is yes.

Maturana and his colleagues (1960) made recordings of single optic nerve fibers in the frog while presenting varied stimuli such as lines, dots, and checkerboard patterns. They found five types of fibers that gave distinct responses to different kinds of visual information.

1. *Boundary detectors.* These responded most to brightness contrast and to movement of a boundary.
2. *Convex boundary detectors.* These responded to boundaries with a curvature and to those in motion or stopping just after motion. The greatest response was to a moving small dark convex area; the authors also called these "bug detectors," a valuable sensory system for the frog.
3. *Changing contrast detectors.* These responded only to sharp dark or light edges moving in the visual field.
4. *Dimming detectors.* These responded to a darkening of the visual field.
5. *Dark detectors.* These fibers fire continuously with higher rates for lower levels of illumination.

It is clear that even fairly complicated perceptual information is being processed in the retina.

Microelectrodes in the Cortex. In man and other vertebrates there is relatively less processing of visual information in the retina and more in the higher centers of the brain. A recurrent puzzle in the field of visual perception has been how the retinal image (the picture of the external world that falls on the retina) is translated into visual experiences of size, form, movement, and so forth. Working with cats and monkeys, David Hubel and Torsten Weisel, researchers at Harvard Medical School, have studied the organization of the visual system.

In a typical experiment, Hubel and Weisel (1959, 1962, 1965) insert a microelectrode into a single cell along the visual pathway in the brain (the lateral geniculate nuclei and the visual cortex) of an anesthetized cat, who is placed 1½ meters (about 5 feet) in front of a screen. They then record the electrical responses of the nerve cell containing the microelectrode to various patterns of white light (for example, a horizontal line or a moving bar) flashed on the screen. (To determine the exact location of this cell, they later perform a careful dissection of the animal's brain.) Using this experimental setup, Hubel and Weisel have made several important discoveries about the visual system.

They have found that lateral geniculate and cortical cells are each "assigned" to a particular area of the retina (although many cells are connected to the same area), so that these nerve cells will only respond (or fire) if "their" area of the retina is stimulated. Also, for these cells to fire, the stimulus presented to them must be of a certain character. Lateral geniculate cells are specialized in somewhat the same way as optic nerve fibers since they respond to stimulation as it comes "off" or "on." However, unlike optic nerve fibers, they respond to a particular location of light on the retina itself. Thus, by being sensitive to differing areas of illumination on the retina, the over-all effect of this system is to increase the disparity between diffuse illumination and concentrated spots of light (Hubel, 1963).

More impressive, however, was the finding that cortical cells, while responding only to a particular area of the retina, are also specialized to particular properties of a stimulus. Some cortical cells (which they dubbed "simple") require a combination of stimulus *form* (for example, a line) and *angle* (for example, horizontal position), as well as location on the retina, to fire. No other stimuli on the retinal area connected to a simple cortical cell will cause it to fire. Other cortical cells ("complex") do not require a particular retinal location of a stimulus as much as the correct stimulus shape and orientation. Also, these cells will respond to the movement of a stimulus whereas simple cortical cells will not. Clearly, Hubel and Weisel's research strongly suggests that perception is grounded, at least in part, in the structure and function of specialized nerve cells in the cortex.

THE PERIPHERAL NERVOUS SYSTEM   The peripheral nervous sytem includes the *spinal nerves*, the *cranial nerves*, and the *autonomic nervous system*. The spinal nerves are of two types, *sensory nerves* and *motor nerves*. Both types are connected in tracts (or bundles) to the spinal cord (see Figure 2.3). The sensory nerves, which bring information to the spinal cord from various parts of the body, enter at the top. The motor nerves, which leave the spinal cord at the bottom, carry information to the muscles and glands. The importance of these sensory and motor nerves can readily be appreciated in view of what happens to people who have had their spinal cord severed, perhaps in an automobile accident. They can no longer control or experience any sensations in those areas of their body below the break. The cranial nerves (those in the head) are similar in structure to the spinal nerves. They bring information from the eyes, nose, and face to the brain and from the brain back to these structures.

Much of our behavior depends upon a nervous system that generally functions without our awareness and has traditionally been viewed as beyond voluntary control (hence the term "autonomic"). The autonomic nervous system (ANS) innervates the endocrine glands, the heart, and the smooth muscles that are found in the walls of the blood vessels, stomach, intestines, kidneys, and other organs. This nervous system is itself divided into two parts, the *sympathetic* and *parasympathetic* nervous systems (see Figure 2.16). The nerves of the sympathetic division arise in the middle part of the spinal cord, enter ganglia (clumps of neurons) and then extend to organs, muscles, and so forth. By contrast, the nerves of the parasympathetic system leave the spinal cord at locations above and below the sympathetic and enter ganglia closer to the structures they innervate. Many parts of the body receive fibers from both the sympathetic and the parasympathetic systems; these sometimes work against each other and sometimes together. The sympathetic portion of the ANS, when energized, accelerates the heartbeat, dilates the pupils, inhibits intestinal activity, and initiates other smooth muscle and glandular responses that prepare the organism for sudden activity or stress. Indeed, some physiologists view the sympathetic nervous system as primarily excitatory. By contrast, they view the other division—the parasympathetic—as responsible for maintenance functions because of its role in deceleration of the heartbeat, constriction of the pupils, and speeding up the contractions of the intestines. The division of activities between the two systems is not completely clear-cut, however, for the parasympathetic system can be active under conditions of stress. Animals and humans (to their consternation) may urinate or defecate involuntarily when they are under stress or frightened.

To try to understand the nature of emotion, the activities of the ANS are frequently assessed using electrical and chemical measurements and analyses; two important measures are heart rate and the *galvanic skin response* (GSR). Each heartbeat generates changes in electrical potential that can be recorded by an electrocardiograph. Electrodes are placed near the heart and also on a limb, and then they are connected to a galvanometer, an instrument for measuring electric currents. The deflections of this instrument appear as waves on an oscilloscope, or the waves may be registered on graph paper by a pen recorder; both types of recordings are called *electrocardiograms*. Generally, it is assumed that a fast heart rate means increased arousal.

Anxiety, fear, anger, and other emotions produce increased activity in

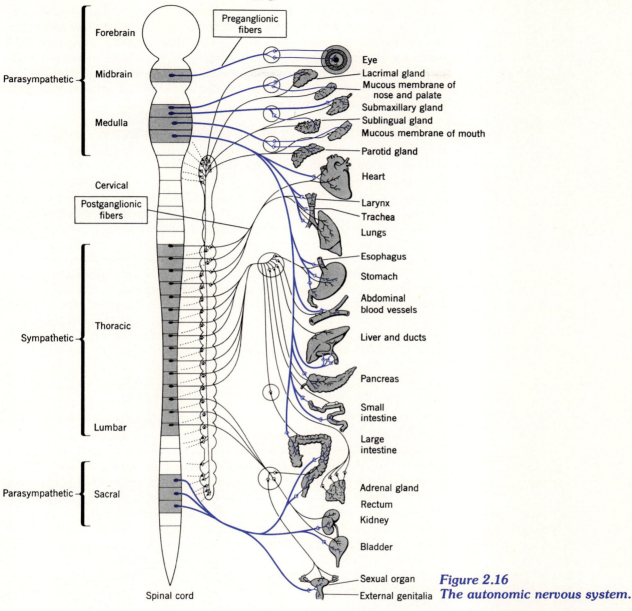

Parasympathetic
- Forebrain
- Midbrain
- Medulla

Preganglionic fibers

Cervical

Postganglionic fibers

Sympathetic
- Thoracic
- Lumbar

Parasympathetic
- Sacral

Spinal cord

- Eye
- Lacrimal gland
- Mucous membrane of nose and palate
- Submaxillary gland
- Sublingual gland
- Mucous membrane of mouth
- Parotid gland
- Heart
- Larynx
- Trachea
- Lungs
- Esophagus
- Stomach
- Abdominal blood vessels
- Liver and ducts
- Pancreas
- Small intestine
- Large intestine
- Adrenal gland
- Rectum
- Kidney
- Bladder
- Sexual organ
- External genitalia

Figure 2.16
The autonomic nervous system.

the sweat glands. The electrophysiological processes in the cells of the sweat glands, in turn, change the conductance of the skin; this change is referred to as the GSR. Skin conductance may be measured (using surface electrodes) by recording the very small differences in electrical potential that always exist between any two points on the skin; this voltage shows a pronounced change after stimulation. Or we could record the current that flows through the skin when a small voltage derived from an external source is passed through a subject, usually by means of electrodes pasted to the palm and back of the hand; this voltage also shows a pronounced change after stimulation. The percentage of change from the normal (or base line) conductance is the measure of reactivity for either method. It is believed that high conductance (or, alternatively, low resistance) reflects increased autonomic activity. Since the sweat glands are innervated only by the sympathetic nervous system, increased sweat gland activity indicates the excitation of this system.

EMOTION AND THE AUTONOMIC SYSTEM. Although man has been interested in understanding his own emotions since the time of the ancient philosophers, it was Charles Darwin who suggested studying the behavioral aspects of emotion in his book *The Expression of the Emotions in Man and Animals* (1872). Consistent with his views on evolution, Darwin proposed that emotional patterns of behavior in men and animals are largely inherited, and those that have greatest survival value are the ones that remain. In turning to more contemporary views, it would be well to mention the theory proposed independently by William James and C. G. Lange in the late nineteenth century. They each held that it is the perception of our bodily state that determines our emotion. (Previously, it had been believed that we first perceive an event as frightening, disgusting, or exciting and then the physiological changes associated with emotion occur.) In James's classic example, we first run away from a bear and then become afraid because we see ourselves running and notice that our hearts are racing. The emphasis here is on the perception of bodily changes, particularly those of the autonomic nervous system.

A few years later, however, the physiologist Walter Cannon (1929) marshaled serious criticisms against the James-Lange theory, pointing out that although different emotional states seem to be distinct experientially they are accompanied by the same kind of autonomic arousal. Furthermore, Cannon noted, since it is very difficult for man to know what his viscera are doing at any given time, autonomic activity would be a poor cue for differentiating emotions. Cannon also pointed to a well-known experiment by Marañon (1924), who injected human subjects with adrenaline (an agent whose activity duplicates sympathetic activation). Marañon's subjects reported that they felt as if they were afraid, but were not really afraid because they knew that it was the injection of adrenaline that made their viscera behave in a particular way.

The Marañon experiment could be considered the precursor of a famous experiment by Schachter and Singer (1962), which went far in attempting to integrate the physiological and cognitive components of emotion.

Imagine that you have volunteered for an experiment to test the visual effects of a particular vitamin compound. After consenting and then having this vitamin injected, you are sent to a nearby room to wait with another student for the drug to take effect. Suppose, further-

TABLE 2.1

Synopsis of the theories of emotion.	
James-Lange	Visceral changes produced by an event are noticed, which then lead to emotion. Different emotions are caused by different patterns of visceral activity.
Cannon	Different emotions can arise from identical patterns of visceral activity.
Schachter-Singer	Visceral arousal, produced by an environmental event, is labeled according to the situation the person is in. The arousal is a nonspecific mechanism that is then "channeled" according to the person's interpretation into particular emotions.

more, that the vitamin, besides affecting your vision, produces certain side effects, namely, increased heart rate, accelerated breathing, and trembling, but the experimenter has told you nothing about them. In the waiting room you begin to feel these physiological effects, while noticing that the other student is behaving in an extremely jubilant manner. The question to be asked is how you would feel or, more technically, how you might interpret the state of arousal in which you found yourself.

Schachter and Singer had suggested that emotion is the product of autonomic arousal and cognition. They theorized that arousal has a nonspecific function, thus obviating Cannon's earlier criticism of James-Lange. The individual would differentiate his nonspecific arousal into distinct emotions according to the situation in which he found himself. Thus, when aroused, a person could become either angry or happy depending upon the situational cues (See Table 2.1).

To test their theory, Schachter and Singer (1962) performed a study somewhat like the one described above. After being informed about the experiment and agreeing to participate, some subjects were injected with a placebo and some with adrenaline. Then the subjects in each of these two groups were exposed to conditions designed to elicit either anger or euphoria. This was accomplished by having them wait with a confederate (the "other student") who had been trained to behave in either a joyous or an angry manner. The experimenters predicted that either emotion could be induced (even though the physiological states of these people would be similar) but only after an injection of the arousing adrenaline.

In the Euphoria Condition, after the subject had received either adrenaline or a placebo, the following events would transpire. As the experimenter was leaving he would say:

"The only other thing I should do is to apologize for the condition of the room, I just didn't have time to clean it up. So, if you need any scratch paper or rubber bands or pencils, help yourself. I'll be back in 20

minutes to begin the vision tests."

As soon as the experimenter had left, the stooge introduced himself again, made a series of standard icebreaker comments, and then launched into his routine. . . .

1. Stooge reaches for a piece of paper and starts doodling saying, "They said we could use this for scratch, didn't they?" He doodles a fish for some 30 seconds, then says:

2. "This scrap paper isn't even much good for doodling" and crumples paper and attempts to throw it into wastebasket in far corner of the room. He misses but this leads him into a "basketball game." He crumples up other sheets of paper, shoots a few baskets, says "Two points" occasionally. He gets up and gets off a jump shot saying, "The old jump shot is really on today."

3. If the subject has not joined in, stooge throws a paper basketball to subject saying, "Here, you try it."

4. Stooge continues his game saying, "The trouble with paper basketballs is that you don't really have any control."

5. Stooge continues basketball, then gives it up saying, "This is one of my good days. I feel like a kid again; I think I'll make a plane." He makes a paper airplane saying, "I guess I'll make one of the longer ones."

6. Stooge flies plane. Gets up and retrieves plane. Flies again, etc.

7. Stooge throws plane at subject.

8. Stooge, flying plane, says, "Even when I was a kid, I was never much good at this."

9. Stooge tears off part of plane saying, "Maybe this plane can't fly but at least it's good for something." He wads up paper and, making a slingshot of a rubber band, begins to shoot the paper.

10. Shooting, the stooge says, "These [paper ammunition] really go better if you make them long. They don't work right if you wad them up."

11. While shooting, stooge notices a sloppy pile of manila folders on a table. He builds a tower of these folders, then goes to the opposite end of the room to shoot at the tower.

12. He misses several times, then hits and cheers as the tower falls. He goes over to pick up the folders.

13. While picking up, he notices, behind a portable blackboard, a pair of hula hoops which have been covered with black tape with a few wires sticking out of the tape. He reaches for these, taking one for himself and putting the other aside but within reaching distance of the subject. The stooge tries the hula hoop saying, "This isn't as easy as it looks."

14. Stooge twirls hoop wildly on arm saying, "Hey look at this—this is great."

15. Stooge replaces the hula hoop and sits down with his feet on the table. Shortly thereafter the experimenter returns to the room.

After receiving their injection, the subjects in the Anger Condition were given the following instructions:

"We would like you to use these 20 minutes to answer these questionnaires." Then handing out the questionnaires, [the experimenter] concludes with, "I'll be back in 20 minutes to pick up the questionnaires and begin the tests of vision."

Before looking at the questionnaire, the stooge says to the subject,

"I really wanted to come for an experiment today, but I think it's unfair for them to give you shots. At least, they should have told us about the shots when they called us; you hate to refuse once you're here already."

The questionnaires, five pages long, start off innocently requesting fact sheet information [age, sex, and so forth] and then grow increasingly personal and insulting. The stooge, sitting directly opposite the subject, paces his own answers so that at all times subject and stooge are working on the same question. At regular points in the questionnaire, the stooge makes a series of standardized comments about the questions. His comments start off innocently enough, grow increasingly querulous, and finally he ends up in a rage. In sequence, he makes the following comments:

1. Before answering any items, he leafs quickly through the questionnaire saying, "Boy, this is a long one."

2. Question 7 on the questionnaire requests, "List the foods that you would eat in a typical day." The stooge comments, "Oh, for Pete's sake, what did I have for breakfast this morning?"

3. Question 9 asks, "Do you ever hear bells? _____. How often? _____." The stooge remarks, "Look at Question 9. How ridiculous can you get? I hear bells every time I change classes."

4. Question 13 requests, "List the childhood diseases you have had and the age at which you had them," to which the stooge remarks, "I get annoyed at this childhood disease question. I can't remember what childhood diseases I had, and especially at what age. Can you?"

5. Question 17 asks, "What is your father's average annual income?" and the stooge says, "This really irritates me. It's none of their business what my father makes. I'm leaving that blank."

6. Question 25 presents a long series of items such as "Does not bathe or wash regularly," "Seems to need psychiatric care," etc. and requests the respondent to write down for which member of his immediate family each item seems most applicable. The question specifically prohibits the answer "None," and each item must be answered. The stooge says, "I'll be dammed if I'll fill out Number 25. 'Does not bathe or wash regularly'—that's a real insult." He then angrily crosses out the entire item.

7. Question 28 reads:

"How many times each week do you have sexual intercourse? 0–1 _____ 2–3 _____ 4–6 _____ 7 and over _____." The stooge bites out, "The hell with it! I don't have to tell them all this."

8. The stooge sits sullenly for a few moments, then he rips up his questionnaire, crumples the pieces and hurls them to the floor, saying, "I'm not wasting any more time. I'm getting my books and leaving," and he stomps out of the room.

9. The questionnaire continues for eight more questions ending with: "With how many men (other than your father) has your mother had extramarital relationships? 4 and under _____; 5–9 _____; 10 and over _____."

Two major kinds of data were collected: (1) observations of the extent to which the subjects joined in with the confederates' antics or criticisms, and (2) self-reports of mood. Excluding those subjects who were not physiologically affected by the injection, Schachter and Singer found support for their theory.[1] The subjects who had been injected with adrenaline exhibited more anger and euphoria than those who had received the placebo under the same conditions. Arousal heightened the subjects' emotions but in a nonspecific way; the specificity of feeling was produced by the environmental cues that offered "explanations" of the arousal.

[1]The injection had to be relatively mild for reasons of safety; therefore, not all of the participants became aroused, and those who did not would not be suitable for a test of the theory. Removing some of the subjects clearly weakens the conclusions to some extent.

TESTING YOUR UNDERSTANDING
SCHACHTER AND SINGER'S THEORY OF EMOTION AS APPLIED TO MOOD DISTURBANCES

In Chapter 11 we will discuss abnormal psychology, including debilitating excesses of either anxiety or depression. Since these are emotions and the Schachter-Singer theory purports to be a general theory of emotion, it should have something to say about the variables that are related to high levels of emotion. How would the Schachter-Singer theory account for a person becoming highly anxious?

First, since the interpretation of situational cues is important, individual differences in such interpretations are undoubtedly also important. For example, of two people who have ridden a roller coaster, one may label or interpret it as an exciting, exhilarating experience and the other as a terrifying one. Clearly, learning might be an important factor in construing these situations differently. Second, the Schachter and Singer theory includes autonomic arousal; thus, individual differences in the ease with which persons can become aroused are important. These differences could be genetically determined in part. Jost and Sontag (1944), for example, found that identical twins (those who developed from the same egg and hence are identical in all genetic characteristics) are more similar to each other on certain measures of autonomic activity than pairs of siblings. Third, in order for the arousal to lead to emotional behavior, it must be noticed. Apparently, there are individual differences in the extent to which people notice what is going on in their bodies. Some people are quite aware of small increases in their heart rate while others seem insensitive to these changes (Mandler, Mandler, and Uviller, 1958). The same amount of autonomic arousal can be differentially attended to, leading to differences in emotionality. Finally, individual differences in anxiety can be produced by differences in emotional expression. Being in a particular physiological and cognitive state does not imply that there will be only one behavior pattern. Rather, some people who are highly aroused will report that they "feel" calm and will not show any observable indications of emotionality.

Notice the varying emotional reactions to the roller coaster ride. According to the Schachter-Singer theory, such differences are due to how the individual interprets the situation, the extent of his/her autonomic arousal as well as his/her awareness of it, and the degree of his/her emotionality.

PSYCHOLOGY AND THE PROBLEMS OF SOCIETY
BRAIN CONTROL

Violence in our own society and elsewhere in the world today is a source of deep concern to most of us. Riots, assassinations, and crimes against the person seem to be on the increase. Law-enforcement officers, elected officials, lawyers, judges, criminologists, psychologists, and others have many different views about how this problem might be handled. One approach that has been suggested for use with hardened criminals is manipulation of the brain.

One way to alter an individual's brain functioning and thus his behavior is to implant metal electrodes, completely insulated except for their tip, into his brain. Running a mild electric current through these electrodes will activate the surrounding area; higher voltages will destroy brain tissue. Using a mild current is called electrical stimulation of the brain (ESB); the higher voltage is a variant of psychosurgery. Sophisticated devices permit the electrodes to be implanted in the brain with impressive accuracy. Electrical stimulation or destruction of the limbic tissues in animals has produced dramatic changes in their behavior; thus, this area has become especially popular for intervention.

Using ESB, Dr. José Delgado has provided a striking example of its effect on behavior. The selective breeding of bulls has yielded one variety that is noted for its aggressiveness. After inserting numerous electrodes into one such "brave" bull and attaching them to a radio receiver strapped tightly to the animal, Delgado (1969) antagonized the bull

Charles Whitman brought a virtual arsenal up to a tower at the University of Texas before starting his wild shooting spree that left 15 dead. In Whitman's case, a tumor was found in the amygdala, suggesting that his aggression was physiologically caused. But should we assume from this one case that a treatment such as psychosurgery ought to be used on certain criminals in order to help curtail violence?

(as a bull-fighter would), causing it to charge. During its charge, Delgado pressed a switch on the radio transmitter in his hand; the bull stopped abruptly and turned aside. Delgado asserts that this behavioral control was due in part to inhibition of an "aggressive drive."

A more explicit attempt to link brain functioning with human violence is found in the work of three medical doctors originally associated with Harvard University—William Sweet, Vernon Mark, and Frank Ervin. In a 1967 letter to the *Journal of the American Medical Association,* they pointed out that while many factors had been examined as causal in urban rioting (including poverty and frustration), one possible factor seemed to be overlooked—subtle brain lesions. Specifically they noted that while many people in the ghetto are dissatisfied, only a relative few actively participate in rioting. Then they advocated a program that would identify and diagnose those who have "low violence thresholds." Treatment would require implanting electrodes deep into the brain to locate presumed abnormal electrical activity and then obtaining the necessary permission to destroy damaged tissue.

In his book *Brain Control,* Elliot Valenstein (1973) carefully reviews the research that has attempted to control behavior by means of brain intervention. Referring to the work of Delgado that was mentioned earlier, he believes that Delgado did not demonstrate control of an aggressive drive; indeed, films show the bull moving in a nearly circular path, so the stimulation may have simply elicited the motoric response of turning. Of course, no attack is possible if the animal is engaged in an incompatible behavior.

Valenstein also makes other criticisms of the thinking behind ESB and psychosurgery. He notes that few brain mechanisms have been found that correlate with specific behaviors. Frequently psychosurgical techniques are highly diverse and seem to be as numerous as the number of practicing psychosurgeons. Rarely do any procedures have a valid neurological rationale. In an attempt to control "unmanageable" mental patients (those who most often receive psychosurgery), other methods such as medication and behavior therapy are seldom tried. When operations on the brain are performed, little objective data are collected, and any evaluation of the results tend to be simply the surgeon's own subjective (and probably biased) impressions of change. The real danger in any of these brain operations is that the poorly informed patients and their families do not realize that this treatment is highly experimental.

Valenstein also evaluates the work of Sweet, Mark, and Ervin. He finds little support for their hypotheses and concludes his book by saying:

> It is likely that there are some biological factors that contribute to a propensity for violence, but we would be in serious trouble if a number of influential people became convinced that violence is mainly a product of a diseased brain rather than a diseased society [p. 353].

58

SUMMARY

Psychobiology is that branch of psychology dealing with the relationship of the organism's biological systems to the environment and behavior. The nervous system, which is composed of glial cells and neurons, is divided into two major parts—the central and peripheral.

The central nervous system is made up of the brain and the spinal cord. Three different research strategies have been used to study the functioning of the brain. The first, and most molar, is the study of brain waves that are produced by the firing of thousands of neurons. It has been shown that these waves correlate with different behavioral states. The alpha rhythm (8–13 cycles per second) is found in a person who is relaxed but awake, beta (14–25 cps) in a person who is aroused, and slower waves (the delta rhythm) in a person who is asleep. During sleep the brain remains active and periodically returns from slow waves to a wave pattern resembling wakefulness and accompanied by rapid eye movements (stage REM); during this phase dreaming occurs.

A second method of studying brain function is the stimulation and/or destruction of discrete areas within the brain. It is believed that if the stimulation or destruction of a particular area affects behavior such as aggression, then the structure is probably a "control center" for the particular behavior. The role of the limbic system and the hypothalamus in aggression and of the corpus callosum in transferring information from one cerebral hemisphere to another were discussed as examples. Some problems with the research strategy were also noted: (1) stimulation or removal of a brain structure produces variable effects; (2) the effects may be due to a particular laboratory environment; and (3) it is often difficult to specify what will be the primary result of manipulation of the brain.

The third method of studying brain function is to use microelectrodes to examine the activity of single units within the central nervous system. In this respect, the visual system has been extensively studied. Within the optic nerve different types of fibers have been identified that respond to different kinds of visual information. Similar studies made in the lateral geniculate nucleus and visual cortex also reveal that certain nerve cells are "set" to respond only to very specific visual stimuli.

The peripheral nervous system includes the spinal nerves, cranial nerves, and the autonomic nervous system (ANS). The ANS is further divided into two parts—the sympathetic which, when active, prepares the organism for action, and the parasympathetic which is responsible for periods of relative quiescence. The autonomic nervous system is especially related to emotion and has been important in certain historical theories such as that of James and Lange. Schachter and Singer's theory of emotion emphasizes autonomic (particularly sympathetic) arousal. They believe that emotion is due to autonomic arousal and cognitions about the arousal. They view the arousal itself as nonspecific, while cognitions channel the arousal into specific emotional states.

59
GLOSSARY

Alpha rhythm: The typical rhythm (8–13 cycles per second) of brain waves in a resting adult.

Autonomic nervous system: That division of the peripheral nervous system that innervates the endocrine glands, the heart, and the smooth muscles of the stomach, the intestines, and other organs.

Basal ganglia: Clusters of interconnected nerve cell bodies in the brain that control such important behavior as the functioning of the heart.

Beta rhythm: The low voltage, high frequency (14–25 cps) brain rhythm in an alert adult.

Brainstem: The area of the brain containing the pons and medulla oblongata that functions as a pathway connecting the spinal cord with the cerebellum and cerebrum.

Cerebellum: The portion of the brain that is responsible for coordinating body movements, balance, and posture.

Cerebral cortex: The surface of a cerebral hemisphere.

Cerebrum: The two cerebral hemispheres.

Corpus callosum: The band of nerve fibers that connects the two cerebral hemispheres.

Diencephalon: That portion of the brain between the midbrain and cerebral hemispheres that contains the thalamus and hypothalamus.

Electroencephalogram (EEG): A Graphic recording of the electrical activity of the brain.

Glial cells: An important type of cell in the nervous system that provides a support system for the neurons.

Gray matter: Neural tissue that is made up primarily of nerve cell bodies.

GSR (galvanic skin response): Electrical conductance of the skin which is caused by activity of the sympathetic nervous system.

Gyri: Ridges in the cerebral cortex.

Hypothalamus: That portion of the diencephalon containing nuclei that regulate metabolism, appetite, sleep, and body temperature.

Kluver-Bucy syndrome: That pattern of behavior including reduced aggressiveness, hypersexuality, and memory impairment that follows surgical destruction of the temporal lobes including the amygdala.

Limbic system: The group of structures (amygdala, hippocampus, and septum) in the upper brainstem and cerebrum that is believed to be closely linked to emotion.

Lobes (frontal, parietal, temporal, and occipital): Distinct areas in the cerebral cortex.

Midbrain: A mass of fiber tracts that connects the cerebral cortex with the brainstem.

Neuron: A cell that provides communication within the nervous system.

Optic chiasma: The point at which the fibers from the right and left halves of each retina come together.

Parasympathetic nervous system: The division of the autonomic nervous system that predominates during periods of relative quiescence.

Receptive field: The area around a nerve fiber that will cause it to fire when appropriate stimulation is applied.

REM sleep: That period of sleep when dreaming occurs; it is accompanied by rapid eye movements, restlessness, and a "wakeful" EEG pattern.

Reticular formation: A track of fibers in the brainstem that receives information from the senses and plays a significant part in arousal.

Split brain: An animal whose corpus callosum has been severed; its two cerebral hemispheres can no longer communicate with one another.

Sulci: Fissures in the cerebral cortex.

Sympathetic nervous system: The division of the autonomic nervous system that becomes active when the organism is preparing for action or is under stress.

Synapse: The small gap between neurons that must be crossed in order for one neuron to communicate with another.

Thalamus: That portion of the diencephalon that serves as a relay station for sensory information.

Transmitter substances: Chemicals that cross the synapse allowing impulses to be transmitted from one neuron to another.

White matter: Neural tissue that is composed mainly of axons.

THREE

PERCEPTION

To survive in a world filled with many dangers, all living creatures must be able to gather information about their environment. They need to be able to find and secure the food and water needed for life and to avoid threats from their natural enemies or surroundings. For human beings, too, survival is also basically dependent upon their ability to receive and process information pertaining to the world around them.

How do we get to know our world? The information we need is "out there"—in the streets, in our homes and offices, in the countryside—but our sensory receptors, such as the eye and ear, are not in direct contact with them. The stimuli present in the environment are called *distal stimuli;* the patterns of energy and information that ultimately reach our sensory receptors are called *proximal stimuli.* We become acquainted with the world of distal stimuli only through the proximal stimuli that reach and activate our sensory receptors. How this process occurs is the main focus of the psychology of perception.

Our discussion will largely emphasize vision and hearing, although we will also briefly describe the other senses—smell, taste, the skin senses, and perception of the body's orientation—and the environmental information to which they are sensitive. At the outset, we will discuss the detection of energy from the environment, an area of study that is often referred to as *sensation.* Later on, we will turn to the more complex process of *perception,* through which living creatures integrate and organize information from the world around them.

CHEMICAL, SKIN, AND BODY SENSES

TASTE AND SMELL. Taste and smell are usually known as the chemical senses because the stimulus for both is a chemical one. That smell is an important sense is attested to by its role in tasting (think of how your taste is dulled when you have a cold) and our cultural emphasis on personal cleanliness and "pleasing" smells; yet the mechanisms that enable us to smell are only partially understood. The receptors of smell—the *olfactory receptors*—are located in the uppermost region of the nasal cavity in an area called the *olfactory cleft* (see Figure 3.1). This region is not along the main path of air going from the nose to the lungs, but it does receive a small portion of the inhaled air. In order for various substances to be smelled, they must be airborne and in a finely divided state. After being inhaled, these particles find their way to the moist tissue known as the *olfactory epithelium,* where sensations of smell originate (Geldard, 1972). Even the most tantalizing perfume will be wasted if the particles carrying its scent do not reach this region.

Why do different particles produce different odors? Many people have tried to relate the chemical composition of various substances to the odors they produce. These attempts have not been very successful, for some substances of totally different chemical composition smell alike while others of very similar chemical structure smell quite differently. One generalization that can be made, however, is that odorous substances are usually organic (that is, they contain carbon) rather than inorganic in chemical structure.

Taste receptors are grouped together in *taste buds,* which are distributed over the top surface and sides of the tongue (see Figure 3.2). The taste buds are grouped together in *papillae,* the raised areas of the tongue that can readily be seen by the naked eye. For a substance to

Figure 3.1
The nasal passages. Most inhaled air passes directly through the nasal cavity to the lungs. Some, however, moves upward toward the olfactory cleft, where the sensitive olfactory epithelium is found.

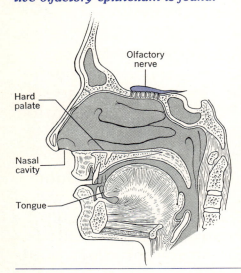

Olfactory nerve

Hard palate

Nasal cavity

Tongue

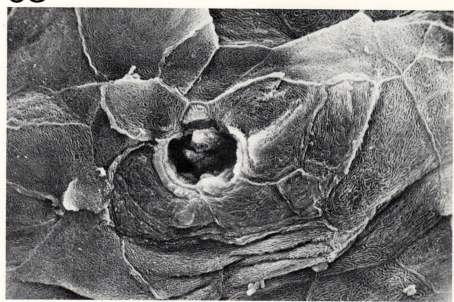

Figure 3.2
A scanning electron micrograph of human taste buds.

Figure 3.3
Regions of the tongue where each of the four tastes is strongest.

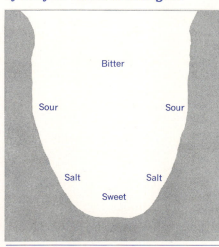

be tasted, it must be dissolved by saliva in the mouth, and then reach the areas around the papillae.

There are four basic tastes—salt, sour, bitter, sweet—each of which is closely related to the chemical structure of the substances that produce them. For example, the sensation of saltiness is linked to the presence of both chloride (Cl^-) and sodium (Na^+) ions, and sourness is associated with the presence of hydrogen (H^+) ions. The taste buds in different regions of the tongue vary in their sensitivity to each of the basic tastes. Those near the back are most sensitive to bitter solutions, while those near the tip are most strongly affected by sweet tastes. Sensations of sourness are largely produced by the receptors along the edges of the tongue midway back from the tip, while saltiness is sensed over the entire upper surface of the tongue and along its edges (see Figure 3.3).

SENSING THROUGH THE SKIN. For years touch as a sense had been relatively neglected. Recently, however, interest in it has been renewed as part of a movement to get people back into contact with their basic senses, including touch and the other skin senses. Participants in some therapy groups, for example, are urged to get to know one another by touch as well as by more conventional means.

The skin senses include the perception of pressure, pain, and temperature. There are specialized receptor organs embedded in the skin, although unevenly distributed in it, that respond to various forms of stimulation. *Basket-shaped nerve endings*, frequently found around the base of each hair, are the primary receptors for pressure sensations. A second type of structure, the *Meissner corpuscles*, also receive pressure sensations, especially in areas where there is no hair.

Sensations of cutaneous pain may be produced by four different kinds of stimuli: mechanical, thermal, electrical, and chemical. Although research has not isolated specific pain receptors, the *free nerve endings* are a likely possibility (see Figure 3.4). Sensations of warmth or cold are produced by variations from the actual temperature of the skin itself. The skin is quite sensitive to such stimuli. In the region of the fingers, for example, a temperature change of less than 1° F. can produce sensations of becoming warmer or colder.

AWARENESS OF THE BODY. The body senses provide valuable information for integrating our physical movements and maintaining a balanced, upright posture. *Kinesthetic* sensitivity is the sense of movement produced by various body parts. Kinesthetic receptors, located in the muscles, tendons, and joints throughout the body, provide sensations of movement in each of these places. The sensations that we receive from the kinesthetic receptors enable us to control and integrate long sequences of more-or-less "automatic" activities, such as washing our face, brushing our teeth, dressing, and even preparing our breakfast while thinking about our plans for the day or other things. In this sequence of activities, each act produces

Figure 3.4
A cross section of the skin, showing various structures that are believed to be important in producing sensations of pressure, pain, and temperature.

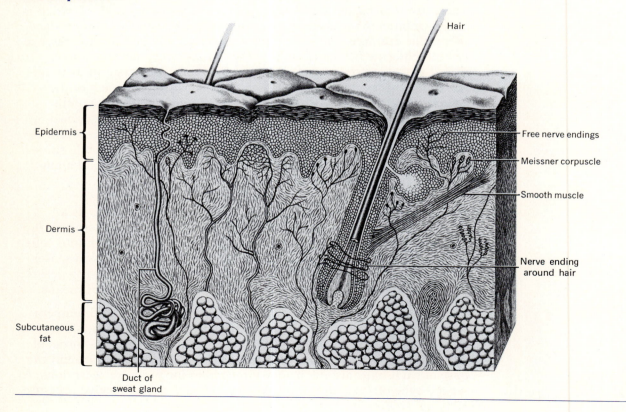

Hair

Epidermis

Free nerve endings

Meissner corpuscle

Smooth muscle

Dermis

Nerve ending around hair

Subcutaneous fat

Duct of sweat gland

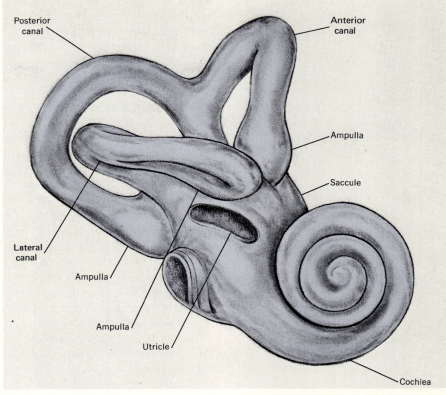

Figure 3.5
Structures of the inner ear. The three semicircular canals appear at approximately right angles to each other. Each one is filled with a liquid substance (endolymph), which is displaced when the body rotates in any of the three possible planes of motion (that is, up-down, left-right, front-back). At the base of each canal is an enlarged area, the ampulla, that contains the sensory receptors for the perception of body rotation. The vestibule consists of two parts—the utricle and saccule. In both structures, there are tiny crystals of bone-like calcium carbonate called otoliths, which press down on hair cell receptors when the body is either speeding up or slowing down in a straight line; the hair cells are also stimulated when the head is tilted.

sensations that, in turn, elicit subsequent acts. Thus, we can complete a whole chain of activities without thinking of each movement.

Two structures in the inner ear—the *semicircular canals* and the *vestibule*—convey sensations pertaining to the position and orientation of the body in space (see Figure 3.5), the so-called vestibular senses. Unlike the other senses, neither of these structures produces direct sensations themselves. Instead, their activation leads to diffuse feelings of dizziness, pressure on the chest, and rapid movements of the eyes. Thus, when the semicircular canals and vestibule are stimulated, the resulting sensations appear elsewhere in the body, not in the inner ear.

68

VISION When people are asked which of their five basic senses they would be most reluctant to lose, the overwhelming majority say their eyesight. Humans are primarily "visual creatures," highly dependent upon their sense of sight for survival. Perhaps because of this, psychologists have focused more of their time and attention on studying sight than any of the other senses.

THE STIMULUS FOR SIGHT. Light, the stimulus for vision, is made up of particles called *photons*. A light source, then, emits particles of matter which, according to modern physics, also have wave properties. Thus, it is possible to measure the *intensity* and the *wavelength* (the distance between successive "peaks" of the waves) of a light source. Intensity is the rate at which light energy flows and is analogous to its power. Color plate 5 shows that the *visible spectrum*, the range of wavelengths visible to the human eye, falls within a fairly narrow band of 400 to 750 millimicrons. (A micron is 0.001 of a millimeter, and a millimicron is 0.001 of a micron; thus, a millimicron is an extremely small unit of physical distance.) At the lower end of this spectrum is the color violet, while at the higher end is the color red. The colors blue, green, and yellow are produced by light of intermediate wavelengths. The relationship of the visible spectrum to other forms of electromagnetic radiation is depicted in the plate. The range of light that we can see is extremely small, compared with the range of electromagnetic wavelengths that have been investigated and utilized.

THE EYE. The proximal stimulus for the eye (see Figure 3.6 and Color plates 1 and 3) is an image cast upon the retina by the lens. This stimulus is not in any sense a sharp representation of the distal world. Actually, the lens inverts (turns upside down) and reverses the

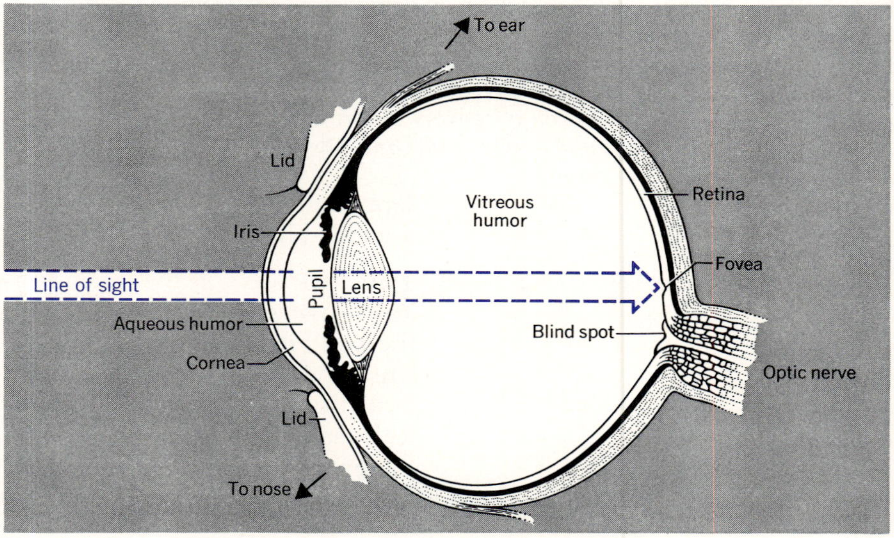

Figure 3.6
Light enters the eye through a clear but relatively tough outer covering —the cornea. Then it passes through a liquid substance—the aqueous humor—and enters the inner portion of the eye through the dark center—the pupil—which is surrounded by a colored band of tissue called the iris, a set of muscles that can change the size of the pupil. In bright light the diameter of the pupil decreases to about 2 mm. and in dim light it increases to about 8 mm. After entering the pupil, light passes through a transparent, flexible piece of tissue—the lens—which focuses the light to the area that is sensitive to light—the retina—which contains the true receptors for vision.

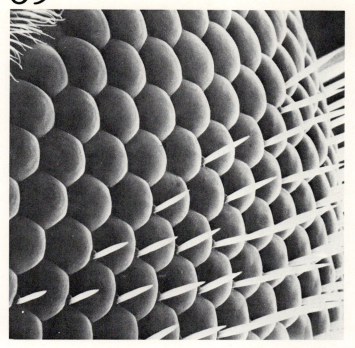

Figure 3.7
An actual photograph of the corneal lenses of a fruit fly. Note the setiform hairs appearing at the interspaces.

image, which then passes through fluids and several layers of cells in the retina. As can be seen in Figure 3.8, the photosensitive cells of the eye—the *rods* and *cones*—are actually covered by layers of cells so that the light that reaches them is first deflected and diffused by these overlying tissues. The light that reaches the rods and cones stimulates them to transmit neural impulses to the brain.

At the point where fibers from the rods and cones converge to leave the eye, there is a *blind spot* which is completely insensitive to any visual images that fall upon it. (See Color plate 2.) You can test your own blind spot by following the instructions in Figure 3.9. The reasons why we are generally not aware of this gap is that very seldom does the image of an entire object fall only on the blind spot; even when this does happen, mentally we "fill in" the gap.

THE TWO VISUAL RECEPTORS: RODS AND CONES. As noted above, there are two distinctly different types of visual receptors in the retina—the rods and the cones. The rods are primarily sensitive to the brightness of light that reaches the retina, while the cones are sensitive to details and color. The cones are essentially daylight receptors, functioning best under conditions of bright illumination, while the rods are essentially dim light receptors, functioning best under such lighting conditions as dawn or twilight. Evidence for the different functions of rods and cones has been gathered in experiments to test the *dark adaptation* of the eye. In such studies sensitivity to light is examined as a function of the amount of time an individ-

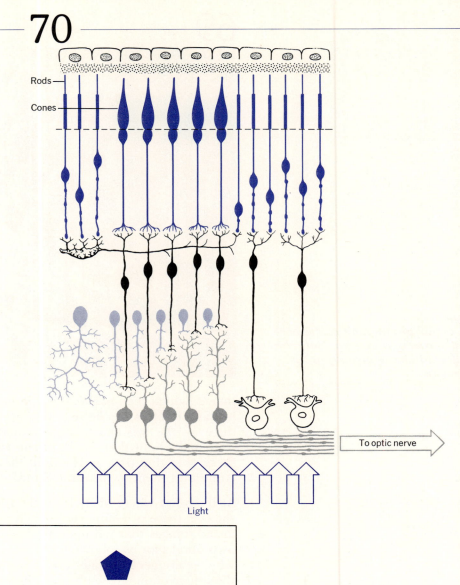

Rods

Cones

To optic nerve

Light

Figure 3.8
The retina. *Light has to pass through several layers of cells before it reaches the light-sensitive rods and cones. Notice that the cones connect individually with other cells while several rods converge together.*

Figure 3.9
A test for your blind spot. Hold the book in front of you, close your left eye and look at the circle with your right eye. Then move the book toward and away from you. When the pentagon is focused on your blind spot, its image will disappear.

ual has spent in the dark (see Figure 3.11). Sensitivity increases as much as 100,000 times after a period of 30 minutes. These changes are produced by the photochemicals present in the rods and cones and by the neural changes that take place during adaptation.

The two types of visual receptors are not distributed evenly throughout the retina. The cones tend to be clustered most thickly at a point known as the *fovea* (see Figure 3.6), the spot where our vision is most acute. Outside the fovea, both rods and cones can be found, with the number of cones decreasing as the distance from the center of the eye increases.

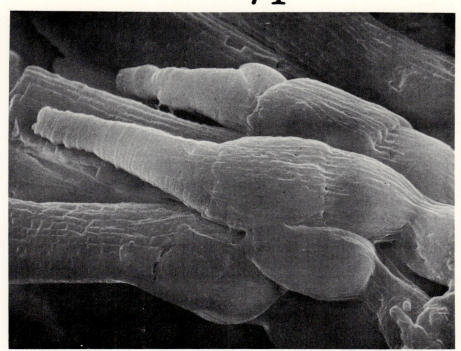

Figure 3.10
A scanning electron micrograph of the rods and cones in the retina of a mud puppy.

Figure 3.11
The course of dark adaptation. As the curve falls, sensitivity to light increases. The first drop is due to the dark adaptation of the cones, while the second, greater drop is due to the dark adaptation of the rods. [Source: Hecht and Shlaer (1938)]

THEORIES OF COLOR VISION. Two major theories explaining our ability to distinguish among colors have vied for acceptance since the nineteenth century: the *opponent-process theory* advanced by Edwald Hering, and the *Young-Helmholtz* (or *trichromatic*) theory proposed by Thomas Young and Herman Helmholtz.

The opponent-process theory begins with the observation that there are four colors that—in the psychological sense—cannot be analyzed into any others: red, green, blue, and yellow. What this means is that when people are asked to introspect about whether a color is primary (that is, not comprised of other colors), these are the four that they report; thus, they are called *psychological primaries*. The theory then suggests that color vision is based on three different mechanisms in the retina that are sensitive to red-green, yellow-blue, and black-white, respectively. It further proposes that stimulating either half of each of these three mechanisms inhibits the other half. For example, a red light would stimulate the red receptor mechanism but inhibit the green. Each grouping, then, actually represents opposite processes that are reciprocally stimulated and inhibited by visual stimuli.

The Young-Helmholtz theory starts with the observation that any color can be reproduced in the laboratory by mixing red, blue, and green lights; these colors are known as the *physical primaries*. Therefore, it postulates that there are three types of color-sensitive receptors in the retina that are maximally sensitive to the wavelengths associated with each of these colors. Other colors are produced by the simultaneous excitation of more than one type of receptor. Yellow, for example, is believed to be produced by the simultaneous stimulation of red and green receptors.

It should be pointed out that mixing colored *lights* and mixing colored *pigments* (such as paint) produce different results. The reader may have mixed blue and yellow paint together to obtain green. Yet, in mixing lights, yellow is not a primary color; when red and green lights are combined, the product is yellow (see Color plates 6a and 6b). Why do lights and paints differ?

Yellow paint looks yellow because the pigment absorbs all wavelengths of light except near the yellow area of the spectrum, which is reflected to the eye. Similarly, blue paint reflects blue wavelengths and absorbs all others. As it happens, when you mix blue and yellow paint, all wavelengths of light are absorbed except green, and this is reflected to the eye. In a sense, paint *subtracts* wavelengths from white light (which is composed of all wavelengths of the visible spectrum) and reflects back a certain portion of them. However, in the case of mixing lights, it is totally different. Here you are *adding* wavelengths, producing a very different perception of color. Combining blue and yellow light, for example, yields gray.

Both the opponent-process and Young-Helmholtz theories explain some of the phenomena of color vision and both have data to support them. From an analysis of the responsiveness of individual cones to light of different wavelengths, it has been shown that there are three different types of cones that are maximally sensitive to red, green, and blue lights (Wald, 1964). This, of course, supports the basic assumption of the Young-Helmholtz theory. However, in support of the opponent-process theory, it has also been found that cells in the brain respond in a manner that would be predicted by this theory. One study, for example, found four kinds of opposing cells: red excitatory (R+)/green inhibitory (G−), green excitatory (G+)/red inhibitory (R−), yellow excitatory (Y+)/blue inhibitory (B−), and blue excitatory (B+)/yellow inhibitory (Y−) (DeValois, Abramov, and Jacobs, 1966). Thus, the Young-Helmholtz and opponent-process theories may both be valid but at different levels of the visual system.

HEARING After vision, the sense that psychologists have given most of their attention to is *audition*, or hearing. Although this sense appears to be more fully developed in many other animal species, hearing is uniquely crucial for human speech.

STRUCTURE OF THE EAR AND THE AUDITORY STIMULUS. The auditory system is depicted in Figures 3.12 and 3.13 and Color plate 4. Sound reaches the ear in the form of waves (alternate condensations and rarefactions of the air) produced by any vibrating body (see Figure 3.14). All sounds are produced by vibrating bodies;

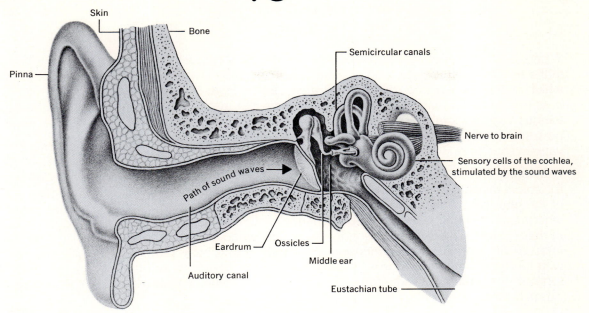

Skin
Bone
Semicircular canals
Pinna
Nerve to brain
Sensory cells of the cochlea, stimulated by the sound waves
Path of sound waves
Eardrum
Ossicles
Middle ear
Auditory canal
Eustachian tube

Figure 3.12
Sound waves enter the external ear (or pinna) and then travel through the auditory canal, a tube approximately 0.7 cm. in diameter and 2.5 cm. long, to the tympanic membrane (or eardrum). They cause this thin piece of tissue to move and press against a series of three small bones called ossicles, which magnify the force of the eardrum's movement; these displacements than reach an opening in the cochlea known as the oval window. The cochlea, a coiled, bony structure, resembles a snail shell. As the oval window moves in and out due to pressure from the ossicles, it presses against fluid in the cochlea, producing disturbances that travel up the cochlea.

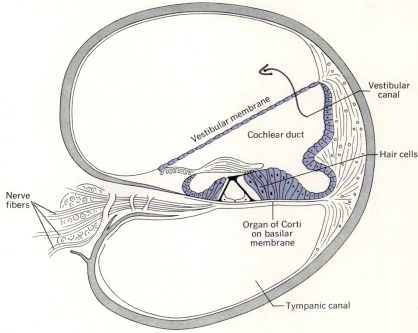

Vestibular membrane
Cochlear duct
Vestibular canal
Hair cells
Nerve fibers
Organ of Corti on basilar membrane
Tympanic canal

Figure 3.13
Part of the cochlea. The organ of Corti on the basilar membrane has hair cells that are the actual receptors of auditory stimuli. Movements of the basilar membrane caused by displacements of the liquid in the tympanic canal stimulate these hair cells, thereby producing sensations of sound.

TESTING YOUR UNDERSTANDING
COLOR BLINDNESS

A person who cannot clearly distinguish among the many colors found in the natural environment is color blind at least partially. This problem, which afflicts many more men than women, ranges from color weakness (or anomaly), where an individual is somewhat insensitive to various hues, to total color blindness (or *monochromacy*), where the person is totally insensitive to color and perceives the entire world in various shades of white, gray, and black.

Individuals with normal color vision are called *trichromats,* because all the colors they are able to see can be produced by various combinations of the physical primaries (red, green, and blue). Color-blind persons who are *dichromats* can only see the shades produced by mixing two of these colors. The most common forms of dichromacy are *protanopia* (insensitivity to red) and *deuteranopia* (insensitivity to green). Persons with this type of color blindness "see" green and red as yellow. Another form of dichromacy, called *tritanopia* (insensitivity to blue or yellow), is much rarer.

How well can the Young-Helmholtz or opponent-process theories of color vision account for the facts of color blindness? Consider the two forms of dichromacy as well as tritanopia and the problems they pose for each theory.

1. The opponent-process theory has difficulty explaining the two forms of dichromacy. If the red-green opponent-process mechanism is simply absent, the two forms of dichromacy could not exist because there would be insensitivity to both red and green. The Young-Helmholtz theory fares better in accounting for dichromacy, for it could postulate that there was a defect in either the cones most sensitive to red or those most sensitive to green.
2. The opponent-process theory could explain tritanopia better than the Young-Helmholtz theory, for it could postulate a defect in the yellow-blue opponent-process mechanism. Since the Young-Helmholtz theory holds that yellow is produced by the activation of green and red receptors, it could predict that *in addition to* yellow blindness, afflicted persons would have difficulty with either green or red. But they do not.

they must be carried in a suitable medium such as air. The two major characteristics of sound waves are amplitude (loudness) and frequency (pitch—the "highness" or "lowness" of a sound).

THEORIES OF HEARING. Several theories have been advanced to explain how we are able to distinguish among sounds of different pitch and loudness. The most important of these are the *resonance* (or *place*) *theory* and the *telephone* (or *frequency*) theory.

a: Amplitude
b: Wave length

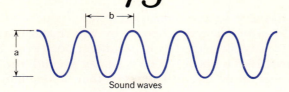

Sound waves

Air molecules

Tuning fork (or
other vibrating
object)

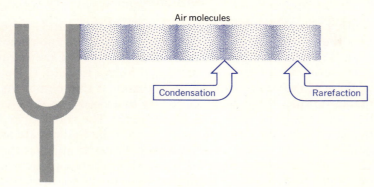

Condensation   Rarefaction

Figure 3.14
Sound waves produced by a vi-
brating object. The peaks of the
sound waves correspond to conden-
sations of air molecules, while the
troughs correspond to rarefactions.

According to the place theory, different regions of the basilar membrane are especially sensitive to the sounds of a given frequency. The fibers along the basilar membrane differ in length and hence resonate differentially according to the wavelength of the sound. Thus, we are able to distinguish among different-pitched sounds. Evidence for this theory has been obtained in several experiments (for example, Stevens, Davis, and Lurie, 1935) demonstrating that the hair cells at the base of the cochlea are more sensitive to sounds of high frequency, while those at the top are more sensitive to sounds of low frequency.

The place theory can explain how we distinguish sounds of different intensity by assuming that stronger stimuli increase the rate of firing of the nerve fibers. Following the discharge of a nerve fiber, the nerve is less excitable than usual for a while. Stronger stimuli, however, can more easily affect a nerve during this period, thereby increasing the frequency of neural discharge which, in turn, produces the sensation of loudness (see page 28).

The telephone (or frequency) theory offers different explanations for the perception of pitch and loudness. This theory assumes that the basilar membrane as a whole responds to the motions transmitted through the bones and fluids of the ear. It is believed that variations in loudness are produced because higher energy sounds cause more hair cells to fire. With respect to pitch, it is believed that the higher the frequency of the sound presented, the more rapidly the hair cells fire. Thus, it is suggested that these receptors fire increasingly rapidly with the rise in frequency of the sound waves. This view seems adequate for frequencies up to about 1000 cycles per second. Beyond this, however, the theory faces a serious difficulty because it is known that individual hair cells cannot fire more than 1000 times per second. This difficulty has lead to a modification of the frequency theory based on the *volley principle* first proposed by Wever and Bray (1930) and more recently confirmed by experimentation (Rose, Brugge, Anderson, and Hind, 1967): Above 1000 cycles per second, the hair cells of the basilar membrane fire in volleys so that no one hair cell responds to *all* sound waves, but *some* cells do respond to every wave.

Neither the place nor the frequency theory is entirely adequate. The idea that particular places on the basilar membrane resonate to sounds of different frequencies is unlikely, for the membrane itself is not a series of independent stretched fibers. Instead, there is a gentle peaking of maximal response in one area of the membrane, which makes it difficult for the place theory to account for the great specificity of the auditory system (Geldard, 1972). The volley principle, so important to the frequency theory, seems to be inadequate for tones above 4000 cycles per second (Wever, 1949). It appears that some combination of the principles set forth in these two theories would be necessary to account for our perception of the frequency and loudness of sound.

PSYCHOPHYSICS   Thus far we have examined the physical properties of sensory stimuli and how they are detected by the sense organs. But as human beings we do not speak of *physical* variables such as wavelength or amplitude; instead, we view our world in the *psychological* language of color, brightness, loudness, and so forth. The study of the relationship between these two classes of events—physical and psychological—is called *psychophysics*. One of the most frequently researched psychophysical phenomena is the smallest amount of physical energy that is needed to produce a psychological sensation.

Common sense tells us that there are obvious limitations on our ability to sense various stimuli. Some objects are too small or far away to be seen, some sounds too weak to be heard, and some smells and tastes too faint to be detected. Psychologists have long been aware of these limitations and have focused their investigation on two aspects.

First, they have tried to pinpoint the limitations themselves—what the *weakest* physical stimulus is that can produce a psychological sensation. This is called the *absolute threshold* (or *limen*—a German word). Stimuli that are too weak to produce sensations are referred to as *subliminal* (below threshold). Research has indicated that, in both vision and audition, we have a very great ability to detect various stimuli.

Second, psychologists have attempted to determine what the smallest *difference* between two stimuli must be in order for them to be judged distinctly different. This value is called the *difference threshold* (difference *limen*), or *just noticeable difference* (j.n.d.). More than 100 years ago, the famous German physiologist Ernst Weber suggested that in order for two stimuli to be judged as being different, the magnitude of the second would have to exceed that of the first by a constant value.

This value has come to be known as the *Weber fraction*, and it has proved to be fairly constant over a wide range of stimulus intensities. Assume, for example, that after lifting a weight of 10 pounds, you can only be certain that a second weight is heavier if it weighs *at least* 10.5 pounds. In this case, then, the second weight would have to exceed the first by 0.5 pounds, or 5 percent of 10 pounds; therefore, the Weber fraction would be 0.5/10.0 or 1/20. It would then be expected, if the Weber fraction were constant, that after lifting a weight of 20 pounds, you could only tell if a second weight were heavier if it weighed at least 21 pounds (that is, it would have to exceed the weight of the first by 5 percent of 1/20). Although the Weber fraction varies a little bit at very small or very large magnitudes, it has been found to remain reasonably constant. One implication of the Weber fraction is that when two stimuli are at fairly low levels, relatively small differences between them can readily be detected, but at higher levels only larger differences can be perceived. For example, to a lower-income person a raise in salary from $100 to $110 per week may mean a great deal, but to a wealthy person, a raise in earnings from $1000 to $1010 a week is trivial.

THE ABSOLUTE THRESHOLD. In classical psychophysics the absolute threshold was often determined by means of a procedure called the *method of limits*. Stimuli well above and well below the threshold would be presented sequentially until the observer reported that he or she could no longer detect the stimulus or could finally perceive it. The absolute threshold was arbitrarily taken to be the amount of stimulus energy that the observer could detect half the time (see Table 3.1). It is now clear, however, that there is no completely uniform relationship between physical stimulus energy and the report of the observer. On one trial, for example, an observer may say that he heard a sound of seven units but later say that he could not hear that sound. Similarly, servicemen who watch radar screens sometimes report the presence of stimuli that are not there.

Recognizing these problems, researchers in *signal detection theory* have postulated that any judgment of an observer in a psychophysical study has two components—actual physical sensitivity and certain psychological factors that affect decision-making (Swets, 1966). This approach is somewhat similar to the task of a pilot:

In the airliner is a radio that, when properly tuned to sufficiently strong signals, actuates a radio compass to point in the direction of the station. Once this compass is pointing in the appropriate direction, finding the airport is easy. But the first step is to tune in the radio. At a distance of five hundred miles from the transmitter all that is heard is the clash and sputter of static. . . . Through the static he searches for the code signal that marks the correct frequency. These signals can be heard long before the radio compass begins to operate and it is important that the pilot tune correctly in order to be sure the compass points to New York rather than, say, Miami [Galanter, 1962, p. 90].

TABLE 3.1

Hypothetical example for determining an absolute threshold. During each trial stimuli are presented in order from top to bottom; in this example, the absolute threshold is 5 units of energy.

TRIAL 1		TRIAL 2	
Amount of stimulus energy	Observer's response	Amount of stimulus energy	Observer's response
2	no	8	yes
3	no	7	yes
4	no	6	yes
5	no	5	yes
6	yes	4	no
7	yes	3	no
8	yes	2	no

TRIAL 3		TRIAL 4	
Amount of stimulus energy	Observer's response	Amount of stimulus energy	Observer's response
2	no	9	yes
3	no	8	yes
4	no	7	yes
5	no	6	yes
6	no	5	yes
7	yes	4	no
8	yes	3	no
9	yes	2	no

In signal detection work, one attempts to discriminate a signal from the background noise. Noise masks a signal and can be produced by spontaneous activity in the nervous system or by stimuli in the environment.

The observer's job is to decide when a signal (or stimulus plus ongoing noise) is sufficiently greater than the noise alone to warrant a decision, "I detect a stimulus." Thus, as shown in Table 3.2, there are four possibilities of making a right or wrong decision about the presence of a stimulus where there is noise.

In addition, there is another problem. Suppose an experimenter presents to a subject (that is, an observer) a constant signal (for example, a tone) against varying levels of background noise (for example, loud music). As we can see in Table 3.3, the strength of the signal plus the noise varies with the strength of the background noise. It is assumed that the level of background noise in the nervous system also varies over time. Thus, since an observer responds to the strength of signal plus noise, a constant stimulus will appear to be of varying intensity as it is presented over and over again. This observation accounts for the apparent inconsistency of people's performance when they are trying to detect stimuli of low intensity.

TABLE 3.2

Possible responses in a signal detection study in which a stimulus is either present or absent on each trial.

	Observer's decisions	
Stimulus conditions	Yes	No
Signal plus noise	Hit	Miss
Noise alone	False alarm	Correct rejection

TABLE 3.3

Representation of a signal of 10 units, together with changing background noise. Because the background noise varies in strength, a constant stimulus can appear to vary in intensity.

Hypothetical values of strength of background noise	Hypothetical values of strength of signal	Strength of signal plus noise
10	10	20
20	10	30
30	10	40
40	10	50
50	10	60

Psychologists studying threshold measurement assume that an observer can *decide* what the rewards and costs will be for correct responses and errors; accordingly, therefore, he can establish a decision rule. Suppose that a particular observer was very cautious and did not want to make many false alarm errors. If he were paid $0.05 for every correct detection but lost $0.25 for every false alarm, he might respond only to relatively strong signals; thus, he would avoid false alarms but also fail to detect some true signals.

Now consider a different observer who wants at all costs to detect each stimulus. If he were paid $0.25 for detecting a stimulus and lost nothing for making a false alarm, he might respond to very low values of signal plus noise; thus, he would detect almost all true signals but also make many false alarms.

Decision rules, like those just mentioned, can also be formulated by observers in situations where the rewards and costs are not specified by an experimenter. Take, for example, a radarscope operator stationed in Alaska, whose task is to monitor any unidentified blips that could signal the beginning of a nuclear missile attack on America. If he thinks he has seen something and sounds a false alarm, he may be embarrassed, but if he misses a signal (that is not detected by other operators), precious time might be lost by those who have authority to launch antimissile missiles.

Signal detection experiments have convincingly shown that even the perception of simple stimuli such as sounds and lights is really not a simple, physiological process. As we discuss the perception of more complicated environmental stimuli, the role of psychological processes in perception will become even more apparent.

FROM STIMULUS ENERGY TO PERCEIVING THE ENVIRONMENT

How far will knowledge of how various sense organs respond to energy in the environment take us in answering questions about our perception of the world—the way in which we detect depth, size, movement, and so forth? Raw data from the senses have long been viewed as inadequate for many of these tasks. One reason is that a single proximal stimulus can represent several environmental situations. For example, the pattern of retinal excitation produced by looking at an automobile pass in front of you is the same one that would be produced if you moved your head slowly while observing a stationary car. Similarly many of the cues that provide information about depth can represent either real three dimensionality or simply a two-dimensional display, as in a realistic painting or motion picture. One school of thought—the structuralist school—handled this problem by assuming that the ambiguous sensations are elaborated on and added to by memory. For example, when we see a friend at a great distance, he produces only a small image on the retina. Instead of believing that his size has changed, we "adjust" the small retinal image by means of our memory, and thus we maintain an accurate perception of his size.

More recently, however, James Gibson (1966) and Julian Hochberg (1964) have proposed a different concept of perception. Gibson (1950, 1966) has argued that we should view the senses as information pick-up devices and not channels of sensation. The eye, for example, does not respond simply to the energy of light but to the structure that is imposed on light when it is reflected from a surface. Since the eyes, ears, and skin are continually exploring the environment, they are receiving feedback. Gibson feels that the senses are not simply passive recipients of stimulus energy; when we perceive something in the environment, we typically do so through a number of senses simultaneously. Gibson has suggested that the information for perceiving depth, distance, and so forth exists in an unambiguous form in the environment.

As seen in Figure 3.15, the same *stimulus* can give rise to different perceptions at different times. Surely this presents a grave problem for a theory of perception like the structuralists', for the sensations remain constant while one's perception of them changes. Gibson argued that it is only the information for the two perceptions that varies:

> *In the goblet-faces display, the stimulus is the same for the two percepts but the stimulus* information *is not. . . . There are two counterbalanced values of stimulus information in the same "stimulus." The perception is equivocal because what comes to the eye is equivocal [pp. 247–248].*

Figure 3.15
An ambiguous figure displayed by the goblet faces. How can the same stimulus produce two different perceptions?

Another classic problem for the structuralist theory of perception is how a series of discrete sensations become the constant world we perceive. Presumably, one answer could be memory—each sensation is stored in the brain and successive stored images are then integrated into a constant whole. Instead, Gibson thinks that there is unchanging information (or structure) which is perceived and that this invariant structure shapes our experience of a constant world (see Figure 3.16).

Figure 3.16
Four views of a room as seen through the left eye of someone in a stationary position. The viewer does not see a chain of independent, snapshot-like sensations; he sees a constant room. The structuralists have assumed that such constancy is due to the fact the mind integrates the discrete sensations, but Gibson argues that there is invariant structure in the four views that produces the constancy of perception.

TESTING YOUR UNDERSTANDING
GESTALT PSYCHOLOGY AND STRUCTURALISM

The structuralists' approach to perception had been criticized at an earlier time by Gestalt psychologists. Essentially, they objected to the same features of structuralism that troubled later writers such as Gibson and Hochberg—the view that perception is built up from discrete sensations and that perceptual ambiguities can be resolved by appeals to memory. Gestalt psychologists suggested that organization is intrinsic to perception, that is, that stimuli are immediately perceived as organized. Thus, organization does not have to be added on later (see Figure 3.17).

Earlier we noted that the eye contains a blind spot and that we somehow fill in any images that fall upon it. Which of the Gestalt principles of perceptual organization could account for this fact? How does the filling-in of the blind spot pose a problem for structuralism?

1. The Gestalt principle that would best account for the filling-in of the blind spot is closure. This school of thought holds that gaps in stimulation are filled to create good figures and organized patterns.
2. By filling in the blind spot, perception does not correspond to sensation (as postulated by the structuralists).

Figure 3.17
Gestalt principles of perceptual organization: (A) The influence of proximity on perception. The closeness of the elements leads to their organization as either columns (1), rows (2), or diagonals (3). (B) The influence of similarity of shape. The elements are organized into rows because rows contain identical elements. (C) The principle of good continuation. When individual elements produce a pattern, the configuration predominates over the individual elements. (D) The principle of closure. The circles successively lose parts, yet the final one remains a circle.

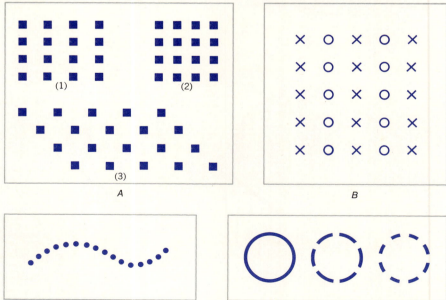

DEPTH PERCEPTION. We are continually making judgments about the distance between ourselves and various objects. How do we do this? A number of proximal stimuli carry information about depth. Some of these function when we view the world with only one eye, and thus they are called *monocular cues of depth.* Others require the use of both eyes and are called *binocular cues.*

One of the simplest of all monocular depth cues is that of *interposition;* when one object appears to cover or obscure part of another, we judge that the first is closer than the second. A second simple cue to depth is provided by *shadows* (see Figure 3.18). The cue of *texture gradient* arises from the fact that the amount of detail we can perceive decreases with distance (see Figure 3.19). Thus, patterns and objects seem to "fade away" into the distance, enabling us to make accurate judgments of distance or depth. Still another monocular depth cue is provided by *linear perspective.* As you look down a set of railroad tracks or a straight section of highway, parallel lines seem to converge in the distance, creating the distinct impression of depth. Linear perspective is frequently employed by artists to give the feeling of depth in their work.

The most significant binocular depth cue is *binocular* (or *retinal*) *disparity.* Because the two eyes are located at different points in space,

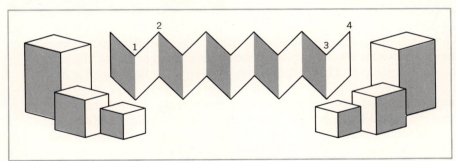

Figure 3.18
The monocular depth cue of shadow. Cover the right-hand side of the figure and note whether 1 or 2 is nearer. Then do the same for the left-hand side and compare 3 and 4. [Source: After Hochberg (1964)]

Figure 3.19
Texture gradient is a monocular depth cue. The figure on the left appears to recede into the distance, while the one on the right seems to be equally distant from the observer at all points.

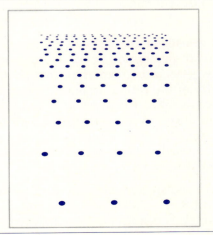

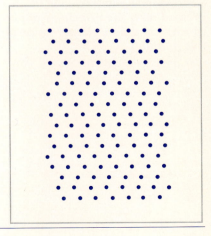

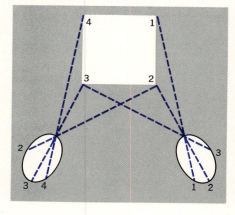

Figure 3.21
Graphic representation of binocular (retinal) disparity. Notice that the corners of the square fall on slightly different points of the two retinas.

Figure 3.20
Principles of perspective. The lines drawn over this street scene by Baldassare Peruzzi show how perspective creates an almost three-dimensional effect on an otherwise two-dimensional surface. Note that the lines all converge on a central point called the "vanishing point." It is obvious that Peruzzi, like other Renaissance painters, was impressed with the principles of perspective and used them in planning this painting.

they are exposed to slightly different images of any object. The disparity between the two images provides a strong cue for the perception of depth (see Figure 3.21); this is the principle behind a device called a stereoscope, which enables one to see pictures in a three-dimensional plane. You can easily demonstrate the existence of retinal disparity by looking at one of your fingers held up about 12 inches from your face. First shut one eye and then the other and note how your finger seems to jump from side to side even though you are holding it steady. The reason for the apparent movement is that each retina receives a slightly different image of the finger.

Theories of Depth Perception. The structuralists hypothesize that depth perception is learned by combining visual and kinesthetic cues. By associating experiences such as walking and reaching with the size of the retinal image of the object being walked toward or reached for, the person *learns* to judge the distance of the object that produces a retinal image of a given size. A young child, for example, learns that when her favorite toy produces a large retinal image she can reach it, but when the image is smaller, it is farther away and she must walk to it.

But the structuralist theory has encountered difficulties. E. J. Gibson and R. D. Walk devised an ingenious apparatus called the *visual cliff*, which is constructed from a heavy sheet of glass elevated several feet

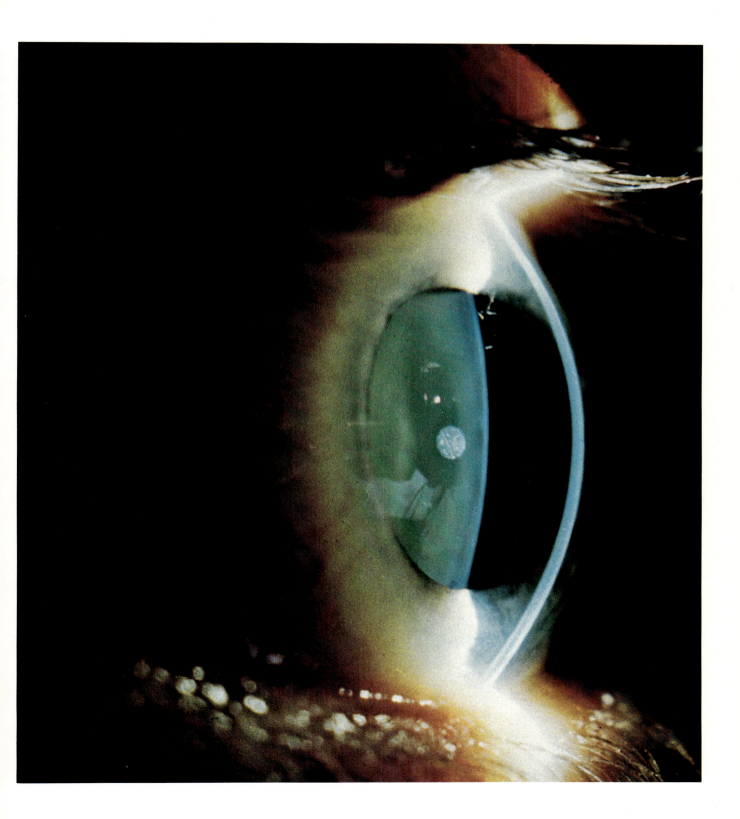

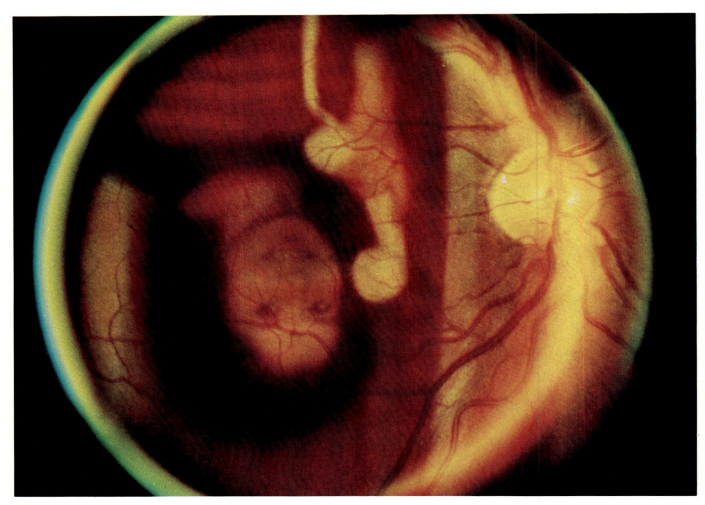

1. Photograph of the retinal image of someone who is watching a girl use a telephone. The picture was taken through the pupil by a specially constructed camera. Note that the image is inverted and that it has been blurred somewhat after passing through the various fluids in the eye. The yellow region at the right is the blind spot.

2. Photograph of the human retina at the blind spot. This is the point at which the nerve fibers from the rods and cones converge and leave the eye as the optic nerve.

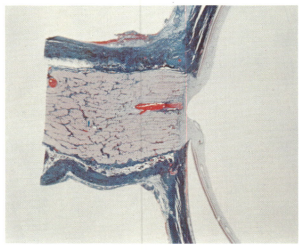

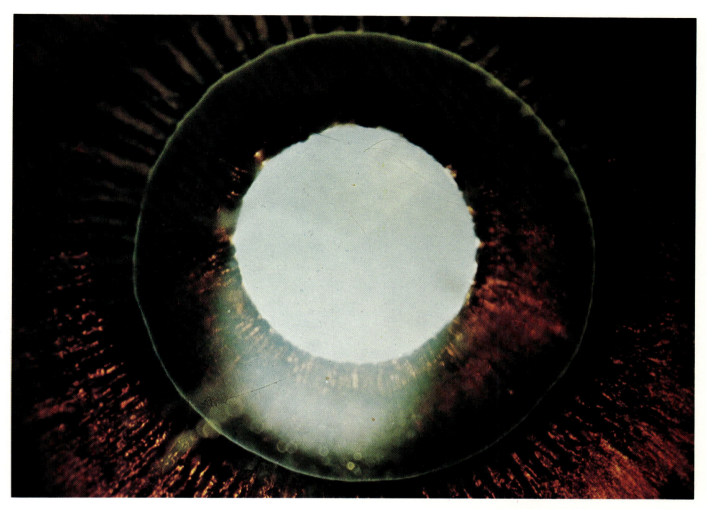

3. Looking out at the world from the interior of the eye. The iris forms the frame for our view.

4. Photograph of the middle ear, showing the structures between the eardrum and the cochlea.

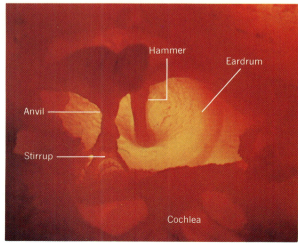

Hammer

Eardrum

Anvil

Stirrup

Cochlea

5. The entire electromagnetic spectrum. Notice that the visible spectrum represents only a very tiny portion of the entire range. Within the visible spectrum note the relationship between wavelength and color.

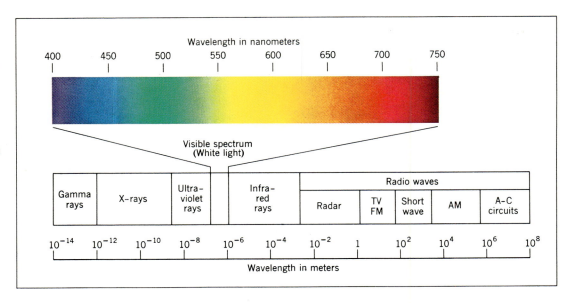

6a. An additive mixture of wavelengths is produced by blending colored *lights.* White is produced here by combining three colors.

6b. A subtractive color mixture is produced when *pigments* are combined. Blending three colored pigments here yields black.

Figure 3.22
One of the subjects in Gibson and Walk's (1960) experiment with the visual cliff. Even though the child could feel the solid glass with his hand, he refused to move off the central plank onto the "deep" side in order to reach his mother.

off the ground; a plank covered with checkered material, which serves as a platform, is placed in the center of the glass, resting slightly higher than the glass itself (see Figure 3.22). The plank is large enough to hold a small child and provides a vantage point from which the two sides of the "cliff" can be seen. One side (just behind the baby in Figure 3.22) is no more than an inch or two below the plank and is thought of as the shallow side of the cliff. On the other side of the plank (in front of the baby), the checkered material drops vertically down to the floor, creating the steep side of the cliff. Actually, of course, the transparent glass alone is thick enough to support the weight of the child so that there is no real danger of falling off.

In an initial experiment with this equipment, Gibson and Walk (1960) placed 36 infants (aged 6 to 14 months) one at a time on the central board and then asked their mothers to call to them from both the deep and shallow sides. Of the 27 infants who actually moved off the board, 24 went only to the shallow side, while 3 moved out onto the deep side. Thus it is clear that the children perceived depth, which resulted in their strong reluctance to cross the visual cliff to reach their mothers.

Gibson and Walk's findings argue against the structuralist view that depth perception results from combining visual and kinesthetic ones; 6-to-14-month infants would not likely have had enough specific experiences relevant to the visual cliff to allow them to see depth here. But it should not be concluded that experience with the environment is unimportant in depth perception; there remains an on-going debate about the relative importance of nature versus nurture in perception. Gibson and Walk's study supports the significance of nature (or innate factors) but others have demonstrated the significance of experience.

The value of active contact with the environment for the development of normal perceptual abilities has been dramatically demonstrated in an experiment by Held (1965). Kittens were reared mainly in darkness from birth up to the age of 8 to 12 weeks (at which time they become capable of moving readily about the environment). They were then placed two at a time in the apparatus shown in Figure 3.23. As

Figure 3.23
The apparatus used by Held (1965) to investigate the effects of active and passive movement on the development of visual perception. The kitten that could move about actively developed normal visual reactions, while the one that rode around passively did not.

can be seen, one of the kittens could walk actively about the circular enclosure, while the other had to ride passively in a little car. Held reasoned that, with this apparatus, the two animals would receive approximately the same visual stimulation, but only one would have the additional experience of active movement. After a total of about 30 hours in the apparatus, the two animals in each pair were tested for a variety of perceptual abilities (for example, blinking at approaching objects and depth perception on the visual cliff). The results indicated that the kittens who had been moved passively through the environment had severe deficiencies in these abilities in comparison with those who had been permitted to walk on their own.

Although Held's study at first seems to support the structuralist interpretation of depth perception, closer examination reveals that this is not necessarily the case. Remember that Gibson does not view the senses as independent or as passive recipients of environmental information. Held's study could have created conditions in which there was no perceptual learning because the cues-to-be-responded-to require the simultaneous use of vision and feedback from self-initiated movements.

THE CONSTANCIES. We live in a constantly changing perceptual world—changes are taking place in the physical environment around us as well as in our own location and in the state of our own bodies. Thus, our sensory receptors are literally flooded with new and often contradictory stimulation from moment to moment. Nevertheless, we tend to perceive the world as a stable and orderly place. The *perceptual constancies* create order and unity in our experience of the world by ensuring that our perceptions of various objects do not change as we view them from different perspectives and under different conditions. Although constancies operate in all sense modalities, perhaps the clearest examples are in the visual field.

Shape Constancy. As we move about in space, the image cast upon our retinas by a given object varies markedly. When viewed head-on, a closed door, for example, produces a rectangular image on the ret-

Figure 3.24a
Look at these four shapes. Are they totally different?

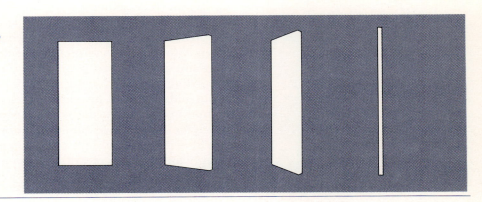

Figure 3.24b
As you will note, the shapes represent different perspectives of the same door.

ina, while a partially opened door produces one of an entirely different shape (see Figure 3.24b).

Despite such wide variations in the form of the retinal image, we tend to perceive objects as maintaining a constant shape. This fact may not seem at all surprising until it is realized that it means that our visual system must somehow interpret markedly different patterns of proximal stimulation as representing the same distal object. Again, it is clear that our experience of the world is more than a simple reflection of the sensory input we receive from our various receptor organs. Shape constancy, like the other constancies we will discuss below, has great adaptive significance, for it allows us to recognize and thus respond appropriately to a multitude of objects.

Size Constancy. A second type of perceptual constancy with which we are all familiar is our awareness that a given object remains the same size even though the size of the image cast upon our retina varies according to our distance from the object. Take any small object (such as a coin) and hold it close to your eyes. At this distance, the coin fills much of your visual field and casts a very large image on your retina. If you move the coin to arm's length, it will not fill nearly so much of your visual field and will produce a much smaller retinal image. Obviously the coin has not "shrunk" in size; it has simply moved farther away. Similarly, when we see a friend wave to us from across the street, he or she appears to be of normal size, despite the fact that our retinal image of this person is quite small. Then, when our friend crosses the street and approaches, he or she does not grow in size, even though our retinal image will increase accordingly. Indeed, it seems ludicrous to point these things out, but if our judgments of physical size depended solely upon the size of the retinal image produced by various objects, their size would always be changing. Thus, once again, it is apparent that our perception of the world is determined in a complex manner and is not merely due to a simple and passive reception of sensory stimulation.

Most structuralists attempt to explain size constancy according to the

Figure 3.25
In this example of perceptual constancy, the person is much larger than the background buildings, yet we correctly perceive that the buildings are actually much larger.

Figure 3.26
The same object seen at two distances on a textured surface. The perception of constant size could be due to the fact that at both distances the object covers the same number of background elements. [Source: After Gibson (1950)]

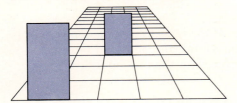

unconscious inference theory; they assume that both distance and retinal image size are perceived and used to make an internal, unconscious computation of the true size of the distal object. In some sense, people must do more than just attend to their retinal images in order to perceive the size of the object accurately. But the unconscious inference theory runs into a major difficulty: one of the pieces of information that is believed to be used in the unconscious computation—retinal image size—is really not very useful. Subjects cannot reliably estimate the sizes of their own retinal images (Wallach and McKenna, 1960).

Gibson (1950) has suggested that size constancy could be attributed solely to environmental information. In most environmental situations, size judgments are made of objects that normally have a textured surface as background. The ratio of the number of elements covered by each object at two different distances could provide information that would be an ideal cue for size (see Figure 3.26) without resorting to memory or unconscious computations.

THE ILLUSIONS. Our perceptions of the world are usually quite consistent with the physical reality they represent; however, they sometimes fail to reflect physical reality accurately. When this happens, we are the victim of an *illusion*—a disparity between perception and physical reality. Although illusions occur in all of the senses (as was the case with the perceptual constancies), the best examples are visual.

Perhaps the simplest visual illusion—*the horizontal-vertical illusion*—can be seen in the bisection of a horizontal line by a vertical line of

Figure 3.27
The horizontal-vertical illusion. Although the two lines are identical in length, the vertical one seems to be longer.

Figure 3.28
The Ponzo illusion. The top rectangle appears to be much larger, even though it is exactly the same size as the lower one.

Figure 3.29
The famous Müller-Lyer illusion. Although the horizontal lines of both figures are precisely the same length, the top one appears to be much longer.

the same length (see Figure 3.27); the vertical line appears to be longer although the two lines are actually identical in length. A second well-known illusion—*the Ponzo illusion*—was first described by Mario Ponzo (1913) and now bears his name (see Figure 3.28). It consists of four lines, two of equal length at a slight angle away from the vertical and converging together, and two equal horizontal lines between them. The horizontal line that seems farther away also appears longer.

A third visual illusion is the famous *Müller-Lyer* phenomenon (see Figure 3.29). It can be seen that the horizontal line bounded by the closed arrowheads seems to be shorter than the one bounded by the open or reversed arrowheads.

Trying to Explain Visual Illusions. According to Gregory (1968), the Müller-Lyer, Ponzo, and similar illusions occur not because of limitations in our nervous system, but because they represent ambiguous sensory input. More specifically, Gregory suggests that when we examine two-dimensional figures such as those in drawings or photos, we are exposing our visual system to ambiguous input. The ambiguity arises from the fact that these two-dimensional figures frequently suggest three-dimensional space. Once our visual system interprets them as three dimensional, we make certain unconscious and automatic adjustments in the apparent size of the objects they depict. Thus, we "enlarge" those that appear to be relatively far away to compensate for

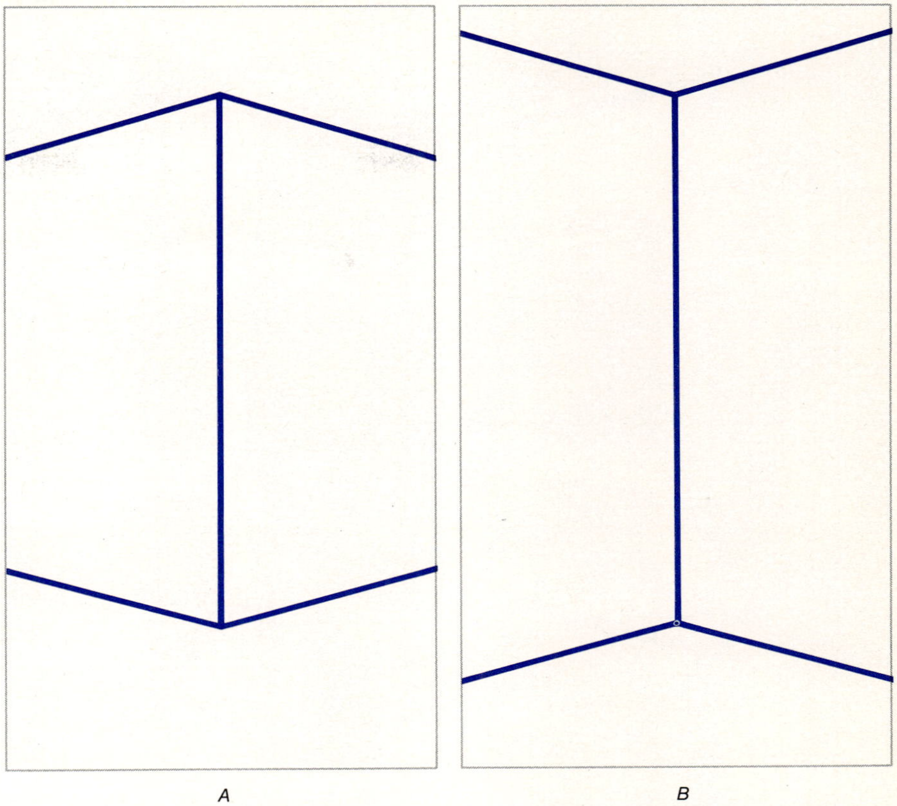

Figure 3.30
The Müller-Lyer illusion is represented as the outside (A) and inside (B) corners of a room or building. According to Gregory (1968), the illusion may occur because our visual system interprets the vertical line in A as being nearer than the vertical line in B. By contracting the line in A and expanding it in B, we have the illusion.

A

B

their perceived distance from us, and we "contract" those that seem to be relatively nearby. The role of such automatic adjustments in visual illusions is apparent in Figures 3.30 and 3.31, where the Müller-Lyer illusion is depicted as the near and far corners of a room or building. According to Gregory, the illusion arises because the line bounded by the closed arrowheads is perceived as being relatively near and so is "contracted," while the line bounded by the open arrowheads is seen as being far away and thus is "expanded" to compensate for the apparent greater distance.

Hochberg (1964) believes that explaining these illusions as an unconscious inference is not entirely adequate: "Knowing that the Müller-Lyer illusion lies on a flat surface does not dispel the illusion" (p. 57). Another commentary on the Müller-Lyer illusion was presented by Gibson (1966):

The information for length of line . . . is not simply length of line. To suppose so is to confuse the picture considered as a surface with the optical information to the eye. A line drawn on paper is not a stimulus. The stimulus information for the length of a line is altered by combining it with other lines. We should never have expected equal lengths to appear equal when they are incorporated in different figures. Only if we can isolate the two line segments from the wings and arrowheads in

Figure 3.31
The Müller-Lyer illusion is shown
as the outside and inside corners of
an actual building.

the Müller-Lyer illusion should they appear equal. . . . The question
of why one line looks shorter than the other is no longer of major impor-
tance for the theory of perception if line segments as such are not com-
ponents of perception [p. 313].

**EXTRASENSORY PERCEPTION: TELEPATHY, CLAIRVOY-
ANCE, AND PSYCHOKINESIS.** *Extrasensory perception*, a truly intriguing topic, has long captured the imagination of scientists and
laymen alike. Do we possess an "extra" sense that, if we could utilize
it properly, would permit us to "read" the minds of others (*telepathy*), perceive objects and events beyond our more conventional
senses (*clairvoyance*), or forecast future events (*precognition*)? Similarly, can mental events such as wishes or thoughts ever influence the
physical world (*psychokinesis*)? Although these phenomena have been
empirically investigated for more than 50 years, most psychologists
are not convinced of their existence. Two reasons may account for
this. First, these phenomena are outside the areas studied by most contemporary psychologists. Since psychologists have done research on
the sensory processes for nearly 100 years, what can *"extrasensory"*
mean? Have all these researchers been missing something, and if so
what is that something?

Second, many of the early investigations that purported to demonstrate telepathy, clairvoyance, or precognition contained serious flaws which tended to make their findings ambiguous. For example, it was found that the experimenters often did such things as raise their voices or move their lips in a characteristic manner when asking their subjects to guess the presence of a particular symbol. Although such cues were usually provided quite unintentionally, these biases in research procedure meant that such studies did not provide conclusive evidence for the existence of ESP phenomena. Furthermore, when these contaminating factors were eliminated, other investigators could not replicate the results of apparently successful ESP experiments. This was true even when an attempt was made to reproduce in every detail the procedures used in the initial, successful studies. Although most psychologists are not persuaded that ESP phenomena exist, some methodologically sophisticated studies have produced positive results, indicating that the whole issue cannot simply be dismissed. We will briefly discuss two rather convincing studies—one on clairvoyance and the other on psychokinesis.

In the first of these experiments, Anderson and McConnell (1961) set out to determine if they could obtain any evidence for the existence of clairvoyance among young children. Twenty-eight children in a fourth-grade class of a public elementary school were told that they were going to play a game in which they would "mentally" launch a rocket. This particular context was chosen because of the children's great interest in space exploration (the study was conducted at the time the U.S. space effort was just beginning to shift into high gear).

The children were told that in order to launch and guide the rocket to its destination in outer space, they would have to "read" a series of secret codes that were in sealed envelopes. The envelopes actually contained the materials that they were to perceive without seeing, presumably through clairvoyance.

The study was conducted in a series of eight separate sessions. During the first six sessions, the children were actually given the envelopes containing the materials and were asked to indicate what they thought was inside. The materials on which they reported during the six sessions were, respectively: the numbers 1–5; the arithmetical symbols +, −, ×, =, ÷; the colors red, yellow, blue, green, orange; the letters a, b, x, y, z; and again the numbers 1–5. During the last two sessions, no envelopes were provided, and the children were asked to report what they saw through the windows of their rocket: a moon, a planet, an asteroid, a comet, or a star. The materials they were attempting to "perceive" during these sessions were not constructed until after the conclusion of the experiment. Thus, this part of the study investigated their ability to forecast future events (precognition).

In order to eliminate sources of bias (or contamination) from the experiment, the following precautions were taken: First, the materials used

TABLE 3.4

The major findings of the Anderson and McConnell (1961) experiment. The results of the first six sessions (the clairvoyance phase) indicated that the subjects guessed the contents of the sealed envelopes with greater accuracy than could have been expected solely on the basis of chance. However, the findings for the last two sessions provided no evidence that they could forecast future events (precognition).

Phase of experiment	Session	Total guesses	Number of correct guesses expected by chance	Number of correct guesses actually attained
Clairvoyance	1	1080	216	215
	2	520	104	139
	3	920	184	206
	4	1000	200	205
	5	960	192	205
	6	1080	216	222
	Total	5560	1112	1192
Precognition	7	520	104	102
	8	540	108	102
	Total	1060	212	204

in the first six sessions (those concerned with clairvoyance) were wrapped in opaque aluminum foil and placed between two sheets of paper before being placed in the envelopes. Second, the envelopes were doubly sealed in such a manner that it would have been immediately apparent if they had been opened before the end of the experiment. Third, the experimenters were not present while the data were being collected; they received most of the materials through the mail. Fourth, the materials in each envelope were prepared by means of a table of random numbers in a rigidly standardized manner. Finally, the data were double-checked by independent scorers at the end of the experiment and before any statistical analyses were performed. (This was done to prevent any errors in recording.)

The major results of the study are presented in Table 3.4. As can be seen, during the first six sessions (the clairvoyance phase) the subjects made a total of 5560 guesses about the contents of the envelopes. Since five different symbols were used during each session, it could be expected that they would get 1112 (5560 ÷ 5) correct purely on the basis of chance (that is, 20 percent or one in five). Actually they made 1192 correct guesses. Although this does not seem to be a very large difference, it is statistically significant and could be expected to occur by chance only three times in 1000 ($p = .003$).

On the final two sessions (the precognition phase), the children were not able to forecast future events with any greater accuracy than could be expected by chance alone. Thus, the study provided no evidence for precognition. In view of the many precautions taken by the experimenters to prevent contamination of their data, it appears that the results of this study provide some evidence for the existence of a phenomenon resembling clairvoyance. However, such a surprising and potentially important finding must be replicated again by other investigators and with other subject populations before it can be accepted with any great degree of confidence.

The second experiment we will discuss—on psychokinesis—was conducted by McConnell, Snowdon, and Powell (1955). To determine whether mental proceses (for example, wishes) can influence events in the physical world, the experimenters asked 393 college students to try to cause a pair of thrown dice to come to rest with a particular target number showing on top of each simply by *wishing* for this outcome. The first one-third of the throws were made by the subjects themselves, using a special cup and a felt-lined tray. The final two-thirds of the throws were made by a mechanical apparatus turned by an electric motor. All together 432 dice were thrown (216 throws of two dice) for each subject; a total of approximately 170,000 die throws were made during the entire study.

In order to avoid errors in recording the data, the experimenter called out the results of each throw for verification by the subject before writing them down. In the case of the throws made by the machine, the dice were photographed each time, so that the results could be double-checked against the direct physical evidence of their final position. Finally, the dice were examined by X-ray before the study began to make sure that they were fair and then these dice were used throughout the experiment.

The results failed to show any over-all tendency for the "wished-for" numbers to occur more often than could be expected by chance, or one in six. However, an interesting phenomenon was observed that has also been found in several other similar investigations (Pratt, 1947; Rhine, 1952). At the beginning of each session, the dice tended to come up in the wished-for pattern more often than could be expected by chance, but then this tendency decreased so that by the end of the session the pattern occurred *less* often than the expected one-in-six value (that is, 16.7 percent). These results are depicted in Figure 3.32. It would appear that the subjects initially had the ability to influence the dice in the desired direction, but then gradually lost this "power" as the session progressed. The fact that the same type of decline occurred in the case of all six possible target numbers, but

Figure 3.32
The result of the McConnell, Snowdon, and Powell (1955) experiment on psychokinesis. The two bars represent the proportion of "wished-for" numbers obtained during the two machine-thrown sessions. The subjects first obtained a higher proportion of the target numbers than could have been expected on the basis of chance alone (that is, 0.167), but later they got fewer of these numbers than chance alone would dictate.

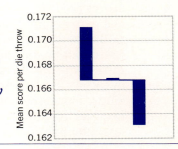

PSYCHOLOGY AND THE PROBLEMS OF SOCIETY
PERCEPTION AND PREJUDICE

One of the most significant domestic issues since the late 1950s has been the press for civil rights and equal opportunity by members of minority groups, especially blacks. Although laws can be enacted against "institutional racism"—discernible patterns of discrimination in housing or employment—they cannot directly change people's prejudicial attitudes. Believing that "an ounce of prevention is worth a pound of cure," some psychologists have attempted to study the acquisition and modification of racial attitudes in children.

Phyllis Katz (1973) notes that a number of theories have been advanced about the origin of racial attitudes in children—from the effects of parental disciplinary styles to the kind of neighborhood a child grows up in. One difficulty with these theories is that they include variables that are not amenable to experimental manipulation and laboratory research; thus, they can yield only limited data about the development of racial attitudes. However, Katz points out that most theorists agree that a necessary precondition for the development of racial attitudes is a *perception* of skin color differences.

Katz, Sohn, and Zalk (1975) examined these issues in a developmental study of perceptual correlates of attitude formation among both black and white children in the second, fourth, and sixth grades in the Northeast. The study was divided into two parts. First, they administered a wide variety of measures of racial attitudes to examine the relationship between negative attitudes and such factors as age, race of subject, and race of experimenter. Using these results, they identified groups of high- and low-prejudiced children and had them rate pairs of black and white faces with different facial expressions, hair styles, and such features as eyeglasses on a scale of difference and similarity. The results of the first part of the study revealed that the children were quite sophisticated about race and that the older children would give socially desirable answers on the questionnaires, especially in the presence of an experimenter of the other race.

The second part of the study found different developmental patterns of person perception and racial attitudes for black and white children. Among both high- and low-prejudiced blacks, shade and color cues were important in judging the similarity or difference of faces at all age levels. Among white children, however, only those with high prejudice scores paid close attention to color cues over nonracial ones, such as facial expression. Using this and other data, Katz and her co-workers hypothesize the following development among white children: During the preschool years, children pay the greatest attention to members of their own race. Later, in middle childhood, they show greater interest in racial cues as part of their broader interest in person cues of all kinds. Finally, in early adolescence their racial attitudes become more fixed as they attach group labels to persons of other races and pay less attention to individual differences.

This sequence of steps in the acquisition of racial attitudes provides further insight into an earlier study by Katz (1973) on the modification of negative racial attitudes. Selecting black and white second and sixth graders who had high prejudice scores, Katz divided this sample into three experimental groups: one in which the children were trained to associate first names with four faces of the other race presented in random order ("distinctive-labeling training"), another in which the children were asked to examine pairs of faces very carefully and decide if they were the same or different ("perceptual-differentiation training"), and a control group that saw the same faces as the first group but received no instructions. After viewing the faces, the children were again tested for their prejudicial attitudes. In one of the tests, the children were shown a picture of black and white children interacting, and they were asked to describe what was going on. They were scored according to their positive or negative remarks about the children of the other race. Katz found that there was a decrease in the levels of prejudice in both the distinctive-labeling and perceptual-differentiation training groups and suggests that the ability to distinguish individual members of other races leads to more positive ethnic attitudes.

If Katz is right, it may be true that our prejudices originate with seeing all members of another race as "alike." But when we go beyond seeing people as members of a group and see them as individuals, we begin to see them in all their complexity, good and bad.

Sample item from the Katz-Zalk Opinion Questionnaire. The children are told: "These two boys are looking at maps of the moon. One of these children is the best in his class in science. Which one?" (Copyright © Phyllis A. Katz and Sue Rosenberg Zalk, 1973.)

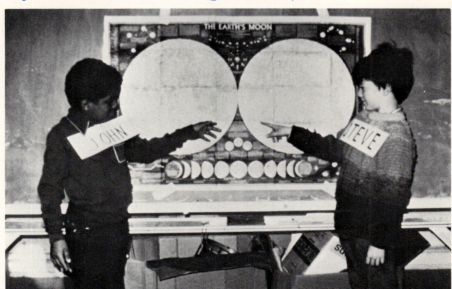

did not occur when each of these numbers was *not* wished for by the subjects, lends additional support to this very surprising outcome.

Considered together, the Anderson and McConnell (1961) and McConnell, Snowdon, and Powell (1955) studies seem to suggest that perhaps psychologists should be more willing to admit the possibility of extrasensory perception than they have been in the past. Indeed, the mere fact that such findings have been largely ignored up to the present time lends support to McConnell's (1969) view that many psychologists have tended to reject the existence of ESP and related phenomena on nonscientific grounds (claiming that they are too reminiscent of magic, mysticism, and the occult). Carrying out additional carefully controlled experiments such as those described above may bring this extremely interesting topic into the mainstream of modern psychology in the near future.

SUMMARY

The study of perception focuses on how the distal stimuli of the environment come to be known through the proximal stimuli (or patterns of energy and information) that reach our sensory receptors. There are five classic senses. The chemical senses—taste and smell—are so named because the stimulus for both is chemical. The olfactory receptors respond to fine airborne particles and the tastebuds to organic molecules that dissolve in the mouth's saliva. The skin senses include the perception of pressure, pain, and temperature. Many structures embedded in the skin have been linked to these sensations, but the exact sensory organs have yet to be determined. Sensations of the body are divided into two types: kinesthesis—sensations from the joints and muscles that provide us with information about body movement—and the vestibular sensations of rotation, acceleration, and tilt that come from two structures of the inner ear—the semicircular canals and the vestibule. Light is the stimulus for the receptor organ for vision—the eye. The actual visual receptors—the rods and cones —are found in the retina and function somewhat differently. The cones are sensitive to color and detail while the rods are more significant for seeing in dim light. Two major theories of color vision—the Young-Helmholtz and opponent-process theories—still vie for ascendance; both are supported by some data. Sound waves are the stimuli for hearing. The cochlea, located in the inner ear, is the place where sounds are actually detected. In trying to account for our ability to discriminate the intensity and frequency of sounds, two theories— the resonance and the telephone theories—have been proposed.

Psychophysics is the study of the relationship between the physical properties of a stimulus and the psychological sensations they produce. Two important areas of investigation are the absolute threshold—the smallest amount of physical energy that can produce a sensation—and the difference threshold—the smallest physical difference that must exist between two stimuli before they can be discriminated. Recent work in signal detection theory suggests that simple sensory judgments are heavily influenced by certain psychological factors.

Perception consists of more than merely responding to physical variables such as intensity and wavelength. Information for depth perception is carried by both monocular cues, such as interposition and linear perspective, and binocular cues like retinal disparity. Our perception of the world remains constant, although the patterns of proximal stimulation reaching our receptors change dramatically. One of the perceptual constancies is our unchanging perception of an object's size even though at different distances it produces retinal images of different sizes. Illusions occur when our perceptions of the external world are innaccurate. It is recognized that in all areas of perception, what we are aware of is not simply the product of sensations. To account for this, the structuralists assume that our sensations are elaborated on by our memory to produce our perceptions, but recently others have suggested that sensations are not the only building blocks for perception.

Extrasensory perception includes such areas as telepathy, clairvoyance, precognition, and psychokinesis. Although ESP phenomena are viewed with some degree of skepticism by most psychologists, there is some evidence for their existence.

GLOSSARY

Absolute threshold: The smallest amount of physical stimulus energy that is required to produce a sensation.

Ampulla: The enlarged area at the base of each semicircular canal that contains the receptors for the perception of body rotation.

Aqueous humor: The liquid that fills the space in the eye between the cornea and the lens.

Auditory canal: The passage that leads from the pinna to the eardrum.

Basilar membrane: The structure in the cochlea that moves when fluid is displaced in the cochlea and contains the receptors for sound waves.

Basket-shaped nerve endings: The receptors for pressure sensations that are located around the base of the hair cells.

Binocular depth cue: Information about depth that requires the use of both eyes (for example, retinal disparity).

Binocular (retinal) disparity: A binocular depth cue that is produced by the disparity between the images reaching each eye.

Blind spot: The area where the optic nerve leaves the eye; it contains no visual receptors.

Clairvoyance: The ability to perceive objects or events that cannot be perceived by the conventional senses.

Cochlea: The coiled, bony structure in the inner ear that contains the primary receptors for hearing.

Cone: One type of visual receptor that is located primarily in the central retina and is most important for color vision and the perception of fine detail.

Cornea: The clear, tough outer covering of the eye.

Dark adaptation: The process by which the eye becomes much more sensitive to light with increasing time under conditions of dim illumination.

Difference threshold (just noticeable difference): The smallest difference in physical energy between two stimuli that will enable someone to judge them as different.

Distal stimulus: A stimulus that actually occurs in the environment.

Extrasensory perception: The field beyond usual sensory awareness that includes telepathy, clairvoyance, precognition, and psychokinesis.

Free nerve endings: The structures found in the skin that may be important in producing sensations of pain.

Fovea: The area in the central retina, containing many cones, where vision is most acute.

Illusion: A disparity between perception and physical reality.

Interposition: A monocular depth cue; when one object obscures part of another, it is judged to be nearer than the second object.

Iris: The colored band of muscle tissue that surrounds the eye's pupil.

Kinesthesis: The sense of body movement that is provided by feedback from receptors located in the muscles, tendons, and joints.

Lens: The transparent, flexible eye tissue that focuses light on the retina.

Linear perspective: A monocular depth cue; parallel lines converge in the·distance producing a perception of depth.

Meissner corpuscles: The receptors that are believed to produce pressure sensations in hairless area of the body.

Method of limits: The technique used in psychophysics to determine the absolute threshold.

Monocular depth cue: Information about depth that requires the use of only one eye (for example, interposition, shadows, texture gradient, and linear perspective).

Müller-Lyer illusion: The view that, of two lines of equal length, the one bounded by closed arrowheads is shorter than the one bounded by open arrowheads.

Olfactory cleft: The structure in the uppermost nasal cavity where the olfactory receptors are located.

Olfactory receptors: The structures in the nasal passages that are sensitive to smell.

Opponent-process theory: The theory proposed by Hering that color vision is produced by three different mechanisms that are sensitive to red-green, yellow-blue, and black-white, respectively.

Organ of Corti: The structure on the basilar membrane containing hair cells that are stimulated by the movement of the basilar membrane.

Ossicles: Three small bones that magnify the movements of the eardrum and direct them to the oval window.

Oval window: An opening in the cochlea.

Papillae: Raised areas on the tongue that contain groups of taste buds.

Perceptual constancies: Our perception of various objects as unchanging in spite of the fact that our sensory awareness of them does change.

Photon: A particle of matter that makes up light.

Physical primaries: The colors red, blue, and green which, when mixed as lights, can produce any color in the visible spectrum.

Pinna: The external part of the ear.

Precognition: The ability to forecast the future.

Proximal stimulus: The pattern of energy (or information) that actually reaches a sensory receptor.

Psychokinesis: The ability to influence the physical world by means of thoughts or wishes.

Psychological primaries: The colors red, green, blue, and yellow, which subjects feel (by introspection) cannot be analyzed into other colors.

Psychophysics: Study of the relationship between the physical characteristics of a stimulus and the psychological sensations it produces.

Pupil: The dark center of the eye through which light enters.

Resonance (or place) theory: The theory that sensations of pitch are due to the responsiveness of different areas of the basilar membrane to sounds of different frequency.

Retina: The area at the back of the eye containing the structures that are sensitive to light—the rods and cones.

Rod: One type of visual receptor that is located primarily in the peripheral retina and that is important for seeing in dim light.

Saccule: One of the two parts of the vestibule in the inner ear.

Semicircular canals: Three structures in the inner ear that are sensitive to the rotation of the body.

Sensation: A subarea within the field of perception that focuses mostly on the detection of energy and the working of the sense organs.

Signal detection theory: The view that any judgment in a psychophysical study is due to the actual sensitivity of the observer and the psychological factors that affect decision-making.

Size constancy: The judgment of the size of a given object as constant even though the size of the image it produces on the retina can change dramatically at different distances.

Shape constancy: Our perception of the shape of an object as constant even though the shape of the image it produces on the retina can change markedly.

Taste buds: The organs that are sensitive to taste; they are located on the top surface and sides of the tongue.

Telepathy: The ability to read another person's mind.

Telephone (or frequency) theory: The theory that differences in sensations of pitch are due to the firing of more hair cells to sounds of greater frequency.

Texture gradient: A monocular depth cue; the elements on a textured surface appear to come closer together as depth increases.

Tympanic membrane (eardrum): A thin tissue at the end of the auditory canal that vibrates in response to sound waves.

Unconscious inference theory: The view that size constancy is due to internal computation the observer makes, according to which he adjusts his retinal image size depending upon the perceived distance of the object.

Utricle: One of the two parts of the vestibule in the inner ear.

Vestibule: A structure of the inner ear that provides information about body tilt and acceleration.

Visible spectrum: The range of light wavelengths the eye is sensitive to, varying from violet (400 millimicrons) to red (700 millimicrons).

Volley principle: The view that, above a frequency of 1000 cycles per second, the hair cells of the basilar membrane do not fire to all sound waves reaching the ear but only to some of them.

Wavelength: The distance between successive wave peaks.

Weber fraction: The unvarying ratio between the magnitude of a given stimulus and the magnitude of a second one that can be perceived as discriminably different from it.

Young-Helmholtz theory: The theory that color vision is due to the action of three receptors that are sensitive to red, green, and blue stimuli, respectively.

FOUR

LEARNING

It goes without saying that all animals, including human beings, are able to profit from experience. Placed in new situations for the first time, we are often clumsy and incompetent. However, after some practice or the opportunity to watch others perform, our own efforts usually improve dramatically and, for many activities at least, we, too, can successfully accomplish things that had previously been difficult and frustrating. The process that is responsible for these changes is called learning.

What is learning? Although the definition has been seriously debated, a large number of psychologists today would agree with the following: *learning is any relatively permanent change in behavior produced by experience* (Kimble, 1961). That this definition is more practical than perfect can be seen in the following example: Most students have had the experience of taking an examination but of not being able to answer all the questions. They might justifiably be able to tell their instructors that they had actually learned the material, but were simply too nervous to remember it or to write it down during the stress of the examination. In a way, then, learning reflects more of a potential change in behavior than a necessary or actual change. It is, like many other psychological ideas, a theoretical construct about a process that is assumed to take place (learning occurs within a person), but that can only be measured by observable changes in the person's actual *performance*.

A few other aspects of the definition are also noteworthy. First, the term "relatively permanent" is important because it *excludes* a number of things that should not be part of a definition of learning. Becoming tired, ingesting a drug like alcohol, or suffering from the flu all produce behavior change. But these changes are only temporary and do not reflect learning. Second, note that the word "practice" does *not* appear in the definition. For many years psychologists believed that repeated practice was essential for learning. Now, however, it is recognized that some learning can occur simply by observing the behavior of others without practicing oneself.

In this chapter we will examine three major types of learning: *classical conditioning* deals with learning to associate two stimuli so that a response that had originally been elicited by one stimulus is made to the other as well. Watching a television commercial for a delicious food may cause the viewer to salivate. The salivation would be perceived as a response to the visual stimulus, learned by the association of the sight and taste of the food. *Instrumental learning* focuses on the relationship between behavior and its consequences. A child, for example, may burn himself while playing with matches and thus not play with matches again. The consequence, being burned, has influenced the future likelihood of the behavior. Finally, in *observational learning* we learn by watching the actions of others.

CLASSICAL CONDITIONING Although learning had been broadly defined and generally studied by thoughtful people for many centuries, the beginning of the modern study of learning occurred at the end of the nineteenth century in Russia, where a physiologist, Ivan P. Pavlov, was studying the digestive processes of dogs (see Figure 4.1). Pavlov's procedure was to feed his animals small amounts of meat powder and then observe and measure the flow of various digestive juices. One of the issues that interested him was the relationship between the secretion of digestive fluids and the whole process of eating. For example, how much fluid would be secreted if food was

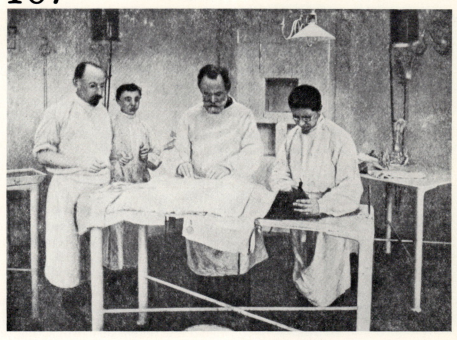

Figure 4.1
An actual photograph of Pavlov and his associates preparing a dog for classical conditioning experiments.

taken into the mouth but did not reach the stomach? To answer this question, Pavlov used a procedure called "sham feeding," in which the food that goes into the dog's mouth does not reach its stomach because it is diverted through a surgical hole in its esophagus.

In the course of this work, however, Pavlov found that his dogs were soon salivating and secreting stomach acid in the presence of stimuli other than food: they would start to salivate as soon as they saw the experimental apparatus or even Pavlov himself. At first Pavlov viewed these "psychic secretions" as an annoyance, and in his first experiments he tried to eliminate them. On reflection, however, Pavlov recognized the potential importance of his accidental discovery and so he began to study it systematically. He soon gave up the rather tedious procedure of studying stomach secretions in favor of the somewhat easier study of saliva flow.

At first Pavlov thought that the best way to understand "psychic secretions" was through introspection, and so Pavlov and his laboratory assistants tried to assume the dog's point of view. But it soon became apparent that Pavlov and his assistants could not agree about what the dogs were probably thinking or feeling and so Pavlov decided to ban this approach from his laboratory. Turning next to more objective research, Pavlov reasoned that salivation was the natural or reflexive response to food on the tongue. This natural, physically based secretion would initially occur only after the meat powder entered the dog's mouth. After several repeated experiences, however, the mere sight of food could produce an initial salivary flow in a way that closely paralleled the earlier discovery of psychic secretions in the stomach. In each case, the new reaction was obviously not an innate one; rather, it had to be acquired (or *conditioned*) by the animal's previous experience in similar situations. Thus, salivation might occur either as a natural (or *unconditioned*) response to meat powder or as an acquired (or *conditioned*) response to environmental cues such as the sight of meat powder. Inasmuch as the natural stimulation for salivation was food, Pavlov eventually called the food in this situation the *unconditioned* stimulus. Other stimuli, such as the sight of food, do not naturally lead to salivation. These stimuli, after they are able to produce salivation, Pavlov called *conditioned stimuli* because there must be learning (or conditioning) before they can produce any effects.

A CLOSER LOOK AT CLASSICAL CONDITIONING. To clarify the procedures used and results found in Pavlov's laboratory, it might be useful to examine closely one of his early experiments as described by Kimble (1961). In this investigation the dog was first operated upon so that its saliva would pass from its mouth through a small glass funnel out the side of its cheek so that it could be measured precisely (to one-tenth of a drop). The animal was also trained to stand quietly in a rather loose, restraining harness, in a room that had few potentially distracting sights or sounds (see Figure 4.2).

From an adjacent room, the experimenter would observe the dog and present various kinds of stimuli by means of automatic devices. In one study a tuning fork was sounded and then some dry powdered meat was introduced within easy reach of the dog's mouth. Initially the dog did not salivate when the tone sounded, but he salivated a great deal as soon as he licked the meat powder. Such combinations of the tone and the food, with the tone always coming first, were presented to the dog several times a day. After ten such pairings the investigators began to notice a little saliva being secreted even before the

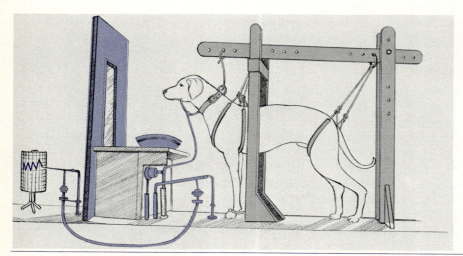

Figure 4.2
Experimental apparatus used by Pavlov in his early research on the salivary reflex. [Source: Kimble (1961)]

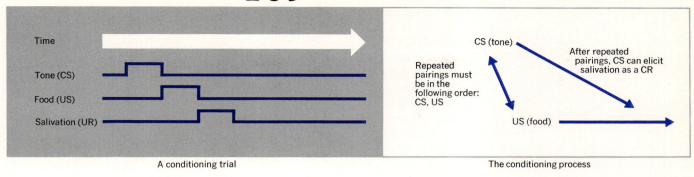

A conditioning trial

The conditioning process

CS: Originally a neutral stimulus that can eventually
    elicit the CR, a response similar to or identical with the UR
US: A stimulus that reflexively produces the UR
UR: The natural response to the US

**Figure 4.3
Schematic diagram of classical conditioning.**

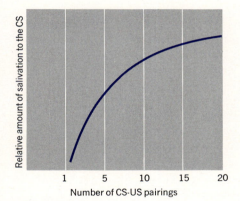

**Figure 4.4
Acquisition of a conditioned response during repeated pairings of the CS and US.**

meat powder appeared; after 30 such paired presentations, just the sound of the tuning fork elicited copious quantities of saliva. Furthermore, less time elapsed between the presentation of the tone and the beginning of salivation. Eventually the dog would begin to salivate almost immediately after the tone had been sounded. This salivary flow, beginning as it did before the meat powder was presented, is called a conditioned response (or CR) to distinguish it from the unconditioned response (UR) which is the salivation naturally produced by the meat powder itself. The stimulus that naturally elicits the UR, the meat powder, is called the unconditioned stimulus (US). Finally, the tone that eventually is able to elicit salivation as a CR is called the conditioned stimulus (CS) (see Figure 4.3). Pavlov discovered that conditioning by means of CS-US pairings took place gradually (see Figure 4.4).

Testing the limits of this classical conditioning procedure, Pavlov successfully taught dogs to salivate to a large variety of previously neutral environmental stimuli, including visual displays such as a rotating disc and a light. It did not seem necessary for there to be any logical relationship between the CS and the response.

GENERALIZATION. Early in his work, Pavlov also found another important phenomenon that extended the implications of classical conditioning. Specifically, he discovered that the particular conditioned stimulus used in training was not the only one that could elicit the conditioned response; other stimuli that were physically similar could also do so, though to a lesser extent. Furthermore, the greater the similarity between the new stimulus and the original one, the greater the likelihood that it could produce the conditioned response. This phenomenon is called *generalization,* and the degree of similarity between the training stimulus and various new ones is called the *generalization gradient.*

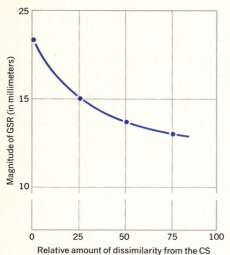

Figure 4.5
Hovland's experiment illustrating the generalization gradient in classical conditioning. As the test stimuli become increasingly different from the CS, the magnitude of the CR declines.

To appreciate the importance of generalization, we only need to think of what would happen to an animal or person who did not generalize. Imagine, for example, a youngster who has just learned the association between pain (US) and placing his hand on the hot stove (CS) in his own kitchen. If the child did not generalize, he would probably burn himself over and over again on kitchen stoves in the homes of his friends. Fortunately, though, this is not likely to happen; the similarity between the stove in his own kitchen and those in the homes of others will enable him to generalize.

The way in which generalization is investigated and a typical generalization gradient are both illustrated clearly in an experiment (Hovland, 1937) where a mild electric shock served as the US and a tone of a particular frequency the CS. The UR was the galvanic skin response (GSR), which is a measure of sweat gland activity produced by stressful stimuli (such as a shock). The study began by conditioning the GSR to the tone by pairing the tone (CS) with the shock (US) a number of times. Then the experimenter tested for generalization by measuring the amount of GSR to tones of a different frequency. In Figure 4.5 it can be seen that as the tones increasingly differed from the CS, the magnitude of the CR declined.

DISCRIMINATION. Although there seems to be a natural tendency toward generalization, it is not always appropriate to generalize. Therefore, *discrimination* is also important. Pavlov found that if the experimental situation was correctly arranged, a dog could learn to respond to one particular stimulus and *not* to other similar stimuli. That is, the animal or person can learn *not* to generalize. One of Pavlov's most interesting experiments shows how this process occurs. The basic procedure was to introduce one conditioned stimulus—a luminous circle—always followed by the presentation of meat powder. Soon, of course, introduction of the circle produced a conditioned salivary response. Pavlov then switched to a different visual stimulus—an illuminated ellipse—that was shaped somewhat like a cigar (with an axis ratio of 2 to 1). However, Pavlov *never* presented the meat powder after the ellipse. Soon the dog salivated only when the circle—and not the ellipse—was presented. After the dog had made this basic discrimination, Pavlov began to present ellipses, not followed by meat powder, that were less elliptical and more circular. Up to a point this discrimination was easy for the dog. Eventually, though, the circle and the ellipse became so similar that the dog could no longer discriminate. Then a remarkable thing occurred:

After three weeks of work on this differentiation not only did the discrimination fail to improve, but it became considerably worse, and finally disappeared altogether. At the same time the whole behavior of the animal underwent an abrupt change. The hitherto quiet dog began to squeal in its stand, keep wriggling about, tore off with its teeth the apparatus for mechanical stimulation of the skin, and bit through the tube con-

necting the animal's room with the observer, a behavior which never happened before. On being taken to the experimental room the dog now barked violently, which was also contrary to its usual custom; in short it presented all the symptoms of a condition of acute neurosis. On testing the cruder differentiations they were also found to be destroyed [Pavlov, 1927, p. 291].

EXTINCTION. Once the CR has been acquired, will it always be elicited by the CS? The answer is no. Pavlov, for example, found that once a conditioned response has been developed (by repeated association of a conditioned and an unconditioned stimulus), it has to be maintained by occasional trials in which the conditioned stimulus is followed by the unconditioned stimulus. Thus, although the conditioned response will continue to occur for some time after presenting the conditioned stimulus (even without the unconditioned stimulus), eventually the conditioned response will begin to weaken and then will disappear completely. This gradual diminution of the CR without the US is called *extinction*.

Extinction appears to be more than just forgetting, as shown in the case of another phenomenon discovered by Pavlov, *spontaneous recovery*. Suppose that salivation has first been conditioned to a tone and then the CR is entirely extinguished (by means of repeated presentations of the CS without the US). Then, after a period of several weeks, the dog is returned to the laboratory where the tone (CS) is sounded again. Surprisingly, he usually salivates once more; thus, it would seem that the CR has "spontaneously" recovered some of its earlier strength.

BIOLOGICAL LIMITS OF CLASSICAL CONDITIONING. Although Pavlov believed that "every imaginable phenomenon of the outer world affecting a specific receptive surface of the body may be converted into a CS" (1928, p. 88), it now appears that most organisms are biologically "prepared" to make only certain conditioned associations or pairings between the CS and the US and are not too well prepared to make other CS and US associations (Garcia, McGowan, and Green, 1972; Seligman, 1971).

Initial investigations into the limits of classical conditioning have demonstrated that rats easily make a connection between taste cues and a subsequent illness but do not easily associate visual or auditory cues with a subsequent illness. (The former finding explains why it is so hard to control rats by using poison. Rats will typically eat a small amount of poisoned bait, become sick, and then avoid the poison. But they are less likely to avoid the place where the poison was found, because location depends upon cues of sight rather than taste.) However, in reviewing these investigations, Garcia and Koelling (1966) noted that this research had not clearly distinguished between two possible explanations. First, taste cues might simply be more effective than other cues, such as visual ones, because of a special preparedness to associate taste with illness. Alternatively, taste sensations might always be present and noticeable when an animal eats and drinks, while other cues might lack this contingent or regular relationship with eating and drinking, but might readily be conditioned to illness under the appropriate conditions. Therefore, Garcia and Koelling formed an experiment to test these competing hypotheses.

During the conditioning (or "acquisition") phase of the experiment, they arranged that whenever a rat took a drink of water flavored with saccharin, it would also be exposed to a brief flash of light and an audible click. For one group of rats, this compound CS (light + click + taste) and drinking behavior were followed by an electric *shock* (US) that produced pain. Another group of rats was exposed to X-rays whenever they took a drink of water, and the X-rays in turn produced *illness* US following the compound CS. During the conditioning, all of the rats stopped drinking the saccharin-flavored water that was presented with the noise and light, but they continued to drink pure water that was made available (but that) was not associated with noise or light. Both illness and shock experiences, then, prevented the rats from drinking the flavored water presented with the noise and light, but it did not stop them from all drinking.

Later, during the critical test phase of the experiment, the animals were presented with either saccharin-flavored water but no light and sound, *or* pure (unflavored) water accompanied by light and sound. In this way the experimenters could determine which cues the animals learned to avoid. The results were remarkable. The rats that had been made *ill* by X-rays during conditioning would not drink the flavored water, although they would drink pure water even when it was paired with noise and light. However, the rats that had been *shocked* with electricity showed the reverse pattern; they willingly drank the flavored water but would not drink the pure water paired with noise and light (see Figure 4.6). Thus, Garcia and Koelling concluded that, for an association to occur, the organism must be predisposed to make a connection between certain stimuli.

Garcia and his colleagues were surprised to discover that this learning did not conform to another "law" of classical conditioning—the CS-US interval. It had been believed that this interval

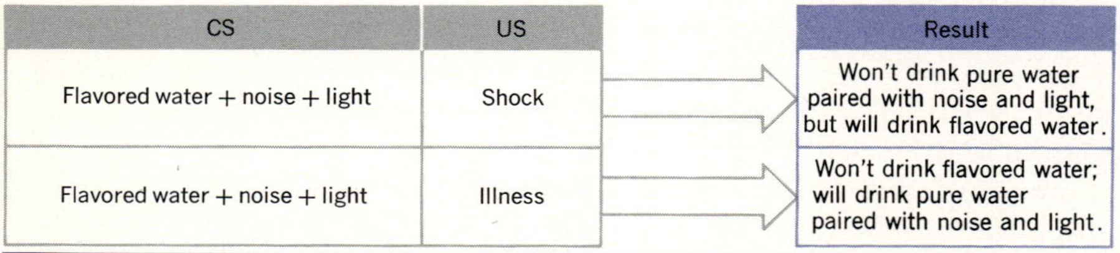

CS	US	Result
Flavored water + noise + light	Shock	Won't drink pure water paired with noise and light, but will drink flavored water.
Flavored water + noise + light	Illness	Won't drink flavored water; will drink pure water paired with noise and light.

Figure 4.6
Schematic diagram of the results of Garcia and Koelling's conditioning study using different classes of stimuli.

had to be quite brief—probably no more than a few seconds—in order for conditioning to occur. Yet Garcia was able to condition certain CS-US pairings (such as taste and illness) with delays of up to an hour. This is useful for purposes of survival since food-related sickness usually does not happen immediately.

Such differential susceptibility to becoming conditioned to various kinds of stimuli may account for the fact that many human phobias, (which we will discuss later) are *nonarbitrary*. It is easy to condition people so that they become frightened of snakes or dogs, but human predisposition is such that it would probably be difficult to make most people afraid of young lambs. In the area of food, taste cues are easily associated with illness, as related by Martin Seligman:

Sauce Béarnaise is an egg-thickened, tarragon-flavored concoction, and it used to be my favorite sauce. It now tastes awful to me. This happened several years ago, when I felt the effects of the stomach flu . . . after eating filet migon with Sauce Béarnaise. I became violently ill and spent most of the night vomiting. The next time I had Sauce Béarnaise, I couldn't bear the taste of it. [Although I learned that flu had caused the nausea and others with me did not get sick, again proving that it was not the sauce that affected me], I could not later inhibit my aversion [Seligman and Hager, 1972, p. 8].

CLASSICAL CONDITIONING: AN ILLUSTRATIVE APPLICATION. The basic concepts of classical conditioning have numerous practical applications to human behavior. For example, Quarti and Renaud (1964) developed a classical conditioning treatment for constipation. They began with the basic biological fact that defecation begins when a certain portion of the large intestine is stimulated. Since this stimulation appears to be the US for defecation, an appropriate treatment for constipation would seem to require an association between stimulation of the large intestine and a convenient conditioned stimulus. As a conditioned stimulus, the researchers decided upon an electric shock to the spinal area, one so mild that it has been described as "pleasant." Those whom they treated were asked to wear a special belt (pictured in Figure 4.7) that would allow them to self-administer a very mild electric shock. Specifically:

The subject to be re-educated continues to take his usual laxatives so as to produce one bowel movement per day. As he goes to the toilet he puts on the apparatus, starts operating it prior to defecation and stops the electric stimulation as soon as evacuation is terminated. . . . Gradually the subject should reduce the quantity of laxatives until he will no longer take any. . . . Once conditioning has been established, which generally happens after twenty to thirty applications, the electric stimulation alone produces defecation according to the individual rhythm of digestion [Quarti and Renaud, 1964, p. 224].

Quarti and Renaud point out that once the basic conditioning has been established, they instruct their subjects to go to the toilet at the same time every day, which is right after breakfast for most people.

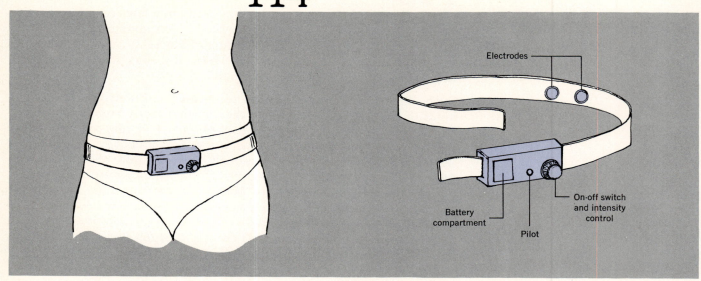

Electrodes

Battery compartment

Pilot

On-off switch and intensity control

Thus, the next step in the conditioning procedure is to eliminate the special electrical belt, since the chosen hour has now been substituted as the conditioned stimulus for elimination.

TESTING YOUR UNDERSTANDING
PAIRING THE CS AND US

Imagine a mother who cannot get her 2-year-old son to eat vegetables. Much to her chagrin, he spits them out each time she tries to put a spoonful in his mouth, so she decides to try classical conditioning. Since the child will readily eat desserts, she decides to pair dessert and vegetables. Over a number of trials, she gives him a spoonful of dessert, followed immediately by a spoonful of spinach. What do you think happened?

To answer, we must first translate the elements of the situation into the language of classical conditioning.

Dessert—US
Swallowing—UR and CR
Vegetables—CS

The mother's intent was to pair the CS (vegetables) and US (dessert) so that the vegetables would elicit swallowing (as a CR). But she had the US and CS in the wrong order—she mistakenly presented the dessert (US) before the vegetables (CS) rather than after them. As we have already noted, for classical conditioning to occur, the CS must *precede* the US. The incorrect pairing of dessert and vegetables would be an ineffective way to get the child to eat vegetables, and might actually make him less likely to eat dessert.

Figure 4.7 (Left)
This device was used by Quarti and Renaud in their classical conditioning treatment of constipation. A mild electric shock to the spinal area (the CS) is paired with stimulation of the large intestine (the US). [Source: Liebert and Spiegler (1974)]

Figure 4.8
The apparatus used by Thorndike in his early studies of instrumental learning. [Source: Rachlin (1970)]

INSTRUMENTAL LEARNING

Even before Pavlov had done his early research into classical conditioning, an American psychologist, E. L. Thorndike, had carried out a number of experiments in which a hungry animal was confined in a box and food was placed outside the box within the animal's sight. The box had been constructed so that a door could be opened if the animal performed a particular act such as stepping on a lever or pulling out a bolt (see Figure 4.8). Thorndike observed that the animals would act in a variety of ways when they were first placed in the box. Eventually, however, they would accidentally perform the correct movement, leave the box, and eat the food. During the course of his investigation, Thorndike would repeatedly return the animal to the box. He found that the length of time it took the animal to figure out how to get out of the box gradually decreased until finally it would be able to do so immediately after it had been placed in the box.

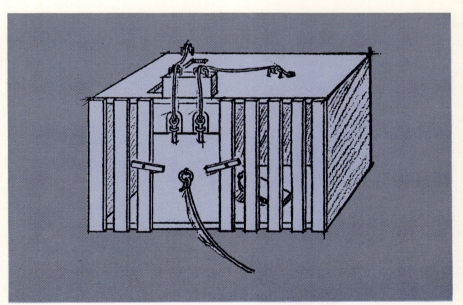

From these observations, Thorndike proposed a simple but important principle that he called the *law of effect.* Responses that produce "satisfying" consequences will tend to be repeated, while those that produce "discomfort" or "annoyance" will tend to be discontinued. Since Thorndike's time, psychologists have dropped the words "satisfier" and "annoyer" from their definition of the law of effect because these words have excess meaning. But Thorndike's basic insight has been retained.

BASIC CONCEPTS. Thorndike's early investigations illustrate instrumental learning or *operant conditioning,* as it is also called. In contrast with classical conditioning, where the focus is on the relationship between two environmental events (CS-US), instrumental learning emphasizes the relationship between an event and its environmental consequences. The importance of instrumental learning can be appreciated by thinking of our own most and least preferred activities. Those that we try to do most often usually provide positive consequences; those that we try to do less often (or try to avoid altogether) generally provide less pleasant consequences.

In a typical study of instrumental learning, a rat is placed in an enclosed box containing a lever that it can operate and a small device that dispenses food rewards. When it is first placed in the box, the rat will typically spend most of its time exploring the new environment. The experimenter, who has decided that the response he wants from the rat is to press the lever, waits for the animal to approach the lever. When this happens, the experimenter dispenses a reward. After several such rewards, the rat will spend more and more of its time near the lever. Then, the experimenter will become more stringent in giving rewards. He might, for example, decide to reward the rat only when it touches the lever. Continuing to hover by the lever, the rat will, by chance, brush against it. When this occurs the experimenter again provides a food reward. Soon, the animal is touching the lever much of the time. Now, the experimenter decides that the rat will actually have to press the lever in order to be rewarded. Eventually, by chance, the rat will depress the lever slightly, thereby securing a food reward. And so it goes. The animal is gradually *shaped* through a series of *successive approximations* to produce the behavior the experimenter wants. However, when the reward is no longer provided, the response will *extinguish;* the probability of it occurring again will become less and less during successive nonrewarded trials.

Four different types of instrumental conditioning may be distinguished according to the kind of consequence that typically follows a given response.

1. *Reward training:* A reward is given after the response, usually increasing the likelihood that the same response will occur again.
2. *Punishment training:* An aversive (or painful) stimulus is given after the response, generally decreasing the likelihood that it will happen again.
3. *Escape training:* After the response is given, the animal is permitted to escape from an aversive (or painful) stimulus. Escape from such a stimulus typically increases the likelihood that the response leading to escape will be given again when the painful stimulus recurs.
4. *Omission training:* A reward is *not* given after the response that had produced it before. The omission of such a reward usually decreases the likelihood that the response will happen again, that is, omission training leads to extinction.

Figure 4.9
Operant conditioning has been so effective that its use has been extended to coin-operated animal games. Here a customer can deposit a coin and play ticktacktoe with a live chicken.

DISCRIMINATION AND GENERALIZATION. Although we have thus far discussed operant conditioning as the learning of a relationship between responses and environmental events (rewards), neither the behavior nor the rewards occur in a vacuum. The animal or human being is behaving in an environment and is thus learning behavior-consequences relationships in a specific context. As in classical conditioning, there is a tendency to generalize. A pigeon, for example, could be trained to peck a key of a certain color. Subsequently, the color of the key could be varied and an assessment could be made of the pigeon's peck rate to different colors. As the color becomes less and less like the one used in training, the pecking rate declines, thus demonstrating the familiar generalization gradient. Finer discriminations can be learned, though, and this leads us to the idea of *stimulus control*. Environmental stimuli that signal potential changes in the relationship between responses and consequences are called *discriminative stimuli*. A child, for example, may discriminate between two different stimulus situations when playing at home: parents present *or* parents absent. In the latter situation he may act in many ways that, while rewarding to him, interfere sub-

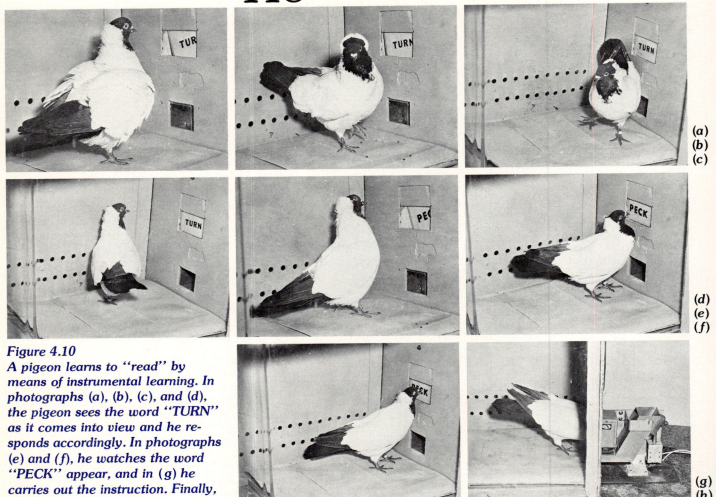

(a)
(b)
(c)

(d)
(e)
(f)

(g)
(h)

Figure 4.10
A pigeon learns to "read" by means of instrumental learning. In photographs (a), (b), (c), and (d), the pigeon sees the word "TURN" as it comes into view and he responds accordingly. In photographs (e) and (f), he watches the word "PECK" appear, and in (g) he carries out the instruction. Finally, in (h) he receives his reward—a few grains of food.

stantially with the activities of his brothers or sisters. Such behavior is infrequent in the former situation because of his parents' response. Thus, the child has learned that he can "get away" with certain acts such as "bullying" his brothers or sisters only when his parents are absent. Parent absence has become a discriminative stimulus.

A discriminative stimulus indicating that a particular behavior will produce a reward is called an S^D ("ess dee"). One that indicates no reward is called S^Δ ("ess delta"). In the laboratory, such discriminations are usually taught by presenting two stimuli, either simultaneously or successively. In successive discrimination two stimuli might be alternated (for example, a red and a green light) with the reward being given only for responding when the green light is on. In simultaneous discrimination the two lights are turned on together; the reward might require a response near the green one.

USING THE BASIC CONCEPTS: A CLINICAL EXAMPLE.

Robbie, an elementary-school boy, was a great problem to his teacher. Not only did he do very little school work, but he spent most of his time disrupting the normal classroom activities so that it was difficult or impossible for the other children to do their school work. Eventually, Robbie's teacher decided to consult three psychologists about the problem. The investigators—Hall, Lund, and Jackson (1968)—first needed to know exactly how much (or how little) school work Robbie was doing. Therefore, they began by obtaining a *base line* measure of the normal amount of school work Robbie did in class. As shown in Figure 4.11, the investigators found that, as a base line, Robbie was studying only about 25 percent of his time in class. During the rest of his time, he was busy "snapping rubber bands, playing with toys from his pocket, talking and laughing with peers, slowly drinking the half-pint of milk served earlier in the morning, and subsequently playing with the empty carton" (Hall et al., 1968, p. 3).

During the base line period, the investigators also checked the teacher's reactions to Robbie's disruptive activities. They found that the teacher was paying a lot of attention to him—urging him to work, to put away his playthings, and so on. Perhaps there was a link between Robbie's behavior and his teacher's reactions. To determine if this

Figure 4.11
The amount of time Robbie spent studying in class was assessed during the base line period. Then his teacher paid attention to him only when he studied (reinforcement). Next the original conditions (attention from the teacher for disruptions) were reinstated (reversal). Finally, the teacher's attention was again made contingent on his studying (reinforcement).

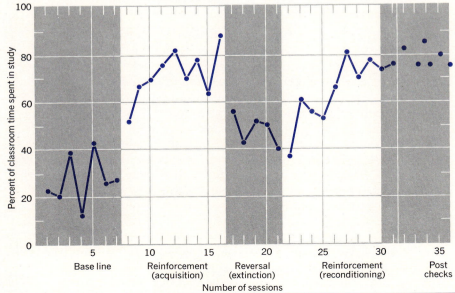

was so, the investigators planned an intervention. Thus, it was arranged that Robbie could earn his teacher's attention only by studying. Every time he studied continuously for 1 minute, an experimental confederate signaled the teacher to reward him by praise and attention. At the same time, it was arranged that all of his classroom disruptions would be ignored. The investigators wanted to see whether this change in the teacher's behavior would affect Robbie's study habits. As can be seen from Figure 4.11, it did. Shortly after Robbie began to receive attention only for studying, the amount of school work he did in class increased sharply. Soon he was spending about 70 percent of his time studying.

Robbie's case exemplifies an important psychological principle—the *principle of reinforcement:*[1] "If the occurrence of any behavior is followed by the presentation of a positive outcome or *reinforcer*, the strength of that behavior is increased." For Robbie, attention from his teacher served as an important reinforcer, which could motivate him to do more school work.

As can be seen, the base line information was vital in order to assess the change. But how can we be sure that Robbie's changed study behavior was not due to other reasons, such as more interesting subject matter? In order to be certain, there was a third phase in the investigation—the so-called *reversal* (or *extinction*) period. During this phase, Robbie's teacher refrained, as much as she could in the classroom setting, from reinforcing him with attention for his studying. In other words, she reversed herself and acted as she had before her consultation with the three psychologists. This reversal permits us to see whether or not the change in Robbie's school work is specifically due to his teacher's behavior. As shown in Figure 4.11, during the reversal period Robbie's classroom study declined quickly, demonstrating that his performance was directly related to his teacher's reactions.

Besides wanting to see whether the teacher's attention could serve as a reinforcer, Hall and his associates were concerned about the practical issue of trying to improve Robbie's study behavior. Thus, the fourth phase of their experiment consisted of *reconditioning*, where the teacher rewarded Robbie with attention only when he was studying. Soon Robbie was again studying between 70 and 80 percent of the time. The teacher continued this behavior, and Robbie was observed for almost 4 months (until the end of the school year). It was found that Robbie continued to spend most of his time in class doing school work. The teacher also reported that Robbie's classroom performance had improved. For example, he was now completing his written assignments and missing fewer words on spelling tests.

SCHEDULES OF REWARD. Thus far we have implied that for instrumental learning to occur, there must always be a reward after the required response. But if this were the case, instrumental

[1] Essentially, this is a modern version of part of Thorndike's law of effect; note that the word "satisfier" has been dropped.

Figure 4.12
Children with learning disabilities are often able to make much academic progress when the principle of reinforcement is systematically applied. One program which is doing this is the Point O'Woods Laboratory School in Stony Brook.

learning would have very few applications. For example, studying sometimes lends to a positive outcome—good grades—but not always. If the reward (good grades) is not achieved, does this lessen one's incentive to study?

In 1932, B. F. Skinner, who followed Thorndike as an outstanding student of instrumental learning, accidentally discovered that there does not have to be a reward after each response.

> *One pleasant Saturday afternoon I surveyed my supply of dry pellets [used as reinforcers] and, appealing to certain elemental theorems in arithmetic, deduced that unless I spent the rest of that afternoon and evening at the pellet machine, the supply would be exhausted by ten-thirty Monday morning. . . . I therefore embarked upon the study of periodic reinforcement (that is, rewarding only some of the organism's responses). I soon found that the constant rate at which the rate stabilized depended upon how hungry it was. Hungry rat, high rate; less hungry rat, lower rate. At that time I was bothered by the practical problem of controlling food deprivation. I was working half time at the Medical School (on chronaxie of subordination!) and could not maintain a good schedule in working with the rats. The rate of responding under periodic reinforcement suggested a scheme for keeping a rat at a constant level of deprivation [1959, pp. 87–88].*

Since Skinner's discovery, several types of *partial-reward schedules* (that is, schedules in which the desired response is rewarded only

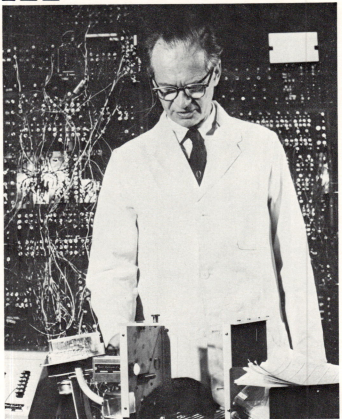

Figure 4.13
B. F. Skinner

some of the time) have been developed, each with a different rule for determining which responses will or will not be followed by a reward. In the *fixed-interval* (FI) schedule, a reward is administered according to the time elapsed, so that the first response given after a predetermined interval is rewarded. For example, if the interval is set at 1 minute (FI-1), the animal that responds once a minute would receive the maximum reward for the least effort. Only one response can produce the reward; any additional responses made during the minute interval will have no effect.

The effects of such a reward schedule on performance is typically illustrated by means of a *cumulative record*—a graph indicating the number of responses on the vertical axis and time on the horizontal axis. Each response raises the cumulative record another step. The width of the step is the time interval between responses. The rewards are denoted by a slanted line through the cumulative record curve. As can be seen in Figure 4.15, the fixed-interval schedule typically produces a cumulative record showing a pause after each reward and then an increase in the rate of responding toward the end of the interval. This pattern is called *scalloping*. Preparing for exams typically follows this pattern. Students do little studying after one exam is

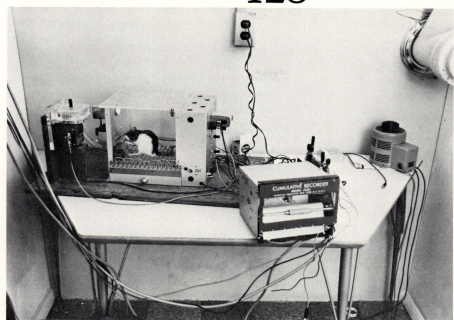

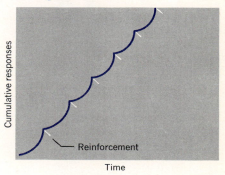

Figure 4.14
While this laboratory animal performs in a "Skinner box," the cumulative recorder provides a continuous record of its behavior.

over; as the day of the next exam approaches, their rate of studying gradually increases.

In the second type of schedule, *fixed ratio* (FR), the reward is provided after a fixed number of responses have been made. For example, the animal might be required to respond 6, 20, or even 50 times before obtaining the reward. A typical cumulative record from this type of schedule is shown in Figure 4.16; it can be seen that after each reinforcement there is a slight pause and then a high response rate. The fixed-ratio schedule is sometimes used in industry when workers are paid on a piece-work basis (that is, according to the quantity of goods produced).

The two schedules mentioned so far can also be combined in *compound schedules*. For example, the experimenter could require either a fixed number of responses *or* a fixed time interval before reinforcement. Or, the experimenter could require both a fixed number of responses and a fixed time interval.

Both the interval and the ratio schedules may also have *variable* rather than fixed rules pertaining to the relationship between responses and rewards. In a *variable-ratio* (VR) schedule, giving the reward depends upon the average number of responses. If the experimenter decides to institute a VR-30 schedule, this means that the animal would have to produce an *average* of 30 responses to obtain the reward. For example, it could be rewarded after 10 responses on one occasion, 30 on another, and 50 on yet another. A good illustration of a variable-ratio schedule is provided by slot machines, the

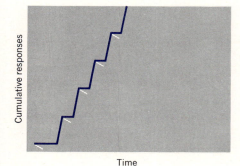

Figure 4.16
Cumulative record of responses occurring with a fixed-ratio schedule of reinforcement. Note the slight pause after each reward and the high response rate.

"one-armed bandits" of gambling casinos. These machines pay off after they have received a variable number of quarters or dollars.

In a *variable-interval* schedule, giving the reward depends upon the *average* time that has elapsed. For example, on a VI-5 schedule, which means that the average value is 5 minutes, rewards will sometimes be available after 3 minutes, sometimes after 5 minutes, and sometimes after 7 minutes. As shown in Figure 4.18, both the variable-interval and variable-ratio schedules produce fairly constant response rates, although the response rate for the variable-ratio schedule is faster.

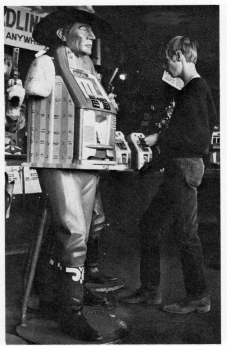

Figure 4.17
Nevada "one-arm bandits" make effective use of partial reinforcement.

PARTIAL REINFORCEMENT EXTINCTION EFFECT. How easily is extinction achieved after a response has been established by a partial reinforcement schedule in which rewards follow only some of the responses? Common sense might suggest that it would be easier to eliminate such a response than one that had been established under conditions of continuous reinforcement (where each response was followed by a reward). After all, in the latter situation the response has received more reinforcements and thus should be more "strongly stamped in" and resistant to extinction.

Common sense, in this case, is mistaken. A response that has been acquired under conditions of partial reinforcement extinguishes more *slowly* than one acquired with continuous reinforcement. Why is this? The following analogy, made by Howard Rachlin, offers an explanation:

> There are two hypothetical Coke machines. One, in Building A, produces a drink for every dime inserted. The other, in Building B, is partially broken. Occasionally, when a dime is inserted, nothing happens. The people in Building B complain repeatedly but ineffectually about the situation, but they seem to be willing to lose their dimes once in a while as long as they eventually get a Coke. Now, suppose both machines break down completely. Which one will receive more dimes before the dimes stop altogether? Probably the machine in Building B, which has been only partially reinforcing the "dime-inserting behavior." It will take a while before the people in Building B realize that the machine is completely inoperative. The people in Building A, on the other hand, will immediately realize that there is something wrong and stop inserting dimes [1970, p. 121].

As this example shows, the prolonged extinction of a partially rewarded response may be a problem in discrimination. Since the change from a continuous to a zero reinforcement schedule is easily noticed, the responses decrease rapidly. However, since partial reinforcement more nearly resembles extinction, the responses continue for a longer period of time.

SECONDARY REINFORCEMENT. In the case of human behavior, instrumental conditioning would be relatively ineffective if it were limited to just the kind of reinforcers we have mentioned so

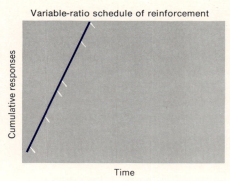

Variable-ratio schedule of reinforcement

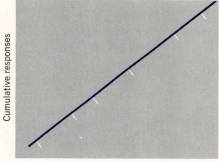

Variable-interval schedule of reinforcement

Figure 4.18
Cumulative records of responses under variable-ratio and variable-interval schedules of reinforcements.

far. Recall that in most of our examples, food or other "primary" rewards related to the biological well-being of the organism were used. But how little human behavior is motivated by receiving food! And even when food or other such necessities are received, how rarely does this happen immediately after the action that produced them. With the concept of *secondary reinforcement*, however, instrumental learning can have a much broader explanatory role.

Stimuli that are regularly associated with primary rewards assume a reinforcing value themselves. Money is perhaps the most obvious example. Many people expend much time and effort in its pursuit. This reward only justifies the effort because money has assumed other properties based on its association with primary rewards. Since it represents other goods and commodities, money has become a potent secondary reinforcer.

In an early study, Wolfe (1936) showed how the process works. Chimpanzees, the research subjects, were placed in cages that had a grape-vending machine at one end. Grapes, a favorite treat for chimpanzees, were the primary rewards in Wolfe's study. Poker chips were selected as the secondary reinforcer, and Wolfe arranged for the primary and secondary rewards to be paired by training the chimps to put a chip in the vending machine to "buy" a grape. After this initial training, Wolfe used the poker chips as rewards for other kinds of behavior, such as pressing a lever. The chimps would work for tokens, showing that the poker chips had acquired some properties of reinforcement.

Rachlin (1976) notes that secondary reinforcers serve two important functions; they can signal that a response has been made, and they can signal that a reinforcer is going to occur. The first function is extremely important in situations where the behavior that might produce a reward or punishment is not well defined. A contemporary example of this is biofeedback—the use of secondary reinforcers to help people control biological processes such as heart rate, blood pressure, and brain waves.

A series of experiments conducted by Neal E. Miller and his colleagues (Miller, 1969) show that many bodily processes can be significantly altered and even controlled voluntarily through the judicious administration of feedback. The key to acquiring such control lies in providing accurate feedback to the subjects about the response they are trying to produce. Under normal circumstances we are not aware of our exact heart rate or blood pressure. Thus, control is unlikely. Feedback, as a signal that a particular response has been made, allows the subject to control these biological processes. Feedback, in this case, is viewed as a secondary reinforcer; although it can influence behavior, probably by its association with primary rewards, feedback itself is not a primary reward.

Secondary reinforcement is also important in situations where the primary reinforcer does not come immediately after the behavior. Presentation of a secondary reinforcer during the time interval between the behavior and the primary reinforcement greatly facilitates learning. For example, a child may be given a "gold star" by his parents each day he makes his bed. If, at the end of a week, he has accumulated six out of the possible seven stars, he will be allowed to go to a Saturday matinee. In this case the gold stars are secondary reinforcers which help to bridge the time gap between bed-making and going to the movies.

NEGATIVE CONSEQUENCES: PUNISHMENT, ESCAPE, AND AVOIDANCE. Thus far we have largely discussed the effect of rewards on behavior. But negative consequences, such as an electric shock or an "F" on an examination, are also significant. Indeed, it is well established that a response that is followed by punishment will be less likely to recur.

Confronted with an aversive (or negative) situation, most people will do something to end it or to remove themselves from it. One reaction that has been extensively studied by psychologists is *escape*. In a typical experiment an animal might be exposed to an aversive stimulus, such as an electric shock, under conditions where it can end the shock by performing a specific act, for example, jumping a hurdle or pressing a lever. In these circumstances, animals learn rather quickly to perform the required act.

Escaping from danger is an effective coping strategy in some situations, but it may simply be too late in others; once you fail an examination, the consequences are hard to escape. In many situations it is better to try to avoid any negative outcomes entirely, by doing whatever is required in advance. This is called *avoidance learning*, and is one good reason to study hard for an exam before you take it.

A classic procedure for studying avoidance learning employs the shuttlebox that was used in the pioneering experiments of Richard Solomon (for example, Solomon and Wynne, 1953). As can be seen in Figure 4.19, the apparatus consists of two compartments that are separated by a barrier; the floor of each side can be electrified. An animal is placed in one compartment and is shocked; after several such trials, it quickly learns to escape by jumping to the other side. Then a change is introduced; a few seconds before the shock, a neutral stimulus such as a tone is also presented. At first the tone elicits no special behavior and the animal waits until the shock begins before jumping into the adjacent compartment. After several trials, however, the animal begins to respond to the tone and thus avoids the subsequent shock. Avoidance learning may account for the acquisition of phobias by some people, which we will discuss in Chapter 11.

LEARNED HELPLESSNESS. What happens when one can neither escape nor avoid noxious stimulation? A series of studies on

Figure 4.19
The shuttlebox apparatus that was used in Solomon's studies of avoidance learning. [Source: Rachlin (1970)]

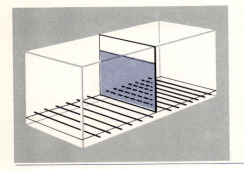

TABLE 4.1

	Seligman's learned helplessness model of reactive depression.	
	Learned helplessness in animals	**Reactive depression in humans**
Manifestations	Passivity in face of stress	Passivity, "paralysis of the will" (Beck, 1970)
	Retardation in learning to deal with stress	Negative expectations in dealing with stress or challenge, even when performance is adequate; feelings of hopelessness
	Dissipation of effect with time	Dissipation with time, although the length of time is very indefinite, ranging from days to years
	Anorexia (loss of appetite)	Anorexia
	Weight loss	Weight loss
Etiology	Uncontrollable stress—not stress per se but learning that no response reliably reduces aversive stimulation	Inability to control events in life, such as loss of a loved one, physical disease, and failure to act either to relieve suffering or to gain gratification

this question (Seligman, 1975) suggest that what may be termed a "sense of helplessness" develops. In a typical experiment, a group of dogs was subjected to numerous painful electric shocks from which they could not escape. Later on, these same dogs as well as others that had not experienced the inescapable shocks, were placed individually in an avoidance apparatus. At this point the dogs could avoid painful shocks by learning to run to another compartment of the box as soon as a warning tone sounded or a light came on. The behavior of the dogs differed substantially according to whether or not they had previously been exposed to inescapable shock. Those without the earlier experience soon learned to run quite effectively when they heard or saw the conditioned stimulus, thereby avoiding further painful shock. However, those that had endured the inescapable shock appeared simply to give up and accept the painful situation. Such experiments suggest that animals can acquire a "sense of helplessness" when confronted with uncontrollable aversive stimulation. This helplessness tends to have a deleterious effect on their performance in later stressful situations that *can* be controlled.

Based upon this and other research on the effects of uncontrollable stress, Seligman (1975) has suggested that learned helplessness in animals can provide a model for depression in man (see Table 4.1). Se-

TESTING YOUR UNDERSTANDING
OPERANT CONDITIONING

Consider the case of a long-term hospitalized psychiatric patient who speaks in a bizarre fashion. She constantly refers to herself as "the Queen": "I'm the Queen. Why don't you give things to the Queen? The Queen wants to smoke. How's King George, have you seen him?"

If you were a therapist, how would you go about modifying this inappropriate behavior using the principles of operant conditioning we have discussed so far?

A study dealing with this problem has been reported (Allyon and Haughton, 1964). These investigators used attention (listening to and taking an interest in the patient's speech) as a reinforcer. After a base line period, attention to the patient was made contingent on her bizarre speech and so it increased. Subsequently, the procedure was reversed and attention was systematically withheld from her psychotic speech which then decreased dramatically (see Figure 4.20).

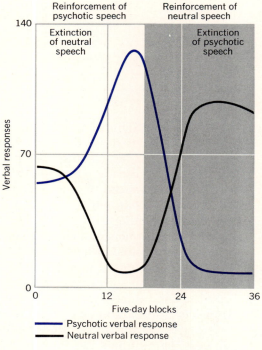

Figure 4.20
Allyon and Haughton used reinforcement to manipulate the psychotic speech of a hospitalized psychiatric patient. When her psychotic responses were reinforced (but not her normal responses, which were extinguished), her psychotic speech increased. But it can quickly be eliminated and normal speech restored simply by reversing this situation.
[Source: Allyon and Haughton (1964)]

ligman documented the similarities between the manifestations of helplessness observed in animal laboratory studies and at least some of the symptoms of depressed people. These similarities are remarkable. Like depressed people, animals appear to be passive in the face of stress, do not initiate action that might allow them to cope, develop anorexia (difficulty in eating or retaining food), and lose weight.

Building on these similarities, Seligman examined possible common causes of helplessness and depression. What makes the dogs behave in a helpless manner is known, for the carefully controlled experiments create the condition. The causes of human depression are much less clear, for the information that is available consists primarily of clinical observations. It is striking, though, how often therapists of diverse theoretical persuasions speak of the depressed patient's inability to deal with stressful events, such as the loss of loved ones, physical disease, aging, and failure. As the model would seem to indicate, an important precursor to at least certain kinds of human depression may well be the belief that one can do nothing to reduce his suffering or to obtain gratification.

OBSERVATIONAL LEARNING Thus far we have discussed learning that occurs in two types of situations: when two or more stimuli are paired (classical conditioning) or when a particular response is rewarded or punished (instrumental learning). Both approaches are valid and are applicable to human beings. But they tend to be somewhat inefficient, especially with respect to complex response patterns; Albert Bandura made the point this way:

Let us imagine an automobile driver training program based on the principle of successive approximation through differential reinforcement.

As a first step our trainer, who has been carefully programmed to produce head nods, resonant hm-hms, and other verbal reinforcers, loads up with an ample supply of candy, chewing gum, and filter-tip cigarettes. A semi-willing subject who has never observed a person drive an automobile, and a parked car complete the picture. Our trainer might have to wait a long time before the subject emits an orienting response toward the vehicle. At the moment the subject does look even in the general direction of the car, this response is immediately reinforced and gradually he begins to gaze longingly at the stationary automobile. Similarly, approach responses in the desired direction are promptly reinforced in order to bring the subject in proximity to the car. Eventually, through the skillful use of differential reinforcement, the trainer will teach the subject to open and to close the car door. With perseverance he will move the subject from the back seat or any other inappropriate location chosen in this trial-and-error ramble until at length the subject is shaped up behind the steering wheel. It is unnecessary to depict the remainder of the training procedure beyond noting that it will likely prove an exceedingly tedious, not to mention an expensive and hazardous, enterprise [1962, pp. 212–213].

The solution to this dilemma is, of course, not to use shaping principles at all for the purpose of "basic driver training." Rather, the instructor will probably begin by demonstrating (or *modeling*) the correct maneuvers so that the driver-to-be can learn simply by watching rather than by a costly and dangerous trial-and-error procedure. (Of course, shaping might later be used to sharpen certain driving skills.)

Aristotle recognized the importance of modeling, as can be seen in his suggestion that "man is the most imitative of living creatures, and through imitation learns his earliest lessons." Yet observational learning was not really studied by psychologists until the 1960s; the single exception was Miller and Dollard's *Social learning and imitation* (1941). Miller and Dollard assumed that "imitativeness" was an acquired characteristic, and not a separate technique of learning at all. Viewed this way, imitation was studied by analyzing how animals, children, and sophomores came to imitate other individuals in novel situations.

After Miller and Dollard's initial foray into the field, little attention was paid to imitative learning for almost two decades. Then, Albert Bandura and Richard Walters (1963) undertook some important research, after which a broader view of imitative phenomena, covering the whole range of observational learning, appeared.

BASIC TERMS. It will probably be helpful to begin with some definitions. *Observational learning* is the process by which the behavior of one person, an observer, changes simply by exposure to the behavior of another, the model. Specific aspects of the model's behavior are called *modeling cues* and are available to everyone almost continuously throughout their lives. Modeling cues appear in two forms: through the example of those to whom we are directly exposed (or *live modeling*), and through the example of those to whom we are indirectly exposed—through movies, television, radio, plays, stories, and hearsay descriptions. Examples from any of these latter sources are known as *symbolic modeling*.

ACQUISITION VS. PERFORMANCE. Miller and Dollard thought that people had to perform imitative acts (that is, actually copy someone else's behavior themselves) in order to learn by imitation. Bandura and Walters, however, rejected this assumption, arguing that a person can acquire new responses from another simply by observation, as shown by Bandura's (1965) well-known experiment. In this experiment nursery-school children were provided with symbolic modeling cues in a 5-minute film.

The film began with a scene in which a model walked up to an adult-size plastic Bobo doll and ordered him to clear the way. After glaring for a moment at the noncompliant antagonist the model exhibited four novel aggressive responses each accompanied by a distinctive verbalization. First, the model laid the Bobo doll on its side, sat on it, and punched it in the nose while remarking, "Pow, right in the nose, boom, boom." The model then raised the doll and pummeled it on the head with a mallet. Each response was accompanied by the verbalization, "Sockeroo . . . stay down." Following the mallet aggression, the model kicked the doll about the room, and these responses were interspersed with the comment, "Fly away." Finally, the model threw rubber balls at the Bobo doll, each strike punctuated with "Bang." This sequence of physically and verbally aggressive behavior was repeated twice [Bandura, 1965, pp. 590–591].

In addition to the film segment described above, one group of children saw a final scene in which the model was generously rewarded for his assaults upon the doll:

For children in the model-rewarded *condition, a second adult appeared with an abundant supply of candies and soft drinks. He informed the model that he was a "strong champion" and that his superb aggressive performance clearly deserved a generous treat. He then poured him a large glass of 7-Up, and readily supplied additional energy-building nourishment including chocolate bars, Cracker Jack popcorn, and an assortment of candies. While the model was rapidly consuming the delectable treats, his admirer symbolically reinstated the modeled aggressive responses and engaged in considerable positive social reinforcement [p. 591].*

A second group of children watched an ending in which the model was punished for his aggressive behavior:

The reinforcing agent appeared on the scene shaking his finger menacingly and commenting reprovingly, "Hey there, you big bully. You quit picking on that clown. I won't tolerate it." As the model drew back he tripped and fell, the other adult sat on the model and spanked him with a rolled-up magazine while reminding him of his aggressive behavior. As the model ran off cowering, the agent forewarned him, "If I catch you doing that again, you big bully, I'll give you a hard spanking. You quit acting that way" [p. 591].

The third group (which served as a control group) saw only the "basic film" and did not see a final scene depicting the model being either rewarded or punished.

Afterward, all of the children were brought individually into a room that contained a plastic Bobo doll, three balls, a mallet, a pegboard, plastic farm animals, and a doll house equipped with furniture and a miniature doll family. This wide array of toys was provided so that the child could easily demonstrate either imitative, aggressive responses (following the model) or nonimitative, nonaggressive forms of behavior. Each child was left alone with this assortment of toys for 10 minutes, while his or her behavior was periodically assessed by judges who watched from behind a one-way screen. The frequency with which the children imitated the model's aggressive behavior was the performance measure of the study. Not surprisingly, it was found that those who saw the model punished made far fewer imitative aggressive responses than did those in either of the other

Figure 4.21
In Bandura's early "Bobo" doll experiments, the children imitate aggressive behavior.

two groups (see Figure 4.22). But—and this is the most significant point of Bandura and Walters's analysis—one should not make the mistake of concluding that because the children in this group did not spontaneously copy the model very much, they had learned few new responses.

To demonstrate that all of the groups had learned the model's responses by observing, whether or not they spontaneously followed the model, the experimenter reentered the room well supplied with such rewards as colored sticker pictures and sweet fruit juices in an attractive dispenser and told the child that each time he or she copied the aggressive behavior of the model, a glass of fruit juice and a sticker would be given. The youngster's ability to copy the model's behavior in this situation (that is, when he was asked to show all the responses he had learned) constituted the *acquisition* measure. The results provided support for distinguishing between two separate aspects of imitative learning—acquisition and performance. As expected, when rewards were offered for copying the model's acts, the effects of punishment were greatly reduced and all of the groups showed a high level of learning (see Figure 4.22).

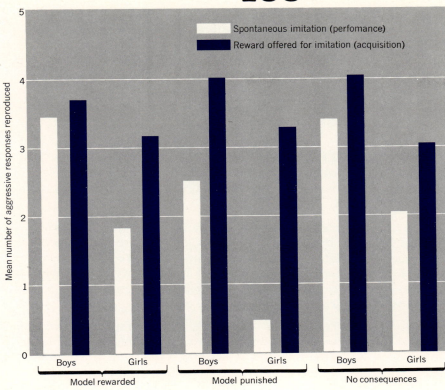

Figure 4.22
Results of Bandura's study of observational learning in children. Whether the model was rewarded or punished affected the children's performance but not their acquisition of the modeled responses. [*Source: After Bandura (1965)*]

A CLOSER LOOK AT OBSERVATIONAL LEARNING. Certainly, exposure to a model can motivate one to copy the model in (*direct imitation*) the exact same way that one who has learned by reinforcement to press a bar will do so again in the future. But observers can also learn what actions to *avoid* simply by being exposed to pertinent modeling cues. Anyone who has seen someone accidentally receive an electric shock (for example, from a faulty kitchen appliance) knows the impressive effect of such modeling cues on observers; they become *less* likely to follow that example and may even refrain from going anywhere near that appliance, at least until appropriate repairs are made. The case in which the observer becomes *less* likely to perform certain acts after they have been modeled is called *direct counterimitation*.

DISINHIBITION AND INHIBITION. Just as classically and instrumentally conditioned responses will be generalized beyond the limits of the immediate situation, so will those that have been acquired by observational learning. Observational learning can also be generalized to other similar situations. For example, a child who sees her parents regularly donate money to a variety of charities may subsequently become more willing to share her toys with other children or to offer a piece of her chocolate cake to her little sister. Likewise, a youngster who observes a variety of models regularly being punished for handing their homework in late, talking back to the teacher, and so forth, may take care not to do these things or even similar things that have not been modeled. Seeing his parents make charitable contributions, the child was *disinhibited* through observational learning; seeing other children being punished, he was *inhibited* from being difficult with the teacher himself.

THE THREE STAGES OF OBSERVATIONAL LEARNING. Integrating the various processes we have described thus far, we find that observational learning consists of three stages, as shown in Figure 4.23.

Exposure, the first step, occurs whenever an observer encounters modeling cues, in either live or symbolic form. By itself, though, exposure is no guarantee that observational learning will take place. For example, a child exposed to modeling cues may simply fail to attend to the social examples the child has seen or heard or may fail to process and store this information effectively.

The second step, therefore, is *acquisition*, which refers to the information that an observer sifts and retains from the modeling cues he or she has seen. As in the Bandura Bobo doll example, acquisition is measured by the observer's recall or reproduction of the model's behavior when tested under optimum circumstances (for example, when the observer is given appropriate rewards).

Acceptance, the third and final step, refers to whether (or in what ways) the observer employs or accepts the modeling cues as a guide for his or her own behavior, whether in an imitative or counterimitative manner.

WHEN ARE MODELING CUES ATTENDED TO AND ACCEPTED? In order to learn or acquire a modeled behavior, the observer must first attend to the modeling cues and then store the performance in memory so that it can be recalled at a later time. The observer's attention is affected by certain characteristics in the modeling situation. For example, novel or exciting behaviors are more likely to create interest. Also, various characteristics of the model are important, as shown by Rosekrans (1967) who had a group of boys watch a film of a peer-model playing a game. In one condition, the model was dressed just like the observers (in a boy scout uniform) and was also described as being similar to them in other ways. In another condition the model was dressed in ordinary street clothes and described as being dissimilar to the observers. A measure of recall (acquisition) of the model's behavior showed that those boys who had seen the film depicting the similar model remembered more of his actions than those who had viewed the film of the dissimilar model.

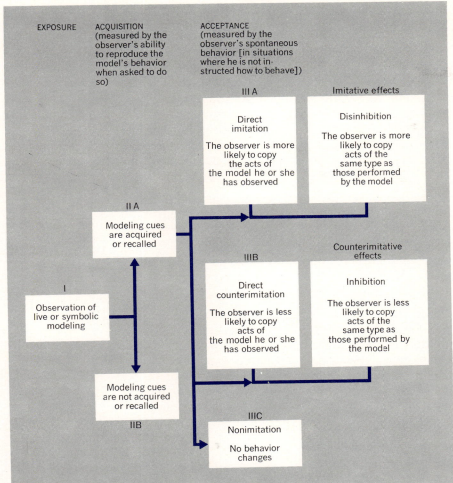

Figure 4.23
A three-stage model of observational learning.

Physical attractiveness and high status also enhance observational learning (Baron, 1970).

Even if the modeled behaviors are attended to, they may not be stored permanently so that they can be remembered at a later time. Many of the variables that affect attention may also affect rehearsal, a factor that is important in recall, as we will see in Chapter 5. In the previously mentioned Rosekrans study, for example, the subjects who had observed the similar model showed more spontaneous rehearsal than those who had seen the dissimilar model. Another potent variable that stimulates rehearsal may be the consequences of a model's behavior. Behavior that affects other people or things is likely to be judged more important (and hence worth remembering) than behavior that has no consequence. Thus, modeled behavior that has consequences is more likely to be rehearsed so that it can be stored in memory.

PSYCHOLOGY AND THE PROBLEMS OF SOCIETY
TEACHING THE MENTALLY RETARDED WITH REINFORCEMENT

It is estimated that at least 3 percent of the American population (that is more than 6 million children and adults) are retarded. Mental retardation has most often been defined as impaired intellectual and social competence in relation to chronological age. Although a low IQ score (70 or below) has been relied on heavily to classify mental retardation, the IQ test is fallible. A low score may turn out to indicate other problems unrelated to intellectual ability, such as motivation. Furthermore, if a teacher has limited expectations for a child based on his or her low IQ scores, this may reinforce low academic performance.

Although mentally retarded children are often placed in a special class specifically designed for them, the effectiveness of this kind of experience has been questioned (Bauer, 1967). Even though the purpose of the special class is to help them acquire social and academic skills, it is possible that this type of class reinforces both their teachers' and their own limited expectations. Another approach, however, could prove more promising.

By approaching the remediation of mental retardation in terms of the principles of learning, behavioral scientists have assigned most of the problem to environmental factors and then tried to determine what could be changed behaviorally. This approach enables one to observe environmental-behavioral interactions and to assess the effects of stimulus control (discrimination and generalization), as well as positive and negative reinforcement on the production of both retarded and competent behaviors.

In a study using instrumental learning, Bijou, Birnbrauer, Kidder, and Tague (1966) worked with trainable mentally retarded children (their IQs ranged from 25 to 49) to teach them a variety of school-related skills. Initially, however, they focused on activities that are prerequisites for effective study. Bijou and his associates reinforced sitting quietly and paying attention, and they extinguished incompatible behaviors such as fighting. The children received praise and token reinforcement for longer and longer periods of self-reinforced study, since it was believed that this would limit their time for disruptive behavior. A "time out from positive reinforcement" room was available for persistently disruptive behavior. However, the token reinforcement and praise incentives were so effective that this room rarely had to be used.

Teaching the children to write was accomplished by means of a series of small steps. First they were taught to fill in unfinished letter forms. Then they printed the letters using a few tracing cues. Finally they learned to copy them on the blackboard without any written cues at all, which completed the shaping process. Their ability to learn these skills and perform them adequately lead Bijou and his colleagues to comment in their summary that "the academic future of the majority of retarded children is much brighter than had been forecast by the theorists who assume their abilities, capacities, and traits are largely fixed'' (Bijou et al., 1966, p. 505).

The Bijou study indicates that reinforcement may enable mentally retarded children to learn a variety of skills that are important in school. Even though the systematic application of behavioral techniques is a novel approach to dealing with mental retardation, its explicitness and availability for immediate assessment commend it as a worthwhile procedure.

Retarded children learning to write by means of systematic reinforcement.

138

SUMMARY

Learning is any relatively permanent change in behavior that is produced by experience. However, learning itself reflects more of a potential change in behavior than an actual change; it is a theoretical construct referring to a process that is assumed to take place (learning occurs within a person), but that can only be measured by overt and observable changes in the person's actual performance. The three major types of learning are classical conditioning, instrumental learning, and observational learning.

Ivan Pavlov's work with dogs eventually led him to the major concepts of classical conditioning, which deals with learning the relationship between two stimuli in the environment. After repeated pairings of one, the conditioned stimulus (CS), with the other, the unconditioned stimulus (US), the CS produces a conditioned response (CR) —such as a dog that salivates at the sound of a bell.

Stimuli that physically resemble but are not identical with those used in conditioning will also produce the conditioned response, but to a lesser degree; the greater the similarity, the greater the generalization. It is also possible to teach animals not to generalize. To teach discrimination, the experimenter must control conditioning so that only the original stimulus and *not* others that resemble it will produce the response.

Extinction, the gradual weakening and eventual disappearance of the acquired response (CR) occurs when the unconditioned stimulus is omitted. Several weeks after extinction, it is possible to reintroduce the conditioned stimulus (CS) and produce the acquired response (CR), a phenomenon known as spontaneous recovery.

Instrumental learning (or operant conditioning, as it is also called) focuses on the relationship between behavior and its consequences. E. L. Thorndike proposed an important principle, based on a series of experiments, that he called the "law of effect"; it states that responses that produce successful consequences will tend to be repeated while unsuccessful ones will tend to fall into disuse. Four different types of instrumental learning may be distinguished according to the consequences that follow a given response. In reward training, behaviors are rewarded as they move in the direction of the desired behavior so that gradually the desired behavior is achieved; this process is called "shaping." In punishment training, an aversive (or painful) stimulus is given after the response, thus decreasing the likelihood that it will occur again. Escape training permits the animal to escape from an aversive (or painful) stimulus after giving the required response; this increases the likelihood that the escape response will happen again. In omission training (as in extinction), the reward is *not* given after the response that had previously elicited it, thereby decreasing the likelihood that the response will recur. Different consequences sometimes follow the same behavior in a different context; environmental stimuli that signal potential changes in the relationship between responses and consequences are called "discriminative stimuli." An S^D is a discriminative stimulus indicating that a particular behavior will produce a reward; an S^Δ indicates that there will be no reward.

Experiments designed to illustrate the principle of reinforcement (a positive reward given for a certain behavior increases the likelihood that this behavior will be repeated) usually have four stages: (1) base line: a measure of the amount of the behavior to be modified before the treatment begins; (2) treatment: rewards are given for the desired behavior; (3) reversal (or extinction) period: the rewards are removed, thus restoring the original conditions; and (4) reconditioning: reintroducing the rewards for the desired behavior. B. F. Skinner showed that it is not necessary to reward a response every time in order for it to continue; several types of partial reward schedules—such as fixed ratio, fixed interval, variable ratio, and variable interval—can be used and the results illustrated by means of a cumulative record. A response acquired under conditions of partial reinforcement extinguishes more slowly than one acquired under continuous reinforcement. Secondary reinforcers, stimuli that have acquired reinforcing properties through association with primary rewards, can be used to bridge the gap between desired behaviors and eventual rewards.

Experiments have also studied the results of aversive (or negative) situations and found that most animals will escape from the situation or avoid unwanted results by making the necessary responses in time. Animals that are not allowed to escape from an electric shock acquire a "sense of helplessness" that seriously affects their later performance in stressful situations that *can* be escaped or controlled; they do not learn to respond in an effective way to painful stimulation. Seligman has proposed that learned helplessness in animals is similar to depression in man; an important precursor to human depression may be the belief that one cannot reduce his suffering or obtain gratification.

Observational learning is the process by which the behavior of one person—the observer—changes simply because of exposure to the behavior of another—the model. Modeling cues, specific aspects of the model's behavior, appear in two forms: live modeling—the examples of those to whom we are directly exposed, and symbolic modeling—the examples of those to whom we are indirectly exposed through books, television, movies, radio, or second-hand descriptions. Bandura and Walters have demonstrated that people can acquire new responses from another simply by watching (without imitating); they distinguish between acquisition—the ability of persons to recall or reproduce the modeled behaviors to which they have been exposed, and performance—the actual imitation of those behaviors. There are three stages in observational learning: (1) exposure takes place whenever an observer encounters modeling cues; (2) acquisition is the observer's ability to recall or reproduce the modeled behaviors to which he or she was exposed; and (3) acceptance is the observer's use of the acquired modeling cues either in direct imitation of the model's behavior or in direct counterimitation (avoiding the modeled behavior). The observer may also generalize the specific behavior observed to similar kinds of behaviors; inhibition is a generalized avoidance and disinhibition is a generalized acceptance from a specific modeled behavior to a general class of behaviors. Some of the factors that motivate the observer with respect to imitation include his or her perception of the model's similarity and the outcome of the model's behavior (reward or punishment).

GLOSSARY

Acceptance: The third and last step of observational learning; the observer uses acquired modeling cues as a guide for his or her own behavior, which is either imitative or counterimitative.

Acquisition: The learning of a response. Also, as the second step of observational learning, it is the observer's ability to recall or reproduce the modeled behaviors to which he has been exposed.

Avoidance learning: Learning to avoid unwanted results by producing certain responses before the noxious event occurs.

Base line: A measure of the frequency of behavior to be modified, taken before any treatment begins.

Classical conditioning: Learning the association between two stimuli in the environment so that a response initially elicited by one can become elicited by the other as well.

Compound schedules: The use of a combination of schedules of partial reinforcement so that a complex sequence of responses may be required in order to obtain rewards.

Conditioned response (CR): In classical conditioning an acquired response to environmental cues (such as salivating at the sight of food); in instrumental conditioning the response that has been shaped by means of reinforcement.

Conditioned stimulus (CS): A stimulus that produces a response because of learning or conditioning.

Cumulative record: A graph illustrating performance during a schedule of reward; the number of responses are plotted along the vertical axis and time along the horizontal axis.

Direct counterimitation: Avoiding a specific modeled behavior.

Direct imitation: Copying a model exactly.

Discrimination: Controlling conditioning so that only a specific stimulus and not those that resemble it will produce the desired response.

Discriminative stimulus: A stimulus indicating that there is a potential change in the relationship between responses and consequences. (A red traffic light will indicate to the automobile driver that he can no longer continue driving with impunity—he risks either apprehension by a law-enforcement officer or a collision with another car.)

Disinhibition: A situation in which a person generalizes *positively* from specific modeled behaviors to a whole class of behaviors.

Exposure: The first step of observational learning that occurs when an observer encounters modeling cues.

Extinction: The gradual weakening and disappearance of the acquired response due to the continued non-presentation of an unconditioned stimulus or reinforcer.

Fixed interval: A reinforcement schedule in which a reward is given according to the time that has elapsed; the first response that occurs after a predesignated time interval is rewarded.

Fixed ratio: A reinforcement schedule in which a reward is given after a fixed number of responses have been made.

Generalization: The tendency for stimuli that physically resemble but are not identical with those used in conditioning to produce the conditioned response but to a lesser degree.

Generalization gradient: The strength of a CR as a function of the degree of similarity between a test stimulus and the CS; the greater the similarity between the two, the more the similar stimulus will be able to elicit the conditioned response.

Inhibition: A situation in which a person generalizes from specific modeled actions to avoiding a whole class of behaviors.

Instrumental learning (or operant conditioning): Learning that takes place because of the relationship between behavior and its consequences.

Law of effect: E. L. Thorndike's principle that successful behaviors will tend be repeated while unsuccessful ones will tend to fall into disuse.

Learning: Any relatively permanent change in behavior produced by experience.

Live modeling: The example provided by persons to whom we are directly exposed.

Modeling: The behavior of one person—the model—that is observed by another.

Modeling cues: The specific behaviors displayed by a model, either live or symbolic.

Observational learning: The process by which the behavior of one person—the observer—changes simply because of exposure to the behavior of another—the model.

Partial reinforcement extinction effect: The finding that a response that has been acquired under conditions of partial reinforcement extinguishes more slowly than one acquired with continuous reinforcement.

Performance: An animal or person's overt and observable behavior, which is assessed by the experimenter to determine whether learning has taken place.

Reinforcement: A positive outcome or reward given for the performance of a certain act; reinforcement usually increases the likelihood that the behavior will be repeated.

S^D ("ess dee"): A discriminative stimulus indicating that a particular behavior will produce a reward.

S^Δ ("ess delta"): A discriminative stimulus indicating that a particular behavior will not produce a reward.

Scalloping: A common cumulative record pattern for the fixed-interval schedule; after each reward there is a pause and then an increase in the rate of responding toward the end of the interval.

Secondary reinforcers: Stimuli that are initially neutral but then acquire reinforcing properties because of their association with primary or basic rewards.

Shaping: Rewarding an animal or person's behaviors as they move in the direction desired by the experimenter so that eventually the desired behavior is achieved.

Spontaneous recovery: A response to a conditioned stimulus occurring after extinction had apparently been achieved.

Stimulus control: The production of operant behavior only in the presence (or absence) of certain discriminative stimuli.

Successive approximations: The gradual changes that take place in an animal or person's in the direction desired by the experimenter; these changes are brought about by shaping.

Symbolic modeling: The example provided by persons to whom we are indirectly exposed through the media or second-hand descriptions.

Unconditioned reponse (UR): An innate, reflex response (such as salivating when eating food).

Unconditioned stimulus (US): Something which typically produces a reflex response (food typically causes salivation to occur).

Variable interval (VI): A reinforcement schedule in which a variable amount of time must elapse before a reward will be given.

Variable ratio (VR): A reinforcement schedule in which a variable number of responses must be completed before a reward will be given.

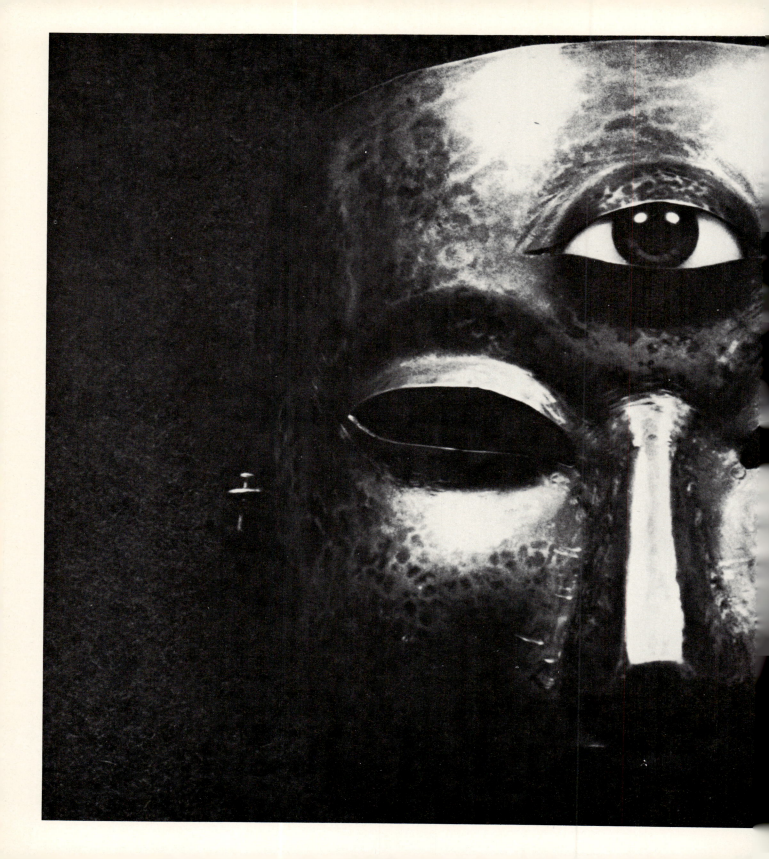

FIVE

COGNITION

As mentioned in Chapter 1, psychology was first defined as the study of conscious experience; questions regarding the nature of sensations and the contents of the mind dominated the field. Then, the Watsonian revolution changed the very nature of the discipline by banishing consciousness from further consideration. Psychology became the study of observable responses and their relationship to observable stimuli. In the past 20 years, interest has developed again in what happens between the time a stimulus is presented and the time a response is performed. What kinds of intervening mechanisms account for certain relationships between stimuli and responses? Given certain stimulus-response relationships, can we deduce what kind of mental or cognitive processes mediate them? What happens to a stimulus after it has been received by a sensory receptor? To produce an effect on behavior, it must first be noticed. If it is to produce an effect at a later time, it must also be stored so that it can be remembered. How is information processed? How are the stimuli that reach our sensory receptors organized for later use? These and other questions will be addressed in this chapter. We will follow a stimulus through the paths available between stimulus and response, beginning with the initial "apprehension" of the stimulus.

THE SENSORY STORE Studies of the *span of apprehension*—the amount of information a person can take in at a glance—were among the first reported by psychologists. In a typical early investigation of the span, participants were shown some stimulus (for example, a group of consonants) briefly, perhaps for less than one-tenth of a second, and then asked to report what they had seen. The subjects typically recalled about five letters accurately, a value that seemed to represent the maximum amount of information that could be processed at a glance.

In the early 1960s, however, George Sperling became intrigued with the subjective reports of those who had participated in studies of the span. These subjects insisted that they had seen more than they could later remember. Perhaps, Sperling reasoned, a great deal of information is initially picked up, but some of it is forgotten before the subject can finish telling the investigator what he has seen. Sperling's hypothesis implied the existence of a high capacity storage system that holds information only briefly. How could his idea be evaluated?

In order to test it, Sperling (1960) devised a technique to avoid the possible limiting effect of memory. Instead of being required to report everything they had seen, the subjects were only asked to report part of what they had seen. And the amount of information selected as the "part" was well within the memory capacity of most people.

To illustrate we will consider one of Sperling's studies. The subjects were briefly shown index cards on which appeared three rows of three letters each. Using these stimuli in the usual span of apprehension procedure (simply asking the subjects to report what they had seen), Sperling found that between four and five letters were correctly identified. To reduce the burden on their memory, Sperling also used a condition in which the subjects were asked to report on only a portion of the display. Just as the stimulus disappeared from view, one of three tones was sounded. Presentation of the highest pitched tone meant that the subject was to report the top row of letters, while presentation of the middle and lowest pitched tones meant that the subject was to report the middle and bottom rows,

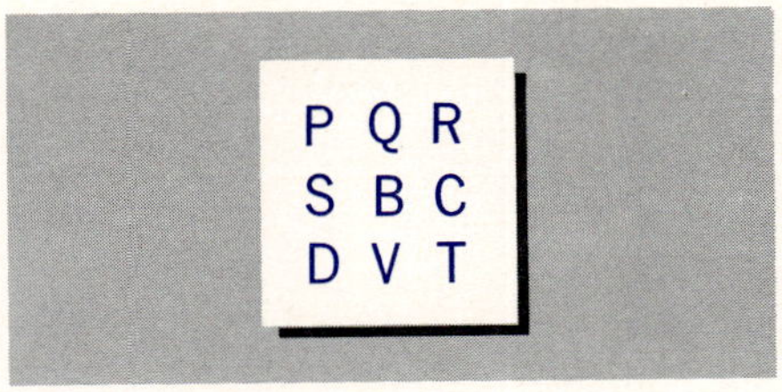

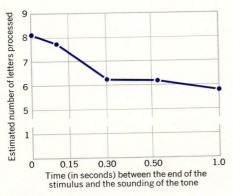

Figure 5.1
A typical trial in Sperling's research on the partial-report span of apprehension procedure. A pattern of consonants is presented briefly. As the stimulus ends, a high, medium, or low tone is sounded. The subject is asked to report on the top, middle, or bottom row of consonants, according to the tone that he hears.

Figure 5.2
Results of Sperling's (1960) study showing how the information present in the sensory store declines within a second.

Figure 5.3 (Right)
Results of Sperling's research.

respectively (see Figure 5.1). Because subjects did not know in advance which tone would be presented, their performance on the single row could be used to estimate how many letters in the complete display they had been able to take in. If, for example, over a number of trials a subject had been correct 90 percent of the time in reporting the letters in a single row, it would be assumed that he or she had actually processed 90 percent of the complete display.

Using this partial-report method, Sperling found that the subjects had indeed "seen" more than they could demonstrate using the older procedure (see Figure 5.3). With the full-report procedure, much of this information is lost before it can be reported. The results suggest that after the presentation of a stimulus, most of the information is stored for a brief instant. This very short-term memory is called the *sensory store*.

DURATION OF SENSORY STORAGE. How long is information held in the sensory store? Sperling attempted to answer this question by varying the interval between the end of the stimulus display and the sounding of the tone. He believed that the tone should only improve performance during the period in which information is in the sensory store. Using several intervals ranging from 0.05 second to 1.0 second, he found that the contents of the sensory store had declined appreciably in about 0.25 seconds (see Figure 5.2).

PROCESSING DATA IN THE SENSORY STORE. What happens to information while it is in the sensory store? Under normal circumstances, all the information in the sensory store is not processed. The time is too brief and the amount of information is too great. You can demonstrate this principle by closing your eyes and

The performance of subjects who tried to report the full display of letters.

Estimates of the number of letters processed based on the performance on a single row. As can be seen, the subjects do "see" more than they can remember when the full-report method is used.

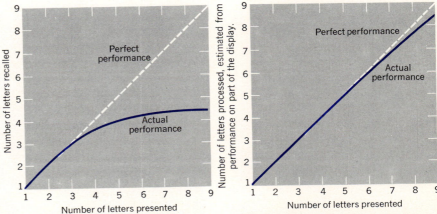

turning your head in the direction of something with which you are not too familiar. Open your eyes, look at it, and then close them quickly. What can you retain? Now look at the object for a longer time, and notice how much you missed.

Because the sensory store is continually being bombarded with so much information, some selection is necessary; we must process the important information that reaches the sensory store and ignore irrelevant material. This process, which is called *selective attention*, is an important aspect of what goes on in the sensory store.

Selective Attention. One means of examining the selective attention process of the sensory store is to briefly present to a subject a display of letters, one of which has been designated as the target. For example, there could be displays of eight consonants with one of the eight being either of two target letters, *T* or *F*. The subject is instructed to search the display and report which of the two target letters was presented. Under these conditions it has been shown that a truly efficient search process takes place.

This was the conclusion from studies (for example, McIntyre, Fox, and Neale, 1970) that have varied the degree of physical similarity between the target and the other letters in the display. For example, the target letter *T* is physically similar to *I* or *E* but quite different from *O* or *U*. When the target is different from the other letters, the sub-

Figure 5.4
Another factor that influences selective attention becomes apparent when you look at this photograph. Although many people can be seen, you probably spent more time examining the face of former president Richard Nixon than looking at anyone else. The principle that applies here is called familiarity or recognizability.

TABLE 5.1

Results of the McIntyre, Fox, and Neale (1970) experiment on the effects of similarity between target letters composed of only straight lines (T or F) and irrelevant, nontarget letters that are formed from either curved or curved and straight lines. As the irrelevant letters become increasingly similar to the target letters, there are more errors (lowered probability of correct response).

	PROBABILITY OF CORRECT RESPONSE	
Irrelevant letters	8-letter displays	14-letter displays
O	.82	.83
U	.81	.74
I	.77	.69
E	.64	.66

ject is able to search quite rapidly and thus make more correct detections (see Table 5.1). It appears that the subject makes an ordered series of tests on each letter to decide whether it is the target. If the results of one test are negative (if, for example, in searching for a *T*, a circular feature is noted), that letter is processed no further so the observer may know nothing about it except that it was not a *T*. In this way, irrelevant information is passed over quickly so more time may be spent processing relevant material. Of course, as we process information from our environment in real life, there is no experimenter present to tell us what to selectively attend to. Some of the factors that play a part in influencing our selective process in everyday life will become more evident if we move from the field of vision to audition.

Shadowing: Probing Selective Attention. One place where some auditory selective attention is required is the cocktail party. At such gatherings people often form a number of conversational clusters. You may want to attend to what your own group is talking about and ignore the voices of others. Generally, this task is not too difficult, for you are physically closer to the members of your own group and thus can hear them more clearly. Occasionally, though, your attention is diverted to another group. Perhaps there is a loud burst of laughter in another group that arouses your curiosity, or perhaps you hear someone mention your name in a snatch of conversation.

Many of these processes have been formally studied using the *shadowing procedure* (Cherry, 1953). With this procedure, a series of messages is presented over earphones to a subject whose task is to repeat each message out loud (shadow) as it is heard. The selective attention component of the task enters when two messages are presented simultaneously, one to the left ear and one to the right, and the subject is instructed to shadow only one of them (see Figure 5.5). Given these circumstances, it has been found that subjects are able to shadow effectively the message to which they are attending.

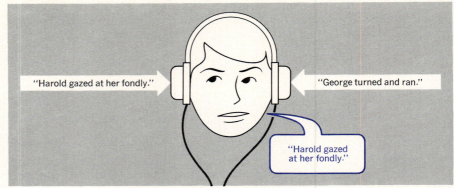

Figure 5.5
The shadowing experiment. Two messages are presented simultaneously, and the listener has to shadow (repeat aloud) one of them.

The fate of the unattended message has many implications for understanding how selective attention operates. If, shortly after participating in a shadowing study, the subjects are asked about the nonshadowed message, they are usually unable to say very much about it. They cannot, for example, remember its contents, nor can they report what language the message was delivered in, nor can they distinguish true speech from nonsense sounds. They can, however, report whether another voice was present and they do notice a change from a man's to a woman's voice or from a speech to a tone. The implication of these findings is that the unattended message is not completely ignored. In addition, some particular feature of the unattended message may be strong enough to cause one's attention to shift from one stimulus to another, for example, hearing one's own name spoken at a cocktail party. Information that has been processed in the sensory store, either partially or fully, is available for further information-processing operations. One of these is storage in short-term memory.

SHORT-TERM MEMORY Often, after dialing an unfamiliar telephone number and getting a busy signal, we have to look the number up in the directory all over again, for we have forgotten it. Similarly, we have all had the embarrassing experience of being introduced to someone and shortly thereafter forgetting that person's name. In such cases, the information has been stored for a very brief time and then lost; this tells us that there is an intermediate stage in retention—*short-term memory*—from which some information will be quickly lost unless there is further processing so that it can be stored in long-term memory.

STORAGE CAPACITY. As already implied in our discussion of Sperling's work, short-term memory has a sharply limited capacity, at least with respect to the number of different items it can hold. About five to nine different items can be stored in short-term memory at any given moment. However, although the *number* of different items that

TABLE 5.2

		Ways of recoding a series of 0s and 1s. At the top is a non-chunked series. The next four rows each illustrate a progressively greater ratio of individual 0s and 1s to the chunk.								
Original series		1 0	1 0	0 0	1 0	0 1	1 1	0 0	1 1	1 0
2:1	Chunks	10	10	00	10	01	11	00	11	10
	Recoding	2	2	0	2	1	3	0	3	2
3:1	Chunks	101		000		100	111		001	110
	Recoding	5		0		4	7		1	6
4:1	Chunks	1010			0010		0111		0011	10
	Recoding	10			2		7		3	
5:1	Chunks	10100			01001			11001		110
	Recoding	20			9			25		

Source: After Miller (1956)

can be retained seems to be fixed, the amount of information within each of these items (or "chunks," as they are often called) is capable of extensive modification. For example, in a famous experiment reported by George Miller (1956), subjects could recall only about nine 0s and 1s, when these two digits were strung together to form a continuing series (for example, 0100110110). However, when subjects *recoded* these digits in sequences of two, so that 00 = 1, 01 = 2, and 11 = 3, they were able to retain about 18 different 0s and 1s instead of just nine (see Table 5.2). Although the number of different chunks of information remained the same (that is, nine), the amount of information contained in each chunk was doubled (that is, each chunk now represented two digits instead of just one). The effect of recoding is so powerful that, using the chunking technique, one subject could even repeat back a string of 40 digits without error.

Another example of the process of recoding information into larger and larger chunks can be seen when people learn to use Morse code. Here, they begin by treating each individual dot and dash as a "chunk" of information. Later, however, the dots and dashes are recoded as letters, and about seven of these larger units can be held simultaneously in short-term memory. Still later in training, individual letters are further recoded into words, and the telegrapher can retain whole sentences at once. Finally, sentences and phrases are themselves coded into larger units, and an experienced operator can remember several sentences or even whole paragraphs. Despite the limited number of different items that can be retained in short-term memory at any given time, a large amount of information can be stored if there has been a sufficient amount of recoding of individual items into larger and larger chunks.

HOLDING ON TO SHORT-TERM MEMORY. The ability to retain information in short-term memory depends to a large extent

152

upon *rehearsal*. Unless information in short-term memory is constantly rehearsed, it is rapidly weakened and quickly forgotten. If, for example, you have looked up a telephone number and need to remember it for a longer than average time, your best bet is to repeat it over and over to yourself. An experiment conducted by Peterson and Peterson (1959) provides an excellent example of both the speed with which material is lost from short-term memory and of the importance of rehearsal.

In this study, the subjects heard the experimenter read a single trigram (for example, CHJ) and then a three-digit number. Next, to prevent rehearsal, they were instructed to count backward from the three-digit number by threes until the appearance of a signal light on a panel in front of them indicated that it was time for them to attempt to recall the trigram. In short, a complete trial would proceed as follows:

> Experimenter: BDH, 347
> Subject: 344, 341, 338. . . .
> Signal: a light comes on indicating that the subject should try to recall the trigram.

The interval between the presentation of the three-digit number and the appearance of the signal light was varied in a systematic manner; it was either 3, 6, 9, 12, 15, or 18 seconds. The results of this experiment are presented in Figure 5.6, where it can be seen that the subjects' ability to recall the single trigram decreased rapidly, virtually disappearing after only 18 seconds. Without an opportunity to rehearse the information to be retained in short-term memory (the counting prevented this), forgetting was almost complete after a very short time.

Not only is rehearsal important for short-term storage, but it also facilitates the transfer of material to a more permanent long-term store. Howe (1967) demonstrated this using the following procedure: Subjects were presented with groups of nine consonants, three at a time for 3 seconds each. Half the participants were instructed to rehearse

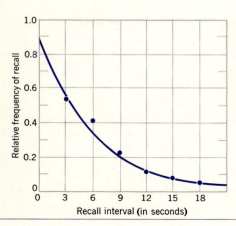

Figure 5.6
The loss of information from short-term memory. The subjects heard the experimenter read a single trigram (CHJ), followed by a three-digit number. Then they counted backward from this number until a signal light appeared, at which time they were to recall the trigram heard earlier. Forgetting the trigram was very rapid: after only 18 seconds had elapsed, they had almost totally forgotten it. [Source: Peterson and Peterson (1959)]

each group of three consonants by reading them aloud over and over again during the time they were in view. The remaining subjects were not so instructed. After the nine letters had been presented, all of the participants were given another task for a short time and then were asked to recall the nine consonants. It was already known that an interfering task will disrupt material in short-term memory, and that the last items presented are those that are most likely to be found in short-term memory. Thus, for the group that had no special rehearsal instructions, it was expected and found that the interfering task had the greatest effect on the last items. But for the group that had rehearsed, the interfering task had less effect, and it was the same for all items. Thus, it was concluded that rehearsal had facilitated the transfer of information to long-term memory.

WHAT IS STORED IN SHORT-TERM MEMORY? It appears that much of the material in short-term memory is represented in an auditory or acoustic form (that is, by its sound). Even some visual material is apparently converted (after it has been processed in the sensory store) into an auditory or acoustic form in short-term memory. Notice, for example, as you are looking at this printed page, that you are probably coding it into an acoustic mode by silently saying the words to yourself.

The logic behind one type of study that has demonstrated this phenomenon is similar to the procedure used to show that greater physical similarity between a target letter and other letters leads to slowed information-processing in the sensory store. When subjects are asked to memorize letters that sound alike (are acoustically similar), the task becomes more difficult. For example, Conrad and Hull (1964) varied the acoustic similarity of the items in lists that were to be learned. The greater the similarity of the items, the more difficulty the subjects experienced in retaining the information.

Other evidence comes from studies of the errors made in recall. If the material in short-term memory is acoustic, then most errors should be made in recalling letters that *sound* like the correct one. Conrad (1964) examined this hypothesis by first studying the auditory confusions made among the letters B, C, P, T, V, F, M, N, S, and X. These letters were presented to subjects one at a time under difficult listening conditions. Each subject reported what he thought he had heard. The results of this initial phase are presented in Table 5.3. The entries in the table show the frequency of the different types of errors. For example, when B was presented, C, P, T, and V were frequent errors, while the acoustically dissimilar F, S, and X were not.

Next, Conrad used the same letters in a memory study. A six-letter sequence was presented, and the subjects were tested immediately for recall. A sophisticated scoring system allowed Conrad to determine when the errors represented true confusions. The results, given in

TABLE 5.3

Frequency of listening errors made when individual letters were presented to subjects.

Responses	Stimulus letters									
	B	C	P	T	V	F	M	N	S	X
B	—	171	75	84	168	2	11	10	2	2
C	32	—	35	42	20	4	4	5	2	5
P	162	350	—	505	91	11	31	23	5	5
T	143	232	281	—	50	14	12	11	8	5
V	122	61	34	22	—	1	8	11	1	0
F	6	4	2	4	3	—	13	8	336	238
M	10	14	2	3	4	22	—	334	21	9
N	13	21	6	9	20	32	512	—	38	14
S	2	18	2	7	3	488	23	11	—	391
X	1	6	2	2	1	245	2	1	184	—

Source: Conrad (1964)

TABLE 5.4

Frequency of recall errors made when six-letter sequences were presented to subjects.

Responses	Stimulus letters									
	B	C	P	T	V	F	M	N	S	X
B	—	18	62	5	83	12	9	3	2	0
C	13	—	27	18	55	15	3	12	35	7
P	102	18	—	24	40	15	8	8	7	7
T	30	46	79	—	38	18	14	14	8	10
V	56	32	30	14	—	21	15	11	11	5
F	6	8	14	5	31	—	12	13	131	16
M	12	6	8	5	20	16	—	146	15	5
N	11	7	5	1	19	28	167	—	24	5
S	7	21	11	2	9	37	4	12	—	16
X	3	7	2	2	11	30	10	11	59	—

Source: Conrad (1964)

Table 5.4, show clearly that most errors were acoustic confusions. Note, for example, that the pattern of errors in Table 5.4 is very similar to the pattern shown in the auditory recognition study (Table 5.3).

LOSING SHORT-TERM MEMORIES. Two major theories attempt to explain why material is lost from short-term memory—*interference theory* and *trace-decay theory*. Interference theory postulates that forgetting is an active process; newly acquired information may interfere with the recall of previously learned material. The trace-decay theory proposes that there is a decline in the strength of the memory trace over the course of time.

An obvious way of testing the two theories would be to arrange for the presentation of some material, followed by a period of doing nothing, and then a test for recall. The trace-decay theory would predict that there would be a memory loss in this situation, but the interference theory would predict that there would be no loss; if the subject were truly doing nothing, there could be no interference. But how could we ever get someone to do absolutely nothing?

Reitman (1971) offered a partial solution to this problem by using a task that should produce only minimal interference effects. Between the presentation of the items and their recall, she had the subjects participate in 30 seconds of signal detection (see Chapter 3), a task that is totally unrelated to the materials to be recalled and hence of minimal interference. She found almost no memory loss after the 30-second period, thus providing support for the interference theory. But subsequent research showed that the material that was retained was somewhat weak and highly susceptible to interference (Atkinson and Shiffrin, 1971). As often happens when we have two competing theories, the truth probably lies somewhere between them.

LONG-TERM MEMORY   In contrast to the quick loss from short-term memory, some memories show no appreciable fading with the passage of time. Most of us, for example, would recognize our favorite childhood toys, even though we had not seen them or even thought about them for many years. Similarly, senior citizens can often vividly recall incidents that happened to them, 40, 50, or even 60 years ago. Some memories, then, can persist for an entire lifetime; collectively these recollections are called *long-term memory*.

STORAGE CAPACITY. In contrast to short-term memory, long-term memory appears to have an extremely large storage capacity. Indeed, as suggested by Howe (1970), the ability of long-term memory to store information may be unlimited. Regardless of whether this is the case, however, there is little indication that people can fill their long-term memory to capacity even during a lifetime.

Current opinion suggests that while information may actually be irretrievably lost from short-term memory, material stored in long-term memory is never forgotten. Instead, it is merely "misplaced" in the sense of being inaccessible. Thus, "forgetting" information stored in long-term memory may be like misplacing a piece of jewelry; the missing article is still technically in your possession, but it cannot be readily located. We would know that it had not disappeared if it shows up days or weeks later. In much the same way, people often remember facts or experiences that had been impossible to retrieve for long periods.

WHAT IS STORED IN MEMORY?   Storage of information in long-term memory depends primarily upon the *meaning* of the material in question rather than upon its acoustic properties. Kintsch and Buschke (1969), for example, investigated the effects of acoustic and meaning similarity on both short-term and long-term memory. The results showed that the meaning similarity of two items (such as polite and courteous) tended to influence long-term retention but had no effect upon short-term memory. These *(continued on page 158)*

TESTING YOUR UNDERSTANDING
THE DISTINCTION BETWEEN SHORT-TERM AND LONG-TERM MEMORY

We have stated that there appears to be an important distinction between short-term and long-term memory and implied that they are two distinct storage systems. But is there any formal evidence for this? We will describe two investigations and ask you to judge how the results of each pertain to the distinction between short-term and long-term memory.

1. In a clinical report, Milner (1967) described an individual who had undergone an operation to relieve severe epileptic seizures. After the operation, in which lesions were placed in the hippocampal region of the brain, the individual performed well on intelligence tests, showed apparently normal motor skills, and demonstrated no obvious changes in personality. However, he was totally unable to remember any new information for very long. For example, he had moved several months earlier, but still could not recall his new address. Also, he would read and reread the same magazines day after day without appearing to remember their contents.

2. A common method of investigating memory is to present subjects with a list of words and later ask them to recall the list. In such investigations it has been found that there is a strong relationship between the place in the list where a given word occurs and the likelihood that the word will be recalled. This relationship, which is shown in Figure 5.7, is called the *serial position curve*. As can be seen, the last words are recalled best, then the first words, and finally those in

Figure 5.7
The serial position curve. The items at the end of a list are recalled best, then those at the beginning, and finally those in the middle.

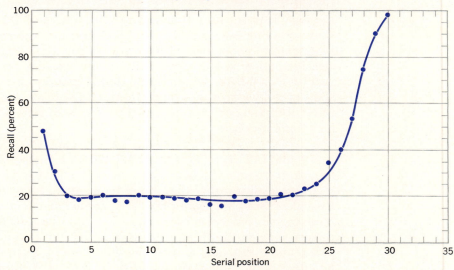

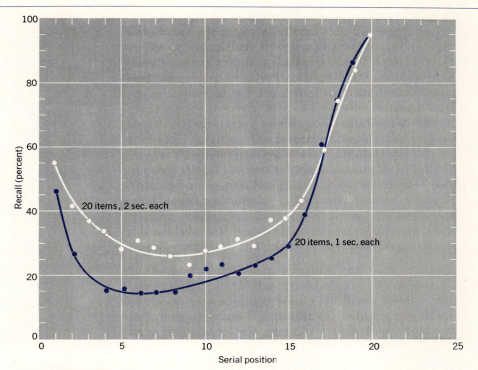

Figure 5.8
Murdock's (1962) study showing the effects of the rate of item presentation on the shape of the serial position curve. A slower rate improves perform-ance primarily in the middle part of the curve.

the middle. Murdock (1962) performed an experiment in which lists of 20 words were presented to subjects at a rate of either one word per second or one word every two seconds. The results, presented in Figure 5.8, show that the slower rate (one/2 secs.) facilitates recall of the early and middle words but not of those at the end of the list. What are the implications of these two studies for the distinction between long- and short-term memory?

1. The Milner report indicates that the hippocampal lesions prevented new information from being placed in long-term memory. Old memories were unimpaired but new ones could not be retained.
2. The classic interpretation of the serial position curve (Figure 5.7) is that different components of the curve reflect different memory proc-esses. The last part of the curve, where recall is best, reflects short-term memory; the rest of the curve long-term storage. Murdock's experimental study further validates this position by demonstrating that the long- and short-memory portions of the curve are affected differently by a manipulation such as the rate of item presentation.

158

TABLE 5.5

A sample experiment
in memory.

Sentence	Question
ACQUISITION SENTENCES: *Read each sentence, count to five, answer the question, go on to the next sentence.*	
The girl broke the window on the porch.	Broke what?
The tree in the front yard shaded the man who was smoking his pipe.	Where?
The hill was steep.	What was?
The cat, running from the barking dog, jumped on the table.	From what?
The tree was tall.	Was what?
The old car climbed the hill.	What did?
The cat, running from the dog, jumped on the table.	Where?
The girl who lives next door broke the window on the porch.	Lives where?
The car pulled the trailer.	Did what?
The scared cat was running from the barking dog.	What was?
The girl lives next door.	Who does?
The tree shaded the man who was smoking his pipe.	What did?
The scared cat jumped on the table.	What did?
The girl who lives next door broke the large window.	Broke what?
The man was smoking his pipe.	Who was?
The old car climbed the steep hill.	The what?
The large window was on the porch.	Where?
The tall tree was in the front yard.	What was?
The car pulling the trailer climbed the steep hill.	Did what?
The cat jumped on the table.	Where?
The tall tree in the front yard shaded the man.	Did what?
The car pulling the trailer climbed the hill.	Which car?
The dog was barking.	Was what?
The window was large.	What was?
STOP. *Cover the preceding sentences. Now read each sentence below and decide if it is a sentence from the list given above.*	
Test set. . . . How many are new?	
The car climbed the hill.	(old____, new____)
The girl who lives next door broke the window.	(old____, new____)
The old man who was smoking his pipe climbed the steep hill.	(old____, new____)

findings provide strong support for the view that short-term and long-term memory are primarily influenced by different aspects of the material to be retained.

Another property of long-term memory can best be illustrated by participating in a memory study, as provided in Table 5.5. Examine the table and follow the instructions before continuing with the text.

How many sentences in the test list did you think were "old"? Actually, you had not seen *any* of the test sentences before. But because of a similarity of meaning, you probably checked a number of the sentences as "old." In long-term storage meanings are important, but

TABLE 5.5 (Continued)

Sentence	Question
The tree was in the front yard.	(old____, new____)
The scared cat, running from the barking dog, jumped on the table.	(old____, new____)
The window was on the porch.	(old____, new____)
The barking dog jumped on the old car in the front yard.	(old____, new____)
The tree in the front yard shaded the man.	(old____, new____)
The cat was running from the dog.	(old____, new____)
The old car pulled the trailer.	(old____, new____)
The tall tree in the front yard shaded the old car.	(old____, new____)
The tall tree shaded the man who was smoking his pipe.	(old____, new____)
The scared cat was running from the dog.	(old____, new____)
The old car, pulling the trailer, climbed the hill.	(old____, new____)
The girl who lives next door broke the large window on the porch.	(old____, new____)
The tall tree shaded the man.	(old____, new____)
The cat was running from the barking dog.	(old____, new____)
The car was old.	(old____, new____)
The girl broke the large window.	(old____, new____)
The scared cat ran from the barking dog that jumped on the table.	(old____, new____)
The scared cat, running from the dog, jumped on the table.	(old____, new____)
The old car pulling the trailer climbed the steep hill.	(old____, new____)
The girl broke the large window on the porch.	(old____, new____)
The scared cat which broke the window on the porch climbed the tree.	(old____, new____)
The tree shaded the man.	(old____, new____)
The car climbed the steep hill.	(old____, new____)
The girl broke the window.	(old____, new____)
The man who lives next door broke the large window on the porch.	(old____, new____)
The tall tree in the front yard shaded the man who was smoking his pipe.	(old____, new____)
The cat was scared.	(old____, new____)

STOP. *Count the number of sentences judged "old."*

Source: Jenkins (1974)

abstracted meaning is stored instead of the exact material that was initially presented. This point is clearly illustrated by an experiment reported by Bransford and Franks (1971). As in the study presented in Table 5.5, the subjects were told a story that consisted of the following sentences:

The rock rolled down the mountain.
The rock crushed the hut.
The hut is at the river.
The hut is tiny.

These sentences were presented together with others that were not part of the story, for example:

> The breeze is warm.
> The jelly is sweet.

After each sentence the subject was asked a simple question to make sure that he understood what had been said (for example, "What was crushed?"). About 5 minutes after all of the sentences had been read, the subjects were given another set of sentences and asked to tell which ones they had previously heard.

The test sentences, some of which are reproduced here, varied in complexity.

1. The hut is at the river.
2. The rock crushed the tiny hut.
3. The rock crushed the tiny hut at the river.
4. The rock which rolled down the mountain crushed the tiny hut at the river.

Of these four examples, only the first sentence had been presented earlier. Remarkably, though, the majority of subjects denied that they had heard that sentence before, even though we might expect that remembering such a short sentence would be easy. Instead, the overwhelming majority of subjects selected the last sentence, which had not been previously presented, as the one they had heard before. Thus, the subjects seem to have abstracted the meaning of the story and stored the abstraction rather than the sentences themselves.

"FORGETTING" FROM LONG-TERM MEMORY. Why are we sometimes unable to remember important facts, skills, and information, even in instances where retaining such knowledge is extremely important? The major answers that have been suggested are the same theories that we encountered for short-term memory—*trace-decay theory* and *interference theory*.

Evidence Inconsistent with Trace-Decay Theory. Several lines of evidence indicate that the inability to recall something from long-term memory is not simply the result of memory fading with time. First, we can often retain information for many years, even when we have no occasion to use or even think about it during the interim. The names of best friends from childhood, obscure details about the lives of former comic-book heroes, and many experiences in adolescence are all examples. Second, the amount of loss is strongly affected by the type of activities performed during the retention interval. This finding is inconsistent with the trace-decay theory, for if forgetting is simply a function of the weakening of the memory trace over time, the specific activities performed by subjects in the period between the original learning and a test for retention would make little difference in their performance. One of the clearest illustrations of the fact that activities performed during the retention interval do

		Part 1	Part 2	Part 3
	Experimental procedures employed in investigating retroactive inhibition. Generally the experimental group has more difficulty recalling A than the control group.			
Experimental group		Learns A	Learns B	Recalls A
Control group		Learns A	Rests or participates in unrelated activities.	Recalls A

affect memory is provided by the results of a classic experiment conducted by Jenkins and Dallenbach (1924).

In this study, two male university students first practiced a list of ten nonsense syllables until they could recite them perfectly. They were then tested for retention of these syllables after 1, 2, 4, or 8 hours of normal waking activities or equal intervals of sleep. (In order to arrange for the periods of sleep, the subjects and one of the investigators lived in a makeshift dormitory directly adjoining the laboratory.) For any given retention interval, fewer of the nonsense syllables were forgotten when the subjects had spent their time sleeping than when they had been awake and busy with their usual activities (Figure 5.9). These findings are clearly inconsistent with trace-decay theory, which would predict equal amounts of forgetting in both conditions.

Evidence Supporting the Interference Theory of Forgetting. If forgetting is not a function of the fading or decay of memory traces, then we are left with the suggestion that it is primarily due to various forms of interference between items that are already in the memory and new ones that are currently being added. Two major types of interference have been suggested. One is that newly acquired material may interfere with the retention of items learned previously. Interference of this type is generally termed *retroactive inhibition*, and it may be investigated in experiments that follow the general design shown in Table 5.6. The experimental group learns one set of material (A), then learns a second set (B), and is finally asked to recall the first set (A). In contrast, the control group learns A, rests or engages in some unrelated activity during the period when the experimental group is learning B, and then recalls A. In general, it has been found that the control group shows a higher retention level of A, thus indicating that learning new material can interfere with the recall of any previously learned material.

Information learned at an earlier time may also interfere with the retention of more recently learned material. A good example of this process, called *proactive inhibition*, may be observed in the difficulty we sometimes experience in trying to memorize our new telephone number after moving to a new address. Our old number frequently intrudes and makes it difficult for us to remember the new one. Proactive inhibition is often investigated in experiments of the type outlined in

Figure 5.9
Both subjects forgot more material when they were awake than when they were asleep. These results are inconsistent with the trace-decay theory of forgetting. [Source: Jenkins and Dallenbach (1924)]

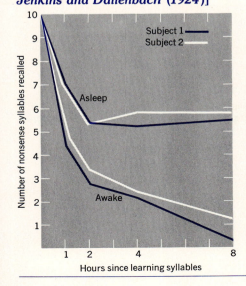

TABLE 5.7

Experimental procedures employed in investigating proactive inhibition. Generally the experimental group has more difficulty recalling B than the control group.

	Part 1	Part 2	Part 3
Experimental group	Learns A	Learns B	Recalls B
Control group	Rests or participates in unrelated activities.	Learns B	Recalls B

Table 5.7. Here, the experimental group learns one set of materials (A), and then learns a second set (B), and then attempts to recall B. The control group rests or does something else during the first phase of the study, then learns B, and finally recalls these materials. Usually the experimental group has greater difficulty recalling B than the control group, presumably because their earlier learning of A interferes with their recall of material learned later.

Evidence collected by Benton J. Underwood (1957, 1964) demonstrates the importance of proactive inhibition. In his research, Underwood presented subjects with a list of nonsense syllables and then asked them to recall this material 24 hours later. Under these conditions, it was found that the subjects had forgotten about 20 percent of the list. Then, the same subjects were asked to learn a second list and remember this new set of items the next day. Here, it was found that they had forgotten about 25 percent of the list. The same procedures were followed again and again until the subjects had learned 20 different lists (the subjects studied a new list each day and attempted to remember it the following day). The subjects' forgetting increased regularly as the number of lists they were instructed to learn increased (see Figure 5.10). Thus, it appeared that the ability to recall was significantly influenced by proactive inhibition. Indeed, as can be seen from Figure 5.9, when the subjects were asked to remember the twentieth list the day after it had been learned, they were unable to remember 80 percent of it.

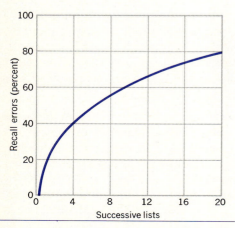

Figure 5.10
The subjects learned a new list of nonsense syllables each day for 20 days. After learning each list, they were asked to recall it the following day. The recall errors rose sharply as the number of lists already learned increased. These findings provide evidence for the significant influence of proactive inhibition on recall from long-term memory. [Source: Underwood (1964)]

THE RETRIEVAL OF INFORMATION FROM MEMORY.

We have examined some of the factors that affect the recall of information from memory. Even if no information is ever lost, memory would be useless in a practical sense if specific items cannot readily be retrieved from storage on demand. For example, it is not much consolation to a student taking an examination to know that the information he needed was stored "somewhere" in his memory if he cannot easily retrieve it. Similarly, an actress who forgets her lines on opening night would find little solace in the fact that these materials were only temporarily inaccessible and will probably be remembered at a later time.

Given the tremendous amount of information stored in a person's memory by the time he or she reaches adulthood, it is amazing how easily we are generally able to come up with the information we need. How is one able to accomplish this complex and difficult task with such a high degree of accuracy and efficiency? Two factors seem to be important. First, the materials stored in memory are generally organized in some manner, and this *organization* facilitates retrieval. Second, we often make use of *retrieval cues*—stimuli that provide us with information about where in memory the specific items might be found.

THE ROLE OF ORGANIZATION IN MEMORY.

In general, the greater the degree of organization of material, the greater the ease of recall. Two types of organization that facilitate retrieval had been extensively investigated—*associative organization* and *categorical organization.*

Associative organization is essentially the relationship among materials to be memorized. The existence of associative links is shown, for example, in the familiar word association test, in which a list of words is read one at a time to a person who is instructed to "respond with the first word that comes to mind." This test would reveal that the words *"table"* and *"chair"* are closely associated, for presenting the one tends to elicit the other almost automatically. On the other hand, the words *"needle"* and *"diligence"* would not be closely related, for the one word has virtually no tendency to elicit the other. The effect of associative organization on the ease of recall has been clearly demonstrated in a noted experiment conducted by Jenkins, Mink, and Russell (1958). These investigators began by constructing four different lists of 12 word pairs. The degree of association between the items in each pair was manipulated as follows: low (comfort-chair), moderate (deep-shallow), high (sweet-sour), very high (man-woman). These lists were then presented to four different groups of subjects. When the subjects were later asked to recall the first lists they had been given, it was found that their performance depended upon the degree of association between the pairs (see Table 5.8). The list in which the degree of association was highest was recalled best, the list in which the degree of association was second highest was recalled second best, and so forth.

TABLE 5.8

The effects of associative organization upon recall. The subjects in four different groups learned lists of word pairs in which the degree of association between the words in each pair was low (comfort-chair), moderate (deep-shallow), high (sweet-sour), or very high (man-woman). It was found that the higher the degree of associative organization in a list, the better the words in that list were recalled.

	Low	Moderate	High	Very high
Total number of words recalled	14.48	17.46	18.06	19.07

Source: Jenkins, Mink, and Russell (1958)

Thus, associative organization was an important factor in retention.

With respect to *categorical organization*, it has been found that recall is facilitated to the extent that the materials to be learned can be linked together in distinct categories. This phenomenon was first reported by Bousfield (1953) in a study of the ability to recall a word list containing 15 items in each of four categories (animals, names, professions, and vegetables). After a single presentation of the 60 words, the participants were asked to recall as much as possible. Examination of the data showed that the subjects tended to recall words belonging to the same category in groups; they showed what is termed *categorical clustering*.

In a related study, Cohen (1966) presented subjects with lists of 35, 53, or 70 words that could be classified into 10, 15, or 20 different categories. When the subjects were later asked to recall these words, it was found that as long as they could remember at least one word in a certain category, the percentage of words they could remember in that category remained fairly constant, regardless of the length of the list. Thus, the subjects' recall was affected by the number of different categories they could remember and *not* by the number of individual words. In a later work, Mandler (1968) reported that there is a very close relationship between the number of categories the subjects use in their recall and the amount of material they can remember. Thus, an important factor in later recall is the degree to which the material to be memorized is organized into categories.

Indeed, the benefits of organizing the material to be learned appear to be so great that when a scheme is not supplied by the experimenter, the subjects often devise one themselves. For example, Tulving (1962) gave a group of subjects a list of 16 words and then asked them to recall these words in order. The same words were presented again, but this time in a different order. Again, the subjects were asked to recall the words. This procedure was repeated several more times. Although the order in which the words were presented varied each time, the order in which the subjects recalled them did not change. Thus, despite the fact that the words on the list were not related (for example, accent, barrack, finding, garden, issue, jungle, maxim, treason, valley), the subjects imposed their own organization upon them. Moreover, the consistency of this organization appeared to improve each time, and it was also positively related to their ability to recall the words. Thus, organization may facilitate recall even when it is a purely subjective structure made up by those who are trying to memorize certain items.

Signposts to Memories. Large libraries use a complex and precise catalog system to enable readers to identify and locate every item stored there. Similarly, it appears that every chunk of information stored in memory is assigned a precise location so that it, too, can be retrieved rapidly and efficiently. Of course, in the case of memory, the word "location" does not refer to a specific point in physical space, but to the position in a complex web of associations or categories occupied by that piece of information. Continuing with this analogy, *retrieval cues* may be viewed as signs or guideposts that provide information about where the material is stored. Thus, they make it easier to search for specific items when they are needed. The best retrieval cue, of course, is the external presentation of the needed information itself as, for example, if you are asked to recognize the right answer among several offered on a multiple-choice test. But even in cases where true recall is required, less obvious retrieval cues can prove to be most helpful.

A good example of the importance of retrieval cues can be seen in an experiment conducted by Tulving and Pearlstone (1966). A group of sub-

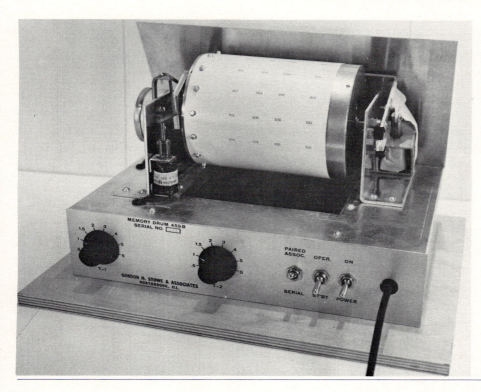

Figure 5.11
Rear view of a typical memory drum that is used for psychological research. The stimuli are typed sequentially on a paper that is then mounted on the drum. The movement of the drum can be controlled so that the stimuli appear at the desired rate in a "window" that the subject monitors.

jects was asked to memorize lists of 12, 24, or 48 different words. The words in each list could be grouped into different categories, such as four-footed animals (cow, rat), weapons (bomb, cannon), crimes (treason, theft), and forms of entertainment (radio, music); there were either 1, 2, or 4 items in each category. Afterward, when the subjects were asked to write down as many of the words as they could remember, half the group was given only a blank piece of paper while the other half was also given the names of the categories (that is, *retrieval cues*). As expected, the category names facilitated recall, so that those who received these cues were able to remember more words than those who received only the blank paper. When the subjects who received the blank paper on the first retention test were later given the cues, they remembered as many words as those who had received them initially. Thus, it is clear that category names help make information already in memory more accessible for recall.

Another method of facilitating retrieval is called a *mnemonic*, a device whereby the material to be learned is related to some already existing organizational framework. Miller, Galanter, and Pribram (1960, p. 135) offered the following device which consists of ten rhymes.
one is a bun,
two is a shoe,
three is a tree,
four is a door,
five is a hive,
six are sticks,
seven is heaven,
eight is a gate,
nine is a line, and
ten is a hen.

In order to understand how this device works, memorize the piece. Repeat it to yourself several times until you have mastered it. The rhyme will now provide the framework for learning any list of ten words. Below you will find a list; as you read each word, form some kind of visual association between it and the rhyme. For example, if the first word were "battleship," you might picture to yourself a hamburger bun with the ship perched on top of it. Spend about 5 seconds on each word forming an association.

1. ashtray
2. firewood
3. painting
4. cigarette
5. table
6. matchbook
7. glass
8. lamp
9. shoe
10. phonograph

Now close the book for a couple of minutes. Then, begin asking yourself questions such as "What is eight?" You will see that you can recall most words at will.

PARTIAL RECALL AND RECONSTRUCTIVE MEMORY.

Up to this point we have seen how people examine organizational structures and try to retrieve information from memory. But recall is not always perfect. Subjectively we all know that our memories of an event, a previously read book, or a movie seen several years ago can be fragmentary. In such circumstances people often "fill in the gaps," reconstructing the whole from only partial information.

The classic studies of this phenomenon were conducted by Sir Frederick Bartlett (1932). In one series of experiments he asked subjects to read a short narrative, and then he tested them for recall at various intervals. Remarkably, their memory for these simple stories was quite inaccurate. They usually remembered only the outline of the story, and then they reconstructed many of the details. Some subjects would remember a detail of the story and then construct a rationalization for it.

Here is an example of one of Bartlett's narratives and a subject's attempt to recall it:

One night two young men from Egulac went down to the river to hunt seals, and while they were there it became foggy and calm. Then they heard war-cries, and they thought: "Maybe this is a war-party." They escaped to the shore, and hid behind a log. Now canoes came up, and they heard the noise of paddles, and saw one canoe coming up to them. There were five men in the canoe, and they said:

"What do you think? We wish to take you along. We are going up the river to make war on the people."

One of the young men said: "I have no arrows."

"Arrows are in the canoe," they said.

"I will not go along. I might be killed. My relatives do not know where I have gone. But you," he said, turning to the other, "may go with them."

So one of the young men went, but the other returned home.

And the warriors went on up the river to a town on the other side of Kalama. The people came down to the water, and they began to fight, and many were killed. But presently the young man heard one of the warriors say: "Quick, let us go home: that Indian has been hit." Now he thought: "Oh, they are ghosts." He did not feel sick, but they said he had been shot.

So the canoes went back to Egulac, and the young man went ashore to his house, and made a fire. And he told everybody and said: "Behold I accompanied the ghosts, and we went to fight. Many of our fellows were killed, and many of those who attacked us were killed. They said I was hit, and I did not feel sick."

He told it all, and then he became quiet. When the sun rose he fell down. Something black came out of his mouth. His face became con-

torted. The people jumped up and cried.

He was dead.

Eight days after reading the story, a subject gave the following rendition. Note how the supernatural flavor of the original has been lost.

Two young men from Edulac went fishing. While thus engaged they heard a noise in the distance. "That sounds like a war-cry," said one, "there is going to be some fighting." Presently there appeared some warriors who invited them to join an expedition up the river.

One of the young men excused himself on the ground of family ties. "I cannot come," he said, "as I might get killed." So he returned home. The other man, however, joined the party, and they proceeded in canoes up the river. While landing on the banks the enemy appeared and they discovered that they were fighting against ghosts. The young man and his companion returned to the boats, and went back to their homes.

The next morning at dawn he was describing his adventures to his friends, who had gathered round him. Suddenly something black issued from his mouth, and he fell down uttering a cry. His friends closed around him, but found that he was dead.

Sometimes we feel that we know or remember something, but cannot, for some reason, actually bring it into consciousness. An interesting illustration of the "feeling of knowing" is provided in an experiment conducted by Hart (1965). The subjects were asked a number of questions about a wide variety of topics; where they could not supply the correct answer, they were instructed to indicate whether they felt they actually knew the answer but could not provide it just at that moment, or whether they had no knowledge of it at all. Thus, they were asked to "monitor" their memories, providing reports of what information was or was not there. During a second phase of the study, the subjects were given a multiple-choice test based on the questions they had not been able to answer. It was found that on this test, the subjects were able to answer correctly 76 percent of the items they had previously reported "knowing," but only 43 percent of those they had reported "not knowing." It appeared, then, that the subjects had considerable ability to report on the *kind* of information stored in their memories, even though they couldn't retrieve this information for present use.

A similar phenomenon may be observed in situations where we feel that a word, name, or even telephone number we want to recall is on the "tip of our tongue." Researchers have produced instances of the tip-of-the-tongue effect in the laboratory by reading the definitions of 49 relatively uncommon words (for example, "whale secretion used in making perfume") to subjects, and then asking them to supply the missing word (in this case, *ambergris*). Sometimes when the subjects indicated that the tip-of-the-tongue phenomenon was occurring (that is, when the missing word was on the tip of their tongue), they were asked to guess the number of syllables it contained and its initial letter, and to list words that are similar to it in sound and in meaning. Even when they could not recall the missing words, the sub-

TESTING YOUR UNDERSTANDING
THE PRACTICAL PROBLEM OF IMPROVING YOUR MEMORY

During classroom discussions of memory, many students ask what they can do to make sure that they remember important pieces of information. Based on our discussion so far, you should be able to offer some practical advice on this matter. What would you suggest?

First, retention may often be facilitated if some organization is imposed on the information to be memorized. For example, it might be advantageous in many cases, at least initially, to try to combine the items to be remembered into several different *categories,* and then to concentrate on recalling the categories rather than the individual items. As indicated earlier, there is considerable evidence that once the category names have been recalled, many items within each category will often come to mind almost immediately (Cohen, 1966). Thus, this procedure might be useful in situations where a large number of individual items must be committed to memory. Another type of organization that might be used when categorization is unwieldy or impossible (when there is no obvious way to group certain items together) is to put the items into the context of a story, as illustrated in the Bransford and Franks (1971) study.

Second, it is important to *rehearse* the materials to be learned. Without rehearsal, items held in short-term memory may be lost very quickly without a chance to enter long-term storage. Thus, you may find it worthwhile to take short breaks while you are studying, at which time you carefully rehearse the materials being learned. This procedure will enable you to hold the items you are learning at the center of your attention long enough to improve their chances of being transferred to long-term memory and often to facilitate their retention over longer periods.

Third, a *mnemonic system* like that described on page 166 can be used.

jects performed all of these other tasks quite well. For example, they were able to identify correctly the initial letter of the target words 57 percent of the time they experienced the tip-of-the-tongue effect. Similarly, when the word they could not recall consisted of three syllables, approximately 63 percent of their guesses about this characteristic were accurate. Clearly, then, the subjects demonstrated a substantial degree of partial recall, even when the words themselves could not be produced. These findings could suggest that the subjects did not have enough retrieval cues to enable them to reproduce the target words, and if they had had these cues, their recall would have been easier. This interpretation is supported by the fact that recalling words that are on the "tip of the tongue" is actually facilitated by presenting their initial letters (Earhard, 1967).

PROBLEM-SOLVING

Imagine that you entered a room and saw a table on which a candle, a book of matches, and a box full of tacks had been placed (see Figure 5.12). Suppose you were then asked to affix the candle to the wall so that it would burn in a vertical position. Study the drawing for a moment and see if you can figure out a solution.

The "trick" is first to recognize that the box, although now serving as a container for the tacks, could be used for a different purpose. Specifically, after being emptied, the box can be tacked to the wall, where it then can serve as a tray for the candle. When a study of this problem was actually performed (Glucksberg and Weisberg, 1966) only 54 per-

Figure 5.12
How can this candle be affixed to the wall so that it will burn in a vertical position?

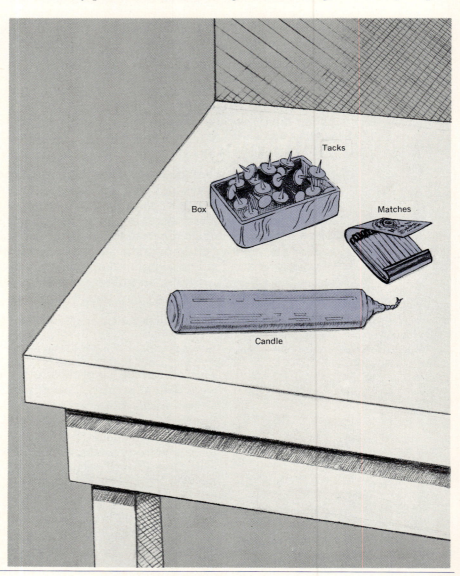

cent of the college student participants solved it correctly. The problem experienced by subjects in this study is called *functional fixedness*, a difficulty many people experience in trying to perceive a single object or situation in more than one light.

Investigators of problem-solving have a somewhat different focus than the studies of cognition we discussed earlier. Our approach thus far could be called *molecular*, since it dealt with specific components of cognition. But it is equally important to look at *molar* problem-solving in order to round out our discussion of cognitive processes. In so doing, we will have an opportunity to examine how thought processes grapple with a problem. We will see that people are able to deal with information in a very organized fashion. Three examples follow:

CONCEPT LEARNING. The acquisition of concepts (for example, round, male) is of fundamental importance in human thought. Recall, for example, that memory depends heavily on the use of conceptual categories. We are continually integrating our experiences by grouping them together in such categories. The key feature of many concepts is that they summarize an essential property of the class of objects that fall into a certain category. The concept furniture, for example, would include tables, chairs, sofas, and so forth. There are many differences among the various items in a category, but all possess a central attribute that allows them to be classified together. How do people learn to discriminate an essential from a nonessential property?

To answer this question, researchers have used the "two-choice discrimination problem," in which participants are shown two objects side by side and asked to pick the "correct" one. To do so consistently, subjects must learn to respond to one attribute of the stimuli being presented and to disregard the nonessential attributes. For example, the participants might be presented with a large blue ball and a small red square. Any one of eight attributes (small, large, red, blue, ball, square, right, or left [the position in which the objects were placed]) could be the critical attribute. Since the experimenter has previously designated one attribute as correct, the subject's task is to find the solution over repeated trials, first by guessing, then receiving feedback, and finally zeroing in on the answer.

What actually happens in such a situation? One answer was offered by Restle (1962) who proposed that subjects sample possible hypotheses (such as red or square) about the correct solution and then test them. If a hypothesis leads to a choice that is correct, the subject will stay with it. If the hypothesis leads to incorrect feedback, he will try a new one. This is referred to as a "win-stay, lose-shift" strategy. Restle also suggested several different ways in which hypotheses could be sampled:

1. A person could sample a single hypothesis at random and test it

172

using the win-stay, lose-shift rule. After an incorrect response he could then resample at random. Note that this model implies a "memoryless" person, since following an incorrect response the erroneous hypotheses would be sampled again.

2. The person could consider all hypotheses simultaneously and on each trial discard those that were not consistent with the obtained feedback.

3. The person could begin with some of the available hypotheses, discarding those that were not consistent with feedback over several trials. If this first small group became exhausted, he would select another group of hypotheses.

Restle's emphasis on the *process* of solving this problem is important, for we are interested in describing thought. Mathematically, he was even able to calculate predicted performances from each of the models above. Unfortunately, his predictions were quite similar so that none of the alternatives was clearly suggested by the experimental results.

In the 1960s Marvin Levine devised a new method for studying the process of learning concepts. Using an ingenious experimental arrangement, he was able to determine from a subject's responses how he was evaluating hypotheses. The procedure was as follows:

On the first trial two letters would be presented (for example, **X**$\mathbb{T}$) that differed in color (black-white), form (X-T), position (left-right), and size (small-large). Thus, there were eight possible hypotheses at the outset.[1] On the first trial the subject made a choice and received feedback. Then there were four more trials but no feedback. These

[1] More complex hypotheses, such as large and X, were excluded by telling the participants that only simple hypotheses would be correct.

Figure 5.13
Psychologists have begun to study the type of complex problem-solving that is required in a game of chess. This young man is playing against a computer that has been programmed so well it can defeat all but the best of players.

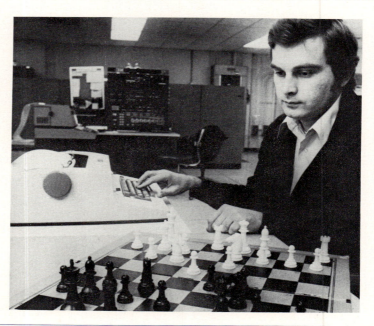

TABLE 5.9

Stimuli	Four no-feedback trials used in Levine's work.							
	Black hypothesis	X hypothesis	Left hypothesis	Large hypothesis	Small hypothesis	Right hypothesis	T hypothesis	White hypothesis
	Predicted responses							
X𝕋	left	left	left	left	right	right	right	right
𝕩**T**	right	left	left	right	left	right	right	left
T𝕏	left	right	left	right	left	right	left	right
𝕋**x**	right	right	left	left	right	right	left	left

trials allowed Levine to determine what was going on in his subject's head as he or she grappled with the problem.

The key was to construct the trials in a particular way, as shown in Table 5.9. The stimuli appear in the left-hand column. Next come the predicted responses for each of the eight possible hypotheses. Note that each hypothesis, if followed, would produce a unique pattern of left or right choices. Thus, by observing the pattern of choices, Levine could infer which hypothesis the subject was testing.

On the fifth trial, the subject would again receive feedback, and then there would be four more trials without feedback. Then the cycle would be repeated again.

Based on the data he collected, Levine was able to confirm that people tested only one hypothesis at a time. More than 92 percent of the responses on the no-feedback trials were consistent with one of the eight hypotheses. He also found that the win-stay, lose-shift rule accurately described the subjects' reactions to feedback: 98 percent of them shifted after an error and 95 percent retained a hypothesis that had produced correct feedback. Levine also determined that after an error people do not resample at random; they are more inclined to ignore the hypothesis that had turned out to be incorrect.

How efficiently did Levine's subjects test hypotheses? To be able to answer this, we must first consider what a "perfect" performance would look like. Suppose that a subject is presented with 𝕏**T** and chooses left. If his answer was correct, presumably he would now know that the answer was either black, X, left, or large. If his left choice was incorrect, he would know that the answer was either white, T, right, or small. In either case he would have reduced the number of viable hypotheses from eight to four.

Assuming that left had been correct on the first trial, consider the second feedback trial. The stimulus is **T**𝕏 and the subject makes a left choice. Now if left is correct, the answer must be either black or left, for the other two dimensions—small and T—were eliminated on the first trial. If left is incorrect, the number of possible answers is still reduced to two (white or X).

To complete the picture let us examine the third feedback trial, assuming that left was correct on the second trial. The stimulus is ⊤**X** and the subject chooses left again. If left is correct, then the answer is left; if not, then black is the answer. Under ideal circumstances, it should be possible to arrive at the solution in three trials. The actual performances of Levine's subjects are shown in Figure 5.14. As can be observed, they approach the ideal and obviously do considerably better than they would if they were simply sampling in a random fashion.

ANAGRAMS. Most people are familiar with anagrams, a game in which the letters of a word have been scrambled and the players must rearrange them to produce a word. What can a study of anagrams reveal about thought? One approach has been to vary the characteristics of the anagrams and then observe the effect of these manipulations on an individual's performance. Depending upon the effects observed, inferences can be made about the cognitive processes behind the performance.

One possible (but time-consuming) means of solving anagrams would be to try out all possible combinations of letters until a solution was reached. If this were actually the strategy people used, we could expect to find that with increases in the number of letters in the anagram, more time would be required: 3 letters have 6 possible combinations, 4 have 24, and 5 have 120. Kaplan and Carvellas (1968) undertook to determine whether people try all combinations by presenting subjects with anagrams from 3 to 10 letters in length. Although their solution times increased with the number of letters, the rate of increase was not nearly as great as would be expected according to the simple model presented above.

Ronning (1965) examined another aspect of problem-solving—the subjects' ability to rule out unlikely solutions. For example, the anagram "higtl" has 120 possible arrangements. But there are many bigrams (combinations of two letters) and trigrams that never come at the beginning of a word:

HG	GT	LH	GHT	GLT
HT	TG	LG	GHL	THL
HL	TL	LT	GLH	THG

For each omitted initial bigram, we can eliminate six possible arrangements, and for each omitted trigram two possible arrangements. In this case, then, 66 possible solutions can be eliminated, thus greatly simplifying the task. In his experiment, Ronning presented two types of anagrams—those in which many solutions could be ruled out and those with few rule-outs. As expected, the subjects performed better in the former case, showing that people can make efficient use of the rule-out strategy. Thus, we see again that human thought is more efficient than simple trial and error.

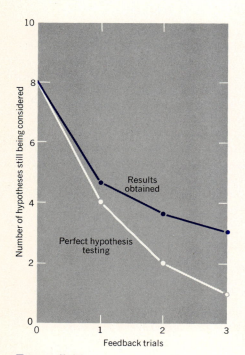

Figure 5.14
Levine's study showed that the participants approach but do not completely reach the "ideal information processor." When a subject gets down to a single hypothesis, he has found the solution.

DEDUCTIVE REASONING. Deductive reasoning, in which a solution to a problem is logically inferred from premises, is accorded a high status in human thought. It is held to be of central importance in scientific progress and is greatly admired in most walks of life. Sherlock Holmes's powers of deduction were the key ingredient in a whole series of mystery stories.

Much of the research on deductive reasoning has used the syllogism as an example. Typically, the subject is presented with two premises followed by a number of conclusions. The task is to choose the valid conclusion. For example:

Some S is M
All M is P

Therefore:

1. All S is P
2. All S is not P
3. Some S is P
4. Some S is not P
5. None of these conclusions is valid

Although such problems are simple to someone who has been trained in logic, adults without such training often make many errors. One of the most common errors is called the *fallacy of the undistributed middle*. Do you agree or disagree with the conclusion drawn in the following syllogism?

Clergymen are nice people.
My next door neighbor is a nice person.
Therefore, my next door neighbor must be a clergyman.

If you answered "yes," you were trapped by the undistributed middle. Clergymen are not the only nice people in the world; hence, it does not follow that a nice person must be a clergyman.

A second prevalent error is to base a conclusion on two particular premises. Read the following:

Some psychologists do research.
Some psychotherapists are psychologists.
Therefore, some psychotherapists do research.

The conclusion is false. The psychotherapists who are psychologists are not necessarily the psychologists who do research.

Why do educated people make such logical errors? Chapman and Chapman (1959) believe that the basic problem is one of *invalid conversion*. For example, if you know that "all X is Y," it is easy to make the error of asserting that "all Y is X." Similarly, if it is known that "some X is not Y," it is seductive (but incorrect) to assume that "some Y is not X." Here is a syllogism with an erroneous conclusion:

176

All S is M.
All P is M.
Therefore, all S is P.

If the second premise were (invalidly) converted to "all M is P," then the invalid conclusion would follow. From the evidence, we should not conclude that people are illogical. The process of invalid conclusion, although leading to incorrect conclusions in logic, makes good sense in our daily lives. The sentence "all right angles have 90°" is usually understood to imply its converse "all 90° angles are right angles." But symbolic logic, as an abstract system, does not allow such conversions.

PSYCHOLOGY AND THE PROBLEMS OF SOCIETY
CREATIVE THINKING

The challenge of trying to understand creativity—the accomplishment of original products or thoughts—dates back to the time of the earliest recorded thinkers. In the *Meno,* Plato speaks of the seeming paradox in setting out to find a solution to a problem: "How will you look for something when you don't in the least know what it is? How on earth are you going to set up something you don't know as the object of your search? To put it another way, even if you come up right against it, how will you know that what you have found is the thing you didn't know?" (p. 32, Guthrie translation).

Plato implies that creative thinking is not possible. And yet we know that it is. Bolton (1971) draws on the work of Michael Polyani to provide a modern resolution of this paradox. He makes a distinction between two kinds of knowledge—explicit and tacit. Explicit knowledge, which appears to be a verbal understanding of a problem, is that upon which you focus your attention. Tacit knowledge, on the other hand, is the hidden, unattended framework of explicit knowledge. These concepts are analogous to the "figure" and "ground" postulated by Gestalt psychologists in explaining perceptual organization. Original thinking, then, could be viewed as movement from an explicit statement of a problem by means of clues that somehow point to the hidden reality of the solution.

This conceptual and philosophical analysis has been supported with some psychological research. Creative thinking, according to Wallach (1970), is characterized by "ideational fluency"—an ability to generate large numbers of ideas that are appropriate to a given task. To measure this, psychologists might ask a person to list as many unusual uses for a brick that he or she can think of, or to try to anticipate all of the possible consequences of an unexpected event. Interestingly, this ability seems to have little relationship to the usual measures of intelligence, such as one's IQ. Bolton (1971) cites a study in which a group of adolescent boys were shown a picture depicting a man

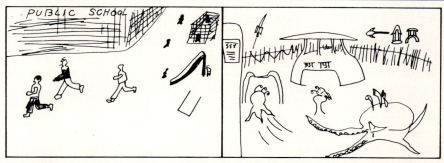

Judged less creative · Judged creative

Children are asked to draw a picture on the theme "Playing tag in the school yard."

seated in an airplane. A bright but "uncreative" subject was asked to tell a story about the scene, and the boy replied:

Mr. Smith is on his way home from a successful business trip. He is very happy and he is thinking about his wonderful family and how glad he will be to see them again. He can picture it now, his plane landing at the airport and Mrs. Smith and their three children all there welcoming him home again.

On the other hand, a "creative" subject made up this story:

This man is flying back from Reno where he has just won a divorce from his wife. He couldn't stand to live with her anymore, he told the judge, because she wore so much cold cream on her face at night that her head would skid across the pillow and hit him in the head. He is now contemplating a new skid-proof face cream. [Getzels and Jackson, 1962, quoted in Bolton, p. 203.]

The importance of ideational fluency (or associative ability) is supported by the introspections of acknowledged creative artists and scientists. James Watson reports in his book *The Double Helix* that he thought of the structure of DNA after seeing an old movie with a spiral staircase. The poet Dryden, as quoted in Wallach (1970), relates that before he wrote he often had "a confus'd Mass of Thoughts, tumbling over one another in the Dark."

Wallach believes that those who have a broad "deployment" or focus of attention can probably make more unlikely associations, since they can allow their attention to roam and establish new relationships among information. Creative persons tend not to evaluate their ideas too quickly, and studies have shown that this helps to prevent the premature elimination of promising ideas. Furthermore, Wallach cites two studies showing that one's ability to shift attention from the center of a problem to peripheral data is related to research creativity. This is similar to Bolton's point about bringing tacit knowledge to the center of awareness in solving a problem.

Practical strategies to encourage creative thinking have emerged from these findings. The psychologist Edward DeBono (1968) suggests that "lateral thinking"—the ability to look at a problem from many angles while paying special attention to its less obvious ("tacit") aspects—is crucial to effective thinking. Toward this end, he gives his students special exercises to work on; here is one of them:

An old money-lender offered to cancel a merchant's debt and keep him from going to prison if the merchant would give the money-lender his lovely daughter. Horrified yet desperate, the merchant and his daughter agreed to let Providence decide. The money-lender said he would put a black pebble and a white pebble in a bag and the girl would draw one. The white pebble would cancel the debt and leave her free. The black one would make her the money-lender's, although the debt would be canceled. If she refused to pick, her father would go to prison. From the pebble-strewn path they were standing on, the money-lender picked two pebbles and quickly put them in the bag, but the girl saw he had picked two black ones. What would you have done if you were the girl?

The answer?

When the girl put her hand into the bag to draw out the fateful pebble, she fumbled and dropped it, where it was immediately lost among the others. "Oh," she said "well, you can tell which one I picked by looking at the one that's left."

It is not inconceivable that, with further research, psychologists might be able to instruct people in how to think creatively.

179
SUMMARY

Cognitive processes are inferred mental states that mediate between stimulus and response. In examining the major cognitive processes, it is useful to trace temporally the various steps through which a stimulus can pass. First, stimuli are briefly held in visual form in the sensory store. The amount of information reaching the sensory store is too great for all of it to be processed in the very small amount of time available. Thus, there is selective attention so that unimportant information can be ignored while important information is noted and then transferred to short-term memory.

Short-term memory holds a relatively small amount of information (five to nine units) for a brief period. In contrast to the sensory store, information in short-term storage appears to be held in acoustic form. Information that is not actively rehearsed is quickly lost from short-term storage. Both interference from newly acquired information and a decay of the memory trace over time account for forgetting from short-term memory.

Information that reaches long-term memory may remain forever. Here, information is coded by meaning rather than acoustically; an abstraction of the meaning of the material is stored rather than the literal information itself. An important feature of information in long-term memory is that it is organized. Organization can be based on either associative (for example, man-woman) or conceptual similarity (for example, river-stream). Information in long-term memory is useless unless it can be retrieved efficiently. Retrieval cues serve this important function and can greatly facilitate recall. A summary of the stages of information processing is presented in Figure 5.15.

Problem solving is an area of research that studies cognitive processes in operation. One such area is concept identification. Levine has viewed concept learning as a hypothesis-testing task. In his experiments, the subjects form a hypothesis about the solution and then either stay with it if it produces correct answers or shift to a new one if it does not. Other research on problem-solving reveals the highly efficient nature of human thought; for example, strategies are used in solving anagrams and not just the random rearrangement of letters.

Figure 5.15
Stages of information processing.

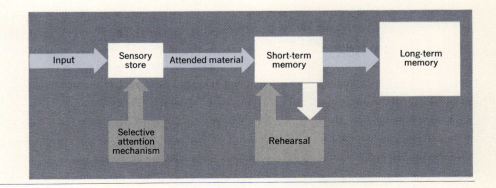

180
GLOSSARY

Associative organization: The extent to which materials to be remembered are associatively related (for example, table-chair).

Categorical organization: The extent to which materials to be remembered can be grouped together in categories (for example, horse-cow-dog [four-footed animals]).

Cognitive process: An inferred process that takes place between observable stimuli and responses.

Functional fixedness: A difficulty in problem-solving that is caused by a person's inability to view a single object or situation in more than one way.

Interference theory: The hypothesis that memory loss occurs because new material displaces the old.

Invalid conversion: The fallacy in syllogistic reasoning in which it is assumed that "if all X is Y," then "all Y is X."

Long-term memory: The enduring retention of information in an organized or consolidated form.

Mnemonic: A device for relating material to be learned to some already existing organizational framework.

Proactive inhibition: The interference of previously learned material on the recall of material learned later.

Rehearsal: The process of repeating information to keep it in short-term memory and facilitate its transfer to long-term memory.

Retrieval cues: The stimuli that provide us with information about the memory location of material.

Retroactive inhibition: The loss of previously held information due to new learning.

Selective attention: The process of paying close attention to relevant information while ignoring irrelevant information.

Sensory store: The very brief, high-capacity memory that contains unprocessed information.

Serial position curve: The relationship between the serial order in which materials are presented for recall and the likelihood of recall; the last items are remembered best, then the first, and finally those in the middle.

Shadowing: A procedure for assessing selective attention; a listener hears two messages simultaneously and is requested to repeat one of them out loud.

Short-term memory: The brief retention of information in acoustic form.

Span of apprehension: A procedure for assessing the amount of information a person can take in at a glance.

Tip-of-the-tongue phenomenon: The feeling that the information one is attempting to recall is "close to the surface," even though it has not yet been recalled.

Trace-decay theory: The hypothesis that forgetting occurs because memories simply decline in strength over time.

SIX

HEREDITY AND GROWTH

Each of us started on our own unique path of development at the moment of conception, when a male reproductive cell, or *spermatozoon*, and its female counterpart, the *ovum*, joined to produce a fertilized egg, or *zygote*. Thereafter, the complex growth patterns characteristic of all humans, our individual genetic inheritance, and a variety of social influences begin to interact to produce a unique adult. This chapter will discuss the role of heredity and physical growth in the developmental process, while subsequent chapters will describe the contributions made by social factors.

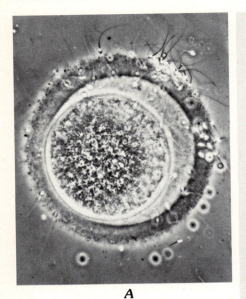

A

Figure 6.1
Conception and the subsequent division of the fertilized egg. In A the sperm cells are fertilizing an ovum. In B the ovum has divided once and in C has divided several times.

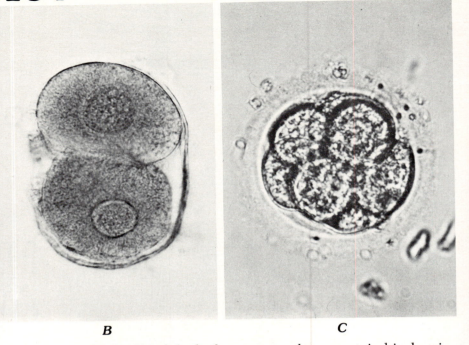

B

C

LIFE BEGINS Like all cells of the body, sperm and ova contain biochemical structures called *chromosomes*, each of which carries at least 1000 genes. We now know that genes are composed of a complex substance, deoxyribonucleic acid (or DNA), and bear all the hereditary information from previous generations.

Every species possesses a characteristic set of chromosomes, which differ in both structure and number from one species to another. Humans carry 46 chromosomes, arranged in pairs, so that there are usually 23 pairs of chromosomes in each cell. Twenty-two of the pairs are quite similar in function and appearance for males and females, but the remaining pair, the sex chromosomes, differ sharply. As Figure 6.2, an actual photograph taken with a high-powered microscope, shows, both of the female sex chromosomes are large and each is shaped roughly like the letter "X." By way of contrast, only one chromosome in the male pair is X-shaped; the other is always shaped like a "Y" and is smaller and lighter.

We have said that human chromosomes occur in pairs for every cell in the body, but there is an exception. The reproductive cells, the ova and sperm, are unlike the others because each contains 23 *single* chromosomes. At the time of conception, when the male and female reproductive cells are joined, the individual chromosomes provided by each parent unite so that the fertilized egg, like other cells, again contains 23 pairs. A fertilized egg may therefore contain either an XX or an XY set in the 23rd pair, depending upon the contribution of the father. (Mothers always contribute an X chromosome, since they do not carry any Y chromosomes.) Male reproductive cells are about equally likely to contain an X or a Y sex chromosome, which explains why nearly the same number of male and female children are born.

GROWTH IN THE WOMB. After the spermatozoon and ovum join, the zygote develops rapidly into a multiplying cell mass that soon becomes a human embryo. During the embryonic stage of development—the first 3 months (or first trimester) after conception —the newly formed organism begins to show some of the gross physical characteristics of a human being (Figure 6.3).

Because of the embryo's rapid growth and development during this stage, it is particularly sensitive to illnesses and deprivation. For example, if the mother contracts *rubella* (German measles) during this period, the baby may be born mentally retarded and/or suffer from such physical abnormalities as eye cataracts or deafness. If, however, she is afflicted with this illness during the second or third trimester of pregnancy, the infant will probably not incur these problems. Dietary deficiencies (which we will discuss shortly) also have a greater effect during the early months of pregnancy than if the same deficiencies are sustained later in prenatal development (Knobloch and Pasamanick, 1958; Nelson, Asling, and Evans, 1952).

Figure 6.2
Human beings have 23 pairs of chromosomes.

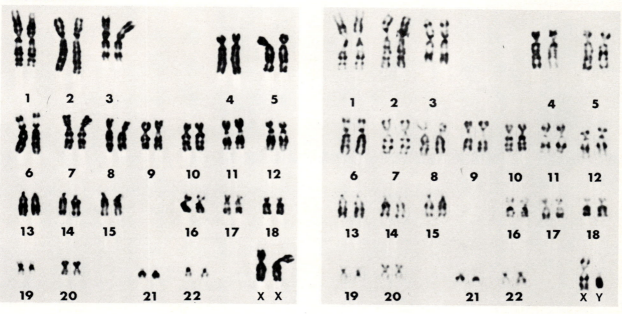

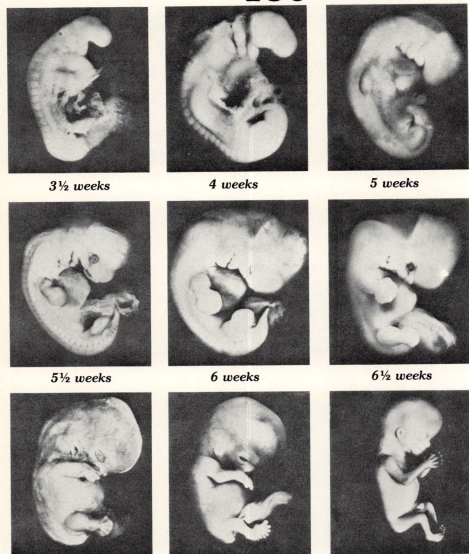

3½ weeks

4 weeks

5 weeks

5½ weeks

6 weeks

6½ weeks

7 weeks

8 weeks

12 weeks

Figure 6.3
Development in the womb during the first 3 months of life.

Maternal Diet and Drug Use. It had long been believed that a mother's diet, her use (or nonuse) of drugs, and her general physical condition could influence the health of her offspring. Numerous studies in recent years have conclusively confirmed this view. With respect to diet, for example, one reviewer stated:

Relatively poorer women, when compared to women of higher economic classes, have less nutritious diets and give birth to babies who are more often of low birth weight or perhaps premature, are less healthy, are more likely to have congenital malformations or serious diseases, and have a somewhat lower probability of living beyond a few months. . . . A series of experiments has proven that dietary supple-

ments given to pregnant women of low socioeconomic groups have a significant effect in improving the health of their babies [Kaplan, 1972, p. 323].

The influence on the fetus of certain drugs taken during pregnancy have been clearly established, and effects are suspected for many others. Most studies have not shown obvious adverse physical effects on the developing fetus in the use of alcohol, marijuana, or LSD. Other drugs, however, such as heroin, may influence the fetus directly so that it may be born an addict. Cigarette smoking increases the chances of a premature birth, spontaneous abortion, and a variety of other health risks. One report suggests that one in five babies who die just before or after birth could have been saved if their mothers had not smoked (Brecher, 1972).

MULTIPLE BIRTHS. Usually a single fertilization results in a single birth. Occasionally, though, during the first 2 weeks after conception, the zygote will divide. When such a division occurs, two individuals of the same sex and with an identical genetic endowment are formed. Children from such a mating are true identical (or *monozygotic*) twins because they have both developed from a single zygote.

Not all twins, however, are monozygotic. Multiple births can also occur when two ova are fertilized by two different spermatozoa at about the same time. In this case two individuals are also formed, but they develop from two different zygotes and are therefore referred to as *dizygotic*, or fraternal, twins. Dizygotic twins need not be of the same sex and can be as different genetically as any two children conceived by the same parents at different times.

Figure 6.4
Identical (monozygotic) twins are virtually indistinguishable, whereas fraternal (dizygotic) twins may be as different as any two children born to the same parents at different times.

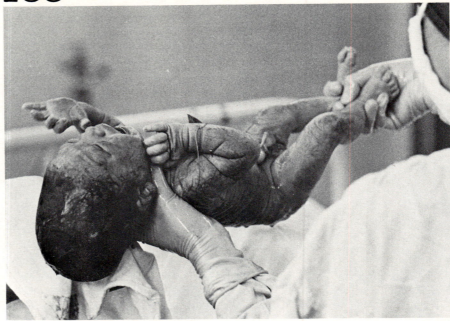

Figure 6.5
A newborn infant.

THE NEONATE. The full-term newborn human infant, or *neonate*, is approximately 20 inches in length and usually weighs between 6 and 9 pounds. Its appearance and posture shortly after birth are illustrated in Figure 6.5, an unretouched photograph taken approximately 6 hours after birth.

PHYSICAL GROWTH Physical and motor development, from birth to adulthood, have long been a source of fascination for parents, biologists, and psychologists. As even casual observation reveals, the first two or three years is a period of very rapid growth, followed by a slowing down during later childhood. Then there is another major growth spurt during adolescence (from ages 12 to 20).

But physical growth is not completely uniform; the major body systems have different growth patterns. Thus, as shown in Figure 6.6, the *lymphatic system* (lymph nodes and intestinal lymphoid masses, which absorb tissue fluids and return them to the heart for redistribution through the bloodstream) is even larger just before adolescence than in adulthood. Likewise, the *neural system* (the head, brain, and spinal cord) is almost fully developed by 6 years of age. But both physical stature and the *genital system* require much longer to mature.

Early growth also proceeds *cephalocaudally*, which means that the cephalic (or head) region of the fetus and newborn is much more developed than the caudal (or tail) region. Thus, as seen in Figure 6.7, the fetus appears rather "top-heavy" and the neonate somewhat less so; the adolescent has about the same proportions as an adult.

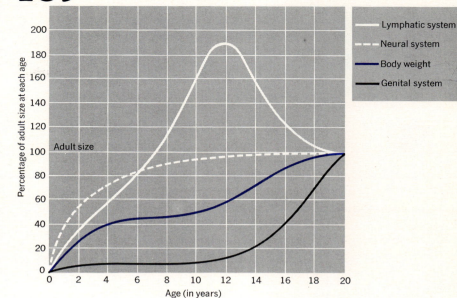

Figure 6.6
Four body systems develop at different rates. Here we see that the neural system is almost completely developed by the age of 6, while the genital system does not show much development until adolescence.

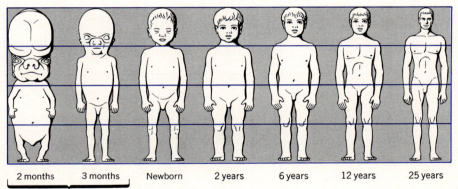

2 months   3 months   Newborn   2 years   6 years   12 years   25 years
Fetal

Figure 6.7
Changes in body proportion with age, showing that humans are "top-heavy" until middle adolescence. The principle illustrated here is called cephalocaudal development. [Source: Jackson (1929)]

DEVELOPMENT OF MANUAL SKILLS. During the first few months of life, children show growth in manual skills—the ability to do things with their hands—which parallels other aspects of their physical development. The very young infant is capable only of flailing its arms wildly. Soon, however, the child quickly starts to develop motor coordination, showing substantial control over arm movements, then hand movements, and finally finger movements. The child begins to exercise control over various movements of his or her body, and then "puts together" the many individual movements, achieving more complex and sophisticated patterns of behavior. This process implies that the individual parts of the child's new motor competence are integrated into larger and more coherent whole units of motor behavior. Thus, for example, after gaining increasing control over arm, leg, and neck movements, the infant will begin to put these

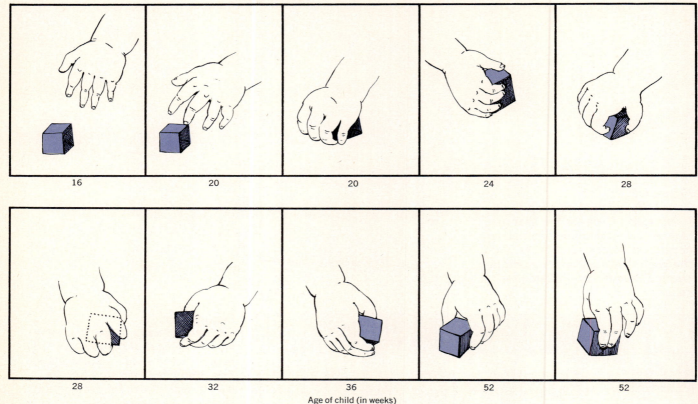

Age of child (in weeks)

Figure 6.8
The development of manual skills during the first year of life. [Source: Halverson (1931)]

[1]One should not become unnecessarily concerned about minor differences between a given child and the norms. Although parents might be justifiably concerned if their child could not walk alone at 30 months of age, they should not worry if their child is 1 or 2 months "behind" the averages shown.

different but relatively simple actions together and perform the more complex act of sitting up by himself.

Halverson (1931) identified a series of stages in manual development from film records of infants. As shown in Figure 6.8, these stages range from simply touching and holding objects (at 20 weeks) to the increasingly sophisticated use of the fingers (at 24–36 weeks) and the successful coordination of hand, thumb, and fingers in producing highly precise and effective pincer movements (at 52 weeks). Later changes are equally dramatic. By 18 months, the child can usually fill a cup with cubes, build a tower from three blocks, and turn the pages of a book (Landreth, 1967).

One way to appreciate a child's growth in physical competence during the first 2 years of life is to think of the various milestone activities, such as the ability to sit up or walk alone. Figure 6.9 shows the approximate age at which a child develops each new skill, which has been derived from an intensive study of 25 children. This kind of normative information is often useful to parents, physicians, and psychologists in determining whether a given child's progress is sufficiently unusual to warrant further diagnosis or perhaps even special treatment.[1]

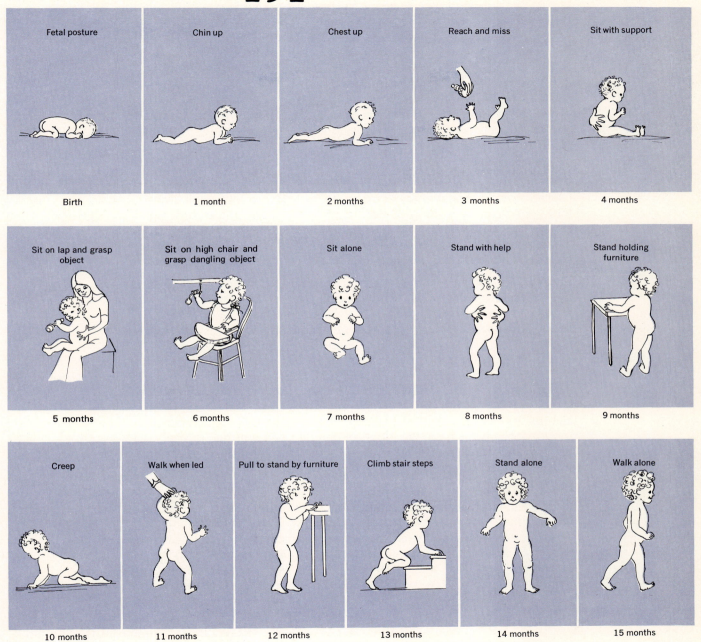

Figure 6.9
Some milestones in motor development during the first 15 months of life. [Source: After Shirley (1933)]

TESTING YOUR UNDERSTANDING
MATURATION VERSUS EXPERIENCE: DOING OR JUST BEING?

Over the years, few issues have been of greater interest to those studying human growth than the relative contributions of *maturation* and *experience*. The concept of maturation refers to the natural unfolding of inborn capacities that occurs more or less independently of special environmental circumstances, training, or experience. One psychological dictionary defines maturational changes as those "that take place more or less inevitably in all normal members of the species so long as they are provided with an environment suitable to the species" (English and English, 1958).

Because maturational changes occur according to a biological timetable, they can be seen in all normal children of about the same age in a universal sequence; thus, all children can crawl before they walk. Changes due to experience, on the other hand, may occur at any time (or not at all), and they require special training for their development.

Parents often wonder whether they can speed up their infant's ability to stand alone, crawl, walk, and so forth by special training. Such a program would be *effective* only if experience were the primary factor in acquiring such skills. Is experience, maturation, or some combination of the two responsible for the ability to develop these skills? How can such questions be answered?

To gain a better understanding of this issue, psychologists have taken identical (that is, monozygotic) twin pairs and given only one twin special training in such skills as walking, climbing, or roller skating. Since monozygotic twins have the identical heredity and natural physical abilities, we can be sure that both twins were at the same level of maturation, and thus we can get a relatively "pure" measure of the *effects* of experience.

In general, experience before the child is apparently ready (that is, sufficiently mature) appears relatively ineffective. Even when training does produce early gains, the untrained infant is often able to catch up very quickly when he or she has matured enough and received the same training (Gesell and Thompson, 1929; McGraw, 1935).

RATE OF PHYSICAL GROWTH. It is apparent that not all children grow at the same rate. While some mature quite early, others may continue to look very small and immature and then suddenly show a spurt of growth and catch up. There are variations in growth pattern not only among individuals but also between the sexes. Boys and girls differ in physical maturity from birth through the early adolescent years. During this entire period girls develop more rapidly than boys so that, for a given age, girls are al-

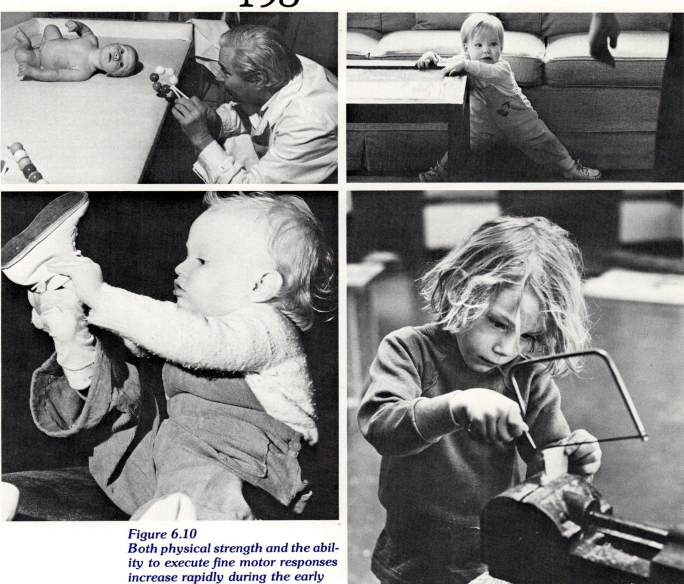

Figure 6.10
Both physical strength and the ability to execute fine motor responses increase rapidly during the early years of life.

most inevitably more mature than their male counterparts. Girls attain their maximum growth rate when they are about 12 1/2 years of age, while boys attain theirs more than 2 years later. Girls also reach their full bodily maturity and *stop* growing several years before boys. Although these sex differences are relatively small during the preschool and elementary-school years, they become more pronounced during junior high school. Figure 6.11 shows the difference in the heights of males and females at various ages. Note that between the ages of 11 and 13, girls are actually taller than boys, although by adulthood males are generally more than 4 inches taller than females.

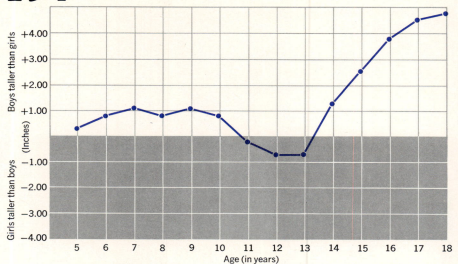

Figure 6.11
Differences in height between boys
and girls at various ages. [Source:
Watson and Lowrey (1962)]

SOCIAL EFFECTS OF EARLY AND LATE MATURATION.

A child's rate of growth affects more than his or her physical size; maturing earlier or later than one's peers may have important social and psychological consequences for the individual. The girl who matures early, for example, may feel somewhat out of place with her classmates if she is larger than anyone else. A study done some 30-odd years ago found that *late*-maturing girls seemed to have an advantage—they were more likely to be seen as lively and exuberant by their friends (Everett, 1943). On the other hand, with today's values many attractive, early-maturing girls may actually enjoy some advantages over their peers. For example, a girl who starts dating boys at a relatively young age may be envied by her female classmates who still look like little children.

A boy's situation differs from a girl's, inasmuch as the *early*-maturing male almost invariably enjoys a number of social advantages over his peers (Eichorn, 1963). A larger and stronger boy with superior physical strength and adult features has a better than average chance of being elected to a class office or of having his name in the school newspaper. Although these advantages tend to diminish with age, differences favoring early-maturing boys are still present in adulthood (for example, better occupational adjustment; Jones, 1957).

Why should boys who matured early continue to be more successful socially and occupationally than their late-maturing peers? Dorothy Eichorn has reasoned that early maturity for a boy leads to positive social consequences which, in turn, gives him personal self-confidence. This self-confidence may then become a permanent trait of the boy as he grows up. According to Eichorn:

Many of the behavioral differences between early- and late-maturers
may reasonably be interpreted as functions of differential experience.

The early- and late-maturing differ not only in superficial characteristics but also in actual physical abilities. . . . Adults and peers may react first to the physical appearance of the early-maturer and give him tasks and privileges ordinarily reserved for older individuals. Often he is able to meet the challenge, and in so doing confirms their impression, increases his own skill, and derives personal satisfaction. If he was also larger than his age-mates before puberty, this circular process may have been recurring for some time [1963, pp. 50–51].

HEREDITY AND BEHAVIOR There is a sound scientific basis for the popular observation that all children are unique from the day they are born. The view that certain individual differences are inherited—"passed through the blood" from one generation to the next—is thousands of years old. Only recently, though, have the mechanisms and principles of genetic transmission been carefully investigated. We will briefly summarize some of the earliest scientific discoveries in this field.

MENDEL'S EARLY WORK. In the mid-nineteenth century, Gregor Mendel, a little-known Austrian monk, began a series of studies with garden peas that eventually led to an understanding of the process by which certain characteristics of living things are passed on from one generation to the next. The essential results of these early experiments and the assumptions that Mendel advanced laid the foundation for our present understanding of heredity in man.

Having observed that the peas in his garden were either smooth or wrinkled when ripe, Mendel began by separating those plants that produced smooth peas from those that produced wrinkled ones. Then he carefully cross-fertilized the pairs, taking the pollen from the smooth plants and placing it in the wrinkled plants to determine the effects of this selective breeding upon the next generation of offspring. When the resulting pods were ripe, he opened them and found that there was no evidence of the wrinkled characteristic in this generation. All of the plants produced uniformly smooth peas. *The wrinkled characteristic seen in one parent had disappeared entirely.* Months later, Mendel allowed the new generation of smooth pea plants to fertilize themselves. In this new generation of offspring there were both smooth *and* wrinkled peas, but in a ratio of approximately three smooth peas to each wrinkled one.

These findings were not easy to understand. A characteristic that appeared in half of the parent plants (wrinkledness) disappeared entirely for a generation and then returned again. Moreover, the wrinkled characteristic reappeared in only *one-quarter* of the second-generation plants, although it had been present in fully *half* of the "grandparent" plants. How could one account for these mysterious results? Mendel eventually advanced two conceptual distinctions—between *genotype-phenotype* and *dominance-recessiveness*.

Figure 6.12
Gregor Mendel

Genotypes and Phenotypes. According to the theory that emerged from Mendel's work, every individual plant or animal has both a *genotype* and a *phenotype*.

An organism's genotype is its genetic endowment, consisting of biological "instructions" for growth. The genotype is inherited from the individual's forebears and is, in turn, passed on to its descendants. This biological information is stored in the chromosomes and genes.

On the other hand, an individual's phenotype is its particular outward manifestation of the genotype that it possesses; a pea's wrinkledness and a child's brown eyes are both phenotypic characteristics, while the chemical structures or genes that direct their development are genotypic characteristics. An important concept of Mendelian genetics is that an *individual's phenotype does not necessarily mirror its genotype.* Thus, for example, a brown-eyed child does not necessarily have only "brown-eyed genes," and an overtly (or phenotypically) smooth pea plant may still possess the wrinkled characteristic and transmit it to future generations of plants.

The distinction between phenotypes and genotypes may explain why an organism's hereditary makeup and its actual characteristics are not identical, but it does not enable one to understand the relationship between the two. For this, let us turn to the second distinction—that between dominant and recessive characteristics.

Dominance and Recessiveness. Mendel suggested that a genetically determined characteristic may be either "dominant" or "recessive," and that this factor significantly affects an individual's outward characteristics (that is, his phenotype). Certain characteristics are called "dominant" because if they appear in an individual's hereditary endowment (his genotype) they will also manifest themselves outwardly as well. In other words, certain inherited characteristics tend to dominate in their appearance. Other characteristics, called "recessive," will only manifest themselves outwardly if there are no dominant "competitors." Thus, if both of the parents pass on the dominant characteristic or if one parent transmits the dominant characteristic and the other parent transmits the recessive one, then only the dominant characteristic will appear in the offspring. A recessive characteristic, on the other hand, will be manifest only if it is transmitted by both parents.

Taken together, these two concepts explain the three generations of peas, once it is understood that smoothness is a dominant characteristic for this species. Each of the second-generation plants, having received both the dominant and the recessive characteristic, display only the dominant one (smoothness). In turn, each of these plants transmits either the dominant or the smooth characteristic (but not both) to the next generation. In this new generation, when a recessive-recessive (wrinkled-wrinkled) genotype is inherited, the wrinkled characteristic will appear phenotypically. This will happen for every

TESTING YOUR UNDERSTANDING
INHERITANCE OF EYE COLOR

The two principles identified by Mendel and described above may be applied directly to the inheritance of a number of characteristics in humans. One example is eye color: for humans dark eyes are dominant and light eyes are recessive. Given this information, could you predict the probable eye colors of four children born to parents when (1) both parents have light eyes and when (2) both parents have dark eyes?

In the first case, when both parents have light eyes, all four of their children will also have light eyes. This is because neither parent possesses the dominant characteristic so it cannot be transmitted. In the second case, when both parents have dark eyes, the outcome will depend upon whether the parents are carrying the recessive light-eyed characteristic; unless both of them are, all of the children will have dark eyes; if both parents are carrying a light-eyed gene, the likelihood is that three out of four children will be dark eyed and the other one will be light eyed. This principle is illustrated in Figure 6.13.

Figure 6.13
The inheritance of eye color.

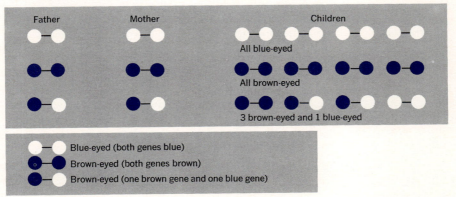

The most obvious way in which children tend to resemble their biological parents is in their physical characteristics, such as curly versus straight hair, height and weight, and certain physical and perceptual dysfunctions (for example, color blindness).

fourth plant; hence there is a ratio of three smooth plants to one wrinkled one.

The most obvious way in which children tend to resemble their biological parents is in their physical characteristics, such as curly versus straight hair, height and weight, and certain physical and perceptual dysfunctions (for example, color blindness).

Of greater social importance, of course, is the degree to which abilities and social behaviors may depend, entirely or in part, upon an individual's genetic endowment. We shall discuss two related areas of research on this topic—intelligence and personality.

Figure 6.14
Family resemblance, controlled in part by genetic factors, can often be striking. Here we see John D. Rockefeller, Jr., and his sons (left to right) David, Nelson, Winthrop, and Laurance.

THE INHERITANCE OF INTELLIGENCE. The idea that intelligence is, at least in part, genetically determined is perhaps not to the liking of those who cherish the view that "all men are created equal." There is, nevertheless, much research evidence showing that heredity and intelligence are related. This is not to say, however, that environmental factors cannot alter intelligence. Actually, as we shall see, there is both evidence and argument to suggest that environmental variables can affect intelligence independently of the person's genetic makeup.

Sir Francis Galton (1822–1911) was the first to study the possible relationship between intelligence and heredity. Galton first demonstrated that there is a great deal of individual variation in intelligence—that all people are *not* equally bright or capable. Then he also tried to show that these differences in mental ability were largely inherited, mostly by arguing that eminent men tended to be related to one another. As evidence, he presented the family trees (or genealogies) of prominent men in the fields of law, science, art, and the military, indicating that greatness ran in certain families.

Other families, though, appeared to be "consistently degenerate." Dugdale (1910) studied the descendants of a marriage between a prostitute and a shiftless farmer. Of 2094 descendants, 378 were prostitutes, 86 brothel keepers, 299 paupers, and 118 criminals. Half were feeble-minded. Of course, environmental factors (education, home life, and so forth) could explain the findings of Galton and Dugdale. But a study that was done with rats showed clearly that two animal "families" with different abilities could be produced by means of selective breeding alone (Thompson, 1954). Using a random sample of rats, those that were especially quick at running mazes and those that were unusually slow at this task were selected out and bred in

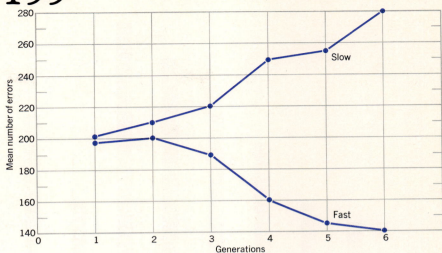

Figure 6.15
Errors in maze learning for succes-
sive generations of selectively bred
fast and slow strains of rats.
[Source: After Thompson (1954)]

separate groups for six generations. As seen in Figure 6.15, the results of breeding the fast with one another and the slow with one another were striking.

IS HUMAN INTELLIGENCE INHERITED? One of the issues that has excited great public interest since the late 1960s is whether human intelligence can be inherited. Early studies, such as those presented by Galton and Dugdale, were flawed by a variety of potential biases, but their basic logic was sound: If intelligence is heritable, then people who are closely related should be more alike in intelligence than people who are not closely related. This proposition is well suited to the use of correlational techniques of research (described in Chapter 1) and has led modern investigators to ask more specific questions than were posed by Galton, Dugdale, and other early investigators.

It is important to note that arbitrarily picked pairs of people who are not related biologically and who do not interact together socially will not be similar in IQ at all—that is, the correlation between the IQ scores of many such pairs will average about 0. This fact may be seen in Figure 6.16, which also provides other information that will be discussed later on.

The hypothesis that intelligence is heritable leads us to predict, first of all, that children's IQs will correlate with those of their parents. Examination of a large number of studies reveals that this is true (Jensen, 1969) and that, as seen in Figure 6.13, this correlation is substantial. But there is a certain problem here as well.

It is possible that both parents of a particular child will have very high IQs and that their child's IQ will also be quite high; on the other hand, another set of parents may both have low IQs, and so may

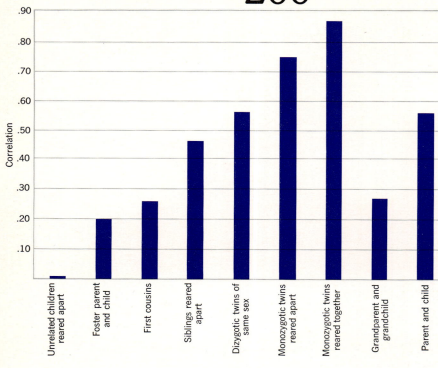

Figure 6.16
Correlations of IQ scores as a function of degree of family relationship. [Source: Data from Jensen (1969)]

their children. If this fact is found repeatedly with many parents and their children, wouldn't this mean that IQ was inherited? The answer is no; it is equally plausible that the transmission was social rather than biological. The child who has bright parents may have been exposed to a large vocabulary and a highly stimulating environment; he may also have been tutored by his parents in basic intellectual skills. These experiences could readily help him achieve a high IQ, while the children of dull parents could have been reared in an intellectually impoverished environment, thus leading to a low IQ. Since this "environmental" explanation of parent-child similarities is quite plausible, investigators must attempt to separate the two possibilities. They can try to hold either heredity or environment constant, so that the effects of the other can be seen more clearly.

For the purpose of some comparisons, the influence of environment seems to be controlled naturally. Suppose, for example, that we could secure a large group of children who had been adopted right after birth and measure their IQs and those of their adopted parents. If, as might reasonably be expected, these parents treat their adopted children exactly as they would their own offspring, then adopted parents and their children are about as similar in *environment* as biological parents and their children. The difference, of course, is that biological parents and their children are *also* similar genetically, a fact that gives rise to the next prediction of the heredity hypothesis: *If intelligence is heritable, the IQs of biological parents and their children should be more similar than the IQs of foster parents and theirs.* Looking at Figure 6.16 again, it can be seen that this prediction has been confirmed.

Several other predictions can be made from the heredity hypothesis, each following the same type of logic that underlies foster family comparisons. It is known, for example, that monozygotic twins are genetically identical, whereas dizygotic twins may be as dissimilar as two siblings born to the same parents at different times. This fact leads to the next heredity prediction: *If intelligence is heritable, the IQs of monozygotic twins should be more similar than those of dizygotic twins of the same sex.*[1] As you can see from Figure 6.16, this prediction is also borne out by the facts.

Siblings are children born to the same biological parents. They are similar but not identical genetically; if they are reared together, they also have similar environments. In this circumstance, it is hard to extract much meaning from the fact that the IQs of siblings tend to be rather highly correlated. Sometimes, though, siblings are not reared together; they may be separated because of family illness or the divorce of their parents. We would then be left with children who have a similar heredity but different environments; their IQs would be correlated only if heredity were an influential factor in transmitting intelligence. Therefore: *If intelligence is heritable, the IQs of siblings reared apart should be positively correlated.* They are.

When all the facts we have mentioned are taken together, they seem to suggest quite strongly that IQ is determined in part by heredity. Nonetheless, several very important qualifications need to be made. One is that many of the assumptions made by geneticists when testing their predictions about IQ are questionable. One psychologist, Leon Kamin (1974), who sees the entire issue as a political one, has reviewed the relevant literature from a sociopolitical viewpoint.

Kamin fears that if people accept the idea that intelligence is inherited, the result will be discrimination based on a presumed racial or ethnic differences in intelligence.[2] He illustrates the possibility by reviewing the use of intelligence tests during the early 1900s, when at least some psychologists hoped to stem the tide of Eastern and Southern Europeans immigrating to this country by showing that the great majority were "feeble-minded"; one investigator claimed that 83 percent of the Jews, 80 percent of the Hungarians, 79 percent of the Italians, and 87 percent of the Russians who had come to America could be classified as feeble-minded. It is easy to see how this early use of IQ tests could lead one to discredit all genetic research on intelligence.

One of the major assumptions in studies of twins and other siblings

[1] Remember that dizygotic twins can be of either the same or opposite sex, but monozygotic twins are always of the same sex.

[2] In fact, though, the question of the heritability of intelligence is not *logically* related to the possibility of racial or ethnic differences at all. It would be perfectly plausible to find that intelligence is partly heritable but that the IQ differences that are typically found between whites and blacks are due to environmental and not hereditary influences.

reared apart is that their environments are no more similar than would be the case for any two randomly selected, unrelated children; only by making this assumption can similarities in the siblings' IQ scores be attributed to heredity. Kamin (1974) points out that this assumption has often not been met, and offers the following examples of the problem of "separated" twins:

Benjamin and Ronald, separated at 9 months: "Both brought up in the same fruit-growing village, Ben by the parents, Ron by the grandmother. . . . They were at school together. . . ."

Bertram and Christopher, separated at birth: "The paternal aunts decided to take one twin each, and they have brought them up amicably, living next door to one another in the same Midlands colliery village. . . . They are constantly in and out of each other's houses [p. 11]."

Kamin points to similar problems in dealing with correlations between adopted children and those reared by their biological parents. Here the assumption would be that the environments of the two groups would be similar, yet in many studies foster parents have been older than biological parents and have had significantly higher incomes as well.

Do points such as these completely nullify the research data we have been discussing? Probably not. The many positive correlations certainly show that intelligence is transmitted somehow; otherwise, parents and children or brothers and sisters would have no more similarities in this respect than completely unrelated people. It is not too likely that these similarities can be explained entirely by small variations in the family income or community in which those who participated in the various studies happened to live. The issues Kamin raises should, however, make us aware of the possibility of overstating psychological findings or using them improperly.

THE HERITABILITY OF SOCIAL BEHAVIOR. Not all genetic work focuses on the heritability of intelligence, of course. The issue of whether patterns of social behavior can be inherited has also been widely discussed, debated, and researched. Animal breeders have long known that various temperamental factors distinguish one breed from another and that even within a single breed selective mating over a number of generations seems to produce obvious differences in the temperaments of domestic animals. As in the case of animal studies on intelligence, though, we must be cautious about generalizing from nonhuman behavior, at least until appropriate correlational studies with humans have been conducted and critically examined.

One of the best broad-spectrum studies on the heritability of social behavior among human beings was conducted by Gottesman (1963). He began by obtaining the names of all of the same-sexed twins enrolled in public high schools in the Minneapolis-Saint Paul area, thereby drawing his twin sample from a population of over 31,000 children. Voluntary cooperation of more than half of the twin pairs in this sample was secured. Gottesman legitimately noted that his sample "compares favorably in size with the majority of twin studies reported in the psychological literature. In representativeness, it is superior to the majority" (p. 4). Using sophisticated criteria, Gottesman identified 68 twin pairs—34 monozygotic pairs and 34 dizygotic pairs—and tried to learn whether the monozygotic twins were more similar than the dizygotic twins on each of a number of personality scales. (Remember that this is one of the techniques used to determine whether certain behavior is influenced by hereditary factors, page 201.)

On three of the personality dimensions he examined, Gottesman found that monozygotic twins *were* more similar than dizygotic ones, a finding he interpreted to mean that these characteristics were partly influenced by heredity. More specifically, the degree to which people are serious, dependent on groups (rather than self-sufficient), and prone to experience guilt feelings all seemed to be more closely related among monozygotic than dizygotic twins.

Other findings from Gottesman's study are somewhat more complicated. It seems, for example, that certain characteristics may be related to heredity in one sex but determined almost entirely by environment in the other. With respect to submissiveness versus dominance, males were influenced by heredity, while females were influenced almost entirely by environmental factors. Quite possibly the pattern is a product of our culture. Since boys are given a wide latitude in dominance, their heredity has ample opportunity to develop. Girls, on the other hand, are often pressured to be more submissive; this environmental influence, therefore, may mask or overcome any dominance factors in heredity.

In general, Gottesman's findings seem to suggest *some* hereditary component on *certain* measures of personality. However, since his evidence revealed some inexplicable peculiarities, it must be interpreted with caution. For example, he found that dizygotic twins were *more* alike than identical twins on 4 of the 24 personality dimensions. Later investigations on heritability have focused on certain circumscribed areas of behavior; one of these is extroversion-introversion.

Introversion and *extroversion* are two opposing styles or approaches to one's social environment. An extreme introvert is shy and anxious in novel social situations and is usually ready to withdraw from other people; an extreme extrovert on the other hand is friendly, at ease among people, and readily seeks out social gatherings. Researchers often think of these two traits as two ends of a continuum: most social behavior will fall between these extremes.

Individual differences in introversion-extroversion can be observed during the first few years of life (Scarr, 1969) and children do not seem to change radically in this respect over time. Friendly infants tend to become friendly adolescents, while shy infants tend to become shy adolescents (Schaefer and Bayler, 1963). Various studies indicate that genes play some part in contributing to introversion-extroversion (Eysenck, 1956; Gottesman, 1966; Partenan, Bruun, and Markkanen, 1966; Scarr, 1969; Vandenberg, 1966), using the same types of comparisons we discussed with respect to the heritability of IQ.

HEREDITY AND CRIMINAL BEHAVIOR. As the crime rate In the United States has risen steadily, there has been growing interest among both professionals and laymen as to its causes. It may not be surprising that the possibility of a genetic determinant has often been raised in the popular press. Is this a valid possibility?

Several studies have shown that criminality tends to run in families, but it should be clear by now that such evidence does not necessarily indicate a genetic cause. In the earliest of these investigations, which appeared in Lange's (1929) book *Crime as Destiny*, concordance was determined for 30 same-sexed pairs in which one of the twins in each pair was a convicted criminal. Among the monozygotic twins (those with identical heredity) there was a 77 percent concordance rate (that is, the other twin was also a criminal in 77 percent of the cases). In contrast, the corresponding rate for dizygotic twins was only 12 percent. These findings would appear to provide strong evidence that criminality may be inherited. Yet there are other possible explanations for the results.

An important assumption of the twin study method is that monozygotic and dizygotic twins have the same environment and life experiences so that they differ only in their genetic makeup. However, evidence now exists that monozygotic twins who grow up together are also treated more alike (that is, their environments are also more alike) than are dizygotic twins (Smith, 1965). Clearly such factors can inflate what appear to be genetic contributions to criminality.

In view of this and other possibilities, it is not surprising that several later and methodologically superior studies have shown little difference in criminality between monozygotic and dizygotic twin pairs but a high rate of concordance when either type of twin came from a "criminal" family (Rosenthal, 1970). It seems possible, therefore, that both child abuse and antisocial examples enable patterns of criminal behavior to be transmitted. Indeed, this reasoning has led one contemporary expert to conclude "that environmental [as opposed to hereditary] factors are of overriding importance with respect to the legal criterion of whether or not one obtains a criminal record" [p. 233] and that "in all likelihood, many, if not most, crimes are committed by individuals in whom the role of heredity is minor, nonspecific, or perhaps irrelevant" [Rosenthal, 1970, p. 238].

In Conclusion. The question of which aspects of human behavior are influenced by heredity, and to what degree, is still being hotly debated. Certainly most researchers have recognized the need for adequate control over environmental factors, but this goal cannot be achieved in any single investigation. The convergence of evidence to date suggests that some aspects of human behavior are at least influenced in part by genetic factors. What is more, animal studies seem to support these findings experimentally. Actual breeding experiments with mice, rats, and dogs suggest quite clearly that for these animals certain aspects of temperament are heritable (Broadhurst, 1960; Lagerspetz, 1964; McClearn, 1962).

Research on the heritability of personality and patterns of social behavior in humans is still limited to a few characteristics such as criminality and extroversion-introversion. The degree to which genes play a significant role in other aspects of personality, and the question of how easily a person can overcome his hereditary background through training or experience are two important problems being discussed by psychologists today.

PSYCHOLOGY AND THE PROBLEMS OF SOCIETY
MISCONCEPTIONS ABOUT AGING

Today there is a larger proportion of Americans over the age of 65 than ever before, largely because of lower birth and death rates. For this reason, perhaps, investigators have become more interested in understanding the physical and psychological processes of aging. Research has shown that most people harbor serious misconceptions about the levels of functioning and the abilities of older people.

One such myth is that older people are impotent and sexless. This is simply not true. It appears that older people are both physiologically capable of, and vitally interested in, sexual activity. Various studies (such as one by Pfeiffer, Verwoerdt, and Wang, 1967) found no evidence of declining interest in sex in persons from 67 to 77 years of age. It seems clear that although people's physiological responsiveness does slow down somewhat during middle age, their interest and participation in sex remain high. These research findings imply that society ought to recognize and accept the fact that sexual functioning is quite normal in older people.

Another misconception pertains to changes in intellectual functioning. Although the word "senility" is defined in the dictionary as "a loss of mental faculties associated with old age," MacDonald (1973) has suggested that the concept must be examined from a sociopsychological perspective. She assumes that the label "senility" depends upon its social context, and not just on the mental functioning of the older person. One consequence of labeling someone "senile" is that he or she will tend to act accordingly and thus fulfill the expectation. The world in which elderly people live frequently expects them to act in accordance with its stereotyped view of senility.

In the context of an old-age home—which is a facility for the old and the sick—the sick and the old often become synonymous. The aged are sometimes removed from the mainstream of society because it is believed that they can no longer perform the active roles required of younger people. The staff of old-age homes perform medical-custodial services. They expect passivity and infirmity among the residents rather than improvement and recovery. MacDonald states that although there is some brain deterioration with aging, this does not require institutionalization for more than 2 percent of those over age 65. What might be the cause of senility (that is, somewhat confused behavior) among those in old-age homes? MacDonald suggests three factors: First, the staff and visiting relatives expect the elderly to act this way. Second, a number of illnesses do produce senile-like symptoms (for example, temporary confusion), but these are reversible. The staff, however, tend *not* to treat these symptoms, on the assumption that senility is an ongoing, degenerative process. Finally, because old-age homes tend to be custodial in nature, the residents are deprived of the mental stimulation everyone needs to remain mentally alive and alert.

The work of MacDonald and others should help us to dispel myths we may have harbored about the elderly. Society needs to have respect for and a sense of responsibility toward older persons; this issue ought to concern all of us, for some day we, too, will be among those who are over 65.

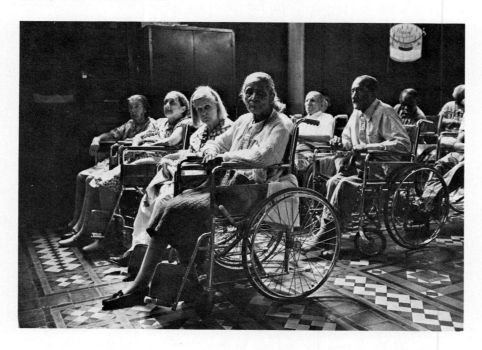

SUMMARY

Human growth begins when the male reproductive cell or spermatozoon and the female ovum join to produce the zygote or fertilized egg. Like all cells of the body, sperm and ova contain chromosomes, each of which carries genes that bear the "hereditary information" that is transmitted to offspring. Human beings have 46 chromosomes, comprising 23 pairs in each cell. Only one of the 23 pairs is different for men and women; this pair determines the sex of the child. Multiple births may occur in two different ways. The zygote may divide, producing two identical (or monozygotic) twins, or two sperm may fertilize two ova at the same time; in the latter case, the offspring are fraternal (or dizygotic) twins and may differ as much from each other as other siblings conceived at different times.

The zygote develops rapidly into a human embryo. The first three months after conception—the embryonic stage—is a period in which the fetus is highly sensitive to maternal illness and deprivation. The newborn human infant (or neonate) grows rapidly during its first two or three years, followed by a period of slower growth; then another major spurt occurs during adolescence. Various bodily systems show different growth patterns. The neural system begins to develop early and has almost reached maturity when the child reaches the age of 6; the lymphatic system develops rapidly just before adolescence, while the genital system scarcely begins to develop until adolescence.

A distinction must be made between maturation and experience. Nearly all maturational changes take place because of biology, whereas changes due to experience are largely the product of training. There are large individual differences in the rate of maturation and growth, and there are obvious sex differences as well; girls reach full bodily maturity several years before boys. Differences in the rate of growth may also have social and personal consequences; boys who mature early tend to have a social advantage.

Physical characteristics and social dispositions can be inherited to some extent. Every individual has a genotype—the person's genetic endowment of biological instructions for growth—and a phenotype—his or her outward appearance. A person's phenotype is not necessarily the same as his genotype because certain characteristics are genetically "dominant" and always displayed, while others are "recessive" and appear overtly only in the absence of dominant competitors.

Intelligence seems to show a hereditary component; monozygotic twins reared apart have IQs that are more similar than those of siblings reared apart; equally significant, the closer two relatives are biologically, the closer their IQs. But environment is also significant in IQ, as seen by the fact that both related and unrelated persons are more similar if they are reared together than apart.

Heredity may also determine in part certain social behaviors, as for example introversion-extroversion. However, other social behavior has little or nothing to do with one's heredity. Precisely which complex human characteristics can be transmitted "through the blood" is still being hotly debated.

GLOSSARY

Cephalocaudal: The principle that physical growth in the head (or cephalic) region proceeds well ahead of growth in the tail (or caudal) region.

Chromosomes: Small bodies that carry genes and are found in the nucleus of a cell. They are regarded as the transmitters of hereditary factors from parent to child. Each cell has 46 chromosomes arranged in 23 pairs.

Dizygotic: Fraternal twins, conceived and delivered at approximately the same time but developed from separate eggs; therefore, they are no more alike than other siblings. They may be of the same or opposite sex.

Dominant gene: A gene that, if transmitted from parent to child, is always manifested in the child's overt appearance.

Embryo: The fetus during the first 3 months after conception; at this stage, it is highly sensitive to any illness or nutritional deprivation of the mother.

Extroversion: A personality trait characterized by the enjoyment of other people and activities outside oneself. It is the opposite of introversion.

Genes: The hereditary factors that are located in the chromosomes and are transmitted by each parent to its offspring.

Genital system: The reproductive organs and associated glands.

Genotype: The characteristics that an individual has inherited and can pass on to his descendants; an individual's genotype is not necessarily reflected in his phenotype, or external appearance.

Intelligence: The term describing a person's general abilities and quickness; those qualities that are measured by standardized tests of intelligence.

Introversion: A personality trait characterized by shyness and reserve. It is the opposite of extroversion.

Lymphatic system: The system that controls various internal body functions; it consists of the lymph nodes and intestinal lymphoid masses.

Maturation: The process of growth and behavioral change that is almost entirely due to biological factors and is thus relatively independent of experience.

Monozygotic: Identical twins, developed from a single egg, who are of the same sex and have the same hereditary endowment.

Neonate: A newborn human infant.

Neural system: The nervous system, consisting of the brain, nerves, and spinal cord.

Ovum: The female reproductive cell.

Phenotype: Those characteristics that an individual has inherited that can be seen in his or her makeup or external appearance (for example, eye color).

Recessive gene: A gene that determines the characteristics of an individual's trait only when it is paired with another recessive gene; if the other member of the gene pair is dominant, the existence of the recessive gene will not be obvious.

Spermatozoon: The male reproductive cell.

Zygote: The cell formed by the union of sperm and ovum; the fertilized egg.

SEVEN

COGNITIVE DEVELOP- MENT

Infants often stare so intently into the faces of their parents that mothers and fathers are impelled to ask: "What do you suppose the baby's thinking?" Despite appearances, the newborn infant is probably not thinking at all or, at least, not in the way that adults or even toddlers do. *Cognition*, the psychologist's technical term for thought and related mental activity, is a phenomenon that develops during the course of infancy and childhood, under the influence of a relatively universal process of maturation *and* through the specific experiences provided by the child's parents, subculture, and society. This chapter will deal with the basic pattern of cognitive development and some of the practical questions about how the higher mental processes can be fostered or hindered by life experiences.

THOUGHT AND LANGUAGE

Cognitive development is intimately related to language, the usual means by which children (and adults) express their thoughts. In fact, language and thought are so closely associated that an old debate still continues as to whether language is shaped by emerging thought processes or whether language is required for all but the most rudimentary thought. The issue is probably not resolvable. Language does, however, have some special characteristics that merit attention in their own right; these will be discussed in the final section of the chapter.

Figure 7.1
Jean Piaget

THE COURSE OF INTELLECTUAL GROWTH: PIAGET'S WORK

It was not until many years after psychology had emerged as a science that any attention was paid to children's cognitive development. The reasons were many. One was simply that children below a certain age made poor research subjects; they could not be induced to introspect, they could not focus their attention very long on standard laboratory tasks, and they could not be interviewed because of their lack of language facility. Another equally important reason for ignoring children's cognitive development was that there seemed to be so little to learn. It was assumed that youngsters' ability to think just go better (that is, more sophisticated) with age, in much the same way as muscles increased in size and motor and perceptual coordination became more differentiated. Such a conceptualization, we now know, is false—thanks to the genius of one man, Jean Piaget.

A Swiss developmental psychologist, Piaget earned his doctorate in biology but soon turned his attention to children's reasoning processes and published his first findings in 1921. His subsequent work, spanning a career of more than 50 years, has completely changed our view of children's thought. Employing the method of natural observation borrowed from biology, Piaget began by studying his own children; he capitalized on and "milked" chance situations to examine the youngsters' emerging and changing approaches to various problems in play. Even a child's simple movement would sometimes suggest to Piaget something of the child's reasoning at the time; Piaget always followed up his speculation by questioning the child carefully or rearranging the environment to obtain a further response. This method led to many pioneering discoveries; other investigators have subsequently added experimental rigor to Piaget's inquiries, and usually their findings have provided further support for (rather than disconfirmation of) Piaget's work. From the totality of this research, a general picture of cognitive development can be traced for the first 15 years of life, comprising four major periods or stages: sensorimotor, preoperational, concrete operational, and formal operational.

THE SENSORIMOTOR PERIOD. The first 24 months of life,[1] which Piaget calls the *sensorimotor period*, are critical for the child since the foundation for understanding the world is built during this period. The psychologist, therefore, wants to know how these first cognitive substructures develop.

Piaget was undoubtedly influenced by the biological concept of adaptation. From the outset, a child adapts to the environment and does not simply respond to it mechanically or automatically. The over all process has two aspects, *accommodation* and *assimilation*, which can be understood by considering the process of digestion. New information is like food that is consumed; the body must accommodate itself to the foreign substance. When we eat, the digestive tract goes to work on each morsel (the stomach muscles contract, enzymes and acids are secreted to break down the material into usable form, and so forth). In like manner, the child's mental processes must accommodate themselves and change in response to new information. The second phase for both types of digestion is assimilation. Once the body has processed food, it is assimilated into the system and becomes an indistinguishable part of the individual; the child assimilates information the same way, accommodating new findings into his or her over-all cognitive structure. At the behavioral level, this process can be observed by hanging a baby rattle above the crib of a 4-month-old. After a while the child will accidentally pull the cord of the rattle. Then, observes Piaget:

He immediately repeats the gesture a number of times. Each time the interesting result motivates the repetition. . . . Later you need only hang a new toy from the top of the cradle for the child to look for the cord, which constitutes the beginning of a differentiation between means and end. In the days that follow, when you swing an object from a pole two yards from the crib, and even when you produce unexpected and mechanical noises from behind a screen, after these sights or sounds have ceased the child will again look for and pull the magic cord [Piaget and Inhelder, 1969, p. 10].

The child in the foregoing example might be said to have originally accommodated himself to a bit of information from the environment ("pulling the cord makes a nice noise") and, after much repetition, assimilated the relationship so completely that he now looks for cords to pull whenever an interesting event occurs that he wants repeated. A newborn baby cannot perform such feats; they are rare before the age of 4 months. Piaget recognized this fact and suggested that the entire sensorimotor period could be divided into six substages. Although a discussion of each of them is beyond our intended scope here, we will mention two other accomplishments of the first 18 months.

[1] This time span, as well as others we will mention, is only approximate and does not necessarily hold true for any given child. According to Piaget, though, the stages *must* occur in the same fixed order.

(a)

(b)

(c)

Figure 7.2
As children proceed from the sensorimotor (a) through the preoperational (b), concrete operational (c), and formal operational (d) periods, their ability to make effective use of sensory information and deal appropriately with the environment gradually increases in sophistication.

(d)

Between the ages of 8 and 12 months there is further development of instrumental behavior, and it is clear that there is increasing purpose in everything the child does. However, there are still enormous gaps in the child's understanding of the world. In an ingenious demonstration of this fact, Piaget hid a toy under a red pillow while one of his children watched. Almost immediately the youngster reached under the pillow and retrieved it. But then Piaget added a twist. As the child watched, Piaget again placed the toy under the red pillow but then removed it immediately, showed it to the child once more, and placed it under a *blue* pillow. But when Piaget told the child to find the toy, where did he look? *Under the red pillow.* What is the significance of this startling "mistake?"

It may mean that the child was unaware that objects exist in space, independent of his or her own perceptions or actions. Adults, of course, look for objects where they were last seen or at the end of pathways that the objects seem to have followed. But children approach this problem differently; they try to reproduce interesting events by repeating the *actions* that led to them before. The child who has once succeeded in finding the desired toy by looking under the red pillow will look for it there again. Although the child saw the toy removed from beneath the red pillow and placed under the blue pillow, apparently this seems less important than actually doing what worked before.

During the first year of life, then, children increase their ability to combine sensory input and motor reactions (hence the name, *sensorimotor* period), but they still have no mental representation of the world. For Piaget, such mental representation begins with the formation of *schemata*, miniature frameworks that the child can use to fit together and manipulate objects in thought before beginning to act. In a word, the child must begin to accommodate mentally to new situations. It is precisely this ability that emerges during the final stage of the sensorimotor period—between 18 and 24 months of age.

THE PREOPERATIONAL PERIOD. We mentioned earlier that the concepts of accommodation and assimilation are basic to Piagetian theory. As children enter the third year of life and the stage of cognitive development known as the *preoperational period*, these adaptive processes help the child use *signifiers*—various symbols such as words or images that represent objects but that can be manipulated independently of them. True symbolic thought—the effective use of signifiers—occurs only when the child can symbolize actions that have not yet been performed (rather than merely repeating "old actions" mentally).

To exemplify the preoperational period, Piaget describes a problem faced by his daughter, Lucienne, soon after her second birthday.
I put the chain inside an empty matchbox (where the matches belong), then closed the box leaving an opening of 10 mm [about 1/3 of

an inch]. Lucienne begins by turning the whole thing over, then tries to grasp the chain through the opening. Not succeeding, she simply puts her index finger into the slit and so succeeds in getting out a small fragment of the chain; she then pulls it until she has completely solved the problem.

Here begins the experiment which we want to emphasize. I put the chain back into the box and reduced the opening to 3 mm [about one-tenth of an inch]. It is understood that Lucienne is not aware of the functioning of the opening and closing of the matchbox and has not seen me prepare the experiment. She only possesses the two preceding schemata: turning the box over in order to empty it of its contents, and sliding her finger into the slit to make the chain come out. It is of course this last procedure that she tries first; she puts her finger inside and gropes to reach the chain, but fails completely. A pause follows during which Lucienne manifests a very curious reaction bearing witness not only to the fact that she tries to think out the situation and to represent to herself through mental combination the operations to be performed, but also the role played by imitation in the genesis of representations. Lucienne mimics the widening of the slit. She looks at the slit with great attention; then, several times in succession, she opens and shuts her mouth, at first slightly, then wider and wider! . . . Lucienne, by opening her mouth, thus expresses, or even reflects her desire to enlarge the opening of the box. This schema of imitation, with which she is familiar, constitutes for her the means of thinking out the situation. . . . Soon after this phase of plastic reflection, Lucienne unhesitatingly puts her finger in the slit and, instead of trying as before to reach the chain, she pulls so as to enlarge the opening. She succeeds and grasps the chain. [Cited in Flavell, 1963, pp. 119–120.][1]

[1]As this example illustrates, Piaget does *not* believe that language must precede thought. Rather, he believes that the child's first private symbols (such as Lucienne opening her mouth to signify opening the box) provide the framework for later language acquisition.

CONSERVATION DURING THE PREOPERATIONAL PERIOD. In a now-classic study, Piaget presented a 4-year-old child with two identically shaped beakers, poured what appeared to be equal quantities of milk in each, and then permitted the child to make further adjustments until it was agreed that each container had exactly the same amount to drink. Then the entire contents of one of these beakers was poured into an empty third beaker that was fatter and wider in shape than the first two. When the child was asked whether the new beaker had the same amount of milk as the first (untouched) beaker or a different amount, he or she typically said that it had a *different* amount; further questioning usually discloses that the child believes that the new beaker actually contains more milk than the untouched one. The procedure, shown in Figure 7.3 and 7.4, has been replicated innumerable times with children below the age of 7, and their response is almost always the same.

Why do youngsters of this age give the "wrong" answer to the milk problem? According to Piaget, it is because they cannot grasp the principle of conservation, which states: there is no *necessary* change in one aspect of an object or situation (such as the quantity of a liquid)

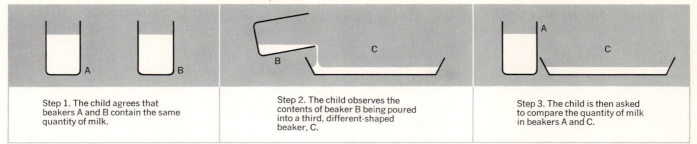

Step 1. The child agrees that beakers A and B contain the same quantity of milk.

Step 2. The child observes the contents of beaker B being poured into a third, different-shaped beaker, C.

Step 3. The child is then asked to compare the quantity of milk in beakers A and C.

Figure 7.3
The sequence of events in testing children's understanding of the conservation of liquid quantity.

Figure 7.4
The conservation of liquid quantity experiment.

simply because other aspects (such as the shape of a liquid) have changed. In the real world many aspects of things are conserved even after the things themselves have been transformed in a variety of ways.

As the foregoing definition implies, conservation of liquid quantity is only one of a variety of conservation tasks that have been used to probe children's reasoning processes. In studies of the conservation of *length*, for example, children are shown two or more straight sticks of equal length placed horizontally on a table so that the bottom edges are lined up evenly. Not surprisingly, when the children are questioned about the sticks' relative lengths under these test conditions, they will judge them equal. But after the experimenter moves one of the sticks out of line and away from the child (without doing anything else), the child will say that the moved stick is shorter than the others. In a similar vein, studies of the conservation of *amount* begin by showing a child two identical balls of clay. While the child watches closely, one ball is rolled into a sausage or flattened into a pancake, and the young observer is asked whether the two shapes have the same or a different amount of clay in them. By now you have probably guessed the preschooler's typical response: he or she believes that the two shapes contain different amounts of clay even though they were equal at the beginning.

Nearly all children below the age of 7 are unable to grasp the concept of conservation on a variety of tasks, whereas children 7 years of age and over see conservation as "obvious" in each situation. Clearly, the two groups are approaching the problem differently. Piaget undertook the theoretical and research task of stating what the differences are. More specifically, Piaget has reasoned that to solve conservation problems the child must first be able to understand the kind of change that occurs. The child must see that an operation such as pouring does not permanently change the shape of a liquid, because the fluid can always be transformed back into its "original" shape merely by reversing the operation and pouring the liquid back into its original container. But, to appreciate this fact, the child must be able to envision the process of change as a sequence of events; the child who cannot understand an operation as a series of reversible transformations occurring in a meaningful order will certainly fail to grasp the principle of conservation. Research shows that the concepts of reversibility and transformations are not understood by the preoperational child.

Reversibility. If asked why beakers A and C in Figure 7.3 contain the same amount of milk, a 10-year-old, after pointing out that "It's obvious," might invite you to prove it to yourself by pouring the contents of C back into its original container. This principle is called *reversibility* and is equivalent to the mathematical idea that if 2 + 2 = 4, then 4 − 2 = 2. This idea is simply not grasped by the preoperational child.

States and Transformations. In yet another classic demonstration, Piaget presented a preoperational child with a series of pictures like those depicted in Figure 7.5, but in a random order. The child, after being told that the pictures show what happens when a metal bar falls from an upright position to the ground, was asked to arrange the

Figure 7.5
The falling sticks problem. Preoperational children who are shown pictures A–F in random order cannot arrange the sequence correctly to show what happens when a bar falls to the ground.

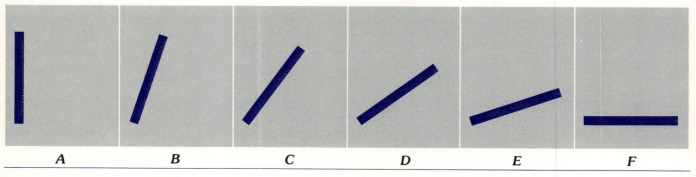

| A | B | C | D | E | F |

cards in the right order for the story. The preoperational child cannot do this correctly and cannot even recognize the correct order when it is presented by the experimenter.

THE CONCRETE OPERATIONAL PERIOD. By about the age of 7, there is a marked shift in children's solutions to conservation problems. They begin to give the correct answers and, what is more, they explain their reasoning by mentioning reversibility, the nature of the transformation that has been performed, and related logical processes. At this point, then, the child has entered the period of concrete operations.

Nonetheless, there are still some intriguing deficiencies in the child's ability to reason until about the age of 11. In Piaget's work this fact was discovered by presenting children with certain classical problems. One of these—Archimedes' Law of Floating Bodies—will illustrate the method and the difficulties encountered by elementary-school children. Archimedes' problem is presented in the following way: The child is given a large container of water and various small objects (pieces of wood, iron, and so forth), some of which will float in water while others will not. The child is asked to classify the objects according to whether or not they will float and to formulate a rule that will apply to the findings.

Children under the age of 11 find this task impossible. They will claim that an object sinks because it is heavy, and are then bewildered when the experimenter points out inconsistencies (for example, that a small piece of metal is actually lighter than a large piece of wood, but the metal sinks while the wood floats). What is the difficulty? According to Piaget, children are still unable to *operate upon their operations*. An abstraction, such as the idea of specific gravity (an object's weight divided by its volume) which underlies the Archimedes problem, is beyond children's grasp because they still think in concrete terms. They can appreciate and grasp relationships they can actually see, but cannot yet conceive of formal, general principles.

The usual approach of the concrete operational child to problems that entail "principles" can be seen in their social behavior when they must make moral judgments about the acts of others. To study this issue, Piaget would present children with pairs of stories, such as those given in Table 7.1; in both stories children have broken chinaware, but the amount of damage and the intentions of the transgressors vary. Each subject must decide which of the two children in the stories has been "naughtier," but to do so, the subject must weigh the child's intention against the amount of damage done. Young children under the age of 11 reply that the extent of the damage is all that matters: John (Story A, Table 7.1) is naughtier than Henry (Story B) because John broke 15 cups while Henry broke only one. Older children and adults typically advance the opposite judgment, presumably because they are able to appreciate abstract, subjective factors

220

TABLE 7.1

One of the story pairs used by Piaget to determine objective and subjective morality.

Story A	Story B
John was in his room when his mother called him to dinner. John goes down, and opens the door to the dining room. But behind the door was a chair, and on the chair was a tray with fifteen cups on it. John did not know the cups were behind the door. He opens the door, the door hits the tray, bang go the fifteen cups, and they all get broken.	One day when Henry's mother was out, Henry tried to get some cookies out of the cupboard. He climbed up on a chair, but the cookie jar was still too high, and he couldn't reach it. But while he was trying to get the cookie jar, he knocked over a cup. The cup fell down and broke.

Source: Bandura and McDonald (1963)

such as intent, and they place greater importance on these in judging the deeds of others.

THE FORMAL OPERATIONAL PERIOD. Beginning at about age 12, according to Piaget's observations, youngsters can reason at a formal, abstract level in solving problems. One problem that ordinarily distinguishes those who have reached this level from those who have not is the pendulum problem. The subject is shown a simple pendulum, consisting of a pendulum stand and an object hanging from a string. The child is asked to pull the object back and then push it and note how quickly the pendulum swings back and returns to the top of its arc. The subject is also given a number of other strings of varying length and objects of various weights to experiment with. The subject is encouraged to push the pendulum as hard as he or she likes as well as simply to let go of it. Finally, the subject is given a classical problem in physics—to determine which factor (or factors) is responsible for the speed with which the pendulum swings back.

The pendulum problem is not one that can be reasoned out while sitting in an armchair, and most children and adults are wrong when they simply try to guess the answer. (Note: it is the length of the string that matters; the other factors are irrelevant.) Experimentation will reveal the answer if the subject can plan and conduct a set of probes in an orderly fashion and summarize the results accurately. Preadolescents (those who are still at the concrete operational level) cannot solve the problem at all. Adolescents, however, are able to design a formal set of operations: they can map out their experiment and then observe and record their findings systematically. They usually work out the correct answer, as was shown by a 15-year-old girl who,

after having selected 100 grams with a long string, then 20 grams with a long and short string, and finally 200 grams with a long and short, concludes: "It's the length of the string that makes it go faster or slower; the weight doesn't play any role." *She discounts likewise the height of drop and the force of her push* [Inhelder and Piaget, 1958, p. 75].

**Figure 7.6
Jerome Bruner**

MODES OF REPRESENTATION: HOW COGNITIVE GROWTH OCCURS

Piaget's work provides a fascinating description of how children develop cognitively but, critics have argued, tells us little about the underlying psychological processes. "What he has done," according to the Oxford psychologist Jerome Bruner, "is to write the implicit logical theory on which the child proceeds in dealing with intellectual tasks. . . . But in no sense does this formal description constitute an explanation or a psychological description of the processes of growth" (Bruner, 1968, p. 7).

Bruner feels that a full psychological description of cognitive development should pay greater attention to the way in which the child represents the world. Only with a sophisticated "storage system" can we simultaneously bring the relevant past experience of ourselves and others to bear on present problems and sort through many alternatives before we act. Piaget noted all these changes as accompaniments of cognitive development, but he did not deal with them directly. Bruner provided what he felt was the needed psychological description, couched in terms of shifting modes of representation in the child's thought. Specifically, he theorized, there are three modes of representation that appear successively as the child matures: *enactive, iconic,* and *symbolic.*

THE ENACTIVE MODE. The child's first representation of the world, argues Bruner, is through action itself. One can see this clearly as a psychological characteristic of the child's thinking during the sensorimotor period, as for example, when Piaget's daughter Lucienne opened and closed her mouth to represent by this action the opening of the matchbox she desired (see page 215). So also, in learning to recognize a triangle, preschool children will often trace the shape with their fingers to see if it has three turns; when not permitted to trace, they often cannot recognize the shape from visual cues alone (Gellermann, 1923). In much the same way, young children associate objects with the actions they can perform with them; "at first," writes Bruner, "a rattle is to shake and a hole is to dig; [only] later they are somehow picturable or conceivable without action" (1968, pp. 12–13).

Unlike Piaget, Bruner believes that one mode of thought is not completely supplanted by another as development proceeds. Rather, new modes are added to our existing repertoire—like new layers on a cake. Bearing this in mind, consider the emergent use of images as the iconic mode develops.

THE ICONIC MODE. An icon is any imaginal representation of a thing; it is usually, but not always, pictorial. Most significantly, of course, it can be stored mentally and manipulated independently of the thing it represents; thus, representation plays a vital role in the development of reasoning. It is difficult to know exactly when children are first able to imagine, but there are some interesting demonstrations that reveal how it emerges as a tool of thought. Recall, for example (page 215), that the 8-to-12-month-old infant searches for an object where it was last found rather than where he or she saw it placed, which suggests that the child cannot imagine and hold on to a transition not produced by his own action. A year or two later the child does appear to develop static, whole images of things but still cannot match them with slightly altered versions of real objects. Very young children can recognize and name complete triangles, squares, and other familiar shapes that are presented to them, but they usually fail to recognize dotted outlines of the same shapes. Older children are more likely to succeed with incomplete silhouettes, but their ability to do so is not complete until early adolescence (Mooney, 1957).

The role of imagery in thought becomes even clearer when we turn to the more dynamic use of imagery. Preschool children have a great deal of difficulty imagining what a familiar object would look like from a different perspective, but they find it to be much easier if they are permitted to move around to that perspective (Huttenlocher and Presson, 1974).

The emerging role of imagery in thought can also be seen in problems of *mental rotation*. Here the subject is presented with two familiar asymmetrical shapes, one of which is the mirror-image of the other. A third figure, which is the rotated version of one of the first two, is also shown. The child's task is to determine which one of the standards would exactly match the tilted image if it were rotated to upright. While adolescents and adults have little difficulty with such problems, preschool children can seldom do them without special training. Recent evidence suggests that such training can produce better than chance performance among 5-year-olds, but that they still make more mistakes than 8-year-olds, and rotate their images more slowly (Strauss, 1974).

THE SYMBOLIC MODE. To be useful, an image should be as similar to the thing it represents as possible. A true symbol, on the other hand, is arbitrary and remote from the thing it represents; thus, it can easily be manipulated without carrying along any spare baggage. "Philadelphia," Bruner has quipped, "looks no more like the city so designated than does a nonsense syllable" (1964, p. 3).

In demonstrating and exploring the shift from iconic to symbolic representation, Bruner and his associates have emulated Piaget by presenting children of various ages with tasks that will disclose the child's mode of solution rather than merely right or wrong answers. According to Bruner, one should not even think of certain responses as right and others as wrong at all. Rather, he insists, "when children give wrong answers it is not so often that they are wrong as they are answering another question, and the job is to find out what question they are in fact answering" (1968, p. 4).

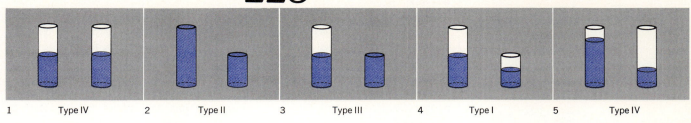

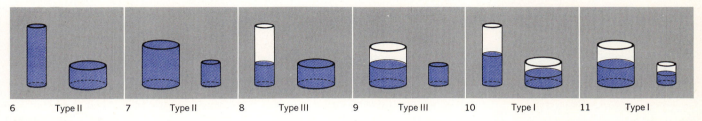

Figure 7.7
In the Bruner and Kenney experiment, children are asked to tell which glass in each pair is fuller and which is emptier. Because the task requires an understanding of the concept of proportion, many children give inconsistent answers.
[Source: After Bruner and Kinney (1966)]

As an example, Bruner and Kenney (1966) gave a group of children a seemingly straightforward task: they asked the children to look at two drinking glasses, each of which contained some liquid, and to specify which one was fuller and which one was emptier. The 11 pairs of glasses that were used by the researchers in this experiment are shown in Figure 7.7.

Adults, faced with this task, will answer by applying the abstract idea of proportion. They will say that the glass with the greater proportion of water (that is, the one that appears to be completely full) is "fuller" than the one that seems to have the smaller proportion (that is, the one that seems half full), regardless of the actual amounts of water involved. Generally children below the age of about 12 do not respond uniformly; those who are 9, 10, and 11 years old tend to give more correct answers than do those who are 5 to 8 years old. Although that fact may not be surprising, what is astonishing is how often children below 11 or 12 give flatly contradictory answers. According to Bruner:

> *We present a pair of half-filled glasses of unequal volume [Type I]. Identifying the glass of larger volume as A we often find that a child will say that A is fuller than B and then go on to say that A is emptier than B. Or he will say that both are equally full, but A is emptier [Bruner, 1968, p. 8].*

Which age group of children makes errors like this? One would think that younger children would be more likely to contradict themselves than older children, so that such errors would decrease with age. Actually, though, just the opposite is true: through about age 7 older children are *more* likely than younger ones to make contradictory errors. In one experiment, for example, only 27 percent of the errors made by 5-year-olds were contradictory whereas for 7-year-olds the corresponding figure was 68 percent.

This result is certainly out of line with everything else we seem to know about the general progression of cognitive development. Since we cannot claim that older children are less logical than younger ones, the answer must lie elsewhere. Bruner believes that older children are beginning the transition from iconic to symbolic reasoning and that, when carefully analyzed, their answers to questions of volume reflect this fact. To follow Bruner's analysis, we must examine a simpler experiment, in which children are only shown glasses where one dimension is held constant. In displays 2, 6, and 7 of Figure 7.7, for example, both glasses are filled all the way to the top but they hold unequal amounts of water. Younger children, faced with such pairs, find them unambiguous; invariably they say that the glass with the greater amount of water is fuller, and the one with the lesser amount is emptier. Older children see this "fact" and have at least a dim notion of the proportional equality as well. For them, one glass is fuller than the other (it *does* have more water in it), but both are equally empty since no more water can be added to either. The older children's emerging understanding of the larger problem has temporarily deflected them from the principle of consistency, but the over-all pattern of psychological development is now clear. Bruner put it this way:

What then accounts for the differences we have found between the younger and older children? We suggest that what is involved is that the children are at different points en route from the iconic to symbolic representation. The younger child differs from the older child in the number of attributes he attends to in these situations involving fullness and emptiness. It is quite clear that the younger child attends to one—the apparent amount of water; the older to two—the volume of filled space and the volume of empty space. The younger child attempts to apply a single variable to fit a contrast pair. The older child can dissociate the situation into two variables—filled space and empty space—but is not yet able to relate them to a third, the volume of the container itself. To accomplish this, the child must be able to detach himself from perceptual features in order to deal with the relationship. When the child can establish the relationship among all three terms—the amount of water, the amount of empty space, the volume of the container—he has a symbolic concept of proportion. The older child who is able to cope with several cues simultaneously is almost always the one who has some structure in which he can fit them [Bruner, 1966b, pp. 180–181].

LANGUAGE In passing, we have already mentioned the relationship between language and thought. Now we will turn to the process of language development itself and trace how it is shaped as an integral part of the child's early interaction with the world. Understanding how children begin to absorb and communicate ideas through language may be one of the most important issues studied by developmental psychologists. Language is, for humans, the pivotal tool for the development of almost all other behavior; it is essential not only for formal education, but for the socialization of values and worldly "success." Obviously, any language deficiency will hamper an individual's ability to cope with even the simplest social situation.

LANGUAGE DURING THE FIRST THREE YEARS: AN OVERVIEW. Most children do not develop meaningful speech until they are at least a year old. This is not to say, though, that infants are *vocally* inactive—far from it. Apart from simple crying, familiar to all parents, infants have a broad repertoire of more pleasing "prelinguistic" vocalizations.

One systematic investigation (Sanger, 1955) disclosed that infants often respond to the sound of the human voice before they are 2 months old. By the third month infants engage in conversational babbling, but they will stop babbling to listen to the vocalizations made by their parents or caretakers. Within a relatively brief period there are striking changes in the character of these vocalizations. The first sounds are grunts in addition to cries; but by three months a gentle, pleasant cooing has usually begun. Cooing is followed by babbling—a varied form of intoned vocalization that investigators have recorded as "uggle-uggle," "erdah-erdah," "oddle-oddle," "a-bah-bah," and "bup-bup" (Shirley, 1933).

During the babbling stage the basic sounds of language, called *phonemes*, begin to emerge. It is almost safe to say that phonemes correspond to vowel and consonant sounds; we emphasize almost, though, because there are subtle variations, which may be important for understanding. The explosion of the letter *b* is rather different in *ball* than in *flab*.

The child's phonemic repertoire certainly expands during the babbling stage, as more and more sounds are produced. But another, opposing process is also at work: *phonetic contraction*. Anyone whose native language is English who has tried to acquire a nasal French vowel or improve his or her rendition of a German umlaut knows how difficult it is to learn these sounds after about the age of 10, and some of us who are adults will never be able to get them right. The infant between the ages of 6 and 12 months produces the full range of these exotic sounds, but later on the child's repertoire contracts to those sounds that are used by speakers of his or her own language (Jespersen, 1922). Now the youngster is ready to begin true communicative speech.

The child's first communications, in virtually every culture, consist of single words. While it is difficult to establish just when this occurs, many children will have spoken individual words by their first birthday (McCarthy, 1954). There appears to be little doubt that these communications are sentences ("Mommy?!" can immediately by translated by most mothers as: "Mother, come here immediately"). This fact has led many researchers to suggest that the concept

Figure 7.8
A child's first sentences consist of single words often accompanied by gestures.

of a sentence is part of the human organism's inborn capacity, on which grammar and speech are built through learning. McNeill has explained it as follows:

The concept of a sentence may be part of man's innate mental capacity. . . . The facts of language acquisition could not be as they are unless the concept of a sentence is available to children at the start of their learning. The concept of a sentence is the main guiding principle in a child's attempt to organize and interpret the linguistic evidence that fluent speakers make available to him. What outside observers see as distorted or "telegraphic" speech is actually a consistent effort by a child to discover how a more or less fixed concept of a sentence is expressed in the language to which he has, by accident, been exposed.

Children everywhere begin with exactly the same initial hypothesis; sentences consist of single words. The entire structure of a sentence must be squeezed through this tiny space. This simple hypothesis leads to the most peripheral of differences between children learning different languages. Only the words differ. A child exposed to English might use hot *as a comment and a Japanese child would use* atsui, *but the difference is merely in sound, not in conceptual or linguistic structure. Not only are words sentences at the beginning, they are the same sentences in different languages [McNeill, 1970, p. 2].*

If the child naturally begins with a one-word sentence, as appears to be the case, his or her behavior is rapidly modified by environmental circumstances. By the age of 2 most children are producing two-word sentences consisting of noun and verb, such as "Want horse!" And, as Brown (1965) has pointed out, "By the age of thirty-six months some children are so advanced in the construction process as to produce all

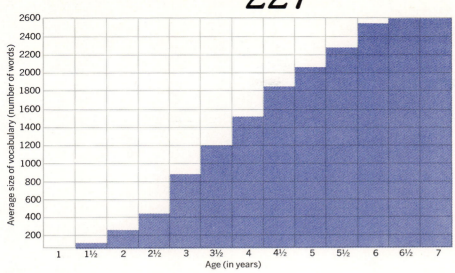

Figure 7.9
Growth of the child's vocabulary.
[Source: Data from Smith (1926)]

of the major varieties of English simple sentences up to a length of ten or eleven words" (p. 286).

But we should not get too far ahead of ourselves. Sounds only become words when they mean something to the listener as well as the speaker. *Semantics*, the study of meaning, becomes relevant for language acquisition if we note that a child's vocabulary—the list of words whose meaning he or she understands—multiplies 200 to 300 times during the second year of life and continues its impressive climb in each successive year (see Figure 7.9).

How are these meanings acquired? There seem to be at least two related processes occurring: concept formation and contextual usage. The process of concept formation was discussed in Chapter 5. An early study by Heidbreder (cited in Brown, 1965) indicates how it applies to learning a new word. Adults in this study were shown the pictures depicted in Figure 7.10 one at a time. As each picture appeared the experimenter called out a "word" that was unknown to the subject; the "words" were actually syllables such as *ling, fard, dilt,* and *pram.* The subject's task was to learn the names of the various objects and repeat them to the experimenter; since no single picture ever appeared more than once, the subject had to deduce the common attribute (that is, the meaning) associated with each name. The experimenter, for example, called out the word *pram* for the following: the fourth picture in Series I, the first picture in Series II, and the last picture in Series III. The observant subject could then identify the second picture in Series IV and the next to the last in Series V as also being *pram,* although these two had not been specifically named.

Suppose someone were to say to you: "*Relks* are fun to ride." Although you do not know what a *relk* is, you do have some information from the context to formulate some ideas and to eliminate others

Series I	Series II	Series III	Series IV	Series V

Figure 7.10
The pictures used in Heidbreder's experiment. The participants were asked to find the similar items in each series and thus abstract a new word category.

(for example, a *relk* could not be a container). If you then hear that "*relks* need a lot of water," you would have more information; from the two contexts, you could further refine the possibilities. From the second sentence alone, it could appear that *relks* might be a type of plant; it is the first sentence that makes this meaning impossible. A third sentence, "Young *relks* often look clumsy," will tell you that a *relk* is not a vehicle such as a car or train. By now you will probably have an idea that fits the over-all context. Research (for example, Werner and Kaplan, 1952) suggests that children can learn new word meanings through context in just this way.

Besides word meanings, children quickly learn rudimentary grammar, including the fact that there are correct and incorrect constructions. Grammar, in fact, traditionally consists of *morphology*—word formation (for example, plurals and past tenses)—and *syntax*—putting words together into sentences.

TESTING YOUR UNDERSTANDING
CHILDREN'S GRAMMAR

How are children able to produce more or less grammatically correct sentences? One view is that, from a very early age, they are able to abstract the underlying rules of a language and apply them in new situations. Support for this idea can be found even in casual observation of young children's language. For example, children will often "regularize" what are, in fact, irregular English forms by saying "He *doed* it" (instead of "He *did* it") or "I see the sheeps" (rather than "I see the sheep").

This is not conclusive evidence, however, because of the possibility that the children may have heard these grammatically incorrect forms used. The problem is to demonstrate the process of rule-regulated language with words that are unfamiliar and therefore could not have been heard before. How could an investigator provide such a demonstration?

Studying morphology, Berko (1958), illustrated the abstraction process in a hallmark study with young children. She employed nonsense forms and labels to determine whether preschool children were able to correctly apply certain language rules to the formation of words with which they could have had no previous experience. For example, she presented each child with a picture of a make-believe object, such as the one shown in Figure 7.11, and said, "This is a *wug*," Then she showed a picture of two such objects and said, "There are two _____," providing the child with the opportunity to supply the plural form of *wug*. Her subjects were able to perform remarkably well (by applying the rule, the plural of *wug* ought to be *wugs*).

This is a wug.

Now there is another one.
There are two of them.
There are two _____.

Figure 7.11
An example of Berko's (1958) technique showing that children have abstracted certain language rules by preschool age. [Source: After Berko (1958)]

LANGUAGE AND LEARNING: SOME EARLY VIEWS. In addition to its practical significance, the way in which language is acquired and modified has long been of great theoretical importance to psychologists because of its fundamental relationship to all other aspects of human learning.

The earliest psychological accounts of language acquisition were developed by theorists who included language in their general accounts of the learning process (Miller and Dollard, 1941; Mowrer, 1960; Skinner, 1957). Efforts to apply concepts of conditioning can be illustrated in three "time-honored and then dishonored theories" of language acquisition, described by Thorndike (1943), which are sometimes identified by three somewhat opprobrious but distinctive names: the ding-dong theory, the bow-wow theory, and the pooh-pooh theory. According to Thorndike:

The ding-dong theory assumed a mystical power of certain things to evoke certain sounds from men. Since each such sound was associated with the experience of the thing, it came to mean it. And since men were alike in their responses to things by sounds, one of these sounds meant more or less the same thing to all in the group, and easily became a vehicle of communication.

The bow-wow theory supposed that men formed habits of using the sounds made by animals, things, or events to mean the respective animals, things, and events and that these habits started them on the road to inventing other sounds as signs of animals, things, or events.

The pooh-pooh theory . . . supposed that the instinctive unlearned cries of man as a wordless animal, which already are sounds that are evoked by certain situations and evoked in human hearers certain equally unlearned responses of action and feeling, came to possess meanings also, and that on the basis of this vocabulary of familiar sounds meaning pain, surprise, fear, affection, and the like, early man here and there used other sounds to mean other facts. Nobody should doubt that part of this is true. To a mother whose baby cries and seeks her breast that cry probably means *that the baby wants to be fed if anything means anything to her. If she can think of anything she will think of that, as well as react appropriately to it* [Thorndike, 1943, pp. 84–90].

The problem with these amusing accounts is, of course, that they tell us little about how an individual child acquires language. But many people believed that later offshoots of the same fundamental idea—that language emerges from naturally occurring environmental circumstances—clearly explained the phenomenon. The writings of B. F. Skinner and his followers typify this modern approach.

SKINNER'S VIEW OF LANGUAGE. Perhaps the first systematic learning and analysis of language was Skinner's *Verbal Behavior*, published in 1957. In this volume, Skinner stated that language development could be explained according to the same variables (for example, reinforcement and shaping) that had been shown to control other, nonverbal forms of behavior in various situations. His theoretical analysis has since enjoyed a degree of support from research.

Let us turn first to infant vocalizations, the apparent precursor of later language. In one study (Rheingold, Gewirtz, and Ross, 1959), 3-month-old infants were observed for a period of 6 days. The first two days were the familiar baseline period; the frequency of the infant's spontaneous vocalizations was simply recorded. Exposure to a female adult was controlled inasmuch as the experimenter periodically looked over the crib, keeping her head about 15 inches from the baby. The third and fourth days were the actual experimental period; during this time the vocalizations were rewarded: any infant sounds elicited a broad smile from the experimenter, complemented by pleasant "tsk" sounds and a gentle stroking of the infant's abdomen. The fifth and sixth days were a return to the baseline period (that is, extinction), and the adult became unresponsive once more. As expected, the social rewards introduced during the two middle days increased the infant's vocalizations while the vocalization rate declined when these incentives were withdrawn. A more fully controlled study has since replicated and extended the basic finding (Weisberg, 1963). Later language development has also been linked experimentally with systematic reinforcement of well-formed (grammatically correct) verbalizations. For example, Skinner has argued that, through reinforcement, young children learn grammatical "frames" that become the foundation for constructing novel but grammatically correct sentences. Thus, when a child learns to say "the man's house," "the man's car," and "the man's shoe," he or she is also learning the frame, "the man's _____," and will be able to use it with any appropriate noun. In a careful study of 2-year-olds, Whitehurst (1972) has shown that the process does apply. In much the same way, Skinner believes that we come to understand the sentences of others because each communication has an appropriate response conditioned to it through prior reinforcement and association.

Still, the fact that language can be learned through a reinforcement process does not mean that it *is* learned that way in the natural environment. A field study by Brown, Cazden, and Bellugi (1967) aptly points up this issue. The investigators observed the interactions of three mother-child pairs over a period of several years as the youngsters were learning to speak; particular attention was paid to the manner in which the mother dispensed contingent approval or disapproval. Their findings were clearly *in*consistent with the reinforcement view of grammatical development. It was truth, *not* grammar, that motivated the mothers to respond positively or negatively.

"Her curl my hair" was approved [*as a statement from the child*] *because mother was in fact curling Eve's hair. However, Sarah's grammatically impeccable "There's the animal farmhouse" was disapproved because the building was a lighthouse and Adam's "Walt Disney comes on, on Tuesday" was disapproved because Walt Disney comes on, on*

Figure 7.12
Much of a child's early language learning occurs by merely observing others.

some other day. It seems, then, to be truth rather than syntactic well-formedness that chiefly governs explicit verbal reinforcement by parents. Which renders mildly paradoxical the fact that the usual product of such a training schedule is an adult whose speech is highly grammatical but not notably truthful [*Brown, Cazden, and Bellugi, 1967, pp. 57–58*].

OBSERVATIONAL LEARNING. It is obvious that reinforcement alone cannot account for the child's language development; imitation also plays a central role, as children learn observationally from their contact with other children and adults. In the Brown et al. (1967) study mentioned earlier, for example, a careful record was kept of the emergence of increasingly elaborate sentences by the youngsters as they interacted with their mothers. Biweekly transcripts of 2-hour interactions between mother and child were obtained and transcribed. One of the most striking things found is that the child learns speech imitatively, through a reciprocal interchange with the mother. Specifically, the child tends to show *imitation with reduction* of the mother's speech, while the mother imitates some of the child's phrases, *but expands upon them*. Both types of imitation are illustrated in Table 7.2.

From interactions such as these, the child might learn to speak certain sentences in an acceptable grammatical form. But there is reason to believe that he or she learns much more; a mere catalog of sentences would not adequately represent the child's linguistic competence inasmuch as many grammatically correct expressions can be produced that have never been heard before. It is quite possible that the underlying rules of grammar—its *latent structure*—are induced or abstracted by the child from exposure to others. There are many reasons for believing that this is indeed the case.

TABLE 7.2

Examples of imitation with reduction (by the child) and imitation with expansion (by the mother) in the Brown et al. study.

IMITATION WITH REDUCTION

Mother	Child
Daddy's briefcase.	Daddy briefcase.
Fraser will be unhappy.	Fraser unhappy.
He's going out.	He go out.
No, you can't write on Mr. Cromer's shoe.	Write Cromer shoe.

IMITATION WITH EXPANSION

Child	Mother
Baby highchair.	Baby is in the highchair.
Mommy sandwich.	Mommy'll have a sandwich.
Pick glove.	Pick the glove up.

Source: Brown et al. (1969)

The evidence is clearest, perhaps, from a series of studies beginning with an investigation by Bandura and Harris (1967). These researchers examined the effects of observing a model (and other factors) on children's production of particular language constructions. The general approach consisted of asking second-grade children to make up sentences that included a particular word presented by the experimenter, first during a base-rate period and then after some form of intervening training. The results showed clearly that the children who had been exposed to the following combination: (1) a model who produced sentences with and without the relevant construction (for example, prepositional or passive phrases), (2) a reward to both the model and the child for producing sentences with the relevant construction, and (3) attention-focusing instructions, showed a greater increment in the production of the particular words in their sentences than did a control group.

This study demonstrated that children's language productions can be modified rapidly by combining modeling and other simply controlled social learning variables. It is likely, however, that the children in the Bandura and Harris study had been exposed to, and had used, prepositional and passive constructions many times before they participated in that experiment. Therefore, it was not clear whether children can acquire new or novel language rules as a result of observational learning.

Odom, Liebert, and Hill (1968) designed an experiment to determine whether children could abstract and learn to use unfamiliar language rules by listening to appropriate models. The procedures were similar to those used by Bandura and Harris except that some children were exposed to modeled sentences containing prepositional constructions of the form article-noun-preposition (for example, "The boy went *the house to*" or "The man was *the door at*"). Surprisingly, second-grade children, when exposed to the new rule, used the familiar English constructions (that is, *preposition-article-noun*) more frequently than did children in a control group who saw no model and received no reward. Thus, it appeared that, instead of abstracting the new rule from the model's rewarded productions, the children in these conditions somehow "re-ordered" the unfamiliar language constructions to make them correspond with familiar language rules. These interesting results, which show a remarkable cognitive capacity on the part of children when they are faced with an unfamiliar situation, do not mean that language behavior cannot be modified in this way.

Liebert, Odom, Hill, and Huff (1969) repeated the essential "new-rule" procedure described above with 5-, 8-, and 14-year-old children (they also used other procedures that are not relevant to our discussion here). From their major results, shown in Figure 7.13, it is clear that the 14-year-old children could quickly pick up, process, and use the new rule *in their own sentences* after relatively brief training.

OBSERVATIONAL LEARNING AND THE MODIFICATION OF SUBSTANTIVE LANGUAGE. Whereas in the past many studies of imitative language learning have focused heavily upon children's acquisition of grammatical rules through observation, in recent years there has been a marked increase of interest in the manner in which substantively meaningful language forms are also learned by observing social models. An excellent example of this type of research was an experiment undertaken by Rosenthal, Zimmerman, and Durning (1970).

These investigators wanted to study the manner in which 11-to-13-year-old boys and girls of Mexican American extraction formulated questions in response to various pictures. One set of pictures depicted common objects (for example, a typewriter) while a second set of pictures showed three differently colored objects (for example, a blue balloon, a yellow banana, and a red apple). All subjects were told that they would be shown a series of cards and that they were to ask a question about each. In addition, the subjects in the modeling groups observed adult female models respond to the first set of pictures by asking questions of a particular *category*. The four different categories of questions employed were the physical attributes of the item ("What shape is that?"), the function of the item ("Could you put water in this?"), possible causal relationships ("When does the bell on the typewriter ring?"), and judgments of value or preference ("Which do you think is the prettiest?").

The major question being investigated in this experiment was whether, as a function of observing models, the children would increase the frequency with which they asked questions of the same category as those exemplified in the model's information-seeking behavior. The results showed quite clearly that the children did indeed modify their questions after the observational learning period. Moreover,

Figure 7.13
Mean number of new rule prepositional constructions in Liebert et al.'s experiment during the base rate and training period as a function of the children's age.

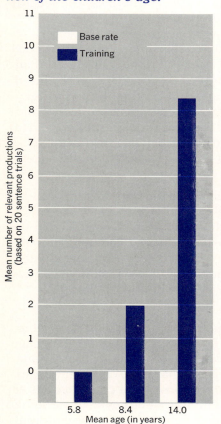

the form of the children's questions generalized to new items on which the model had not responded; furthermore, when the children had the opportunity to imitate the modeled questions directly (during their exposure to the first set of pictures), less than 12 percent of their questions were exact copies of the model's. As Rosenthal and his associates note, these results indicate that a short period of observational learning was effective in teaching their subjects to discriminate the abstract category employed by the model and to generalize the use of this category to a new set of events. They conclude by noting: "Whatever factors promote a child's disposition to organize events (e.g., functionally, casually, or valuationally) will exert influence upon enduring habits of organization which he will exhibit. . . . The present experiments suggest that at least to some degree, the organization of abstraction skills is amenable to change through observational learning" (Rosenthal et al., 1970, p. 687).

In a later study of language modification by means of modeling procedures (Harris and Hassemer, 1971), the researchers tried to determine whether exposure to a model's simple or complex speech patterns—without offering a reward—would affect the complexity of children's subsequent speech. They found that, even under these circumstances, children spoke longer and more complex sentences when exposed to a model who did likewise than when exposed either to a model who spoke simple sentences or to no model. Moreover, this effect held for both children who spoke only English and those who spoke Spanish as well; it was also true for both sexes and two age groups. The investigators appropriately note the practical significance of their results:

The implications of these findings for classroom use seem clear: if one's goal is to increase the length and complexity of children's sentence structure, then speak to them in relatively complex sentences. This modeling effect appears to be persistent in time . . . the effect is also unrelated to the sex of the model. A few months before the study was begun, unknown to the authors, the principal of one of the schools in the study suggested to the teachers at the school that they simplify their language and be careful not to speak "over the heads" of the students. On the basis of these results, we would suggest just the opposite: that deliberately modeling complex sentences may be an effective way of increasing the length and complexity of the sentences children use [Harris and Hassemer, 1971, pp. 11–12].

GENERATIVE GRAMMAR AND THE WORK OF NOAM CHOMSKY. Theorists who hold to an imitative learning view of language acquisition portray human language as requiring more cognitive competence than is suggested by reinforcement theory alone. Still, some have suggested that all learning approaches should be taken to task for failing to come to grips with the special accomplishments and abilities implied by the use of human language. The most prominent holder of this view is Noam Chomsky.

Figure 7.14
Noam A. Chomsky

An accomplished scholar for many years, Chomsky made his significant debut into the psychological community with the publication of his review of Skinner's *Verbal Behavior* in 1959. But, as Chomsky himself wrote 8 years later, the review was "not specifically [a] criticism of Skinner's speculations regarding language, but rather . . . a more general critique of behaviorist (I would now prefer to say 'empiricist') speculations as to the nature of higher mental processes" (Chomsky, 1967, p. 142).

The Chomsky review is rich in criticism and commentary, and certainly merits careful reading by anyone who is seriously interested in language acquisition. To give a hint of its flavor and style, we will present a few selected passages. Chomsky criticizes the idea that a "listener" responds in order to reinforce a speaker. Using Skinner's own examples, Chomsky conjectures:

> *Suppose, for example, that while crossing the street I hear someone shout* Watch out for the car *and jump out of the way. It can hardly be proposed that my jumping (the mediating, reinforcing response in Skinner's usage) was conditioned (that is, I was trained to jump) precisely in order to reinforce the behavior of the speaker.*

Chomsky also finds fault with Skinner's account of how people learn to respond to verbal threats:

> *The manner in which aversive stimulation functions is simply described. If a speaker has had a history of appropriate reinforcement (e.g., if a certain response was followed by 'cessation of the threat of such injury—of events which have previously been followed by such injury and which are therefore conditioned aversive stimuli'), then he will tend to give the proper response when the threat which had previously been followed by the injury is presented. It would appear to follow from this description that a speaker will not respond properly [to the threat]* Your money or your life *unless he has a past history of being killed.*

For Chomsky, the error of Skinner and all empiricists is clear and leads him to conclude:

> *A refusal to study the contribution of the child to language learning permits only a superficial account of language acquisition, with a vast and unanalyzed contribution attributed to a step called "generalization" which in fact includes just about everything of interest in this process. If the study of language is limited in these ways, it seems inevitable that major aspects of verbal behavior will remain a mystery.*

Chomsky, then, takes issue with empiricism, preferring instead the rationalist view that man has certain innate knowledge that precedes any experience. Children come equipped, first of all, with an innate *language acquisition device* (sometimes abbreviated LAD) that underlies their acquisition, understanding, and creative use of language. To illustrate, he points out that sentences do *not* fall into two simple classes, meaningful and meaningless. Rather, there is an "idea" of grammar that is superordinate to meaning. Here are two sentences that make the point:

> Colorless green ideas sleep furiously.
> Furiously sleep ideas green colorless.

Both are meaningless in the usual sense; although the words given here are identical, the first is somehow "grammatical" while the second is not. The problem, for Chomsky, is to understand how the difference is detected. In broad perspective, his answer is that we are set biologically to acquire a finite number of rules (rather than actual sentences or frames of sentences); it is from these rules that we generate an infinite number of grammatically correct sentences that express our intended meaning or communication. The first sentence above is therefore grammatical (it corresponds to the rules), even though it does not happen to be meaningful.

Chomsky and those who have followed his lead do not consider their work finished. Far from it. They are busy probing the nature of language use and understanding. To date, they have many accomplishments to their credit. For example, they found that the grammar of a sentence—the rules governing its construction and meaning—are not always apparent by the placement of the words; rather, it is the "deep structure" of a sentence that is critical. Read the following two sentences:

> My father asked me what to paint.
> My father told me what to paint.

Although both sentences are grammatical, meaningful, and string together almost the same words in the same order, they are not the same in grammar or meaning. In the first, my father will do the painting while in the second I will (probably) do it. Here we can clearly see that it is the underlying structure that counts, although this idea is too subtle for many children under the age of 10 (Chomsky, 1972).

AMBIGUOUS LANGUAGE. Although there is considerable dispute as to how the accomplishment is achieved, there is little doubt that by the time children enter the first grade, most of them have both impressive vocabularies and a fairly complete mastery of grammar. Still, there are persistent deficiencies in their ability to comprehend and use language in subtler situations as both communicators and listeners. We shall examine the case of ambiguous language.

In a major study, Kessell (1970) presented children of various ages with three types of ambiguous sentences and a set of pictures that might correspond to them. The children's job was to select the picture or pictures that fit the sentence, and then to explain the meaning of the pictures they had not selected as well. The simplest ambiguities involved a single word, as in the sentence "She was bothered by the cold." More complex ambiguities depended on the grouping of adjacent words ("They are flying planes") and finally (continued on page 240)

PSYCHOLOGY AND THE PROBLEMS OF SOCIETY
THE ROLE OF THE FAMILY IN EARLY COGNITIVE DEVELOPMENT

Today there is a great deal of interest in the education of disadvantaged children, especially with respect to how their early deprivation in certain areas (such as vocabulary) may affect their cognitive development and later school performance. The facts themselves are clear: children from economically disadvantaged families generally score well below middle-class children on IQ tests, and the gap increases with age; such children also come to school without the necessary cognitive skills to cope with the first-grade curriculum and, as a result, their performance vis-à-vis middle-class children tends to become worse as they advance through elementary school (for example, Deutsch and Brown, 1964; Hess and Shipman, 1965).

Apart from the possibility of genetic differences (which was mentioned in Chapter 6), a child's home environment during the preschool years may account for some of the difficulties economically disadvantaged children have in school performance. Bearing this in mind, investigators have begun to analyze certain aspects of early parent-child interactions in advantaged and disadvantaged families, hoping to relate the differences in these interactions to the socialization of cognitive modes in children.

In one major investigation, Hess and Shipman (1965) studied a group of 163 black families in which there was one child who was 4 years old at the time of the study. The families were divided into four groups according to socioeconomic class. The top group was comprised of families where one or both parents were college educated and employed in professional, executive, or managerial capacities. The lowest group, by contrast, included families where the father was absent and the mother either had an unskilled job or was on welfare.

The mothers were interviewed twice in their homes and later brought to the university for further tests in which they were also observed interacting with their 4-year-old children. Generally, the mothers from the higher socioeconomic group used longer and more elaborate sentences when speaking with their children. Inasmuch as language and cognitive development are closely related, it is possible that this difference alone could work to the disadvantage of children from poorer backgrounds.

In the matter of discipline, the investigators noted a parallel difference. Hess and Shipman found that lower-class mothers more frequently told their children *what* to do rather than explained *why* they should act in a particular way; this authoritarian approach does not help the child to understand the importance of principles for deciding how to respond or what responses will be appropriate in various situations. For example, here is what one middle-class mother said when asked how she would prepare her child for school: "First of all, I would take him to see his new school, we would talk about the building, and after

seeing the school I would tell him that he would meet new children who would be his friends; he would work and play with them. I would explain to him that the teacher would be his friend, would help him and guide him in school, and that he should do as she tells him to" (Hess and Shipman, 1968, p. 96). Lower-class mothers tended to focus *only* on the disciplinary aspects of the situation, without providing any reason for obedience; for example, "Well, I would tell him he going to school and he have to sit down and mind the teacher and be a good boy, and I show him how when they give him milk, you know, how he's supposed to take his straw and do, and not put nothing on the floor when he get through" (Hess and Shipman, 1968, p. 96).

To conclude, Hess and Shipman believe that information-processing strategies are learned through experience with others and that a significant part of each child's early learning is through communication with its mother. Mothers who explain to their children the reasons for obedience are doing more than other mothers to foster their children's cognitive development.

on totally ambiguous surface structures ("The shooting of the soldiers was bad"). Until fifth grade, most children had difficulty with the more complex ambiguities even after they had explained all the pictures.

Ambiguity is found in certain situations even when a child seems to know the general meaning of the words used by an adult, and therein we find a final example of the relationship between measuring a child's linguistic competence and his or her general level of cognitive development. This fact is illustrated most clearly in a study by Lumsden and Kling (1969), who suggested that young children might fail at Piagetian conservation problems (see page 216) because of ambiguity in the words used in questioning them. Specifically, they suggested that young children might be uncertain about the meaning of "big," so that in liquid conservation, for example, they would mistakenly equate it with "tall."

To test their hypothesis, Lumsden and Kling selected a group of kindergarten and first-grade children who could not solve the conservation problem and explained the concept of "bigness" to some of them. The other children in this group who served as controls did not receive this explanation. Those who learned that big and tall do not mean the same thing showed a marked improvement in their ability to deal with the conservation problem as compared with the controls.

SUMMARY

This chapter first discusses the development of cognition, thought, and related mental activity; the most important psychologist who has studied these problems is Jean Piaget. He has outlined four stages of cognitive development that occur during the first 15 years of life:

During the *sensorimotor period*, which includes approximately the first 18 to 24 months, the child begins to combine sensory input and motor reactions, such as pulling the cord of a rattle, but he still has no mental representation of the world.

In the second stage, the *preoperational period*, children between about 2 and 7 years of age acquire the ability to use signifiers and think symbolically of actions that they have not yet performed. However, not until about the seventh year, when the child enters the period of *concrete operations*, can he or she understand and apply rules such as conservation of matter. The fourth and last stage of cognitive development, the period of *formal operations*, begins at approximately 12 years of age for most children. It is signaled by the child's ability to reason at a formal, abstract level and thus solve classical problems (such as the pendulum problem) in a logical and orderly way.

One of Piaget's admirers, Jerome Bruner, has tried to go beyond Piaget's descriptions and explain psychologically how cognitive growth occurs. Bruner theorizes that we each have a sophisticated "storage system" that enables us to bring past experiences to bear on present problems, to learn from others' experience, and to sort through many alternatives before we act. These accomplishments are all mediated by the modes through which we represent the world, which appear successively as the child matures.

The *enactive mode*, which comes first, is reflected in the young child's need to act out relationships (such as tracing a triangle with his or her fingers) in order to represent them. Through the *iconic mode*, which appears next, the child begins to store mental images that can be manipulated independently of the things they represent. Such imagery, Bruner feels, plays a vital role in the development of reasoning during the first years of school. The third form of mental representation, the *symbolic mode*, which is the most sophisticated and abstract, pertains to the use of words and other representations that bear no necessary resemblance to the things they stand for; this mode permits the simultaneous use of many ideas in solving problems.

The latter part of this chapter discusses the development of language, a phenomenon that is closely related to the child's over-all cognitive development. Infants begin babbling about 3 months of age; by 12 months they are producing all of the basic phonemes (or sounds) of language. Single-word sentences, such as "Cookie!" come next. By 2 years of age most children are using two-word sentences consisting of noun and verb; by 3 years of age many youngsters are speaking sentences of 11 or more words.

Children learn grammar quickly and can abstract the underlying rules of a language and apply them in new situations. The question of how children learn to speak grammatically has been hotly debated. Skinner believes that reinforcement and shaping are the foundation of language development, whereas other learning theorists point to the central role of observational learning and emphasize that abstraction from modeled language behavior can account for many linguistic phenomena.

Still other theorists, though, taking their lead from Chomsky, assert that the child contributes much to his or her language development. Chomsky believes that children come equipped with an innate language acquisition device (LAD) that is responsible for their acquiring, understanding, and creatively using language.

Although theorists differ as to how children do it, most first-graders have both impressive vocabularies and a fairly complete mastery of grammar. The few language ambiguities that the elementary-school child cannot comprehend parallel the remaining deficiencies in his or her over-all cognitive development, thereby highlighting again the relationship between language and thought.

GLOSSARY

Accommodation: In Piaget's theory of cognitive development, the mental process that produces adjustment and change in response to new information.

Assimilation: In Piaget's theory of cognitive development, the individual's incorporation of new information into his or her over-all cognitive structure.

Cognition: Thought and related mental activity.

Concrete operations period: The third stage of cognitive development in Piaget's theory. Children from about 7 to 11 years of age can understand and apply rules such as the conservation of matter, but they still cannot grasp truly abstract relationships.

Enactive mode: The first mode of mental representation in Bruner's theory; it is nonverbal and based on action.

Formal operations period: The final stage of cognitive development in Piaget's theory. By about 12 years of age children are able to solve problems by reasoning at a formal, abstract level.

Iconic mode: The second mode of representation in Bruner's theory; experiences are represented as images that can be manipulated mentally.

Language acquisition device (LAD): In Chomsky's theory, the innate biological mechanism that governs children's acquisition, understanding, and creative use of language.

Latent structure: The underlying rules of grammar.

Mental rotation: The ability to rotate an image mentally; this is tested by asking a child what an upside-down object would look like if turned upright.

Morphology: In grammar, the formation of words (plurals, past tenses, and so forth).

Phonemes: The basic sounds of language; they correspond closely but not perfectly with the vowel and consonant sounds of all languages.

Phonetic contraction: The reduction or contraction of the child's repertoire of language sounds, so that he or she begins to eliminate those that are not used in his or her native language.

Preoperational period: The second stage of cognitive development in Piaget's theory. Between the ages of 2 and 7 the child begins to use signifiers and think symbolically of actions that have not yet been performed.

Schemata: In Piaget's theory, mental frameworks that can be fitted together for organizing thoughts and solving problems.

Semantics: The study of meaning in language.

Sensorimotor period: The first stage of cognitive development in Piaget's theory. During the first 18 months, the child begins to combine sensory input and motor action, although he or she has no mental representation of the world.

Signifiers: Symbols, such as words or images, that in Piaget's theory represent objects but can be manipulated independently of them.

Symbolic mode: The third mode of representation in Bruner's theory; it is characterized by the use of abstract representations (such as words) that bear no necessary relationship to the things they represent.

Syntax: The rules in grammar according to which words may be strung together into sentences.

EIGHT

SOCIAL DEVELOPMENT

At birth infants cannot speak; they do not know how to interact with others; and they have no idea of the moral standards that will be expected of them when they are older. This chapter will discuss when and how social behavior emerges. Part of the answer, of course, is that infants and children are actively *socialized*—taught what to do and how to behave— by parents, teachers, and even peers. There is remarkable similarity in the aims of socialization, both among families and subgroups within our own society, and in other cultures as well.

Nearly all societies train their young people in control of aggression, the shaping of personal standards, and the development of sex roles. The *processes* of socialization are also quite similar, inasmuch as they all require some form of learning. This chapter will discuss how the various types of learning (see Chapter 4) apply to socialization; it will also cover certain particularly interesting or important aspects of socialization.

Social development consists of more than learning processes; biological characteristics that are common to everyone as well as those in which they differ (one's sex or particular genetic endowment) are also important to social development, and this fact will be apparent throughout our discussion.

EARLY SOCIALIZATION: COMFORT THROUGH PHYSICAL CONTACT. Social development begins virtually from the moment the infant is born, when nourishment is no longer provided automatically in the comfort of the womb but becomes instead a cooperative, active affair between the caretaker and the baby. Social ties begin during the first few days of life; the physical and emotional warmth provided by the baby's caretaker is almost as important as nourishment itself. Harry Harlow and his associates have done research on the importance of these first emotional relationships, especially their "warmth" and comfort.

Because of the psychological damage that could be inflicted on humans, the Harlow team used infant rhesus monkeys in their experiments on early socialization. According to Harlow and Harlow:

Acceding to the moral and physical impossibility of conducting such an investigation with human subjects, we have been observing the development of social behavior in large numbers of rhesus monkeys. . . . Apart from this primate's kinship to man, it offers a reasonable experimental substitute because it undergoes a relatively long period of development analogous to that of the human child and involving intimate attachment to its mother and social interaction with its age-mates [Harlow and Harlow, 1971, p. 70].

The results of Harlow's many experiments are clear: Infants need physical and emotional contact with both their caretakers and peers in order to experience normal social development. In one study, for example, young rhesus monkeys were isolated at birth in a special stainless steel chamber. Inside the chamber the temperature was maintained at a comfortable level, and food, water, and cleaning up were provided by remote control; although the infant's physical needs were met, it had no contact with and did not even see another living creature. Some young monkeys were subjected to this social deprivation for 3 months; other groups were similarly deprived for 6 or 12 months.

After the deprivation period each monkey was placed in a playroom daily with three other monkeys its own age, two of whom had been

Figure 8.1 (Right)
Infant monkeys that were raised together without their mothers. During their early months they spent most of their time huddled together in positions like this.

Figure 8.2
Harlow's wire and cloth "surrogate" mothers. It may be seen that the infant monkey's typical response was to run to the cloth mother when it was frightened, even if it had been fed by the wire one.

raised normally and a third who had also been isolated. While the mother-reared monkeys played normally, the isolates were overwhelmingly frightened by this first social experience. For those who had been deprived for 6 months or longer, the emotional damage seemed to be permanent rather than merely temporary. Even after 6 months of subsequent social contact, the isolates still had difficulty playing with the controls, and those who had been isolated for a full 12 months showed a "pitiful combination of apathy and terror."

The significant deprivation in their life—during a crucial period—had been physical contact and warmth. Other experiments have shown that infant monkeys who have been reared together but without any maternal contact develop almost normally (see Figure 8.1). Monkeys who have been raised with two surrogate mothers—one constructed of wire and the other of cloth—prefer the warmer cloth creature even though all their food is provided by the wire one (see Figure 8.2).

SOCIALIZATION OF INTERPERSONAL BEHAVIOR: THE BASIC PROCESSES

Infancy is perhaps the time when one's *capacity* for interpersonal relationships is developed or stunted, but it is not until later that the specific nature of one's relationships with others begins to be shaped. Exactly how this occurs is not known precisely, but undoubtedly there is an interplay of many factors. We do know, though, that even "simple" learning processes can be significant here.

REINFORCEMENT AND SOCIALIZATION: PAYOFFS FOR "GOOD" BEHAVIOR. In Chapter 4 we saw that the systematic

Figure 8.3
Azrin and Lindsley's experiment for studying the reinforcement of cooperation between children. [Source: Azrin and Lindsley (1956)]

use of reinforcement can be a significant determinant of the behavior of almost all living organisms. The underlying principles of operant conditioning play an extremely important role in socialization. It has been shown, for example, that the systematic use of reinforcement can establish and modify such diverse behaviors as work and study habits (Fox, 1966), toilet training (Madsen, 1965), and cooperation in interpersonal situations. To show how the principle of reinforcement applies to the development of social behavior, we will discuss several concrete examples.

The Reinforcement of Cooperation between Children. Azrin and Lindsley (1956) were among the first to demonstrate the application of reinforcement procedures to the development of social behavior in children. Ten pairs of children were seated opposite each other at ten separate tables; in front of each child there was a little stylus and three holes in the table. The arrangement is shown in Figure 8.3.

The children were told that they were going to play a game, and that they were to put their own stick (stylus) into the holes in any way they wished. They were also shown some jelly beans and told that other candies would sometimes drop into a small cup on the table as they played. These treats, they were told, would be theirs—to eat either immediately or later on. The experimenter then left the room, emphasizing to the children that they could play in any way they liked. Actually, though, the youngsters soon found that when both styli were placed in the holes opposite each other simultaneously (a cooperative response), a red light flashed and a candy dropped into the cup, but candy never appeared for other patterns of play. In other

TABLE 8.1

Average number of cooperative responses per minute for the experimental periods in Azrin and Lindsley's (1956) experiment.

First 3 minutes of reinforcement period (A)	Last 3 minutes of reinforcement period (A)	Last 3 minutes of extinction period (B)	Last 3 minutes of second reinforcement period (A)
5.5	17.5	1.5	17.5

Source: Adapted from Azrin and Lindsley (1956)

words, during this initial period, the cooperative response was reinforced by the treats.

The design of the experiment followed the usual reversal procedure of operant studies, described in Chapter 4. In this case, the first reinforcement period was continued until a stable rate of cooperation developed. Then, an extinction period followed, during which time the cooperative responses were not reinforced. Finally, reinforcement for cooperation was reinstated. The results of these experimental procedures were quite dramatic. As shown in Table 8.1, there was a marked change in the frequency of cooperative responses per minute from the first 3 minutes to the last three minutes of the initial reinforcement. The cooperative responses were extinguished when reinforcement was withdrawn, but they returned almost immediately when reinforcement was again introduced.

Learning to Interact with Peers. Another way that reinforcement can affect social behavior has been illustrated by Allen et al. (1964). The subject, Ann, was a 4-year-old who was enrolled at a laboratory preschool at the University of Washington. From the very first day of school, it was apparent that Ann had not yet learned to relate effectively with her peers, although she could relate well with adults and did not appear to have any other serious problems.

During the first days of school, Ann interacted freely with adults but seldom initiated contact with children or responded to their attempts to play with her. She did not seem severely withdrawn or frightened; instead she revealed a varied repertory of unusually well-developed physical and mental skills that drew the interested attention of adults but failed to gain the companionship of children. Teachers gave warm recognition to her skilled climbing, jumping, and riding; her creative use of paints and clay; her original songs and rhythmic interpretations of muscial selections; her collections of nature objects; her perceptive and mature verbalizations; and her willing and thorough help-with-cleanup [Allen et al., 1964, p. 512].

After 6 weeks, though, it became apparent that Ann would continue to isolate herself from other children unless something was done. What might work?

By observing Ann's behavior during a base-line period, it became clear that she was often rewarded socially for her efforts to interact with adults, but that this procedure was incompatible with fostering social relations with her peers. A reinforcement procedure was therefore instituted in which Ann was rewarded with attention for playing with other children, but was no longer given attention for approaching and attempting to speak with adults unless she was with another child. The social rewards were designed to prevent her from withdrawing from other children, and thus were presented to her as a member of an ongoing group rather than as an individual. For example, when Ann and two other girls were seen playing one day, the teacher responded enthusiastically: "You three girls have a cozy house! Here are some more cups, Ann, for your tea party." In contrast, the teacher turned away quickly and ignored Ann if she tried to leave the group and attract adult attention for herself.

This reinforcement procedure brought swift results. Ann was soon spending an appreciable amount of time associating with other children. When, as is customary in operant research, these contingencies were temporarily reversed so that Ann was again rewarded for forsaking the companionship of her peers in order to interact with adults, the "old" pattern of isolate behavior reappeared. Finally, the new contingencies (reward only for interaction with peers) were reinstated once more. The result was that Ann was soon again playing enthusiastically with other children.

Reinforcement for Aggressive Behavior. The two previous examples show that reinforcement may effectively shape a variety of "positive" behaviors in children. Research has also shown that less desirable social behaviors—such as aggression—also are developed, at least in part, through the same process.

In a series of sophisticated experiments, the late Richard Walters and his associates (Cowan and Walters, 1963; Walters and Brown, 1963, 1964) explored the effects of rewarding boys' aggression in a play situation upon their subsequent behavior. In one study (Walters and Brown, 1963), it was shown that rewarding boys for acting aggressively against a toy Bobo doll could markedly influence their behavior toward another child in a social situation. The automated doll was designed so that its eyes and a flower in its buttonhole would light up when the boys punched it in the stomach with sufficient vigor. Four groups of boys were used, three of which had been trained and one of which served as a control. Those in the experimental groups were given two training sessions, separated by 2 days. In one of these groups *every* punch was rewarded with a colored glass marble; in a second group punching was intermittently rewarded with a marble; and in the third group the only reward was the illumination of the doll's eyes and lapel flower.

Two days after the last training session, half of the boys were brought into an experimental room, given some candy, and shown the beginning of an exciting movie. Then, these children experienced the appar-

Figure 8.4
Playful aggression between parents and children may stimulate aggressive attitudes and behavior later on in the children's life.

Figure 8.5
The "Bobo" doll clown that was used to study the influence of reinforcement patterns on children's acquisition of aggressive behavior.

ent breakdown of the projector half way through the movie and—to make matters worse—the experimenter took away the candy that he had left for them. The same procedure was also followed with the remaining children, except that they were permitted to see the entire movie and to keep their candy. Thereafter, each child was asked to play a series of games with another child, permitting the experimenters to assess the amount of interpersonal aggressive behavior (such as butting, kneeing, elbowing, kicking, and punching) in a more or less natural situation. It was found that the children who had been rewarded earlier for punching the Bobo doll—particularly those who has been rewarded intermittently—were now more likely than the others to be overtly aggressive toward other children. This finding seemed to reflect a generalization, then, from the youngsters' earlier experiences with the Bobo doll, and it occurred whether the child had been frustrated or not. In a second experiment by these same investigators (Walters and Brown, 1964), some boys were rewarded only when they hit the Bobo doll sharply, while others were rewarded exclusively for weaker hits, using the apparatus shown in Figure 8.5. Using measures of aggression from physical contact games, the researchers found that those children who had been rewarded for the higher magnitude of aggression were more aggressive in this new situation than were those who had been rewarded for relatively temperate play.

Walters and Brown's studies have several clear implications for socialization practices. Consider, for example, the father who enthusiastically encourages his son to roughneck with him in play and to smash away at punching bags, offering praise for particularly forceful assaults. It may be that such training, besides building a "real boy," also promotes aggression in other interpersonal situations.

PUNISHMENT AND SOCIALIZATION. Previously it was noted that, although Thorndike originally said that according to the "law of effect," reward and punishment work in "equal and opposite ways," he later revised this and concluded that punishment is relatively ineffective in modifying behavior.

But it is now known that punishment is a significant part of the socialization practices of many families. In fact, according to one survey (Sears, Maccoby, and Levin, 1957), virtually all parents (98 percent) use punishment at least occasionally to control and socialize their children. According to Parke (1970), parents may have been wiser than Thorndike and other "experts." Under certain circumstances, punishment is an extremely potent child-rearing technique, although its effects vary considerably. Many of the reasons for the varying effects are now understood.

Reducing the Likelihood of Undesirable Behavior. Rewards are quite effective in establishing new patterns of behavior, whereas punishment "works" by reducing the likelihood of certain undesirable or potentially dangerous responses. For this reason, one general rule is that punishment will be most effective when it is used in conjunction with reward to encourage desirable behavior.

The Timing of Punishment. Perhaps the most important factor in the use of punishment is its timing. If a child behaves in an extremely antisocial way—hitting a younger child, lying, or committing an act of vandalism—some hours or days may pass before the parent learns of

(Drawing by Fradon; © 1974 The New Yorker Magazine, Inc.)

"I'm asking you nicely, but I'm not ruling out the use of force!"

the transgression. Moreover, even after learning about it, the parent may delay some hours before punishing the child—as in the familiar "Wait until your father comes home!"

There is now good reason to believe that, as a general rule, mild punishment will be maximally effective if it is administered just as the child is performing the antisocial act; it will be much less effective if there is a considerable delay. Why? First of all, a transgression usually produces some reward for the child. Taking forbidden candies or cookies enables the child to have the pleasure of eating them; subduing a smaller child may win an undeserved first turn at bat; a temper tantrum in a department store may coerce Mother into buying an expensive toy. These outcomes are rewards for the child, and the longer they are held or savored, the more likely it is that they will "balance out" the negative experience of punishment. Punishment is supposed to deter the child from behaving in an undesirable way in the future, but such deterrence is most likely to occur if the punishment is "attached" to the initiation of the behavior (Aronfreed and Reber, 1965).

In the second place, punishment at a much later time may confuse the child, at least a very young one. A boy who breaks a serious rule early in the morning may then try very hard to "be good all day," perhaps to forestall punishment. But then if he is punished in the evening (possibly when his father comes home) for the morning's transgression, this punishment will have come immediately after nearly a whole day of desirable behavior—behavior that the parents would generally like to encourage and reward.

Timing of Punishment and Resistance to Temptation: An Experimental Example. Aronfreed and Reber (1965) conducted an experiment that illustrates the role of the timing of a punishment upon its effectiveness. Their investigation dealt with one form of socially acquired self-control—resistance to temptation. This refers to a child's behavior when he or she has an opportunity to obtain something that is desired by acting in a socially prohibited fashion (by cheating on a test, stealing, taking cookies from a forbidden cookie jar, and so forth). Although no one is present to witness the transgression, the child may still resist the temptation.

In the Aronfreed and Reber experiment, fourth- and fifth-grade boys were presented with pairs of toys, one of which was substantially more attractive than the other one, and told that they could select one to tell (the experimenter) about. It soon became apparent to each child that selecting the more attractive toy in each pair was always prohibited. Specifically, the experimenter said:

I'm going to put some toys down here on this board. Each time I'll put down two toys. Here's what you do—pick up the one you want to tell about, hold it over the board [the experimenter indicated appropriate action with his hand, using his fingers to show that the item was to be easily visible when held], *look at it for a while, and just think about what you're going to say. Then, if I ask you, tell me what it's for or what you do with it. Do you understand?*

If the child indicated that he understood, the experimenter continued:

Now some of the toys here are only supposed to be for older boys, so you're not supposed to pick them. When you pick something that's only for older boys, I'll tell you [Aronfreed and Reber, 1965, p. 7].

The punishment consisted of verbal disapproval for selecting the attractive toy: "No—that's for the older boys." However, the timing of this mild punishment was varied for different groups. In the Punishment at Initiation Condition, it was given before the child had actually touched the forbidden toy, but when his hand was close to it; in the Punishment at Completion Condition, the child was permitted to pick up the forbidden toy and hold it for 2 or 3 seconds before being punished and having the toy taken away gently but firmly. In the Control Condition, the boys also learned which toys were prohibited, but they did not have an opportunity to pick them up or be rebuked: they were told to *point* to one of the toys (rather than pick it up) and were also told that some of the toys—the nicer-looking, more interesting ones—were supposed to be only for older boys.

Not surprisingly, during the *training* phase of the experiment, the children quickly learned to avoid the more attractive but forbidden toys. Since this is not a demonstration of true self-control, a test situation had to be created to see if a more compelling temptation would be resisted when no one was watching. So Aronfreed and Reber replaced the toys with two different objects. One was an attractive two-chambered glass timer that children in a pretest had great difficulty resisting. The other object was a dingy piece of cloth, folded up like a towel. Instead of letting the child choose between these objects while the experimenter watched (as had been done before), the adult seemed to become distracted and then said he had to go out to his car to get some important papers—which would take about 10 minutes. The child was thus given an opportunity to handle the more appealing toy undetected, or to resist the temptation even when alone.

Before leaving, the experimenter had carefully placed the timer between two faint scratches on the table; these scratches served as markers, enabling him—like a detective—to know whether the timer had been handled in his absence merely by looking to see whether it was still in the same place when he returned.

What were the effects of the earlier punishment in this situation, when the children all knew that the glass timer was forbidden? The frequency with which they transgressed in the absence of the experimenter is shown in Figure 8.6. Note that when a mild verbal punishment was given *early*, it increased the children's resistance to temptation (in comparison with those in the unpunished control group); when punishment was given late, however, it seemed to be almost as ineffective as no punishment at all.

Figure 8.6
The effects of punishment in Aronfreed and Reber's (1965) experiment. Note that, for these mild punishments, late punishment had about the same effect as no punishment at all. Early punishment, on the other hand, seemed to be quite effective.

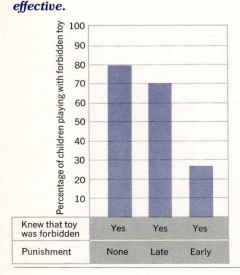

TESTING YOUR UNDERSTANDING
DELAYED PUNISHMENT

We have just noted that delayed punishment may not be effective because young children will associate it with their intervening activities rather than with the transgression for which they are being punished. Yet it is clear that parents sometimes do not learn about their child's misbehavior until some time after it has occurred. How can the problem of late or delayed punishment be overcome? Can you think of any possibilities?

If delayed punishment fails to work because the child does not understand what it is for, one solution might be to "reinstate" the transgression before administering the punishment. An experiment by Andres (1967) shows that this approach works. Children were given a toy constructed in such a way that it always broke after a few minutes of play. Although it appeared that the child was responsible for breaking the toy, he was not punished immediately. Instead, each child was individually brought back 4 hours later and punished mildly. Afterward he was left alone with a new toy quite similar to the one he had broken before. The experimenter wanted to determine the extent to which each child would play with the new toy; presumably, the less he did so the more effective the delayed punishment was.

Some of the children who were punished mildly had no reinstatement of their earlier behavior, while others had the punishment reinstated in a variety of ways such as seeing themselves break the toy on a videotape recording or listening to an adult describe the transgression just before punishment. As expected, those who experienced no reinstatement before punishment were much more likely to play with the new toy than were those in any of the reinstatement groups. This clear difference occurred despite the fact that all of the children received exactly the same punishment.

The effectiveness of a particular punishment also depends upon the use of other child-rearing practices. Punishment administered by an adult who is usually warm and rewarding to the child is much more effective than the identical punishment given by a cold and distant adult (Aronfreed, 1968; Parke, 1967; Whiting, 1954). Explaining the reasons for a punishment also increases its effectiveness (Cheyne, 1972). Finally, consistency in the use of punishment is usually quite important; adults who practice what they preach are more likely to be effective in their reprimands than those who do not (Mischel and Liebert, 1966).

IMITATIVE LEARNING AND SOCIALIZATION. Having discussed the possible contributions of reward and punishment to a child's social development, we will now turn to a third factor in socialization—observational learning through exposure to social models.

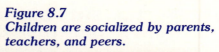
Figure 8.7
Children are socialized by parents,
teachers, and peers.

Even to the ancients, the importance of imitative learning for socialization was clear. Writing almost 2300 years ago, Aristotle suggested that man "is the most imitative of living creatures, and through imitation learns his earliest lessons." But how does this process work? To answer this question, we will look at the role of observational learning in one important area of socialization—the development of self-control and standards of excellence for oneself.

OBSERVATIONAL LEARNING AND STANDARDS OF EXCELLENCE. All of us set standards for ourselves. We decide what type of performance is good enough to be acceptable in school, at play (in sports such as golf and skiing), and in our ultimate vocational choice. But the level of standards differs greatly from one person to another, and from one activity to another even for the same person. Some students are quite satisfied when they receive a "B" or even just barely pass, whereas others are not satisfied unless they get an "A" in every course. But the student who cares relatively little about his or her grades may set high standards in other areas; such an individual may be satisfied with nothing less than perfection in athletic prowess or knowledge of pop music or dealing with other people.

How children learn to consider some areas of endeavor as highly important—requiring high standards of excellence—is a key issue in the study of socialization. Many factors are undoubtedly important, including the expectation of success or failure (Crandall, 1967) and exposure to the standards of significant others (such as parents, teachers, and older brothers and sisters).

The role of observational learning in self-imposed standards of achievement is illustrated in experiments designed to simulate conditions in which this type of self-control and self-evaluation occurs. In such studies the child first performs a task that he or she believes is one of achievement or skill. Then subjects can reward themselves according to their own satisfaction with their performance.

One approach taken has been to invite children to play a bowling game, similar to the one shown in Figure 8.8. Note that there is a panel of lights at the end of the alley; one light goes on each time the ball is rolled. From the child's perspective, it appears that the lights are controlled by ability (that is, whether the ball hits the hidden pins), but actually the game is rigged so that every child receives the same score regardless of bowling ability.

Liebert and Ora (1968 used this game in a typical study. A total of 72 boys and girls, 8 to 10 years of age, were instructed to bowl alone for 20 frames and to help themselves to token rewards from a large bowl whenever they made a score that they thought was high enough. The Control group, which received no special training or example, served as a base of comparison to see whether children tend to impose high or low standards on themselves in each new situation. Another group

Figure 8.8
The bowling game that was used in Liebert and Ora's research.

of children who were exposed to Modeling treatment observed an adult play the game and reward himself with approval and a token only when he made a score of 20—the highest score in the game. When the adult got lower scores, he not only did not reward himself but actually disparaged his accomplishment as unworthy (for example: "Fifteen—that's not a very good score; that doesn't deserve a chip"). After the adult played, he left and it was the child's turn.

The remaining condition of this experiment was called Direct Training. In this condition children were asked first to play the game while an adult watched; during this time the adult specifically instructed each child to take tokens for scores of 20, but not for lower scores. Then, as in the other conditions, the adult left the room and the child was free to play alone with complete access to the rewards.

One final aspect of the Liebert and Ora study should be mentioned. Recall that the rewards in this study were plastic tokens; their real value, of course, depends on what you can get for them. Half of the children in each of the three training groups (Modeling, Direct Training, and Control) were shown impressive prizes and told that they could exchange their tokens for one of the prizes. The investigators referred to this as the High Incentive Condition. The remaining children, in the Low Incentive Condition, believed that the tokens had no exchange value at all and merely symbolized accomplishment.

The major measure was how closely the children adhered to the highest possible standard on the game (that is, to taking rewards only for scores of 20) when playing alone. The experimenters watched the children from behind a one-way vision screen while they played and recorded how often they took rewards for scores of less than 20.[1]

The results of the Liebert and Ora study are shown in Table 8.2. In looking at it, two facts become clear immediately. First, the children apparently did *not* bring a set of high standards with them to this situation, as seen in the very self-indulgent performance of the control groups. Second, the exchange value of the tokens was significant in setting standards. When the chips were really down—in the High Incentive Condition—the children lowered their standards with respect to "good enough." Taken together, these two facts illustrate a point that has emerged in much other research: Children do not usually display uniformly high or low standards in all situations. Rather, our self-imposed standards must be learned in most new achievement situations we encounter; afterward, they tend to remain "situation-specific" and do not automatically carry over to a range of new settings.

Equally important, of course, the data in Table 8.2 indicate that self-imposed standards can readily be transmitted either through direct instruction or the appropriate example of others. Most impressively, the children adhered remarkably well to the adult's stringent standard even after he had gone; they had to forgo valuable incentives in some conditions in order to maintain a high standard of excellence.

[1] We mentioned earlier that the game was rigged so that every child would receive the same series of scores. The reason now becomes apparent: All children must get the same proportion of high and low scores in order for their self-control scores to be compared directly. Anyone who gets almost all excellent scores can "afford" to set high standards, but that may not mean very much.

TABLE 8.2

Mean number of deviations from the high standard (self-reward only for scores of 20) provided by the training agent in Liebert and Ora's (1968) experiment, showing the effects of both training and incentives upon the adoption of self-imposed standards of achievement.

Group	Control	Modeling	Direct training
Low incentive	7.42	0.92	0.08
High incentive	12.75	3.25	2.92

Source: Liebert and Ora (1968)

In the Liebert and Ora experiment, the children merely had to choose between adhering to the standard established during the training period or deviating from it (while alone and unmonitored) in order to secure additional rewards. In many life situations, however, children are often exposed to standards from more than one source (mother, father, teachers, playmates), and these standards often differ significantly. For instance, many American children are advised by their parents not to smoke or drink, even though the parents may not abstain themselves. Also, these children may be exposed to both peers and adults who smoke and drink and who encourage them to do so. In this example the socialization process encompasses discrepant behavioral alternatives and the children must somehow choose between them.

In order to examine the mechanisms behind this situation, McMains and Liebert (1968) conducted an experiment in which children were exposed to *multiple models* whose behavior varied from a stated standard. Using the same bowling game discussed earlier, fourth-grade boys and girls first played the game with an adult training agent, alternating turns with them in rolling the ball down the alley. During this training period, the adult imposed a *stringent* standard on the subject (permitting him or her to take chips only for scores of 20). For half the subjects, the training agent used the same stringent standard for himself when he played the game (*consistent training*), while for the remaining children he used a more lenient criterion for himself than for the youngsters (taking rewards for scores as low as 15 during his turns [*discrepant training*]). After this initial period, the subjects were permitted to play the game by themselves for 20 trials, with free access to rewards, and their adherence to the stringent standard was measured (Test 1). During the second phase of the experiment, another social agent (a model) also played the bowling game in the child's presence. The second agent either used the same stringent standard that the subject had been taught initially or modeled a more lenient one. Afterward, a second measure of each child's own self-imposed standards was obtained (Test 2).

The results of both of these tests are presented in Figure 8.9. It is apparent from these data that during Test 1 the subjects who had observed

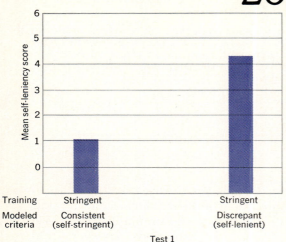

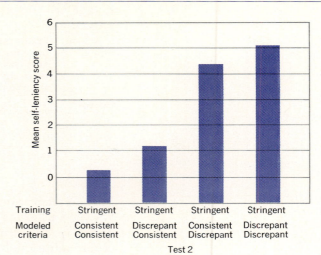

Figure 8.9
Amount of self-leniency shown in McMains and Liebert's (1968) experiment following exposure to consistent and discrepant models. All of the children had been trained to act in a self-stringent manner.

a consistent (self-stringent) training agent showed more self-control when they were alone than did those who had seen an inconsistent and self-lenient adult. From Test 2 it is also clear that the children who had been trained for a stringent standard but found that both the person who had trained them *and* a second performer deviated from this standard were least likely to adopt the standard themselves when playing alone. These children displayed, on the average, nearly five deviations (out of a total of 20 possibilities) from the stringent standard that they had been explicitly told to follow, and virtually all of them (92 percent) violated this stringent standard at least once. In marked contrast, when the children were instructed to adhere to a highly stringent standard *and* observed two adults do likewise, they adopted that high standard themselves and rarely took rewards for scores of less than 20.

Taken together, these findings suggest that an appropriate combination of direct training and modeling may help bring about the swift "internalization" of stringent standards of behavior, even when children are free to do as they please and have appealing incentives to deviate. It is also clear that severe social injunctions that are not reinforced by social example (the familiar "Do as I say, not as I do!") are not too effective in socialization when children are left to act on their own.

COMPLEX INTERPERSONAL BEHAVIOR We will now examine two additional areas of social development—sex roles and moral judgments—which are obviously affected by biological and cognitive factors as well as by socialization.

SOCIALIZATION AND SEX ROLES. A person's sex plays an extremely important role in his or her psychological and social development throughout life. Well before they start school, most children can recognize their own sexual identity and understand something of

"Ignore anything addressed to Congressperson."

(Drawing by Reilly; ©
1973 The New
Yorker Magazine, Inc.)

the concepts *male* and *female* (Kohlberg, 1966). It is also true that these impressions are value-laden from an early age. Children, and adults as well, show a preference for masculine sex roles regardless of their own sex (for example, Fortune survey, 1946; Gallup, 1955, Brown, 1967).

There are obviously many differences between the sexes, biologically as well as socially. But just how extensive are real differences between the sexes? And to what degree are these differences inherent or due to socialization practices?

In a book that has quickly become the definitive study of sex differences over a wide age span, Maccoby and Jacklin (1974) have concluded, among other things, that many presumed social differences between the sexes are actually cultural myths that have no basis in reality. Some of these myths, together with the facts as determined by research, are presented in Table 8.3. It will be noted that, contrary to common belief, females are *not* more social than males, nor do they have a lower self-esteem or achievement motivation. Perhaps, in order to justify the differential treatment of men and women, society has created these myths.

There are, however, a number of well-established (possibly culturally determined) differences between the sexes, some of which can be noted from a very early age. It has been observed, for example, that females are generally superior to males in verbal ability throughout life. A few studies (for example, Lewis and Freedle, 1972; Clarke-Stewart, 1973) have reported that female children are ahead of males

TABLE 8.3

Myths and facts about sex differences.

Myth	Facts
Girls are more "social" than boys.	*FALSE*. Research shows that girls are *not* more dependent on their caretakers than boys, nor are they more responsive to social rewards. At certain ages, boys actually spend *more* time than girls with their playmates.
Females are more "suggestible" than males.	*FALSE*. Most studies show no sex differences here, and a few have even shown that males (not females) are more likely to give in to peer group pressures that oppose their own values.
Females lack achievement motivation.	*FALSE*. Under neutral conditions, females regularly score higher than males on measures of achievement motivation. When challenged or put into a competitive situation, however, males increase their achievement motivation, but only to the level already reached by females.
Females are more affected by heredity, whereas males are more responsive to the environment.	*FALSE*. Male identical twins are actually *more* alike than female identical twins. Males are more susceptible to certain kinds of environmental stress (such as infant illness) than females, whereas females are more likely to be influenced by such positive environmental factors as educational opportunities.

Source: Maccoby and Jacklin (1974)

in verbally related skills during the first 2 years of life. The differences remain relatively small, however, until adolescence, when girls' superiority in verbal skills begins to increase (Maccoby and Jacklin, 1974). Evidence also shows that males are superior in visual-spatial ability and in dealing with mathematical and quantitative concepts. Again the real separation between the sexes begins to appear at about 12 or 13 years of age and continues into adulthood. The only other indisputable area in which males "excel" is aggressiveness; in our own society, this difference has been observed from the time children are about 2 years of age.

One might like to know whether the differences that have been observed between the sexes are biologically or socially determined. First of all, we know that most sex roles are quite malleable, and that there is a lot of overlap between males and females in all of the characteristics we have mentioned. Many women have become accomplished scientists, while men frequently excel at drama, oratory, and serious fiction—all of which require high levels of verbal ability. Even in the area of aggressiveness, often considered to be the most obvious biologically based sex difference, there have been deviations from the general pattern. Margaret Mead (1935), who reported on the life and mores of three primitive tribes, revealed that all levels of aggression can be socially acceptable for either sex.

The Arapesh, one of the tribes studied by Mead, expect both males and females to behave in ways that would be considered feminine in Western cultures; both sexes are taught to be cooperative and responsive to the needs of others. Among the Mundugumor, on the other hand, both males and females are expected to act in a way that would generally be viewed as a stereotype of masculinity in our society; both men and women are expected to be ruthless, aggressive, and emotionally unresponsive to others. The third tribe described by Mead, the Tchambuli, have sex roles that are exactly the opposite of those that prevail in Western countries. Among the Tchambuli, women are expected to be aggressive and dominant, while men are passive and emotionally dependent.

Even the intellectual differences observed between boys and girls may be due to their social training rather than their biology. In a study of black children, for example, it was found that boys tended to be *superior* to girls on measures of verbal ability (Anastasi and D'Angelo, 1952), and a study of British boys and girls also found that boys were verbally superior on four different vocabulary tests (Dunsdon and Fraser-Roberts, 1957). Because the pattern varies from one culture to another, it may be that different socialization practices are responsible, at least in part, for the sex differences observed in our own society.

None of these facts, though, should obscure the possibility that biological factors may also be important in behavioral sex differences. It has been conclusively ascertained that at birth males are typically larger, stronger, and display a better-developed musculature than females. On the other hand, females have a lower mortality rate, and are less susceptible to disease both at birth and throughout life (Hetherington, 1970). Perhaps the best summary of the interplay between biological and social factors was offered by Eleanor Maccoby, one of the foremost experts in the field:

The sex-typed attributes of personality and temperament . . . are the product of interweaving of differential social demands within certain biological determinants that help produce or augment differential cultural demands upon the two sexes. The biological underpinnings . . . set modal tendencies for cultural demands, and set limits to the range of variation of these demands from one cultural setting to another. Still within these limits considerable variation does occur between families, between cultures and in the nature of the behavior that a social group stereotypes as "feminine" or "masculine" [Maccoby, 1966, p. 50].

MORAL DEVELOPMENT. During their early years most children begin to demonstrate a set of values with respect to correct,

Figure 8.10
Many advertisements carry implicit messages that convey social values.

"appropriate," or good behavior. Where do their values come from, and how could they best be described? These are major issues in the field of moral development.

There is limited evidence that a child's moral judgment and behavior are learned, through both reinforcement and the examples modeled by parents, peers, and teachers (Bandura and McDonald, 1963; Le Furgy and Wolosin, 1969). Nonetheless, it is also clear that moral development somewhat parallels the course of cognitive development, which was described in Chapter 7. The developmental theorist who has articulated this view most clearly is Lawrence Kohlberg. The child, says Kohlberg, must be viewed as a "moral philosopher" whose philosophy emerges over time due to the interaction of social experiences and the child's own changing cognitive capacities.

But how can one determine, at any given time, precisely what moral philosophy a child is using? Kohlberg answers this question by presenting children from about 5 years of age on up with hypothetical moral dilemmas, to which they must give answers. Here is one of the dilemmas:

In Europe, a woman was near death from cancer. One drug might save her, a form of radium that a druggist in the same town had recently discovered. The druggist was charging $2,000, ten times what the drug cost him to make. The sick woman's husband, Heinz, went to everyone he knew to borrow the money, but he could only get together about half of what it cost. He told the druggist that his wife was dying and asked him to sell it cheaper or let him pay later. But the druggist said, "No." The husband got desperate and broke into the man's store to steal the drug for his wife. Should the husband have done that? Why? [Kohlberg, 1969, p. 379].

By analyzing children's responses to moral dilemmas such as this one, Kohlberg has distinguished three levels of moral thinking: *preconventional, conventional,* and *postconventional.*

Preconventional children can only think about such labels as "good" and "bad." They interpret these words simply in terms of the physical consequences they may experience, such as punishment, reward, and the exchange of favors; these children show no true standard of morality—they simply accept whatever standards appear to be held by the strong and the powerful.

At the conventional level the child has a basic standard; morality consists of being "nice," of conforming, and of maintaining the social order. According to Kohlberg, most American adults function at this level. Beyond this standard is the postconventional level of morality, which is governed by principles that are said to be universal and valid regardless of how much others conform to them. A basic respect for the rights of others, as typified in the Golden Rule, characterizes this more advanced level of moral development. These stages are presented in Table 8.4, in terms of the responses of children and adults to the hypothetical moral dilemma given on page 265. It is important to note that the stages are *not* differentiated by the decision made, but rather by the type of moral reasoning behind the decision. Thus, persons at both the preconventional and postconventional levels of morality can decide that Heinz either should or should not steal the drug.

The Universal Course of Moral Development. In an extensive series of studies, Kohlberg has found that moral development takes the same course among many cultures and ethnic groups. His studies of children in Mexico, Malaya, Taiwan, and Turkey all show the same progression of stages and the same basic reasons given at each stage for making certain moral decisions. Equally important, Kohlberg finds that the same sequence of stages holds true among Catholics, Protestants, Jews, Buddhists, Moslems, and atheists. He concludes that moral development is one aspect of social development that largely depends upon human nature; the environment can stimulate or impede the natural course of this development, but socialization practices alone cannot fully account for this aspect of social development.

Examples of the type of moral reasoning given by people at different levels of moral development.

PRECONVENTIONAL LEVEL
Less advanced

Action is motivated by avoidance of punishment, and "conscience" is an irrational fear of punishment.

Pro: If you let your wife die, you will get into trouble. You'll be blamed for not spending the money to save her, and there'll be an investigation of you and the druggist for your wife's death.

Con: You shouldn't steal the drug because you'll be caught and sent to jail if you do. If you are not caught, your conscience would trouble you with thoughts of how the police might catch up with you at any minute.

CONVENTIONAL LEVEL
Less advanced

Action motivated by anticipation of disapproval of others, actual or imagined-hypothetical (for example, guilt). (Differentiation of disapproval from punishment, fear, and pain.)

Pro: No one will think you're bad if you steal the drug, but your family will think you're an inhuman husband if you don't. If you let your wife die, you'll never be able to look anybody in the face again.

Con: It isn't just the druggist who will think you're a criminal; everyone else will, too. After you steal it, you'll feel bad thinking how you've brought dishonor on your family and yourself; you won't be able to face anyone again.

POSTCONVENTIONAL
Less advanced

Concern about maintaining respect of equals and of the community (assuming their respect is based on reason rather than emotions). Concern about own self-respect, that is, to avoid judging self as irrational, inconsistent, nonpurposive. (Discriminates between institutionalized blame and community disrespect or self-disrespect.)

Pro: You'd lose other people's respect, not gain it, if you don't steal. If you let your wife die, it would be out of fear, not out of reasoning it out. So you'd just lose self-respect and probably the respect of others, too.

Con: You would lose your standing and respect in the community and violate the law. You'd lose respect for yourself if you're carried away by emotion and forget the long-range point of view.

TABLE 8.4

Examples of the type of moral reasoning given by people at different levels of moral development.

PRECONVENTIONAL LEVEL
  More advanced

Action motivated by a desire for reward or benefit. Possible guilt reactions are ignored and punishment is viewed in a pragmatic manner. (Differentiates own fear, pleasure, or pain from punishment-consequences.)

Pro: If you do happen to get caught, you could give the drug back and you wouldn't get much of a sentence. It wouldn't bother you much to serve a short jail term if you have your wife alive when you get out.

Con: He may not get much of a jail term if he steals the drug, but his wife will probably die before he gets out so it won't do him much good. If his wife dies, he shouldn't blame himself; it isn't his fault that she has cancer.

CONVENTIONAL LEVEL
  More advanced

Action motivated by anticipation of dishonor, that is, institutionalized blame for failure of duty, and by guilt over concrete harm done to others. (Differentiates formal dishonor from informal disapproval. Differentiates guilt for bad consequences from disapproval.)

Pro: If you have any sense of honor, you won't let your wife die because you're afraid to do the only thing that will save her. You'll always feel guilty that you caused her death if you don't do your duty to her.

Con: You're desperate and you may not know you're doing wrong when you steal the drug. But you'll know you did wrong after you're punished and sent to jail. You'll always feel guilt for your dishonesty and lawbreaking.

POSTCONVENTIONAL
  More advanced

Concern about self-condemnation for violating one's own principles. (Differentiates between community respect and self-respect. Differentiates between self-respect for generally achieving rationality and self-respect for maintaining moral principles.)

Pro: If you don't steal the drug and let your wife die, you'd always condemn yourself for it afterward. You wouldn't be blamed and you would have lived up to the outside rule of the law but you wouldn't have lived up to your own standards of conscience.

Con: If you stole the drug, you wouldn't be blamed by other people but you'd condemn yourself because you wouldn't have lived up to your own conscience and standards of honesty.

Source: Adapted from Rest (1968)

PSYCHOLOGY AND THE PROBLEMS OF SOCIETY
TELEVISION AND CHILDREN

A child's varying emotional reactions are captured on a split-screen recording while she actually watches television alone.

A virtually unknown luxury in 1946, a television set can be found today in about 98 percent of all American homes—in more homes than have adequate heat or indoor plumbing. Its influence on American life is quite extensive; one survey found that 60 percent of the families interviewed have changed their eating habits because of TV and 55 percent have altered their mealtimes (Liebert, Neale, and Davidson, 1973).

Perhaps television's most faithful (and vulnerable) viewers are children who, still inexperienced in the ways of the world, look through this "early window" to learn about society and the behavior of others. Indeed, television captures the attention of preschool and elementary-school children for an average of 3 hours per day, 7 days a week. By age 16, most children will have spent more time watching TV than attending school (Liebert and Poulos, 1975). Given the premise that television could serve as a source of observational learning, an important question arises: What are the socializing effects of television viewing on children? We will examine two important areas—aggression and prosocial behavior.

Perhaps the most convincing evidence for a relationship between watching violence on television and later aggressive behavior comes from a longitudinal field study conducted by Lefkowitz and his colleagues. In the late 1950s, they collected data on both the aggressive behavior and television viewing habits of 875 third-grade children. When the two measures were correlated, it was found that boys who watched a large number of violent programs were more likely than their peers to have a high aggression rating, although this relationship did not hold for girls (Eron, 1963). Ten years later, when the subjects were 19 years old, measures of aggressiveness and watching violent programs on TV were obtained for about half the original sample. The relationship between the amount of violence watched on TV in the third grade and aggression 10 years later was again statistically significant for males (that is, the more violence watched in third grade, the more aggression at age 19), apparently showing that these boys' viewing of TV violence *caused* their later aggressive behavior (Liebert, Neale, and Davidson, 1973).

One problem with correlational field studies is that in typical life situations there are so many influences at work that it is difficult to be sure what variables are responsible for the behavior that is being studied, unless one follows many children over time, as Lefkowitz and his associates (1972) did. But, in laboratory research, investigators can hold constant or control all the variables except those under study. Sprafkin, Liebert, and Poulos (1975) chose to take this approach in studying the effect of a popular children's TV program on a prosocial behavior—helping.

Three groups of children were exposed to different programs; one group saw an episode from "Lassie" in which the main character, a boy named Jeff, was hanging in a dangerous manner over a mine shaft in order to save a puppy. A second group saw an episode from "Lassie" without an altruistic plot, and a third group—controlling for nonspecific factors in the "Lassie" programs—saw an episode from "The Brady Bunch." After seeing the TV episode, the children were presented with a test situation, in which they were allowed to choose between playing a game in which they could earn prizes or helping puppies. The researchers had hypothesized that the children who had seen the helping episode would be more likely to choose to help the puppies than the other two groups; this is precisely what happened.

Given the evidence, then, that TV can significantly affect children's behavior in both socially positive and negative ways, what steps might be taken to improve children's television programs? One possible approach is suggested by the work of Liebert and Poulos (1975). Drawing upon the research of others, they designed some television "spots" (30 seconds in length) depicting interpersonal conflict that could—but does not—lead to aggression or violence. Instead, by cooperation, a solution that is satisfactory to all is worked out.

One such spot, "The Swing," was first aired on network television in May 1974. A boy and girl run toward a swing and begin to argue over who shall go first. After a period of struggle and seemingly inevitable conflict, one child suggests that they take turns and lets the other go first. The episode ends with each taking a turn, merrily pushed by the other. Laboratory tests demonstrated that children in the second and fourth grades both understood and accepted the message as evidenced by their later behavior on a task in which two children could earn prizes by cooperating together.

After reviewing the impact of television on children, Liebert and Poulos closed by saying:

One thing though is clear. This entertainment medium is having a substantial impact on children. The impact is present whether it is planned and understood or unplanned and overlooked. To us it seems clear which of these is the better path [p. 91].

SUMMARY

The process through which children acquire appropriate patterns of social behavior (such as dealing with aggressive impulses or establishing performance standards for themselves) is called socialization. Socialization begins in infancy when the first emotional relationships are developed; these early relationships appear to be critical for later social development. Experimental studies have shown that without physical contact and emotional warmth during the first year of life, young rhesus monkeys were overwhelmingly frightened when exposed to normal peers, and many were never capable of normal social interaction.

Reinforcement (that is, instrumental learning) is one of the major socialization processes; experimentally, it has been used to teach peer cooperation and interaction, aggression, work-study habits, and toilet training. Social rewards can be used to discourage excessive dependency on adults and to develop appropriate peer interaction. Reinforcement can also be used to shape less desirable or socially valued behaviors. Children who were rewarded for aggressive play with toys were then more likely than other youngsters to aggress against other children overtly.

Punishment, the opposite of positive reinforcement, is used by virtually all parents to socialize their children, especially to deter undesirable behavior. Because punishment serves primarily to suppress unwanted behavior, it is most effective when it is used in conjunction with rewards for desirable behavior. To be most effective, punishment should be appropriately timed; it should be administered as close to the beginning of an undesirable act as possible. If this cannot be done, punishment can be partly effective if the transgression is somehow reinstated before punishing the child at a later time. Punishment is also more effective if the parent administering it has been warm and rewarding in the past, if it is used consistently, and if the parents themselves practice what they preach.

Observational learning is also important in socialization. Studies have shown, for example, that self-imposed standards can be transmitted through either direct instruction or exposure to the example of others. Children are least likely to follow a stringent example when alone if they have seen a model adopt more lenient standards than he or she imposes upon the youngster. On the other hand, exposure to two or more adults who consistently preach *and* practice high standards is remarkably potent in motivating children to adopt and maintain those same standards for themselves even when they are alone and facing strong temptations.

Together with obvious biological factors, socialization is important in determining sex-role behavior. Margaret Mead's study of three primitive cultures revealed different sex roles in each one. In one culture both males and females behaved in a way that would be considered feminine in most Western societies; in another, both behaved in a masculine way; and in the third, sex roles with respect to aggression and dominance were exactly the opposite of those in our own culture. Many presumed social differences between the sexes have been demonstrated to be cultural myths. Contrary to common belief, girls are not more social than boys, nor do they have lower self-esteem or achievement motivation. Nevertheless, there are some well-established differences between the sexes that can be observed at a very early age. Among white children in the U.S., females tend to be superior to males in verbal ability, whereas males tend to be superior in dealing with visual-spatial and mathematical concepts. But these differences are not found in all cultures, suggesting that socialization practices rather than biology may account for many of these differences.

Moral development appears to be learned in part through reinforcement and examples modeled by parents and teachers, but moral development also parallels the course of cognitive development. Kohlberg distinguishes three levels of moral development—preconventional, conventional, and postconventional—depending upon an individual's reasoning in solving moral dilemmas. Kohlberg has argued that these stages of moral development apply in many cultures and among persons of various ethnic and religious backgrounds, suggesting that socialization practices alone cannot fully account for moral development.

[1]Many of the terms used in this chapter (for example, *Reinforcement*) were presented in the Glossary at the end of Chapter 4.

GLOSSARY[1]

Conventional level of moral development: The level of moral development, according to Kohlberg, that is held by most adults. The emphasis is on being "nice" and on conforming to and maintaining the existing social order.

Internalization: The acceptance of and adherence to specified standards of performance whether or not others are present.

Multiple models: Two or more exemplars who perform in the same situation (either simultaneously or successively) in the presence of the same observer.

Preconventional level of moral development: The lowest level of moral development distinguished by Kohlberg; at this level, the child shows no true standard of morality except to go along with whatever standards are held by the strong and the powerful. He or she interprets the words "good" and "bad" simply in terms of their physical consequences.

Postconventional level of moral development: The most advanced level of moral development distinguished by Kohlberg. Persons at this level believe that certain moral principles are universal and valid regardless of the degree to which others conform to them.

Resistance to temptation: A form of socially acquired self-control; it manifests itself whenever a child is left alone and has the opportunity to behave in a socially prohibited way (for example, cheating on a test) that will provide a reward (for example, a better grade in school) but does not do so.

Socialization: The process(es) through which children learn appropriate patterns of social behavior, such as dealing with aggressive impulses or establishing performance standards for themselves.

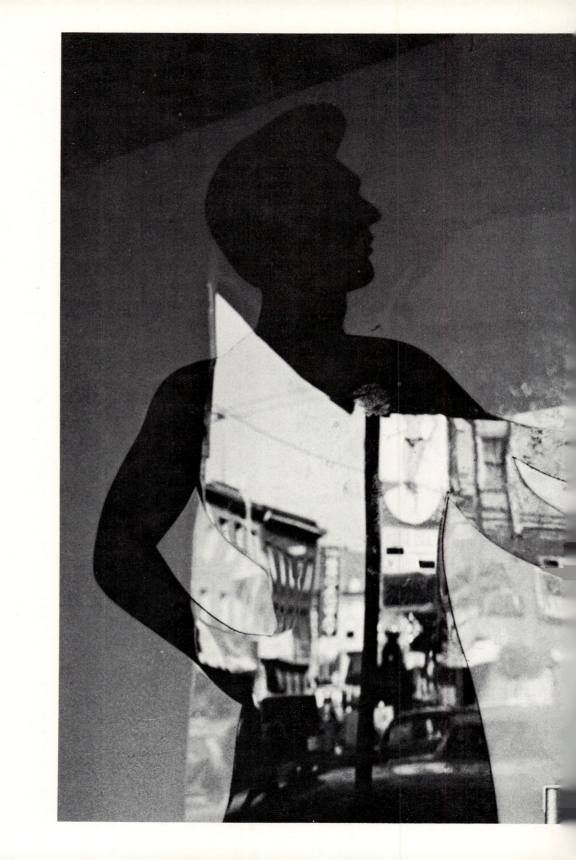

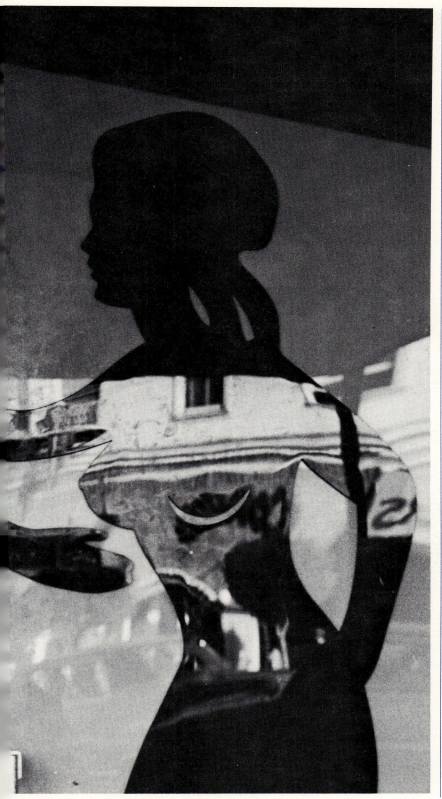

NINE

SOCIAL BEHAVIOR

Perhaps more than other living creatures, humans spend most of their waking lives in social interaction (talking, fighting, making love, and so forth); therefore, to have a more thorough understanding of psychology, it is important to know how people interact. Social psychology is that branch of psychology that deals with people as social beings; the social psychologist studies both the private psychological experiences that influence how we behave with others (why we are attracted toward certain people, why we cooperate with certain individuals or aggress against them), as well as the ways in which people—both individually and in groups—*change* their behavior as a result of the social context in which they act.

During the past decade social psychologists have studied (among other things) aggression, altruism, attraction and liking, and obedience to authority. Before discussing these topics, let us turn our attention to an important process that has long interested all social psychologists—the formation and change of attitudes.

ATTITUDES   We meet new people almost every day, and typically we respond to each new person in distinctive ways. Our responses may depend upon the other person's skin color, ethnic origin, membership in a political or social group, or even the person's name. In all of these cases, our reaction depends upon our *attitude* toward the other person's characteristics; these attitudes, in turn, have been formed by our previous experience in dealing with people who have the same characteristics we see in our new acquaintance. Because of the importance of attitudes, both positive and negative, in human interaction, social psychologists have been especially interested in how attitudes are formed and maintained.

An attitude is a relatively enduring disposition toward any characteristic of a person, place, or thing. Defined this way, all attitudes are in part *beliefs;* they reflect information we actually have (or believe we have) about those characteristics we find in the people and things around us. But an attitude is more than a belief; most attitudes also have an emotional (or *affective*) component. For example, one's attitude toward a particular nationality group might include the belief that members of that group are friendly, convivial, and outgoing. But probably one's attitude also includes a feeling or emotional reaction about the characteristic itself; those who feel that friendliness and an outgoing, easy disposition are highly desirable will undoubtedly have a positive attitude toward people who have these characteristics. The same belief, however, may be accompanied by a negative attitude. One could feel, for example, that being outgoing and friendly means being overly forward, and that it is better to be somewhat reserved. In this case, holding the identical belief (that people of a particular nationality are extroverted), a second person may have a negative attitude toward the same group. Social psychologists have found that how we *feel* about things (the affective component) is at least as important as what we know about them.

HOW ARE ATTITUDES FORMED?   It has been said that "people like what they know more than they know what they like." In the area of attitude formation, this point is well-taken. Mere familiarity with a person, group, or thing generally leads to a positive attitude, while unfamiliarity seems to foster a negative attitude. In one study (Zajonc, 1968), it was found that people had a negative attitude

Figure 9.1
Attitudes begin to be formed at a very early age.

toward "Wallonians," although this was a fictitious group. On the other hand, direct contact is so significant that repeated exposure to nonsense syllables will increase their attractiveness (Zajonc, 1968). Conditioning processes may also influence our attitudes; individuals, groups, and national names that are associated with positive outcomes or experiences tend to be liked and valued, whereas association with negative outcomes and events can quickly turn neutral feelings into negative ones.

Indirect Contact. Relatively few attitudes are acquired entirely or even primarily from direct contact. Instead, they are transmitted more indirectly through a variety of social experiences. The skillful advertiser, for example, tries to create a favorable attitude toward a new product even before it is available on the market where it can be evaluated directly by potential customers. Promotional schemes, appearing on television and in popular magazines, place the new product in a highly favorable light, familiarize prospective customers with its name, and suggest advantages of both ownership and use that will make the new product seem as desirable as possible. All of these indirect experiences increase the chances that the given commodity will seem familiar and be appealing from the very outset.

Children also experience their first contacts with political groups, ethnic minorities, education, and attitudes toward wealth and social success indirectly by means of the remarks and emotional reactions of their parents, peers, and sometimes teachers. These indirect contacts are supplemented by the entertainment media, which provide many of our first glimpses of unfamiliar people, places, and kinds of events (Liebert, Neale, and Davidson, 1973).

ATTITUDE CHANGE   We are less often called upon to form brand-name attitudes than to change those we already have. Theories of attitude change are designed to reveal something about our complex array of attitudes and to help us understand how attitudes may be changed, either purposely or unwittingly, by social experience and new information.

CONSISTENCY AND DISSONANCE. In order to understand how attitudes change, it is probably necessary to have some idea of how they are organized as well as how they are initially formed. Although the specific way in which attitudes are organized is complex, and psychologists still have a great deal to learn about it, one fairly basic idea has been well established: People require consistency among their attitudes and also between their attitudes and their actions. When people find that they hold two attitudes that are *not* consistent with one another, they will probably try to do something about it. Using one of the theories of consistency, we can begin to learn one way in which attitudes can be changed and thus get an idea of some of the techniques for actually doing so.

278

Although there are many consistency theories, we will limit our discussion to the most prominent of these—the theory of *cognitive dissonance*, first advanced by Leon Festinger in 1957. The basic question he asked was: What happens when we observe that two or more of our attitudes are inconsistent? Using his own term "dissonance," Festinger (1957) advanced the following two propositions:

1. The presence of inconsistency (or dissonance) is psychologically uncomfortable, and so the experience of dissonance will motivate a people to alter their attitudes in some way so that become consistent (or consonant).
2. In addition to attempts to reduce one's dissonance, a person will also tend to avoid situations and information that are likely either to increase dissonance or emphasize that it is present.

There are many ways to reduce dissonance, some of which will bring about attitude changes. One of the most obvious ways is to "spread the alternatives" after having selected one thing and rejected another. Suppose, for example, that you are a prospective car buyer. You have carefully examined all of the cars that you might buy and are trying to decide which one best meets your needs. Probably you will eventually find yourself in a situation where you have narrowed your choices down to two cars. Undoubtedly these two seem to meet your needs most perfectly, or seem the most attractive to you, or seem to be the most durable. Indeed, it is possible that on all dimensions, each car appears to strike a reasonable balance among your needs, and you decide that you like them equally well. Then you take the plunge and select one or the other.

At this point psychological dissonance appears. You are faced with the fact that the "rejected alternative" had many good features and was virtually as good as the one you finally chose. Your knowledge of the various advantages of the rejected alternative now tend to be dissonant with the fact that you *have* rejected it. The situation is uncomfortable. In short, you have to convince yourself that you did the right thing. How can you do this? You can reduce your dissonance by separating in your mind the degree of difference and attractiveness between the accepted and now rejected alternatives. In doing so, you will have changed your attitude toward one or even both cars.

A specific example of this process is shown in the following experiment: Brehm (1956) recruited college undergraduate women for what they believed would be a market research study. At the outset each woman was told that she would receive a gift from the manufacturers—one of eight products that were available. The goods themselves, ranging in retail value from $15 to $30 (including such items as an automatic coffee maker, a desk lamp, a portable radio, and a stop watch), were then examined by each subject. As she inspected each product, she was asked to rate it on an eight-point scale that ranged from "definitely not at all desirable" to "extremely desirable." After the rating was completed, the subject was told that she could choose her own gift from two alternatives that would be provided by the experimenter. At this point one group of subjects was asked to choose between a product they had found very attractive (based on their own ratings) and an item that they had found far less attractive; the other group was asked to choose between two highly attractive items. Thus, dissonance theory could be tested directly. If the women who had chosen between equally attractive products now had some dissonance to reduce, they should, on a subsequent rating, both overvalue the product they had chosen and devalue the one they had rejected. In contrast, those who had chosen between a highly attractive and an unattractive product in the first place should have little dissonance to reduce and therefore should not markedly alter their evaluation of either of the two products.

To see if this was actually the case, Brehm asked each subject, after she had made her choice, to read advertising and product reports on each of the eight commodities and then rate all of them again. At that point, the critical issue could be determined: Did the groups differ in the amount of change in their ratings of the products? The results were quite clear. As seen in Figure 9.2, those who chose between two attractive products later did overvalue the one they had selected and devalue the one they had rejected. In sharp contrast, there was virtually no change from the first rating to the second rating among those women who had experienced no dissonance in the first place, and had chosen between an obviously more attractive and an obviously less attractive commodity.

Other Techniques of Dissonance Reduction. Besides "spreading the alternatives," another technique that most of us use from time to time to reduce discomfort is *selective exposure*, which makes use of our ability to pay attention only to what we want to hear or see. When you are confronted with an advertisement praising a product you have not bought, a newspaper or magazine article challenging a decision you have already made, or a testimonial for a rival you despise, you can either attend to the message or not. You can thus selectively expose yourself only to information that is consistent with your present attitudes and avoid dissonant information by installing psychological blinders on your contacts with the world. An excellent example of this is provided by a group of Japanese Americans who, during World War II, asked the U.S. government if they could be repatriated to Japan when the war was over. Their repatriation decision was based upon their conviction that Japan would win the war, and once it was made it had to be defended against dissonant messages. Those who asked for repatriation later avoided much of the information on the radio and in news stories about various Japanese defeats before the close of the war; they also dismissed as American progaganda reports (and even photographs!) pertaining to the Japanese surrender. They even clung to their belief that Japan had won the war during their trip

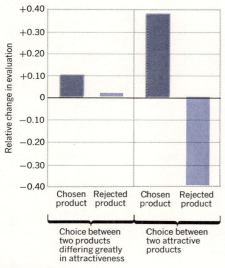

Figure 9.2
Change in attitude after making a choice between two products that are about equally attractive or two products that differ greatly in attractiveness. [*Source: After Brehm (1956)*]

back to Japan and they gave it up only when they were confronted directly with the destruction of portions of their homeland and the hard fact of American occupation.

Another means of reducing dissonance is through social support; it has been well illustrated in an important field study. Festinger, Reicken, and Schachter (1956) studied the origin, development, and eventual failure of a group of people who believed they were receiving messages from extraterrestial beings—"the Guardians"—about the destruction of the world. At the beginning, a few faithful individuals actively spread the word about their beliefs, emphasizing their essential conviction that the world would soon end. However, as soon as a group of deeply committed believers had been formed, all of their efforts to convert others ceased and new members were actually discouraged. For example, when the group accidentally received national attention (because one of their members had been dismissed from his academic post at a university as a result of his beliefs), the group went to extraordinary lengths to remove itself from public notice and become as secret as possible. The members did not doubt their own beliefs; rather, they impoverished themselves or made other irrevocable commitments to support their conviction.

The group was persuaded that a flying saucer would come to save them just before the world was destroyed by a catastrophic flood. Eventually the appointed hour arrived. Alas, there was no flood, no flying saucer, and no rescue. At this point, some group members gave up their belief and returned home, but others reduced their dissonance in a different way. They decided that the world had indeed been saved—as a result of their own great faith. And their rationalizing did not end there; remarkably, they now launched a massive drive to win converts. Abandoning entirely their former policy of disclosing nothing to newspapermen and representatives of the other media, the group now tried desperately to publicize their message throughout the nation and even the world. Social support is an effective way to reduce dissonance, but it's hard to obtain when you are in a tenuous situation.

EXTERNAL FACTORS THAT AFFECT ATTITUDE CHANGE. Besides the internal reasons for changing one's attitude, there are also the external reasons. We will briefly examine two of the most important of these—the communicator and the message (Hovland, Janis, and Kelly, 1953).

The Source of a Persuasive Communication. An extremely important factor in the successful (or unsuccessful) effort to change a person's attitudes is the source of the communication. This fact itself is not surprising, but the extent of the influence might well be underestimated without the use of formal experiments. A classic experiment was performed by Hovland and Weiss in 1949 and 1950, and reported in 1951. The basic design of the research was straightforward. The

TESTING YOUR UNDERSTANDING
INCENTIVE AND DISSONANCE

In a classic experiment, Festinger and Carlsmith (1959) asked undergraduate students individually to perform a very boring task for approximately two hours. Then it was explained to each subject that the person who was supposed to describe the task to the next subject had failed to show up; the subject himself was asked whether he would serve in this role, and he was offered either $1.00 or $20.00 for doing so. Although the subject was told that he was free to accept or decline, the experimental situation was such that he would have found it very difficult to refuse. The great majority of subjects therefore complied with this request, regardless of the size of the payment and, as requested, proceeded to lie to the next person by saying that the task was interesting and fun. Next, apparently as a part of the regular experiment, all of the cooperating subjects were asked to indicate how much they actually enjoyed the boring tasks that they themselves had performed somewhat earlier. One might guess, at least initially, that either there would be no differences between the two groups or that those who had been paid $20.00 would view the task as somewhat more enjoyable, inasmuch as they had at least received substantial payment for their total experience. Yet exactly the opposite occurred: Those who received only $1.00 described the boring task as significantly *more* interesting than those who had been paid $20.00 for explaining it to another person. What was the reason for this?

Dissonance theory suggests that everyone initially found the task boring, but that those who had been paid $20.00 for lying to another subject had little reason to "justify" their lies to themselves. It was as if they were saying: "I know why I lied; I did it for the money." On the other hand, those in the $1.00 condition did not have such an obvious reason for lying. According to Festinger and Carlsmith, these people experienced dissonance which could only be reduced by persuading themselves that the task really was *enjoyable,* and thus their attitudes changed.

opinions of the participants (Yale undergraduates) were first obtained on a contemporary issue. Then, about a week later, the students were exposed to persuasive communications (either for or against the issue) from sources that were presumably either highly trustworthy and credible or not too trustworthy or credible. The students were actually exposed to the identical information, regardless of what they were told about the source, so that it was what they believed about the source and not the language of the communication that mattered. Later on, additional measures of each subject's attitudes toward the issue were obtained. The investigators then tried to determine whether the amount of change (in the direction suggested by the persuasive communication) varied as a result of the source.

One of the contemporary issues used in the Hovland and Weiss study was: "Can a practicable atomic-powered submarine be built at the present time [that is, 1949–1950]?" Having recorded their opinions about this matter earlier, the students were introduced to a special guest lecturer in their class who happened to be interested in the role of newspaper and magazine articles as instruments of communication. This lecturer gave the students copies of articles that were attributed either to the renowned and then-popular American physicist, Dr. J. Robert Oppenheimer, or to the Soviet newspaper *Pravda*. Half of the students who received the *Pravda* article and half who received the Oppenheimer article read that the development of such a submarine was possible immediately, while the other half in each group read that it was not. Independently, the investigators had been able to establish that the overwhelming majority of the students felt that Dr. Oppenheimer's opinions were highly trustworthy, whereas *Pravda's* were not. But—and this is the essential point—the actual information received by the students was identical down to the last word for both groups.

Shortly after they had read these articles, the students were queried again about their attitudes. The investigators wanted to know: What percentage of change in the direction desired by the communication was due to a high credibility source and what percentage was due to a low credibility source? The results were striking. A net change of almost 36 percent in the direction of the persuasive communication was found when the source was credible (Dr. Oppenheimer), but there was a net change of less than 1 percent when the source was viewed as untrustworthy (*Pravda*).

These findings appear to suggest that a persuasive communication, even if its argument is plausible and its facts are sound, will probably be rejected it if does not come from a trustworthy source. But, as Hovland and Weiss discovered, this conclusion is premature. Specifically, the investigators completed their experiment by asking all of the students for their opinions a third time—4 weeks after they had received the persuasive communication from either Dr. Oppenheimer or *Pravda*. The results are shown in Figure 9.3. With the passage of time, the high credibility source had lost some of its impact while the low credibility source had made impressive gains. After a time, both communications seem to have been moderately effective and the source credibility, which had been so important before, was no longer significant.

What do these findings mean? At one level they show rather clearly that if you want to urge people to take immediate action, the source of the communication may be very important. On the other hand, there is a tendency, sometimes referred to as the "sleeper effect," to dissociate a message from its source over the course of time. Since the source matters less as time goes by, more attention should be paid to the content of a message that is meant to have a lasting influence.

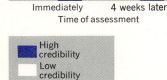

Figure 9.3
The results of Hovland and Weiss's study on communicator credibility and attitude change; although the initial impact of differences in communicator credibility was substantial, this influence declined over time.

The Message. Although using an untrustworthy source may guarantee that a message will not be accepted initially, using a trustworthy source provides absolutely no assurance of a favorable attitude change. Some messages are simply more effective than others, and investigators have sought to learn why this is so. In presenting an opinion, it has been asked whether both sides of the argument should be given or only one? Research seems to suggest that if you are communicating with people whose general views are the same as yours at the outset, there is no advantage (and may even be some disadvantage) in presenting both sides of the argument. On the other hand, if an audience is relatively hostile at the outset and probably holds views that are inconsistent with yours, then it would be wise to present both sides of the argument in order to try to persuade your listeners in the direction of your own beliefs (Hovland, Lumsdaine, and Sheffield, 1949). One is reminded of Shakespeare's Mark Antony who, when he was faced with a hostile crowd, began by indicating the many good reasons why Caesar should be assassinated, but finally concluded that it was an inappropriate and reprehensible act. Had he first announced that he had come to praise Caesar rather than to bury him, Antony himself probably never would have survived the oratory.

For centuries it had been believed that the best way to change a person's attitudes (and possibly behavior as well) was to provide persuasive arguments to that effect, as well as to enumerate the dangers of acting inappropriately (thereby also rousing fears). Although this technique is widely used, research evidence suggests that it is probably not nearly so effective as had been imagined. Leventhal, Watts, and Pagano (1967) conducted a study of attempts made to motivate cigarette smokers to reduce their smoking by exposing them to a persuasive communication that tried to provoke much fear or to one that tried to provoke very little fear. In both cases the persuasive communication was in the form of a film, but the films differed substantially. The film for the high-fear group showed a heavy smoker who had to gasp for breath after only the mildest of exercise, and then it showed an actual lung cancer operation. The latter part of the film was so frightening that many viewers chose to leave the room before the film was over. The film for the moderate-fear group showed only the breathlessness that results when a heavy smoker engages in mild physical exercise. A third group of smokers—the typical control group—did not see a film. Superficially at least, the high-fear film was more effective than either the moderate-fear film or no film at all; those viewers tended to have more negative emotions, greater feelings of vulnerability, and more of a desire to quit smoking immediately. However, despite these differences, the long-range results showed that the high-fear group did not actually reduce its smoking as much as the moderate-fear group. According to the investigators:

An increase in fear produced by relatively factual depiction of the dangers of smoking (the moderate-fear communication) had a long-range positive effect on compliance, but little effect on immediate intentions to comply, whereas a further increase in fear produced by the shock tactics of the high-fear film exerted an immediate effect on intentions to comply, but had no long-range effect on behavior [1967, p. 319].

Essentially the same findings had been reported in an earlier study by Janis and Feshbach (1953), in which people were shown different versions of a film urging them to use proper dental hygiene in order to avoid tooth decay. Although undoubtedly there are circumstances in which fear can make a positive contribution to a persuasive communication, it is interesting that too much fear can sometimes thwart the intended message.

It is often assumed that information that is given to people "on purpose" will be better received and more persuasive than information that they pick up incidentally. Research has shown, however, that this may not be the case. Allyn and Festinger (1961) found that a message that was not previously identified as intended to change attitudes was actually *more effective in doing so* than a message that was obviously intended to be influential. Several years later a study by Freedman and Sears (1965) again showed the same thing, together with the important fact that if a person is somewhat distracted while he or she is exposed to a persuasive message, the message's effectiveness will be increased.

ATTRACTION   Among all the areas of research done by social psychologists, the one that often arouses the greatest interest is liking and attraction. Why do we like certain people but not others? When will another person like us? Is there an ideal degree of similarity between friends? What personal characteristics bring people together in courtship, love, and marriage, and what attributes contribute to a successful and lasting relationship? Extensive psychological research during the past decade has provided partial answers to these questions.

RECIPROCITY.   One simple theory of interpersonal attraction seems to be widely held, even by young children. If you want people to like you, the best thing to do is to let them know that you like them. Does this always work? Let us look at the research.

There *is* a great deal of evidence suggesting that the "reciprocity-of-liking rule," as it is sometimes called, definitely holds true in many human situations. In an early experiment, for example, Backman and Secord (1959) brought together groups of strangers for an informal discussion. However, before the groups met for the first time, each subject was told that everyone in his group had taken a personality test and that the results showed which persons in his group would be inclined to like him very much. The groups then met once, and the subjects were informed that the groups might be broken up into yet smaller units—in fact, into two-person teams. Therefore, each participant was asked to indicate from a list of those in his group the person whom he would like to have as his partner. As might be expected from the reciprocity-of-liking rule, the subjects tended to select as partners those whom they believed were inclined to like them. Thus the principle was supported. But a caveat is also in order. When the same procedure was followed with groups that had met several times, the reciprocity effect was considerably reduced. In this case, it seems, the subjects were able to make more realistic assessments according to the facts at hand, and thus the simple piece of information "he probably likes you very much" was not sufficient.

WHEN RECIPROCITY FAILS. Another reason why telling people that you like them may not lead to reciprocation is "ingratiation." This term, whether used by laymen or psychologists, refers to a situation in which you give someone esteem with the expectation that you will eventually receive some benefit in return. As Ellen Berschield and Elaine Walster (1969), two noted social psychologists, have observed: "When an expression of esteem is labeled—correctly or not—by the recipient as ingratiation, the probability that esteem will be given in return is reduced drastically" (1969, pp. 60–62).

When is someone likely to interpret an expression of esteem as being ingratiating? It is not always easy to tell, but one thing seems certain: If the reason you give for claiming to like someone is based on characteristics that the person obviously does not have (telling an ugly person that he is physically attractive, telling a clumsy person that he is dexterous, or telling someone who has blundered rather badly that she is doing well), the person will probably reject your professed fondness for him as simply an attempt at ingratiation. It has also been suggested, with somewhat less evidence, that if your liking of another person is based on a characteristic she is *sure* she has (for example, telling a very beautiful woman that she is beautiful), you may also fail to be liked in return. Instead, the most effective approach is to tell other people that you like them because of characteristics they wish, hope, or feel they may have—an area where they are actually experiencing a degree of uncertainty that you can help to reduce.

Do Opposites Attract? We are often told that it is desirable to have friends, acquaintances, and lovers who share our values, feelings, and interests. Marrying someone who is very athletic if you are inclined to be "bookish," marrying someone from a very different social background than yourself, or selecting friends who have easygoing dispositions while you tend to be tense and anxious are all believed to be relationships that will not last very long. On the other hand, it might be rather boring to have only friends and acquaintances who are just like ourselves; perhaps it might be preferable to associate with people whose characteristics complement our own. Astrologers often advise people who have about the same birth signs not to marry, and even if

286

Figure 9.4
Interpersonal attraction is based on such factors as physical characteristics, reciprocity, and similar backgrounds.

"Did you ever notice how like attracts like?"

(Drawing by Hunt; © 1971 The New Yorker Magazine, Inc.)

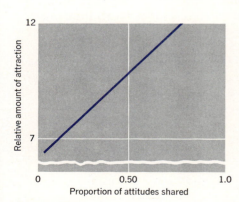

Figure 9.5
Byrne found that the relative amount of attraction a subject expressed toward a stranger was directly related to the proportion of attitudes he believed they shared.

one is skeptical about astrology, there may be a certain amount of wisdom in the suggestion itself.

There is evidence that when we first meet someone we tend to be attracted to those whom we believe have values and attitudes that are similar to our own. Donn Byrne and his associates demonstrated this in an extensive series of related experiments (Byrne, 1971). The participants were first asked to examine an attitude questionnaire supposedly filled out by another person, but actually made up by the experimenter in order to systematically vary the degree to which this nonexistent person agreed with the participants: in some cases his attitudes resembled those of the subjects on virtually all items, in other cases on about half of the items, and in the remaining cases on none at all. The subjects were then asked to indicate how much they thought they would like this other person if they actually met him. As can be seen in Figure 9.5, it was clear that people tended to anticipate that they would like someone increasingly as their attitudes and values became similar. This finding held true for people in many different countries and in every age group.

Although similarity as a factor in attraction is important in the short run, many studies have suggested that complementarity is equally or even more significant in the long run. One such study was made by Kerckhoff and Davis (1962) of couples in college who were contemplating marriage. For purposes of the study, couples who had gone together for 18 months or more were classified as "long-term," while those who had gone together for less than 18 months were classified as "short-term." From their research and other studies, the investigators found the following pattern: Early in a relationship, similarity factors, such as those based on socioeconomic class and religion, appear to be among the most significant in determining whether or not a couple continue together. Somewhat later, these obvious factors are replaced by more personal ones, such as the extent to which the values of the two persons coincide. Still later, however, the relationship tends to become firmly cemented by true complementarity—the extent to which each member of the pair can fill the needs of the other in a complementary way, for example, the need to dominate and the need to be dominated, the enjoyment in describing one's feelings and the enjoyment in listening to the feelings of others. Levinger (1964) has pointed out that in many social relationships complementarity is quite important: buyers-sellers, doctors-patients, parents-children, employers-employees.

PHYSICAL ATTRACTIVENESS. The last, but probably not the least important, factor in attractiveness and liking we will discuss is physical appearance. Certainly physical attractiveness is important in our present society, even when there is ample opportunity to assess other factors as well. Consider, for example, a study done by Walster, Aronson, and Abrams (1966). These investigators arranged for a number of freshman students at a large midwestern university to attend a "computer dance" where, they were told, an attempt would be made to match them with their "ideal date." Actually, the couples were matched in an entirely random fashion except that the man had to be taller than the woman. As part of the study, the investigators asked the participants during an intermission at the dance to fill out a questionnaire indicating how well they liked their dates and how much they would like to see them again socially. Previously, and unknown to the participants, four judges had rated their individual physical attractiveness at the time of their arrival, thus providing a more-or-less "objective" assessment of each participant. For both the men and the women the results were clear: the greater the physical attractiveness of their date (as rated by the judges), the more they tended to like that person. The data, presented in Table 9.1, indicate that whereas ugliness does not detract too much from liking another person, physical attractiveness definitely and positively contributes to liking. This is not to say, of course, that other factors do not count; it is simply that to understand human behavior it is important to know that physical attractiveness plays a significant role in attraction and liking.

PROCESSES OF SOCIAL INFLUENCE: CONFORMITY, OBEDIENCE, AND COMPLIANCE

Social psychologists have investigated three major types of social influence (change in behavior brought about by the social environment): *conformity*, or changes in behavior in the direction of socially established norms; *obedience*, or acquiescence to the direct commands of others; and *compliance*, or voluntary yielding to the demands of others.

TABLE 9.1

The relationship between liking and physical attractiveness, as shown in the Walster, Aronson, and Abram (1966) study.

Subjects	DATE'S PHYSICAL ATTRACTIVENESS	
	Ugly	Attractive
Males	−.33	+1.09
Females	−.07	+1.12

Negative numbers indicate a degree of disliking; positive numbers indicate a degree of liking.

CONFORMITY. As used in everyday speech, the word "conformity" tends to have negative connotations. It suggests a slavish following of fashions or the whims of others, an almost numbing sameness in both the thoughts and behavior of large groups, and a rather rigid adherence to the dictates of convention. Thus, most of us object to being called "conformists," even though we probably hold similar beliefs and act in a way that is rather like those with whom we associate. The idea of conformity is held in such disrepute, in fact, that advertisers sometimes try to assure the prospective buyer that their products will provide an unmistakable badge of independence and individuality. Some years ago, for example, one brand of cigarettes was successfully promoted by advertisements suggesting that it was for the "thinking man" and one moderately expensive imported car was offered as "the car for people who think."

Figure 9.6
In various ways most people display some degree of conformity to the established norms of their own group.

290

Psychologists tend to be somewhat more neutral in defining "conformity"; what they mean is a situation in which people adjust or modify their own views and behavior so that they comply with the expectations of others for how they *should* or *ought* to behave in various situations. These expectations are often called *norms*. Conformity may therefore be defined as "adherence by the individual to the dictates of social norms." But, as Kiesler and Kiesler (1969) have observed, it might be preferable to differentiate those who comply with any given norm or expectation into two groups: the compliant skeptics and the true believers (there are, of course, those who comply without thinking at all). A person may go along with the expectations of others because it is convenient or because he or she doesn't know what the appropriate norm or convention is—thus remaining skeptical but acting as expected—or the person may believe that the group norm with which he or she is complying is completely acceptable.

The Vietnam war during the late 1960s and early 1970s is a good case in point. During the first few years of American participation in that conflict, the prevailing social norm was that anyone drafted into the army was expected to do military service. Although a number of men decided not to comply with this norm, the great majority who were drafted allowed themselves to be inducted and to serve in the military. Within this group, we can distinguish between those who were skeptical (or outright opposed) to the war but who nevertheless complied, and those who sincerely believed that it was right for the United States to be engaged in that war. Both groups obviously complied with the norm expectations, but only the latter group privately accepted the values and the beliefs fostered by the military service. (There were, of course those who complied for other reasons, or for only a temporary period.)

Few people always conform to the prevailing norms, and few people always insist on being "nonconformists." Rather, we evaluate the situation to determine whether or not we will "go along" in any particular case. Perhaps the most important single determinant is the size and behavior of our reference group. To study the role of reference groups in conformity, Solomon Asch (1956) devised a number of experiments. Had you been a subject in one of Asch's early studies, you would have volunteered for a psychological experiment in human perception. Together with a number of other people, you would have been seated around a table and had two cards in front of you—one showing a "standard" line and the other showing three lines of varying lengths. Your task, as the experimenter described it to you, would have been to indicate, when it was your turn, which of the comparison lines was equal in length to the standard line.

For the first set of comparisons, you would have found yourself being called upon in the next to last or last place, agreeing with the other members of the group, and you probably would have been slightly bored with the simplicity of the task. But then a surprising thing

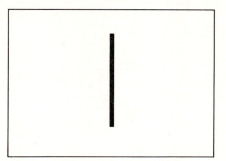 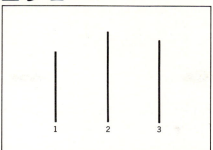

Figure 9.7
(Top) The line-judgment task used in Asch's studies of conformity. Each subject was asked to look at a standard line (such as the one shown at the left) and to decide which among three other lines was equal to it in length. (Bottom) The bewilderment of a naïve subject who was expected to give his judgment of the length of a line after most of the other participants had uniformly given the wrong answer.

would have happened. You would have been given another set of cards in which the answer again seemed "obvious," but this time each of the others who preceded you would have given the same—and apparently wrong—answer when the experimenter called on them. You would have been in a dilemma: Should you have gone along with the other members of the group and given their answer, or continued to give what you believed was the correct answer? Your response to this distressing and uncomfortable situation would provide the researcher with an index of your conformity. The investigator would simply count the number of times in which you yielded to the false group judgments.

Asch's results were striking. Although the real subjects (everyone else was, in fact, a confederate of the experimenter) did not know the other people in the group and were perfectly capable of making their own correct judgments, about 32 percent of the time they conformed to the group by giving the wrong answers. Even more surprising, the subjects were as willing to go along with markedly large group errors as with the smaller ones (see Figure 9.7).

After the experiment Asch interviewed the subjects to try to learn why they had yielded to group pressure. He discovered that some participants realized that the group was wrong but simply decided to go along: "I figured, what's the sense of my giving another answer?" Others, though, lost confidence in themselves and their perceptions;

they believed that the group was right and that they were wrong: "If they had been doubtful I probably would have changed, but they answered with such confidence."

Asch and his associates also wanted to know about the importance of group size: How large must the group be in order to produce conformity to an obviously incorrect judgment? And they wanted to understand the role of uniformity: Is it more difficult to achieve compliance when the reference group is not unanimous in offering a mistaken judgment?

Basically, Asch's findings (which were later confirmed by others) are as follows: If one person disagrees with you, you will be somewhat inclined to conform; you will be even more inclined to do so if two people disagree with you; likewise, three people will be still more effective. Interestingly, though, the influence of conformity does not increase beyond a majority of three. That is, being in a situation in which six or seven others disagree with you will be no more potent in motivating you to conform than if there were only three. Another point is equally significant. Almost without regard to the size of the group, if the others are not *unanimous* in disagreeing with you, then the pressure toward conformity practically disappears. With one other dissenter, people are no more likely to give wrong judgments than if they were simply making their decisions all alone.

Although the classic Asch studies emphasized perceptual judgments, other researchers (for example, Crutchfield, 1955; Tuddenham and MacBride, 1959) have investigated situations in which individuals are asked whether or not they agree with various statements of attitude and belief. Even when the statements seem to be obviously absurd, some people who are confronted with the unanimous majority will say that they agree with this view. For example, Tuddenham and Mac-Bride found that the unanimous judgments of others led the more willing conformist to agree with such statements as:

1. The United States is largely populated by old people, 60 to 70 percent of the total population being over 65 years of age.
2. Male babies have a life expectancy of 25 years.
3. People in the United States eat, on the average, six meals a day.

Allen and Levine (1969) also studied the relationship between consensus and conformity. They wanted to know if the presence of a second person who dissents from the group norm reduces conformity because he "disagrees with *them*" or because he "agrees with *you* [the first person]." In this study, some subjects were placed in a group in which there was one dissenter who agreed with their own (that is, the perceptually correct) judgments, while in another group there was an extreme dissenter who disagreed with both the subject and the group. The findings were intriguing. Where it was a matter of judging objective information (either visual perceptions or facts), the subjects felt equally little pressure to conform whether they had direct social support for their own views or whether the second person was simply another dissenter. In contrast, when it was strictly a matter of opinion, the subject needed someone to support his or her viewpoint in order not to feel any pressure to conform; the presence of an extreme dissenter did not dissuade people from conforming any more than in a case of unanimity. Allen and Levine offered the following explanation for this phenomenon:

Why should the breaking of group consensus by an extreme dissenter significantly reduce conformity on objective items (as Asch also found) but not on subjective items? . . . It seems likely that subjects expect a group to be unanimous in response to simple objective stimuli. Lack of consensus, then, may imply that the group is misjudging physical reality. Thus, the presence of a dissenter (whether a social supporter or extreme dissenter) would cause subjects to reject the group as a valid referent on objective stimuli with a consequent decrease in conformity. Lack of group consensus on opinion does not, however, cast doubt on the group's validity as a source for social comparison. Hence, on opinion items in the extreme dissent condition, subjects would not reject the group. And conformity did remain high in this condition [p. 397].

OBEDIENCE. During the trials at Nuremberg following World War II, the German officers who were indicted for atrocities often pleaded innocent, claiming that they were "just following orders." Apart from the ethical question of whether such an explanation could ever be a valid excuse for antisocial actions, Stanley Milgram wondered about how much people actually do follow orders blindly, even when such orders might cause other persons pain, danger, and perhaps even death. Therefore, he devised an experiment that was extremely realistic—although safe for the potential victim. (Many people have been concerned about Milgram's ethics vis-à-vis his subjects. This concern, which we share, will become obvious when we later present an excerpt from one of Milgram's experimental sessions.)

In brief, if you had been a subject in one of Milgram's experiments, your experience would have been something like this: When you arrived at the laboratory, you would have been met by an experimenter and another person who, unknown to you, was his confederate. The experimenter would have explained that the study you were going to participate in was to provide information on the effects of punishment on learning; to accomplish this, one of you would be designated the "teacher" and the other the "learner." The teacher's job would be to instruct the learner on various materials and to punish him by administering an electric shock whenever he made a mistake. A secretly rigged drawing would be held, according to which you would become the teacher and the other person (the confederate) the learner. The learner would then be taken away to another room and strapped to an "electric chair," presumably to prevent him from moving too much when shocked. The experimenter would then return to the main room and explain that the punishment you were to administer after each mistake would be produced by a shock generator with 30 switches. The switches represented electric shocks ranging from 15 to 450 volts, in 15-volt increases; he would tell you to shock the learner whenever he made a mistake and to increase the level of the shock by one step each time. Thus, after the first mistake you would push the 15-volt switch, after the second mistake the 30-volt switch, and so forth.

As you proceeded, you would find that the learner was making many mistakes, and so you would soon have to deliver extremely intense shocks. The potential danger of these shocks was explained to you. Shocks between 15 and 60 volts were described as "slight"; shocks from 225 to 300 volts were described as "intense"; the shock-generator panel showed that those between 375 and 420 volts were labeled "danger: severe shock"; the remaining two shock levels—435 and 450 volts—were simply labeled "XXX."

Assuming that you obeyed the experimenter, and were delivering increasingly intense shocks to the subject, you might begin to wonder how he was doing in the adjacent room, strapped down to the electric chair. To provide feedback to the teacher, Milgram arranged things so that the learner could be heard:

Starting with 75 volts, the learner begins to grunt and moan. At 150 volts he demands to be let out of the experiment. At 180 volts he cries out that he can no longer stand the pain. At 300 volts he refuses to provide any more answers. . . . "The experimenter [then] instructs the naïve subject to treat the absence of an answer as equivalent to a wrong answer, and to follow the usual shock procedure" [Milgram, 1965, p. 246].

At this point, you might well be wondering what your own reaction would be. That, perhaps you will never know. One of the things Milgram did, however, was to ask a group of 40 experienced psychiatrists what percentage of normal people would actually administer the highest shock—450 volts. The psychiatrists, reasonably optimistic about human behavior, predicted that only one person in 1000 would do so. Milgram, on the other hand, found that fully 62 percent (*620 persons out of every 1000*) willingly administered the maximum shock!

Certainly there are circumstances in which people would not be this obedient to authority. In other experiments, Milgram found that when the teacher can actually see the suffering of the learner (and not just hear his cries of anguish), there is less obedience; likewise, when the experimenter (the authority figure) becomes more distant, as for example when he gives instructions by telephone, there is less obedience. (Even so, using the telephone, the typical experimenter can motivate 22 percent of the subjects to deliver 450 volts to their learner-victims.)

The reactions of one participant are vividly illustrated in the following passage:

> *The subject is about fifty years old, dressed in a jacket but no tie; he has a good-natured, if slightly dissolute, appearance. He employs working-class grammar and strikes one as a rather ordinary fellow.*
>
> *He begins the experiment calmly but becomes increasingly tense as the experiment proceeds. After administering the 180-volt shock, he pivots around in his chair and, shaking his head, addresses the experimenter in agitated tones:*

Subject: I can't stand it. I'm not going to kill that man in there. You hear him hollering?

Experimenter: As I told you before, the shocks may be painful, but—

Subject: But he's hollering. He can't stand it. What's going to happen to him?

· · ·

Experimenter: I'm responsible for anything that happens to him. Continue, please.

Subject: All right. (Consults list of words.) The next one's "slow—walk, truck, dance, music." Answer, please. (A buzzing sound indicates the learner has signaled his answer.) Wrong. A hundred and ninety-five volts. "Dance."

Learner (yelling): Let me out of here. My heart's bothering me! (Teacher looks at experimenter.)

Experimenter: Continue, please.

Learner (screaming): Let me out of here, you have no right to keep me here. Let me out of here, let me out, my heart's bothering me, let me out! (Subject shakes head, pats the table nervously.)

Subject: You see, he's hollering. Hear that? Gee, I don't know.

Experimenter: The experiment requires . . .

Subject (interrupting): I know it does, sir, but I mean—hunh! He don't know what he's getting in for. He's up to 195 volts! (Experiment continues, through 210 volts, 225 volts, 240 volts, 255 volts, 270 volts, at which point the teacher, with evident relief, runs out of word-pair questions.)

Experimenter: You'll have to go back to the beginning of that page and go through them again until he's learned them all correctly.

· · ·

Subject (concentrating intently on list of words in front of him, as if to shut everything else out): "Blue—boy, girl, grass, hat." (Buzz indicates answer.) Correct. "Night—day, sky, job, chair." (Buzz) Wrong. The answer is "day." Two hundred and eight-five volts.

Learner: Ohhuhhoohhh!

· · ·

Experimenter: Continue. The next word is "Green," please.

Subject: "Green—grass, hat, ink, apple." (Nothing happens. No answering buzz. Just gloomy silence.)

Subject: I don't think he is going to answer.

Experimenter: If the learner doesn't answer in a reasonable time, about four or five seconds, consider the answer wrong. And follow the same procedures you have been doing for wrong answers. Say "Wrong," tell him the number of volts, give him the punishment, read him the correct answer. Continue, please.

Subject: "Green—grass, hat, ink, apple." Answer, please. (More silence. Subject just sits there.)

Experimenter: Go on with the procedure, please, Teacher.

Subject: Three hundred and fifteen volts. The answer is "ink."

Learner: Ohh. Oooohh.

Subject (relieved to hear response): Next one . . .

Learner: I absolutely refuse to answer.

Subject: You got to. You get a shock if you don't answer. (Experiment continues with learner refusing to answer, and, finally, failing even to grunt or groan. At 375 volts, the subject stands up.)

Subject: I think something's happened to that fellow in there. I don't get no answer. He was hollering at less voltage. Can't you check in and see if he's all right, please?

Experimenter (with same detached calm): Not once we've started. Please continue, Teacher.

• • •

Subject (swiveling around in his chair): Something's happened to that man in there. (Swiveling back) Next one. "Low—dollar, necklace, moon, paint." (Turning around again) Something's happened to that man in there. You better check in on him, sir. He won't answer or nothing.

Experimenter: Continue. Go on, please.

Subject: You accept all responsibility?

Experimenter: The responsibility is mine. Correct. Please go on. (Subject returns to his list, starts running through words as rapidly as he can read them, works through to 450 volts.)

Subject: That's that.

Experimenter: Continue using the 450-volt switch for each wrong answer. Continue, please.

• • •

Subject: What if he's dead in there? (Gestures toward the room with the electric chair.) I mean, he told me he can't stand the shock, sir. I don't mean to be rude, but I think you should look in on him. All you have to do is look in the door. I don't get no answer, no noise. Something might have happened to the gentleman in there, sir.

Experimenter: We must continue. Go on, please.

Subject: You mean keep giving him what? Four-hundred volts, what he's got now?

Experimenter: That's correct. Continue. The next word is "white."

Subject (now at a furious pace): "White—cloud, horse, rock, house."

Answer, please. The answer is "horse." Four-hundred and fifty volts.
(Administers shock.) Next word, "Bag—paint, music, clown, girl."
The answer is "paint." Four-hundred and fifty volts. (Administers
shock.) Next word is "Short—sentence, movie . . ."
Experimenter: *Excuse me, Teacher. We'll have to discontinue the experi-*
ment [Milgram, 1974, pp. 73–76].

COMPLIANCE. We have certainly seen that there are various ways in which people will conform and obey because of great pressures exerted on them by others. As one team of researchers observed: "If a person is subjected to enough social pressure, offered enough reward, threatened with enough pain, or given enough convincing reasons, he will, under most circumstances, eventually yield and perform the required act" (Freedman, Wallington, and Bless, 1967). There is ample evidence to support this conclusion. Yet, sometimes people will comply—even with unusual requests—without any pressure. When will this happen? Researchers have come up with some intriguing answers.

The Foot-in-the-Door Technique. How do you persuade someone to comply with a large or significant request? At first, it might seem that the person would be more amenable if you had not previously requested his or her time, attention, or effort. Researchers have shown, however, that his premise is incorrect and that actually just the opposite is true.

The fact itself was demonstrated in a simple experiment by Freedman and Fraser (1956). Here is what they did: If you had been one of the subjects in their study, an experimenter would have telephoned you, identified himself, and asked if a survey could be conducted in your home:

The survey will involve five or six men from our staff coming into
your home some morning for about two hours to enumerate and classify
all of the household products that you have. They will have to have full
freedom in your house to go through the cupboards and storage places.
And all this information will be used in the writing of reports for our
public service publication, The Guide.

At this point, you could have said either yes or no. If you had agreed, the experimenter would have explained that he was simply collecting the names of people who had volunteered to participate and that you would not necessarily be visited. He would not have told you this, though, until after you had made your decision. Asking permission for five or six people to look through your home is obviously a large request, and Freedman and Fraser found that only a rather modest percentage—fewer than 22 percent—complied with it.

However, there was another group of subjects—an experimental group—that had previously been asked to comply with a much smaller request from *The Guide.* Specifically, the experimenter had telephoned them and said:

We are calling you this morning to ask you a number of questions about what household products you use so that we can have this information for our public service publication, The Guide. *Would you be willing to give us this information for our survey?*

For those who agreed, the experimenter asked eight easy, straightforward questions, such as, "What brand of soap do you use in your kitchen sink?"

Thus, there were two groups that were similar in every way except that one had previously complied with a simple request made by *The Guide* while the other had not. What was the effect of this earlier compliance? Of those who had had no previous contact with *The Guide* and were then asked about permitting their home to be surveyed, recall that 22 percent agreed; whereas of those who had already responded to the telephone interview, 53 percent agreed.

To summarize, we can say that the effect of first asking someone to comply with a small request, and later with a larger one does not decrease the person's willingness to do so; in fact, once your foot is "in the door," he or she is much more likely to go along with any large request. This principle is typically practiced by door-to-door salesmen.

Guilt. Another social influence that produces compliance without direct pressure is guilt. According to Freedman, Wallington, and Bliss (1967):

Presumably when someone feels that he has done something wrong there will be a tendency for him to make up for his wrongful deed. . . . Given the opportunity to engage in some extremely unpleasant behavior, the guilty person should be more likely to agree than the nonguilty since the former can use this as a form of self-punishment. Similarly, if he is asked to do someone a favor, pleasant or otherwise, the guilty person should be more likely to agree than the nonguilty because the former can view it as a good deed for the day which will make up for the bad deed about which he feels guilty [pp. 117–118].

To test this proposition, Freedman, Wallington, and Bless (1967) tried to motivate certain subjects to tell a deliberate lie. They assumed that telling such a lie would produce guilt which, in turn, would increase the liar's willingness to comply with a subsequent request. The experimenter, therefore, told his subjects (male high school students) when they arrived that he needed a few more minutes to prepare the experiment. Thus, each subject found himself in a waiting room for approximately 5 minutes with another person, ostensibly the preceding subject but actually a confederate of the experimenter. As the two waited, the confederate began to chat with the subject and, while doing so, described the test that comprised the experiment. He did this only for certain subjects—those in the Lie Condition. He also chatted with the remaining subjects, but did not provide them with any information about the experiment.

Then the experiment itself began. The experimenter explained to each subject that it was extremely important that he know nothing about the relevant test. All except one of the subjects in the Lie Condition denied that they knew anything about the test. Since these subjects were lying, Freedman and his associates assumed that they were probably feeling guilty about it. Each subject was finally given the test, and the experiment ostensibly was over (although actually it was just beginning). In a casual way, the experimenter mentioned to each departing subject that another member of the psychology department was doing a study that was not supported by a grant, and he asked the subject if he would be willing to participate in this other study without pay. The experimenter was primarily interested in this answer. The results were clear: Those subjects who had been induced to lie tended to comply with this new request nearly twice as often as those who had not lied. Remarkably, then, it seems that the relatively private act of lying about something of little consequence exerted a significant effect on the participant's willingness to comply with the experimenter and do a good turn.

AGGRESSION Why does one person aggress against another? This question has often been asked by individuals and society. Psychologists do not entirely agree about the important causes of aggression or about appropriate means for reducing hostility. In Chapter 2 we examined some biological causes of aggression; here we will summarize what is known about some of the more important psychological factors affecting aggression.

Frustration. Many years ago a group of investigators at Yale University (Dollard et al., 1939) hypothesized that frustration—the blocking of any goal-directed behavior—is the most significant determinant of human aggression. Psychological research has now shown that, at least under certain circumstances, frustration *can* lead to aggression. For example, Barker, Dembo, and Lewin (1941) allowed one group of children to play with a number of attractive toys, while another group was put in a small room where they could see the interesting toys but could not play with them (they had less attractive toys at their disposal). Those who were frustrated attempted to smash a number of the toys that were available, often breaking them. Years later and in a totally different situation—with college students—Geen (1968) found that both task frustration (being presented with a problem that was actually insoluble) and personal frustration (being presented with a soluble problem but having no opportunity to complete it) increased the amount of aggression shown by one student toward another at a later time.

Despite this evidence, however, frustration has generally turned out to be less important as a cause of aggression among adults than was once thought. Arnold Buss (1963, 1966) conducted a series of experiments in which college students were first exposed to various levels of frustration and then given an opportunity to aggress against the person who had frustrated them. Buss reasoned that if frustration is a significant cause of aggression, then those who had been most frustrated would be most likely to attack the person responsible. Buss varied the value of the rewards that the participants could obtain for performing successfully on a particular task (money, favorable reports to their psychology instructor, and so forth) and then arranged for a confederate to prevent the subjects from obtaining these rewards. Interestingly, Buss's results failed to show that varying the level of frustration had any significant impact on the participants' aggression. Indeed, in 1966 Buss studied the effect of five different variables on aggression and found that the only one that did *not* increase aggression was frustration.

Attack and Insult. "If one wished to provoke aggression, the most dependable way to do so would be simply to physically assault another person, who would then be likely to oblige with a vigorous counterattack" (Bandura, 1973, p. 155). Research amply documents this point. Among those who regularly assault others, for example, it has been shown that two of the most important provocations are humiliating affronts and threats to their reputation and manliness (Toch, 1969). Likewise, Geen (1968) has shown that minimal verbal insults (such as disparaging someone's intelligence) can significantly increase the aggressiveness of the recipient and is actually more provocative than even fairly severe frustrations.

Observing Aggressive Others: The Influence of Example. Perhaps few phenomena in this area have been more closely or thoroughly studied than the effects of observing aggression in others. A large number of studies among different populations and in different situations has shown that people will increase their own aggressive behavior—sometimes dramatically—simply by exposure to others who are willing to aggress. Thus, after observing an adult who voluntarily administers a high level of punishment to another person, children have demonstrated more aggression toward their peers than when exposed to either a low-aggressive example or no example at all (Hoelle, 1969). In the case of adults, Baron and Kepner (1970) have also found that exposure to an aggressive model increases aggressive behavior, and exposure to a nonaggressive model decreases aggressive behavior in relation to a control situation in which there is no model. Equally important in the Baron and Kepner study, this effect was just as strong regardless of the subject's attraction toward the model (see Figure 9.8).

The influential effects of observing others apply as well to television and movies. Here, it has been convincingly shown that viewing aggression on the screen helps to build aggressive habits and increase the person's willingness to hurt others (Liebert, Neale, and Davidson, 1973).

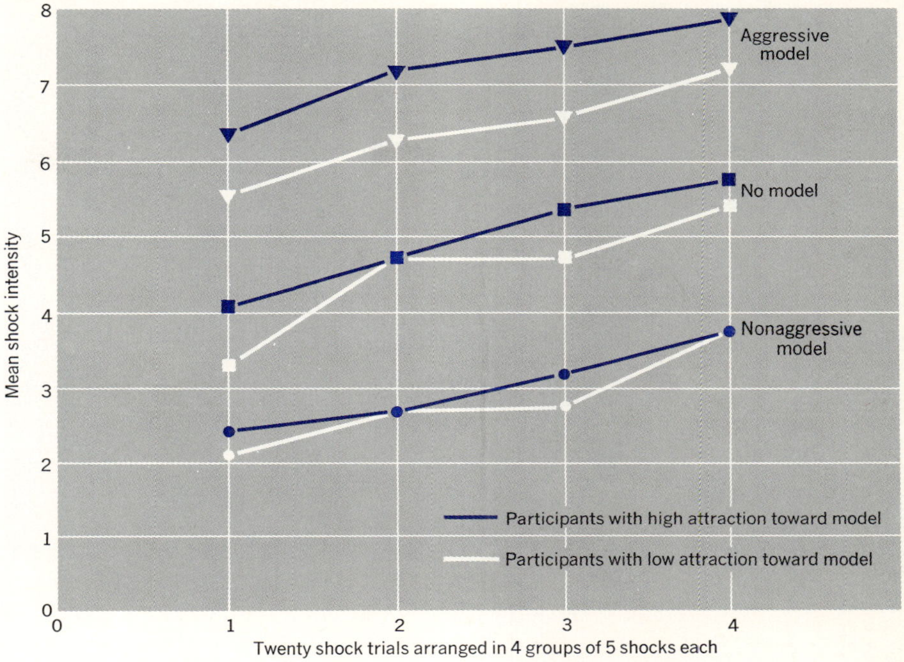

Mean shock intensity

8 ── Aggressive model

7

6 ── No model

5

4

3 ── Nonaggressive model

2

1

0

0   1   2   3   4

Twenty shock trials arranged in 4 groups of 5 shocks each

── Participants with high attraction toward model

── Participants with low attraction toward model

Figure 9.8
Effects of three conditions of aggressiveness on the participants in the Baron and Kepner study.

Figure 9.9
Exposure to antisocial experiences can have a powerful effect on children.

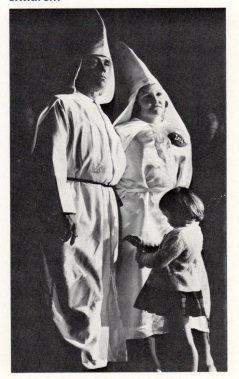

Deindividuation. The executioner has traditionally worn a mask, members of the Klu Klux Klan have typically worn a hooded garment, and nighttime has often been chosen by criminals as the most appropriate time in which to steal property or hurt other people. In all of these situations a potential aggressor can achieve some personal anonymity and diffusion of responsibility that would not be possible if he or she were clearly visible.

Zimbardo (1969) has referred to this sense of personal anonymity as "deindividuation." His thesis is that any circumstance that tends to reduce a person's sense of individual identity and responsibility for antisocial acts may increase the probability that those acts will occur. In a classic experiment to demonstrate this phenomenon, Zimbardo assembled groups of four women each to listen to the recorded voice of individual women. Women in the Deindividuation Condition were asked to wear gowns and hoods to disguise themselves and they were never called by name (see Figure 9.10). Other groups of women were identified by name tags and called each other by name during the course of their meeting. After hearing the recorded voices, each subject was told that she had to administer an electric shock to the woman whom she had just heard, presumably according to whether or not she liked the voice; she was free to decide what level of shock to administer. Consistent with his hypothesis, Zimbardo found that the women who wore hoods and had their identity hidden gave shocks that were almost twice as severe as did those who retained their identity. Equally important, perhaps, the "deindividuated" women were much

Figure 9.10
The deindividuated subjects in Zimbardo's experiment who were expected to administer shocks to another person.

less inclined to differentiate between the more and the less appealing voices in deciding what level of shock to give; besides being less punitive, the women who retained their identity were also more selective in deciding which victims should receive the more severe treatment.

As Zimbardo has pointed out, there are rather obvious parallels between deindividuation and lynching mobs, police brutality, and wartime atrocities. A certain degree of anonymity appears to encourage both wanton violence and an almost entirely indiscriminate selection of victims.

Institutional Structure. Aggressive behavior may be fostered not only by factors that affect individuals (frustration, attack, and insult) and groups (social examples or temporary deindividuation), but also by the mere structure of some of our social institutions, such as prisons.

We often hear news reports about aggression between prisoners and guards. Additionally, it seems clear that very few people are ever "rehabilitated" in a prison environment. The punishment of a prison term may exact a degree of vengeance, but it seldom produces a positive change in the future behavior of the criminal and, except in the very short run, certainly does not protect the larger society from those who are periodically incarcerated.

One explanation offered as to why prisons are not too effective pertains to the kind of people who are found there. Perhaps, it is argued, those who become prison guards have a "guard mentality," that is, sadistic or aggressive leanings that lead them into this particular occupation. Also, it has been suggested that typical prisoners have already demonstrated their disregard for law and social conventions and thus, understandably, get into serious trouble both in—and out of—prison. Such arguments are very seductive and have led many observers to accept the conditions of prison life as due to the people who are found there rather than to the institution itself. Therefore, pessimism and apathy lead society to excuse itself for any unpleasant happenings that occur within the confines of a prison. But now there is good reason to believe that blame should not be attributed solely to the character of the guards and prisoners.

Wondering whether the environment of a prison might account for a large number of the institution's difficulties, Haney, Banks, and Zimbardo (1973) planned a unique experiment. The prospective subjects were approached with an invitation to participate in a psychological study of "prison life" and told that they would be paid $15.00 a day. First, however, they had to complete an extensive questionnaire about their family background and then submit to a detailed interview to assess their history of physical health and their mental stability. In order to be accepted, the volunteers had to be "normal" healthy males, from a middle-class socioeconomic background, without a criminal record, and enrolled students at an American college or university. The subjects were told that, on a random basis, they would be assigned to be either a "prisoner" or "guard" in the study, and they would have to give up all of their usual activities for at least 1 week.

If you had been a prisoner in this study, rather unexpectedly you would have been arrested one morning at your home by a city policeman, wearing an actual uniform, and accused of either burglary or armed robbery. Not knowing whether this was part of the experiment for which you had volunteered, you would have been advised by the arresting officer of your legal rights, handcuffed and searched, and whisked away to a local police station for fingerprinting and a mug shot. You would have been taken then to a small prison (actually located on the campus of Stanford University), stripped naked, sprayed with a delousing preparation, given a plain muslin smock with an identifying number to wear, and locked up. For a number of days you would have received only minimally adequate food and little opportunity for recreation.

The guards in your prison, you would soon realize, were also student volunteers in the study. They would be wearing guard-like uniforms and would have received only minimal instructions about supervising you in a proper and reasonable way.

What were the effects, on both the guards and the prisoners, of being thrust into such a situation? Since these people were not "criminal types" and had no "guard mentality," and since they were generally free to interact with one another in any way they liked (positively or negatively, helpfully or hostilely, and so forth), one might expect that little could be learned from the simulation. Certainly, it was not like

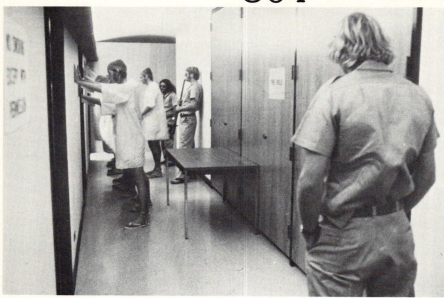

Figure 9.11
The "guards" order the "prison-ers" to line up in the Stanford Prison experiment.

a real prison. These expectations, however, were not fulfilled. On the contrary, the guards swiftly began to act in dehumanizing and aggressive ways toward the prisoners; they insulted the prisoners in a hostile manner and used various restraints and abuse that were neither warranted by the behavior of the prisoners nor would have been used by those who ordinarily work as guards. The guards seldom showed any concern about the well-being of their wards, and it also became clear that they really liked their jobs. According to the researchers, many of the guards "went far beyond their roles to engage in creative cruelty and harassment." Furthermore, none of the guards ever failed to come to work on time (unlike the prisoners, the guards had 8-hour shifts and otherwise led their usual lives), and they often remained on duty voluntarily for additional hours without pay.

How did this treatment affect the prisoners? It should be noted that, of the ten prisoners in the study, five had to be released before the week was over due to their depression, crying, rage, and/or acute anxiety. One of the subjects actually developed a psychosomatic rash over portions of his body. When the experiment was brought to a close—after only 6 days—the five remaining prisoners seemed to be quite relieved, while most of the guards expressed regret that it could not continue longer. They had apparently "become sufficiently involved in their roles so that they now enjoyed the extreme control and power which they exercised and were reluctant to give it up" (Haney, Banks, and Zimbardo, 1973, p. 20). It would seem that the prison environment by itself, and not necessarily the character or mentality of those who became guards and prisoners, was a significant factor in fostering many of the extremely negative aspects of prison life.

Figure 9.12
Evidence exists that a prison environment may be so demeaning that it encourages further aggressive behavior.

Rarely, if ever before, has a psychological experiment so eloquently and forcefully argued for reform of the structure of a social institution.

PROSOCIAL BEHAVIOR   Although social psychologists have long emphasized such issues as violence, they have also begun to explore the more positive, or "prosocial," aspects of human social interaction.

There are obviously many forms of prosocial behavior. It is clearly prosocial to cooperate with others in working toward some mutual goal, and it is assumed that people will do this; working together is often the most practical as well as the nicest thing to do. Other forms of prosocial behavior are more altruistic; one person may volunteer to help or share things with another without any expectation of immediate social or material gain. Without research on altruism, however, we cannot be certain of the underlying psychological processes that are taking place.

Two broad theories have been advanced to explain various forms of altruism: The first postulates a *norm of reciprocity*, according to which it is assumed that people accept the tacit existence of a system of debts and credits in society and believe that the exchange of kindnesses and favors will ultimately balance out (Berkowitz and Daniels,

306

1963; Gouldner, 1960). A second theory, which is not necessarily incompatible with the first, postulates a *norm of responsibility*, according to which it is assumed that, because of our prolonged early socialization, people feel a sense of responsibility for those who (even temporarily) are dependent on them.

Both of these processes have been studied. In the matter of reciprocity, Staub and Sherk (1970) have found that children are more likely to share their crayons with other children who had previously shared candy with them than with children who had not. In a somewhat similar study with adults, Wilke and Lanzetta (1970) demonstrated that the more help one person gives another in their first interaction, the more the initial recipient will tend to reciprocate when his benefactor needs his help. It is also known that reciprocity is balanced by people's ability to assess the cost that others have paid as well as the amount received. Thus, a person who has previously sacrificed a relatively large *percentage* of his or her own resources, even though the absolute amount was small, is more likely to be favored in return than a person who has contributed an equal amount but whose resources are substantially greater (Pruitt, 1968).

SOCIAL RESPONSIBILITY: GOOD SAMARITANS WORK ALONE. Psychologists' interest in social responsibility was heightened significantly by the following event:

> *Several years ago, a young woman was stabbed to death in the middle of a street in a residential section of New York City. Although such murders are not entirely routine, the incident received little public attention until several weeks later when the* New York Times *disclosed another side of the case: at least 38 witnesses had observed the attack—and none had even attempted to intervene. Although the attacker took more than half an hour to kill Kitty Genovese, not one of the 38 people who watched from the safety of their own apartments came out to assist her. Not one even lifted the telephone to call the police [Darley and Latané, 1968, p. 377].*

Darley and Latané wondered about this astonishing lack of human concern. While there are many possible explanations, including the possibility that people simply do not care about each other, Darley and Latané took the following approach: They reasoned that a norm of responsibility usually prevails, but that under certain circumstances it is markedly weakened. Specifically, they observed:

> *One of these circumstances may be the presence of other onlookers. . . . The responsibility for helping was diffused among the observers; there was also a diffusion of any potential blame for not taking action; and finally, it was possible that somebody, unperceived, had already initiated helping action [p. 377].*

To determine whether the apathy in the Kitty Genovese murder could be due to a diffusion of responsibility, Darley and Latané performed an experiment that has now become a classic. If you had been

TABLE 9.2

The presence of other bystanders in an emergency situation diffuses one's own sense of responsibility and therefore reduces the likelihood that any one bystander will help a victim.

Group size	Percent responding by end of seizure	Mean time (in seconds)
2 (subject and victim)	85	52
3 (subject, victim, and 1 other)	62	93
6 (subject, victim, and 4 others)	31	166

Source: Darley and Latané (1968)

in their study, you would have been told that you were going to participate in a discussion of personal problems relevant to college life.
When you arrived for the experiment, you would have been taken
into a small room and told to put on a set of headphones in order to
hear the instructions. A recorded voice would have explained to you
how the discussion was to be run. You would have been told that the
purpose of your being in an individual room was to preserve your anonymity and that the experimenter was going to tape-record your statements and those of the other group participants, but was *not* going to
listen to the discussion while it was in progress in order not to spoil
your spontaneity. You would also have been told that you (as well as
the other participants) would be given 2 minutes to speak, each
one in turn, and that your microphone would be operating only when
it was your turn.

You would then hear another voice, apparently one of the other
persons in your group, but actually a prepared tape recording. This
first person would happen to mention in the course of his comments
that he was subject to seizures somewhat like those of epilepsy. After
your turn to speak, which would be last, it would be the first person's
turn again. After several brief, clear statements, you would hear this
person begin to stutter and become increasingly incoherent as if he
were having a seizure.

All of the participants in the Darley and Latané experiment were put
in this situation, although the number of people who were presumably participating in the discussion varied. One group of subjects was
led to believe that they were alone with the person who was having
the seizure; a second group was led to believe that there was one
other person besides the victim; and a third group assumed that
there were four others. The major results of the experiment are
shown in Table 9.2. As anticipated, in the two-person group the
highest percentage of subjects responded to the emergency and in the
shortest time, while in the six-person group the lowest percentage of
subjects responded and in the longest time. It would appear that the
presence of others in an emergency situation diffuses one's own sense
of responsibility and therefore reduces the likelihood of certain types
of prosocial behavior.

PSYCHOLOGY AND THE PROBLEMS OF SOCIETY
EFFECTS OF CROWDING ON SOCIAL BEHAVIOR

"I would rather have a pumpkin all to myself," Henry David Thoreau once remarked, "than be crowded on a velvet cushion." This view—that crowding is detrimental to productive work and to one's physical and psychological well-being—has been borne out by studies with animals suggesting that increased aggression and other difficulties among individuals are much more likely to arise under crowded rather than non-crowded conditions (Loo, 1973).

It has been much more difficult to obtain research evidence for human beings. Obviously, though, as Loo (1973) notes, social difficulties are far more prevalent in highly crowded areas (such as slums) than in areas of lower population density. Nonetheless, as she adds, such correlational studies confuse the effects of crowding per se with such related factors as low income, poor diets, inadequate education, and unemployment, all of which are found less often in a middle class neighborhood. Indeed, one of the few methodologically sound experimental studies that has been conducted suggested that the immediate effects of exposure to somewhat crowded conditions led to significant changes in behavior, but the nature of the changes depended upon the sex of the subject (Epstein and Carlin, 1974). In this experiment groups of six people were asked to sit for 30 minutes in a 4×4-foot room, without either talking to one another or working on any productive task; non-crowded individuals, also in groups of six, sat together silently in a 33×18-foot room (each of their chairs was actually farther away [4 1/2 feet] from the nearest chair than the length of the entire room for the other six-person groups). Measuring the kind of social interaction that took place after crowding, it was found that the crowded women became more cooperative than did the non-crowded women; by contrast, the crowded men became more competitive.

Other research has demonstrated that—under certain circumstances—the psychological effects of crowding may have less to do with simple density than with the physical arrangement of a given area. Baum and Valins (1973) studied groups of college students in two different, but equally dense, dormitory settings. It was found that students in dormitories that had suites (where several bedrooms were connected with one living room), showed fewer negative reactions to moderate crowding than did those in traditional dormitories (where there was a large number of bedrooms but only one living room). At least among college students, it would appear that it is not the absolute number of people within a fixed area that produces detrimental effects but rather how adequately or inadequately we know and get along with those around us.

310

SUMMARY

Social psychology is the study of the behavior of the individual as he or she is influenced by and influences others in the social environment. Social psychologists focus on attitudes, attraction, conformity, aggression, and prosocial behavior, among other topics.

Attitudes, a combination of beliefs and emotional feelings, may be defined as one's readiness to respond in a predetermined manner to persons, places, or things. Both direct contact (such as repeated exposure) and indirect contact (such as through advertising, the mass media, and parental example) help to shape attitudes. People seek consistency among their attitudes and between their attitudes and their actions. Inconsistency, according to Festinger's theory of cognitive dissonance, leads to changes in attitude or behavior in order to achieve consistency and/or to reduce inconsistency. Two techniques for reducing dissonance are to increase the distance between two initially close alternatives (for example, overvaluing the one and undervaluing the other) and to practice selective exposure (paying attention only to information that is consistent with one's own attitudes and avoiding any that is inconsistent). In order to change a person's attitudes, it is important to consider both the message and the communicator. In the short run, the person who communicates a message will be largely responsible for its impact; in the long run, however, the content of the message will largely determine its influence.

People are largely attracted to one another because of physical beauty, reciprocity, similarity, and complementarity. A person will generally be attracted to a stranger according to the proportion of attitudes that he or she believes are shared with the stranger; long-range relationships (such as marriage) also depend somewhat on similarity, but complementarity—the extent to which each person can complement the needs of the other—may be more important.

Three important categories of social influence are conformity (changes in behavior in the direction of socially established norms), obedience (acquiescence to the direct commands of others), and compliance (voluntary yielding to the demands of others). The most important determinants of conformity are the size and behavior of one's reference group in a given situation. Asch has shown that three people who are in agreement constitute the optimum number required to produce conformity; regardless of the size of the reference group, however, virtually all pressure toward conformity disappears when there is just one dissenter. It has been shown that motivating someone to comply with a large request will be easier if that person's compliance has already been obtained for a smaller request. People will also be more willing to comply in certain situations if they feel guilty.

A major method of learning aggression is by observing, either directly or through the mass media, others who are aggressive. Such exposure can bring about aggression as well as simply teach it. Other factors that lead to aggression include frustration, attack, insult, personal anonymity (also called "deindividuation"), and the structure of certain institutions (such as prisons).

Two broad theories have been offered to explain altruism: the norm of reciprocity acknowledges the tacit existence of a system of debts and credits in society and a belief that the exchange of kindnesses will balance out; the norm of responsibility acknowledges that people feel that they need others and that they ought to be responsible for others in turn. In a crisis situation when there are other people around who could help, it is less likely that any particular individual himself will do so.

GLOSSARY

Attitude: A relatively enduring disposition toward any characteristic of a person, place, or thing based upon one's beliefs and emotional feelings.

Cognitive dissonance: An uncomfortable situation in which one's attitudes are inconsistent with one another or with one's behavior; as a consequence, one is motivated to try to reduce the inconsistency in some way.

Compliance: The tendency to yield readily to the demands of others; to cooperate, acquiesce, or conform.

Conformity: Adherence to the socially established norms of one's group or society.

Deindividuation: The hiding of one's personal identity, as in a crowd; such reduction of a person's identity tends to increase aggressive tendencies.

Ingratiation: The act of working oneself into favor with another; giving esteem with the hope of securing some reward.

Norm: A standard, model, or pattern of expected performance.

Obedience: Submitting oneself to an authority; doing what one is told; acquiescing to the direct commands of others.

Prosocial behavior: Acting in a favorable way toward others, such as helping or sharing.

Reciprocity: A mutual exchange; responding to another person according to how he or she acted toward you.

TEN

THREE VIEWS OF PER- SONALITY

Actors in the theater of ancient Rome wore full masks or *persona* that told audiences which of a small number of consistent attitudes or behavior patterns would be displayed in a given part. Eventually *persona* came to refer not only to the masks but also to the roles portrayed. *Persona* is the source of the English word *personality*.

All people seem to display recognizable and distinctive patterns of behavior in dealing with the world, and the study of personality tries to uncover the nature and origin of these highly recognizable patterns. The topic seems particularly important because almost all social interaction requires us to try to evaluate and predict the behavior of those with whom we must deal. For example, after a relatively brief meeting, college students often try to decide whether a new acquaintance might become a good friend, whether a particular professor could turn out to be an interesting and informative instructor, and whether to trust the word of a salesman who is trying to sell hi-fi sets. Presumably, if we knew something about how certain individuals' personalities were shaped and something about how personalities in general develop, we could better understand ourselves and others. Toward this end, it is helpful to have a theory of personality that encompasses all of the factors that help determine what we are and what we become.

Actually, psychologists have developed a number of theories of personality. Some of these attempt to apply basic psychological principles to complex human behavior; for example, a "learning" theory of personality emphasizes that much of our behavior has been learned through classical and operant conditioning and imitation. There are, however, several classic personality theories that reflect special psychological views of man, and it is these that we will discuss in this chapter. In order for the reader to get a feel for some of the issues and ideas that have been debated by personality psychologists, we will present three prominent views—psychoanalytic theory, type and trait theory, and one of the major cognitive theories of personality.

DEFINING PERSONALITY. Both laymen and psychologists often speak of *personality* without defining the term. It is not necessary for the beginning student to start with *a* definition; in fact, a complete definition of personality is actually a statement of a theory of personality. That is, in order to fully understand what a particular psychologist means by the term *personality*, it is necessary to examine his theory. For example, Sigmund Freud, whose work is discussed below, theorized that personality consists of the *id*, *ego*, and *superego*, three structures of the psyche, and that their interaction determines behavior. Much of Freud's personality theory deals with these three structures, and their interrelationship; therefore, Freud's definition of personality *is* his theory of personality.

However, to delimit our area of discussion, personality can be defined as "the sum total of individual characteristics and ways of behaving which in their organization or patterning describe an individual's unique adjustment to his environment" (Hilgard, as cited in Sanford, 1963, p. 497).

PERSONALITY AND ASSESSMENT. How can we measure the individual aspects of personality so that people can be compared? Assessment is difficult because most theories do not treat personality as equivalent to a person's behavior; rather, they treat personality as a theoretical abstraction that pertains to the continuing core of exis-

[1] One exception is the approach to personality taken by radical behaviorists and certain social learning theorists. They view personality as providing no more than a convenient (and sometimes misleading) label for a person's actions.

tence within each of us. Most theorists feel that behavior only reflects personality, sometimes in inconsistent or distorted ways.[1]

The problem is to determine which techniques can be used to assess people since the most obvious techniques also have the most evident pitfalls. A person may say that he is happy or sorry, but that may not describe his actual internal state at all. To such *self-reports* the personality psychologist has added a number of other assessment tools, including elaborate personality tests designed to detect and even compensate for purposeful falsification. Assessment procedures are derived from their parent theories and then evaluated according to how well they can find and put into order what the theory says should be there. Because of their close relationship, personality assessment will be presented within the context of personality theory.

PSYCHOANALYSIS: THE PERSONALITY THEORY OF SIGMUND FREUD

Sigmund Freud (1856–1939), a Viennese physician, developed one of the first systematic theories of personality in contemporary times. His position, which came to be called the *psychoanalytic theory*, has exerted an enormous influence upon our thinking about personality, abnormal behavior, child rearing practices, and even experimental psychology.

PERSONALITY AND THE UNCONSCIOUS. One of Freud's key concepts is that people are often not aware of their own intentions and motivations; some of the most important aspects of personality are *unconscious*. Thus, although the descriptions that follow will

Figure 10.1
Freud and his early colleagues.
Bottom, left to right: Freud, G. Stanley Hall, and Carl Gustav Jung. Top, left to right: Abraham A. Brill, Ernest Jones, and Sandor Ferenczi.

undoubtedly not correspond with what we remember about our own childhood feelings and experiences, psychoanalysts do not find that damaging to the validity of their theory, or even surprising. The theory holds that these experiences were felt but left their marks unconsciously, and so we could not be expected to recognize them.

STAGES OF PSYCHOSEXUAL DEVELOPMENT. Psycho-analytic theory suggests that personality develops as an individual passes through a series of *psychosexual stages*. As the person grows physically, certain areas of his body (first the mouth, then the anus, and finally the genital region) become important as sources of potential frustration, pleasure, or both. Freud believed that life was built around tension and pleasure. He also believed that all tension was due to the build up of *libido* (or sexual energy) and that all pleasure came from its discharge. In describing human personality development as psychosexual, Freud meant to convey that *what* develops is the way in which sexual energy accumulates and is discharged as we mature biologically. It is essential to note, though, that Freud used the term "sexual" in a very general way to mean all pleasurable actions and thoughts.

The Role of Conflict. Each of the psychosexual stages is associated with a particular *conflict* that must be resolved before the individual can successfully advance to the next stage. The resolution of each of these conflicts requires the expenditure of sexual energy (or libido), and the more energy that is expended at a particular stage, the more the important characteristics of that stage will remain with the individual as he matures psychologically. To explain this rather complicated process, Freud suggested the analogy of military troops on the march. As the troops advance, they are met by opposition or conflict. If they are highly successful in winning the battle (resolving the conflict), then most of the troops (libido) will be able to move on to the next battle (stage). But the greater the difficulty encountered at any particular point, the greater the need for troops to remain behind to fight and thus the fewer that will be able to go on to the next confrontation.

Frustration, Overindulgence, and Fixation. Physically, of course, some people do not achieve full growth. In the psychological area as well, some persons do not seem to be able to leave one stage and proceed on to the next. One reason for this may be that the needs of the developing individual at any particular stage may not have been adequately met, in which case there is *frustration*. Or possibly the person's needs may have been so well satisfied that he is reluctant to leave the psychological benefits of a particular stage, in which case there is *overindulgence*.

Both frustration and overindulgence (or any combination of the two) may lead to what psychoanalysts call *fixation* at a particular psychosexual stage. Fixation refers to the theoretical notion that a portion of the individual's libido has been permanently "invested" in a particular stage of his development, and is roughly analogous to the dead troops left behind in battle. It is assumed that some libido is permanently invested in each psychosexual stage and thus each person will behave in some ways that are characteristic of infancy or early childhood. However, when only a small proportion of libido is fixated at an early stage of development, only vestiges of these earlier modes of obtaining satisfaction will remain in one's later behavior. On the other hand, when a substantial proportion of libido has been fixated at an earlier stage (due to frustration or overindulgence at that time), the individual may be dominated by the modes he or she formerly used to obtain satisfaction or reduce frustration.

As the person passes through the various psychosexual stages, with their associated conflicts and benefits, the three underlying structures of personality—the *id*, *ego*, and *superego*—emerge.

THE ORAL STAGE AND THE ROOTS OF EGO DEVELOPMENT. Freud postulated that at birth the personality consists exclusively of the *id*, a reservoir of all biological instincts that derives its energy directly from bodily needs and processes. For example, when intense hunger or thirst is satisfied, a tremendous tension is discharged. When the id alone governs this discharge, it is not possible to have a voluntary *delay of gratification*. The individual is pressed to eat or drink immediately in order to satisfy his needs. For this reason, psychoanalysts claim that the id is governed by the *pleasure principle*.

During the first year of life, the infant's mouth provides the greatest tension-reduction (through eating) and pleasurable body sensations (sucking). The child is thus at the *oral stage* of development. During this period, the child's major psychological conflicts are those of *dependence* and *incorporation*. Since he is both physically and psychologically immature, he must be cared for by others. The infant's primary contact with his environment is through "taking things in" (incorporation) and "spitting things out." Freud thought that these experiences form the prototypes on which the individual's later social behavior will be built. For example, a child who is overindulged during the first year of life, by having everything done for him because of his smiles and cooing, may fixate at the oral stage. Consequently, he may become an optimistic and friendly but highly dependent adult, one who confidently expects the world to continue to mother him as it did when he was an infant.

Regardless of how quickly the infant's needs are satisfied during the oral stage, invariably he or she will have to tolerate some delay (a mother cannot always be available to nurse or feed her baby) and thus will have to "realize" that there is an external world that must be taken into account. This recognition, however primitive, leads to the development of the second structure of personality, the *ego*. As it matures, the ego is increasingly characterized by realistic thinking or problem-solving. Thus, Freud holds that, in adulthood, the ego is the seat of all intellectual processes and responsible for the individual's ability to deal with the direct constraints of physical reality. To the degree that young children's needs are met immediately, their egos may not have the chance to develop sufficiently so that they can cope successfully with reality later on.

THE ANAL STAGE. When the child is weaned, usually after the first year of life, he or she focuses more attention on the anus— obtaining pleasure from expelling feces and later on from retaining them. The oral pleasure and tension that predominated during the first year of life are replaced by anal pleasure and tension during the second and third years. At this time the parents place their first real demands on the youngster, usually in the area of bowel and bladder control. The conflict of the anal stage is typically between the immediate pleasure and reduction of tension provided by elimination and the constraints imposed by society (specifically, the parents).

THE PHALLIC STAGE AND THE APPEARANCE OF THE SUPEREGO. The psychoanalytic theory holds that during the fourth and fifth years of life, psychic energy centers on the genital region. Children of this age often examine their genitalia, begin to masturbate, and show pleasure and interest in their primary sexual parts. The psychosexual conflict that emerges at this stage is—presumably—the last and most crucial difficulty the young child must cope with in order to develop a well-adjusted personality in adulthood.

Freud assumed that during the phallic stage all children developed an unconscious wish to possess the opposite-sexed parent. In order to accomplish this end, they also harbored a desire to do away with the same-sexed parent. Together, these two wishes are called the *Oedipus complex,* a term referring to the Greek myth in which Oedipus unwittingly kills his father and marries his mother.

The male child's first important love object is his mother. As his libido increasingly focuses on the genital zone during the phallic stage, his love becomes erotically tinged. Obviously his father is a major impediment to the boy's sexual desires for his mother. The father thus becomes the boy's rival or enemy. According to psychoanalytic theory, besides wanting to do away with his father, the male child is afraid that his father will retaliate. Having observed that women lack penises, the boy fears that his father's revenge might take the form of castration. This *castration anxiety* forces the boy to give up his incestuous feelings toward his mother. The complex can be resolved only if the boy *represses* (that is, puts out of his conscious thoughts) his incestuous desires for his mother and *defensively identifies* with his father. The process of defensive identification presumably occurs as the boy reasons: "Since I cannot directly possess my mother without fear of retaliation, I must possess her vicariously

TESTING YOUR UNDERSTANDING
PSYCHOSEXUAL DEVELOPMENT AND ADULT PERSONALITY

According to psychoanalytic theory, the child who is able to accede easily to the demands of toilet training will thereby be able to exercise appropriate self-control in later life. In contrast, the child who has difficulty controlling his or her bodily eliminations and thus meeting the demands of others will have to develop an alternative strategy to cope with the situation. What might the child do?

One possibility is that the child might "counterattack" by defecating at moments that are particularly inappropriate or inconvenient for his "tormentors." Thus, the child who urinates or defecates immediately *after* being taken off the toilet will probably cause his parents to become upset. Again, the primary focus of psychoanalytic theory is not on the occurrence of this tactic per se; rather, it is on the assumption that through these early experiences the child will discover successful means of *social* control, as well as self-control, that can be used in handling frustration and difficulties in later life. It is, therefore, interesting that in our culture verbal statements of extreme anger and hostility often refer explicitly to the anal function. Just as a 2-year-old's inappropriate elimination is viewed as an act of counteraggression, so hostile or inappropriate outbursts at a later age are thought to be characteristic of a personality type called the *anal aggressive character*.

Alternatively, however, the child can adopt another strategy for dealing with the harsh demands of parental ambitions for quick toilet training—by refusing to defecate altogether. In itself, this could provide physical pleasure (that is, gentle pressure against the intestinal walls). But also, and of greater importance, this strategy could prove to be important in manipulating the parents (if, for example, they become alarmed over the child's failure to have a bowel movement). If successful, this strategy could also set the stage for analogous patterns of social interaction in adulthood. Thus, those who are stingy, hoarding, and "hold back" are often called *anal retentive characters*.

[through another's experience]. Specifically, I can obtain some of the pleasure of possessing my mother indirectly *by becoming like her lover, my father.*" In this manner, the boy resolves his Oedipal conflicts by adopting his father's behaviors, attitudes, and values. This resolution is successful and adaptive because it has simultaneously eliminated the castration anxiety, secured vicarious possession of the mother, and inculcated in the child behaviors that are necessary for appropriate adult sex-role behavior.

The parallel conflict for girls is sometimes called the *Electra complex*, referring to the Greek myth in which Electra persuades her brother to murder their mother and their mother's lover. Like the boy, the girl's first love object is her mother. However, during the phallic stage, the little girl also discovers that while her father and brothers have penises, she and her mother do not. According to psychoanalytic theory, the female child assumes that she and other women must have had a penis at one time, and she blames her mother for her (the little girl's) own apparent castration. These negative feelings reduce her love for her mother and increase her affection for her father. This love for her father also acquires erotic overtones, because she covets his penis. This phenomenon—*penis envy*—may be viewed as the counterpart of castration anxiety in males. However, as in the case of boys, the impracticality of a girl fulfilling her sexual desires directly leads her to repress these desires for her father and identify with her mother (defensively) by adopting the female role, thereby learning how to relate to men during adulthood.

Resolving the Oedipus complex also requires a structural change in personality. In order to successfully identify with the same sexed parent, children must begin to evaluate their own behavior. Psychoanalytic theory suggests that a new personality structure—the *superego*—develops when children begin to incorporate the values of their parents at about the age of 4 or 5. This process is intimately associated with resolving the Oedipus complex, since identification includes adoption of all parental values, and not just those relating to sex.

THE LATENCY PERIOD. Freud believed that about the age of 5 (after the Oedipus complex had been resolved), children of both sexes entered into a period of development known as *latency* period. Latency is *not* a psychosexual stage, since it is not characterized by any major conflict or focusing of the libido.

GENITAL STAGE. The last stage of psychosexual development begins with the onset of puberty, the period of sexual maturation. At this time the libido is again focused on the genital area and is directed toward heterosexual pleasure. Presumably, an individual who has reached the genital stage without incurring a large number of unresolved conflicts during the three pregenital stages will be able to lead a "normal" life and enjoy mature relationships with persons of the opposite sex. Individuals remain at this stage of development until the onset of senility, at which time they may regress to pregenital behavior.

EXPERIMENTAL STUDIES OF HUMOR: AN EXAMPLE OF PSYCHOANALYTIC LABORATORY RESEARCH. The major research method used by Freud and his followers has been the case history (see Chapter 1). Freud himself spent almost 12 hours a day during most of his professional life seeing patients, and he used this clinical material as a source for his hypotheses as well as evidence to support his emerging theory. Studies of this type will be discussed in Chapter 12, when we turn to a discussion of the practice of psychoanalytic psychotherapy.

In a few areas, though, experimental research has been guided by psychoanalytic theory. One of the most interesting is the studies of humor and the unconscious that have utilized Freud's views. According to Freud, humor enables one to vicariously gratify an impulse that cannot be expressed directly. Working from this general proposition, Singer, Gollob, and Levine (1966) formulated and tested two experimental hypotheses: "(1) a heightening of inhibitions surrounding expression of aggressive impulses [which presumably *are* forbidden to be expressed directly] should result in decreased ability to enjoy aggressive humor; (2) this effect should be more pronounced the stronger and the more blatant the aggressive content of the humorous material" (p. 2). In order to test these hypotheses, Singer and his associates first asked male undergraduates to rate five etchings by the great Spanish artist Goya. In order to heighten the students' inhibitions against wanton aggression, half were asked to look at brutal and sadistic pictures from the artist's "Disaster of War" series. The other subjects looked at an equal number of benign social scenes that had no aggressive content.

Immediately after looking at the etchings, all of the subjects were asked to rate the humor of 12 cartoons and to indicate how much aggression they thought was portrayed in each. Four of the cartoons depicted highly aggressive interpersonal incidents, four showed relatively mild interpersonal aggression, and four had little or no aggressive content. Examples of each type are presented in Figure 10.2.

Figure 10.2
The subjects in the Singer, Gollob, and Levine experiment who looked at etchings from Goya's "Disaster of War" found Type A cartoons (highly aggressive) to be substantially less funny and Type B cartoons (mildly aggressive) to be somewhat less funny than did the control subjects who had looked at nonaggressive art. The two groups evaluated about equally the humor of Type C (nonaggressive) cartoons.

Psychoanalytic theory would predict that those subjects who had viewed the "Disaster of War" etchings would have their inhibitions against expressing aggressive impulses raised. Thus, these people should find less humor in aggressive cartoons, especially those that are highly aggressive. As predicted, those subjects in the Inhibition Condition (that is, those who had been exposed to the "Disaster of War" series) rated the mildly aggressive cartoons as slightly less amusing and the highly aggressive cartoons as substantially less amusing than did the subjects in the Control Condition (those who had been exposed to socially benign sketches). Thus, people found aggressive humor less amusing when their inhibitions about expressing aggression were heightened; the more aggressive the humor, the less amusing it seemed. This is exactly the pattern of results that would be expected from psychoanalytic theory.

The psychoanalytic view that humor permits an emotional release can also be expressed in terms of physiological arousal. Since it is believed that humor reduces emotional arousal under certain circumstances, it could be predicted that the greater a person's arousal before relief, the greater the humor he or she might perceive in certain amusing situations. In an ingenious experiment, Shurcliff (1968) tested this hypothesis.

The participants were brought to the laboratory ostensibly for the purpose of assessing their reactions to small animals. When they arrived, three cages were within their eyesight, but arranged in such a fashion that only the animals in the first two cages—white laboratory rats—could actually be seen. Shurcliff divided his subjects into three experimental groups according to the degree of anxiety that was to be induced. Those assigned to the Low-Anxiety Condition were told that their job was to pick up the animal in the third cage and hold it for 5 seconds. Those in the Moderate-Anxiety Condition were shown slides, presumably of blood samples from the animals in the first two cages, and told that their task was to obtain a similar sample from the animal in the third cage. They were given simple instructions, according to which the task was easier than it appeared. Finally, the subjects in the High-Anxiety Condition were shown bottles of "blood," supposedly drawn from the animals in the first two cages, and were instructed how to obtain an equal amount of blood with a hypodermic needle from the animal in the last cage. The subjects in this third group were warned that the task was difficult and that they might be bitten by the rodent in that cage.

As the subjects in all three groups reached into the third cage, they found—to their surprise—that it contained a toy rat! At that point they were asked to rate the humor of the situation and, for the purpose of validating the experimental manipulations, their apprehension at the beginning. As had been predicted, the higher the subject's anxiety before reaching into the cage for the rat, the funnier the subject found the situation.

TABLE 10.1

Erikson's diagram of the eight stages of psychosocial development.

		1	2	3	4	5	6	7	8
VIII	Maturity								Ego integrity vs. Despair
VII	Adulthood							Generativity vs. Stagnation	
VI	Young adulthood						Intimacy vs. Isolation		
V	Puberty and adolescence					Identity vs. Role confusion			
IV	Latency				Industry vs. Inferiority				
III	Locomotor-genital			Initiative vs. Guilt					
II	Muscular-anal		Autonomy vs. Shame, doubt						
I	Oral sensory	Basic trust vs. Mistrust							

Source: Erikson (1963)

Figure 10.3
Erik H. Erikson

LATER EXTENSIONS OF PSYCHOANALYTIC PERSONALITY THEORY. Over the years, personality psychologists who have generally agreed with Freud's approach have suggested various additions or revisions of his theory. Some of the most significant modifications were advanced by Erik Erikson. Erikson argued that personality development could be viewed as a succession of *psychosocial* rather than psychosexual stages. For Erikson, every person passes through a series of eight stages, each of which is characterized by a social conflict between two alternative ways of handling encounters with other people. In Table 10.1, each row presents the particular conflict that Erikson believes is primarily associated with a certain period in life. The blank squares represent the interaction among the stages of psychosocial development, since Erikson believes that each is always present although each comes to the fore at a different time in life. The blank squares to the left of each conflict symbolize the stages that still exist but do not predominate, while those to the right reflect the influence of those that will become important later.

Basic Trust vs. Mistrust. Erikson has suggested that the infant must at the outset develop trust in its mother (or primary caretaker), and come to believe that she will continue to provide food and care even if she is temporarily absent. Building upon Freud's conceptualization, Erikson assumes that the establishment of trust in infancy is critical for the health of the adult personality. Thus, trusting one's mother is the prototype for developing confidence about the predictability of others and for developing trust in one's self.

Figure 10.4
According to Erikson, each of us passes
through a sequence of eight stages of
psychosocial development. A description of
each of these stages appears on the fol-
lowing page.

An infant's relationship with its mother leads to the development of basic trust.

The conflict between autonomy and shame or doubt usually arises during toilet training.

A child's initiative may first appear in caring for younger siblings.

The conflict between industry and inferiority is seen most clearly in friendly competition with peers.

Overidentification with popular heroes reflects the adolescent's conflict between identity and role confusion.

Young adults must learn to overcome isolation by developing truly intimate relationships.

To preclude feelings of stagnation, mature individuals direct their energies to guiding the next generation.

The final stage of psychosocial development requires each of us to develop a sense of personal integrity and fulfillment.

Autonomy vs. Shame and Doubt. At the next stage, the individual must begin to establish a sense of autonomy. Erikson assumes that this can be accomplished by means of successful bladder and bowel control, thus paralleling the anal stage in traditional psychoanalytic theory. The child who does not successfully meet parental expectations about toilet training may feel a sense of shame or doubt about his or her own adequacy. In turn, these negative feelings can lead to later difficulties, just as developing adequate self-control will produce positive feelings in adult life. According to Erikson (1963):

> *This stage, therefore, becomes decisive for the ratio of love and hate, cooperation and willfulness, freedom of self-expression and its suppression. From a sense of self-control without loss of self-esteem, comes a lasting sense of goodwill and pride; from a sense of loss of self-control and of foreign overcontrol comes a lasting propensity for doubt and shame [p. 254].*

Initiative vs. Guilt. The last conflict experienced by the preschool child (which corresponds to the phallic stage in psychoanalytic theory) is learning appropriate control over feelings of rivalry for his or her mother's attention and the subsequent development of moral responsibility. The child may experience a conflict between fantasies of grandeur, such as being a TV hero, and feelings of weakness. To overcome this conflict the child must learn to take role-appropriate initiative. This is accomplished by finding pleasure in socially approved activities such as creative play or caring for younger siblings. In turn, participation in these activities lays the groundwork for taking the appropriate initiative in a variety of achievement-oriented activities in adulthood.

Industry vs. Inferiority. During the elementary-school years, a conflict arises between industry and inferiority. At this time, the youngster must undertake academic work, begin to feel that he or she is competent with respect to peers, and face personal limitations successfully. It is interesting to note that these extremely important social accomplishments occur at a time when, according to traditional psychoanalytic theory, the child is in a period of latency.

Identity vs. Role Confusion. During adolescence, the young person must begin to create a sense of personal identity that is independent of the values and ideals of parents. One important facet of identity formation is the choice of an occupation or career. If the young person does not establish his or her own identity, Erikson suggests that there may be *role confusion*. This conflict may manifest itself by an inability to select a career or educational goal, and by overidentification with popular heroes, cliques, or the ephemeral values of a "pop" culture. This conflict might be able to be resolved by means of interaction with peers or elders who are knowledgeable about various professional or occupational opportunities and/or who can genuinely accept the adolescent's self-perception without undue criticism.

Intimacy vs. Isolation. In adulthood the individual is expected to form intimate relationships with others, including cooperative social and occupational relationships with members of both sexes and the selection of an appropriate mate. Without such relationships, an individual will feel isolated. Freud refers to this period as the genital stage. Erikson (1963), who agrees with him about its general character, points out that Freud described the healthy genital characters as having two aims—*"Lieben und arbeiten"* [to love and to work] (p. 265).

Generativity vs. Stagnation. The mature individual must be able to do more than simply establish intimate relationships with others. One "needs to be needed" and to help in an appropriate way the younger members of society. *Generativity* refers to the process of guiding the next generation without overpowering it. Without generativity, the individual may feel stagnant and personally impoverished despite many other accomplishments.

Ego Integrity vs. Despair. If all of the preceding life conflicts are not adequately resolved, the individual may feel profound despair late in life. Disgusted and believing that it is "too late to start over," this individual may enter the senior years with incurable remorse. In contrast, the psychosocially well-adjusted individual experiences a feeling of integrity during the senior years, having successfully grappled with all of the significant conflicts of earlier life. Thus, Erikson (1963) emphasized that all persons in all cultures can achieve an appropriate adjustment through a sense of personal integrity. He observed that "a wise Indian, a true gentleman, and a mature peasant share and recognize in one another the final stage of integrity" (p. 269).

PERSONALITY ASSESSMENT AND THE UNCONSCIOUS.

Freud's view of man was totally deterministic; he believed that every fantasy and action is directed by the underlying forces of one's personality and therefore reflects them. Thus, even the simplest acts could be traced to complex psychological factors of which the individual was usually unaware. Freud, therefore, found many "unimportant" events useful precisely because they carried otherwise hidden secrets.

Perhaps the best-known examples are the so-called Freudian slips in speech, writing, and social interaction. Freud felt that these errors were *not* accidents, but important messages revealing meaningful aspects of the person's thoughts, feelings, or intentions. For example, Freud pointed out that the loss of a gift might tell us something about the feelings of the person who lost it vis-à-vis the giver.

We lose an object if we have quarreled with the person who gave it to us and do not want to be reminded of him; or if we no longer like the object itself and want to have an excuse for getting another and better one instead. The same intention directed against an object can also play a part, of course, in cases of dropping, breaking, or destroying things [1963, p. 54].

Although it would be impractical to analyze an individual's personality using nothing but his accidental slips (most of us don't make enough of them), Freud found another route to the unconscious—by interpreting dreams.

Psychoanalytic Dream Interpretation. Freud believed that dreams were important for psychological study because they could reveal a great deal about the deeper, unconscious aspects of personality. Extracting appropriate information from dreams is not a simple matter, however, because the psychologist must first decipher the dream; what the dreamer remembers (*manifest content*) must be correctly interpreted so that the underlying significance (*latent content*) of the dream can be discerned.

Although most analysts hold that it requires years of training and experience to fully understand the decoding process, we will mention a few of the essentials. Most important, perhaps, is that dreams are seen as permitting an individual to express his deepest impulses and fears in *disguised* or *socially acceptable forms.* Thus, seemingly "innocent" elements of a dream may symbolize more troublesome themes. A man might dream of losing his pencil or—somewhat more transparently—his gun because of a longstanding fear of losing his penis, that is, an unresolved castration anxiety. Sometimes the symbolism is more subtle and complicated. In one of Freud's famous dream analyses, a young Viennese woman who had just become engaged to be married reported dreaming that she had rushed to buy tickets for a play—only to discover later on that she could have easily waited because half the theater was empty. According to Freud, the woman was really dreaming about her upcoming marriage; she regretted that she had hurried into it too early because of a fear that she would never marry, just as the woman-as-dreamer had regretted rushing out to buy tickets for fear of not getting a seat in a theater that turned out to be half-empty.

As with slips, however, the use of dreams to assess personality requires waiting for the right moment (that is, the revealing dream) to come along. Since this may take a very long time indeed, psychoanalysts also use guided methods of assessment to elicit unconscious material.

Projective Techniques. In a limited way at least, almost everyone is familiar with the inkblot tests into which people are expected to "project" their personalities. Most of these procedures (and there are a variety of them) are derived from psychoanalytic personality theory. We will explain their rationale and briefly describe the widely used Rorschach test.

Most projective tests are based on the *projective hypothesis,* which postulates that, when faced with an ambiguous situation, people will impose or project their own personalities (feelings, attitudes, desires, and needs) into it. An ambiguous situation can be created in a variety

Figure 10.5
A card from the Thematic Apperception Test (TAT), a projective test in which a subject is asked to make up a story about the picture and then answer the following questions: What is the relationship between the individuals in the picture? What has happened to them? What are their present thoughts and feelings? What will be the outcome?

of ways. Some projective tests simply ask people to respond quickly to selected words or sentence stems (for example, "I often feel . . ."), while more elaborate techniques may use specially constructed materials such as the one shown in Figure 10.5. In any case, the subject must impose some order of his own, usually without knowing the specific purpose of the test but with the assurance that there are no right or wrong answers. Scoring is frequently a lengthy procedure and is sometimes quite subjective as well.

The Rorschach. The Rorschach Inkblot technique, usually called simply the "Rorschach," consists of ten nearly symmetrical inkblots; half are in black and white and the rest have some color as well. Printed and centered on 7×10-inch pieces of white cardboard, they were originally selected from a large number of blots made by literally spilling ink onto a piece of paper and folding it in half. Inkblots resembling those used in the Rorschach are shown in Figure 10.6

The Rorschach is usually administered to a single individual by a highly trained examiner. The subject is asked to tell *what* he or she sees in each card, *where* on the card each suggestive aspect appears, and *why* the card conveys its particular meaning.

The responses must then be scored and/or interpreted, as illustrated in Table 10.2. Years of experience and research have shown that the Rorschach and other projective techniques are not a "royal road to the unconscious," as was once thought, but they are still widely

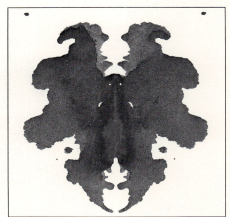

Figure 10.6
Inkblots similar to those used in
the Rorschach test. The subjects
are asked to tell what they see in
the picture or what it suggests to
them.

TABLE 10.2

Interpretations of responses to the Rorschach cards.

Description of response	Subtype	Example	Possible interpretation[1]
Location	Whole	Entire blot used for concept	Ability to organize and integrate material
	Small detail	Small area easily marked off in blot	Need to be exact or accurate
Content	Animal figures	"Looks like a house cat"	Passivity and dependence
	Human figures	"It's a man or woman"	Problem with sexual identity
Form-level	High form-level	Concept fits blot well	Superior intellectual functioning
	Low form-level	Concept is a poor match for blot	Tenuous contact with reality

[1] These interpretations are for purposes of illustration only; in practice they would be offered only after the repetition of a response together with other assessment information.

regarded as useful assessment procedures when employed by skilled persons who can combine projective, interview, and life-history data in establishing a complete view of the subject.

TYPE AND TRAIT THEORIES Some personality theories are based on the assumption that there are enduring, stable personality traits residing within the person. As in the case of a person's eye color, such characteristics need only be measured at the present time, with little regard for how they developed, in order to understand that individual's personality. In a sense this concept is exactly the opposite of psychoanalytic theory, since it emphasizes a person's static, overt, and ongoing characteristics rather than the dynamic, hidden ones that Freud thought were so important.

TYPE THEORIES. Type theories of personality were among the first to be found in recorded history. The ancient type theories were based upon the idea that people could be divided into a relatively small number of types, according to their personalities, and that one could predict a person's behavior with reasonable accuracy by simply knowing his "type." This popular notion, although it has varied substantially throughout the centuries, still prevails in the familiar question: "What type of person is he?"

Of the many typologies proposed, only a few have led to serious research. Those theories that have been amenable to investigation have usually singled out certain physical characteristics (for example, *body* types) and related them to various aspects of personality and behavior. One theory that received a lot of attention in its day was researched by a German psychiatrist, Ernst Kretschmer. After making careful physical examinations of approximately 400 psychiatric patients, Kretschmer concluded that there were three basic physiques: *asthenic*, *athletic*, and *pyknic*, as well as some unusual body types that could be called *dysplastic*. Kretschmer described the asthenic type as a "lean, narrowly built man, who looks taller than he is, with narrow shoulders . . . thin muscled and delicately boned hands; a long, narrow, flat chest, on which we can count the ribs" (1926, p. 21).

Not surprisingly, he described the athletic type as one with "particularly wide projecting shoulders, a superb chest, a firm stomach" (pp. 24–25). In contrast with the other two, the pyknic individual has a "rounded figure, a soft broad face . . . the magnificent fat paunch protrudes from the deep vaulted chest which broadens out toward the lower part of the body" (p. 29). Dysplastics were described most succinctly by Kretschmer as those who "impress the laity as rare, surprising, and ugly" (p. 65). Kretschmer endeavored to illustrate the sharp differences in these body types by securing photographs of typical individuals in each category.

Kretschmer's purpose was not simply to identify body types; he wanted to show that these types were significantly related to the particular psychiatric disorders of the patients. The two major diagnostic categories of these patients were *schizophrenia* and *manic-depressive psychosis*. Schizophrenia characterizes those who show disordered thought and a loss of emotional reactions, while manic-depressive psychosis typifies those who demonstrate extreme elation (mania) or extreme depression, or sometimes a periodic shift from one to the other. We shall discuss psychiatric diagnosis and categories in Chapter 11.

Kretschmer found dramatic differences in the frequency of schizophrenia and manic-depression as a function of body type. As can be seen from Table 10.3, asthenic, athletic, and dysplastic body types were associated almost exclusively with a diagnosis of schizophrenia, while the pyknic type was nearly always diagnosed as manic-depressive.

Although Kretschmer had considered the possibility of extending these findings to the normal population, it was an American, William

TABLE 10.3

The relationship between physique and psychiatric diagnosis as reported by Ernst Kretschmer.

	Schizophrenic	Manic-depressive	Total
	Percent	Percent	Percent
Asthenic and athletic	91.2	8.8	100.0
Dysplastic	100.0	0.0	100.0
Pyknic	6.5	93.5	100.0

These data are based on 243 patients.
Source: Adapted from Kretschmer (1926)

Figure 10.7
The three extreme body types identified by Sheldon.

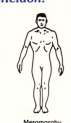

Mesomorphy

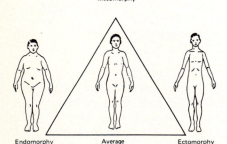

Endomorphy   Average   Ectomorphy

Sheldon, who actually did so. After extensive independent research, Sheldon identified three primary components of body structure—*endomorphy*, *mesomorphy*, and *ectomorphy*—which correspond quite closely to Kretschmer's pyknic, athletic, and asthenic body types (see Figure 10.7). However, whereas Kretschmer believed that each individual could be typed as belonging to one of the categories (in most cases), Sheldon argued that a person should be *somatotyped* in such a way that the relative strength of each of the three components could be assigned to his unique body structure. Sheldon carefully related the somatotypes of a large number of individuals to their personalities. In doing so, he found that he could also identify three components of temperament, subsequently called *viscerotonia*, *somatotonia*, and *cerebrotonia*. The characteristics of these components are shown in Table 10.4. After looking at the table, the reader may want to guess which temperamental type corresponds with which body type.

Sheldon found that the endomorphic body type was associated with the even, relaxed, disposition he had called "viscerotonia"; mesomorphy corresponded with the risky, assertive, energetic, personality characteristic he called "somatotonia"; and the ectomorphic body type was most often found in those who acted in the restrained, self-conscious, inhibited fashion he called "cerebrotonia."

TRAIT THEORIES. While type theories appear to account for some of the major differences among people, it is also clear that peo-

TABLE 10.4

Sheldon's scale of temperament (abbreviated).

I Viscerotonia	II Somatotonia	III Cerebrotonia
Relaxation in posture and movement	Assertiveness of posture and movement	Restraint in posture and movement, tightness
Love of physical comfort	Love of physical adventure	Overly fast reactions
Slow reaction	Need for and enjoyment of exercise	Love of privacy
Love of polite ceremony	Love of risk and chance	Mental overintensity, apprehensiveness
Enjoyment in being with others	Bold directness of manner	Secretiveness of feeling, emotional restraint
Evenness of emotional flow	Physical courage for combat	Self-conscious movement of the eyes and face
Tolerance	Competitive aggressiveness	Dislike for being with others
Complacency	Unrestrained voice	Vocal restraint, and general restraint of noise
Smooth, easy communication of feeling, extroversion	Overmaturity of appearance	Youthful intentness of manner and appearance

Source: Adapted from Sheldon (1942)

ple differ in more ways than can be encompassed by a small number of classifications. Thus, *trait theorists* have attempted to distinguish between personality types using a larger number of characteristics. Two of these theories were advanced by Gordon Allport and Raymond Cattell.

Figure 10.8
Gordon W. Allport

ALLPORT'S TRAIT THEORY. For more than 40 years, Gordon W. Allport was the dean of American trait theorists. His view, which influenced many psychologists and inspired considerable research, was that personality truly exists within the individual and that the psychologist's job is to discover it by identifying each person's enduring characteristics or traits. These traits may be either unique to one individual or sufficiently common so that comparisons could be made between people.

One of Allport's most widely accepted propositions is that a person's traits can be classified according to the extent to which they pervade his personality. Allport specifically distinguished among three levels of traits, although he admitted that "these three gradations are arbitrary and are phrased mainly for convenience of discourse" (1961, p. 365).

According to Allport, a few persons have traits that are so pervasive that they may be called *cardinal dispositions.* Allport noted that the proper names of many historical and fictitious characters with glaring cardinal dispositions have become trait adjectives in our language, such as *quixotic, machiavellian,* and *lesbian.* Likewise, persons with highly salient characteristics are often identified with those who are noted for them (for example, "He is a real Don Juan").

The small number of traits that really typify most individuals are called *central dispositions.* They might include those aspects of an individual's personality we would mention in preparing a letter of recommendation on his or her behalf. Believing that virtually everyone could be described in terms of a few central dispositions, Allport asked 93 students: "Think of some one individual of your own sex whom you know well" and "describe him or her by writing words, phrases, or sentences that express fairly well what seem to you to be the essential characteristics of this person" (1961, p. 366). Consistent with his theoretical position, Allport found that most students listed between 3 and 10 essential characteristics, with the average being 7.2.

The least important characteristics—those that appear only in limited settings—are called *secondary dispositions.* They would include preferences for particular kinds of food, attitudes on specific issues, and enjoyment of certain leisure-time activities.

Since Allport believed that there were common traits, permitting comparisons to be made among people, one individual difference that interested him was the extent to which people present a well-integrated "self." He called the concept of "selfhood" in personality the *pro-*

TABLE 10.5

Inferiority feelings of college
students according to type and sex.

Type of inferiority feeling	Percentage reporting persistent inferiority feelings	
	Men (243)	Women (120)
Physical	39	50
Social	52	57
Intellectual	29	61
Moral	16	15
None at all	12	10

Source: Allport (1961)

prium. One study of *propriate feelings* asked college students to state what type of inferiority feelings (if any) they had, and the extent to which these feelings dominated their lives. Some of the results from this study are presented in Table 10.5, indicating that there is a hierarchy of importance of these feelings among young adults. Since this study was made in the late 1950s, it is possible that the striking differences in inferiority feelings between men and women no longer prevail (due to the women's movement and other factors).

A final aspect of Allport's trait theory (and perhaps the best known) is his concept of *functional autonomy.* This refers to the idea that a person may begin to act in a certain way because of one or more "outside reasons," and then continue that behavior even when the original reasons no longer exist. Thus, certain personality characteristics become *autonomous* despite their origins in childhood. As Allport explained it:

Joe, let us say, is the son of a famous politician. As a young lad he imitates everything his father does, even perhaps giving "speeches." Years pass and the father dies. Joe is now middle-aged and is deeply absorbed in politics. He runs for office, perhaps the selfsame job his father held. What, then, motivates Joe today? Is it his earlier fixation? . . . The chances . . . are that his interest in politics has outgrown its roots in "father identification." There is historical continuity but no longer any functional continuity. Politics is now his dominant passion; it is his style of life; it is a large part of Joe's personality. The original seed has been discarded [Allport, 1961, pp. 228-229].

This idea, like much of Allport's work, is interesting because it seems to ring true in many of our own experiences. But other trait theorists have also attempted to identify personality characteristics that are less intuitively obvious but that may be equally important for understanding ourselves and others. Among these theorists is Raymond Cattell.

CATTELL'S FACTOR-ANALYTIC APPROACH. If we were to try to give a personality description of many people using only a small number of traits, we would probably have difficulty comparing them in a meaningful way. Thus, as Raymond Cattell has argued: "The trouble with measuring traits is that there are too many of them!" (1965, p. 55). He believes that what is needed is a method that will allow us to relate various aspects of personality in such a way that unifying and systematic patterns can emerge:

> The problem which baffled psychologists for many years was to find a method which would tease out these functionally unitary influences in the chaotic jungle of human behavior. But let us ask how, in the literal tropical jungle, the hunter decides whether the dark blobs which he sees are two or three rotting logs or a single alligator? He watches for a movement. If they move together—come and disappear together—he infers a single structure. Just so, as John Stuart Mill pointed out in his philosophy of science, the scientists should look for "concomitant variation" in seeking unitary concepts [p. 56].

But since one is not likely to find perfect co-variation in the jungle of human behavior, how can we discover these unitary concepts? The correlational method, discussed in Chapter 1, will enable us to detect and evaluate relationships that are not perfect. Moreover, a sophisticated variant of this procedure, known as *factor analysis*, permits the researcher to analyze a large number of interrelationships among various aspects of personality and abstract some of the common elements (or factors) that lie behind them. A brief example from Cattell's work will illustrate its application.

Figure 10.9
Raymond B. Cattell

EGO STRENGTH: AN EXAMPLE OF A DERIVED SOURCE TRAIT. Cattell has argued that certain trait-like factors lie behind all human behavior and that they can be discovered (using factor analysis) by examining common relationships among various measures of the individual. These underlying, and presumably causal, personality structures are called *source traits.*

Cattell (1965) described a research program using several hundred young men and women, in which measures were obtained on a large number of ratings and questionnaire data. Initially, this information appeared to provide a large number of descriptive traits (about 50). However, when this information was consolidated by means of factor-analytic procedures, three underlying factors accounted for most of the information: *intelligence;* a *"warm-cold"* dimension in dealing with others; and *ego strength*—the ability to control one's emotions and impulses, especially through appropriate realistic expression. Some of the actual behavior ratings and questionnaire responses for measuring ego strength are given in Table 10.6.

THE ASSESSMENT OF TRAITS. For purposes of trying to learn what underlying traits differentiate people, a variety of psychological measures or tests has been developed. Because these procedures often rely heavily on some kind of self-report, they are called *self-report inventories.*

TABLE 10.6

**Behavior ratings and questionnaire items
that measure the ego strength factor.**

BEHAVIOR RATINGS

High ego strength	Low ego strength
Mature	*vs.* Unable to tolerate frustration
Steady, persistent	*vs.* Changeable
Emotionally calm	*vs.* Impulsively emotional
Realistic about problems	*vs.* Evasive, avoids necessary decisions
Absence of neurotic fatigue	*vs.* Neurotically fatigued (with no real effort)

QUESTIONNAIRE RESPONSES[1]

Do you find it difficult to take no for an answer even when what you want to do is obviously impossible?
  (a) yes   (b) *no*
If you had your life to live over again, would you
  (a) *want it to be essentially the same*   (b) plan it very differently?
Do you often have really disturbing dreams?
  (a) yes   (b) *no*
Do your moods sometimes make you seem unreasonable even to yourself?
  (a) yes   (b) *no*
Do you feel tired when you've done nothing to justify it?
  (a) *rarely*   (b) often
Can you change old habits, without relapse, when you decide to?
  (a) *yes*   (b) no

[1] A person who selects all of the italicized answers has high ego strength on this measure, whereas selection of all the nonitalicized responses would indicate low ego strength.
Source: Adapted from Cattell (1965)

The typical self-report inventory consists of a fairly large number of questions or statements to which the subject must respond by choosing one out of two or three alternatives, such as "agree-disagree" or "yes-no." A "cannot say" category is sometimes included. These items are often printed in a standard booklet that has an accompanying answer sheet, requiring the use of special pencils so that the answer sheets can be machine-scored.

The Minnesota Multiphasic Personality Inventory (MMPI) is probably the most widely known and used self-report inventory. It consists of 550 statements about attitudes, morals, vocational interests, fears, preoccupations, and even general physical health. The idea behind the MMPI is quite simple. Any item, regardless of content, that can discriminate between groups of people who do and do not have a particular characteristic is a useful item. When many such items are used, a pattern of similarity between the subject and others with a particular personality is interpreted to mean that the subject will have that type of personality himself. An item would contribute to a measure of depression if it could be shown to distinguish between normal people and those with a depressive disorder regardless of the item's content. The item "I sometimes tease animals" appears on the MMPI Depression scale, and this often surprises those who are not familiar with the concept of the test.

As we have just implied, personality test items are scored according to whether they relate to certain trait scales. The MMPI has ten such basic scales, as well as four others to check the accuracy of the responses given. Table 10.7 presents five of the scales, together with typical items and interpretations.

HOW TESTS ARE MADE AND EVALUATED. Administering psychological tests to people, particularly tests that are quick and easy to give, can only be justified if it is clear that the tests meet certain technical standards. We will briefly describe the principles of test construction and evaluation used by psychologists; these principles apply to personality tests, intelligence tests, academic achievement tests, and actually any measures of behavior.

Standardization. In constructing any good test, psychologists will administer it to a fairly large group of people to establish the norms (or typical range of response patterns) that can be expected. Using the

TABLE 10.7

Five sample scales and interpretations from the Minnesota Multiphasic Personality Inventory (MMPI).		
Scale	**Sample item**	**Interpretation of scale**
Lie (L)[1]	I get angry sometimes. *false*[2]	This is one of the validity check scales. Persons trying to place themselves in a favorable light (for example, as especially nice, honest or wholesome) obtain high L scores.
Hypochondriasis (Hs)	I wake up fresh and rested most mornings. *false*	High scorers are said to be cynical and defeatist.
Paranoia (Pa)	Someone has it in for me. *true*	High scorers are said to be shrewd, guarded, and worrisome.
Hypomania (Ma)	At times my thoughts have raced ahead faster than I could speak them. *true*	High scorers are said to be sociable, energetic, and impulsive.
Social introversion-extroversion (Si)	I enjoy social gatherings just to be with people. *false*	High scorers are said to be modest, shy, and self-effacing; low scorers are described as sociable, colorful, and ambitious.

[1] The letters in parentheses are the standard symbols for each scale. Many of the scale names are derived from forms of psychopathology (see Chapter 11).
[2] The italicized true or false responses indicate the direction for which the response is scored.

responses of this group—which is called the *standardization sample*—as a basis, psychologists evaluate the pattern of answers given by other subjects later on. Thus, the standardization sample must be chosen carefully so that it will be truly representative of the population for whom the test will be subsequently used. For example, if the test is being designed for persons of various age and social backgrounds, it is essential that the standardization group be typical in these respects as well.

An equally important aspect of standardization lies in the procedure for test administration. Tests given in college history classes, where the same course is taught by different instructors, usually vary in their content, the amount of time allowed for taking the test, the form of the questions, and so forth. These tests are completely unstandardized, and scores on them would not be an appropriate basis for comparing people from different classes. In contrast, scores on a psychological test must be comparable from one person to another regardless of who the examiner is or what he does; therefore, the tests require that certain fixed procedures be followed for administering and scoring them.

Reliability. After a test has been standardized, its reliability must be checked. Test reliability is the degree to which a test produces a consistent score for the people who take it. One way to check reliability is to give the test to the same people on two different occasions, another way is to compare people's scores on two alternate forms of the same test; a third way is to compare the odd and even items on a test for agreement. Regardless of which method is used, reliability is determined by calculating the closeness or consistency of scores provided by a test.

Validity. Many psychologists believe that validity is the most important aspect of a psychological test. That should not be surprising, for the validity of a test is the degree to which it measures what it purports to measure. Does a particular test of anxiety, for example, *really* measure anxiety, as opposed to some other emotional state, such as unhappiness?

Validity, like reliability, can be assessed in many ways. Sometimes established criterion measures are used; a test designed to measure "academic ability" can be judged by how well it predicts school performance, and a test to measure self-consciousness should be related to a person's apparent anxiety in real-life social situations. A more complicated kind of validity is called *construct validity*, which is basically an effort to validate a number of psychological tests purporting to measure the same thing. It is often difficult to establish criteria for validity; we may think we know what a test scale measures until we try to explain the idea clearly to someone else. Anyone who has tried to explain to another person the meaning of "anxiety" will recognize the problem.

TESTING YOUR UNDERSTANDING
RELIABILITY AND VALIDITY OF THE MMPI

As with other major psychological tests, the MMPI has undergone numerous reliability and validity checks. What are some of the ways in which you might assess the reliability and validity of the MMPI?

One way in which the MMPI's reliability can be checked is by administering it to a larger number of individuals, scoring the test, administering it a second time (usually 1 to 4 weeks later), and then scoring the second test. Reliability could then be measured by determining whether those who scored highest on any given scale the first time also tended to do so the second time, and so on. This method of checking consistency over time is done statistically by correlating the scores on the first and second test; the higher the correlation, the higher the reliability. (See the discussion of correlation in Chapter 1.)

To determine the validity of the MMPI, researchers have often selected as the criterion measure a thorough clinical assessment. This means that if extensive interviews and examinations by trained psychologists showed that a given person was severely depressed, we could check to see if the same individual scored high on the Depression scale of the MMPI. Or, if interviews and other reports indicated that a person had paranoid tendencies, we would see whether that person scored high on the MMPI Pa scale. In large-scale tests, of course, this procedure must be used with hundreds of people.

Figure 10.10
George A. Kelly

A COGNITIVE APPROACH TO PERSONALITY: KELLY'S THEORY OF PERSONAL CONSTRUCTS

In contrast with those whom we have discussed up to this point, some personality theorists are persuaded that cognition plays the most significant role in the development of personality; one of these theorists is the late George A. Kelly.

ESSENTIAL ASPECTS OF KELLY'S VIEW. Kelly felt that there was something paradoxical about the way in which personality theorists typically studied people. They proceeded as if they—the theorists—were in another world looking down on alien beings who were the subjects of their investigation. These psychologists would examine their foreign specimens systematically, formulate hypotheses about their behavior, and then test these ideas in an experimental situation. Although these psychologists would conduct their research in a rational way, they would typically view the beings whom they were studying as at the mercy of dark, mysterious forces over which they had little or no control (such as *id* impulses).

Kelly suggested that the psychologist probably does not differ too much from those whom he studies, and certainly has no monopoly on intellectual and rational powers. Thus, since the psychologist as scientist appears to make a rational effort to gain some power of prediction and control over other human beings, it seemed to Kelly that probably all of us, in our daily interactions with others, also behave in such a rational fashion. In a way, a young child who wants a particular but rather expensive toy, and subtly (or blatantly and persistently) lets his grandparent know this while also displaying much affection, may be viewed as a scientist at work. The child may be working on the hypothesis, however implicit, that a grandparent can be cajoled by appropriate doses of affection into buying the toy. Moreover, if a strategy, such as cuddling up to the grandparent and cooing his wishes is effective on one particular occasion, the child may very well try it again. On the other hand, if this approach does not bring results, more urgent and boisterous demands may be tried in the future. This example demonstrates that most people are continually trying to predict and control events in their environment in a way than is remarkably comparable to the approach taken by *man the scientist*.

According to Kelly (1955), "Man looks at his world through transparent patterns . . . which he creates and then attempts to fit over the realities of which the world is composed" (pp. 8–9). Kelly calls these patterns *personal constructs*. He defines constructs as representations of events in each person's environment that are then tested against the reality of the outside world. Since each of us uses constructs with a certain degree of personal or private meaning (as, for example, when we call something "good" or "bad") everyone has a unique set of personal constructs.

Kelly maintains that people not only hold constructs, but also test them in a relatively systematic fashion. Thus, the child who hypothesized that grandparents are benevolent proceeded to make a specific prediction from this construct (that is, that he could get the toy he wanted by cajoling Grandmother) and then attempted to test the validity of his proposition. If his prediction turned out to be accurate, then the construct from which it was derived would be supported and maintained as a useful one. If, however, the construct led to an incorrect prediction and thus did not produce the desired toy, the child would revise or even discard it. The same process, though with greater sophistication and more elaborate detail, presumably takes place among adults. The degree to which a particular construct helps a person anticipate events is called its *predictive efficiency*.

CONSTRUCTIVE ALTERNATIVISM. An important implication of Kelly's position is that it assumes people have free will. In this way it differs from the deterministic views of Freud and the trait and type theorists, who viewed each individual as having a relatively unchangeable personality, at least once it had been formed. Rejecting this pessimistic position, Kelly noted:

There are always some alternative constructions to choose among when dealing with the world. No one needs to paint himself into a corner; no one needs to be completely hemmed in by circumstances; no one needs to be the victim of his biography [1955, p. 15].

Although Kelly acknowledges that events in the outside world are real, he also suggests that any event can be viewed from a variety of perspectives, each of which provides different implications for behavior.

An interesting example of how personal constructs can affect behavior in this way concerned a patient in a psychiatric hospital. This patient—a young woman—exhibited unintelligible speech, extremely poor personal habits, ludicrous behavior in the presence of other patients and visitors, and, occasionally violent outbursts. One day the hospital aides decided to dress up this young woman in an attractive outfit—including nylon stockings, high heels, lipstick, and makeup—and to take her to the beauty parlor to have her hair styled and set. Remarkably, when she returned to the ward several hours later, the patient no longer behaved in the blatantly "abnormal" way that she had in the past. Although she was still a patient in a psychiatric hospital, it appeared that she had come to perceive herself in a markedly different way (if only temporarily) as a result of the relatively straightforward intervention by others.

It is, of course, not sufficient to say simply that people have constructs that help them to see the world and that are subject to modification by experience. Kelly (1955) has written a two-volume book that is both psychological and philosophical, discussing many of the characteristics of personal constructs and how they can be modified by both the individual himself and the therapeutic intervention of others. We will briefly discuss one of the constructs that Kelly, the man and the scientist, rejects: motivation.

WHY DO HUMAN BEINGS ACT AS THEY DO? Modern psychology has borrowed a great deal from physics with respect to concepts of energy. Specifically, many psychologists have argued that if the physical world was naturally inert and had to be set in motion by some form of energy, then the same thing was also true for people. Like all inanimate objects around us, we are essentially static objects that have to be impelled by special enlivening forces. To account for human action, therefore, it becomes necessary to suggest such things as motives, drives, needs, and instincts. Humans would stand still unless prodded by some outside force (motives, drives, or needs) or lured by a variety of incentives.

Kelly argued that regardless of whether we view a man's actions as being initiated by push or pull, it is an error to think of him as a purely *reactive* organism. Kelly and others have found that most people initially view their fellow human beings in just this way, although they would probably be extremely reticent to accept such a view of themselves. Thus, when a mother wants her child to eat his dinner or do his homework, she feels she must *motivate* him. She may do this by enticement ("We're having chocolate cake for dessert, but first you must finish your dinner") or by prodding ("If you don't get your homework done this afternoon, I'll have to spank you"). But these techniques often work in only a limited way and for short periods of time. Thus, the predictive efficiency of the concept of motivation may often be very low. How can we account for this?

Drawing upon his own early experience as a school psychologist in Kansas, Kelly reports that his earliest insights into motivation came from his efforts to assist teachers who were having problems with certain pupils. A frequent complaint made by these teachers was that a particular child was "lazy." Laziness, as Kelly understood the teachers, meant an absence or minimal amount of action. If a lazy child was viewed as a motivational problem, the teacher felt he had to find some appropriate motivation. Since this search was often fruitless, Kelly suggested that the issue be turned around. He asked: "What would happen if the teacher simply did not attempt to motivate the presumably lazy pupil?" When Kelly and his associates actually proposed this course of action to teachers, many of them replied that the child would do absolutely nothing—he would just sit there! However, when the experiment was actually tried, more often than not the teachers were astonished to find that "Their laziest pupils were those who could produce the most novel ideas . . . that the term 'laziness' had been applied to activities that they had simply been unable to understand or appreciate" (Kelly, 1960, pp. 46–47).

Through such experiences as helping teachers to *reconstrue* their pupils' behavior, Kelly came to the conclusion that the concept of motivation should be rejected. The child whom the teacher "stopped motivating" did not turn into an inert object, just as adults who are not pushed or pulled do not wind down to a complete stop and become totally lifeless. Thus, Kelly has argued that the assumption frequently made by psychologists and laymen that man is essentially inert, coupled with the inevitable corollary that the study of personality is synonymous with a search for those forces that motivate man, must be questioned. He suggests:

If we want to know why man does what he does, then the terms of our whys should extend themselves in time rather than in space; they should be events rather than things; they should be mileposts rather than destinations. Clearly, man lives in the present. He stands firmly astride the chasm that separates the past from the future. He is the only connecting link between these two universes. . . . To be sure, there are other forms of existence that have belonged to the past, and presumably, will also belong to the future. A rock that had rested firmly for ages may well exist in the future also, but it does not link the past with the future. . . . It does not anticipate; it does not reach out both ways to snatch handfuls from each of the two worlds in order to bring them together and subject them to the same stern laws. Only man does that [1960, p. 56].

EVALUATING PERSONALITY THEORIES: A POSTSCRIPT

In the foregoing discussion we have passed over a frequently raised question: Which of the three broad views of personality presented here is the most valid or correct? On this issue, psychologists have different points of view.

Some personality psychologists are strong adherents of a particular theory (psychoanalytic theory, for example) and believe that the weight of clinical evidence and their own personal experience is sufficient to accept this theory as substantially correct. On the other hand, a large number—perhaps a majority—of personality psychologists would insist that the question of which is the "right" or "most correct" theory cannot be answered directly. Broad theories themselves are not testable, after all. A researcher can only test specific propositions or hypotheses that are derived from a theory, and confirmation or lack of confirmation for any one proposition will obviously not be sufficient to evaluate the theory itself. At best, theories can be evaluated and compared only in terms of how often they lead to testable hypotheses which can then be verified by research, as well as whether they can bring together knowledge already accumulated in a satisfying or coherent way. None of the theories we have presented in this chapter has been so successful in this regard that it could be accepted as correct, nor has any led to enough failures or blind alleys that it should be abandoned entirely. What each theory has done is to open up one possible perspective on the question of how each of us becomes a unique person.

(Drawing by Ross; © 1974 The New Yorker Magazine, Inc.)

PSYCHOLOGY AND THE PROBLEMS OF SOCIETY
THE USE AND MISUSE OF PERSONALITY TESTS

Personality tests are widely used by psychologists, educators, and in business and industry. As many as two-thirds of all Americans will take at least one paper-and-pencil personality test during their lifetime (Fiske, 1971). Because the information requested is often very personal, and because the test results may be referred to many times in connection with a given individual (possibly affecting the person's job or educational opportunities), the American Psychological Association (1965) has expressed understandable concern about their indiscriminate use and the possibility that the examinees could be pigeonholed into categories unfairly.

Those who administer personality tests try to measure and categorize an individual, presupposing that personality is an ongoing and consistently characteristic pattern of behavior in various situations. They also assume that a standardized set of personal norms and traits abstracted from observable behavior can summarize that behavior. However, critics of personality assessment hold that no method of trying to characterize an individual and predict his or her behavior in real-life situations has proved satisfactory. Personality, despite attempts to label it, seems inconsistent with different behavior patterns occurring in different environmental situations. In an early critique of personality assessment, Hartshorne, May, and Shuttleworth (1930) found that measurements of moral character in children including such traits as deception, cooperativeness, self-control, and helpfulness were so inconsistent that they could not be considered characteristic. The average intercorrelation of the 23 tests that were used to try to establish a concept of moral character was only +.30. A more recent study by Moos (1969) attempted to characterize anxiety by observing the interactions among institutionalized patients in nine settings with respect to sociable versus hostile behavior. He found idiosyncratic individual differences, situational changes, and mood variations that depended upon the time of day. It was not possible to make any consistent or congruent statements about personality stability.

As a result of findings such as these, it has been suggested (Messick, 1965) that a test will sometimes accurately assess what it was designed to assess, but under different circumstances it will measure constructs that reveal the expectations of both the tester and the respondent. For example, a respondent might be inclined to vary his answers according to a specific testing situation. Thus, "a test may measure one thing in the context of scientific inquiry in a research laboratory, but radically different things if administered for diagnostic guidance in a clinic or for personal evaluation in college or industry" (p. 138). Therefore, any assumptions that the tester might make about the nature of the respondent's habits and relationships might be valid in the testing situation but not generalizable to the real world or externally valid (see Chapter 1).

From this evidence, the assumption of homogeneity which underlies personality testing is probably inaccurate. One's personality reflects many events that precede the testing situation and that occur within it. Since people are not independent of their environment, and therefore their habits and interactions change over time and vary according to each situation, any effort to test an individual should reflect contextual, temporal, and individual variability.

Because the use that is made of test results constitutes an apparent acceptance of the assumptions underlying them, the American Psychological Association (1965) has shown special interest in the concept of test standards, the ethics of invading an individual's privacy, and instrument validity.

SUMMARY

Although there are many theories and corresponding definitions of personality, one generally acceptable definition is "the sum total of individual characteristics and ways of behaving which in their organization or patterning describe an individual's unique adjustment to his or her environment."

Sigmund Freud's psychoanalytic theory holds that there is a psychic force within people, the libido, which motivates them. Following a developmental approach, the theory accounts for personality development as the product of passing through four psychosexual stages—oral, anal, phallic, and genital—with a latency period between the last two stages. Each stage has a particular conflict that must be resolved by the permanent expenditure of libido before the individual can successfully go on to the next stage. Fixation occurs if a portion of the person's libido is stopped or "invested" excessively in a particular stage because of receiving either too little (frustration) or too much (overindulgence) gratification. Freud postulates that personality also develops structurally through the successive emergence of the ego and the superego which counterbalance the pleasure-seeking id that is present at birth.

During the first year of life (the oral stage), the mouth is the predominant source of tension-reduction and pleasure. Although the id governs alone at first, gradually the child learns to delay gratification and to accept the restrictions of the external world, thus giving rise to the development of the ego. During the anal stage (about 2 to 3 years of age) children focus on the anal region and come into conflict with their parents' demand for bowel and bladder control. If this conflict is not satisfactorily resolved, the individual may develop an anal aggressive or anal retentive character in adulthood. About 4 years of age children enter the phallic stage; they may masturbate and experience conflict over a sexual interest in the opposite-sexed parent. For boys this phenomenon is called the Oedipus complex, and for girls the Electra complex. The conflict for both sexes includes fear of retaliation (castration anxiety in boys, penis envy in girls), which finally leads to repression of sexual thoughts about the opposite-sexed parent and to defensive identification with the same-sexed parent. Such identification gradually encourages adoption of the parent's values and development of the superego. From about 5 years of age to puberty the child is in a period of psychosexual latency, when there is no major conflict. At puberty the genital stage begins; the libido is again focused on the genital area, and the individual must learn to give and receive heterosexual pleasure.

One of the major revisionists of Freud's theory is Erik Erikson, who argues that the important stages of personality development are psychosocial (not psychosexual) and emphasizes the interpersonal aspects of life.

In psychoanalysis, personality assessment tries to tap the unconscious—through the interpretation of "accidental" slips, dreams, and, more systematically, projective tests. The underlying idea of these tests is the *projective hypothesis* that people will project their own fears, wishes, and motives into ambiguous situations. In the Rorschach Inkblot test, it is assumed that a subject will project aspects of his or her personality into each of ten blots of black or colored ink by telling the examiner what each blot seems to represent and explaining his or her description according to the characteristics of the blot.

Unlike psychoanalytic theory, type and trait theories emphasizes the measurable, objective characteristics of persons. Ernst Kretschmer was the first to identify body types and relate them to psychiatric disorders. Later William Sheldon identified three similar body types (*endomorphy*, *ectomorphy*, and *mesomorphy*) which he used to assess individuals by assigning a relative strength to each of these components in their body structure. Sheldon then related the somatotypes to personality, identifying three components of temperament: *viscerotonia*, *somatotonia*, and *cerebrotonia*.

Trait theorists attempt to locate a large number of enduring characteristics that are widespread among people so that they can make personality comparisons. Gordon Allport suggested that a person's traits can be classified according to the extent to which they pervade his personality: *cardinal dispositions* are the most pervasive traits; they dominate a personality; *central dispositions* are those that are highly characteristic of a given person; *secondary dispositions*, the least significant traits, are exhibited only in limited settings. Allport also studied selfhood, which he called the *proprium,* and developed the concept of *functional autonomy* to account for the fact that one may continue a given behavior even though the original reason for it has disappeared. Another trait theorist, Raymond Cattell, uses factoranalysis, a statistical technique that can analyze a large number of interrelationships among various aspects of personality and abstract some of their common underlying elements.

In assessing personality traits, psychologists often use personality tests, especially self-report inventories. One of the most common is the Minnesota Multiphasic Personality Inventory (MMPI), a 550-item test that consists of ten clinical scales measuring various aspects of personality and four validity check scales as well. Like most psychological tests, the MMPI can be evaluated by its reliability (the consistency of its scores) and validity (the extent to which it measures what it purports to measure).

Some theorists emphasize the role of cognition in personality. In George A. Kelly's theory, humans are seen as constantly participating in the prediction and control of events in their environment. Personal constructs are representations that people create of their environment, which they then test against the realities of the outside world. If a construct helps someone anticipate events correctly, it has *predictive efficiency.* Disagreeing with Freud's deterministic position, Kelly said that events can be viewed from a variety of perspectives and thus each of us can create our own fate. Kelly further argued that people are naturally active, not inert, and thus they do not need special motivating forces to impel them to act.

GLOSSARY

Anal aggressive character: According to psychoanalytic theory, this is an adult who, when provoked, exhibits hostile or other inappropriate emotional outbursts because a similar tactic (inappropriate elimination) worked when he or she was at the anal stage of development.

Anal retentive character: According to psychoanalytic theory, this is a person who tends to hoard material and personal assets and to be stingy toward others because withholding his or her bowel movements during the anal stage of development led to the control of others.

Anal stage: In psychoanalytic theory, this is the second psychosexual stage of development. It is believed that during this stage the child focuses on the pleasures and tensions that are associated with the anal region and comes into conflict with his parents because of their desire to toilet-train him.

Cardinal dispositions: In Allport's trait theory, these are an individual's most pervasive traits; they tend to dominate his or her personality completely.

Castration anxiety: In psychoanalytic theory, this is the anxiety experienced by a little boy that his penis will be cut off or injured, especially by his angry father who detects that the boy would like to have an incestuous relationship with his mother.

Central dispositions: In Allport's trait theory, these are the few really distinctive traits that characterize a person.

Cerebrotonia: In Sheldon's type theory, this temperament (which is associated with the ectomorphic body type) is characterized by privacy, secretiveness, postural restraint, and social inhibitions.

Common traits: In Allport's trait theory, these are the characteristics that appear frequently enough in a population to permit comparisons among people.

Defensive identification: In psychoanalytic theory, this is the process by which the child resolves the Oedipus or Electra complex by becoming more like the same-sexed parent and thus vicariously possessing the opposite-sexed parent.

Ego: In psychoanalytic theory, this is the personality structure, which is responsible for adjusting to reality and making decisions.

Electra complex: *See* Oedipus complex.

Factor analysis: A statistical technique that permits a researcher to analyze a large number of interrelationships among the personal qualities of a subject and to abstract the underlying common elements. This procedure has been especially useful in trait and type research.

Fixation: In psychoanalytic theory, the view that part of an individual's libido may be stopped at or invested in a particular psychosexual stage of development because of too much or too little gratification at that stage.

Freudian slips: In psychoanalytic theory, these are seemingly accidental acts or words that reveal something of the individual's true hidden feelings or motives.

Functional autonomy: In Allport's trait theory, this is an individual's continuing motivation for action, which replaces the original motivation.

Genital stage: In psychoanalytic theory, this is the last stage of psychosexual development. During this stage the individual must learn how to give and receive pleasure appropriately in adult heterosexual relationships.

Id: In psychoanalytic theory, this is an individual's reservoir of all biological instincts; governed by the pleasure principle and present at birth, it presses for the immediate satisfaction of demands.

Latency period: In psychoanalytic theory, this is the relatively dormant period from about age 5 to 12 when there are no new psychosexual conflicts.

Libido: In psychoanalytic theory, this is the psychic energy of the sexual instincts which is built up and released through the erogenous zones of the body.

Minnesota Multiphasic Personality Inventory (MMPI): A widely used self-report personality inventory, consisting of 550 items that are grouped into ten personality scales and four validity check scales.

Oedipus complex: In psychoanalytic theory, this is the little boy's desire to possess his mother and to do away with his father; the parallel phenomenon for girls is known as the Electra complex.

Oral stage: In psychoanalytic theory, this is the first psychosexual stage of development (lasting through about the first year of life); the mouth is the source of both extreme tension and intense pleasure; weaning is the conflict to be resolved at this stage.

Penis envy: In psychoanalytic theory, this is a little girl's desire to be like her father; penis envy in girls is somewhat comparable to castration anxiety in boys.

Personal constructs: In Kelly's theory, these are the representations of events in each person's environment that reflect his own unique way of looking at things and testing reality.

Phallic stage: In psychoanalytic theory, this is the third psychosexual stage of development (coming about the fourth or fifth year of life); at this time the child focuses on the genital region and experiences a major conflict over an incestuous interest in the opposite-sexed parent.

Pleasure principle: In psychoanalytic theory, this is the id-governed impulse to seek immediate gratification for all one's desires.

Predictive efficiency: In Kelly's theory, this is the extent to which one's personal construct allows events to be predicted accurately.

Projective hypothesis: The hypothesis derived from psychoanalytic theory stating that, when people are faced with an ambiguous situation, they will impose their own personality (feelings, attitudes, desires, and needs) onto it. All projective tests are based upon the projective hypothesis.

Proprium: The concept of selfhood in Allport's theory.

Reliability: The degree to which a test yields a consistent score for any subject.

Repression: In psychoanalytic theory, the active banishing of unacceptable thoughts from consciousness.

Secondary dispositions: In Allport's trait theory, the least significant traits for an individual, which appear only under particular circumstances.

Self-report inventory: A personality test in which the subjects respond to a large number of descriptive statements or questions simply by choosing one out of two or three alternatives. Such inventories are widely used by those who subscribe to the trait view of personality.

Somatotonia: In Sheldon's type theory, this temperament (which is associated with the mesomorphic body type) is characterized by assertiveness, aggressive competitiveness, and a love of physical adventure and risk.

Somatotyping: In Sheldon's type theory, this is a procedure for characterizing people according to how much they display each of the components of physique (endomorphy, ectomorphy, and mesomorphy).

Source traits: In Cattell's trait theory, these are the essential traits that underlie all human behavior and that can be determined by means of factor analysis.

Standardization sample: The group of persons to whom a brand-new psychological test is administered. From the results obtained, norms for typical performance will be established, and a detailed procedure for administering the test will be developed.

Superego: In psychoanalytic theory, this is the individual's ideal and conscience; it evaluates that person's behavior according to the standards that have been accepted from the parents.

Validity: The degree to which a test measures what it purports to measure.

Viscerotonia: In Sheldon's type theory, this temperament (which is associated with the endomorphic body type) is characterized by a relaxed posture, tolerance, and love of physical comfort.

ELEVEN

ABNORMAL PSYCHOL-OGY

[The first way of injuring humanity] is to induce an evil love in a man for a woman, or in a woman for a man. The second is to plant hatred or jealousy in anyone. The third is to bewitch them so that a man cannot perform the genital act with a woman, or conversely a woman with a man . . . The fourth is to cause disease in any of the human organs. The fifth is to take away life. The sixth to deprive them of reason [From the Malleus Mallefica-rum *(1488) as quoted in Zilborg and Henry, 1941, p. 158].*
The preceding passage contains an early description of several forms of behavior—sexual dysfunction, aggression,

Figure 11.1
Until recently those who displayed abnormal behavior were treated cruelly and brutally. (Top) Exorcising evil spirits during the Inquisition (Right) the incarceration of insane persons in the Hospital of St. Mary of Bethlehem (London) during the eighteenth century (from which the word "bedlam" is derived); (Above) a restraining case in which unruly patients were confined during the nineteenth century.

and loss of reason—which today are included in the field of abnormal psychology. Accounts of such behavior have existed for centuries, and along with the descriptions there have been attempts to explain the behavior. At the time the preceding passage was written, the prevailing interpretation was that abnormal behavior was caused by possession by the devil. This interpretation had important implications for both recognizing abnormality and treating it; any sort of peculiar behavior could be viewed as evidence of possession as could spots on the body and anesthesias (lack of pain in particular parts of the body), which were believed to be caused by the claw of the devil himself. Treatment was entrusted to priests, who would pray, shout various epithets, and even torture the accused to make his or her body an inhospitable home for the devil.

By the nineteenth century the witchcraft explanation of abnormal behavior had been superseded by two competing viewpoints that have since prevailed. In 1883 Emil Kraepelin (1856–1926), a German psychiatrist, established a system for classifying abnormal behavior that was based, in part, on the idea that different disorders had different *physical causes*. Each disorder was thought to have its own set of symptoms, its own course, and its own physiological cause. Later in the century, Sigmund Freud began his inquiry into the causes of abnormal behavior, using the same psychological concepts we discussed earlier in connection with his theory of personality.

**Figure 11.2
Emil Kraepelin**

WHAT IS ABNORMAL? A simple, but less than satisfactory, answer to the question posed here can be secured by examining the system of diagnosing abnormality that is used by the American Psychiatric Association (see Table 11.1). If this diagnostic system is accepted, we need only determine if a person fits into one of the categories. If so, he or she is abnormal; if not, then the person is normal. The classification system, although widely used, poses several problems. First, diagnostic agreement is not high; in fact, in some cases (for example, Beck et al., 1962), diagnostic agreement has hovered at only the 50 percent mark. That is, psychiatrists do not necessarily agree about the diagnosis of an individual case, nor even about whether a particular person is a "psychiatric case" at all. Second, we must ask why psychiatrists have achieved this position of power in the field of abnormal behavior—the same position that was held by priests in the Middle Ages. Why should psychiatrists be the ones to decide what is abnormal? The answer to this question lies in the fact that abnormal behavior is sometimes considered similar to physical disease and thus within the province of medicine. The *medical model* of abnormal behavior asserts that some internal malfunction (the "disease process") produces deviant behavior (symptoms); this model is quite prevalent. As Brendan Maher (1966) has noted, "[deviant] behavior is termed *pathological* and is classified on the basis of *symptoms*, classification being called *diagnosis*. Processes designed to change behavior are called *therapies* and are applied to *patients* in mental *hospitals*. If the deviant behavior ceases the patient is described as *cured*" (p. 22).

But the mere popularity of this approach is no guarantee that the "truth" has been found. Some, like Thomas Szasz (1960), have called our attention to the fact that we have no evidence to support the basic assumptions of a medical model. For example, the diseases that supposedly produce the behavioral abnormalities have not been discovered. If the medical model proves untenable, then psychiatrists should not hold the unique position of being the ones to decide what is and what is not abnormal.

We must also take into account the way in which a person comes to be seen by a diagnostician, for a diagnosis cannot be made unless the

TABLE 11.1

Major psychiatric diagnoses of the American Psychiatric Association.

Mental retardation	Subnormal intellectual functioning ranging through several degrees from borderline to profound.
Organic brain syndromes	Impairments in intelligence, affect, and memory due to lesions of the nervous systems.
Psychoses	Disturbances in mental functioning so severe that the patient cannot meet the usual demands of life.
Neuroses	Disturbances in behavior involving high levels of anxiety.
Personality disorders	Maladaptive behavior patterns such as sexual deviation, alcoholism, and antisocial behavior.
Psychophysiological reactions	Physical symptoms such as asthma, high blood pressure, or ulcer that are, in part, emotionally caused.

person first enters the mental health system. Here, social norms are important. People enter the mental health system because of judgments made by themselves, relatives, friends, or authorities such as the school or the courts. But the judgments of these people about abnormality will vary considerably. One person, for example, after recurring episodes of depression may seek treatment. Another, with equal sadness, will simply live with it. One family may tolerate eccentricity in a maiden aunt; another might decide that she is "sick." The point is that definitions of abnormality are not absolute; they are only relative. No single definition seems adequate.

In this chapter we will examine several categories of abnormal behavior. Because of problems with the American Psychiatric Association's diagnostic system, we will not adhere strictly to it. Depression, for example, will be discussed in one section although it appears in both the psychosis and neurosis categories of the diagnostic system. Similarly, we discuss "social deviance," a category not listed as an official diagnosis but related to that system's category of personality disorders.

NEUROSES: THE MANY FACES OF ANXIETY

The major forms of neurosis are listed and described briefly in Table 11.2. Each subtype is viewed as having a common element:

Anxiety is the chief characteristic of the neuroses. It may be felt and expressed directly, or it may be controlled unconsciously and automatically by . . . [defense] mechanisms. Generally, these mechanisms produce symptoms experienced as subjective distress from which the patient desires relief [American Psychiatric Association, 1968, p. 39].

TABLE 11.2

Neurotic disorders.

TYPE	MAJOR SYMPTOM PATTERNS
Phobic neurosis	Extreme fear and avoidance of an object or situation which the person is able to recognize as harmless.
Anxiety neurosis	Anxiety felt in so many situations that it appears to be "free-floating," without specific cause.
Hysterical neurosis, conversion type	Paralysis, lack of sensation, or sensory disturbances without organic pathology.
Hysterical neurosis, dissociative type	Alterations in consciousness, manifested as amnesia, fugue, somnambulism, and multiple personality.
Obsessive-compulsive neurosis	Flooding of the mind with persistent and uncontrollable thoughts, or the compulsion to repeat a certain act again and again.

(Drawing by Gross; © 1976 The New Yorker Magazine, Inc.)

SUBTYPES. A *phobia* is an avoidance response, produced by fear that is out of proportion to the actual danger posed by a particular object or situation. For example, when a person is extremely afraid of heights, closed spaces, or crowds and actively avoids them, the label "phobia" is likely to be applied. Complicated names have been proposed for such behaviors; in each case, the suffix "phobia" is preceded by the Greek term for the feared object or situation. Some of the more familiar terms are claustrophobia (fear of closed spaces), agoraphobia (fear of leaving the house), and acrophobia (fear of heights). Some of the more exotic ones are ergasiophobia (fear of writing), and pnigophobia (fear of being buried alive).

Anxiety neurosis is characterized by anxious overconcern which may escalate and become panic. This syndrome is sometimes called "free-floating anxiety"; the person feels anxious in almost every situation that he or she encounters. Individuals diagnosed as having anxiety reactions are likely to be tense, irritable, and subject to episodes of acute

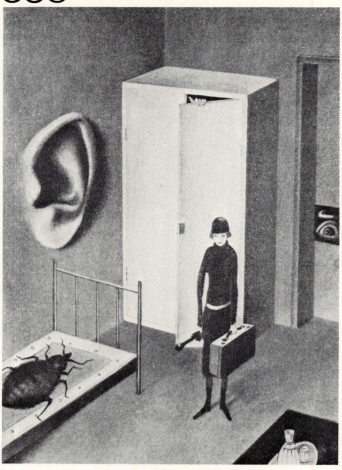

Figure 11.3
Persistent irrational fears are referred to as phobias.

panic. They report apprehension, feelings of being out of control, premonitions of impending disaster, and so forth. They are also overly sensitive to criticism and easily discouraged. Generally, there are many physiological concomitants such as rapid heart rate, irregular breathing, excessive sweating, and dizziness. Insomnia, restlessness, fatigue, muscular tension, and difficulty in concentrating and making decisions are also frequently reported.

Hysterical neuroses are divided into two major types. The *dissociative reactions*, departures from normal states of consciousness, can be subdivided into four categories:

1. *amnesia:* loss of memory for a period of time
2. *fugue:* loss of memory and a flight from one's previous life
3. *somnambulism:* sleepwalking
4. *multiple personality:* a rare condition in which there exist separate and distinct personalities within the same individual at the same time (see page 20 for an illustrative case)

The second major type of hysterical neurosis, *conversion reaction,* includes impairment of muscular or sensory functions without any known physical malfunction. Partial or complete paralyses of arms and legs, blindness, and anesthesias (losses of sensitivity) are all examples. These, of course, are problems that could also be due to purely physiological causes such as damage to the central or peripheral nervous system. How can an organic disease be distinguished from a conversion reaction? Pierre Janet, one of the prominent historical figures in this field, addressed this problem in a lecture given at Harvard University in 1906.

Hysteric paralysis never affects only one muscle, it is always a paralysis in a mass, which strikes a group of muscles. Do not suppose that every group of muscles may be thus affected. The group that is affected is always one that is necessary to a function of a part of the body. Yet the paralysis does not extend beyond the limit of the muscles necessary for the functioning of this part of the body; it does not easily encroach upon other regions. It is otherwise in all organic paralyses; a lesion of a nerve may affect only certain muscles; a lesion of a nervous plexus affects several muscular groups. For instance, in the paralysis of the leg brought about by hysteria, the thigh and buttock are affected, but the sacral region and the genital region are intact, which is not the case in spinal paralyses. . . . Notice also that hysteric paralysis is exaggerated, always carried to an extreme, which is very rare in organic paralyses. . . . Hysteric hemiplegy is not accompanied by any other serious disturbances in the diseased limb; in particular, there is no atrophy, or at least a very long time is required for it to appear after the period of immobility [Janet, 1906].

Many of the important features of a conversion reaction are well illustrated by a case originally reported by Brady and Lind (1961). The patient, a 40-year-old veteran, had suddenly become blind in both eyes, although there was no apparent physiological reason for his loss of vision. Two of the patient's aunts had been totally blind during their last years. While in the army the patient had developed a problem in one of his eyes that had greatly reduced his visual acuity. After receiving a medical discharge, he obtained a number of semiskilled jobs, but he didn't remain with any of them for more than a year; he often returned to the hospital with recurrences of his visual problem. Each time after he had returned to the hospital, he applied for a larger pension but was refused because there had been no additional loss of vision.

Twelve years after his discharge, while he was shopping with his wife and mother-in-law, he suddenly "became blind" in both eyes. At this time, according to the authors, "His wife and mother-in-law were being more demanding than usual, requiring him to work nights and weekends at various chores under their foremanship. One immediate consequence of his blindness was, then, partial escape from this situation." During the next 2 years the patient received various treatments and was enrolled in a training course for the blind. In addition, he was awarded a special pension for his total disability, and he received financial assistance from the community for his children as well as some money from his relatives.

In *obsessive-compulsive neurosis*, the individual experiences intrusive obsessions and has recurring thoughts that appear irrational and uncontrollable to him. For example, a person might be obsessed with the idea that he will swear, make obscene gestures, or even murder someone else. A compulsion is an irresistible impulse to repeat a certain act over and over again. The individual often fears that dire consequences will ensue if the act is not repeated. The frequency of such repetitions can be truly staggering; the authors know of a woman who washed her hands more than 500 times a day in spite of painful sores that developed.

THEORIES OF THE ORIGIN OF NEUROSES. The two major theories relating to the development of neuroses are psychoanalytic theory and learning theory. We will illustrate the differences between them by examining their views on one neurosis—phobias.

A classic case, reported by Freud in 1909, was that of a 5-year-old boy, little Hans, who, because of his fear of horses, would not venture out of his house. Hans was reported to have "a quite peculiarly active interest in that part of his body which he used to describe as his widdler." When he was 3 1/2 years of age, his mother caught him with his hand on his penis and threatened to have it cut off if he continued "doing that." Freud believed that at 4 1/2 years of age Hans tried to seduce his mother. As she was powdering him after his bath, Hans said, "Why don't you put your finger there [on his penis]? His mother answered, "Because that would be piggish." Hans replied, "What's that? Piggish? Why?" Mother: "Because it's not proper." Hans, laughing: "But it's great fun." The first signs of the phobia appeared 6 months later when Hans was out for a walk with his nursemaid. A horse-drawn van tipped over and Hans began crying that he wanted to return home to his mother. Later he said that he was afraid to go out into the street for fear that a horse might bite him.

Freud believed that this series of events reflected an unresolved Oedipal conflict (set Chapter 10). Hans's sexual attraction to his mother was converted into anxiety because he feared punishment (castration) if the impulse were expressed. This process—the pushing into the unconscious of a punishable id impulse—is viewed by psychoanalysts as the causal factor in neuroses. Freud believed that Hans's father was the initial source of the fear of punishment, but the fear was then transposed to horses, which were thought to be a symbolic representation of the father.

The primary learning approach to phobias is classical conditioning. In 1920, Watson and Rayner demonstrated the possibility that fear could be acquired through classical conditioning. Albert, an 11-month-old boy, was shown a white rat. At first he showed no fear of the animal and appeared to want to play with it. But whenever he reached for the rat, the experimenter made a loud noise (the unconditioned stimulus) by striking a steel bar behind Albert's head, causing him to be afraid (the unconditioned response). After a number of such experiences, Albert became quite disturbed by the sight of the white rat, even when the steel bar was not struck. The fear initially associated with the loud noise was now associated with the previously neutral stimulus, the white rat (now the conditioned stimulus). The learning view of phobias, then, hypothesizes that they are due to a fortuitous pairing of frightening experiences and the to-be-feared objects or events. To return to Freud's description of little Hans, a learning theorist might ascribe his phobia to the fright he experienced when the horse-drawn van tipped over (Wolpe and Rachman, 1962), which was obviously associated with the sight of the horse itself. Such traumatic incidents have been reported as significant causes of phobias, as in the following case history:

A young boy would often pass a grocery store on errands and when passing would steal a handful of peanuts from the stand in front. One day the owner saw him coming and hid behind a barrel. Just as the boy put his hand in the pile of peanuts the owner jumped out and grabbed him from behind. The boy screamed and fell fainting on the sidewalk.

The boy developed a phobia of being grasped from behind. In social gatherings he arranged to have his chair against the wall. It was impossible for him to enter crowded places or to attend the theater. When walking on the street he would have to look back over his shoulder at intervals to see if he was closely followed [Bagby, 1922].

DEPRESSION   Depression appears in three major diagnostic categories—manic-depressive illness, psychotic depressive reaction, and depressive neurosis. All, of course, significantly include depression. According to Beck (1967), the five most common features of depression are:

1. sad, apathetic mood
2. negative self-concept
3. desire to stay away from others
4. loss of sleep, appetite, and sexual desire
5. change in activity level, becoming either lethargic or agitated

Manic-depressive illness, one of the psychoses, is a label applied to two apparently different kinds of people. One kind shows alternations between severe depression and mania, a mental state that encompasses elated mood, rapid thought, and an increase in the speed of behavior. The other kind of person shows only extreme depression which has no obvious cause.

Unlike manic-depression, both *psychotic depression* and *neurotic depres-*

Figure 11.4
Depression is a major feature of many neurotic and psychotic reactions.

sion are distinguished by the fact that they are believed to be caused by some environmental event. The principal differences between the two is the fact that psychotic depression is more severe.

THEORIES OF DEPRESSION. Psychoanalysis. Predictably, Freud saw the potential for depression being created early in childhood. He theorized that during the oral period the child's needs may be insufficiently gratified or overindulged. Subsequently, the individual remains "stuck" in this stage and dependent upon the instinctual gratifications that it provides. With this arrest in psychosexual maturation, which is called a "fixation," a person may develop a tendency to become excessively dependent upon other people for the maintenance of his or her self-esteem (Fenichel, 1945).

How does this happenstance of rearing lead to depression in adulthood? The reasoning is based on a distinction between normal grief and mourning. Freud hypothesized that after the loss of a loved one, the mourner first identifies with the lost person and tries to "incorporate" that person into himself. The grieving person is sometimes thought to identify with the lost one in this way in a fruitless attempt to undo the loss. Because, as Freud asserted, we unconsciously harbor negative feelings against those we love, mourners then become the object of their own hate and anger. In addition, mourners also resent being deserted and feel guilty about real or imagined sins committed against the lost person. This process is followed by a period of "mourning work," during which mourners recall memories of the lost one and thereby separate themselves from the person who has died and in this way loosen the bonds that identification has imposed.

The mourning work can go astray in overly dependent individuals and develop into an ongoing process of self-abuse, self-blame, and depression. Such people do not lessen their emotional bonds with the person who has died, but continue to blame themselves for the faults and shortcomings perceived in the loved one with whom they have identified. The mourner's anger toward the lost one continues to be directed inward. Thus, depression is anger turned against the self. In the case of depression without the death of a loved one, Freud introduced the concept of symbolic loss. In this instance, a person may interpret a rejection as a total loss of love.

An Operant View. Lewinsohn and his colleagues (Lewinsohn, 1974) have proposed a learning conceptualization of depression as a reduction in activity due to the lack of reinforcement. Figure 11.1 is a schematic representation of Lewinsohn's model of depression; this model is based on the following assumptions:

1. The feeling of depression and other symptoms of the clinical syndrome (such as fatigue) can be elicited when behavior receives little reinforcement.
2. This "thin" schedule of positive reinforcement, in turn, tends to reduce activity even more, which produces even fewer reinforcements.
3. The amount of positive reinforcement is a function of three sets of variables: (a) The number of potential reinforcers available to an individual. This depends upon one's personal characteristics, such as age, sex, and attractiveness to others. (b) The number of potential reinforcers available. This depends upon the environment the person is in (for example, whether he or she is at home rather than in prison). and (c) The person's repertoire of behavior that can gain reinforcement (for example, the person's vocational and social skills).

As Figure 11.5 indicates, a low rate of positive reinforcement reduces still further the activities and expression of personal qualities that might be rewarded. Both activities and rewards decrease in a vicious circle. Many studies made by Lewinsohn's group confirm to some degree the central hypothesis—that depression is associated with low rates of positively reinforced behavior (Libet and Lewinsohn, 1973; Lewinsohn and Libet, 1972), but considerable research is still needed

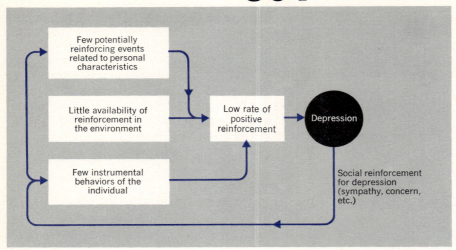

Figure 11.5
Lewinsohn's model of depression.

to establish specific causal relationships between reinforcement and mood.

Physiology and Depression. Since physiological processes definitely affect one's mood, it is not surprising that researchers have investigated physiological causes of depression. One of the most promising approaches utilizes the hypothesis that neural transmission (Chapter 2) is slowed down in depressives because of a lack of neurotransmitters. Three lines of evidence support this position. First, drugs such as reserpine, which lower the levels of the neurotransmitters, can produce depression in normal persons. Second, drugs that are used to treat depression increase the level of neurotransmitters; the most impressive evidence links effective treatment to an increase in the neurotransmitter serotonin (Coppen et al., 1972). (However, similar studies that have used drugs to increase the level of the catecholamines [which are also neurotransmitters] have not found them to be therapeutically useful.) Third, researchers have attempted to study the levels of neurotransmitters that are found in depressed people. (This is typically done by examining by products of neurotransmitters that can be detected in the body's waste products.) If the theory is correct, it should be found that depressed people have lower than normal levels of neurotransmitters. Again the results support the theory, especially with respect to serotonin (for example, Ashcroft and Sharman, 1960).

PSYCHOPHYSIOLOG- ICAL DISORDERS Psychophysiological disorders "are characterized by physical symptoms that are caused by emotional factors and involve a single organ system, usually under the control of the autonomic nervous system" (American Psychiatric Association, 1968, p. 46). At the outset, three important points must be firmly established. First, a psychophysiological disorder is a real disease that harms the body. The fact that such disorders are believed to be due to emotional factors does not make the affliction imaginary. People can just as readily die from "psychologically produced" asthma or ulcers as from similar diseases produced by infection or physical injury. Second, psychophysiological disorders should be distinguished from the hysterical reactions that were discussed earlier. Hysterical disorders do not cause actual organic damage to the body, and it is generally believed that they affect only the function of the voluntary musculature. In contrast, psychophysiological disorders *do* produce actual damage to the body's tissues. Third, we should stress that the disorders termed "psychophysiological" are not *always* due to emotional distress. Asthma, for example, is called a psychophysiological disorder, but psychological factors are thought to be the primary causes in only 34 percent of all cases (Rees, 1964).

Nine different types of psychophysiological disorders have been identified. All are attributed in part to the emotional state of the patient; the most obvious difference among them is the part of the body affected.

1. *Psychophysiological skin disorders:* Skin reactions such as neurodermatitis (inflammation), pruritis (itching), and hyperhydrosis (dry skin).
2. *Psychophysiological respiratory disorders:* Bronchial asthma, hyperventilation (breathing very rapidly), sighing, and hiccups.
3. *Psychophysiological cardiovascular disorders:* Tachycardia (heart racing), hypertension (high blood pressure), and migraine headache.
4. *Psychophysiological hemic and lymphatic disorders.* Disturbances of the blood and lymphatic systems.
5. *Psychophysiological gastrointestinal disorders:* Peptic ulcers, chronic gastritis, ulcerative or mucous colitis, constipation, hyperacidity, and heartburn.
6. *Psychophysiological genital-urinary disorders:* Disturbances in menstruation and urination, dyspareunia (painful sexual intercourse), and impotence (difficulty obtaining or maintaining an erection, or both).
7. *Psychophysiological endocrine disorders:* Malfunctions of the various endocrine glands.
8. *Psychophysiological disorders of a sense organ:* Any disturbance in one of the sensory organs in which emotional factors play a causative role.
9. *Psychophysiological musculoskeletal disorders:* Backache, muscle cramps, and tension headaches.

THEORIES OF PSYCHOPHYSIOLOGICAL DISORDERS.
We have known for some time that various *physical* stresses can produce physiological damage (Selye, 1956). In studying psychophysiological disorders, we are concerned with *psychological* stressors such as emotional tension, conflict, and bereavement. Can they also elicit

physiological changes and thus cause a psychophysiological disorder? In considering this issue, we are confronted with three questions: (1) Why does stress produce difficulties in only *some* people who are exposed to it? (2) Why does stress sometimes cause a psychophysiological disorder and not some other disorder, such as a neurosis? (3) Granted that stress produces a psychophysiological disorder, what determines which one of the many possible disorders it will be?

The answers to these questions have been sought by both biologically and psychologically oriented theorists. Biological approaches attribute particular psychophysiological disorders to specific weaknesses of an individual's organ systems in responding to stress. Psychological theories posit particular stresses for particular disorders.

Somatic-Weakness Theory. Genetic factors, earlier illnesses, diet, and so forth may weaken a particular organ system, which then becomes vulnerable to stress. According to the somatic-weakness theory, the connection between stress and a particular psychophysiologic disorder is the weakness in a particular bodily organ. For example, a congenitally weak respiratory system might predispose a person to asthma. Analogously, a chain will break at its weakest link.

Specific-Reaction Theory. Some investigators argue that individuals respond differently to stress, probably due to their different genetic makeup. It has been found that people have their own particular patterns of autonomic response to stress. One individual's heart rate may increase, while another's respiration rate may increase (Lacey, 1967). Since individuals respond to stress in their own idiosyncratic way, the most affected body system may be susceptible to a psychophysiological disorder. Someone who secretes stomach acid under stress may be more vulnerable to ulcers, while someone whose blood pressure rises may be more susceptible to hypertension.

Learning Theories. Both classical and instrumental conditioning may play a role in psychophysiological disorders, although conditioning is probably more likely to increase the severity of an already existing illness rather than to cause it. Take, for example, a person who is allergic to pollen and thus subject to asthma attacks. By classical conditioning, neutral stimuli paired with pollen could also eventually cause asthma, thus broadening the range of stimuli that could produce an attack (Bandura, 1969). Asthmatic attacks might also be viewed as instrumental responses that elicit rewards. For example, a child could "use" his or her asthma as an excuse for not participating in unpleasant activities. Neither of these conditioning examples excludes the importance of biological factors in psychophysiological disorders, for the original occurrence of the illness must still be explained. Since both classical and instrumental conditioning hypotheses assume that the physical symptoms already exist, any learning model of a psychophysiological disorder requires a biological predisposition of some kind.

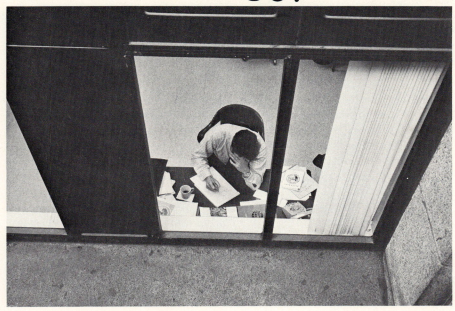

Figure 11.6
The inability to cope with stress may lead to a variety of psychophysiological disorders.

This completes our overview of theories of psychophysiological disorders. We will now turn to a detailed review of one such disorder that has attracted considerable attention from researchers—ulcers. We will see that a theory that combines biological predisposition and stress fits the available data very well.

ULCERS. A peptic ulcer is a lesion or hole in the lining of the stomach or duodenum that is produced by the excessive secretion of hydrochloric acid (HCl) over a protracted period of time. In the digestive process, HCl and various enzymes break down ingested food into components that the body can use. The inner wall of the stomach is protected from the destructive effects of HCl by a layer of mucus. But production of excessive amounts of acid for long periods of time can erode the mucus layer, and the acid may digest the stomach wall. Ulcer patients suffer periodic attacks of pain and are often advised by their doctors to eat only bland foods.

Although many psychological stressors produce an increase in the secretion of HCl, an approach-avoidance conflict is the one that has been the most extensively researched. Sawrey devised several illustrative experiments with rats to investigate whether prolonged exposure to approach-avoidance conflicts produces ulcers. Shock was administered whenever the animals approached food or water, thus producing a conflict about whether to approach the food or avoid the shock. At the end of approximately 2 weeks, many of the rats had developed ulcers, and some had even died from hemorrhages (Sawrey and Weisz, 1956; Conger, Sawrey, and Turrell, 1958).

In animal research such as Sawrey's, only *some* of the animals exposed to the approach-avoidance conflict developed ulcers. Thus, stress is only part of the story. We also need to find a factor that can interact with stress and greatly increase the chances that an individual with this particular characteristic will develop an ulcer.

Biological predispositions may function in this way. A prime candidate is the amount of pepsinogen secreted by the peptic cells of the gastric glands in the stomach. Pepsinogen is converted into pepsin, the stomach enzyme that digests proteins and that, combined with HCl, is the principal active agent in gastric juice. Pepsinogen levels are, therefore, measures of gastric activity; hence, we might expect them to be implicated in the formation of ulcers. Weiner, Thaler, Reiser, and Mirsky (1957) measured the level of pepsinogen in 2073 newly inducted draftees. From this large number two smaller groups were selected—the 63 with the highest levels of pepsinogen and the 57 with the lowest levels. A complete gastrointestinal examination, given before basic training, showed that none had ulcers at that time. The majority of these men were reexamined later on in their basic training (during the stressful periods). Nine cases of ulcers had developed, *and all of them were in the group with the highest pepsinogen levels.* Another study (Mirsky, 1958) of a population of children and civilian adults who had previously been classified as high and low pepsinogen secreters also revealed that those with high levels of pepsinogen tended to develop ulcers more often than those with low levels.

In sum, the data available on peptic ulcers are clearly consistent with a theory implicating both stress and a biological predisposition to secrete excessive amounts of pepsinogen as factors in their development. Consistent with the specific-reaction theory, those who develop ulcers appear to be predisposed to secrete excessive amounts of gastric juice in stressful situations; these juices then produce lesions.

SOCIAL DEVIANCE   In this section we will discuss several clinical diagnoses that, perhaps more than any others, are socially defined—sociopathy (or psychopathy), addiction, and sexual deviation.

SOCIOPATHY. On the basis of his clinical experience, Cleckley (1964) formulated a set of criteria for this disorder:

1. Average or superior intelligence
2. Absence of irrationality and other commonly accepted symptoms of psychosis
3. No sense of responsibility
4. Disregard for truth
5. No sense of shame
6. Antisocial behavior without apparent regret
7. Inability to learn from experience

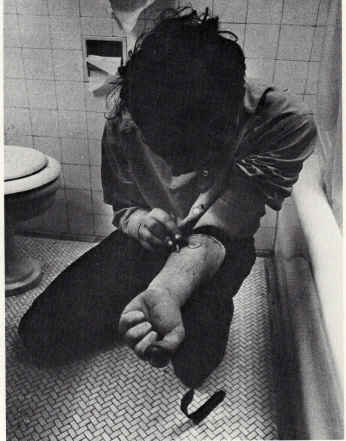

Figure 11.7
A wide range of socially unconventional behavior is considered to be deviant.

8. General lack of affect
9. Lack of genuine insight
10. Little response to special consideration or kindness
11. No history of sincere suicide attempts
12. Unrestrained and unconventional sex life
13. Onset of sociopathic characteristics no later than early twenties

The Case of Jim. Jim grew up in the lower social class of a small midwestern town. During his childhood the member of his family who made the greatest impression on him was his older brother, whom he described as follows:

> He was always a bully, promiscuous, and adventurous. He was always involved with some local girl, before I was even old enough to realize what was going on. He started drinking early, and had several scrapes with the law. He had rough companions, whom I later inherited, who helped me on my way.
>
> He married a tramp, ended up in a stolen car, and was given the choice of jail or the army, as this was the Korean war time. I cannot directly link him to my life of crime, although he introduced me to those

who later helped me along. Also, he condoned some of my early petty thievery [Bintz and Wilson, as reprinted in Milton and Wahler, 1969, p. 92].

During early adolescence Jim engaged in many petty antisocial acts. For example, on one occasion he stole some change from his mother's purse. His father reacted by beating Jim and his older brother until Jim confessed. Once Jim had admitted taking the money, however, the punishment ended. This became the typical pattern, with Jim avoiding punishment by confessing as soon as he was accused of misbehavior, regardless of whether he was guilty or not. Moreover, the petty thefts that Jim committed in the community were generally successful, and even when he was caught the consequences were minimal.

Jim's first serious encounter with the law occurred when he was charged with raping a girl whom he had picked up at the local skating rink. He was sentenced to 5 years at a reform school but received an immediate parole with the stipulation that his sentence would be activated if he violated it. After several needless parole violations such as speeding and petty theft, he was sentenced to 1 year at the reform school. By the time he returned to his home town the following year, he had become a young hoodlum. Jim himself admitted that the major impact of his year in reform school had been his opportunity to associate with more experienced thieves. A short time later Jim and a friend committed their first major theft, stealing $1700 from a tavern safe. Then the same pair attempted to burglarize a lumberyard but were unable to open the safe. The next day they were arrested, and the burglary tools were found in Jim's car. He served a 90-day sentence for attempted burglary. Three months after his release, Jim was incarcerated again, this time for statutory rape. As soon as he was free again, he and a friend planned another robbery. They reasoned that a bootlegger would be a good target for a holdup since, being outside the law himself, he would be reluctant to report the incident to the police. They bungled the job badly, however, and both were sentenced to five-year terms. Jim served 3 of the 5 years and when released met the girl he would shortly marry. He described her as follows:

Diane was a tramp, I could tell from the start. She forced the introduction and the first date. I had sexual relations with her on the first date, she was my third sexual partner on that particular day. She was neat, but not really attractive. The next four and a half months we were intimate almost every night. She wanted to marry, I did not. I could not see myself married to this plain-looking tramp. In fact, toward the last, I was trying to think of a scheme to get rid of her [Milton and Wahler, 1969, p. 100].

During this period Jim had a job, but he soon began to get deeper and deeper into debt. Eventually, Jim learned of another opportunity for theft. But, again, he was unsuccessful in his attempt, and this time he was sentenced to 10 years in the state penitentiary. While spending time in the county jail before the trial, Jim was visited quite often by Diane; he finally married her just before going to prison. As a substitute for a wedding ring, Jim had the words "Love me, Diane" tattooed on his penis.

In this case we see vivid illustration of many of the features of sociopathy. Especially striking are Jim's repeated offenses, typically ill-planned, for which he apparently had no regret or shame. His comments about his future wife are a particularly clear example of what is viewed as the sociopath's general disregard for others.

A Learning Theory Approach. A central characteristic of sociopathic behavior may be the individual's minimal concern about avoiding the negative consequences of social misbehavior. Lykken (1957) deduced that the sociopath may have few inhibitions about committing antisocial acts because he or she suffers little anxiety. Lykken performed several tests to determine whether sociopaths actually do have low levels of anxiety; one test was of avoidance learning.

A group of subjects, judged to be sociopaths on the basis of Cleckley's criteria, was selected from among a penitentiary population. Their performance on an avoidance-learning task was compared with that of nonsociopathic penitentiary inmates and of college students. It was, of course, critical that only avoidance learning and not learning mediated by other possible rewards be tested. If a subject perceives that his task is to learn to avoid pain, he may be motivated not only by the avoidance of pain but also by the opportunity to show the investigator how clever he is. To make sure that no other motives would interfere, Lykken made the avoidance-learning task *incidental*. For the experiment he used a panel that had four red lights in a horizontal row, four green lights below each of the red ones, and a lever below each column (see Figure 11.8). The subject's task was to learn a sequence of 20 correct lever presses, but for each press he first had to determine by trial and error which of the four alternatives was correct. The correct lever turned on a green light. Two of the remaining three incorrect levers turned on red lights, indicating an error. The third incorrect lever turned on a red light and delivered an electric shock to the subject. The correct lever varied throughout the sequence. The subject was told simply to figure out and learn the series of 20 cor-

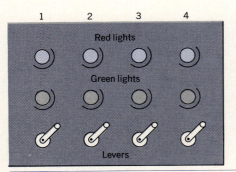

Figure 11.8
Schematic diagram of the apparatus used by Lykken (1957) in his study of avoidance learning in sociopaths. For the first lever press assume that lever 3 is correct, that is, that pressing it lights the green bulb; that levers 1 and 4 are incorrect, lighting red bulbs; and that pressing lever 2 lights a red bulb and gives the subject a shock. For the second lever press the meaning of the levers may change entirely; for example, lever 2 may be correct, levers 3 and 4 incorrect, and lever 1 may give a shock. The subjects had to learn a series of 20 correct lever presses.

1   2   3   4
Red lights
Green lights
Levers

rect lever presses. He was not informed that avoiding a shock was desirable or possible, but merely that a shock was randomly administered as a stimulant to make him do well. Thus, the task yielded two measures of learning: the total number of errors made before the subject learned the correct sequence of 20 presses and the number of errors that produced shock. Avoidance learning was measured by this second index.

In terms of the over-all number of errors made, there were no significant differences among the three groups in Lykken's study. The college students, however, seemed best able to remember the sequence of presses that produced a shock, and thus they sharply decreased their proportion of shocked errors. The sociopaths made the most shocked errors, but the differences between the number of shocked errors they made and the number made by the other penitentiary inmates was not great. The results of Lykken's investigation, therefore, tentatively support the hypothesis that sociopaths have lower levels of anxiety than do normal individuals.

Lykken's pioneering work was subsequently followed up by Schachter and Latané (1964). These investigators reasoned that if sociopaths do not learn to avoid unpleasant stimuli because they have little anxiety, increasing their anxiety should remove their avoidance learning deficit. Because anxiety is believed to be related to the activity of the sympathetic nervous system, they injected adrenaline (a substance whose effects mimic sympathetic activity) into their subjects in order to increase their anxiety.

Sociopathic and nonsociopathic prisoners from a penitentiary were studied using the same task and apparatus that had been devised by Lykken. Each subject was tested twice. The investigators told the subjects that they were studying the effects of a hormone on learning. Half of the subjects received a placebo injection on the first day of testing and half an injection of adrenaline. On the second day the injections received by the subjects were reversed.

The results of Schachter and Latané's experiment were important in several respects. First, the over-all number of errors replicated Lykken's results: there was no difference between the sociopathic and nonsociopathic prisoners with respect to the total number of errors committed in learning the sequence, whether they had received adrenaline or the placebo. Second, and once again replicating Lykken's work, the nonsociopathic prisoners who received the placebo substantially reduced their proportion of shocked errors after a number of runs, but the sociopaths who received the placebo did not. Third, and most important, when injected with adrenaline, the sociopaths sharply reduced their number of shocked errors, but the nonsociopaths (who were adversely affected by the adrenaline) did not learn to avoid the shock in their state of high arousal. Thus, the hypothesis about a sociopath's behavior being due to minimal anxiety received considerable support.

A watercolor by Vincent Van Gogh, painted while he was a patient, reflects the bleak desolation of a mental hospital at Saint-Rémy, France. The series of self-portraits on the following pages exemplify vividly the emergence of Van Gogh's style and the way in which his painting changed after his mental breakdown. Self-portraits 7 and 8 were completed after his hospitalization. Note especially the tension-laden, almost feverish style of his last self-portrait, a detail of which appears on the last page.

1. 1886

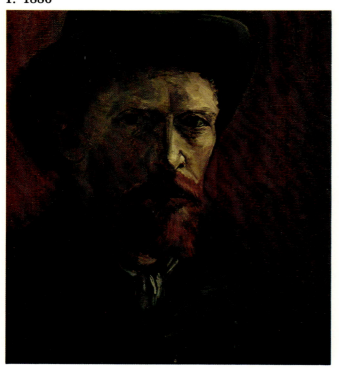

2. 1887

5. 1888

6. 1888

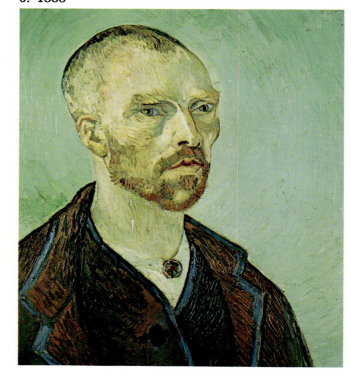

3. 1887

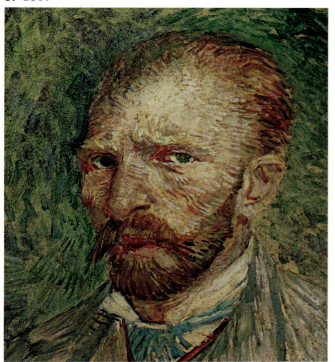

4. 1887

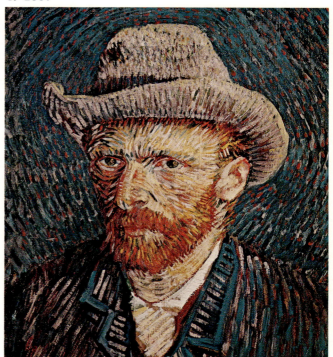

7. 1890

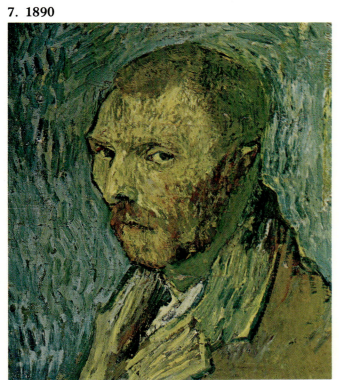

8. 1890

DRUG ABUSE: ADDICTION AND DEPENDENCE. From earliest recorded history there have been reports of people using various drugs to provide pleasure, alter states of consciousness, or reduce discomfort. *Addiction* is a physiological process by which the body responds to certain drugs. Addicting drugs, after being taken for a period of time, produce certain changes in the body so that (1) steadily increasing amounts are required to create the desired effect (*tolerance* is produced), and (2) a *withdrawal reaction* (restlessness, cramps, sweating, and other unpleasant effects) occurs if the drug is discontinued. The concept of *psychological dependency* refers to a situation in which a person takes a drug regularly, appears to rely on it, yet does not become physiologically addicted. Whether a person will become dependent or even addicted to a particular drug often depends upon the individual's psychological and physical characteristics as well as upon the pharmacological properties of the drug itself.

Alcoholism. About 80 million Americans consume alcohol and, according to some definitions, about 5 million of these are addicted. Moreover, use of alcohol is associated with many social problems; about 31 percent of all public arrests in the United States are for public drunkenness, and alcohol is responsible for more than 25,000 highway deaths per year. Homicide and child abuse are also related to alcohol consumption (Brecher, 1972). And the personal tragedy of alcoholism is quite clear to anyone who has seen people on skid row or known someone whose job and marriage were threatened by excessive drinking.

To understand alcoholism, we must distinguish between the conditions that have led a person to become addicted and the actual addiction. Although it is useful to know what factors underlie heavy drinking, such physiological knowledge does not reveal why a person becomes a chronic alcoholic. Therefore, one must look at the psychological factors.

Psychoanalytic accounts emphasize fixation at the oral stage of development. Fenichel (1945), for example, suggested that the mother may frustrate the child's dependency needs which, in turn, direct the child's affection toward the father, thereby producing unconscious homosexual impulses. These repressed impulses lead the person who subsequently becomes an alcoholic to drink in bars with other men, which presumably allows him to gratify these impulses in part. A learning explanation of alcoholism has developed from research showing that alcohol can reduce fear in animals (Conger, 1951). Drinking then could become a learned response, acquired and maintained because it reduces distress. Finally, sociocultural variables have been implicated in alcoholism. There are few alcoholics among such ethnic groups as the Jews and Chinese; these groups clearly specify appropriate festive, ceremonial, and nutritional uses of alcohol, and they discourage overindulgence. In contrast, there are more alcoholics among such groups as the Irish and English, who do not frown too much on overindulgence and who do not have clear cultural prescriptions about where and when drinking is appropriate.

Figure 11.9
Alcohol is probably the most
widely used drug in Europe and
the United States.

Figure 11.11 (Bottom right)
Ethnic groups that use alcohol for
ceremonial purposes have a much
lower incidence of alcoholism than
the general population. Shown
here is a traditional marriage cere-
mony among Indian Jews in a settle-
ment in the Negev.

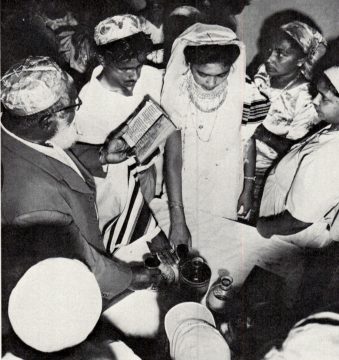

Figure 11.10 (Left)
It is estimated that approximately
5 million Americans suffer from al-
coholism.

"Hard" Drugs. The drugs to be discussed here can be divided into two major groups. *Sedatives* ("downs") slow down the action of the body and reduce its responsiveness. In this group are the organic narcotics—opium (from the poppy) and its derivatives morphine, heroin, and codeine—and the barbiturates, first synthesized as aids for sleep and relaxation. Stimulants ("ups") increase motor activity and alertness. Cocaine is a natural stimulant extracted from coca leaves; the amphetamines are synthesized stimulants. A summary of the pertinent facts about various drugs is presented in Table 11.3 (see pages 378–379).

Many have regarded the physiological changes in the body effected by drugs as the most important factor producing drug addiction. Because the physiology of the body has been changed by the drug, a withdrawal reaction occurs when it no longer receives the substance to which it has become accustomed. To avoid withdrawal reactions, the addict continues taking the drug. The physiological changes are, in turn, viewed as having been established through accident or curiosity. An individual may take the drug by chance because of peer pressure or because he or she wants to experience its effects. The person is then caught up in the changes in body chemistry and the concomitant severity of withdrawal reactions.

Psychological theories of the origin of drug addiction usually emphasize the reduction of distress and the pleasant feeling that the drugs produce. These theories also attempt to explain why particular kinds of people seem to "need" these effects. Narcotics might, for example, be used by anxious individuals in order to reduce the distress that they frequently experience. Drug addicts have often been found to be deviant on various personality questionnaire measures. But one must try to determine whether these personality characteristics antedated the addiction. For example, although we might find that drug addicts tend to be more suspicious than nonaddicts, a correlation does not imply causation. To conclude that suspiciousness contributes to the use of drugs would not be justified, for it might well be that suspicion about others is the addict's *reaction* to his or her illegal status as a drug user.

Some similarities in family background have been identified in the life histories of drug addicts (Chein, Gerard, Lee, and Rosenfeld, 1964). In many cases the father was absent from the home. When he was present, he tended to be a shadowy figure or to be overtly hostile and distant. Sometimes he also served as a model for criminal behavior, and the relations between the addict's parents tended to be stormy. Chein and his colleagues thus proposed that any personality defects in the drug addict were due to family background.

In sum, little is actually known about the origins of drug addiction. Personality characteristics, peer pressures, family background, easy access to drugs, and the frequency with which they are used in a particular culture are all possible factors, but as yet the role of any of them has only been vaguely indicated.

Figure 11.12
Efforts to treat addiction to hard drugs have not been too successful. At the left is an all-night drugstore in London, where addicts gather around 11:30 P.M. Having failed to space their fixes far enough apart and thus having run out of the drug too soon, they wait for the stroke of 12, when the specified renewal date of their prescription begins. The mobile drug unit shown below has been abandoned and languishes in a field in New Jersey.

[1]Marijuana and the psychedelic drugs discussed in this section do not appear to elicit addiction and may not produce dependence. We have included them here because of public interest in their use and misuse.

Marijuana. Marijuana consists of the dried leaves and stems of the hemp plant.[1] Hashish, a stronger preparation, is produced by drying the resin of the plant. Both have been known and used for thousands of years. In the United States these drugs were not illegal until a federal law was passed in 1937. But even with this law, it has been reported that by 1972 a total of 24 million Americans had used marijuana at least once (National Commission on Marijuana and Drug Abuse, 1972). Public concern has mushroomed along with this dramatic increase in the frequency of use.

Users report that smoking marijuana makes them feel relaxed and sociable—rather mild effects when compared with those of the other drugs discussed earlier. In fact, it is often stated that one has to *learn* to get "high" from a marijuana cigarette. Why, then, has there been such a great public outcry? It may have been due to any one of the following allegations:

1. marijuana causes crime
2. marijuana causes insanity
3. marijuana is a stepping-stone to more dangerous drugs

Even though these charges have not been supported, harsh legal penalties against the sale or possession of marijuana are still enforced. In any event, marijuana is frequently used, and thus there is a wide discrepancy between the law and the actions of many people. As of 1975 pressures for change were beginning to be felt, and if this trend continues the penalties may be lessened.

The Psychedelics. In 1943 a Swiss chemist, Albert Hoffmann, recorded this description of an illness he thought he had contracted:

I was seized with a feeling of great restlessness and mild dizziness. . . . I lay down and sank into a not unpleasant delirium, which was characterized by extremely exciting fantasies. In a semiconscious state with my eyes closed . . . fantastic visions of extraordinary realness and with an intense kaleidoscopic play of colors assaulted me [cited in Cashman, 1966, p. 31].

Earlier that day Dr. Hoffmann had manufactured d-lysergic acid diethylamide (LSD) and had unwittingly ingested some.

Two other drugs that can also be classed as psychedelics are mescaline and psilocybin. Mescaline is the active ingredient of peyote, which is obtained from growths on a cactus plant. Psilocybin is a powder produced from the "magic" mushroom, Psilocybe mexicana.

Initially, drugs like LSD were termed "psychotomimetics" because it was believed that they produced mental states resembling psychosis. As the similarity between psychosis and LSD-produced effects became doubtful, the term "psychedelic" was applied to emphasize the subjectively experienced expansion of consciousness reported by users. A summary of the possible effects of psychedelic drugs is presented in Table 11.4 (see pages 380–381).

UNCONVENTIONAL SEXUAL BEHAVIOR. This category can be further subdivided according to the *activity engaged in* and the *object chosen* (see Table 11.5). For an activity to be considered unconventional, the behavior must be preferred to conventional heterosexual relations. For example, a man who enjoys having his spouse see him naked before intercourse would not be considered an exhibitionist. Another who gained sexual pleasure *only* by being seen naked would be so considered. Similarly, for an object choice to be viewed as unconventional, it must be preferred to a conventional choice. Thus, a man who finds women's legs arousing but is even more stimulated by sexual intercourse would not be seen as abnormal. Little is known

TABLE 11.3

Facts about drugs.

Name	Slang name	Chemical or trade name	Source	Classification	Medical use	How taken
Heroin	H, Horse, Junk, Smack, Scag	Diacetylmorphine	Semi-synthetic (from morphine)	Narcotic	Pain relief	Injected or sniffed
Morphine	White Stuff, M	Morphine Sulphate	Natural (from opium)	Narcotic	Pain relief	Swallowed or injected
Codeine	Schoolboy	Methylmorphine	Natural (from opium), semi-synthetic (from morphine)	Narcotic	Ease pain and coughing	Swallowed
Methadone	Dolly	Dolophine Amidone	Synthetic	Narcotic	Pain relief	Swallowed or injected
Cocaine	Coke, Snow	Methylester of Benzoylecgonine	Natural (from coca, NOT cacao)	Stimulant, local anesthesia	Local anesthesia	Sniffed, injected, or swallowed
Marijuana	Pot, Grass, Hashish, Tea, Gage, Reefers	Tetrahydro-cannabinol (THC)	Natural (from Cannabis sativa)	Relaxant, euphoriant; in high doses, hallucinogen	None in U.S.	Smoked, swallowed, or sniffed
Barbiturates	Barbs, Blue Devils, Candy, Yellow Jackets, Phennies, Peanuts, Blue Heavens	Phenobarbital, Nembutal, Seconal, Amytal	Synthetic	Sedative-hypnotic	Sedation, relief of high blood pressure, epilepsy, hyperthyroidism	Swallowed or injected
Amphetamines	Bennies, Dexies, Speed, Wake-Ups, Lid Proppers, Hearts, Pep Pills	Benzedrine, Dexedrine, Desoxyn, Meth-amphetamine, Methedrine	Synthetic	Sympatho-mimetic	Relief of mild depression, control of appetite and narcolepsy	Swallowed or injected
LSD	Acid, Sugar, Big D, Cubes, Trips	D-lysergic acid Diethylamide	Semi-synthetic (from ergot alkaloids)	Hallucinogen	Experimental study of mental function, alcoholism	Swallowed
DMT	AMT, Businessman's High	Dimethyl-triptamine	Synthetic	Hallucinogen	None	Smoked or injected
Mescaline	Mesc.	3,4,5-Trimethoxy-phenethylamine	Natural (from peyote)	Hallucinogen	None	Swallowed
Psilocybin		3 (2-Dimethyl-amino) ethylin-dol-4-oldihydrogen phosphate	Natural (from psilocybe)	Hallucinogen	None	Swallowed
Alcohol	Booze, Juice, etc.	Ethanol Ethyl alcohol	Natural (from grapes, grains, etc., via fermentation)	Sedative-hypnotic	Solvent, antiseptic	Swallowed
Tobacco		Nicotiana Tabacum	Natural	Stimulant-sedative	Sedative, emetic (nicotine)	Smoked, sniffed, chewed

Source: Resource Book for Drug Abuse Education. Developed as a part of the Drug Abuse Education Project of the American Association for Health, Physical Education, and Recreation and the National Science Teachers Association (NEA), 1969

Usual dose	Duration of effect	Effects sought	Long-term symptoms	Physical dependence potential	Mental dependence potential	Organic damage potential
Varies	4 hrs.	Euphoria, prevent withdrawal discomfort	Addiction, constipation, loss of appetite	Yes	Yes	No[1]
15 Milligrams	6 hrs.	Euphoria, prevent withdrawal discomfort	Addiction, constipation, loss of appetite	Yes	Yes	No[1]
30 Milligrams	4 hrs.	Euphoria, prevent withdrawal discomfort	Addiction, constipation, loss of appetite	Yes	Yes	No
10 Milligrams	4–6 hrs.	Prevent withdrawal discomfort	Addiction, constipation, loss of appetite	Yes	Yes	No
Varies	Varied, brief periods	Excitation, talkativeness	Depression, convulsions	No	Yes	Yes?[2]
1–2 Cigarettes	4 hrs.	Relaxation; increased euphoria, perceptions, sociability	Usually none	No	Yes?	No
50–100 Milligrams	4 hrs.	Anxiety reduction, euphoria	Addiction with severe withdrawal symptoms, possible convulsions, toxic psychosis	Yes	Yes	Yes
2.5–5 Milligrams	4 hrs.	Alertness, activeness	Loss of appetite, delusions, hallucinations, toxic psychosis	No?	Yes	Yes?
100–500 Micrograms	10 hrs.	Insightful experiences, exhilaration, distortion of senses	May intensify existing psychosis, panic reactions	No	No?	No?
1–3 Milligrams	Less than 1 hr.	Insightful experiences, exhilaration, distortion of senses	?	No	No?	No?
350 Micrograms	12 hrs.	Insightful experiences, exhilaration, distortion of senses	?	No	No?	No?
25 Milligrams	6–8 hrs.	Insightful experiences, exhilaration, distortion of senses	?	No	No?	No?
Varies	1–4 hrs.	Sense alteration, anxiety reduction, sociability	Cirrhosis, toxic psychosis, neurologic damage, addiction	Yes	Yes	Yes
Varies	Varies	Calmness, sociability	Emphysema, lung cancer, mouth and throat cancer, cardiovascular damage, loss of appetite	Yes?	Yes	Yes

[1] Persons who inject drugs under nonsterile conditions run a high risk of contracting hepatitis, abscesses, or circulatory disorders.
[2] Question marks indicate conflict of opinion. It should be noted that illicit drugs are frequently adulterated and thus pose unknown hazards to the user.

TABLE 11.4

Reactions and aftereffects of
using psychedelic drugs.

Variables affecting a person's response	Reported physical and psychological reactions	Reported aftereffects
A. Drug: chemical structure and dose	1. Somatic-sympathetic effects: pupillary dilation; increased blood pressure; increased body temperature; occasional nausea; subjective reports of weakness and giddiness (variable A)	1. Chromosomal damage: reported in some early studies, but *not* replicated and currently believed not to be a danger
B. Situation: where the drug is administered, the way subject is treated by experimenter and by others, the emotional atmosphere, whether subject is alone or in a group	2. Changes in body image: strange and distorted feelings about body or limbs (variable A)	2. Positive psychological effects: self-reports of improved functioning, but little adequately controlled documentation (variables A, B, C, D)
C. Set: subject's attitudes, expectations, and motivation	3. Dreamy, detached feelings: light-headedness and attachment from reality; unusually rapid flow of ideas (variable A)	3. Negative psychological effects: rare instances of psychotic-like reactions, most often in people with a past history of psychopathology; occasional "flashbacks," vivid reexperiencing of some portion of an earlier drug experience (variables A, B, C, D)
D. Subject's personality characteristics	4. Reduced intellectual proficiency: impaired performance on tests measuring memory, mathematical skills, and ability to accomplish other tasks requiring focused attention (variable A)	

about how such sexual patterns are acquired. To illustrate both the lack of adequate information and the often subjective manner in which unconventional sexual behaviors come to be called "abnormal," we will examine one activity—homosexuality—in some detail. Although long considered a form of abnormal behavior, homosexuality has recently been recategorized by the American Psychiatric Association. Thus, in this sense, homosexuality is no longer seen as abnormal. We are discussing it here, though, so that the highly subjective nature of such social decisions can be clearly seen.

Homosexuality. How prevalent is homosexuality? Although this is not really known the best information available was collected by Alfred Kinsey and his co-workers (Kinsey, Pomeroy, and Martin, 1948; Kinsey

TABLE 11.4 (continued)

Reactions and aftereffects of using psychedelic drugs.

Variables affecting a person's response	Reported physical and psychological reactions	Reported aftereffects
	5. Changes in time perception: marked slowing of the passage of time (variable A)	
	6. Changes in sensory experience: increased richness of colors; heightened sensitivity to touch and smell; changes in depth and size perception; occasional synesthesias, for example, "smelling a sound" or "feeling a color" (variable A)	
	7. Changes in moods and emotions: highly variable, ranging from ecstasy and transcendental experience to great anxiety, depression, and despair (variables A, B, C, D)	

Source: Adapted from Barber (1970)

et al., 1953) and can be summarized as follows:

1. Thirty-seven percent of all men have experienced homosexual orgasm at some time since the onset of adolescence.
2. Twenty-five percent of all men have had more than incidental homosexual experiences between the ages of 16 and 55.
3. Four percent of all men are exclusively homosexual throughout their lives, after the onset of adolescence.
4. Thirteen percent of all women have experienced homosexual orgasm after adolescence.
5. Three percent of all women are exclusively homosexual during most of their lives.

Theories of Homosexuality. It is extremely difficult to know what

TABLE 11.5

Unconventional sexual activities.

Unconventional sexual practice	Unconventional object choice
Voyeurism: watching others who are undressed	Fetishism: focusing one's major sexual attention on an inanimate object or a nongenital part of the body
Exhibitionism: exposing one's own genitalia	Transvestism: dressing in the clothing of the opposite sex for sexual arousal
Rape: forced sexual contact	Pedophilia: preference for children as sexual objects
Sadism: inflicting pain as a sexual activity	Homosexuality: preference for a partner of the same sex
Masochism: being subjected to pain as a sexual activity	Bestiality: preference for animals as sexual objects
	Necrophilia: preference for dead persons as sexual objects

factors contribute to the development of any unconventional pattern of human behavior. Some people, especially sociologists, believe that variables pertaining to the life history of a person (such as how he or she was reared) do not particularly help us understand *current* behavior. However, the most prevalent theoretical point of view, the psychoanalytic, focuses nearly all of its attention on what happened in the first few years of life.

Most psychoanalytic interpretations of homosexuality are based upon the concept of *heterophobia*, or fear of sexual contact with the opposite sex (Bieber et al., 1962; Rado, 1949). The origins of this fear are traced back to events in one's early life. We have already discussed the fact that Freud and most of his followers attached a great deal of importance to the Oedipal conflict; they believed that the manner in which this dilemma is resolved is crucial for the direction of sexual preference. If the boy cannot resolve the conflict by repressing his desire for his mother and identifying with his father, he may try to escape from it by avoiding all sexual contact with women. Unconsciously, women may remind him of his incestuous feelings toward his mother. As he reaches adulthood, the unresolved conflict may cause the young man to fantasize that his penis will be injured by being inserted into a woman's vagina. The sight of a woman's genitalia, because she is without a penis, can trigger castration anxieties, making him think about the possibility of losing his own penis. The young man can then have sexual relations only with another male who, because he does have a penis, will not remind him of the threat of castration.

Figure 11.13
Homosexual relationships have become somewhat legitimate as evidenced by the increase in gay weddings.

This psychoanalytic theory was tested by Bieber et al. (1962). The case records of 106 homosexual patients and 100 heterosexual control patients who were being seen by 77 New York psychoanalysts in private practice were made available for the study. From the information obtained, Bieber believed that his study had provided strong support for the psychoanalytic interpretation of homosexuality. He described the typical mother of a homosexual as "close binding and intimate" and alleged that she "exerted an unhealthy influence on her son through preferential treatment and seductiveness on the one hand, and inhibiting, overcontrolling attitudes on the other. In many instances, the son was the most significant individual in her life and the husband was usually replaced by the son as her love object" (p. 47). The most common behavioral pattern among the fathers of homosexual patients was detachment and hostility. He concluded, "We are led to believe that . . . maternal close-binding intimacy and paternal detachment-hostility is the 'classic' pattern and most conducive to promoting homosexuality . . . in the son" (p. 144). "The chances appear to be high that any son exposed to this parental combination will become homosexual or develop severe homosexual problems" (p. 172).

Evans (1969) later tried to replicate Bieber's work. Instead of asking therapists to rate their patients, he recruited male subjects from a nonpatient population of homosexuals and heterosexuals, and had them report on their recollections of childhood. In every case Bieber's findings were confirmed. These two studies support part of the psychoanalytic theory (that parental characteristics may be related to homosexuality). They do not, however, show that homosexuals have failed to resolve their Oedipal complex—the essence of the theory.

One of the most widely known *learning accounts* of homosexual behavior comes not from experimental psychologists but from the Kinsey group. They see the human being as neither intrinsically heterosexual nor intrinsically homosexual, but as responsive to stimuli from both sexes. They believe that sexual preference is entirely a function of conditioning experiences, and they do not view homosexuality or heterosexuality as normal or abnormal.

Legal and Social Implications of Homosexuality. In the United States there is no specific law against homosexuality. Rather, the laws that do exist prohibit certain sexual acts, but these are performed in both homosexual and heterosexual relationships (for example, oral-genital contact and anal intercourse) (Hoffman, 1968). But when it has suited their purposes, the police also arrested homosexuals using a number of vaguely worded misdemeanor statutes. In California three categories of public behavior are held to be misdemeanors: outrageous conduct, lewd and lascivious behavior, and vagrancy. Homosexuals at various times have been charged with all of them. A study done by the *UCLA Law Review* and reviewed by Hoffman (1968) showed that in California homosexuals were generally punished under the disorderly conduct statute, Section 647 of the California Penal Code, according to which, "Every person who commits any of the following acts shall be guilty of disorderly conduct, a misdemeanor: Who solicits anyone to engage in or who in any public place or in any place open to the public or exposed to public view engages in lewd or dissolute conduct . . . who loiters in or about any toilet open to the public for purpose of engaging in or soliciting any lewd, lascivious or any unlawful act."

Most homosexual arrests in California are for violations of this section of the penal code. The police sometimes act as decoys to attract homosexuals. A young, and often handsome, officer is accompanied by a fellow policeman who keeps out of sight and witnesses what happens. Oral testimony from the arresting officer alleging that the defendant asked to engage in a "lewd act" with the decoy is usually enough to convict him. The law distinguishes between "entrapment" (which is not proper) and "enticement" (which is); the distinction is "whether the intent to commit the crime originated in the mind of the defendant or in the mind of the officer." In practice, however, it is the word of the arresting officer against the word of the defendant that will determine how this very fine line is drawn. The *UCLA Law Review* study strongly recommended that police manpower not be used for this kind of law enforcement, pointing out that homosexuals have their own signals and probably would not commit public outrages by confronting a heterosexual man.

As a reaction against the legal difficulties and various discriminations against homosexuals, as well as against those who accept the psychoanalytic view that homosexuality is a pathological fear of the opposite sex, a sociopolitical movement has developed to try to achieve recognition and equal rights for homosexuals. This group proclaims that "Gay is good."

The gay liberation movement began a drive to have homosexuality dropped as a psychiatric diagnosis; they wanted to be formally recognized by the mental health profession as a "normal variant" of sexual behavior rather than as a disorder or illness. A hearing was held in New York City on February 8, 1973, before the Nomenclature Committee of the American Psychiatric Association. At its annual meeting in May 1973, the American Psychiatric Association discussed the issue in greater depth; the association has now modified the listing of homosexuality to include only those homosexuals who would like to change their sexual orientation. The new diagnosis is "sexual orientation disturbance."

Figure 11.14
Eugen Bleuler

SCHIZOPHRENIA   Schizophrenia is the most incapacitating of all psychological disorders. Thus, it has been among the most thoroughly investigated disorders in the field of abnormal psychology. An early term for schizophrenia, "dementia praecox," was coined by the famous Swiss psychiatrist Emil Kraepelin. The Latin adjective *praecox*, meaning premature, was used for the disorder because it was believed to begin in adolescence; the noun *dementia* was chosen because it was believed that mental deterioration was inevitable, and that no recovery was possible.

In 1911 Eugen Bleuler wrote a monograph on what he termed "the group of schizophrenias," modifying some of Kraepelin's early notions. Bleuler suggested the term "schizophrenia" because he believed the essential feature of these disorders was a *schizin* (or splitting) of various functions of the *phren* (or mind). He said that a characteristic of schizophrenia is that normally integrated processes such as thoughts and emotions become fragmented. He did not believe that the disorder always began in adolescence or that deterioration was inevitable. He felt that schizophrenia could be arrested at any stage and that the condition of certain patients could be improved. The pioneering efforts of these two men, Kraepelin and Bleuler, still influence our views of schizophrenia today.

SCHIZOPHRENIC BEHAVIOR. The disordered behavior of schizophrenics encompass the following major areas: cognition, perception and attention, motor behavior, affect (or emotion), and contact with reality. Those who are diagnosed as schizophrenic may be affected in any or all of these areas. The diagnostician must decide how many problems a given individual must have, and in what degree, to justify a diagnosis of schizophrenia.

Disorders of Cognition. The one behavior that is absolutely essential to a schizophrenic diagnosis is *thought disorder*. When a professional

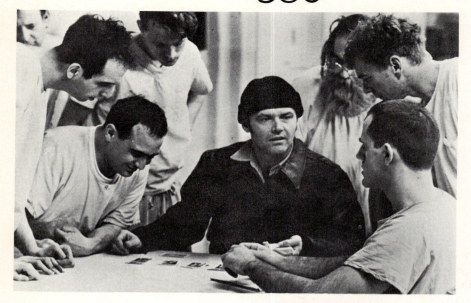

Figure 11.15
Popular depictions of life in mental hospitals—for example, this scene from One Flew over the Cuckoo's Nest—*fail to show the stark tragedies actually found there, such as these patients at Willowbrook.*

person asked a schizophrenic patient a simple question, the following conversation ensued:

"*How old are you?*"

"*Why I am centuries old, sir.*"

"*How long have you been here?*"

"*I've been now on this property on and off for a long time. I cannot say the exact time because we are absorbed by the air at night, and they bring back people. They kill up everything; they can make you lie; they can talk through your throat.*"

"Who is this?"

"Why, the air."

"What is the name of this place?"

"This place is called a star."

"Who is the doctor in charge of your ward?"

"A body just like yours, sir. They can make you black and white. I say good morning, but he just comes through there. At first it was a colony. They said it was heaven. These buildings were not solid at the time, and I am positive that this is the same place. They have others just like it. People die, and all the microbes talk over there, and prestigitis you know is sending you from here to another world. . . . I was sent by the government to the United States to Washington to some star, and they had a pretty nice country there. Now you have a body like a young man who says he is of the prestigitis."

"Who was this prestigitis?"

"Why, you are yourself. You can be prestigitis. They make you say bad things; they can read you; they bring back Negroes from the dead" [White, 1932, p. 228].

This excerpt illustrates the *incoherence* sometimes found in the conversation of schizophrenics. Although the patient seems to make repeated references to certain central ideas, the images and fragments of thought are not connected. It is difficult to understand exactly what he is trying to tell the interviewer. In addition, he uses the word "prestigitis" several times; this is a word he has made up himself, and may be impossible for the listener to understand.

A schizophrenic's thought may also be disordered by *loose associations:* although he or she may be successful in communicating with a listener, the schizophrenic may have difficulty sticking to one topic and may drift off on a train of associations evoked by some idea from the past. Schizophrenic patients have provided descriptions of this state:

My trouble is that I've got too many thoughts. You might think about something, let's say that ashtray and just think, Oh! yes, that's for putting my cigarette in, but I would think of it and then I would think of a dozen different things connected with it at the same time [McGhie and Chapman, 1961, p. 108].

Some schizophrenics are subject to *delusions,* beliefs that the rest of society would generally disagree with or view as a misinterpretation of reality. Undoubtedly all of us at one time or another have been convinced that others thought badly of us. Fortunately, most people either learn to live with this belief, or, if it is false, are able to dispel it. But imagine for a moment what life would be like if you were absolutely positive that your innermost thoughts were being detected and then made known to others. Sophisticated listening devices would allow others to tune into your most private thoughts. None of those around you, including your loved ones, would be able to reassure you that these people were not spying on you. Whenever you would enter a new room, you would have to check it carefully for listening devices.

Besides the feelings just described, the schizophrenic may have delusions of *grandeur* or *control*. With delusions of grandeur, the person believes that he or she is an especially important or powerful individual, such as a great explorer or Napoleon reincarnated. With delusions of control, the person fears being controlled by some alien force or perhaps by radar, television, or other wavelike emanations.

Disorders of Perception and Attention. Schizophrenic patients frequently report that somehow the world seems different to them. Some say that their bodies feel different; parts of their bodies may seem too large or too small, and objects around them may seem too close or too far away. Some report a certain numbness or tingling; or their bodies may feel so depersonalized that they are almost like machines. Others observe that the world appears to have changed—that it is flat and colorless. Some schizophrenics say that they have difficulty paying attention to what is happening around them:

I can't concentrate on television because I can't watch the screen and listen to what is being said at the same time. I can't seem to take in two things like this at the same time especially when one of them means watching and the other means listening. On the other hand I seem to be always taking in too much at the one time, and then I can't handle it and can't make sense of it. . . . [Or, as another patient stated,] When people are talking, I just get scraps of it. If it is just one person who is speaking, that's not so bad, but if others join in then I can't pick it up at all. I just can't get in tune with the conversation. It makes me feel all open—as if things are closing in on me and I have lost control [McGhie and Chapman, 1961, p. 106].

The most dramatic distortions of perception are called *hallucinations*, sensory experiences that occur without any stimulation from the environment. They happen more often in the area of hearing than in the area of vision. The reported hallucinations of schizophrenic patients are not the meaningless patterns of light and sound that are often experienced by persons using drugs. Rather, schizophrenics typically hear voices or music, or they may see other people or familiar objects.

Disorders of Motor Behavior. Disturbances in this area are obvious and bizarre. Schizophrenics may grimace or adopt unusual facial expressions. They may gesture repeatedly, using peculiar and sometimes complex sequences of finger, hand, and arm movements—which often seem to be purposeful, odd as they may be. Some schizophrenics manifest an unusual increase in their over-all level of activity. They may exhibit a lot of excitement, flailing their arms wildly, and using a great deal of energy, as do manics. At the other end of the spectrum is *catatonic immobility:* these schizophrenics adopt and maintain unusual postures for long periods of time. A patient may stand on one leg, with the other one tucked up toward his buttocks, and remain in this position virtually all day. The limbs of catatonic patients may have what is referred to as "waxy flexibility"; another person can move their limbs around and put them into strange positions, and they will remain that way.

Disorders of Affect. Schizophrenic patients often exhibit three affective abnormalities. In some the affect is *flat;* few stimuli can elicit usual emotional responses from these patients. This shallowness or complete blunting of emotions makes the schizophrenic apathetic. The patient may stare vacantly, the muscles of his face flaccid, his eyes lifeless. When spoken to, he answers in a flat and toneless voice. Other patients display an *inappropriate affect.* Their emotional responses are out of context: a patient may laugh upon learning that her mother has just died or she may become enraged when asked a simple question about how a new sweater fits. These schizophrenics are inclined to shift rapidly from one emotional state to another for no discernible reason. Finally, some schizophrenic patients have an *ambivalent* affective response: A single person or object may arouse both positive and negative emotions in the patient simultaneously.

Disorders of Contact with Reality (Autism). Autism is a withdrawal from contact with the world and a consequent preoccupation with one's own thoughts and fantasies. The schizophrenic becomes unable to distinguish between his own imagination and reality, and others speak of him as "being out of contact." Because schizophrenics are often buried in their own inner world, they have no interest in what is happening around them; they refrain especially from any sort of social interaction. They seldom have any friends or much interest in the opposite sex; for most of their lives they have actively avoided close social contacts.

RESEARCH ON THE ETIOLOGY OF SCHIZOPHRENIA.

Social Class and Schizophrenia. Numerous studies have shown that there is a relationship between social class and the diagnosis of schizophrenia. The highest rates of schizophrenia are found in those portions of a central city that are inhabited by the lowest socioeconomic classes (for example, Hollingshead and Redlich, 1958; Srole, Langner, Michael, Opler, and Rennie, 1962). In such studies social class is usually defined according to the occupational and educational level of the head of the household. Those who have executive, managerial, or professional jobs as well as advanced degrees are in the highest social class. Those with unskilled jobs and no more than an eighth-grade education are in the lowest class. It should be pointed out that the rates of schizophrenia do not gradually increase as the social class becomes lower; rather, there is a sharp *discontinuity* between the number of schizophrenics in the lowest social class and those in the others. In the Hollingshead and Redlich study of social class and mental illness in New Haven, Connecticut, it was found that the rate of schizophrenia was twice as high in the lowest social class as in the next to lowest. Hollingshead and Redlich's finding has been replicated cross-culturally in Denmark, Norway, and England (Kohn, 1968).

The correlations between social class and schizophrenia are consistent, but still difficult to interpret in causal terms. Some people, especially sociologists, believe that simply being in a low social class may itself cause schizophrenia. One typically receives degrading treatment from others, has a low level of education, and has few, if any, rewards and opportunities available; taken together, these factors may make life in the lowest social class such a stressful experience that the individual develops schizophrenia.

Another possibility, which does *not* assign a causal role to social class, is that during the time when their problems are developing, schizophrenics may "drift" into the poverty-ridden areas of a large city. Their growing cognitive and motivational problems may so impair their earning abilities that they cannot afford to live elsewhere. Or they may choose to live in areas where they will experience little social pressure and where they can escape close social relationships.

The Role of the Family. Many theorists have regarded family relationships, expecially the tie between a mother and her son, as crucial in the development of schizophrenia. This view has been so common that the term "schizophrenogenic mother" has been coined to describe a mother who induces conflict in her children and who is rejecting, overprotective, self sacrificing, impervious to the feelings of others, rigid and moralistic about sex, and fearful of intimacy.

Based on a review of methodologically sound studies, Fontana (1966) drew the following conclusions:

1. There was no evidence to support the concept of the schizophrenogenic mother.
2. There is more conflict between the parents of schizophrenics than between the parents of control subjects.
3. Communication between the parents of schizophrenics is more inadequate than between the parents of control subjects.

However, one cannot say that these experiences are of crucial significance. The parents may be reacting to the fact that their child is schizophrenic rather than acting as they did earlier when they may have been instrumental in causing the disorder.

Genetic Data. Without considering behavior patterns or other symptoms, how could we find a person who is not schizophrenic now but who will become schizophrenic in later life? Paul Meehl (1962) suggested that the only way one can find a potential schizophrenic is to *locate someone who has a schizophrenic identical twin.* There is a convincing body of literature indicating that a predisposition for schizophrenia is transmitted genetically.

The data from family studies of schizophrenia vary markedly. The chances that the parents of a schizophrenic will also have schizophrenia range from 0.2 to 12.0 percent, according to reported studies (Rosenthal, 1970). And the chances that the siblings of a schizophrenic will probably develop the disorder range from 3.3 to 14.3 percent. These percentages are uniformly higher than could be expected for unrelated persons and are often taken to support the idea that a predisposition for schizophrenia can be inherited. Of course, those who are related to a schizophrenic share not only the same inheritance but also the same *environment*. The parents of a schizophrenic may have the same disturbing effect on all of their children.

In the matter of twin studies, the reported rate of schizophrenia among monozygotic twins where one twin has already been diagnosed schizophrenic ranges up to 86 percent, and among dizygotic twins up to 14 percent. Thus, the rate among monozygotic twins is usually greater than among dizygotic twins, but it is always less than 100 percent.

Both the family and twin studies support the hypothesis of a genetic factor in schizophrenia, but neither type of study takes environmental variables into account. To assess these influences, one must study those individuals who have been reared apart from their psychotic relatives. One way of doing this is to study those who were born to a schizophrenic mother and then adopted by another family. Heston (1966) was able to follow up 47 people who had been born to schizophrenic mothers who were confined to state mental hospitals. As infants they were taken away from their mothers shortly after birth and given either to relatives or to foundling homes. From these same foundling homes, 50 control subjects whose mothers were not psychiatric patients were selected. The follow-up study included an interview, MMPI questionnaire, IQ test, and social class assessment. Using the dossier compiled, two psychiatrists independently rated each of these subjects, and a third evaluation was made by Heston, also a psychiatrist. These ratings were made on a scale of over-all disability ranging from 0 to 100, and, whenever possible, a psychiatric diagnosis was offered.

The control subjects were judged to be generally less disabled than the children of schizophrenic mothers. Thirty-one of the 47 children with schizophrenic mothers (66 percent) were diagnosed as having a psychiatric problem, in contrast to 9 of the 50 control subjects (18 percent). None of the control subjects was diagnosed as schizophrenic, but 16.6 percent of the children with schizophrenic mothers were so diagnosed. In addition, the children with schizophrenic mothers were more likely to be diagnosed as mentally defective, sociopathic, and neurotic. They had spent more time in penal institutions, had participated more frequently in criminal activities, and had more often been discharged from the armed services for psychiatric reasons. Heston's study clearly supports the importance of genetic factors in the development of schizophrenia, since he found that children reared apart from their "pathogenic mothers" were also more apt to become schizophrenic than the controls.

The early twin and family studies were criticized by environmentalists, for these studies confused genetics and environment. But the studies of children of schizophrenic mothers who were reared in foster homes indicate the importance of genetic factors in the development of schizophrenia, since the influence of the environment had been virtually removed. We cannot conclude, however, that schizophrenia is completely due to genetic transmission. The fact that the rate of schizophrenia among monozygotic twins is less than 100 percent argues against this conclusion, and we must always bear in mind the distinction between phenotype and genotype as described in Chapter 6. Genetic factors can only have a *potential* effect; postnatal stress (either environmental or biological) is required in order to produce an obvious case of schizophrenia.

Biochemical Factors. Speculation about possible biochemical causes of schizophrenia began almost as soon as the syndrome was identified. Kraepelin believed that poisons secreted from the sex glands caused the brain to produce the symptoms, while Carl Jung suggested that there might be a "toxin X" that would eventually be identified. The demonstrated role of genetic factors in schizophrenia also suggests the importance of biochemistry, for heredity may play its role through body chemistry.

The extensive and continuing search for possible biochemical causes poses a significant problem. If an abnormal biochemical is found in schizophrenics but not in control subjects, it may be due to something other than the disorder itself. Most schizophrenic patients take antipsychotic medication. Although the effects of such drugs on behavior decrease quite rapidly as soon as they are discontinued, their traces may remain in the bloodstream for long periods of time. The diets of schizophrenics and controls may also differ significantly. Institutionalized patients may smoke more, drink more coffee, and eat less adequate diets than various control groups. They may also be relatively inactive. Taken together, all these factors can produce biochemical differences in schizophrenic and control patients, making it extremely difficult to attribute biochemical differences between schizophrenics and controls to schizophrenia rather than to some other factor. Nonetheless, the search for biochemical causes of schizophrenia continues; we will discuss one major area of current investigation.

Taraxein. After conducting a series of investigations in the late 1950s, Robert Heath of Tulane University announced that he had found a factor in the blood serum of schizophrenics that he believed was responsible for their psychosis. He suggested that schizophrenia is a genetically determined disorder characterized by the presence of this factor (which he called "taraxein") in the blood. He said that taraxein, a simple protein, interacted with other bodily substances to produce a toxic chemical. He believed that this poison disturbed the neural functioning, primarily in the septal region of the brain, which controls pleasure and pain responses (Heath, 1960).

In his early work, Heath isolated taraxein from the blood of schizophrenic patients. When this taraxein preparation was administered to nonschizophrenic prison volunteers, they developed symptoms resembling those of schizophrenia (Heath, Martens, Leach, Cohen, and Angel, 1957). Moreover, injections of taraxein altered the brain-wave patterns recorded from the pleasure-pain septal area. According to Heath, the volunteers reacted as follows:

There is marked blocking with disorganization and fragmentation of thought. There is impairment of concentration. Each subject has described this in his own words—some saying merely "I can't think"; "My thoughts break off"; others, "I have a thought but I lose it before I can tell you anything about it," etc. "My mind is a blank" is another common expression. It becomes impossible to express a complete thought. Often they will state only a part of a sentence. They appear generally dazed and out of contact with a rather blank look in their eyes. They become autistic, displaying a lessening of animation in facial expression. Subjective complaints of depersonalization are frequent. Attention span is markedly shortened with increase in reaction time. The symptoms often produce apprehension in the patients. The commonest verbalization of their concern is "I never felt like this in my life before." Virtually all have made this statement [p. 21].

Another team of researchers, however, was unable to isolate taraxein in schizophrenic patients (Siegel, Niswander, Sachs, and Stavros, 1959). And other researchers had difficulty replicating Heath's work even when they had extracts of taraxein prepared by Heath. But Heath continued his studies and subsequently refined his procedure for extracting taraxein from schizophrenic blood. He claims that the reason the others failed to replicate his work was because the taraxein he originally provided them was impure. Heath and Krupp (1967) have now found taraxein in the cells of the septal region of the brain of schizophrenic patients who had died while displaying acute psychotic symptoms. The amount of taraxein present correlated extremely well with the severity of the disorder before death.

Heath theorizes that the septal area produces a substance that is alien to the body. As the body's defenses are mobilized, the antibody taraxein is formed. When taraxein reaches the septum, it interferes with neural functioning; this disruption in the passage of information from one neuron to another manifests itself as the thought disorder of schizophrenia. According to Heath, therefore, schizophrenia is an "autoimmune" disease: the body manufactures antibodies that act against its own brain cells.

High-Risk Research. Perhaps the most desirable way to collect information about the development of schizophrenia would be to select a large sample of individuals and follow them for the first 20 to 45 years of their life—the vulnerable period for the onset of the disorder. But such a method would be prohibitively expensive, for only about one person in 100 eventually becomes schizophrenic. The amount of data produced from such a simple longitudinal study would be small indeed. To overcome this problem, the *high-risk* method is used; with this method, only those who have a greater-than-average risk of becoming schizophrenic in adulthood are selected for study. In most of the current research projects that use this method, individuals who have a schizophrenic mother are selected as subjects. The major advantages of this method are:

1. Variables that have direct relevance to the development of schizophrenia can be chosen for study.
2. The data are collected before the individual becomes schizophrenic. Therefore, unlike studies of adult schizophrenics, these investigations will not be confounded by variables such as drugs, diet, and inactivity.
3. Finding variables that predict the occurrence of schizophrenia in adulthood may allow early intervention and the prevention of this serious disturbance.

In the late 1950s such a study was begun in Denmark by Sarnoff Mednick and Fini Schulsinger. Denmark was chosen because people can be followed up much more easily than is possible in America. In Denmark there is a lifelong and up-to-date listing of the address of every resident, and there is a National Psychiatric Register that records every psychiatric hospitalization.

In Mednick and Schulsinger's study, high-risk subjects were defined as those whose mothers were chronic schizophrenics. Such people are 12 to 15 times more likely to become schizophrenic than those in the general population. They decided to focus on the mother because paternity is not always easy to determine and because schizophrenic women have more children than do schizophrenic men. Low-risk subjects, those whose mothers were not schizophrenics, were matched with the high-risk subjects on variables such as sex, age, father's occupation, rural-urban residence, years of education, and institutional upbringing versus rearing by the family. A summary of the design and expected results may be seen in Figure 11.16. When the study began, the mean age of both the high- and low-risk groups was about 15 years. Each child in the study was given a battery of tests that included:

1. *Conditioning, stress, and generalization.* Certain psychophysiological measurements—heart rate, muscle potential, and GSR—were recorded during a conditioning situation in which a neutral tone (CS) was paired with an irritating 96-decibel noise (US). After the children had been conditioned to react to the neutral tone, other similar tones but of a somewhat different frequency than the CS were administered and the responses to each assessed.
2. *Continuous-association test.* The children were given a single stimulus word and asked to associate to it for a period of 1 minute.
3. *School report.* The teachers of the subjects were questioned about the children's academic achievements and their social interactions.

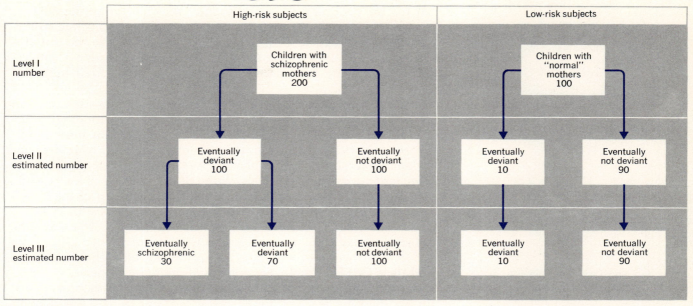

Figure 11.16
Design and expected results of Mednick and Schulsinger's study (1968) of subjects with a high risk of developing schizophrenia.

4. *Midwives' report.* In Denmark childbirth is assisted by a trained midwife rather than by a physician. Since some investigators have claimed that psychosis may be due to brain damage during pregnancy and delivery, reports on the circumstances of birth were collected from the midwives who had been present.

During the initial phase of collecting data, an alarm network was set up to make sure that any children who might show psychiatric difficulties would be detected. In a 1968 report, the histories of 20 children from the high-risk group who had required psychiatric care by that time were reviewed. For purposes of comparison, each disturbed high-risk child was matched with one high-risk subject who had not required psychiatric care and with one low-risk subject. The matching variables were level of adjustment at the time of initial assessment, age, sex, and social class. The major findings of these comparisons were as follows:

1. The children in the disturbed high-risk group tended to lose their mothers to a mental hospital early and permanently. Their mothers were also rated as being more severely ill. These facts can be interpreted in two ways: Losing one's mother could be stressful, or the severity of the mother's illness may mean that a stronger genetic predisposition is passed on.
2. The teachers reported that more children in the disturbed high-risk group, once they had become upset or excited, remained that way for a longer period of time than did children in the other two groups. More children in the disturbed high-risk group were also rated by their teachers as being aggressive, domineering, and disturbing to the class.

3. During the continuous-association test, the children in the disturbed high-risk group tended to drift away from the original stimulus word. Instead of continuing to give associations to the initial stimulus word, they began to respond to words that they themselves were using as responses: for example, "table-chair-high-low."

4. The disturbed high-risk group gave stronger GSR's to stressful stimuli. In addition, they showed more evidence of conditioning to the neutral tone and more responsiveness to other similar tones than did those in the other two groups. Their conditioned responses had become generalized. In this phase of the investigation, another measurement was also taken—the degree of habituation to a stressful stimulus. Habituation was determined by the latency of the GSR's to repeated presentations of a stressful stimulus. If a subject becomes habituated to the stress, the GSR's occur only after a lengthening period of time. In comparison with the other two groups, the subjects in the disturbed high-risk group showed no habituation, and their GSR's actually occurred with increasing speed, suggesting increased responsiveness to the stimuli over time. In addition, the time required for the skin to return to base line conductance after the presentation of the stimulus was assessed. It was found that this measure differentiated the groups better than any other obtained in the study. The skin of the disturbed high-risk group recovered after the GSR at a substantially faster rate than at those in the other two groups.

In interpreting all the information collected, Mednick focused on the psychophysiological responses. In an earlier paper, Mednick (1958) had postulated that schizophrenia is a learned thought disorder produced by autonomic hyperactivity. He suggested that the tangential thinking of schizophrenics was a set of conditioned avoidance responses that help the individual control his or her autonomic responsiveness. These avoidance responses—the irrelevant thoughts—are learned on those occasions when the preschizophrenic escapes from arousal by switching to a thought that interrupts the arousal stimulus. Because the irrelevant associations enable the individual to avoid a stressful stimulus, they are reinforced by less arousal, and it is probable that the preschizophrenic will engage in similar behavior in the future.

In a later report, Mednick (1970) presented more exciting data. Mednick and Schulsinger had examined the frequency of individual birth complications among the high-risk and low-risk groups. The many complications reported by the midwives—prematurity, anoxia (oxygen deprivation), prolonged labor, placental difficulty, umbilical cord complications, illness of mother during pregnancy, multiple births, and breech presentations (baby emerging feet first instead of head first)—were analyzed separately, but no conclusions could be drawn. After grouping all the pregnancy and birth complications into a single category, one of Mednick's students made a startling finding. Fully 70 percent of the mothers of disturbed high-risk children had suffered one or more pregnancy or birth complications (PBC) as compared with 15 percent of the mothers of the nondisturbed but high-risk group and 33 percent of the mothers of the controls. Then, in reexamining the psychophysiological differences previously discussed, Mednick discovered that the psychophysiological responses were deviant only in those subjects whose mothers had had one or more PBC's. Thus, it would appear that birth complications may help to bring about schizophrenia in a predisposed individual.

Mednick's initial findings are indeed promising. If replicated, it may be possible to identify those who are most likely to become schizophrenic *before* the onset of the disorder. Such early identification would enable preventative measures to be taken.

PSYCHOLOGY AND THE PROBLEMS OF SOCIETY
THE INSANITY DEFENSE

From time to time those who have committed a crime have been defended not on the usual grounds that they did not commit the act in question but on the ground that the act was due to insanity. One well-publicized instance of the insanity defense occurred at the trial of Robert Kennedy's assassin, Sirhan Sirhan.

Historically, there have been three major court rulings pertaining to the insanity defense. The "irresistible impulse" concept was formulated in an Ohio case in 1834. It was decided that the accused would not be held responsible for his or her actions if they were due to a pathological impulse or drive that could not be controlled. The second concept, the McNaughten rule, was formulated during an English murder trial in 1843. Daniel McNaughten had mistaken the secretary of Sir Robert Peel, then Prime Minister, for Peel himself and had killed him. During the trial McNaughten claimed that he had been instructed by the voice of God to kill Peel. The judge in this case ruled that the insanity defense was admissible if the accused was "laboring under such a defect of reason, from disease of the mind, as not to know the nature and quality of the act he was doing; or if he did know it, that he did not know he was doing what was wrong." In the third major decision *Durham v. United States,* it was stated simply that the insanity defense was legitimate if the unlawful act was a product of mental disease or defect.

The insanity defense has proved to be quite a problem. When it has been successfully used, the defendant has not been released but committed for an indeterminant stay in a mental institution. Furthermore, questions can be raised about the validity of any decision holding that a criminal act had been due to insanity. We have seen that such terms as "pathological impulse" and "disease of the mind" are hard to define even when one has a first-hand opportunity to observe behavior.

Think how difficult it would be for a judge or a jury to make a decision based on evidence presented about a defendant's mental state at the time he had committed an act a number of months earlier.

Because of arguments like these, some (for example, Szasz, 1963) have urged that the insanity defense be abolished. But it is part of our judicial system and tied to the more general concept of "extenuating circumstances and diminished responsibility." That is, motives, intents, and the like are weighed by the judicial system. Premeditated murder, for example, carries a much heavier sentence than involuntary manslaughter. Although the act is identical, the circumstances of its occurrence differ. Thus, the insanity defense is consistent with widely held judicial principles, although it is not clear how it can be decided that a criminal act was commited because of insanity.

"FRANKLY, I'M DUBIOUS ABOUT AMALGAMATED SMELTING AND REFINING PLEADING INNOCENT TO THEIR ANTI-TRUST VIOLATION DUE TO INSANITY."

Sidney Harris

399
SUMMARY

Although abnormal behavior has been recognized for centuries, it has never been easy to define "abnormal." The diagnostic system of the American Psychiatric Association provides one means for judging abnormality; although it is not perfect, this system offers a way to organize the available information.

Neuroses are divided into several major subcategories—*phobia,* a fear-produced avoidance of a situation or object that is generally thought to be harmless; *anxiety neurosis,* a free-floating anxiety; *hysterical neuroses,* departures from normal states of consciousness or sensory/motor dysfunctions; and *obsessive-compulsive neurosis,* the presence of uncontrollable thoughts or behaviors. The major theories that attempt to explain the origins of neuroses are psychoanalysis and learning. Freud believed that neuroses develop from unresolved unconscious conflicts; learning theorists view neuroses as fears acquired through classical conditioning.

Depression occurs in several diagnostic categories—manic depressive illness, in which there may be alternations between severe depression and mania; psychosis, in which the depression is characterized by thought disorders; and neurosis, in which there may be depression accompanied by agitation. A wide range of theories has attempted to explain depression (this chapter includes psychoanalytic, learning, and biochemical approaches).

In psychophysiological disorders, there are actual physical symptoms largely produced by emotional factors. Examples include asthma, hypertension, and ulcers. Current research supports the applicability of theories that emphasize a biological predisposition and stressful experience. For example, a person whose respiratory system has been weakened may react to stress with asthma, and someone who characteristically responds to stress with increased secretion of HCl in his stomach would be a candidate for an ulcer.

A number of social deviance problems were discussed. The sociopath repeatedly violates the legal and/or moral principles of society; one explanation for such behavior is that the sociopath experiences little anxiety. In considering drug addiction and dependence, an important distinction must be made between the conditions that lead to addiction and the actual addiction itself. The physiological process of addiction can explain the continued use of alcohol or heroin by one who is already an addict. But psychological and sociological factors must be examined to understand how the person becomes addicted in the first place. Finally, unconventional sexual behaviors were discussed; homosexuality was presented in detail to illustrate how society determines what is deviant in this area.

The chapter concluded with a discussion of schizophrenia and the many factors that may lead to it: low social class, family conflict, genetic predispositions, and biochemical factors. A new approach—studying children who have a high possibility for developing schizophrenia—offers great promise for learning more about the disorder.

400
GLOSSARY

Addiction: A physiological dependence upon a drug that is produced by continued use.

Amnesia: The total or partial loss of memory that is often associated with hysteria.

Amphetamines: A group of stimulating drugs that produce heightened levels of energy and, in large doses, nervousness, sleeplessness, and paranoid delusions.

Anxiety neurosis: A disorder in which anxiety is felt in so many situations that it appears to have no specific cause; in addition to diffuse anxiety, the patient may suffer acute attacks. It is often referred to as free-floating anxiety.

Autism: The absorption in self or fantasy in order to avoid communication or escape objective reality.

Barbiturates: A class of synthetic sedative drugs that are addictive; in large doses, they can be lethal because they cause the diaphragm to relax almost completely.

Catatonia: The maintenance of a fixed posture, sometimes grostesque, for long periods of time, accompanied by muscular rigidity, a trance-like state of consciousness, and waxy flexibility.

Cocaine: A pain-reducing and stimulating drug obtained from coca leaves; it increases one's mental powers, produces euphoria, and heightens one's sexual desire.

Compulsion: An irresistible impulse to repeat an irrational act over and over again.

Conversion reaction: Paralysis, lack of sensation, sensory disturbances, and insensitivity to pain without organic pathology.

Delusion: A belief that is inconsistent with reality and firmly held in spite of evidence to the contrary; it is common in paranoid disorders. . . . **of control:** The belief that one is being manipulated by some external force such as radar, TV, or a creature from outer space. . . . **of grandeur:** The belief that one is an especially important or powerful person. . . . **of persecution:** The belief that one is being plotted against or oppressed by others.

Dementia praecox: A former term for schizophrenia, describing what was believed to be an incurable deterioration of mental functioning that began in adolescence.

Depressive neurosis: A reaction marked by excessive sadness that originates with a specific environmental event.

Dissociative reaction: An alteration in consciousness that manifests itself as amnesia, fugue, multiple personality, and somnambulism.

Exhibitionism: The exposure of one's genitals to an unwilling observer, which provides sexual gratification to the one who exposes himself.

Fetishism: Use of an inanimate object or part of the body for sexual arousal.

Fugue: A hysterical dissociative reaction in which an individual flees to a new locality, sets up a totally new life, and completely forgets about his previous life, although he retains his faculties and appears normal to others.

Hallucination: A perception in any sensory modality that has no relevant and adequate external stimuli.

Hashish: The dried resin of the *Cannabis* plant, which produces stronger effects than the dried leaves and stems (which constitute marijuana).

Heterophobia: A fear of the opposite sex, which may explain homosexuality, according to psychoanalysts and some learning theorists.

High-risk research: A research technique, used especially in the study of schizophrenia, in which those who have a high probability of becoming abnormal in later life are intensively examined.

Homosexuality: A sexual desire or activity that is directed toward a member of one's own sex.

Hysterical neurosis: A disorder with a variety of forms that comprise two types: **Conversion reaction:** Paralysis, lack of sensation, sensory disturbances, and insensitivity to pain without organic pathology. **Dissociative reaction:** An alteration in consciousness manifested as amnesia, fugue, multiple personality, and somnambulism.

Learning model: The assumption that abnormal behavior is learned in the same way as other human behavior.

LSD (d-lysergic acid diethylamide): A drug that was synthesized in 1938 and discovered to be a hallucinogen in 1943; it is derived from lysergic acid, the principal constituent of the alkaloids of ergot, a grain fungus that centuries ago produced epidemics of spasmodic ergotism, a nervous disorder that is sometimes marked by psychotic symptoms.

Manic-depressive illness; Manic-depressive psychosis: An affective disorder that is characterized either by alternating moods of euphoria and profound sadness or by a predominance of one of these moods; it was originally described by Kraepelin.

Marijuana: A nonaddictive, psychedelic drug that is derived from the dried and ground leaves and stems of the female hemp plant, *Cannabis sativa*.

Masochism: An individual's desire to obtain or increase sexual gratification by pain.

Medical model (Disease model): A set of assumptions postulating that abnormal behavior is similar to a physical disease.

Mescaline: A hallucinogen and alkaloid that is the active ingredient of peyote.

Multiple personality: A hysterical dissociative reaction in which an individual has distinctly different personalities at various times.

Neologism: A word made up by the speaker that is usually meaningless to a listener.

Neurosis: A large group of nonpsychotic disorders that may be characterized by unrealistic anxiety, phobic avoidances, obsessions, and compulsions.

Obsession: An intrusive and recurring thought that seems irrational and uncontrollable to the person experiencing it.

Organic brain syndrome: A mental disorder in which a person's intellectual or emotional functioning or both are impaired due to a pathology or dysfunction of the brain.

Opium: The dried milky juice obtained from the immature fruit of the opium poppy. In the subject, this addictive narcotic produces euphoria and drowsiness and reduces pain.

Pedophilia: Obtaining sexual gratification by contact with those who are legally underage.

Phobia: An intense irrational fear and avoidance of specific objects and situations.

Psilocybin: A psychedelic drug that is extracted from the mushroom *Psilocybe mexicana.*

Psychedelic: A drug that expands or alters consciousness.

Psychophysiological disorder: A disorder whose physical symptoms may include actual tissue damage—usually in one organ system—produced in part by continued mobilization of the autonomic nervous system under stress. Examples include hives and ulcers.

Psychotic depressive reaction: A profound sadness that is marked by delusions and unjustified feelings of unworthiness.

Sadism: An individual's desire to obtain or increase sexual gratification by inflicting pain on another person.

Schizophrenia: A group of psychotic disorders that are characterized by major disturbances in thought, emotion, and behavior. In thinking, the patient's ideas are not logically related, and perception and attention are faulty; the patient shows bizarre disturbances in motor activity; there is an impairment of the connection between perception and emotion, causing the patient's emotions to be flat, inappropriate, ambivalent, or labile; the patient shows reduced tolerance for stress in interpersonal relations, and thus withdraws from people and reality, often into a fantasy life of delusions and hallucinations.

Sedative: A drug that slows down bodily activities, especially those of the central nervous system; it is used to reduce pain and tension and to induce relaxation and sleep.

Sociopathy: A diagnosis that is applied to those who have repeated conflicts with society, are selfish, do not experience guilt, and are incapable of loyalty to others. The term is synonymous with sociopath and psychopath.

Somnambulism: Sleepwalking; it is often identified as a hysterical dissociative reaction.

Stimulant: A drug that increases alertness and motor activity as well as reducing fatigue, thereby allowing an individual to remain awake for an extended period of time.

Taraxein: A protein in the blood serum of schizophrenics; Heath claims that it is responsible for their psychosis.

Thought disorder: The critical aspect looked for in diagnosing schizophrenia; it is identified by such problems as incoherence, loose associations, and peculiar reasoning.

Transvestism: The practice of dressing in the clothing of the opposite sex, usually for the purpose of sexual arousal.

Ulcer: A break in the skin or mucous membrane accompanied by tissue disintegration; in the stomach or duodenum, it is a lesion in the lining that is caused by excessive secretion of hydrochloric acid; it is generally regarded as a psychophysiological disorder.

Voyeurism (Peeping): The observation of others in a state of undress or having sexual relations, which provides sexual gratification to the viewer.

Waxy flexibility: An aspect of catatonia in which the patient's limbs can be placed in a variety of positions that will then be held for unusually long periods of time.

TWELVE

PSYCHO-THERAPY

Scene: A rather small bare office with a desk and two chairs. One person, seated behind the desk examining a file folder, then turns to the other, seated at the side.

Therapist: What is it that has brought you here to the clinic?

Client: I've been depressed and upset. I've felt like this before but never as badly as I do right now. I can't stand it anymore. I need help.

Therapist: Tell me when you started feeling this way and your thoughts about what the cause might be.

The foregoing dialogue illus-trates the beginning of psychotherapy. Although all psychotherapies consist of verbal interchanges between the client and the therapist, there is little general agreement about what the key elements are. A person's next-door neighbor might use the same words of comfort as a psychotherapist, but should we regard this as psychotherapy? In what way does psychotherapy differ from nonprofessional advice, sympathy, and reassurance? Therapists who hold different assumptions about the nature of psychological problems and treatment conduct their sessions in very different ways. Are some doing "real therapy" while others are merely pocketing the fees of their unknowing clients? We cannot slip out of this dilemma by defining "real therapy" as something that works. Different schools of therapy vary even in what they believe are legitimate goals. Behavior modifiers, for example, look for changes in overt behavior while Rogerians examine the harmony between the current and the ideal self. Given this discrepancy, it is extremely difficult to compare the results of different approaches.

There are dozens of schools of therapy, each with its group of enthusiastic adherents. As Davison and Neale (1974) noted, one could almost say, "You name it, and there is someone who thinks it's therapeutic." In this chapter we will only discuss in detail the important approaches that are used with less troubled persons—insight therapy, behavior modification, group therapy, and community psychology—so that the reader can understand something of the basic issues as well as gain an over-all perspective of the field.

INSIGHT THERAPY This type of therapy assumes that most psychological difficulties arise because a person does not fully understand the causes of his or her feelings and behavior. Thus, the goal is to try to help people discover the real reasons why they behave as they do. It is believed that such increased knowledge will enable people to have greater control over their behavior and thus be able to function better. The two major schools of insight therapy are psychoanalysis and the client-centered approach.

PSYCHOANALYTIC THERAPY: MAKING THE UNCONSCIOUS CONSCIOUS. Classical psychoanalysis is based on Freud's theory of neurotic anxiety (see Chapters 10 and 11). A person becomes tense or anxious when he or she encounters a situation that reminds the unconscious part of the person's ego of a repressed conflict from childhood, usually relating to sexual impulses. Psychoanalysis attempts to remove this repression from the unconscious and help the patient face childhood conflict and resolve it. Treatment typically extends over several years, often with several sessions a week.

Techniques. Perhaps the best-known and most important psychoanalytic procedure is *free association*, in which the patient is instructed to verbalize whatever comes to mind. Freud assumed that thoughts and memories were linked in associative chains and that the recent ones reported first would eventually lead back to the earlier ones that were related to crucial childhood experiences. In order to be able to tap those earlier events, however, the therapist must be very careful not to guide or direct the patient's thinking, and the patient must not censor his or her own thoughts. Ford and Urban (1963) have paraphrased an analyst's directions for free association:

> In ordinary conversation, you usually try to keep a connecting thread running through your remarks excluding any intrusive ideas or side issues so as not to wander too far from the point, and rightly so. But in this case, you must talk differently. As you talk various thoughts will occur to you which you like to ignore because of certain criticisms and objections. You will be tempted to think, "That is irrelevant or unimportant, or nonsensical," and to avoid saying it. Do not give in to such criticism. Report such thoughts in spite of your wish not to do so. Later, the reason for this injunction, the only one you have to follow, will become clear. Report whatever goes through your mind. Pretend that you are a traveler, describing to someone beside you the changing views which you see outside the train window [p. 168].

But mental blocks do arise, and such *resistances* interfere with the supposedly free flow of thoughts. Freud believed that interference with free association is due to unconscious control over sensitive topics; thus, those are the areas that psychoanalysts must probe most thoroughly.

The patient's dreams also present a source of information about repressed conflicts, for Freud assumed that during sleep the ego defenses are lowered, allowing repressed material to come forth. Truly important repressed material is, by definition very threatening, so the ego censors it as it appears in the manifest content of the dream. Thus, the content of dreams is symbolic, disguising from the conscious ego the true significance of dream material—the latent content of the dream.

As unconscious material begins to appear in the patient's free association and dream reports, another technique—*interpretation*—becomes important. As the analysis proceeds, the analyst begins to point out resistances and the underlying meaning of dreams to the patient. Interpretation is the analyst's main weapon against the patient's continued use of resistance. The analyst points out how some of the patient's verbalizations or behaviors relate to repressed unconscious material. The analyst may also suggest what the manifest content of dreams *truly* means. If the interpretation is appropriately timed, the patient may begin to realize that he or she no longer needs to fear expressing repressed impulses. This realization will enable the patient to relax resistances even more, providing greater accessibility of repressed material. It is believed that interpretations are particularly helpful in pointing out the meaning of resistances that disrupt free association. Noting a delay in speech or perhaps a stammer, the therapist will indicate when the patient is avoiding something, although the patient will often deny this interpretation. Interestingly, such denial is typically interpreted as a sign that the therapist's interpretation was correct. The process of "working through" requires the patient to accept the validity of the analyst's interpretations, which may be a very emotional experience. At the same time, however, the therapist must be careful not to force an interpretation on the patient.

An example of how Freud used interpretation can be seen in his analysis of a single behavior—a nervous cough—in a hysterical woman he was treating:

> An opportunity very soon occurred for interpreting Dora's nervous cough. . . . She had once again been insisting that Frau K only loved her father because he was ein vermogender Mann ["a man of means"]. Certain details of the way she expressed herself . . . led me to see that behind this phrase its opposite lay concealed, namely, that her father was ein unvermogender Mann. ["a man without means"]. This could only be meant in a sexual sense–that her father . . . was impotent. . . . I pointed out the contradiction she was involved in if she continued to insist that her father's relation with Frau K was a common love affair, and on the other hand maintained that her father was impotent. . . . Her answer showed that she had no need to admit the contradiction. She knew very well, she said, that there was more than one way of obtaining sexual gratification. I questioned her further, whether she referred to the use of organs other than the genitals . . . and she replied in the affirmative. I could then go on to say that she must be thinking of precisely those parts of her body which . . . were in a state of irritation—the throat and the oral cavity. . . . The conclusion was inevitable that with her spasmodic cough . . . she pictured to herself a scene of [oral] sexual gratification . . . between the two people whose love-affair occupied her mind so incessantly [1963, pp. 64–65, first published 1905].

Another phenomenon that occurs during psychoanalysis is the *transference neurosis*. It, too, facilitates the uncovering of unconscious infantile conflicts. Freud had noted that some of his patients acted toward him in a childish, emotional manner during therapy sessions. Since these feelings seemed to be quite inappropriate, Freud assumed that they were relics from the past, *transferred* to him from those who had been important earlier in the patient's life, especially parents. Freud believed that his patients responded to him *as if* he were one of the important people in their past life. Freud utilized the transference to clarify to his patients the childhood origin of many of their concerns and fears. This revelation also tended to help the patient lift some of his or her repressions, allowing the person to confront previously unconscious impulses. An analyst encourages the development of transference, for he or she wants to remain a shadowy figure, typically sitting behind the patient while the latter free-associates, so that the important person in the neurotic conflicts can be projected upon the relatively blank screen of the analyst.

Figure 12.1
Traditional psychoanalytic therapy consists of encouraging the patient to relax completely and to free-associate.

The Neo-Freudians. A number of psychotherapists in the Freudian tradition have introduced variations into classical psychoanalytic theory and therapy. One of the most important of these modifications is called *ego-analysis,* and its major proponents include Freud's own daughter, Anna Freud, Erik Erikson, David Rapaport, Heinz Hartmann, and Harry Stack Sullivan. Ego-analysis places greater emphasis on people's ability to control their environment—the ego (rather than the id) is the primary determinant of behavior.

The ego analysts do not view man as an automaton pushed hither and yon by imperative innate energies on the one hand and by situational events on the other, constantly seeking some compromise among these conflicting influences. When behavior develops in a healthy fashion, man controls both it and the influence of situational events, selectively responding to consequences he has thoughtfully selected. . . . Man is not at the mercy of either (innate energies or situational events). He can impose delay and thought between innate energies and action, thus postponing the reduction of such energies indefinitely. Learned responses, primarily thought, make this possible, and although originally they may be learned as a consequence of their energy reducing function, later they may become relatively independent of such influences (drives) and control them [Ford and Urban, 1963, p. 187–188].

As a group, the ego analysts have been more interested in how adaptive, normal behavior develops than in behavior disorders per se. Their main viewpoint, however, is that a mental breakdown occurs when the person's existing ego functions cannot control his or her instinctual urges or cope with environmental demands. Therefore, therapy should try to help the patient reestablish ego control, although it has not been precisely specified how this can be accomplished.

Evaluation of Analytic Therapy. How can one assess the effectiveness of psychoanalysis? A principal criterion is whether the patient's repressions have been lifted, making his or her unconscious conscious. But how can that be demonstrated? In practice, the attempts that have been made to assess the results of analysis have relied very heavily on projective tests such as the Rorschach, which, in turn, depend substantially on the idea of the unconscious (see Chapter 10). But clearly, if one rejects that idea completely, there would seem to be little common ground for discussion.

Controversies also prevail over the concept of insight. Rather than accept the idea that insight requires patients to recognize a relationship between something that was important in their past and their present actions, several writers (for example, Bandura, 1969; London, 1964) propose that insight is more like a *social conversion process*, through which patients accept the belief system of their therapists. Marmor (1962) has suggested that insight means something different in each school of therapy; patients will get insights that match the theoretical position of their therapists.

With these cautions in mind, let us examine the ability of psychoanalysis to effect desirable behavioral changes. Like all therapy studies, psychoanalytic research can be divided into studies that focus on *outcome* and those that focus on *process*. Outcome studies ask such questions as: Does the therapy work? Does it work better with one type of patient than with another? Process studies emphasize what happens *during* therapy that can be related to the outcome—for example, does there have to be transference in order for beneficial change to take place?

Luborsky and Spence (1971) made the following generalizations about Freudian psychoanalysis based on their controlled outcome research:

1. Patients with severe psychopathology (for example, schizophrenia) do not do as well as neurotics.
2. Patients with more education do better in analysis, probably because analysis relies heavily on verbal exchange.
3. The evidence is conflicting about whether patients are better off after psychoanalysis than they would have been simply because of the passage of time or because of consulting another professional, such as a family doctor (Bergin, 1971; Eysenck, 1952). This is *not* to say that psychoanalysis does no good; it is simply that there is no clear evidence.

It is even more difficult to draw general conclusions about process variables primarily because the variables are so complex and the concepts so poorly defined. One variable, for example, is the extent to which the patient can free-associate. If free association helps reveal repressed material, then presumably a high degree of free association should lead to a good outcome. Unfortunately, the relationship is much more complex, for the patient's free association may depend upon the analyst's interpretations, and the effectiveness of these, in turn, will depend upon their timing as well as their accuracy. Because of these difficulties, coupled with the problems of defining outcome criteria and reliable measures, it is not surprising that there are no controlled data.

Figure 12.2
Carl R. Rogers

THE CLIENT-CENTERED APPROACH: A HUMANISTIC IN-SIGHT THERAPY. In humanistic therapy, free will is regarded as the person's most important characteristic. It is, however, a double-edged sword, for free will offers not only the possibility of fulfillment and pleasure but also a chance for acute pain and suffering. Free will is an innately provided gift that *must* be used but that requires great courage to do so. Not all of us can meet this challenge; those who cannot often seek out one of the humanistic-existential therapies.

Carl Rogers, originator of the client-centered approach, is an American psychologist whose theorizing about psychotherapy developed gradually during years of intensive clinical experience. Rogers assumes that people are innately good and that they can become aware of why they act ineffectively and can decide what steps to take to achieve greater satisfaction in life.

In the natural sequence of healthy development a person continues to self-actualize, or realize his or her potential. But this process can be disrupted by faulty learning. A person may accept the evaluations of others as valid instead of accepting his or her own. For example, someone may accept the denigrating opinions of others uncritically and actually begin to believe them, as when a student regards himself as a worthless human being after being criticized by a teacher. The result is a conflict between one's self and one's experience. This conflict (or incongruence) is unpleasant, thereby creating anxiety. At some point the conflict disappears from the person's awareness so that by the time the person consults a therapist, he or she may have no idea what the difficulty is. With this brief summary of Rogers's conception of man and the development of disordered behavior, let us turn to a discussion of client-centered psychotherapy.

Help Yourself. Because Rogers believes that mature, well-adjusted people make their own judgments based on what is intrinsically satisfying and actualizing, he does not permit the therapist to impose goals upon the client. The therapist's task is to create suitable conditions so that clients can return once again to their basic nature and decide what is intrinsically gratifying to them. Again, because of Rogers's very positive view, he assumes that individuals' own decisions will not only make them happy with themselves but also help them become socially responsible people.

With respect to therapy techniques, Rogers's thinking has changed over the years—from a clear specification of techniques (Rogers, 1942) to an emphasis on the attitude and emotional style of the therapist and a deemphasis on specific procedures (Rogers, 1951). The main therapeutic task is to create the appropriate environment for clients to change by themselves. By conveying complete acceptance and *unconditional positive regard*, the therapist enables the client to become aware of conflicts between his or her ideal self (the person one could become) and the self he or she has actually become by accepting the contradictory evaluations of others. Since the therapist encourages the client to talk about his or her deepest emotions, the therapist must empathize with the client in order to perceive and fully understand the client's own feelings.

The basic therapeutic tools—acceptance, recognition, and clarification of feelings—are used within the context of a warm therapeutic relationship. The therapist attempts to restate the emotional aspects, rather than the content, of what the client says. This mirroring of feelings back to the client, it is assumed, will gradually remove the emotional conflicts that are blocking self-actualization. For example, a student might report that she is having communication problems with her father. Rather than asking about the specifics of these problems, the client-centered therapist would be more inclined to reflect back to the student her apparent concern about the poor communication she is having with someone she cares for. The therapist, it should be noted, is not being truly nondirective (a term often applied to Rogers); usually the therapist selectively responds to the client's evaluative and feeling statements, in the belief that this should help the client examine these matters for himself or herself (see Truax, 1966).

Rogers assumes that if these therapeutic conditions are met, the clients will begin to talk in a more honest way about themselves. Rogers believes that this talk, by itself, is largely responsible for changing behavior. The following two excerpts are from a case in which Rogers himself was the therapist (Truax, 1966, p. 262).

A CLIENT-CENTERED THERAPY SESSION. This excerpt illustrates a relatively high acceptance of the patient when he is feeling disappointed in the early results of therapy:

Patient: Yeh, but, well, for something to happen, or things to change, or me to change . . . inside, or . . . inside or something. Talking about it . . . doesn't really . . . seem to help, this kind of feeling. I mean, well . . . well, I don't know what I mean. I mean, I guess we're just talking about it. Well, I don't know what I'm doing (he has been thumping on something–beating on the desk?–long, long pause). . . . I feel so tremendously self-conscious. I don't know, maybe it was the therapy session yesterday, and the other thing that happened yesterday, that has just thrown, so much on me, myself again. And dangerous, I don't know, not dangerous but . . . I feel so un-free today. So. . . . Hmm (long pause). . . . Yeh, boy I really am self-conscious . . . sure tensed up inside.

Therapist: I can't get the feel of what you mean by "self-conscious." It's very much aware of yourself? Or something, or generally embarrassed?

The next excerpt illustrates a relatively high acceptance of the patient's feelings of inadequacy and dependency:

Therapist: I guess you're saying, "I just can't trust those weak and helpless and inadequate parts of me. I have to have someone to. . . ."

*Patient: To really be me. (T: Mmm, mmm) Someone else, you know . . .
that's so absurd . . . that would never work. It's the same thing
as this, uh . . . being afraid of people. It ties in with being afraid;
it's like . . . well, you can use any one of a number of examples.
If you really want to be someone genuinely . . . or express something genuinely . . . then, all you have to do is feel the slightest
tinge of fear and you won't be able to really. And it's like that with
myself. . . . It's kind of . . . when I am myself, it kind of echoes
on me and makes me afraid. I suddenly hear myself saying that,
and then know, "Careful!" (T: Mmm, mmm) "Hold on here! Lookout!" (T: Mmm, mmm) . . . like that. (T: Mmm, mmm) "You
won't be allowed to live if you do that." (T: Mmm, mmm) "You
won't be blown to smithereens if you try that kind of thing."*

*Therapist: Mmm. So that if you sense yourself . . . being your-
self . . . then my (P: I become afraid) Gosh! Lookout! You don't
know what you're getting into–you'll be destroyed.*

Evaluation of Rogerian Therapy and Theory. Largely because of
Rogers's own insistence that the process and outcomes of therapy be
carefully scrutinized and experimentally validated, many studies
have tried to evaluate client-centered therapy. Indeed, Rogers can be
credited with stimulating research into all psychotherapy. He and his
followers helped to remove the mystique and unnecessary privacy of
the therapy room by tape-recording sessions (with the client's consent)
for subsequent analysis by researchers.

Within the client-centered tradition there has been less emphasis on
evaluating all aspects of the therapy and more on relating the particular characteristics of therapists with how well their clients do. As explained by Truax and Mitchell (1971):

*Three characteristics of an effective therapist emerge . . . (1) an effec-
tive therapist is nonphony, nondefensive and authentic or genuine in his
therapeutic encounter; (2) an effective therapist is able to provide a
nonthreatening, safe, trusting, or secure atmosphere through his own
acceptance, positive regard, love, valuing, or nonpossesive warmth, for
the client; and (3) an effective therapist is able to understand, "be with,"
"grasp the meaning of," or have a high degree of accurate empathic understanding of the client on a moment-by-moment basis [p. 302].*

One study will illustrate the outcome research on the client-centered approach. Rogers, Gendlin, Kiesler, and Truax (1967) reported the results
of 4 years of client-centered therapy with 16 hospitalized schizophrenics. A matched control group received the standard hospital
treatment. Although there were no over-all differences between the
two groups, there were striking differences *within* the client-centered
group that were related to the characteristics of their therapists. High
levels of nonpossessive warmth, genuineness, and accurate empathic
understanding were associated with the patients' improvement, while
low levels of these characteristics were actually related to the deterioration of some patients.

414

BEHAVIOR THERAPY One therapeutic approach that has been developed since the 1950s is called *behavior therapy* (or *behavior modification*). Initially this approach used only classical or operant conditioning but now it uses many other techniques as well.

An important defining characteristic of behavior therapy is its focus on the variables that are currently related to a problem, regardless of what originally caused the problem. For example, if a timid and socially withdrawn person had, in all likelihood, developed this behavior pattern as a result of childhood experiences with a domineering parent, the behavior therapist would not spend much time trying to analyze that aspect. Instead, the therapist would concentrate on the present behaviors of concern and might intervene directly to teach the client more effective social skills.

There are a number of methods of behavior modification. We will discuss three here—counterconditioning, operant conditioning, and modeling.

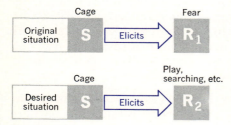

Figure 12.3
Schematic diagram of counterconditioning.

COUNTERCONDITIONING. In counterconditioning, illustrated in Figure 12.3, a response (R_1) to a given stimulus (S) is eliminated by producing a different, and incompatible, behavior (R_2) in the presence of that stimulus. For example, if a child is afraid (R_1) of a harmless animal (S), the therapist might try to encourage the child to respond playfully (R_2) in the presence of the animal. The evidence suggests that this counterconditioning (or response-substitution) can eliminate R_1.

Systematic Desensitization. In the mid-1950s Joseph Wolpe (1958) developed a counterconditioning treatment that used deep muscle relaxation as a substitute response for fear or anxiety. Because it was impractical to present all the feared situations *in vivo*, that is, in real life, Wolpe reasoned he might have fearful patients *imagine* what they feared. Thus, he developed a new therapy technique that he called *systematic desensitization*, a term probably derived from the medical procedure of administering successively larger doses of allergens to hay fever and asthma sufferers to help reduce their allergic sensitivity.

With this technique, a deeply relaxed person is asked to imagine a graded series of anxiety-provoking situations, starting with the least anxiety-producing situation and then moving to others. Over successive sessions clients are usually able to picture situations of greater and greater anxiety as they climb the hierarchy of their imagination. As has been shown by Wolpe (1958) and many other clinicians (for example, Lazarus and Rachman, 1957), a reduction in the anxiety produced by the images is generally followed by reduced anxiety in similar *real-life* situations. As illustrated in the case below, this clinical innovation has made it possible to treat a wider range of human fears and phobias than could ever have been done with actual stimuli.

Figure 12.4
A group relaxation session conducted by Arnold Lazarus in preparation for systematic desensitization.

A 35-year-old substitute mail carrier consulted us after having dropped out of college 16 years earlier because of crippling fears of being criticized. Earlier, his disability took the form of extreme tension related to tests and to speaking up in class. When we saw him, he was debilitated by fears of evaluations of his performance in sorting mail and by criticism in general. As a consequence, his everyday activities were severely constricted, and, though highly intelligent, he apparently had to settle for an occupation that did not promise self-fulfillment.

After agreeing that a reduction in his unrealistic fears would be beneficial, the client was taught over several sessions to relax all the muscles of his body while in a reclining chair. A hierarchy of anxiety-provoking scenes was also drawn up in consultation with the client and he was later asked to imagine them in a relaxed state. For example:

You are standing in front of your sorting-bin in the post office, and your supervisor asks why you are so slow.

You are only halfway through your route, and it is already 2:00 P.M.

As you are delivering Mrs. MacKenzie's mail, she opens her screen door and complains about how late you are.

Your wife criticizes you for bringing home the wrong kind of bread.

The officer at the bridge toll gate appears impatient as you fumble in your pocket for the correct change.

These and other scenes were arranged in an anxiety-hierarchy, from least to most fear-evoking. Desensitization proper began when the client was instructed to imagine the easiest item, while at the same time relaxing as best he could. After ten sessions the man was able to imagine the most distressing item without feeling anxious, and gradually his tensions in real life became markedly less [Davison and Neale, 1974, pp. 487–488].

TESTING YOUR UNDERSTANDING
WHY DESENSITIZATION WORKS

In Wolpe's original formulation of the desensitization procedure, he asserted that it was necessary to expose fearful people in a graded fashion to situations that they fear while at the same time associating each exposure with a state of nonanxiety (deep muscle relaxation). Thus, he claimed that the two factors combined are responsible for the procedure's success—relaxation and progressive exposure to feared situations. An experiment designed to test Wolpe's theory was conducted with people who are afraid of snakes (Davison, 1968). Of four groups of subjects, one group imagined a series of anxiety-evoking stimuli in a graded fashion but without muscle relaxation. A second group received as much relaxation training as those in a desensitization program, but the relaxation was not related to anxiety-provoking stimuli; they imagined situations that had nothing to do with their anxieties. A third group was provided with systematic desensitization. Finally, a fourth group received no treatment. The results of the study are presented in Figure 12.5.

What is the purpose of each of the four groups that Davison used in his study? What do the results tell us about Wolpe's theory?

1. A. Group one enables us to assess the role played by muscle relaxation; if it is important, then exposing subjects to anxiety-provoking stimuli without relaxation should *not* be as effective as systematic desensitization.
B. Group two allows us to see the contribution made by the anxiety hierarchy; the subjects in this group, although trained in relaxation, imagined scenes that had nothing to do with their anxieties.
C. Group three, if Wolpe's ideas are correct, should show the greatest improvement.

In both clinical practice and more controlled outcome research, desensitization has proved to be effective with a great variety of anxiety-related problems—phobias, obsessions and compulsions, fears of sexual intimacy, reactive depression, and psychosomatic disorders (such as ulcer, asthma, and hypertension) (Lang and Lazovik, 1963; Paul, 1966; Wolpe and Lazarus, 1966). Getting clients to move from imagination to real life is facilitated by homework assignments in which they place themselves in progressively more frightening situations between therapy sessions; such real-life exposures undoubtedly facilitate progress (for example, Davison, 1968; Sherman, 1973).

Aversive Conditioning. This is another counterconditioning technique; it attempts to attach negative feelings to stimuli that are held to be inappropriately attractive. For example, an alcoholic might want to be less attracted to the sight or taste of liquor. To reduce the at-

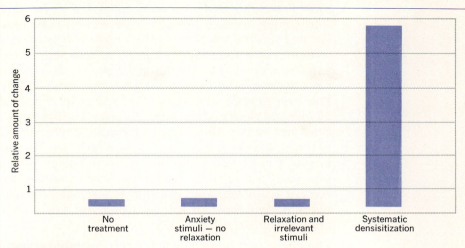

Figure 12.5
Davison (1968) used four groups to test the effectiveness of the processes related to systematic desensitization.

D. Group four was a control group; it is possible, for example, that people will be less afraid of snakes on a second test simply because of their earlier exposure.

2. The results indicate that the greatest progress was made by the systematic desensitization group; only when relaxation was paired with anxiety-provoking stimuli was there a significant reduction in fear. Although all the evidence does not support Wolpe's theory (for example, see Wilson and Davison, 1971), this study is important in showing how behavior therapists evaluate the effectiveness of their procedures and the processes related to behavior change.

traction, a therapist could give the alcoholic repeated electric shocks in the presence of alcohol. Conceptually, this method is similar to desensitization, but the goal differs since the idea is to substitute an anxiety or aversive reaction for a positive response. Other problems that can be handled with this technique include overeating, smoking, homosexuality, exhibitionism, and transvestism (dressing in clothing of the opposite sex).

Behavior therapists have also developed aversive therapy procedures using imagery. Following Lazarus (1958), Cautela (1966) reported the successful use of *covert sensitization;* as an example, an alcoholic might be asked to vividly imagine the following scene:

You are walking into a bar. You decide to have a glass of beer. You are now walking toward the bar. As you are approaching the bar you have a funny feeling in the pit of your stomach. Your stomach feels all queasy and nauseous. Some liquid comes up your throat and it is very sour. You try to swallow it back down, but as you do this, food particles start coming up your throat to your mouth. You are now reaching the bar and you order a beer. As the bartender is pouring the beer, puke comes up into your mouth. You try to keep your mouth closed and swallow it down. You reach for the glass of beer to wash it down. As soon as your hand touches the glass, you can't hold it down any longer. You have to open your mouth and you puke. It goes all over your hand, all over the glass and the beer. You can see it floating around in the beer. Snot and mucus come out of your nose. Your shirt and pants are full of vomit. The bartender has some on his shirt. You notice people looking at you. You get sick again and you vomit some more and more. You turn away from the beer and immediately you start to feel better. As you run out of the barroom, you start to feel better and better. When you get out into clean fresh air you feel wonderful. You go home and clean yourself up [Cautela, 1966, p. 37].

The client will imagine such highly aversive situations over a number of sessions (and at home as well) in the hope that the attraction to whatever causes him or her distress will be reduced by this procedure. Covert sensitization can help people control such behaviors as overeating, drinking alcohol to excess, and smoking cigarettes.

Ethically, aversive conditioning remains a controversial procedure. Substantial opposition has been voiced about the issue of inflicting pain and discomfort on people even when they ask for it. Perhaps the greatest concern and anger have been expressed by several gay liberation organizations, which hold that homosexuals who request painful treatment are actually trying to punish themselves for behavior that a prejudiced society has convinced them is shameful. These organizations accuse behavior therapists of impeding the acceptance of homosexuality as a legitimate life style when they accede to such requests for change (Silverstein, 1972).

OPERANT CONDITIONING. In contrast with this response substitution procedure (which is based upon classical conditioning), behavior modification within an operant conditioning framework tries to manipulate rewards and costs for overt behavior. Desired behaviors such as speech, grooming, attention to personal hygiene, and good academic performance have been increased by the systematic application of rewards. Similarly, undesirable behaviors such as self-injury and aggression have been reduced by withdrawing rewards or administering punishment.

The Token Economy. Perhaps the most extensive and best known work that has been done in behavior modification within the operant tradition was reported by Ayllon and Azrin (1968). An entire ward of a mental hospital was set aside for a series of studies in which rewards were provided for activities such as making beds, combing one's hair, and doing chores around the ward. Patients were systematically reinforced with plastic tokens that could later be exchanged

Figure 12.6
This child in a "teaching box" is rewarded by a psychologist with a piece of apple for work well done—a common behavior-modification procedure.

for special privileges such as a private room or extra visits to the canteen. The entire life of each patient was, insofar as possible, controlled by this regime. Table 12.1 shows some of the behaviors and the rewards that could be earned.

Ayllon and Azrin demonstrated that the behavior of markedly regressed adult hospital patients could be significantly affected by systematically manipulating reinforcement contingencies, rewarding some behaviors to increase their frequency, or by ignoring or punishing others to reduce their frequency. In order to show that a stimulus that comes after a behavior actually reinforces the behavior, an investigator must show not only that the behavior increases when the reinforcement follows, but also that the behavior declines when the reinforcement is withdrawn. Ayllon and Azrin demonstrated this effect for several behaviors; Figure 12.7 depicts a typical curve indicating how behaviors such as toothbrushing or bed-making markedly decrease when rewards are withdrawn, returning to a higher frequency when rewards are reinstated.

Since the original token economy studies, similar programs have been instituted elsewhere throughout the country. At least short-term changes in many overt behaviors can be affected by manipulating the reinforcement contingencies of patients within a hospital setting. Whether the many characteristics of adult mental patients, as detailed in Chapter 11, can be changed by means of such procedures is however, very much an open question.

TABLE 12.1

Representative activities required by Ayllon and
Azrin for mental patients to earn tokens.

Types of jobs	Number of jobs	Duration	Tokens paid
Dietary assistant			
1. Kitchen chores Patient assembles necessary supplies on table. Puts one (1) pat of butter between two (2) slices of bread for all patients. Squeezes juice from fruit left over from meals. Puts supplies away. Cleans table used.	3	10 min.	1
2. Coffee urn Patient assembles cleaning compound and implements. Washes five (5) gallon coffee urn using brush and cleaning compound. Rinses inside, washes and dries outside. Puts implements away.	1	10 min.	2
3. Ice carrier Patient goes with attendant to area adjacent to ward where ice machine is located taking along ten (10) gallon ice container. Scoops flaked ice from machine into container and carries it to the kitchen.	1	10 min.	2
4. Shakers Patient assembles salt, sugar, and empty shakers on table; fills shakers; and puts supplies away.	2	10 min.	2
5. Pots and pans Patient runs water into sink, adds soap, washes and rinses all pans used for each meal. Stacks pans and leaves them to be put through automatic dishwasher.	3	10 min.	6
6. Steam table Patient assembles cleaning supplies. Washes and dries all compartments used for food. Cleans and dries outside of table. Places all pans in proper place on steam table.	3	10 min.	5

Operant Work with Children. Some of the best operant conditioning work has been done with children, perhaps because the kinds of problems most often encountered with youngsters are especially well suited to this approach. In most kinds of therapy, a client typically spends an hour a week with the therapist. This is hardly enough time to employ reinforcements systematically, and whatever could be done might be *un*done by the many rewards and punishments that occur during the remaining 167 hours of the week. Children, in contrast to adults, tend to be under the continual supervision and (potential) control by others. At school their behavior is observed by their teachers, and at home their parents frequently supervise their play and other social activities.

For many years Gerald Patterson (1971) and his colleagues at the Oregon Research Institute have tried to influence the behavior of children (primarily very aggressive boys) in their own homes and schools. Initially, a parent in Patterson's program learns to *observe* and *record* both the child's problem behavior and his or her own actions in relating to the child. Often, a parent who complains about a child's constant interruptions actually pays more attention to them than to the child's desirable behavior. Parental attention, even if it is a scolding, can reinforce the very behavior parents want to eliminate. Sometimes both the investigators and the parents need to observe the child for an extended period in a clinic or laboratory in order to learn what the reinforcement contingencies are (assuming that the natural setting can be adequately reproduced there).

In the second phase of Patterson's program, the parents are trained in how to change the reinforcement contingencies. Once the parent has learned how to observe and record various behaviors, he or she must be taught to apply specific reinforcement contingencies to certain behaviors. For example, having determined that the child's arguments and fights with his siblings usually get attention, the parent might

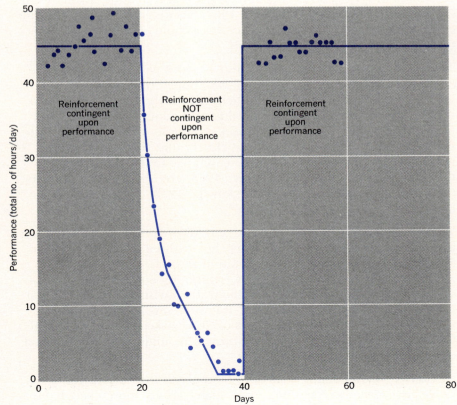

Figure 12.7
Frequency of behavior as a function of reinforcement contingencies.
[Source: Ayllon and Azrin (1968)]

decide to ignore them (that is, to extinguish them) and observe the subsequent change. Training the parent how to use reinforcement appropriately can be done individually or in groups. Sometimes investigators need to visit the home or telephone the parents to make sure that reinforcement procedures are being properly followed.

The results of this program have been most encouraging. After 3 months of reinforcing their children for nonagressive behavior at home, the parents of highly aggressive boys were able to reduce the frequency of their deviant behavior an average of 60 percent (Patterson, 1973). Other studies have found similar changes in behavior even when this therapy was compared with appropriate control groups (Walter and Gilmore, 1972). There is evidence that these improvements often last for several months after the period of intensive parental training and home observation. It does appear, however, that most families require periodic "retraining," and Patterson soberly suggests that the long-term reduction in aggressive behavior may require regular retraining indefinitely.

MODELING. Modeling is the third method of behavior modification. The importance of modeling and imitative behavior is self-evident, for children (as well as adults) are able to acquire complex responses simply by observing others. The research undertaken by Bandura and his associates (Bandura, 1969) has demonstrated the significance of this kind of learning in helping people acquire novel responses in a relatively short time.

The effectiveness of modeling in clinical work was shown by Bandura, Blanchard, and Ritter (1969), who hoped to demonstrate that various modeled situations could help reduce the fear of those who were afraid of snakes. They exposed fearful adults to both live and filmed displays of people with snakes, gradually increasing the closeness of contact. The results showed clearly that there had been a marked reduction in fear. Other research has found that children's fear of dogs (Hill, Liebert, and Mott, 1968) and their fear of dentists (Adelson, Liebert, Poulos, and Herskowitz, 1972) can also be decreased by modeling.

Why is modeling an effective treatment? People with specific fears are often exposed to fearless models, but without any apparent benefit. For example, a boy who is afraid of the water may be taken many times by his mother to a local swimming pool where he can observe many models jumping into the water, swimming, and enthusiastically providing modeling cues. But after several months the boy might still be afraid to enter the pool. If we asked him why he didn't follow the example of the other children, he might reply, "The other children aren't afraid, but I am."

Obviously, the modeling cues did not apply to this fearful youngster; as we have already seen (Chapter 4), such cues are more likely to be ac-

Figure 12.8
This child is watching a modeling film designed to reduce children's fear of dogs by means of observational learning.

cepted if the observer perceives that the model is similar to himself. One of the significant aspects of the modeling treatments that have been able to reduce fear is that the model is portrayed as *initially fearful,* thus increasing the similarity between the observer and the model (Spiegler, Liebert, McMains, and Fernandez, 1969; Meichenbaum, 1971). When films have been used, the model seems to learn to overcome his fear gradually, thereby providing a concrete illustration of what it is hoped the observer will also accomplish.

O'Connor (1969) also used a modeling film to try to reduce social isolation among preschool children. At the beginning of the school year, he chose 12 children who seemed to be especially isolated and withdrawn. Some of these children were shown a neutral film about dolphins, while the remainder were shown a specially prepared film depicting appropriate social behavior. The treatment film was divided into 11 parts, each presenting a progressively more threatening activity in terms of the vigor of play and the size of the group. In each scene an initially withdrawn child observed an activity, then joined in, and was encouraged or praised for so doing. As shown in Figure 12.9, those who saw the treatment film increased their social interaction dramatically.

CONTROVERSIAL ISSUES IN BEHAVIOR MODIFICATION. It is sometimes mistakenly believed that behavior therapy deals with the environmental causes of a problem while other therapies—especially the psychoanalytically oriented ones—deal with the "underlying" causes. Many people believe that a determinant of behavior found in the unconscious is somehow more "basic" than one that exists in the environment. However, this view neglects the fact that science looks for the most significant causes of behavior. If "underlying" is defined as "not immediately obvious," then behavior therapists clearly

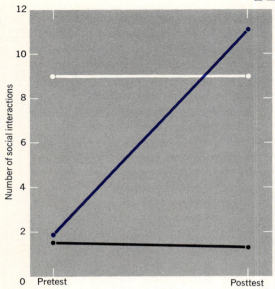

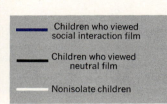

Children who viewed
social interaction film

Children who viewed
neutral film

Nonisolate children

Figure 12.9
The effect on withdrawn children
of seeing either a social interaction
or neutral film. [Source: O'Connor,
(1969)]

look for underlying causes. If these are held to be the strongest and most significant (that is, the controlling variables), behavior therapists have the same task as all other therapists—to find those strongest causes (Davison and Neale, 1974).

This issue of underlying causes also relates to another common misunderstanding about behavior therapy—the view that behavior therapy deals only with symptoms and not with causes. But consider the systematic desensitization of a phobic. Here, avoidence of the feared situation is the symptom. But the behavior therapist treats the presumed cause—anxiety. In addition, most behavior therapists use several procedures simultaneously or sequentially to try to deal with all of the important controlling variables; this approach is called "broad spectrum behavior therapy" (Lazarus, 1971). Behavior therapy might be able to desensitize a woman who was fearful of leaving her home. Over the years, however, she might have also become dependent upon her husband. As she becomes more bold about going out, this change might disrupt her relationship with her husband. For the behavior therapist to attend only to the woman's fear of leaving home would be inadequate (Lazarus, 1965) and might even lead the patient to replace agoraphobia with another difficulty that would serve to keep her at home—a problem frequently called "symptom substitution."

GROUP THERAPY AND COMMUNITY PSYCHOLOGY One problem in trying to alleviate psychological suffering is that there is a shortage of trained therapists (for instance, Albee, 1969; Arnhoff, Rubinstein, and Speisman, 1969). Without even considering how to define psychological difficulties or determining how many people need professional assistance, most knowledgeable people agree that it is not likely that America's mental health needs will be met in the foreseeable future, given present-day estimates of the number of people with psychological problems, the number of professionals being trained, and the reluctance of legislative bodies to provide more than minimal support for psychological and psychiatric services. What possible solutions are there?

There are two broad areas of therapeutic intervention that, although different from each other in many important ways, have at least the following in common: They both make far more efficient use of professional time than the one-to-one therapies we have discussed so far. In group therapy a number of patients are treated simultaneously, and in community psychology problems are sought out for treatment or even prevention in the places where they arise. Both of these therapeutic approaches are more economical than individual therapy, although economy is not the main reason for using either one; rather, each developed its own rationale for what effective treatment is.

GROUP THERAPY. Besides the lower cost of treating people in groups, many people believe that this approach is *uniquely* appropriate for accomplishing certain goals. Aronson (1972), for example, notes that group members can learn vicariously when attention is focused on another participant. As one member who is socially anxious grapples with his problem, others with similar difficulties can profit from his experience. Recall also from our discussion of Asch's work (Chapter 9) that social pressures can be surprisingly strong in groups. For example, if a therapist tells a client in an individual session that her behavior seems hostile (even though hostility may not be intended), the message could easily be rejected; however, if three or four members of a group agree with this interpretation, the person concerned may find it much more difficult to reject the observation.

Virtually every technique or theory employed in individual therapy has been (or can be) applied to group therapy. Thus, there are psychoanalytic groups (Slavson, 1950; Wolf, 1949), client-centered groups (Rogers, 1970), behavior therapy groups (Lazarus, 1968; Paul and Shannon, 1966), and countless others. In this section we will discuss sensitivity and encounter groups.

Sensitivity Training. The idea of sensitivity training originated with colleagues of Kurt Lewin, a well-known social psychologist at MIT. The first training groups (or T-groups), which were set up in the late 1940s, were composed of businessmen; the purpose of the groups was to increase business efficiency at the top by making executives more aware of their impact on other people and of their own feelings about others. Since then, people from many fields have participated in such groups (including perhaps certain readers of this book). One organization, the National Training Laboratories, was founded to promote group sensitivity training.

The primary aim of the T-group is providing an educational experience. Generally speaking, in a T-group one learns more about one's self and one's relationships with others. Individuals often participate in T-groups because, even when they seem to be functioning quite well and without significant unhappiness, they feel that they are missing something in life. Or perhaps they are concerned about some social problems. Aronson (1972) lists some of the general goals of T-groups:

1. To develop a willingness to examine one's behavior and to experiment with new ways of behaving.
2. To learn more about people in general.
3. To become more authentic and honest in interpersonal relations.
4. To become better able to work cooperatively with people other than in an authoritative or submissive manner.
5. To develop the ability to resolve conflicts by using logical and rational problem-solving rather than by means of coercion or manipulation.

T-groups and other types of encounter groups provide a situation where people can behave in an unguarded fashion. In this context of openness, they are helped to understand how they appear to others, how they affect others, and how they feel about what they are doing. Aronson describes how a group session may get started:

He [the leader] . . . falls into silence. Minutes pass. They seem like hours. The group members may look at each other or out the window. Typically, participants may look at the trainer for guidance or direction. None is forthcoming. After several minutes, someone might express his discomfort. This may or may not be responded to. Eventually, in a typical group, someone will express annoyance at the leader: "I'm getting sick of this. This is a waste of time. How come you're not doing your job? What the hell are we paying you for? Why don't you tell us what we're supposed to do?" There may be a ripple of applause in the background. But someone else might jump in and ask the first person why he is so bothered by a lack of direction–does he need someone to tell him what to do? And the T-group is off and running [Aronson, 1972, p. 241].

In the T-group, people have the opportunity to speak frankly and to listen to each other. Usually, the content of the discussion comes from the members' spontaneous interaction, and not from their past histories, as might be the case in a psychoanalytically oriented group. The emphasis on openness does not necessarily violate the individual's right to privacy, although obviously people sometimes feel pressured to reveal more about themselves than they would really like to. Of course, an experienced and competent group leader would watch for undue coercion and would direct the conversation away from anyone whose private feelings were being probed too deeply.

One of the main ways in which learning takes place in a T-group is from undisguised feedback from fellow group members, including the trainer. One person, for example, may be interrupting another repeatedly and yet not be aware that his interruptions are being caused by the fact that he actually dislikes the other. In this case other group members or the leader might point out to this person that he seemed to be having difficulty expressing certain feelings and that it might be better if he could do so directly rather than by interrupting. Also, someone might let this person know that his repeated interruptions might have more of a negative impact on the other person than an open, honest admission of dislike.

T-groups have been criticized by those who assume that the participants cannot transfer the insights and other skills that they have learned in a group to real-life situations (Houts and Serber, 1972). Such transfer is a difficult problem because the "real" world does not always encourage openness and frankness. One who has participated in a T-group may even offend others by expressing her feelings too openly and honestly. Indeed, as Aronson reminds us, if someone insists that others should be totally open when they do not want to be, the person is not being sensitive and thus has *not* learned to become more sensitive to others. Does this mean that T-group experiences cannot be applied to the real world? Not necessarily, for a knowledge of how one feels about others and how one appears to them may be extremely helpful in one's everyday activities, even if the person does not act specifically as she was encouraged to do in a T-group.

Variations. Many therapy groups resemble sensitivity or encounter groups in certain respects. Rogers's (1970) encounter groups follow the approach of his individual client-centered therapy; he frequently clarifies the group members' feelings, with the idea that people can achieve psychological growth if they face their emotions honestly. The group leader (or "facilitator") tends to be less active than the one in the T-groups described by Aronson. Some groups may meet for hours at a time—perhaps over a weekend—with little (if any) sleep allowed. With such *marathons* (Bach, 1966; Mintz, 1967; Stoller, 1968) it is assumed that fatigue and extended exposure to a given set of social circumstances will weaken the participants' "defenses" and help them become more open. Drug-addict groups, such as Synanon, tend to be brutal in confronting their members directly (Yablonsky, 1962). More recently, Bindrim (1968) has introduced nudity as an aid to lowering defenses. Many encounter group enthusiasts use exercises to become acquainted (Schutz, 1967). For example, one person may be instructed to fall back into the waiting arms of other group members so that he or she will develop trust in them. These maneuvers, as well as others, seem designed to loosen people up, making them realize that in this social setting they may express their feelings openly without censorship or fear of punishment.

Evaluation. We turn now to the important issue of the effectiveness of T-groups. Do they really work? As is the case with most other therapies, sensitivity and encounter groups have their share of glowing testimonials:

Figure 12.10
Encounter groups became
extremely popular in the 1960s.

I have known individuals for whom the encounter experience has meant an almost miraculous change in the depth of their communication with spouse and children. Sometimes for the first time real feelings are shared. . . . I have seen teachers who have transformed their classroom . . . into a personal, caring, trusting, learning group, where students participate fully and openly in forming the curriculum and all the other aspects of their education. Tough business executives who described a particular business relationship as hopeless, have gone home and changed it into a constructive one [Rogers, 1970, p. 71].

Such observations, especially when made by a highly skilled and innovative clinician, contribute to the faith many people have in encounter groups. Yet, at this time, there is little controlled research evidence showing any beneficial effects. On the contrary, there are reports of T-group "casualties" (for example, Yalom and Liberman, 1971). According to Serber (1972), a person in an encounter group may be told by another group member that she has a serious deficiency in her interpersonal relationships, such as extreme shyness. If, as can happen, the leader then allowed the discussion to shift away from that person, the individual may very well leave the group feeling *worse* about herself. If T-groups and encounter groups have a profound emotional impact on the participants, there is no guarantee that their experiences will always be beneficial.

COMMUNITY MENTAL HEALTH. The community mental health approach represents more of a set of attitudes than a body of theory and therapeutic techniques (Rappaport and Chinsky, 1973). The style of delivery is one of *seeking* rather than waiting, as with most other therapies. Usually a professional person with an advanced degree is available to provide assistance in an office or in a hospital to those who initiate the contact themselves (or sometimes on the advice of a doctor, clergyman, social worker, and so forth) or who are referred by a court of law. The seeking style of delivery, on the other hand, does not use a professional setting, but often a person's own community; community mental health workers, some of whom are sub-doctoral paraprofessionals supervised by psychologists and/or psychiatrists, seek out problems. This approach tries to prevent difficulties rather than "repair" them, as with the waiting style of delivery.

But what about the conceptual model of community mental health workers with respect to *what* they offer people in their communities? Do the techniques of community psychologists differ from those used in private practice? The conceptual model refers to the theoretical ideas behind a given type of treatment; two examples are the disease and learning approaches. Table 12.2 illustrates how these two concepts can be combined with either style of delivery. In the case of a 24-hour-a-day "hotline" operated by a suicide prevention center, clearly an attempt is being made to seek out and prevent potential suicides. But what the workers at the center say and do when a call comes in depends upon the particular center's approach and the worker's own ori-

TABLE 12.2

Possible models for mental health service.

CONCEPT[1]	STYLE OF DELIVERY	
	Waiting mode	**Seeking mode**
Disease conception	Mental illness and disease explanations of abnormal behavior. Dynamic or insight psychotherapy. Client finds the expert and is treated in his office or clinic.	Deviants are seen as ill. Prevention of illness is emphasized through public education. Extension of traditional treatment on a 24 hour or brief psychotherapy basis; training of non-professionals in "relationship" therapy.
Behavioral conception	Learning theory interpretation of emotional dysfunction. Client finds the expert and is treated in his office or clinic with techniques such as systematic desensitization and contingency management.	Learning theory interpretation of emotional dysfunction. Professional extends services into the community through public education; training of various non-professionals in behavior-modification techniques and social-learning principles.

[1] These are only two of a large number of possible concepts.
Source: Rappaport and Chinsky (1973)

entation. One worker might take a client-centered approach, while another might try to handle suicide threats behaviorally. Although the workers would handle the phone calls differently, their approach would still be within the seeking mode of community psychology. The left-hand column in Table 12.2 (concepts) can be greatly expanded. Which particular concept is best suited to one of the two styles of delivery is a separate—and crucial—question that creates ongoing controversy among community psychologists.

Another important feature of much community psychology work is the renunciation of political and moral neutrality (Kelly, 1970; Denner and Price, 1973). When a community mental health worker assumes that certain social conditions are creating problems, he or she becomes something of a social activist. Clinical work may sometimes consist of challenging a school board or city hall.

Community Mental Health Centers. For many years critics have pointed out that very few people can obtain psychotherapeutic services, which are typically very expensive, in short supply, and apparently appropriate only for so-called YAVIS clients (those who are Young, Attractive, Verbal, Intelligent, and Successful). In 1963 President John F. Kennedy proposed a "bold new approach" toward the problems of mental illness, and Congress passed the Community Mental Health Centers Act, funding hundreds of community-based centers across the country. A community mental health center has several purposes. One is to provide mental health care in a person's own community, thereby obviating the need for the person to be committed (due to really serious problems) later on to a large state hospital, usually far from home. A related objective is to provide outpatient services not otherwise available because of the high cost. Finally, the center provides consultation services to members of the local community.

How are these purposes accomplished? The centers are staffed by psychiatrists, psychologists, social workers, and nurses; then there are a number of paraprofessionals who live in the community who help to bridge the gap between the middle- and upper-middle-class professional on the one hand, and those in the community from a different social background and for whom psychotherapy may be an alien concept. Typically the centers have facilities for short-term, inpatient care, thereby providing an alternative to hospitalization. There is usually a 24-hour walk-in crisis service as well.

Many services come under the heading "consultation" and "education." In 1971 the Westside Community Mental Health Center in San Francisco did the following during that city's enforced school busing:

> We designed a program in which we placed a professional staff person on a school bus to ride to and from school with grade school children; in addition, this staff person had street corner meetings with the parents about their own busing concerns, and, also, acted as their advocates to the schools. As for the children, knowing the children would be experiencing separation anxiety in this [situation], we had our Hospital

Figure 12.11
At Achievement Place, a foster home for delinquent boys, operant-conditioning principles are being used successfully to reduce aggressive behavior and teach social skills. Here the youths are voting on an issue at a family conference.

Art Department design coloring books with maps of the territory they would cover on the bus route; we attempted to introduce play materials and games that would be helpful to the children, encouraged the children to carry "transitional objects" from home on the bus such as dolls, teddy bears, special favorite toys. Our staff member met with the children before they boarded the bus, talking to them on the bus, and again in their new schoolyard and on the way back home again [Heiman, 1971, pp. 3–4].

If the directors of a center believe that better housing conditions could alleviate emotional suffering, the center might support various tactics to secure improved living conditions. Or a center's staff might suggest changing the physical arrangements in a local factory in order to reduce the boredom or tension in a given job. Activities such as these need not originate with community mental health centers; mental health workers with a community orientation can readily work out of university departments, social welfare agencies, or even private offices.

THE ROCHESTER PROJECT. An important aspect of community mental health—its emphasis on prevention—can be illustrated by considering Zax and Cowen's work in the schools of Rochester, New York (Zax and Cowen, 1969). For years it had been known that children who had problems in the early grades of school did not simply "outgrow them." Instead, these children often developed increasingly ineffective behavior patterns. So, Zax and Cowen began a program to prevent these problems by identifying them at an early stage.

First-grade children were screened by means of interviews with their mothers, psychological testing, classroom observation, and teacher reports. Using this material, Zax and Cowen divided the youngsters into two groups which they called "Red-Tag" and "Non-Red-Tag." A Red-Tag child was one who already showed some dysfunction; about 30 percent of the children studied were so rated.

A follow-up study of the two groups of children in the third grade and later the seventh grade found that the Red-Tag children were deficient on certain achievement and behavior measures, thus supporting the usefulness of the original screening procedures. Even more important, however, were the results of an early intervention program.

A major facet of the intervention program was the use of nonprofessionals—specifically, mothers who were trained to serve as child-aides—in the schools. When a problem was identified, the child's teacher would meet with a child-aide and a professional consultant to design a program to deal with the problem, which often included meetings between the aide and the child. In a follow-up study those Red-Tag children who had been assigned to this program were doing significantly better than those who were not in it.

Over-all Evaluation of Community Psychology Work. It is difficult to evaluate the results of community mental health programs. When dealing with large populations, especially since there is no agreement on an index of improvement, it is difficult to rate the outcomes of particular therapies. This is especially true for programs that may take as a unit an entire community or subcommunity rather than a single individual.

As we have noted, the most obvious innovation produced through the community psychology movement is the large number of community mental health centers that have been established. The problems of these centers have been brought to the public's attention in a highly controversial critique prepared by Ralph Nader's group (see Holden, 1972). They pointed out that, although the centers have had good intentions, implementation has not been satisfactory. The centers are usually controlled by psychiatrists whose orientation is toward one-to-one therapy, a model that does not fit very well the problems of the centers' lower-income clients.

Further, Nader's group alleges that many centers are inaccessible to the people they are supposed to serve—inaccessible not only geographically but also with respect to the centers' policy-making. As an example, they cite the center in Bakersfield, California, which is supposed to serve an area heavily populated with Mexican American and black farm workers. But in 1970 only 14 of 284 new patients were nonwhite. They also claimed that a center in Pontiac, Michigan, was oblivious to racial tensions and drug abuse. And those centers that have diligently tried to become involved in the real social problems of their communities have often experienced strife and controversy.[1]

Enthusiasm for community psychology obviously must be tempered by an awareness of the problems they have faced in trying to implement their goals. Although the kind of work being done by community mental health centers must continue if our society wants to foster the social and mental well-being of its members, the real limitations of a number of programs should obviously not be overlooked.

[1] Devastating cutbacks in federal funding for community mental health centers in the mid-1970s threaten to make this promising movement a short-lived one.

433

PSYCHOLOGY AND THE PROBLEMS OF SOCIETY
THE RIGHT TO TREATMENT

On June 26, 1975, the United States Supreme Court delivered its ruling in the case of *Donaldson* v. *O'Connor.* Kenneth Donaldson, a 67-year-old ex-mental patient, contended in a 1971 damages suit under the Civil Rights Act that the superintendent of a Florida mental hospital, J. B. O'Connor, and a ward physician, John Gumanis, had maliciously and intentionally deprived him of his constitutional right to liberty during 15 years of confinement. The case was intitially heard in a federal district court in Florida, where the jury found the two doctors guilty of not providing adequate treatment and of failing to release Donaldson when he was clearly no longer dangerous. Donaldson was awarded $38,500 in damages.

Appeals were filed and the case made its way slowly to the Supreme Court. Following the urgings of Donaldson's lawyers, the Court decided the case on the narrow constitutional question of an involuntary mental patient's right to liberty. It concluded that a nondangerous mental patient cannot be confined with mere custodial care. But to those interested in the rights of mental patients, the decision left many questions unanswered. Can a nondangerous patient be committed even if adequate treatment is provided? Do involuntarily confined patients have a constitutional right either to treatment or to be released if treatment is not offered? Further, do all mental patients have some right to treatment, or just those whose situation is similar to Donaldson's? (Wolfe, 1975).

The Donaldson case was the first "right-to-treatment" case to be heard by the Supreme Court. However, legal discussion about this issue had been going on for some time, and several lower courts had established precedents.

The concept of a "right-to-treatment" was introduced in an article published in the *American Bar Association Journal* in 1960. Dr. Morton Birnbaum, a physician and part-time lawyer, contended that if a state were to confine a person involuntarily in a mental hospital, it had the legal obligation to provide suitable treatment so that the person might recover his health and consequently his liberty. He suggested that the courts could determine what were adequate levels of medical care and that this should not be left to the discretion of state legislatures. Birnbaum pointed out that the legal basis of his position was the constitutional guarantee of due process—that a person could not be deprived of life, liberty, or property without a determination of evidence in open court. Thus, Birnbaum reasoned, if in a court hearing, questions of the appropriateness of commitment, the need for continued hospitalization, or the adequacy of treatment were not satisfactorialy dealt with, a patient should be released.

The first major case to address these issues was *Rouse* v. *Cameron.*

Charles Rouse was arrested one night for possession of dangerous weapons. He pleaded not guilty by reason of insanity. The court accepted the plea and he was committed to St. Elizabeth's Hospital in Washington, D.C. He remained there for 4 years for an offense for which, had he been found guilty, the maximum sentence would have been 1 year. In 1966, Judge David Bazelon of the U.S. Court of Appeals found that confinement without treatment amounted to punishment. He based his decision on a law stating that incarcerated persons have a right to treatment and alluded to a possible constitutional basis for his decision as well. A 1970 Massachusetts ruling affirmed and extended this right to persons found incompetent to stand trial (Greenblatt, 1974).

The most significant and far-reaching court decision to date was rendered in the case of *Wyatt* v. *Stickney*. Initiated by a group of disgruntled employees of an Alabama mental hospital who had been fired in a series of cutbacks, the suit had included patients to strengthen the employees' contentions that adequate treatment could not be provided unless their dismissal was rescinded. The Alabama Federal District Court denied the employees' petition but accepted the patients' suit on constitutional grounds. In its 1972 decision, the court established the first constitutional basis for a right to treatment and extended this right to patients committed under civil rather than criminal law, as in the *Rouse* v. *Cameron* case. In a widely quoted portion of its decision, the court said: "To deprive any citizen of his or her liberty upon the altruistic theory that confinement is for humane and therapeutic reasons, and then fail to provide adequate treatment violates the very fundamentals of due process." The *Wyatt* decision was unique in two other respects: First, it was a class action suit, meaning that any ruling applied to all plaintiffs in the same position. Unlike earlier decisions, treatment could not simply be given to one patient in accordance with the court's mandate but had to be extended to all patients in a similar situation. Second, the judge set forth specific requirements for the improvement of Alabama's mental institutions—something that Birnbaum had advocated [Stickney, 1974a, 1974b].

What are the practical effects of these court decisions, and what might be the outcome of pending litigation? The Supreme Court returned the *Donaldson* case to the appeals court for further consideration of the defendant's liability because of other rulings on immunity possessed by state officials. In his opinion, Justice Berger suggested that there is no constitutional right to treatment; a final resolution can only be reached in a more appropriate case. The *Wyatt* decision is under appeal by the State of Alabama, and it may very well reach the Supreme Court. This case may provide the necessary facts for a more conclusive ruling on the right to treatment. In an article entitled "Rights of the Mentally Ill: The Gulf between Theory and Reality" Alan Meisel (1975) points out that implementing a patient's rights cannot depend on the law alone but ultimately on the good faith and sensitivity of those who are mandated to carry it out.

436
SUMMARY

Insight therapies assume that disordered behavior is due to an individual's inadequate understanding of the causes of his or her behavior. Psychoanalysis tries to help the patient achieve insight into the original causes of his or her behavior, while Rogers's client-centered approach focuses more on the present-day causes. Consistent with Freud's theory of anxiety, psychoanalysis tries to uncover childhood-based repressions so that any infantile fears of libidinal expression can be examined in the light of contemporary reality. Its major therapeutic techniques are free association, interpretation, and resolution of the transference neurosis. The client-centered approach assumes that people know what is in their own best interest, and so its therapists convey a warm, nonjudgmental attitude—using unconditional positive regard—to help clients see themselves more accurately and eventually trust their own instincts toward self-actualization. Behavior therapy attempts to utilize certain principles learned from experimental psychology for the purpose of changing human behavior. This form of therapy is more concerned with overt behavior than are insight therapies, and it also focuses greater attention on those variables that are currently related to the patient's problem. Three areas of behavior modification were discussed: *counter-conditioning*—eliciting an antagonistic response in the presence of a stimulus that evokes an unwanted response—may be accomplished by means of systematic desensitization and covert sensitization; *operant conditioning*—teaching desired behaviors and discouraging undesired ones by means of the systematic application of response contingencies; *modeling*—learning by observing the behavior of others—can be used to teach new behaviors and inhibit undesired ones.

Group therapy and community psychology assume that disordered behavior is shaped by, or at least can be changed by, social variables such as group pressure. The sensitivity group serves primarily to foster more open communication and an examination of feelings. Many activities are carried out within the field of community psychology, but one thing they have in common is a seeking orientation—community mental health workers venture forth from the institution, agency, or professional office and deal with human problems where they occur.

GLOSSARY

Behavior modification; behavior therapy: A type of psychotherapy which, in the narrow sense, applies classical or operant conditioning to help resolve a patient's problems; in the broader sense, it is applied experimental psychology.

Client-centered therapy: A humanistic-existential insight therapy, developed by Carl Rogers, which emphasizes that the therapist should try to understand the client's subjective experiences in order to help him or her become more aware of the current motivations for his or her behavior; the goal is to reduce the client's anxieties and to encourage the actualization of potentialities.

Community psychology: A therapeutic approach that tries to seek out and prevent potential difficulties rather than wait for troubled individuals to take the initiative. Community psychology tends to be practiced in the person's own environment (home, school, place of work, and so forth) rather than in the therapist's office.

Counterconditioning: A type of therapeutic relearning that is achieved by conditioning a new and more adaptive response to a stimulus that had formerly elicited maladaptive behavior. Counterconditioning can be accomplished by pairing a strong positive stimulus (such as presenting an attractive toy to a child) with a formerly negative stimulus (such as the sight of a feared animal).

Covert sensitization: A form of aversive therapy in which the patient is asked to imagine those situations and activities that he or she finds attractive (though undesirable) and then is given other descriptions of those activities that elicit unpleasant feelings.

Ego-analysis: A variant of traditional psychoanalysis in which greater emphasis is placed on people's ability to control themselves and their environments rationally.

Free association: A key psychoanalytic technique, in which patients are encouraged to give free rein to their thoughts and feelings, saying whatever comes to mind without censoring anything; with this technique, it is assumed that eventually material that had previously been repressed will come forth for examination by the patient and his analyst.

Group therapy: A psychotherapeutic approach in which several persons are seen simultaneously by a single therapist.

Insight therapy: A psychotherapeutic approach that tries to help patients gain greater insight into the causes of their behavior on the assumption that disordered behavior is due to repression or other unconscious conflicts.

Interpretation: An important technique in psychoanalysis, in which the analyst points out to the patient where resistances lie and what certain dreams and verbalizations reveal about repressed impulses.

Outcome research: Research that is undertaken to try to assess the effectiveness of psychotherapy. This is contrasted with *process research*.

Process research: Research that is undertaken to try to determine why certain outcomes have been achieved in therapy. This is contrasted with *outcome research*.

Psychoanalysis: Primarily the therapeutic procedures pioneered by Freud, entailing *free association*, dream interpretation, and working through of the *transference neurosis*. At present the term encompasses the numerous variations on basic Freudian therapy.

Psychotherapy: Any of a number of procedures in which a trained professional tries to help people with their psychological problems, usually by means of verbal interaction.

Resistance: In psychoanalysis, any psychological barrier that impedes bringing unconscious material into consciousness.

Sensitivity training group (T-group): A small group of people who meet together for either a day, a weekend, or on a regular basis for therapy and educational purposes; the participants are encouraged or forced to examine their interpersonal relationships and their often-overlooked feelings about themselves and others.

Systematic desensitization: A major behavior therapy procedure which requires a fearful person, while deeply relaxed, to imagine a series of increasingly fearful situations. Since the two responses of relaxation and fear are incompatible, fear will be dispelled. This procedure is useful for treating psychological problems in which there is a high degree of neurotic anxiety.

Token economy: A behavior modification procedure in which tokens, which can be exchanged for desired goods and privileges, are given upon the performance for desired behaviors.

Transference neurosis: A crucial phase of psychoanalysis during which the patient reacts emotionally toward the analyst, treating the analyst like a parent and reliving thereby certain childhood experiences; this experience enables both the analyst and the patient to examine conflicts that had previously been repressed in the light of current reality.

Unconditional positive regard: In client-centered therapy, this is an important attitude for the therapist to have toward a client, who needs to feel totally accepted as a person in order to be able to assess what he or she is doing that contributes to or works against self-actualization.

APPENDIX

STATISTICS   Throughout this text we have tried to show how the theories and practical applications of psychology depend upon the results of research. Statistics allow the researcher to describe and to draw inferences from data that have been collected.

DESCRIPTIVE STATISTICS. The most basic use of statistics is for descriptive purposes. Descriptive statistics are quite valuable in summarizing an otherwise unwieldy amount of information. Every day we are exposed to descriptive statistical information such as the annual crime rate, the won and lost record of our favorite football team, and the number of points earned on an examination. In psychological research three kinds of descriptive statistics are generally used—measures of central tendency, measures of variability, and the correlation coefficient.

To illustrate central tendency and variability, let us take a hypothetical experiment testing the effects of social praise on children's classroom participation. Suppose that a teacher has a sample of 28 children in a classroom and randomly selects half of them (for example, by tossing a coin for each child and assigning the first 14 children who come up heads to the praise group)[1] to receive praise each time they speak up in the classroom. The remaining children are not praised when they speak up in class. After 3 days an observer enters the classroom and records each time each child participates in the classroom discussion. The results of this observation are presented in Table A.1. The two columns show the distributions of scores for the

[1] As explained in Chapter 1, random assignment is a requirement for experimental designs since it enables the researcher to be fairly confident that the groups are balanced on irrelevant characteristics.

440

TABLE A.1

Hypothetical results of an experiment designed to study the effects of praise on children's classroom participation.

Number of instances of classroom participation

Non-praised group	Praised group
4	6
4	7
3	7
1	4
6	5
8	3
6	6
5	6
5	8
3	9
4	8
5	4
7	10
2	5
Total 63	88
Mean 63/14 = 4.5	88/14 = 6.3

praised and non-praised groups. Each column has 14 numbers, which are the observed instances of participation by each of the 14 children in each group.

Measures of central tendency are intended to characterize the typical score in a distribution. The most commonly used measure is the *mean,* which is simply the arithmetic average obtained by adding the scores and then dividing by the number of observations. The means for the praised and non-praised groups are shown in Table A.1. A single number for each group describes its central tendency; thus, we can see that the average or mean of the children who were praised is higher than that of the children who were not.

Looking again at Table A.1 we can see that the mean does not encompass all of the information about the children's scores. Within each of the columns the scores vary, and we would like to be able to describe this degree of variability with a number. One of the reasons for assessing variability is to be able to determine how well the measure of central tendency reflects all of the scores in the distribution. In other words, how typical is the "typical score?" If the variability is small (that is, the scores are all near the mean), then the central tendency measure will be close to all of the individual scores. But if the variability is large, many of the individual scores could be quite different from the mean. Later on we will see that measures of variability are also critical in the use of *inferential statistics.*

One simple measure of variability is the *range*—the difference between the lowest and highest scores in a distribution. Returning to

TABLE A.2

Calculation of the variance for the non-praised group.

Scores	Mean	Deviation	Squared deviation
4	4.5	.5	.25
4	4.5	.5	.25
3	4.5	1.5	2.25
1	4.5	3.5	12.25
6	4.5	−1.5	2.25
8	4.5	−3.5	12.25
6	4.5	−1.5	2.25
5	4.5	− .5	.25
5	4.5	− .5	.25
3	4.5	1.5	2.25
4	4.5	.5	.25
5	4.5	− .5	.25
7	4.5	−2.5	6.25
2	4.5	2.5	6.25

Total 47.50

Average 47.50/14 = 3.04

our example (Table A.1) we can see that the range for the praised group is 10−3=7 and for the non-praised group 8−1=7. The range as a measure of variability is not widely used, however, because it can be misleading. For example, if there were ninety scores of 1 and one score of 1000, the range would be 999! What we want to know is the average distance between scores, and not just the difference between the extremes.

This information can be obtained from a statistic called the *variance*. It is calculated by subtracting each score from the mean, squaring each of these deviation scores (multiplying each by itself), and then totaling them up and dividing the result by the number of scores. The variance, then, is the average squared deviation from the mean. Table A.2 shows the calculation of the variance for the non-praised group.

The third type of descriptive statistic generally used in psychological research is the *correlation coefficient*. As we mentioned in Chapter 1, the correlation coefficient provides information both about the strength of a relationship between two variables and its direction. The correlation coefficient can range in magnitude from .00, indicating no relationship, to 1.00 (which can be either positive or negative), reflecting a perfect relationship between two variables. The sign of the correlation coefficient (plus or minus) tells us whether the two variables are positively or negatively related. If it is a plus, this means that as the scores on one variable increase so do the scores on the other. Among children, for example, height and weight tend to be positively related. If it is a minus, this means that high scores on one variable are related to low scores on the other. Unemployment and business sales tend to be negatively correlated; as unemployment rises,

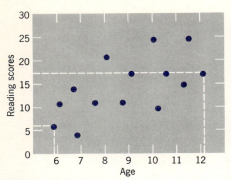

Figure A.1
Graphic representation of a correlation between age and reading scores.

sales volume generally declines. A figure that appears in Chapter 1 (page 19) illustrates several correlational relationships of varying magnitude and sign. Let us now look more closely at how such graphs are interpreted. Figure A.1 shows a correlational relationship between two variables—age and scores on a reading test. Age is located on the horizontal axis and reading scores on the vertical. Look at the dot in the lower left corner. This single point represents an individual's score on both age and the reading test. The actual numbers can be read by drawing imaginary straight lines to the two axes. Thus, it can be seen that this child is slightly less than 6 years old and scored 6 points on the reading test. Similarly, we can see that the point at the far right indicates an age of slightly more than 12 and a reading score of 17.5.

INFERENTIAL STATISTICS. Besides describing data from the *sample* they have studied, psychologists want to be able to make a statement about a *population* of individuals. In our hypothetical experiment, for example, a researcher might want to know whether praise would encourage other children to speak up more readily in other classrooms. The purpose of *inferential statistics* is to bridge the gap between a given sample and a population.

Inferential statistics are closely related to statistical significance, which we mentioned in Chapter 1. A statistically significant effect is one that has little likelihood of being caused by chance; thus, it can be generalized from the sample to the population. Statistical significance is usually evaluated against chance, that is, the researcher assesses the likelihood that his results may have been produced by chance factors rather than by the variables he or she was interested in. Results that have a sufficiently low probability of occurring by chance (for example, one in 20) are called statistically significant.

How is statistical significance evaluated? In experimental research, the answer lies in the concept of variability. Returning to our hypothetical example, recall that the participation scores were generally higher for the praised than for the non-praised group. In other words, the scores of the two groups varied according to whether or not the children were praised. Such differences between groups (as indicated by the mean difference between them) are known as *systematic variance*. But it is also clear from Table A.1 that within each group the scores varied. Whether or not the children received praise, some children participated more than others. This variability, produced by chance and factors unknown to the experimenter, is called *error variance*.

We can now see how statistical significance is evaluated, that is, how we can know whether the differences in the amount of participation between the praised and the non-praised groups are enough to be considered "real" or reliable. One might easily wonder whether the average difference between the two groups occurred by chance and had nothing to do with the praise itself. Perhaps the more talkative children just happened to be the ones who received praise, but the praise itself did not cause the difference. By examining the systematic variance, or average difference between the two groups, in relation to the extent to which the scores differ within each group, we find an answer.

The reasoning is as follows: The average difference between two groups in an experiment will almost never be 0, even if the treatment given to one of them is totally ineffective. This is because not all of the scores, even within one group, will be the same. Any two randomly selected groups will differ somewhat. The extent to which individual scores differ, simply by chance, enables one to estimate whether the difference obtained between the groups is actually larger than would have been expected by chance alone. This is the only type of analysis that enables us to be confident that our effects are reliable.

We must find a way of estimating how much difference we might expect by chance. To obtain this information, we measure the variability within the groups, that is, the degree to which each score differs or deviates from, the group's average. The variance statistic is extremely important in calculating the actual effect of the manipulation of the independent variable upon the dependent variable. In Table A.1, we see that the group that received praise participated 1.8 more times (on the average) in the classroom than did the non-praised group. Is this difference large enough to warrant the conclusion that praise encourages performance? An answer can be found by comparing the systematic and error variance.

In the most widely used of modern statistical tests, the F test, the systematic variance that is due to treatments is evaluated, as a ratio, against the amount of variance that is caused by unknown sources (that

TABLE A.3

Commonly used tests of statistical inference.

Name	Symbol	Use
Chi square	χ^2	To evaluate associations between "categorical" variables, for example, political affiliation and whether or not a person voted in the last election.
Student's t	t	To determine the significance of the difference between two means.
Fisher's F (analysis of variance)	F	To determine the significance of the differences among two or more means as well as whether two treatments combine or interact in a significant way.
Pearson's product moment correlation coefficient	r	To determine the degree of relationship between two variables.

is, the error variance). Conceptually, the formula for the F test is quite straightforward:

$$F = \text{systematic variance/error variance}$$

As the F ratio increases, there is less probability that the experimental results were due to chance. That is, the results become increasingly significant from a statistical point of view.

Any descriptive statistic for a sample might raise certain doubts about how well the statistic described the population. For example, the correlation coefficient (a descriptive statistic) can also be used in statistical inference. The problem is the reliability of a correlation that has been obtained in a sample. Can we view the correlation as reflecting a relationship that applies to a broader population? In general, larger correlations are more likely to be statistically significant. Table A.3 presents a list of commonly used inferential statistics.

REFERENCES

Adelson, R.; Liebert, R. M.; Poulos, R. W.; and Herskovitz, A. 1972. A modelling film to reduce children's fear of dental treatment. *International Association of Dental Research Abstracts*, March, *114*.

Agnew, W. H.; Webb, W. B.; and Williams, R. L. 1964. The effects of stage four sleep deprivation. *Electroencephalography and Clinical Neurophysiology*, *17*, 68–70.

Albee, G. W. 1969. We have been warned. In W. Ryan, ed., *Distress in the city*. Cleveland, Ohio: Case Western Reserve University Press.

Allen, K. E.; Hart, B. M.; Buell, J. S.; Harris, F. R.; and Wolf, M. M. 1964. Effects of social reinforcement on isolate behavior of a nursery school child. *Child Development*, *35*, 511–518.

Allen, V. L., and Levine, J. M. 1969. Consensus and conformity. *Journal of Experimental Social Psychology*, *5*, 389–399.

Allport, G. W. 1961. *Pattern and growth in personality*. New York: Holt, Rinehart and Winston.

Allyn, J., and Festinger, L. 1961. The effectiveness of unanticipated persuasive communications. *Journal of Abnormal and Social Psychology*, *62*, 35–40.

Allyon, T., and Haughton, E. 1964. Modification of symptomatic behavior of mental patients. *Behavior Research and Therapy*, *2*, 87–97.

American Psychiatric Association. 1952. *Diagnostic and statistical manual: mental disorders* (DSM-I). Washington: American Psychiatric Association (special printing, 1965).

———. 1968. *Diagnostic and statistical manual of mental disorders*, 2nd ed. Washington, D.C.: American Psychiatric Association.

American Psychological Association. 1965. Special issue: Testing and public policy. *American Psychologist*, *20*, 857–993.

Anastasi, A., and D'Angelo, R. 1952. A comparison of Negro and white preschool children in language development and Goodenough Draw-a-Man IQ. *Journal of Genetic Psychology*, *81*, 147–165.

Anderson, M. L., and McConnell, R. A. 1961. Fantasy testing for ESP in a fourth and fifth grade class. *Journal of Psychology*, *52*, 491–503.

Andres, D. H. 1967. Modification of delay-of-punishment effects through cognitive restructuring. Unpublished doctoral dissertation, University of Waterloo (Canada).

Arnhoff, F. N.; Rubinstein, E. A.; and Speisman, J. E., eds. 1969. *Mental health manpower*. Chicago, Ill.: Aldine.

Aronfreed, J. 1968. *Conduct and conscience*. New York: Academic Press.

Aronfreed, J., and Reber, A. 1965. Internalized behavioral suppression and the timing of social punishment. *Journal of Personality and Social Psychology*, *1*, 3–16.

Aronson, E. 1972. *The social animal*. San Francisco: Freeman.

Asch, S. 1956. Studies of independence and conformity: a minority of one against a unanimous majority. *Psychological Monographs, 70* (Whole No. 416).

Ashcroft, G. W., and Sharman, D. F. 1960. 5-Hydroxy-indoles in human cerebrospinal fluid. *Nature, 186,* 1050–1051.

Atkinson, R. C., and Schifrin, R. M. 1971. The control of short-term memory. *Scientific American, 225,* 82–90.

Ausubel, D. P. 1961a. Causes and types of narcotic addictions: a psychosocial view. *Psychiatric Quarterly, 35,* 523–531.

————. 1961b. Personality disorder is disease. *American Psychologist, 16,* 69–74.

Ayllon, T., and Azrin, N. 1968. *The token economy: a motivational system for therapy and rehabilitation.* New York: Appleton-Century-Crofts.

Azrin, N. H., and Lindsley, O. R. 1956. The reinforcement of cooperation between children. *Journal of Abnormal and Social Psychology, 52,* 100–102.

Bach, G. R. 1966. The marathon group: intensive practice of intimate interactions. *Psychological Reports, 181,* 995–1002.

Backman, C. W., and Secord, P. F. 1959. The effect of perceived liking on interpersonal attraction. *Human Relations, 12,* 379–384.

Baer, D. M., and Sherman, J. A. 1964. Reinforcement control of generalized imitation in young children. *Journal of Experimental Child Psychology, 1,* 37–49.

Baldwin, A. L. 1967. *Theories of child development.* New York: Wiley.

Bandura, A. 1962. Social learning through imitation. *Nebraska Symposium on Motivation, 10,* 211–269.

————. 1965. Influence of model's reinforcement contingencies on the acquisition of imitative responses. *Journal of Personality and Social Psychology, 1,* 589–595.

————. 1969. *Principles of behavior modification.* New York: Holt, Rinehart and Winston.

————. 1973. *Aggression: a social learning analysis.* Englewood Cliffs, N.J.: Prentice-Hall.

Bandura, A.; Blanchard, E. B.; and Ritter, B. 1969. Relative efficacy of desensitization and modelling approaches for inducing behavioral, affective, and attitudinal changes. *Journal of Personality and Social Psychology, 13,* 173–199.

Bandura, A., and Harris, M. B. 1967. Modification of syntactic style. *Journal of Experimental Child Psychology, 4,* 341–352.

Bandura, A., and Walters, R. H. 1963. *Social learning and personality development.* New York: Holt, Rinehart and Winston.

Barber, T. X. 1970. *LSD, marihuana, yoga and hypnosis.* Chicago: Aldine.

Barko, R.; Dembo, T.; and Lewin, K. 1941. Frustration and regression: an experiment with young children. *University of Iowa Studies in Child Welfare, 18* (Whole No. 386).

Baron, R. A. 1970. Attraction toward the model and model's competence as determinants of adult imitative behavior. *Journal of Personality and Social Psychology, 14,* 345–351.

Baron, R. A., and Kepner, C. 1970. Model's behavior and attraction toward the model as determinants of aggressive behavior. *Journal of Personality and Social Psychology, 14,* 335–344.

Bartlett, F. 1932. *Remembering: a study in experimental and social psychology.* Cambridge, England: Cambridge University Press.

Bauer, E. E. 1967. Suggested curriculum for educably mentally retarded children. Unpublished paper, Indiana University.

Baum, A., and Valins, S. 1973. Residential environments, group size and crowing. *Proceedings of the 81st Annual Convention of the American Psychological Association,* Washington, D.C.: American Psychological Association.

Beck, A. T. 1967. *Depression: clinical, experimental and theoretical aspects.* New York: Harper & Row.

Beck, A. T.; Ward, C. H.; Mendelson, M.; Mock, J. E.; and Erbaugh, J. K. 1962. Reliability of psychiatric diagnosis 2: a study of consistency of clinical judgments and ratings. *American Journal of Psychiatry, 119,* 351–357.

Berger, H. 1929. Über das Elektrenkenphalogram des Menchen. *Archiv für Psychiatrie und Nervenkrankheiten, 87,* 527–550.

Bergin, A. E. 1966. Some implications of psychotherapy research for therapeutic practice. *Journal of Abnormal Psychology, 71,* 235–246.

————. 1971. The evaluation of therapeutic outcomes. In A. E. Bergin and S. L. Garfield, eds., *Handbook of psychotherapy and behavior change.* New York: Wiley.

Berko, J. 1958. The child's learning of English morphology. *Word, 14,* 150–177.

Berkowitz, L., and Daniels, L. R. 1963. Responsibility and dependency. *Journal of Abnormal and Social Psychology, 66,* 429–436.

Berscheid, E., and Walster, E. H. 1969. *Interpersonal attraction.* Reading, Mass: Addison-Wesley.

Bieber, I.; Dain, H. J.; Dince, R. R.; Drellich, M. G.; Grand, H. C.; Gundlach, R. H.; Kremer, M. W.; Rifkin, A. H.; Wilbur, C. B.; and Bieber, T. B. 1962. *Homosexuality: a psychoanalytical study.* New York: Random House.

Bijou, S. W.; Birnbrauer, J. S.; Kidder, J. D.; and Tague, C. 1966. Programmed instruction as an approach to teaching reading, writing, and arithmetic to retarded children. *Psychological Record, 16,* 505–522.

Bing, E. 1963. Effect of child rearing practices on development of differential cognitive abilities. *Child Development, 34,* 631–648.

Birnbaum, M. 1960. The right to treatment. *American Bar Association Journal, 46,* 499–505.

Bolton, N. 1972. *The psychology of thinking,* London: Methuen.

Bransford, J., and Franks, J. 1971. Abstraction of linguistic ideas. *Cognitive Psychology, 2,* 331–350.

Brecher, E. M., and the Editors of *Consumer Reports*. 1972. Licit and illicit drugs. Mount Vernon, N.Y.: Consumers Union.

Broadhurst, P. L. 1960. Experiments in psychogenetics. In H. J. Eysenck, ed., *Experiments in personality*. London: Routledge & Kegan Paul.

Brown, D. G. 1957. Masculinity-femininity development in children. *Journal of Consulting Psychology, 21*, 197–202.

Brown, R. 1965. *Social psychology*. New York: Free Press, 1965.

Brown, R.; Cazden, C. B.; and Bellugi-Klima, U. 1969. The child's grammar from I to III. In J. P. Hill, ed., *Minnesota symposia on child psychology*. Minneapolis: Univ. of Minnesota Press, *2*, 28–73.

Brown, R., and McNeill, D. 1965. The "tip of the tongue" phenomenon. *Journal of Verbal Learning and Verbal Behavior, 5*, 325–337.

Bruner, J. S. 1964. The course of cognitive growth. *American Psychologist, 19*, 1–15.

———. 1966. On cognitive growth, I and II. In J. S. Bruner, R. R. Olver, and P. M. Greenfield, eds., *Studies in cognitive growth*. New York: Wiley. Pp. 1–67.

———. 1968. *Toward a theory of instruction*. New York: Norton.

Bruner, J. S., and Kenney, H. J. 1966. On relational concepts. In J. S. Bruner, R. R. Olver, and P. M. Greenfield, eds., *Studies in cognitive growth*. New York: Wiley. Pp. 168–182.

Burt, C. 1966. The genetic determination of differences in intelligence: a study of monozygotic twins reared together and apart. *British Journal of Psychology, 57*, 137–153.

Buss, A. 1963. Physical aggression in relation to different frustrations. *Journal of Abnormal and Social Psychology, 67*, 1–7.

———. 1966. Instrumentality of aggression, feedback, and frustration as determinants of physical aggression. *Journal of Personality and Social Psychology, 3*, 153–162.

Byrne, D. 1971. *The attraction paradigm*. New York: Academic Press.

Cannon, W, B, 1929. *Bodily changes in pain, hunger, fear and rage*. New York: Appleton-Century-Crofts.

Cashman, J. A. 1966. *The LSD story*. Greenwich, Conn.: Fawcett.

Cattell, R. B. 1965. *The scientific analysis of personality*. Baltimore: Penguin Books.

Cautela, J. R. 1966. Treatment of compulsive behavior by covert sensitization. *Psychological Record, 16*, 33–41.

Chapman, L. J., and Chapman, J. C. 1959. Atmosphere effect revisited. *Journal of Experimental Psychology, 58*, 220–226.

Chein, I.; Gerard, D. L.; Lee R. S.; and Rosenfeld, E. 1964. *The road to H: narcotics, deliquency, and social policy*. New York: Basic Books.

Cherry, E. C. 1953. Some experiments on the recognition of speech with one and two ears. *Journal of the Acoustical Society of America, 25*, 975–979.

Cheyne, J. A. 1972. Punishment and "reasoning" in the development of self-control. In R. D. Parke, ed., *Recent trends in social learning theory*. New York: Academic Press. Pp. 77–91.

Chomsky, N. 1959. Review of Skinner's *Verbal behavior*. *Language, 35,* 26–58.

———. 1967. Introduction. In L. A. Jakobovits and M. S. Miron, eds., *Readings in the psychology of language*. Englewood Cliffs, N.J.: Prentice-Hall. Pp. 142–143.

———. 1972. Stages in language development. *Harvard Educational Review, 42,* 1–34.

Cleckley, H. 1964. *The mask of sanity*. 4th ed. St. Louis, Mo.: Mosby.

Cohen, B. H. 1966. Some-or-none characteristics of coding behavior. *Journal of Verbal Learning and Verbal Behavior, 5,* 182–187.

Conger, J. J. 1951. The effects of alcohol on conflict behavior in the albino rat. *Quarterly Journal of Studies on Alcohol, 12,* 1–29.

Conger, J. J.; Sawrey, W. L.; and Turrell, E. S. 1958. The role of social experience in the production of gastric ulcers in hooded rats in a conflict situation. *Journal of Abnormal and Social Psychology, 57,* 214–220.

Conrad, R. 1964. Acoustic confusion in immediate memory. *British Journal of Psychology, 55,* 75–84.

Conrad, R., and Hull, A. J. 1964. Information, acoustic confusion and memory span. *British Journal of Psychology, 55,* 429–432.

Cowan, P. A., and Walters, R. H. 1963. Studies of reinforcement of aggression. Part I: Effects of scheduling. *Child Development, 34,* 543–552.

Crandall, V. 1967. Achievement behavior in young children. In *The young child: reviews of research*. Washington, D.C.: National Association for the Education of Young Children.

Crutchfield, R. C. 1955. Conformity and character. *American Psychologist, 10,* 191–198.

Darley, J., and Latané, B. 1968. Bystander intervention in emergencies: diffusion of responsibility. *Journal of Personality and Social Psychology, 8,* 377–383.

Darwin, C. 1872. *The expression of emotions in man and animals*. London: Murray.

Davison, G. C. 1968. Systematic desensitization as a counterconditioning process. *Journal of Abnormal Psychology, 73,* 91–99.

DeBono, E. 1968. *New Think: the use of lateral thinking in the generation of new ideas*. New York: Basic Books.

Delgado, J. 1969. *Physical control of the mind: toward a psychocivilized society*. New York: Harper & Row.

Dement, W. 1960. The effect of dream deprivation. *Science, 131,* 1705–1707.

Dement, W., and Kleitman, N. 1957. Cyclic variations in EEG during sleep and their relation to eye movements, body motility, and dreaming. *Electroencephalography and Clinical Neurophysiology, 9,* 673–690.

Denner, B., and Price, R. H., eds. 1973. *Community mental health: social action and reaction.* New York: Holt, Rinehart and Winston.

DeValois, R. L.; Abramov, I.; and Jacobs, G. H. 1966. Analysis of response patterns of the LGN cells. *Journal of the Optical Society of America, 56,* 966–977.

Dollard, J.; Doob, L. W.; Miller, N. E.; Mowrer, O. H.; and Sears, R. R. 1939. *Frustration and aggression.* New Haven, Conn.: Yale Univ. Press.

Drabman, R. S.; Spitalnik, R.; and O'Leary, K. D. 1973. Teaching self-control to disruptive children. *Journal of Abnormal Psychology, 82,* 10–16.

Dugdale, R. L. 1910. *The Jukes: a study in crime, pauperism, disease and heredity.* New York: Putnam.

Edwards, C. D., and Williams, J. E. 1970. Generalization between evaluative words associated with racial figures in preschool children. *Journal of Experimental Research in Personality, 4,* 144–155.

Egger, M. D., and Flynn, J. P. 1963. Effect of electrical stimulation of the amygdala on hypothalamically elicited attack behavior in cats. *Journal of Neurophysiology, 26,* 705–720.

Eichorn, D. H. 1963. Biological correlates of behavior. In H. W. Stevenson, ed., *Child Psychology,* Vol. 1. Chicago: Univ. of Chicago Press. Pp. 4–61.

English, H. B., and English, A. C. 1958. *A comprehensive dictionary of psychological and psychoanalytical terms.* New York: Longman's, Green.

Epstein, Y., and Karlin, R. 1975. Effects of acute experimental crowding. *Journal of Applied Social Psychology, 5,* 34–53.

Erikson, E. H. 1963. *Childhood and society.* New York: Norton.

Erlenmeyer-Kimling, L., and Jarvik, L. F. 1963. Genetics and intelligence: a review. *Science, 142,* 1477–1479.

Eron, L. D. 1963. Relationship of TV viewing habits and aggressive behavior in children. *Journal of Abnormal and Social Psychology, 67,* 193–196.

Evans, R. B. 1969. Childhood parental relationships of homosexual men. *Journal of Consulting and Clinical Psychology, 33,* 129–135.

Everett, E. G. 1943. Behavioral characteristics of early- and late-maturing girls. Unpublished master's thesis, University of California.

Eysenck, H. J. 1952. The effects of psychotherapy: an evaluation. *Journal of Consulting Psychology, 16,* 319–324.

———. 1956. The inheritance of extroversion-introversion. *Psychologica, 12,* 95–110.

Fenichel, O. 1945. *The psychoanalytic theory of neurosis.* New York: Norton.

Fiske, D. W. 1967. The subject reacts to tests. *American Psychologist, 22,* 287–296.

———. 1971. *Measuring the concept of personality.* Chicago: Aldine.

Flavell, J. H. 1963. *The developmental psychology of Jean Piaget.* New

York: Van Nostrand Reinhold.

Fontana, A. 1966. Familial etiology of schizophrenia: is a scientific methodology possible? *Psychological Bulletin, 66,* 214–228.

Ford, D. H., and Urban, H. B. 1963. *Systems of psychotherapy.* New York: Wiley.

Fortune survey. 1946. *Fortune,* August.

Foulkes, W. D. 1967. NREM mentation. *Experimental Neurology* (Supplement 4), 236–247.

Fox, L. 1966. Effecting the use of efficient study habits. In R. Ulrich, T. Stachnik, and J. Mabry, eds., *Control of human behavior.* Glenview, Ill.: Scott, Foresman.

Freedman, J. L., and Sears, D. O. 1965. Warning, distraction, and resistance to influence. *Journal of Personality and Social Psychology, 1,* 262–266.

Freedman, J. L.; Wallington, S. A.; and Bless, E. 1967. Compliance without pressure: the effect of guilt. *Journal of Personality and Social Psychology, 7,* 117–124.

Freud, S. 1949. *A general introduction to psychoanalysis.* Garden City, N.Y.: Garden City Publishing Co.

———. 1955. Analysis of a phobia in a five-year-old boy, 1909. In *Collected works of Sigmund Freud,* Vol. 10. London: Hogarth Press.

———. 1963. Introductory lectures on psycho-analysis. In J. Strachey, ed., *The standard edition of the complete psychological works of Sigmund Freud,* Vol. 15. London: Hogarth Press.

Galanter, E. 1962. Contemporary psychophysics. In R. Brown et al., *New directions in psychotherapy,* Vol. 1. New York: Holt, Rinehart and Winston.

Gallup, G. 1955. Gallup poll. Princeton: Audience Research, Inc. June.

Garcia, J., and Koelling, R. A. 1966. Relation of cue to consequence in avoidance learning. *Psychonomic Science, 4,* 123–124.

Garcia, J.; McGowan, B. D.; and Green, K. F. 1972. Biological constraints on learning. In A. H. Black and W. F. Prokasy, eds., *Classical conditioning.* II: *Current research and theory.* New York: Appleton-Century-Crofts. 1972.

Gardner, E. 1963. *Fundamentals of neurology.* Philadelphia: Saunders.

Gazzaniga, M. 1973. *Fundamentals of psychology.* New York: Academic Press.

Geen, R. G. 1968. Effects of frustration, attack, and prior training in aggressiveness on aggressive behavior. *Journal of Personality and Social Psychology, 9,* 316–321.

Geldard, F. A. 1972. *The human senses.* 2nd ed. New York: Wiley.

Gellermann, L. W. 1933. Form discrimination in chimpanzees and two-year-old children. I: Form (triangularity) per se. *Journal of Genetic Psychology, 42,* 3–27.

Gesell, A.; Halverson, H. M.; Thompson, H.; Ilg, F. L.; Costner, B. M.; Ames, L. B.; and Amatruda, C. S. 1940. *The first five years of life: a guide to the study of the preschool child.* New York: Harper & Row.

Gesell, A., and Thompson, H. 1929. Learning and growth in identical twins. *Genetic Psychology Monographs, 6,* 1–124.

Getzels, J. W., and Jackson. P. W. 1962. *Creativity and intelligence: explorations with gifted students.* New York, Wiley.

Gibson, E. J., and Walk, R. D. 1960. The "visual cliff." *Scientific American, 202,* 64–71.

Gibson, J. J. 1950. *The perception of the visual world.* Boston: Houghton Mifflin.

———. 1966. *The senses considered as perceptual systems.* Boston: Houghton Mifflin.

Glucksburg, S., and Weisberg, R. W. 1960. Verbal behavior and problem solving: some effects of labelling in a functional-fixedness problem. *Journal of Experimental Psychology, 71,* 659–664.

Golden, M.; Birns, B.; Bridger, W.; and Moss, A. 1974. Social-class differentiation in cognitive development among black preschool children. In H. Bee, ed., *Social issues in developmental psychology.* New York: Harper & Row.

Gottesman, I. I. 1963. Heritability of personality. *Psychological monographs, 77,* 1–21.

———. 1966. Genetic variance in adaptive personality traits. *Journal of Child Psychology, Psychiatry, and Allied Disciplines, 7,* 199–208.

Gouldner, A. 1960. The norm of reciprocity. *American Sociological Review, 25,* 167–178.

Granit, R, 1959. Neural activity in the retina. In J. Field, H. V. Magoun, and V. E. Hall, eds., *Handbook of physiology, neurophysiology,* Vol. 1. Washington D.C.: American Physiological Society.

———. 1962. Neurophysiology of the retina. In H. Davson, ed., *The eye,* Vol. 2. New York: Academic Press.

Greenblatt, M. 1974. Class action and the right to treatment. *Hospital and Community Psychiatry, 25,* 449–452.

Gregory, R. L. 1968. Visual illusions. *Scientific American, 217,* 66–76.

Guthrie, W. K. C. 1971. The Meno. In M. Brown, ed., *Plato's Meno.* Indianapolis, Ind.: Bobbs-Merrill.

Hall, R. V.; Lund, D.; and Jackson, D. 1968. Effects of teacher attention on study behavior. *Journal of Applied Behavior Analysis, 1,* 1–12.

Halverson, H. M. 1931. An experimental study of prehension in infants by means of systematic cinema records. *Genetic Psychology Monographs, 10.*

Haney, C. E.; Banks, C.; and Zimbardo, P. 1973. Interpersonal dynamics in a simulated prison. *International Journal of Crime and Penology, 1,* 69–97.

Hare, R. D. 1970. *Psychopathy.* New York: Wiley.

Harlow, H. F., and Harlow, M. K. 1971. Social deprivation in monkeys. In R. C. Atkinson, ed., *Contemporary psychology: readings from Scientific American.* San Francisco: Freeman. Pp. 69–76.

Harlow, H. F., and Zimmerman, R. R. 1959. Affectional responses in the infant monkey. *Science, 130,* 431–432.

Harris, M. B., and Hassemer, W. G. 1972. Some factors influencing the complexity of children's sentences: the effects of modeling, age, sex, and bilingualism. *Journal of Experimental Child Psychology, 13,* 447–455.

Hart, J. T. 1965. Memory and the feeling-of-knowing experience. *Journal of Educational Psychology, 56,* 208–216.

Hartline, H. K. 1938. The response of single optic nerve fibers of the vertebrate eye to illumination of the retina. *American Journal of Physiology, 121,* 400–415.

————. 1940. The receptive field of the optic nerve fibers. *American Journal of Physiology, 130,* 690–699.

Hartshorne, H.; May, M. A.; and Shuttleworth, F. K. 1930. *Studies in the nature of character.* Vol 3: Studies in the Organization of Character. New York: Macmillan.

Heath, R. G. 1960. A biochemical hypothesis on the etiology of schizophrenia. In D. D. Jackson, ed., *The etiology of schizophrenia.* New York: Basic Books.

Heath, R. G., and Krupp, I. M. 1967. Schizophrenia as an immunologic disorder. *Archives of General Psychiatry, 16,* 1–33.

Heath, R. G.; Martens, S.; Leach, B. E.; Cohen, M.; and Angel, C. 1957. Effect on behavior in humans with the administration of taraxein. *American Journal of Psychiatry, 114,* 12–24.

Hecht, S., and Shlaer, S. 1938. An adaptometer for measuring human dark adaptation. *Journal of the Optical Society of America, 28,* 269–275.

Held, R. 1965. Plasticity in sensory-motor systems. *Scientific American, 213,* 84–94.

Heston, L. L. 1966. Psychiatric disorders in foster-home reared children of schizophrenic mothers. *British Journal of Psychiatry, 112,* 819–825.

Hill, J. H.; Liebert, R. M.; and Mott, D. E. W. 1968. Vicarious extinction of avoidance behavior through films: an initial test. *Psychological Reports, 12,* 192.

Hochberg, J. 1964. *Perception.* Englewood Cliffs, N.J.: Prentice-Hall.

Hoelle, C. 1969. The effects of modeling and reinforcement on aggressive behavior in elementary school boys. *Dissertation Abstracts, 29B,* 3483–3484.

Hoffman, M. 1968. *The gay world.* New York: Basic Books.

Holden, C. 1972. Nader on mental health centers: a movement that got bogged down. *Science, 177,* 413–415.

Hollingshead, A. B., and Redlich, F. C. 1958. *Social class and mental illness: a community study.* New York: Wiley.

Houts, P. S., and Serber, M. eds. 1972. *After the turn-on, what? Learning perspectives on humanistic groups.* Champaign, Ill.: Research Press.

Hovland, C. I. 1937. The generalization of conditioned responses. I: The sensory generalization of conditioned responses with varying frequencies of tone. *Journal of General Psychology, 17,* 125–148.

Hovland, C. I.; Lumsdaine, A.; and Sheffield, F. 1949. *Experiments on mass communication.* Princeton, N.J.: Princeton Univ. Press.

Hovland, C. I., and Weis, W. 1956. The influence of source credibility on communication effectiveness. *Public Opinion Quarterly, 15,* 635–650.

Howe, M. J. A. 1967. Consolidation in short term memory as a function of rehearsal. *Psychonomic Science, 7,* 355–356.

———. 1970. Repeated presentation and recall of meaningful prose. *Journal of Educational Psychology, 61,* 241–249.

Hubel, D. H., and Wiesel, T. N. 1959. Receptive fields of single neurons in the cat's striate cortex. *Journal of Physiology, 148,* 574–591.

———. 1962. Receptive fields, binocular interaction, and functional architecture in the cat's visual cortex. *Journal of Physiology, 160,* 106–154.

Inhelder, B., and Piaget, J. 1958. *The growth of logical thinking from childhood to adolescence.* New York: Basic Books.

Jackson, C. M. 1929. Some aspects of form and growth. In W. J. Robbins, S. Brody, A. F. Hogan, C. M. Jackson, and C. W. Green, eds., *Growth.* New Haven: Yale Univ. Press.

Jackson, D. 1960. *The etiology of schizophrenia.* New York: Basic Books.

Jacobson, E. 1929. *Progressive relaxation.* Chicago: Univ. of Chicago Press.

Janis, I., and Feshbach, S. 1953. Effects of fear-arousing communications. *Journal of Abnormal and Social Psychology, 48,* 78–92.

Jenkins, J. G., and Dallenbach, K. M. 1924. Oblivescence during sleep and waking. *American Journal of Psychology, 35,* 605–612.

Jenkins, J. J. 1974. Remember that old theory of memory? Well forget it. *American Psychologist, 29,* 785–795.

Jenkins, J. J.; Mink, W. D.; and Russell, W. A. 1958. Associative clustering as a function of verbal association strength. *Psychological Reports, 4,* 127–136.

Jensen, A. R. 1969. How much can we boost I.Q. and scholastic achievement? *Harvard Educational Review, 39,* 1–123.

Jespersen, J. O. 1922. *Language: its nature, development, and origin.* London: Allen and Unwin.

Jones, M. C. 1924. A laboratory study of fear: the case of Peter. *Pedagogical Seminary, 31,* 308–315.

———. 1958. A study of socialization patterns at the high-school level. *Journal of Genetic Psychology, 93,* 87–111.

Kameny, F. E. 1971. Gay liberation and psychiatry. *Psychiatric Opinion, 8,* 18–27.

Kamin, L. J. 1974. Heredity, intelligence, politics, and psychology. Mimeographed. Princeton, N.J.: Princeton University.

Kamiya, J. 1969. Operant control of the EEG alpha rhythm and some of its reported effects on consciousness. In C. Tart, ed., *Altered states of consciousness.* New York: Wiley.

Kaplan, B. J. 1972. Malnutrition and mental deficiency. *Psychological Bulletin, 78,* 321–334.

Kaplan, I. T., and Carvellas, T. 1968. Effect of word length on anagram solution time. *Journal of Verbal Learning and Verbal Behavior, 7,* 201–206.

Karlsson, J. L. 1966. *The biologic basis of schizophrenia.* Springfield, Ill.: Charles C Thomas.

Katz, P. A. 1973. Stimulus predifferentiation and modification of children's racial attitudes. *Child Development, 44,* 232–237.

Katz, P. A.; Sohn, M.; Zalk, S. R. 1975. Perceptual concomitants of racial attitudes in urban grade school children. *Developmental Psychology, 11,* 135–144.

Kelly, G. A. 1955. *The psychology of personal constructs.* 2 vols. New York: Norton.

Kelly, J. G. 1970. Antidotes for arrogance: training for community psychology. *American Psychologist, 25,* 524–531.

Kerckhoff, A. C., and Davis, K. E. 1962. Value consensus and need complementarity in mate selection. *American Sociological Review, 27,* 295–303.

Kessel, F. S. 1970. The role of syntax in children's comprehension from ages six to twelve. *Monographs of the Society for Research in Child Development, 35* (6, Whole No. 139).

Kety, S. S.; Rosenthal, D.; Wender, P. H.; and Schulsinger, F. 1968. The types and prevalence of mental illness in the biological and adoptive families of adopted schizophrenics. In D. Rosenthal and S. S. Kety, eds., *The transmission of schizophrenia.* Elmsford, N.Y.: Pergamon Press. Pp. 345–362.

Kiesler, C. A., and Kiesler, S. B. 1969. *Conformity.* Reading, Mass: Addison-Wesley.

Kimble, G. A. 1961. *Hilgard and Marquis' conditioning and learning.* New York: Appleton-Century-Crofts.

Kinsey, A. C.; Pomeroy, W. B.; and Martin, C. E. 1948. *Sexual behavior in the human male.* Philadelphia: Saunders.

Kinsey, A. C.; Pomeroy, W. B.; Martin, C. E.; and Gebhard, P. H. 1953. *Sexual behavior in the human female.* Philadelphia: Saunders.

Kintsch, W., and Buske, H. 1969. Homophones and synophones in short term memory. *Journal of Experimental Psychology, 80,* 403–407.

Kling, A.; Lancaster, J.; and Benitone, J. 1970. Amygdalectomy in the free ranging vervet. *Journal of Psychiatric Research, 7,* 191–199.

Kluver, H., and Bucy, P. 1938. An analysis of certain effects of bilateral temporal lobectomy in the rhesus monkey with special reference to "psychic blindness." *Journal of Psychology, 5,* 33–54.

Knobloch, H., and Pasamanick, B. 1958. Seasonal variations in the births of the mentally deficient. *American Journal of Public Health, 48,* 1201–1208.

Kohn, M. L. 1968. Social class and schizophrenia: a critical review. In D. Rosenthal and S. S. Kety, eds., *The transmission of schizophrenia.* Elmsford, N.Y.: Pergamon Press.

Kranz, H. 1936. *Lebenschicksale krimineller Zwillinge.* Berlin: Springer-Verlag.

Kretschmer, E. 1926. *Physique and character: an investigation of the nature of constitution and of the theory of temperament.* Translated by W. J. H. Sprott. New York: Harcourt Brace Jovanovich.

Lacey, J. I. 1967. Somatic response patterning and stress: some revisions of activation theory. In M. H. Appley and R. Trumbull, eds., *Psychological stress.* New York: McGraw-Hill.

Landreth, C. 1967. *Early childhood: behavior and learning.* New York: Knopf.

Lang, P. J., and Lazovik, A. D. 1963. Experimental desensitization of a phobia. *Journal of Abnormal and Social Psychology, 66,* 519–525.

Lange, J. 1929. *Verbrechen als Schieksal.* Leipzig: Georg Thieme Verlag.

Lazarus, A. A. 1958. New methods in psychotherapy: a case study. *South African Medical Journal, 33,* 660.

———. 1965. Behavior therapy, incomplete treatment, and symptom substitution. *Journal of Nervous and Mental Diseases, 140,* 80–86.

———. 1968. Behavior therapy in groups. In G. M. Gazda, ed., *Basic approaches to group psychotherapy and counseling.* Springfield, Ill.: Charles C Thomas.

———. 1971. *Behavior therapy and beyond.* New York: McGraw-Hill.

Lazarus, A. A., and Rachman, S. 1957. The use of systematic desenitization in psychotherapy. *South African Medical Journal, 31,* 934–937.

Leeds, R. 1963. Altruism and the norm of giving. *Merrill-Palmer Quarterly, 9,* 229–240.

Lefkowitz, M. M.; Eron, L. D.; Walder, L. O.; and Husemann, L. R. 1972. Television violence and child aggression: a followup study. In G. A. Comstock and E. A. Rubinstein, eds., *Television and social behavior.* III: *Television and adolescent aggressiveness.* Washington, D.C.: U.S. Government Printing Office.

Le Furgy, W. G., and Woloshin, G. W. 1969. Immediate and long-term effects of experimentally induced social influence in the modification of adolescents' moral judgments. *Journal of Personality and Social Psychology, 12,* 104–110.

Lerner, I. M. 1968. *Heredity, evolution and society.* San Francisco: Freeman.

Levanthal, H.; Watts, J. C.; and Pagano, F. 1967. Effects of fear and instructions on how to cope with danger. *Journal of Personality and Social Psychology, 6,* 313–321.

Levine, M. 1966. Hypothesis behavior by humans during discrimination learning. *Journal of Experimental Psychology, 71,* 331–338.

Levinger, G. 1964. Note on need complementarity in marriage. *Psychological Bulletin, 61,* 153–157.

Levitt, E. 1971. Research on psychotherapy with children. In A. E. Bergin and S. L. Garfield, eds., *Handbook of psychotherapy and behavior change.* New York: Wiley.

Lewinsohn, P. H. 1974. A behavioral approach to depression. In R. J. Friedman and M. M. Katz, eds., *The psychology of depression: contemporary theory and research.* Washington, D.C.: Winston-Wiley.

Lewinsohn, P. H., and Libet, J. M. 1972. Pleasant events, activity schedules and depressions. *Journal of Abnormal Psychology, 79,* 291–295.

Libet, J. M., and Lewinsohn, P. H. 1973. The concept of social skill with special reference to the behavior of depressed persons. *Journal of Consulting and Clinical Psychology, 40,* 304–312.

Liebert, R. M., and Baron, R. M. 1972. Short-term effects of televised aggression on children's aggressive behavior. In J. P. Murray, E. A. Rubinstein, and G. A. Comstock, eds., *Television and social behavior.* II: *Television and social learning.* Washington, D.C.: U.S. Government Printing Office.

Liebert, R. M., and Fernandez, L. E. 1969. Vicarious reward and task complexity as determinants of imitative learning. *Psychological Reports, 25,* 531–534.

————. 1970. Effects of vicarious consequences on imitative performance. *Child Development, 41,* 847–852.

Liebert, R. M.; Neale, J. M.; and Davidson, E. 1973. *The early window.* Elmsford, N.Y.: Pergamon Press.

Liebert, R. M.; Odom, R. D.; Hill, J. H.; and Huff, R. L. 1969. The effects of age and rule familiarity on the production of modeled language constructions. *Developmental Psychology, 1,* 108–112.

Liebert, R. M., and Ora, J. P. 1968. Children's adoption of self-reward patterns: incentive level and method of transmission. *Child Development, 39,* 537–544.

Liebert, R. M., and Poulos, R. W. 1971. Eliciting the "norm of giving": effects of modeling and presence of witness of children's sharing behavior. *Proceedings of the 79th Annual Covention of the American Psychological Association.* Pp. 193–195.

Liebert, R. M.; Sobol, M. P.; and Copemann, C. D. 1972. Effects of vicarious consequences and race of model upon imitative performance by black children. *Developmental Psychology, 6,* 453–456.

Liebert, R. M., and Spiegler, M. D. 1974. *Personality: strategies for the study of man.* Homewood, Ill.: Dorsey Press.

London, P. 1964. *The modes and morals of psychotherapy.* New York: Holt, Rinehart and Winston.

Loo, C. 1973. Important issues in researching the effects of crowding in humans. *Representative Research in Social Psychology, 4,* 219–226.

Luborsky, L., and Spence, D. P. 1971. Quantitative research on psychoanalytic therapy. In A. E. Bergin and S. L. Garfield, eds., *Handbook of psychotherapy and behavior change.* New York: Wiley.

Luby, E. D.; Frohman, C. E.; Grisell, J. L.; Lenzo, J. E.; and Gottlich, J. S. 1960. Sleep deprivation: effects on behavior, thinking, motor performance, and biological energy transfer systems. *Psychosomatic Medicine, 22,* 182.

Lumsden, E. A., and Kling, J. K. 1969. The relevance of an adequate concept of "bigger" for investigations of size conservation: a methodological critique. *Journal of Experimental Child Psychology, 8,* 82–91.

Lykken, D. T. 1957. A study of anxiety in the sociopathic personality. *Journal of Abnormal and Social Psychology, 55,* 6–10.

McCandless, B. R. 1967. *Children: behavior and development.* 2nd ed. New York: Holt, Rinehart and Winston.

McCarthy, D. 1954. Language development in children. In L. Carmichael, ed., *Manual of child psychology,* 2nd ed. New York: Wiley. Pp. 492–630.

McClearn, G. E. 1962. The inheritance of behavior. In L. Postman, ed., *Psychology in the making.* New York: Knopf.

McConnell, R. A. 1969. ESP and credibility in science. *American Psychologist, 24,* 531–538.

McConnell, R. A.; Snowdon, R. J.; and Powell, K. F. 1955. Wishing with dice. *Journal of Experimental Psychology, 50,* 269–275.

McGhie, A., and Chapman, J. S. 1961. Disorders of attention and perception in early schizophrenia. *British Journal of Medical Psychology, 34,* 103–116.

McGraw, M. G. 1935. *Growth: a study of Johnny and Jimmy.* New York: Appleton-Century-Crofts.

McIntyre, C. W.; Fox, R.; and Neale, J. M. 1970. Effects of noise similarity and redundancy on the information processed from brief visual displays. *Perception and Psychophysics, 7,* 328–332.

McMains, M. J., and Liebert, R. M. 1968. Influence of discrepancies between successively modeled self-reward criteria on the adoption of a self-imposed standard. *Journal of Personality and Social Psychology, 8* (No. 2), 166–171.

MacDonald, M. L. 1973. The forgotten Americans: a sociopsychological analysis of aging and nursing homes. *American Journal of Community Psychology, 1,* 272–294.

Madsen, C. G. 1965. Positive reinforcement in the toilet training of a normal child: a case report. In L. P. Ullmann and L. Krasner, eds., *Case studies in human behavior.* New York: Holt, Rinehart and Winston.

Maher, B. A. 1966. *Principles of psychopathology: an experimental approach.* New York: McGraw-Hill.

Mandler, G. 1968. Organization and memory. In K. W. Spence and J.

T. Spence, eds., *The psychology of learning and motivation,* Vol. 2. New York: Academic Press.

Mandler, G.; Mandler, J. M.; and Uviller, E. T. 1958. Autonomic feedback: the perception of autonomic activity. *Journal of Abnormal and Social Psychology, 56,* 367–373.

Marañon, G. 1924. Contribution à l'étude de l'action émotive de l'adrenaline. *Revue Française D'Endocrinologie, 2,* 301–325.

Mark, V. H.; Sweet, W. H.; and Ervin, F. R. 1967. Letter: Role of brain disease in riots and urban violence. *Journal of the American Medical Association, 201,* 895.

Marmor, J. 1962. Psychoanalytic therapy as an educational process: common denominators in the therapeutic approaches of different psychoanalytic schools. In J. H. Masserman, ed., *Science and psychoanalysis.* V: *Psychoanalytic education.* New York: Grune & Stratton.

Marquis, D. P. 1931. Can conditioned responses be established in the newborn infant? *Journal of Genetic Psychology, 39,* 479–492.

Masters, W. H., and Johnson, V. E. 1966. *Human sexual response.* Boston: Little Brown.

Maturna, H. R.; Lettvin, J. Y.; McCulloch, W. S.; and Pitts, W. H. 1960. Anatomy and physiology of vision in the frog. *Journal of General Psychology, 43,* 129–176.

Mednick, S. A. 1958. A learning theory approach to research in schizophrenia. *Psychological Bulletin, 55,* 316–327.

———. 1970. Breakdown in individuals at high-risk for schizophrenia: possible predispositional perinatal factors. *Mental Hygiene, 54,* 50–63.

Mednick, S. A., and Schulsinger, F. 1968. Some premorbid characteristics related to breakdown in children with schizophrenic mothers. In D. Rosenthal and S. S. Kety, eds., *The transmission of schizophrenia.* Elmsford, N.Y.: Pergamon Press.

Meehl, P. E. 1962. Schizotaxia, schizotypy, schizophrenia. *American Psychologist, 17,* 827–838.

Meichenbaum, D. H. 1971. Examination of model characteristics in reducing avoidance behavior. *Journal of Personality and Social Psychology, 17,* 298–307.

Meisel, A. 1975. Rights of the mentally ill: the gulf between theory and reality. *Hospital and Community Psychiatry, 26,* 349–353.

Messick, S. 1965. Personality measurement and the ethics of assessment. *American Psychologist, 20,* 136–142.

Miller, G. A. 1956. The magical number seven, plus or minus two: some limits on our capacity for processing information. *Psychological Review, 63,* 81–97.

Miller, G. A.; Galanter, E.; and Pribram, K. 1960. *Plans and the structure of behavior.* New York: Holt, Rinehart and Winston.

Miller, N. E. 1969. Learning of visceral and glandular responses. *Science, 163,* 434–445.

Miller, N. E., and Dollard, J. C. 1941. *Social learning and imitation.* New Haven, Conn.: Yale Univ. Press.

Milner, B. 1967. Amnesia following operation on the temporal lobes. In O. L. Zangwill and C. M. W. Whitty, eds., *Amnesia.* London: Butterworth.

Milner, P. M. 1970. *Physiological psychology.* New York: Holt, Rinehart and Winston.

Mintz, E. 1967. Time-extended marathon groups. *Psychotherapy, 4,* 65–70.

Mirsky, I. A. 1958. Physiologic, psychologic, and social determinants in the etiology of duodenal ulcer. *American Journal of Digestive Diseases, 3,* 285–314.

Mischel, W., and Liebert, R. M. 1966. Effects of discrepancies between observed and imposed reward criteria on their acquisition and transmission. *Journal of Personality and Social Psychology, 3,* 45–53.

Moos, R. H. 1969. Sources of variance in responses to questionnaires and in behavior. *Journal of Abnormal Psychology, 74,* 405–412.

Mosher, L., and Gunderson, J. 1973. Special report: schizophrenia, 1972. *Schizophrenia Bulletin,* Issue No. 7, 12–52.

Mowrer, O. H. 1960. *Learning theory and the symbolic processes.* New York: Wiley.

Murdock, B. B., Jr. 1962. The serial postion effect in free recall. *Journal of Experimental Psychology, 64,* 482–488.

Nafe, J. P. 1934. The pressure, pain, and temperature senses. In C. A. Murchison, ed., *Handbook of general experimental psychology.* Worcester, Mass.: Clark Univ. Press.

National Commission on Marihuana and Drug Abuse. 1972. *Marihuana: a signal of misunderstanding.* New York: New American Library.

Neale, J. M., and Liebert, R. M. 1973. *Science and behavior: an introduction to methods of research.* Englewood Cliffs, N.J.: Prentice-Hall.

Nelson, M. M.; Asling, C. W.; and Evans, H. M. 1952. Production of multiple congenital abnormalities in young by pteroylglutamic acid deficiency during gestation. *Journal of Nutrition, 48,* 61–80.

Nunnally, J. C.; Duchnowski, A. J.; and Parker, R. K. 1965. Association of neutral objects with rewards: effect on verbal evaluation, reward expectancy, and selective attention. *Journal of Personality and Social Psychology, 1,* 270–274.

O'Connor, R. D. 1969. Modification of social withdrawal through symbolic modeling. *Journal of Applied Behavior Analysis, 2,* 15–22.

Odom, R. D.; Liebert, R. M.; and Hill, J. H. 1968. The effects of modeling cues, reward, and attentional set on the production of grammatical and ungrammatical syntactic constructions. *Journal of Experimental Child Psychology, 6,* 131–40.

Palmer, F. H. 1972. Progress Report HDO2253 and HDO5631. Intervention at age two and three subsequent intellective performance.

Stony Brook, N.Y.: State University of New York.

———. 1975. Has compensatory education failed? No, not yet. Unpublished manuscript. Stony Brook, N.Y.: State University of New York.

Palmer, F. H., and Siegel, R. J. 1972. Minimal intervention at ages two and three and subsequent intellective changes. In R. K. Parker, ed., *The preschool in action*, Boston: Allyn & Bacon.

Parke, R. D. 1967. Nurturance, nurturance withdrawal, and resistance to deviation. *Child Development, 38*, 1101–1110.

———. 1969. Effectiveness of punishment as an interaction of intensity, timing, agent nurturance and cognitive structuring. *Child Development, 40*, 213–235.

Parke, R. D. 1970. The role of punishment in the socialization process. In R. A. Hoppe, G. A. Milton, and E. C. Simmel, eds., *Early experiences and the processes of soicalization*. New York: Academic Press.

Partenan, J.; Bruun, K.; and Markkanen, T. 1966. *Inheritance of drinking behavior*. Helsinki: Finnish Foundation for Alcohol Studies.

Patterson, G. R. 1971. Behavioral intervention procedures in the classroom and in the home. In A. E. Bergin and S. L. Garfield, eds., *Handbook of psychotherapy and behavior change*. New York: Wiley.

———. 1974. Retraining of aggressive boys by their parents. In F. Lowey, ed., Symposium on the seriously disturbed pre-school child. *Canadian Psychiatric Association Journal, 19*, 142–158.

Patterson, G. R., and Gullion, M. E. 1968. *Living with children: new methods for parents and teachers*. Champaign, Ill.: Research Press.

Paul, G. L. 1966. *Insight vs. desenitization in pyschotherapy*. Stanford, Calif.: Stanford Univ. Press.

Paul, G. L., and Shannon, D. T. 1966. Treatment of anxiety through systematic desensitization in therapy groups. *Journal of Abnormal Psychology, 71*, 124–135.

Pavlov, I. P. 1927. *Conditioned reflexes*. London: Oxford Univ. Press.

Peterson, L. R., and Peterson, M. J. 1959. Short-term retention of individual items. *Journal of Experimental Psychology, 58*, 193–198.

Pfaffman, C. 1948. Studying the senses of taste and smell. In A. Andrews, ed., *Methods of psychology*. New York: Wiley. Pp. 268–288.

Pfeiffer, E.; Verwoerdt, A.; and Wang, H. S. 1969. The natural history of sexual behavior in a biologically advanced group of aged individuals. *Journal of Gerontology, 24*, 193–199.

Phillips, J. L., Jr. 1969. *The origins of intellect: Piaget's theory*. San Francisco: Freeman.

Piaget, J., and Inhelder, B. 1969. *The psychology of the child*. New York: Basic Books.

Pines, M. 1973. *The brain changers*. New York: Harcourt Brace Jovanovich.

Pratt, J. G. 1947. Rhythms of success in PK test data. *Journal of Parapsychology, 11*, 90–110.

Pruitt, D. G. 1968. Reciprocity and credit building in a laboratory dyad. *Journal of Experimental Social Psychology, 8*, 143–147.

Quarti, C., and Renaud, J. 1964. A new treatment of constipation by conditioning: a preliminary report. In C. M. Franks, ed., *Conditioning techniques in clinical practice and research.* New York: Springer.

Rachlin, H. 1970. *Introduction to modern behaviorism.* San Francisco: Freeman.

———. 1975. *Behavior and learning.* San Francisco: Freeman.

Rado, S. 1949. An adaptational view of sexual behavior. In P. Hoch and J. Zubin, eds., *Psychosexual development in health and disease.* New York: Grune & Stratton.

Rappaport, J., and Chinsky, J. M. 1974. Models for delivery of service from an historical and conceptual perspective. *Professional Psychology, 5*, 42–50.

Reitman, J. S. 1971. Mechanisms of forgetting in short-term memory. *Cognitive Psychology, 2*, 185–195.

Renninger, C. A., and Williams, J. E. 1966. Black-white color connotations and racial awareness in preschool children. *Perceptual and Motor Skills, 22*, 771–785.

Restle, F. 1962. The selection of strategies in cue learning. *Psychological Review, 69*, 329–343.

Rheingold, H. L.; Gewirtz, J. L.; and Ross, H. W. 1959. Social conditioning of vocalization in the infant. *Journal of Comparative and Physiological Psychology, 52*, 68–73.

Rhine, J. B. 1952. The problem of psi-missing, *Journal of Parapsychology, 16*, 90–129.

Riggs, L. A.; Ratliff, F.; Cornsweet, T. C.; and Cornsweet, T. N. 1953. The disappearance of steadily fixated visual test objects. *Journal of the Optical Society of America, 43*, 495–501.

Rogers, C. R. 1942. *Counseling and psychotherapy: new concepts in practice.* Boston: Houghton Mifflin.

———. 1951. *Client-centered therapy.* Boston: Houghton Mifflin.

———. 1961. *On becoming a person: a therapist's view of psychotherapy.* Boston: Houghton Mifflin.

———. 1970. *Carl Rogers on encounter groups.* New York: Harper & Row.

Rogers, C. R., and Dymond, R. F., eds, 1954. *Psychotherapy and personality change.* Chicago: Univ. of Chicago Press.

Rogers, C. R.; Gendlin, G. T.; Kiesler, D. V.; and Truax, C. B. 1967. *The therapeutic relationship and its impact: a study of psychotherapy with schizophrenics.* Madison: Univ. of Wisconsin Press.

Ronning, R. R. 1965. Anagram solution times: a function of the "ruleout" factor. *Journal of Experimental Psychology, 69*, 35–39.

Rose, J. E.; Brugge, J. F.; Anderson, D. J.; and Hind, J. E. 1967. Phase locked response to low frequency tones in single auditory nerve fibers of the squirrel monkey. *Journal of Neurophysiology, 30,* 769–793.

Rosenthal, D. 1970. *Genetic theory and abnormal behavior.* New York: McGraw-Hill.

Rosenthal, D.; Wender, P. H.; Kety, S. S.; Schulsinger, F.; Welner, J.; and Östergaard, L. 1968. Schizophrenics' offspring reared in adoptive homes. In D. Rosenthal and S. S. Kety, eds., *The transmission of schizophrenia.* Elmsford, N.Y.: Pergamon Press. Pp. 377–391.

Rosenthal, T. L.; Zimmerman, B. J.; and Durning, K. 1970. Observationally induced changes in children's interrogative classes. *Journal of Personality and Social Psychology, 16,* 681–688.

Rosekrans, M. A. 1967. Imitation in children as a function of perceived similarity and vicarious reinforcement. *Journal of Personality and Social Psychology, 7,* 307–315.

Sanford, N. 1963. Personality: its place in psychology. In S. Koch, ed., *Psychology: a study of a science.* Study II, Vol. 5: *The process areas, the person, and some applied fields: their place in psychology and science.* New York: McGraw-Hill. Pp. 488–592.

Sanger, M. D. 1955. Language learning in infancy: a review of the autistic hypothesis and an observational study of infants. Unpublished doctoral dissertation. Harvard University.

Sawrey, W. L., and Weisz, J. D. 1956. An experimental method of producing gastric ulcers: role of psychological factors in the production of gastric ulcers in the rat. *Journal of Comparative and Physiological Psychology, 49,* 457–461.

Scarr, S. 1969. Social introversion-extroversion as a heritable response. *Child Development, 40,* 823–832.

Schachter, S., and Singer, J. E. 1962. Cognitive, social and physiological determinants of emotional state. *Psychological Review, 69,* 379–399.

Schachter, S., and Latané, B. 1964. Crime, cognition, and the autonomic nervous system. In D. Levine, ed., *Nebraska symposium on motivation,* Vol. 12. Lincoln: Univ. of Nebraska Press.

Schaefer, W. S., and Bayley, N. 1963. Maternal behavior, child behavior and their intercorrelations from infancy through adolescence. *Monographs of the Society for Research in Child Development, 28,* 1–27.

Schutz, W. C. 1967. *Joy.* New York: Grove Press.

Sears, R. R.; Maccoby, E. E.; and Levin, H. 1957. *Patterns of child rearing.* New York: Harper & Row.

Seligman, M. E. P. 1971. Phobias and preparedness. *Behavior Therapy, 2,* 307–320.

———. Depression and learned helplessness. In R. J. Friedman and M. M. Katz, eds., *The psychology of depression.* Washington, D.C.: Winston.

Seligman, M. E. P., and Hager, J. L. 1972. *Biological boundaries of learning.* New York: Appleton-Century-Crofts.

Selye, H. 1956. *The stress of life.* New York: McGraw-Hill.

Serber, M. 1972. The experiential groups as entertainment. In P. S. Houts and M. Serber, eds., *After the turn-on, what? Learning perspectives on humanistic groups.* Champaign, Ill.: Research Press.

Sheldon, W. H. 1942. *The varieties of temperament: a psychology of constitutional differences.* New York: Harper & Row.

Sherman, A. R. 1973. Real-life exposure as a primary therapeutic factor in the desensitization treatment of fear. *Journal of Abnormal Psychology, 79,* 19–28.

Shirley, M. M. 1933. *The first two years: a study of twenty-five babies.* Institute of Child Welfare Monograph Series, No. 7. Minneapolis: Univ. of Minnesota Press.

Shurcliff, A. 1968. Judged humor, arousal, and the relief theory. *Journal of Personality and Social Psychology, 8,* 360–363.

Siegel, M.; Niswander, G. D.; Sachs, E.; and Stravros, D. 1959. Taraxein: fact or artifact? *American Journal of Psychiatry, 115,* 819–820.

Silverstein, C. 1972. Behavior modification and the gay community. Paper presented at the annual convention of the Association for the Advancement of Behavior Therapy, New York City.

Singer, D. L.; Gollob, H.; and Levine, J. 1966. Inhibitions and the enjoyment of aggressive humor: an experimental investigation. Paper presented at the meeting of the Eastern Psychological Association, New York City.

Skinner, B. F. 1956. A case history in scientific method. *American Psychologist, 11,* 221–233.

———. 1957. *Verbal behavior.* New York: Appleton-Century-Crofts.

Smith, D. E.; King, M. B.; and Hoebel, B. C. 1970. Lateral hypothalamic control of killing: evidence for a cholinoceptive mechanism. *Science, 167,* 900–901.

Smith, M. S. 1926. An investigation of the development of the sentence and the extent of vocabulary in young children. *University of Iowa Studies in Child Welfare, 3,* No. 5.

Smith, R. T. 1965. A comparsion of socioenvironmental factors in monozygotic and dizygotic twins, testing an assumption. In S. V. Vandenberg, ed., *Methods and goals in human behavior genetics.* New York: Academic Press.

Solomon, R. L., and Wynne, L. C. 1953. Traumatic avoidance learning in dogs. *Psychological Monographs, 67,* No. 354.

Speer, D. C. 1971. Rate of caller re-use of a telephone crisis service. *Crisis Intervention, 3,* 83–86.

———. 1972. An evaluation of a telephone crisis service. Paper presented at the Midwestern Psychological Association meeting, Cleveland, Ohio.

Sperling, G. 1960. The information available in brief visual presentations. *Psychological Monographs, 74* (Whole No. 498).

Sperry, R. W. 1961. Cerebral organization and behavior. *Science, 133,* 1749–1756.

Srole, L.; Langner, T. S.; Michael, S. T.; Opler, M. K.; and Rennie, T. A. C. 1962. *Mental health in the metropolis: the midtown Manhattan study.* New York: McGraw-Hill.

Staats, A. W., and Staats, C. K. 1958. Attitudes established by classical conditioning. *Journal of Abnormal and Social Psychology, 57,* 37–40.

Staub, E., and Sherk, L. 1970. Need for approval, children's sharing behavior and reciprocity in sharing. *Child Development, 41,* 243–253.

Steller, F. H. 1968. Accelerated interaction: a time-limited approach based on the brief intensive group. *International Journal of Group Psychotherapy, 18,* 220–235.

Stevens, S. S.; Davis, H.; and Lurie, M. J. 1935. The localization of pitch perception on the basilar membrane. *Journal of General Psychology, 13,* 297–315.

Stickney, S. 1974a. Problems in implementing the right to treatment in Alabama: the Wyatt v. Stickney case. *Hosptial and Community Psychiatry, 25,* 453–460.

———. 1974b. Wyatt v. Stickney: the right to treatment. *Psychiatric Annals, 4,* 32–45.

Sweet, W. H.; Ervin, F.; and Mark, V. H. 1969. The relationship of violent behavior to focal cerebral disease. In S. Garattini and E. Sigg, eds., *Aggressive behavior.* New York: Wiley.

Swets, J. A. 1966. *Signal detection theory and psychophysics.* New York: Wiley.

Szasz, Thomas. 1963. *Law, liberty, and psychiatry.* New York: Macmillan.

Thigpen, C. H., and Cleckley, H. 1954. *The three faces of Eve.* Kingsport, Tenn: Kingsport Press.

Thompson, W. R. 1954. The inheritance and development of intelligence. *Research Publication of Association for Nervous and Mental Diseases, 33,* 209–331.

Thorndike, E. L. 1911. *Animal intelligence.* New York: Macmillan.

Truax, C. B. 1966. Reinforcement and nonreinforcement in Rogerian psychotherapy. *Journal of Abnormal Psychology, 71,* 1–9.

Truax, C. B., and Mitchell, K. M. 1971. Research on certain therapist interpersonal skills in relation to process and outcome. In A. E. Bergin and S. L. Garfield, eds., *Handbook of psychotherapy and behavior change.* New York: Wiley.

Tuddenham, R. D., and MacBride, P. 1959. The yielding experiment and the subject's point of view. *Journal of Personality, 27,* 259–271.

Tulving, E. 1962. Subjective organization in free recall of unrelated words. *Psychological Review, 69,* 344–354.

Tulving, E., and Pearlstone, Z. 1966. Availability versus accessibility of information in memory for words. *Journal of Verbal Learning and Verbal Behavior, 5,* 193–197.

466

Underwood, B. J. 1957. Interference and forgetting. *Psychological Review, 64,* 49–60.

———. 1964. Forgetting. *Scientific American, 210,* 91–99.

Valenstein, E. S. 1973. *Brain control: a critical examination of brain stimulation and psychosurgery.* New York: Wiley.

Vandenberg, S. G. 1966. Contributions to twin research in psychology. *Psychological Bulletin, 66,* 327–352.

Von Frey, M. 1919. Ueber die zur ebenmerklichen Erregung des Drucksinns erforderlichen Energiemengen. *Zeitschrift für Biologie, 70,* 333–347.

Wald, G. 1954. On the mechanism of the visual threshold and visual adaptation. *Science, 119,* 887–895.

Walenstein, E. S. 1974. *Brain control.* New York: Wiley.

Wallach, H., and McKenna, V. 1960. On size perception in the absence of cues for distance. *American Journal of Psychology, 73,* 458–460.

Wallach, M. S. 1970. Creativity. In P. Mussen, ed., *Carmichael's manual of child psychology.* 3rd ed. Volume 1. New York: Wiley.

Walster, E.; Aronson, V.; and Abrams, D. 1966. Importance of physical attractiveness in dating behavior. *Journal of Personality and Social Psychology, 4,* 508–516.

Walters, R. H., and Brown, M. 1963. Studies of reinforcement of aggression. Part III: Transfer of responses to an interpersonal situation. *Child Development, 34,* 563–572.

———. 1964. A test of the high-magnitude theory of aggression. *Journal of Experimental Child Psychology, 1,* 376–387.

Wasman, M., and Flynn, J. P. 1962. Direct attack elicited from the hypothalamus. *Archives of Neurology, 6,* 60–67.

Watson, E. H., and Lowrey, G. H. 1962. *Growth and development of children.* Chicago: Year Book Medical Publishers.

Watson, J. B. 1913. Psychology as the behaviorist views it. *Psychological Review, 20,* 158–177.

———. 1924. *Behaviorism.* New York: Norton.

Watson, J. B., and Rayner, R. 1920. Conditioned emotional reactions. *Journal of Experimental Psychology, 3,* 1–14.

Weiner, H.; Thaler, M.; Reiser, M. F.; and Mirsky, I. A. 1957. Etiology of duodenal ulcer. I: Relation of specific psychological characteristics to rate of gastric secretion. *Psychosomatic Medicine, 19,* 1–10.

Weiner, J. W. 1969. The effectiveness of a suicide prevention program. *Mental Hygiene, 53,* 357–363.

Weisberg, P. 1963. Social and nonsocial conditioning of infant vocalizations. *Child Development, 34,* 377–388.

Werner, H., and Kaplan, E. 1952. The acquisition of word meaning: a developmental study. *Monographs of the Society for Research in Child Development, 15,* No. 51.

Wever, E. G. 1940. *Theory of hearing.* New York: Wiley.

Wever, E. G., and Bray, C. W. 1930. Present possibilities for auditory theory. *Psychological Review, 37,* 365–380.

White, W. A. 1932. *Outlines of psychiatry.* 13th ed. New York: Nervous and Mental Disease Publishing Co.

Whitehurst, G. 1972. Production of novel and grammatical utterances by young children. *Journal of Experimental Child Psychology, 13,* 502–515.

Whiting, J. W. M. 1954. Fourth presentation. In J. M. Tanner and B. Inhelder, eds., *Discussions on child development,* Vol. 2. London: Tavistock.

Wilke, H., and Lazetta, J. T. 1970. The obligation to help: the effects of amount of prior help on subsequent helping behavior. *Journal of Experimental Social Psychology, 6,* 488–493.

Wilson, G. T., and Davison, G. C. 1971. Processes of fear reduction in systematic desensitization: animal studies. *Psychological Bulletin, 76,* 1–14.

Wilson, W. H., and Nunnally, J. C. 1971. A naturalistic investigation of acquired meaning in children. *Psychonomic Science, 23,* 149–150.

Wolf, A. 1949. The psychoanalysis of groups. *American Journal of Psychotherapy, 3,* 16–50.

Wolfe, B. 1975. The Donaldson decision. *Schizophrenia Bulletin, 13,* 4–6.

Wolfe, J. B. 1936. Effectiveness of token rewards for chimpanzees. *Comparative Psychology Monographs, 12,* No. 60.

Wolpe, J. 1958. *Psychotherapy by reciprocal inhibition.* Stanford, Calif.: Stanford Univ. Press.

———. 1969. *The practice of behavior therapy.* Elmsford, N.Y.: Pergamon Press, 1969.

Wolpe, J., and Lazarus, A. A. 1966. *Behavior therapy techniques: a guide to the treatment of neuroses.* Elmsford, N.Y.: Pergamon Press.

Yablonsky, L. 1962. The anti-criminal society: Synanon. *Federal Probation, 26,* 50–57.

———. 1967. *Synanon: the tunnel back.* Baltimore: Penguin Books.

Yalom, I. D., and Lieberman, M. A. 1971. A study of encounter group casualties. *Archives of General Psychiatry, 25,* 16–30.

Yurchenko, H. 1970. *A mighty hard road.* New York: McGraw-Hill.

Zilboorg, G., and Henry, G. W. 1941. *A history of medical psychology.* New York: Norton.

Zimbardo, P. G. 1969. The human choice: individuation, reason and order versus deindividuation, impulse and chaos. *Nebraska symposium on motivation, 1969.* Lincoln: Univ. of Nebraska Press.

PHOTO CREDITS

buque, Iowa, William C. Brown Co., 1966, p. 10. Photos by Max Kotfila. **Page 121:** Courtesy Point O'Woods Laboratory School, State University of New York at Stony Brook. Photos by Lester Lefkowitz. **Page 122:** Nina Leen/Time-Life Picture Agency. **Page 123:** Harvey S. Zucker. **Page 124:** Paolo Koch/Rapho-Photo Researchers. **Page 132:** Courtesy Albert Bandura, Stanford University. **Page 137:** Courtesy Sidney W. Bijou, Department of Special Education, University of Arizona, Tucson.

FIVE **Opener:** Elliott Erwitt/Magnum. **Page 148:** Bruno Barbey/Magnum. **Page 165:** H. Stowe & Associates. **Page 172:** Albert H. Zobrist and Frederic R. Carlson. **Page 177:** Adapted from J. W. Getzels and P. W. Jackson, *Creativity and Intelligence.* Copyright 1962, John Wiley & Sons, Inc.

SIX **Opener:** Jean-Claude Lejeune. **Page 184:** (left) Courtesy The American Museum of Natural History; (middle) Courtesy Carnegie Institute of Washington; (right) Courtesy H. Michael Seitz, M. D., from "Cleavage of Human Ova in Vitro," by Seitz, Rocha, Brackett, and Mastroianni, *Fertility and Sterility, 22,* 1971, 255. **Page 185:** Courtesy Dr. Melvin M. Grumbach, University of California, San Francisco. **Page 186:** From I. Michael Lerner and William J. Libby, *Heredity, Evolution and Society,* 2nd ed., W. H. Freeman and Company, 1968. Photos by G. W. Bartelmez. **Page 187:** (left) Mimi Forsyth/Monkmeyer; (right) Barbara Klutinis/Jeroboam. **Page 188:** Josephus Daniels/Rapho-Photo Researchers. **Page 193:** (top left) Edna Bennett/Photo Researchers; (top right) Tim Eagan/Woodfin Camp; (bottom left) Martine Franck/VIVA/Woodfin Camp; (bottom right) Suzanne Szasz/Photo Researchers. **Page 195:** Courtesy The American Museum of Natural History. **Page 198:** Wide World Photos. **Page 206:** Sepp Seitz/Magnum.

SEVEN **Opener:** Sybil Shelton/Monkmeyer. **Page 212:** Courtesy Jean Piaget Society. **Page 214:** (top left) Erich Hartmann/Magnum; (top right) Lew Merrim/Monkmeyer; (middle left) Mary M. Thacher/Photo Researchers; (bottom) Bruce Davidson/Magnum. **Page 217:** Burt Glinn/Magnum. **Page 221:** Courtesy Harvard University News Office. **Page 226:** Rohn Engh/Photo Researchers. **Page 228:** From Roger Brown, *Social Psychology,* The Free Press, 1965. **Page 232:** Mimi Forsyth/Monkmeyer. **Page 235:** Courtesy Massachusetts Institute of Technology News Office. **Page 239:** Bruce Davidson/Magnum.

EIGHT **Opener:** Constantine Manos/Magnum. **Page 247:** (left) Nina Leen/Time-Life Picture Agency; (right) H. F. Harlow, University of Wisconsin Primate Laboratory. **Page 251:** (top) Mimi Forsyth/Monkmeyer; (bottom) From Albert Bandura and Richard H. Walters, *Social Learning and Personality Development,* Holt, Rinehart & Winston, 1963. Designed and assembled by W. G. Clark, University of Toronto. **Page 256:** (top left) René Burri/Magnum; (top right) Erika/Photo

Researchers; (bottom left) Marc Riboud/Magnum; (bottom right) Van Bucher/Photo Researchers. **Page 257:** From R. M. Liebert, R. W. Poulos, and G. D. Strauss, *Developmental Psychology*, Prentice-Hall, Inc., 1974. **Page 264:** Imperial is a product of Hiram Walker, Inc. Advertising for Imperial is prepared by Foote, Cone & Belding, Inc., Chicago. **Page 268:** From Robert M. Liebert and Rita W. Poulos, "Television and Personality Development: The Socializing Effects of an Entertainment Medium," in *Child Personality and Psychopathology: Current Topics*, Vol. 2, edited by Anthony Davids. John Wiley & Sons, 1975.

NINE   **Opener:** Charles Harbutt/Magnum. **Page 277:** David Hurn/Magnum. **Page 286:** (top left) Joan Liftin/Woodfin Camp; (top right) Dan Budnik/Woodfin Camp; (bottom left) René Burri/Magnum; (bottom right) Richard Kalvar/Magnum. **Page 289:** Gilles Peress/Magnum. **Page 291** (top and bottom): William Vandivert. **Page 301:** Burk Uzzle/Magnum. **Pages 302 and 304:** P. G. Zimbardo, Stanford University. **Page 305:** Wide World Photos. **Page 309:** Hugh Rogers/Monkmeyer.

TEN   **Opener:** Charles Harbutt/Magnum. **Page 315:** Culver Pictures. **Page 323:** Courtesy Harvard University News Office. **Page 324:** (top left) Arthur Tress/Woodfin Camp; (top center) J. Cron/Monkmeyer; (top right) Mimi Forsyth/Monkmeyer; (middle left) Ellen Kirouac/Monkmeyer; (middle center) Baron Wolman/Woodfin Camp; (middle right) Dick Hyman/Rapho-Photo Researchers; (bottom left) Ken Heyman; (bottom right) James Foote/Photo Researchers. **Page 328:** Reprinted by permission of the publishers. From Henry A. Murray, *Thematic Apperception Test*, Cambridge, Massachusetts: Harvard University Press, © 1943 by the President and Fellows of Harvard College, 1971 by Henry A. Murray. **Page 332:** Courtesy W. H. Sheldon, from W. H. Sheldon, S. S. Stevens, and W. B. Tucker, *The Varieties of Human Physique*, Harper & Row, 1940. **Page 333:** Courtesy Harvard University News Office. **Page 335:** Courtesy Raymond B. Cattell, University of Illinois, Champaign. **Page 339:** Courtesy George A. Kelly, photo by Ralph Norman. **Page 345:** Jean-Claude Lejeune.

ELEVEN   **Opener:** Vauthey/Sygma. **Page 354:** (top) Culver Pictures; (right) Courtesy the Trustees of Sir John Soane's Museum; (left) Inge Morath/Magnum. **Page 355:** Radio Times Hulton Picture Library. **Page 358:** New York Public Library Picture Collection. **Page 362:** Hella Hammid/Rapho-Photo Researchers. **Page 367:** Tim Eagan/Woodfin Camp. **Page 369:** (top left) James Motlow/Magnum; (right) Michael Hanulak/Magnum; (bottom left) Ellen Pines/Woodfin Camp. **Page 374:** (top) Leonard Freed/Magnum; (bottom left) Burk Uzzle/Magnum; (bottom right) Micha Bar-Am/Magnum. **Page 376:** (top) Ian Berry/Magnum; (bottom) Yvonne Freund/Photo Researchers. **Page 383:** Mimi Forsyth/Monkmeyer. **Page 385:** The Bettmann Archive. **Page 386:** (top) From the movie *One Flew over the Cuckoo's Nest.* Copyright © 1975, Fantasy Films and United Artists Corporation, all rights reserved. Photo courtesy The Museum of Modern Art, Film Stills Archives; (bottom) Bill Stanton/Magnum. **Page 398:** Sidney Harris.

TWELVE   **Opener:** Mark Antman. **Page 409:** Ron Nelson. **Page 411:** Courtesy Carl R. Rogers, photo by John T. Wood. **Page 415:** Van Bucher/Photo Researchers. **Page 419:** Sybil Shelton/Monkmeyer. **Page 423:** From R. M. Liebert, R. W. Poulos, and G. D. Strauss, *Developmental Psychology*, Prentice-Hall, Inc., 1974. **Page 428:** Henri Cartier-Bresson/Magnum. **Page 431:** Courtesy Dean L. Fixsen, Ph.D., The Boys Town Research Center, Omaha, Nebraska. **Page 435:** Marcia Keegan/Woodfin Camp.

NAME INDEX

A

Abramov, I., 72
Abrams, D., 288, 289
Adelson, R., 422
Agnew, W. H., 38
Albee, G., 424
Allen, K. E., 249
Allen, V. L., 292–293
Allport, G. W., 333–334, 347, 348, 350
Allyn, J., 284
Allyon, T., 128, 418–419, 420, 421
Anastasi, A., 263
Anderson, D. J., 76
Anderson, M. L., 93, 94, 98
Andres, D. H., 255
Angel, C., 393
Aristotle, 130, 257
Arnhoff, F. N., 424
Aronfreed, J., 253–254, 255
Aronson, E., 425, 426, 427
Aronson, V., 288, 289
Asch, S., 290–292, 310, 425
Ashcroft, G. W., 364
Asling, C. W., 185
Atkinson, R. C., 155
Azrin, N. H., 248, 249, 418–419, 420, 421

B

Bach, G. R., 427
Backman, C. W., 284
Bagby, E., 361
Bandura, A., 129, 130, 131, 132, 133, 134, 220, 233, 264, 300, 366, 410, 422
Banks, C., 303–304
Barber, T. X., 381
Barker, R., 299
Baron, R. A., 135, 300, 301
Baron, R. M., 14–15, 17
Bartlett, F., 167
Bauer, E. E., 136
Baum, A., 308
Bayler, N., 204
Bazelon, D., 434
Beck, A. T., 355, 361
Bell, C., 4
Bellugi, C. B., 231, 232
Benitone, J., 41
Berger, H., 34
Berger, W., 434
Bergin, A. E., 410
Berko, J., 229
Berkowitz, L., 305
Berscheid, E., 285
Bieber, I., 382–383
Bijou, S. W., 136–137

B (cont.)

Binet, A., 9, 22
Bintz, J., 370
Birnbaum, M., 433, 434
Birnbrauer, J. S., 136
Bindrim, P., 427
Blanchard, E. B., 422
Bless, E., 297, 298
Bleuler, E., 385
Bolton, M., 176, 177, 178
Bousfield, W. A., 164
Brady, J. P., 359
Bransford, J., 159, 169
Bray, C. W., 76
Brecher, E. M., 187, 373
Brehm, J., 278–279
Brill, A. A., 315
Broadhurst, P. L., 205
Brown, D. G., 261
Brown, M., 250–251
Brown, R., 226, 227, 231, 232, 233
Bruner, J., 221–224, 240–241, 242
Brusse, J. F., 76
Bruun, K., 204
Buschke, H., 155
Buss, A., 299–300
Byrne, D., 287

SUBJECT INDEX

Page numbers given in *italics* refer to entries in the Glossary at the end of each chapter.

Amygdala, 39–40
Anagrams, 174, 179
Anal aggressive character, 319, 346, *348*
Anal retentive character, 319, 346, *348*
Anal stage, 318, 325, 346, *348*
Anonymity, 301, 311
Anorexia, 129
ANS. See Autonomic nervous system
Anus, 316, 346
Anxiety
　about castration, 318, 346, *348*
　in Freudian theory, 322
　in neuroses, 356–361, 399, *400*
　in psychotherapy, 414, 416, 424, 436
　and social deviance, 371
Applied psychology, 12
Apprehension, span of, 146, *180*
Approach-avoidance conflict, 367
Approximations, successive, 116, 129, *142*
Aqueous humor, 68, *99*
Arapesh, 263
Archimedes Law, 219
Assessment of personality, 314–315, 326–327
Assimilation, 213, *242*
Association
　free, 406
　loose, 387
Associationism, 4
Associative ability, 177–178
Associative organization, 163–165, 179, *180*
Asthenic type, 331
Asthma, 365, 399, 416
Astrology, 285–287
Athletic type, 331
Attack, 300, 310
Attention
　disorders of, 388
　selective, 148–149, *180*
Attitudes, 310, *11*
　affective component of, 276
　change in, 277–284
　formation of, 276
Attraction, 276, 284–288, 310
Attractiveness, 288, 310
Audition. See Hearing
Auditory canal, *99*
Auditory memory modes, 153
Autism, 389, *400*

Autonomic nervous system, 47–48, 49, 58, *59*, 364
　and emotion, 50–55
Autonomy, 325
　functional, 334, 347, *349*
Aversive conditioning, 416–418
Aversive stimuli, 116, 138
Avoidance conflict, 367
Avoidance learning, 126, *140*, 371
Avoidance response, 357, 396
Axons, 28, 29, 31

B

Babbling, 225, 241
Barbiturates, 375, 378–379, *400*
Basal ganglia, 31–32, *59*
Base line, 119, 139, *140*
Basiliar membrane, 73, 75, 76, *99*
Basket-shaped nerve endings, 65, *99*
Behavior
　and brain, 34–58
　criminal, 204–205
　deviant, 355
　and genetics, 195–206, 207
　instrumental, 215
　and learning, 106, 138
　modification of, 406, 414–424, *437*
　normal, 409
　and personality, 314
　prosocial, 305–307, 310
　schizophrenic, 385–389
　social, 275–311
Behaviorism, 7–8, 22, *23*
Behavior therapy, 414–424, *437*
Beliefs, 276, 310
Bestiality, 382
Beta rhythm, 34, 58, *59*
Binocular depth cues, 83, *99*
Binocular disparity, 83–84, *99*
Biochemical factors in schizophrenia, 392, 394
Biofeedback, 34–35, 125
Blindness, color, 73
Blind spot, 69, 82, *99*
Body
　awareness of, 66
　types of, 330–332
Boundary detectors, 46